11/98

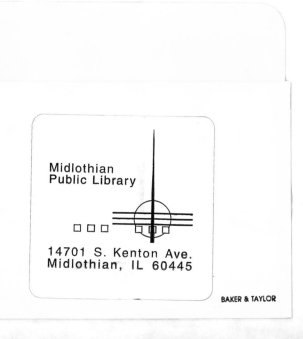

ELVIS
PRESLEY

A LIFE IN MUSIC

THE COMPLETE

RECORDING

SESSIONS

ELVIS
PRESLEY
A LIFE IN MUSIC

THE COMPLETE

RECORDING

SESSIONS

ERNST JORGENSEN

St. Martin's Press
New York

For Tine and Theodor

Grateful acknowledgment for use of illustrations in this book is made to Showtime Archives (Toronto)/Colin Escott, Motion Picture & Television Photo Archive, RCA Record Label Archive, Ger Rijff, Roger Semon, Joseph A. Tunzi/JAT Publishing, and Elvis Presley Enterprises, Inc. Photos taken on April 14, 1956 © Don Cravens/Time Inc. Photos taken on July 2, 1956 © Alfred Wertheimer, All Rights Reserved. Photo taken on April 23, 1977 © Bob Heis.

Library of Congress Cataloging-in-Publication Data

Jorgensen, Ernst.
    Elvis Presley : a life in music / Ernst Jorgensen ; foreword by Peter Guralnick.
        p. cm.
    ISBN 0-312-18572-3
    1. Presley, Elvis, 1935–1977. 2. Rock musicians—United States—Biography. 3. Presley, Evis, 1935–1977—Discography. I. Title.
ML420.P96J65 1998
782.42166'092—dc21
[B]
                                                                        97-42483
                                                                            CIP
                                                                            MN

First Edition: July 1998
10 9 8 7 6 5 4 3 2 1

CONTENTS

ACKNOWLEDGMENTS

It's no understatement to say that this book would not have been possible without the total support of Erik Rasmussen, Alexandra Guralnick, and Peter Guralnick. Should you ever forget how important you were to this project, give me a call and I'll refresh your memories.

Sincere thanks for a great time to St. Martin's Press's own Calvert D. Morgan. You made the final editing a truly exciting exercise. Frankly, there was a time when I thought *I* was the expert. Now I'm not so sure!

Thanks also to:

the late Mary and Felton Jarvis;

Carmen Fanzone of the AF of M in Los Angeles, and Harold Bradley and Buddy Harman of the Nashville union, for work beyond the call of duty;

the many employees of RCA Records who helped me over the years: Joan Deary, Rocco Laginestra, Gregg Geller, Ole Jochimsen, Bruce Hailstalk, Bernadette Moore, Steve Sholes, Joyce Triplett, my good friend Chick Crumpacker and his wife, Bunny, and my great colleague, Roger Semon;

the producers, engineers and musicians: Steve Binder, David Briggs (I think I bored you to death, but you took it well), Tom Brown, Tony Brown, Hayward Bishop, Hal Blaine, James Burton, Kenneth Buttrey, Jerry Carrigan, Al Casey, Floyd Cramer, Jimmy Day, Ray Edenton, D. J. Fontana, Tilman Frank, Emory Gordy, Bones Howe, Jerry Kennedy, Jim Malloy, Charlie McCoy, Bob Moore, Scotty Moore, Mike Moran, Shaun Nielsen, Thorne Nogar, Ron Olson, Al Pachucki, Knox Phillips, Sam Phillips, Sandy Posey, Norbert Putnam, Thurl Ravenscroft, Gordon Stoker, Billy Strange, Sonny Tremmell, Ray Walker, Margaret and Alton Warwick, Richard Weise, Bobby Wood, Chip Young, and Reggie Young;

and others: Freddy Bienstock, Trevor Cajaio, Al Cooley, Joe Esposito, Lamar Fike, Barbara Franchino, Paal Granlund, Johnny Mikkelsen, Bent Moeller, Red and Pat West, Charlie Hodge, Gary Hovey, Gregg Howell, Scott Perry, Randy Pope, Ger Rijff, Shelly Ritter, Bernhard Seibel, Jerry Schilling, Tom Schultheis, Jack Soden, Mike Stoller, Joe Tunzi, Morten Vandborg, Ben Weisman, and Larry Zwisohn.

FOREWORD

PETER GURALNICK

My grandfather taught me a number of important lessons when I was a kid. "Hang in there" was one. "Keep the faith, baby" (after Adam Clayton Powell) was another. The principal point of these sayings, which was the same point I later took from Wilson Pickett's "99½ Won't Do," was that you never gave up; long after others might think the battle over, you kept on. I thought this was a lesson that could not be over-done. But sometimes Ernst Mikael Jorgensen carries it too far.

I first met Ernst over Elvis, naturally. We had been talking and corresponding long-distance for some time when Ernst came to New York to work on the RCA five-CD '50s boxed set, *Elvis: The King Of Rock 'n' Roll.* I had been laboring away at the first volume of my Elvis Presley biography for five years at this point, and Ernst had been upsetting me for the last two or three with pesky questions of fact that invariably threw good stories into doubt. Watching him as he carefully assembled the collection, observing the way in which he refused to give up on all-but-hopeless leads, located long-lost tapes that clearly wanted to stay lost, and painstakingly scrutinized the sound, made me realize he might be just as hard on himself as he was on me. When, some time later, we visited the former RCA studio in New York where Elvis had cut "Hound Dog" and "Don't Be Cruel" (it was now a television teaching studio in a building owned by Baruch University) and Ernst insisted that the pattern of the acoustic tile on the wall pointed conclusively to the fact that publicity pictures had been taken there prior to what we thought to be Elvis's first visit to New York, I realized I was in the presence of either a madman or a great detective. I'm glad to say that subsequent research proved Ernst right, impelling me to select the latter category.

No reader of this book, of course, will have any such doubt. *Elvis Presley: A Life in Music* is a triumph of pure scholarship — but it is much more than that. What is so wonderful about the book is the sense of a story unfolding, the kind of nuanced picture that emerges not from facts alone but from clarity of vision and sharp critical thinking. It is not simply that you will find everything you ever wanted to know about Elvis Presley's recording dates in the pages of this book. This is a tale told with elegance, insight, and discrimination that opens up into much broader territory, arriving inevitably at the nexus between business and creativity.

Even with his magnum opus completed, however, I wouldn't presume to ask Ernst if he is finished with his research. How could he be if he continues to keep in mind the precepts cited above? Ernst will go on with the quest undaunted, I'm sure, maintaining as always his indefatigable calm, apologizing for his impeccable English, saying that he fears America is not yet ready for him (well, he's right there), and embarrassing us not just by the scholarly excellence of his work and the success of the definitive reissue program that he and Roger Semon continue to carry out at RCA, but now by the scope of his critical intelligence as well.

INTRODUCTION

I always felt that someday, somehow, something would happen to change every-thing for me, and I'd daydream about how it would be.
—Elvis Presley, August 1956

I remember those dreams—not Elvis's, but my own: The intense longing for some-thing to happen, for my life to be somehow different from all of its predictable ele-ments, its guarantee of what appeared to be a safe, boring future as a child growing up in Denmark.

Riding to the post office on my bicycle through the snow at five-thirty in the morn-ing, I had plenty of time to dream. As a teenager I had to support myself and my stud-ies at the University of Copenhagen by working as a mailman in the mornings, but it sure wasn't my likely future as a teacher that occupied my mind on those cold morn-ings delivering the mail. What I dreamed was that somehow I would get involved with Elvis Presley's music; that I would come to understand how, when, and why it was made; and that someday, finally, I might come to understand why it seemed to have a greater effect on the world than any other music I knew.

I wasn't old enough to remember Elvis Presley at the start, when he was the contro-versial new American singing sensation of the '50s. You couldn't even buy his records in Denmark until late 1958, and it wasn't until 1963, at the age of thirteen, that I even got a record player. Like so many other Europeans, I was primarily exposed to Elvis's early '60s material, songs like "It's Now Or Never," "Are You Lonesome Tonight?," "Can't Help Falling In Love," and the one that really caught my attention—"Little Sister." To most teenagers, music was very much a question of taking a stance. In my country you were presented with one simple choice—between Elvis Presley and England's Cliff Richard—and if your position didn't define who you were, at least it gave an indication of what kind of person you wanted to be. But all that changed very quickly—soon the choice was the Beatles versus the Rolling Stones—and over the next few years Elvis faded from the scene, leaving only the most diehard fans to admit that they still bought Elvis Presley records.

I wasn't one of those diehards. I bought Stones and Dylan albums, and later, records by the Doors and Jefferson Airplane. But I also started to collect the early Presley records—a treasury of wonderful, unknown music. Soon I'd become fascinated

not just with rock 'n' roll but with the music that rock 'n' roll came from, opening up new doors to country, R&B, and gospel. I had no problem playing Jimi Hendrix back to back with any of Mahalia Jackson's albums.

My other main interests during those years were an insatiable appetite for detective novels and a continuing interest in the history courses I took at school. Somehow all these interests came together in my pursuit of Elvis Presley. I found it impossible simply to dismiss my earliest hero, but I was still faced with the historical contradictions, the mysteries, of his music—the way he could go from the utter ridiculousness of "Old MacDonald" to the masterfulness of "Big Boss Man" within just months. Eventually I found two new friends, Johnny Mikkelsen and Erik Rasmussen, who not only shared my passion for music but were as intrigued by Elvis Presley as I—and who, like myself, were endlessly curious about the absolute contradictions and erratic logic of his recorded work and the way it was released. Together we started to collect information about Elvis's music—only to learn that Elvis's record company and management was enforcing a "no comment" policy. Recording dates, musicians, background information: Everything was off-limits to the public.

My friends and I were not easily dissuaded. Soon I was writing letters to his record company, session musicians, union offices, engineers—practically anybody we thought might have some answers. Maybe one out of ten, at best, would write back, but piece by piece we were able to organize our collections of Presley's recordings and answer many of the questions that we (and, no doubt, plenty of other Elvis fans) had. There were significant breakthroughs when we got hold of all of Steve Sholes's early paperwork; when RCA president Rocco Laginestra asked Joan Deary to send us a complete list of Elvis's master serial numbers; and when Elvis's producer, Felton Jarvis, started to correspond with us. At no time were the three of us prouder than when, in 1974, Felton submitted a complete list of the Stax sessions he had held with Elvis a few months earlier, confiding in three Danish researchers about ten new titles that wouldn't be released for another twelve months.

At a certain stage in such endeavors, you reach a level of notoriety, and doors begin to open a little more easily. For us, that time came only after we had published several small pamphlets' worth of all the information we had accumulated. All of a sudden we began to get responses in the form of additions, corrections, and general encouragement from like-minded folk around the world.

Still dreaming about another life, I finally quit the university for a career in the Danish recording industry, which eventually led me to a job as managing director for BMG's soon-to-be-opened offices in Copenhagen. BMG had acquired RCA Records in 1986, just two years earlier; now I found myself working within the company that *owned* Presley's recordings. Some people at the label already knew about me and my interest in Elvis; indeed, several of BMG's administrative departments were using our latest *Recording Sessions* booklet as their guide to the vast Presley catalog. Two years earlier

I had hooked up with RCA's entrepreneurial, London-based marketing director Roger Semon, whom I assisted in putting together several Presley albums especially for Europe. When we found ourselves working for the same company, we began to express our mutual concerns about the way the Presley catalog was being handled, and to our surprise we found that the new German international management was extremely supportive and encouraging.

The record business is as tumultuous as any other, and after a few years it looked as if both Roger Semon and I were about to leave the company, when another unexpected turn of events occurred. Out of the blue, RCA's New York office asked if we would like to work for them exclusively in restoring the Elvis Presley catalog. Organizing the releases and checking the tapes, a process I've been laboring at for nine years, has given me the opportunity to listen to every tape in the RCA vault; I spent literally thousands of hours cataloging Elvis's music, poring over the snippets of dialogue captured on tape between songs, listening for clues, studying whatever facts and data we could, all in an attempt to reconstruct every aspect of Elvis's recording career. As a consequence I came in contact with many of the people who had worked with Elvis and his music—each new contact another opportunity for more inside information. It is a process we are continuing today, and there's plenty of work left to do.

When Elvis died, it was as if all perspective on his musical career was somehow lost. From the utter ridicule of the tabloids to the almost religious dedication of the most ardent fans, any wish to understand Elvis Presley the singer seemed almost totally obscured by the unavoidable fact of his celebrity and the endless stories about eating habits, girlfriends, drug problems, and more that went with it. During his life, only one substantial biography was published: Jerry Hopkins's *Elvis*. Since August 16, 1977, hundreds of books have appeared, some seeking honestly to explain a popular phenomenon, many simply looking to cash in on that phenomenon or, more often than not, to place the writer at the center of Elvis's life. With Albert Goldman's book these manipulations reached alarming new heights, as facts were rearranged to fit an author's agenda and a rhetoric of contempt was substituted for honest evaluation. It was out of these distortions that my desire first arose to try, as best I could, to set the record—and the records—straight. This book, along with the many reissues Roger Semon and I have produced for RCA/BMG, is the result.

Like any other writer, I will be guilty of mistakes. No doubt I've misinterpreted a few situations or left out nuggets of interesting information. But between the covers of this book is tucked more factual information about Elvis's music and recordings than can be found in any other book. It is an attempt to convey as much as I can about not only the exceptional nature of Elvis's recording career, but also its very normality.

It is as subjective as any other book, I'm sure, but I hope it will give you the opportunity to make up your own mind, to dive into the music and discover for yourself the same endless hours of enjoyment and wonderful listening that I have found. It's my hope and goal that the story I tell in these pages will make it easier to understand the phenomenon of Elvis Presley by illuminating what was at the heart of it: his music.

As the other Elvis (Costello) said: My aim is true.

—Ernst Jorgensen
Denmark, 1997

SESSION DATA KEY

A —— 37. Soundtrack recordings for MGM's *Jailhouse Rock*
April 30, 1957: Radio Recorders, Hollywood

B —— MGM producer: Jeff Alexander
Engineer, Radio Recorders: Thorne Nogar

C —— Guitar: Scotty Moore
Guitar: Elvis Presley
Bass: Bill Black
Bass: Elvis Presley
Drums: D.J. Fontana

Piano: Dudley Brooks
Piano: Mike Stoller
Piano: Elvis Presley
Vocals: The Jordanaires

D —— 4/30, 10 AM–1:45 PM, 2:45–6:10 PM   **H**   **I**

E —— **2001-06 Jailhouse Rock**   **Single A-side** —— **G**
F —— *H2WB 6779   Jerry Leiber/Mike Stoller — Elvis Presley Music*   *47-7035/1957* —— **J**
2001-06 Jailhouse Rock (movie version)   **Essential Elvis**
H2WB 6780   Jerry Leiber/Mike Stoller — Elvis Presley Music   *6738-2-R/1986*
2004-sp Young And Beautiful (movie end)   **Essential Elvis**
Abner Silver/Aaron Schroeder — Gladys Music   *6738-2-R/1986*
2004-22 Young And Beautiful   **Jailhouse Rock**
H2WB 6777   Abner Silver/Aaron Schroeder — Gladys Music   *EPA 4114/1957*
2005-03 Young And Beautiful   **The King Of Rock 'N' Roll**
WPA5 2507   Abner Silver/Aaron Schroeder — Gladys Music   *66050-2/1992*
2006-07 Young And Beautiful (Florita Club version)
Abner Silver/Aaron Schroeder — Gladys Music

A Session heading — Purpose of session, date, venue.

B Technical credits — Producer, engineer.

C Musician credits — Elvis Presley sings lead vocal on all tracks unless otherwise noted. Keyed to specific songs where possible.

D Time: — Duration of session.

E F Matrix number — Master numbers for RCA studio recordings appear in bold type preceding song titles. Soundtrack recordings have two sets of numbers —the primary number assigned by the studio **E**, which precedes the song title in such cases, and an RCA number **F** in italics on the second line.

A two-digit suffix indicates the take number of the master take. Masters marked "sp" are spliced from more than one take; "na" indicates that the number of the master take is unknown; "nm" indicates that none of the takes recorded was selected as a master. Sometimes "tr" appears also, indicating that the listed take is only a backing track for later vocal overdubbing.

G Initial release — Indicates the first appearance of each track on an RCA single (A- or B-side), LP, EP, or CD. No listing indicates an unreleased track.

H Composer — Listings for recordings released by RCA reflect credit as given at time of release. Some songs may be listed as "traditional" in official RCA releases, but given full composer credit in the context of informal or unreleased recordings.

I Publisher — Publisher listings reflect each song's publishing status at the time of each recorded track's release. As a result, publishing information may vary from year to year, and informal or unreleased recordings may not carry publishing information.

J Catalog number — Reflects original RCA release, including year first issued.

Many sessions carry further information about overdubs, "work parts" (re-recordings of song parts for later splicing), additional musicians, and other exceptional circumstances in the notes following each session.

1935–55

MUSIC IN THE AIR

When Elvis Presley was born on January 8, 1935, the music he would one day make famous was already all around him. It was in the churches, in the juke joints, on street corners, on the radio, wherever friends gathered. All of the elements he would eventually incorporate into his music, however he and the passing of time would transform them, were already part of the lifeblood of East Tupelo, Mississippi, and of the American South.

Coming up on thirty-nine years after that January day, Elvis found himself in Memphis's Stax Studios, one of the many musical melting pots that had sprung up in the twenty years since he had first tried singing professionally. Into his head popped a few lines of a half-remembered tune, "Columbus Stockade Blues," and as he had so many times before he crooned them out loud, as much for himself as for anyone else who was listening. His cousin Billy Smith was there, and Elvis joked, "Hey man, that song is old. I did that when I was three years old." Chronologically, at least, it was possible: The song was already well established by 1938, having first been recorded by Thomas Darby and Jimmie Tarlton in 1927, the same year Henry Burr and Al Jolson both had big hits with "Are You Lonesome To-Night?" The music Elvis was absorbing in 1938 and every other year of his childhood, the music he loved and sang and recorded, came from every genre and walk of life.

Nothing meant more to him than the music of the church. In a quote reproduced in the liner notes of his first religious album, his mother, Gladys, recalled, "When Elvis was just a little fellow, he would slide off my lap, run down the aisle, and scramble up to the platform of the church. He would stand looking up at the choir and try to sing with them. He was too little to know the words, of course, but he could carry the tune." While Elvis was still in knee britches, the Golden Gate Quartet was preparing to make their first recordings, including a number of songs Elvis would later sing and record. "I know every religious song ever written," he was known to say. Elvis frequently cited country and western (C&W), rhythm and blues (R&B), and gospel as his musical inspirations, but he also knew and loved the work of pop stars such as Dean Martin and Bing Crosby, and even semioperatic singers such as Mario Lanza. All through his life, in private and professionally, he would hum, sing, play, and record songs dredged up from his musical memory, as if to remind himself and everyone around him of where it had all come from.

It's impossible to be sure exactly when Elvis first decided to become a musician. He recalled later that his father told him, "I haven't met a guitarist who was worth a damn." But it was his father whose lovely baritone voice could be heard around the Presley house throughout Elvis's childhood, singing gospel and country songs. His parents were the ones who gave him his first guitar; his uncles gave him his first few lessons. Perhaps the earliest indication came at the age of ten when he climbed on the stage at the Mississippi-Alabama Fair, stood on a chair, and came in fifth singing Red Foley's "Old Shep" before a talent-show audience. Later, we know, he hung around WELO, Tupelo's radio station, hoping the local celebrity and singer Mississippi Slim would show him a few chords or tell him a few stories about the stars he'd met. By those early teenage years, he seems to have singled music out as his future.

The little family—Vernon, Gladys, and Elvis—moved to Memphis in 1948 and into new musical surroundings. Memphis was cosmopolitan; Beale Street was full of the blues, and the region's radio stations played "race records" featuring the music that became known as rhythm and blues. There are many stories of the teenage Elvis hanging around in various musical spots around town—some substantiated, others not—but everyone remembers hearing him sing and seeing him with his guitar, and many noticed his changing appearance. By his last year in school he'd made a point of setting himself apart from his classmates, assuming a personalized dress code right out of the Lansky Brothers' window. But even as he was starting to align himself with the look of R&B (and honky-tonk) stars, the only things he seems to have sung himself were ballads. After he became famous, he recalled never having "sung a fast song" until his first official recording session. Dixie Locke, his steady girlfriend in those years, remembers hearing nothing from him but songs like "Tomorrow Night" and "My Happiness." At the Lauderdale Courts, where he and his family lived during his early high school days, neighbors heard him sing songs made famous by Bing Crosby, Eddy Arnold, and Joni James. He made passing attempts to get some of the older, more proficient aspiring musicians in the Courts to teach him a thing or two, but it wasn't so easy: His neighbor Lee Denson recalls being forced by his mother (a friend of Gladys) to help Elvis out with a few guitar pointers, and remembers his young pupil's slow progress.

Over the years, most of Elvis's friends and acquaintances came in contact with his shy but always persistent attempts at singing. To them it might have seemed like a dream, but Elvis's wish to become a singer was always more of a hope, a hope to make something good or even glorious out of his undefined future. To many he seemed like a loner, but he was always hanging around, watching, listening—waiting to make his move.

The story of that move is legendary. One day in the summer of 1953, Marion Keisker was sitting at her desk at the Phillips Recording Studio at 706 Union Avenue in Memphis. Out of 706 Union, studio owner and operator Sam Phillips ran a record label called Sun; the Alabama native had opened the facility in 1950, looking to record some of the many African-American players around Memphis and the rich farmland of the Mississippi delta south of the city. What he tapped into was an exploding R&B scene, already one of

America's most exciting. The music had become increasingly popular with the fading popularity of big bands after World War II, and all over the area—in Memphis, across the river in West Memphis, Arkansas, and down in Helena, Arkansas, and Clarksdale, Mississippi—black acts were doing good business luring new and exciting sounds out of their rich blues heritage. Sam Phillips recorded B. B. King, Howlin' Wolf, Junior Parker, Joe Hill Louis, and many others at 706 Union. He had even recorded what would later be deemed the first rock 'n' roll record, Jackie Brenston and Ike Turner's "Rocket 88." The little studio also had a service facility where anyone off the street could make a two-sided acetate record for $8.25. There were other, cheaper, less professional places to make recordings around town, places other young musicians used, but Elvis chose Sun. He would later say that he wanted to surprise his mother. Perhaps; more likely, though, what moved him was his burning, unexpressed desire to make music and to become a star.

Marion Keisker worked for Sam, and with him. She also had her own radio talk show, and a feeling for music. When she asked the nervous, almost unintelligible young man, "What kind of a singer are you?" he responded instantly, "I sing all kinds." "Who do you sound like?" she persisted. "I don't sound like nobody," was his response. He was hoping, he said, that she could recommend someone who was looking for a singer. Maybe he was just trying a little salesmanship; in fact, he sang very little but ballads, and to the untrained ear, we now know, he sounded like plenty of other local C&W singers. To Marion, though, there was something there—a stronger yearning? A deeper passion? A greater determination? Whatever it was, she wanted to keep an eye on it; after the kid had made his acetate she made herself a note: "Good ballad singer. Hold."

1. Private Recordings
1953: Memphis Recording Service (Sun Studio)

Guitar: Elvis Presley

WPA5 2531	**My Happiness**		**The Great Performances**
	Peterson/Bergantine		*2227–1/1990*
WPA5 2532	**That's When Your Heartaches Begin**		**The King Of Rock 'N' Roll**
	Raskin/Brown/Fisher		*66050/1992*

"That's When Your Heartaches Begin" ends (with the words "that's the end") just after what would normally have been a midsong recitation, although it's not clear whether this was intentional.

That day, with only the most fundamental of guitar skills, Elvis strummed and sang a twenty-year-old ballad called "My Happiness," following it up with the 1951 Ink Spots hit "That's When Your Heartaches Begin." The sound must have been exactly what his family, friends, and neighbors had been listening to for years, while the repertoire reflected a music business where the lines of genre, race, and social origin were already being blurred. "My Happiness" had been a pop record, a country record, and a jazz record before Elvis got to it; his version was sung as a kind of half-confident plaint. The other side—a song he'd return to for years—was filled with aspiration. If he had hoped for instant recognition, or for Sam Phillips to come out of the control booth to talk to him, he was sadly disappointed. Marion duly noted his name and number, but weeks and months went by and he heard nothing.

January came—or possibly several months after that; these dates are still elusive—and finding he couldn't stand it anymore he started dropping by the studio to talk with Miss Keisker. Around the same time he tried out for a place with the Songfellows, a kind of apprentice group connected to Memphis's very popular gospel quartet the Blackwood Brothers. He was rejected; he couldn't sing harmony, they said, and that was that. He didn't make any other outright moves to further his career. He never joined a band, or formed his own group, or tried out on the radio. But eventually he did make it back to Sun and paid to cut another acetate.

2. Private Recordings (Sun Studio)
January 4, 1954: Memphis Recording Service

Guitar: Elvis Presley

CPA5 5101	**I'll Never Stand In Your Way** *Hy Heath/Fred Rose*	**Platinum: A Life In Music** *67469–2/1997*
CPA5 5102	**It Wouldn't Be The Same Without You** *Jimmy Wakely/Fred Rose*	

This time he chose a new pop song from Joni James, "I'll Never Stand In Your Way," which was also out in a country version. For the other side he sang "It Wouldn't Be The Same Without You," from a record by the respected country singer Jimmy Wakely. There had been little progress since the last recording. The plaintive, insecure, but strangely passionate voice seemed to hold no commercial promise whatsoever. And so Elvis went back to waiting, stopping by the studio every now and then, determined for something to happen. It *had* to, he wanted it so much.

Then, on June 26, Marion called. Could he be there by three? "I was there by the time she hung up," he later joked; she suspected he'd run all the way, all charged up with the idea that Mr. Phillips might have found something for him.

The previous year, Sun had had a sizable hit with a group called the Prisonaires, all residents of the state penitentiary in Nashville. Their song, "Just Walking In The Rain," had been written by another prisoner; now Sam had a tune from yet another inmate, this time a ballad called "Without You," and he thought it might suit the quiet young singer. It might have, but Elvis couldn't find a way to do it; nevertheless, Sam invited him to keep singing—to let him hear whatever other songs he knew. The older man encouraged the boy, listened and tried to understand him, but when it was all over he didn't really know what to suggest. He only knew there was something there. "I have one real gift," Sam Phillips later said, "and that gift is to look another person in the eye and be able to tell if he has anything to contribute, and if he does, I have the additional gift to free him from whatever is restraining him." It didn't happen that afternoon, but sometime over the next ten days it did. Sam's insight and his patient persistence would help make him one of the most inspired and productive record producers of American vernacular music.

At around the same time a young guitar player, Winfield Scott "Scotty" Moore III, was also hanging around the studio, and eventually Sam gave his band, Doug Poindexter's Starlite Wranglers, a chance to record. Scotty had ambition—he wanted to work in the record business—and Sam liked him a lot. One day over coffee he suggested that Scotty contact a young ballad singer Sam was thinking of recording, to see if they could work something up for a session. Scotty wasn't given any further direction, but he knew that if he wanted to get something going with Sam he should at least give it a shot. He called the young singer and arranged to meet him. Bill Black, the Wranglers' bass player, would come along too; Bill's younger brother, Johnny, was one of the young musicians Elvis had hung around with in Lauderdale Courts, in a loose group that also included Lee Denson and the Burnette Brothers, Johnny and Dorsey.

Because everyone worked during the week, the trio met at Scotty's house the following Sunday and began by working their way through all the songs that Elvis could think of. The two older musicians were left with no distinct impression of his singing ability, but they were impressed with his outrageous appearance. He had arrived dressed in a black shirt, pink pants with a black stripe, white shoes, and a slick hairdo, all sideburns and ducktail. The very next evening, after work, the trio took their rehearsals to the studio, where a determined Sam Phillips seemed ready to get to the bottom of the situation—to try to understand why it was that he couldn't seem to shake the idea of this kid.

3. Studio Sessions for Sun
July 5–6, 1954: Sun Studio, Memphis

Producer/Engineer: Sam Phillips

Guitar: Scotty Moore   Bass: Bill Black
Guitar: Elvis Presley

G2WB 1086-sp	**I Love You Because**	**Elvis Presley**
	Leon Payne—Fred Rose Music	*LPM 1254/1956*
F2WB 8040-na	**That's All Right**	**Single A-side**
	Arthur Crudup—St. Louis Music/Wabash Music	*SUN 209/1954*
EPA3 2742-02	**Harbor Lights**	**Elvis: A Legendary Performer Vol. 2**
	J. Kennedy/H. Williams—Peter Maurice Music Co./Chappell	*CPL1 1349/1976*
F2WB 8041-na	**Blue Moon Of Kentucky**	**Single B-side**
	Bill Monroe—Peer International	*Sun 209/1954*

The RCA master of "I Love You Because" is a splice of takes 2 and 4, leaving out the spoken part. When Elvis transferred to RCA, the company received a tape referred to in Steve Sholes's notes as " 'That's All Right' plus two other selections"; it is unclear whether these "other selections" were Presley recordings.

Back in the studio, this time with Scotty and Bill, Elvis once again tried everything he could think of. Sam recorded him singing Leon Payne's country hit, "I Love You Because," with little success; it wasn't that Elvis was bad (save for the dismal recitation in the middle), but what was the point in Elvis doing the song when it had already been done better? Then, toward the end of the night, Sam was in the control room doing something when he got caught off guard by what would become the most significant musical moment in his, Elvis's, Scotty's, and Bill's lives. Patience might not have been the frenetically busy Sam Phillips's most obvious virtue, but it was one of his most important, as the hours he spent with Elvis and the boys were finally proving. In four years of work with local black musicians, he'd found their talent was frequently obscured by a lifetime of insecurity, and waiting for musicians to shake those feelings of "inferiority" and get beyond their natural fear of failure naturally took patience. Sam had always believed in the amateur spirit; to him it was only with fresh, unjaded nonprofessional musicians that truly creative and innovative work could be done. Now—if he could believe the sound coming over the monitor—his patience was finally paying off. After all his failures, Elvis was starting to warm up.

Scotty and Bill weren't yet comfortable themselves, exactly, but they were falling in right behind Elvis, giving it their best shot, catching up with him as best they could. Clowning around was definitely second nature to both Elvis and Bill, so it shouldn't have been much of a surprise when the two of them started fooling around with a familiar blues song, Arthur "Big Boy" Crudup's "That's All Right." When the normally reserved Scotty joined in, Sam sensed that the patience part of his job was over. This was something truly unexpected, something original; it had a logic of its own, even if Sam recognized elements that were borrowed from his own recordings of Jackie Brenston or Junior Parker. It was the "something different" he'd been looking for, the beat the music had always been lacking, and without hesitating Sam finally made his move. Stopping the group in midverse, he asked them to start over as he pushed the RECORD button on the tape machine. Relaxed and loose at last, Elvis injected a bright, breezy, more melodic feel into the traditional blues, and with only two guitars plus the slap of Bill's bass, a sound came through that got Sam's eyes dancing. Suddenly, they were making a record.

Perhaps they tried other material that night, tried working up other songs in the same vein as "That's All Right." They may have done "Tiger Man," a song Sam had cowritten (under the name Burns) with blues artist Joe Hill Louis and given to Rufus Thomas to record. (We know that in 1970 Elvis kicked off the song with a cryptic introduction: "This was my second record, but not too many people got to hear it.") It may have been before "I Love You Because" that they spent time on "Harbor Lights," but they couldn't get the Hawaiian-inspired pop song right. Eventually, though, they came up with a song even more improbable than "That's All Right"—and just as promising. From a childhood of Saturday nights listening to the Grand Ole Opry, Elvis knew the bluegrass music of Bill Monroe and his Bluegrass Boys. The waltz tempo of "Blue Moon Of Kentucky" was as far from Crudup's rhythm and blues as you could get, but the group straightened the song out, converted it to 4/4 time, and brought the tempo up to that of the earlier number. After an early take Sam enthused, "Fine, man. Hell, that's different. That's a pop song now, nearly 'bout." With a few more takes and a little more refinement, the song edged even further from its country roots and into the domain of

Elvis Presley, Bill Black, and Scotty Moore with Sam Phillips at the Sun control booth.

13

The first Sun publicity portrait: 1954

rhythm and blues. The result was something compatible with "That's All Right," and, more important, the perfect B-side to a record.

Scotty and Bill were sure "they would be run out of town" if the song ever saw the light of day. But Sam knew what he was doing. He rushed a reference record down to the hippest DJ in Memphis and all of America, Dewey Phillips (no relation) of WHBQ. When Dewey played Elvis's record on his "Red, Hot and Blue" show, Elvis was so embarrassed he hid out at the Suzore No. 2 Theater until his mother and father retrieved him. Dewey Phillips was calling: The switchboard at the station had lit up with confirmation of Sam's instincts. This was something new, something worthwhile, a sound they all could run with. All of a sudden, all those old hopes of Elvis's began cropping up as immediate facts and demands in his life. On the strength of the record's "Red, Hot and Blue" reception, the little band, who had never appeared in public, was booked for a guest spot at Memphis's Bon Air Club. Then, before long, Elvis was added to the bottom of a bill headlined by Slim Whitman, on well-known Memphis DJ Bob Neal's "Folk Music" show out at the Overton Park Shell. A flurry of publicity, including a picture and article in the *Memphis Commercial Appeal,* took note of the record's startling local success.

At the Overton Park show, almost overcome by panic, Elvis got through his opening number, but not without another unexpected development: His leg started shaking uncontrollably, just the way he'd seen Statesmen bass singer Jim "Big Chief" Wetherington's do as he worked the crowd. The response from the girls in the audience was instantaneous. All through that summer the record was heard everywhere in Memphis, and through the power of radio it spread to neighboring areas.

4. Studio Sessions for Sun
August 19, 1954: Sun Studio, Memphis

Producer/Engineer: Sam Phillips

Guitar: Scotty Moore   Bass: Bill Black
Guitar: Elvis Presley

F2WB 8117-04   **Blue Moon**   **Elvis Presley**
                Rodgers/Hart—Robbins Music   *LPM 1254/1956*

The tape is dated with a sticker on the plastic reel: "8/19. Wed Nite."

The little Sun Studio became the center of his world, a place where he could stop for companionship, where he could come to try out new ideas. One day he came in wanting to record Rodgers and Hart's "Blue Moon," though where he got the idea is not at all clear. It may have been from Slim Whitman (though Slim hadn't yet cut the song), but music historian Colin Escott suggests that couldn't have been his only influence: "Elvis skips the bridge and the final verse that contains the happy ending, neatly transforming the 32-bar pop classic into an eerie 16-bar blues." It was a fascinating mix of musical styles, but not, Sam finally decided, a record.

It was common record company practice to release a new single every three months, but with a breaking story like Elvis Sam knew he had to watch things closely: The right kind of blockbuster hit, with enough radio support, could stay on the charts for a year or more. It is an indication of the kind of faith Sam Phillips had in Elvis that he put out no new records by any other artist in the wake of Elvis's successful debut— until it was time for a second Presley release.

5. Studio Sessions for Sun
September 10–?, 1954: Sun Studio, Memphis

Producer/Engineer: Sam Phillips

Guitar: Scotty Moore
Guitar: Elvis Presley

Bass: Bill Black

F2WB 8115-07	**Tomorrow Night** *Sam Coslow/Will Grosz—Bourne Company*	**The King Of Rock 'N' Roll** *66050–2/1992*	
-01	**Satisfied** *Martha Carson*		
F2WB 8116-na	**I'll Never Let You Go (Little Darlin')** *Jimmy Wakely—Sunshine Music*	**Elvis Presley** *LPM 1254/1956*	
F2WB 8042-na	**I Don't Care If The Sun Don't Shine** *Mack David—Famous Music*	**Single B-side** *SUN 210/1954*	
F2WB 8118-na	**Just Because** *Bob & Joe Shelton/Sid Robin—Leeds Music*	**Elvis Presley** *LPM 1254/1956*	
F2WB 8043-na	**Good Rockin' Tonight** *Roy Brown—Blue Ridge Pub.*	**Single A-side** *SUN 210/1954*	

The listing for "Tomorrow Night" reflects the first release of the complete, undubbed master, which included a long gap in the middle apparently intended for a guitar solo. The song was first released in 1965 on the RCA album *Elvis For Everyone* (LSP/LPM 3450), in a version overdubbed with guitar, harmonica, and backing vocals. An edited version of the original undubbed master, with the space for the solo edited out, was released on *The Complete Sun Sessions* (6414-2-R). According to Steve Sholes's original notes on the fifteen Sun tapes purchased by RCA, the following number of takes were definitely recorded: "Satisfied," 1; "I'll Never Let You Go," 10; "I Don't Care If The Sun Don't Shine," 3; "Just Because," 17; "Good Rockin' Tonight," 2. There may have been many more, as Sam Phillips recorded over many Presley tapes. The Sun tapes that RCA did receive from these sessions were lost in a vault "clean-out" in 1959.

Long experience, and the previous session, told Sam it would take Elvis a while to adjust once again to the studio environment and find the right mood. So it was only natural to allow the young singer to start with what he loved best: ballads. This time he attempted Lonnie Johnson's "Tomorrow Night," a song he sang all the time at home and with Dixie. But Sam knew this wasn't the kind of song he wanted Elvis to record; Dean Martin, Perry Como, Teresa Brewer, Doris Day, and scores of other popular singers already had that territory covered, all on major labels offering costly promotional support and well-timed television appearances. It wasn't that Elvis didn't sing the song well, for this time he certainly did; the confidence he'd gained could already be heard in his voice, along with an undeniable passion. But like all of Elvis's Sun ballads, "Tomorrow Night" didn't have much of an arrangement; Elvis's voice was almost drowned in echo, and Scotty just plunked along as if they were recording cowboy songs. Trying to explain why he let Elvis cut so many ballads, Sam has said, "I didn't have the heart to stop him."

If Sam ever gave any thought to stopping Elvis from following his nose in the studio, "That's All Right" was there to remind him that the boy needed the freedom to explore, to jump into whatever came to mind. Occasionally something promising, like Martha Carson's "Satisfied," would emerge, only to be dropped as Elvis moved on to another idea. Elvis had sung Jimmy Wakely's "It Wouldn't Be The Same Without You" on his second acetate, and now he selected another Wakely ballad, "I'll Never Let You Go" (originally written for Gene Autry in 1941). He sang straight until the last two choruses, for which he tried leaping into double time; the group worked on the number over and over, but never managed to get the transition from ballad to rhythm song to work quite the way they wanted.

The songs that came to Elvis's mind were as motley a crew as can be imagined, yet each one was drawn from his own experiences. His prodigious memory helped him dredge up songs from the oddest places, and the Dean Martin and Jerry Lewis movie *Scared Stiff* was one. He recalled Martin's rendition of a number called "I Don't Care If The Sun Don't Shine," which had actually been written for *Cinderella* but was never used in the Disney film. The movie version differed from Martin's 1950 recorded version, and it was the screen performance he remembered; he took Martin's approach one step further, speeding the song up, solidifying the beat, and adding an energetic vocal delivery on top. "Just Because," another song from these sessions, is harder to pinpoint. Written in 1933, the song had seen a popular 1948 polka version by Frankie Yankovic, which may well have been the interpretation Elvis heard, but it could just as well have been the Shelton Brothers' original record, or Cliff Carlisle's cover. Whatever the source, the group worked hard to follow Sam's directions on both songs. To spur his artists along, he would often suggest trying a song up-tempo, then changing back to a slower groove. "Just Because" was recorded both ways, but when it was first released by RCA on Elvis's premiere album, it was the fast version that was used.

Still without a real winner, they returned to the formula that had proved so successful on "That's All Right," brushing up and reworking an old R&B number in what was rapidly becoming a distinctive new style. In this case the song was Roy Brown's

"Good Rockin' Tonight," and it was a perfect subject for revision. Sam's vision was centered on rhythm. He was always warning Scotty Moore away from the style of his idol Chet Atkins; pretty fingerpicking was fine for country or pop, but Sam was looking for something a little simpler, a little gutsier. "Good Rockin' Tonight" proved to be a natural follow-up: It came from the same current R&B scene, it was up-tempo, and with Scotty ad-libbing his way into a new style that hammered away at the beat even during the solos, it worked like a charm. It was a convincing demonstration that Elvis's first record was no fluke. This was an emerging talent, taking his next logical step. As soon as the session was over the tape was rushed to Buster Williams's Plastic Products pressing plant over on Chelsea Avenue. "Good Rockin' Tonight" backed with "I Don't Care If The Sun Don't Shine" would be the new single.

But just how far could this little trio go? Sam succeeded in getting them a guest appearance on the Grand Ole Opry in October, where, awed by many of their musician heroes, the three young men performed adequately but got little in the way of enthusiasm from the audience—and failed to get invited back. With the Opry out of the picture Sam turned to the other significant showcase for country-and-western talent, Shreveport's Louisiana Hayride, which was both less choosy and more willing to take risks than its upscale cousin. It was on the Hayride that Hank Williams had first triumphed, along with Webb Pierce, Faron Young, and other big country stars. Just as important as its history, though, was the broadcast signal of sponsoring radio station KWKH, which reached from northwestern Louisiana west into Texas and parts of Arkansas.

6. Live Recordings for "The Louisiana Hayride"
October 16, 1954: The Municipal Auditorium, Shreveport

Guitar: Scotty Moore
Guitar: Elvis Presley

Bass: Bill Black

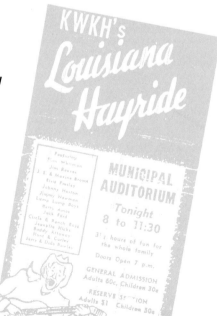

HPA5 6101	**That's All Right**		**Elvis: The Hillbilly Cat**
	Arthur Crudup		*PB 3602/1984*
HPA5 6101	**Blue Moon Of Kentucky**		**Elvis: The Hillbilly Cat**
	Bill Monroe		*PB 3602/1984*

Lucky Strike guest time, now. Just a few weeks ago a young man from Memphis, Tennessee, recorded a song on the Sun label, and in just a matter of a few weeks that record has skyrocketed right up the charts. It's really doing good all over the country. He's only nineteen years old. He has a new distinctive style—Elvis Presley. Let's give him a nice hand.

—Frank Page, announcer for the Louisiana Hayride

He might have been nervous, but his thoroughly confident version of "That's All Right" didn't show it. The audience may well have been surprised that the big sound they'd heard on the record was made by such a humble little trio, but spurred by a week-long radio buildup, they responded to Elvis and his band (now called the Blue Moon Boys) with genuine recognition. When Frank Page asked Elvis how the group had come up with this new style, the nineteen-year-old singer replied with truthful modesty, "We just stumbled upon it," then went on to perform the other side of the record. If he wasn't an overnight sensation, he was at least successful enough for Horace Logan, manager of the Hayride, to offer him a contract. So on November 6 Elvis returned to perform again, this time bringing his parents, who were needed to sign for the underage singer.

Contemporary accounts tell us that on that night Elvis performed, among others, a song called "Sitting On Top Of The World," either the old Delta blues (kept in circulation by Bob Wills well into the '50s) or the pop standard of the same name. And he *was*—proudly straddling a new world he barely knew anything about. With a twelve-month Hayride contract in hand, the three musicians gave up their day jobs to devote themselves full-time to their new career. Scotty and Bill had already resigned from their previous band as the new trio began appearing around Memphis, principally at the Eagle's Nest, a Lamar Avenue complex hosted by popular country DJ Sleepy-Eyed John. The shows they played outside the city often proved disappointing—only thirty-two people came to one show at the Nettleton High School, just outside Jonesboro, Arkansas. But then at the end of November Houston DJ Biff Collie, who liked the new sound, booked them into the Palladium in downtown Houston. When they went over well, he invited them to stay two more nights.

Scotty was acting as the group's manager, but both he and Sam Phillips knew they needed more professional representation, so before long Bob Neal of the Overton Park "Folk Music" show took over not just bookings but artist management as well. As a popular country DJ on strong-signal WMPS, Neal had a considerable following in the many small communities around the city and frequently emceed and promoted shows featuring acts like Elvis and the brother-sister duo Jim Ed and Maxine Brown.

The Blue Moon Boys were making progress. But even as well received as the second record was, it stalled, and with winter coming on Sam Phillips was anxious to get the group back into the studio to try to match the success of the first single.

7. Studio Sessions for Sun
November or December, 1954: Sun Studio, Memphis

Producer/Engineer: Sam Phillips

Guitar: Scotty Moore
Guitar: Elvis Presley

Bass: Bill Black

F2WB 8044-na	**Milcow Blues Boogie**	**Single A-side**
	Kokomo Arnold—Leeds Music	*SUN 215/1955*
F2WB 8045-na	**You're A Heartbreaker**	**Single B-side**
	Jack Sallee—Hill & Range	*SUN 215/1955*

A payment slip of November 15 seems to indicate a session date, but it may be a falsification; December 8 has also been mentioned as a possible date for the session. It's more than likely that other songs were tried out on the session, although apparently no other tapes survive. RCA never received master tapes or outtakes from this session from Sun; their masters were dubbed from a Sun 78.

Little is known about the sessions that led to Elvis's third Sun single. "Milcow Blues Boogie," like the first recordings, was a gutsy blues with a strong beat to which Elvis brought a light, definitely country feel. From a rhythmic point of view, the double-time gimmick worked better here, coming off Elvis's slow-talking intro, than it had in "I'll Never Let You Go," and the record combined charm with an undeniably bluesy flavor. It may be that the A-side sounded too "black" for the majority of Elvis's white audience, but it's just as likely that the opposite problem was what doomed it: Bob Wills, the "King of Western Swing," had been playing it in his own hopped-up version, "Brain Cloudy Blues," since 1946. It's possible, in other words, that this particular batch of race mixing was just too *familiar* for most DJs to notice. Whatever the case, the audience and the DJs were lagging behind; Elvis and his boys, with Sam Phillips, were putting out one classic after another.

New Year's Day 1955 found the Presley trio before a capacity crowd at the Eagle's Hall in Houston. A few days later, in New Boston, Texas, a crowd of five hundred was big enough to attact the attention of a seasoned music man: country singer Eddy Arnold's one-time manager, now working for Hank Snow—"Colonel" Thomas A. Parker. Bob Neal suggested the Colonel come by the following Saturday night to catch the young performer on the Hayride. Parker couldn't have missed the *Billboard* notice about the new group's burgeoning success in both personal appearances and radio play throughout east Texas. Nor would their review of the new single have escaped his attention: Of "Milcow Blues Boogie," they wrote "Presley continues to impress," and they complimented "You're A Heartbreaker" for its slick country style.

8. Radio Recordings
January or February, 1955: Lubbock, Texas

Guitar: Scotty Moore
Guitar: Elvis Presley

Bass: Bill Black

WPA5 2533 **Fool, Fool, Fool**
Nugetre

The King Of Rock 'N' Roll
66050–2/1992

WPA5 2534 **Shake, Rattle And Roll**
Charles Calhoun

The King Of Rock 'N' Roll
66050-2/1992

These recordings were most likely made on January 6, when Elvis played Lubbock for the first time; if not, they are from February 13, when he returned. It was common at the time for artists to visit local radio stations when touring, encouraging the local DJ to play their records, often performing live (or taped) on the air to promote their upcoming shows. Because Elvis and his Blue Moon Boys had so little recorded repertoire, they would supplement their own repertoire with covers like the above, both recent Atlantic singles. "Fool, Fool, Fool" was a number one R&B record by the Clovers in 1951. "Shake, Rattle And Roll" was a 1954 R&B hit in its original version by Big Joe Turner, and a number seven pop hit in its instant cover version by Bill Haley and His Comets. Poor, almost inaudible recordings exist of other Presley shows from early 1955, documenting that the repertoire also included LaVern Baker's "Tweedle Dee" and the Charms' "Hearts Of Stone" (both also covered by the Fontane Sisters), as well as another Clovers song ("Little Mama")—all 1954 releases—and Ray Charles's "I Got A Woman" and the Drifters' "Money Honey," released just weeks before.

The acetate of "Fool, Fool, Fool"
(mislabeled as "What A Fool I Was")

This new recording sensation—the Hillbilly Cat, they were starting to call him—was exploding in the small region around Memphis and the area that the Louisiana Hayride reached, but Bob Neal knew he needed help to make Elvis known beyond those limited borders. When Colonel Parker and his assistant, Tom Diskin, arrived at the Louisiana Hayride, they were met with something very new, very different—something dressed in a rust-colored suit, pink socks, and a purple and black polka-dot tie. Elvis's repertoire, in addition to his recorded tunes, now included current radio hits like "Hearts Of Stone," "Tweedle Dee," and "Shake, Rattle And Roll." What was more astonishing than the music itself, though, was the intensity of his audiences' reactions—particularly the overheated behavior of the girls. This was potential if Tom Parker had ever seen it, and he responded with a modest offer to try Presley out on a Hank Snow package tour set to begin on February 14 in Roswell, New Mexico. It was decided that they would meet before then, at a big show Bob Neal was putting on in Memphis at Ellis Auditorium on February 5, to formalize the arrangement.

With three singles behind him, Sam Phillips knew how important it was to keep putting out product, if only to keep feeding the radio stations "hot" new records to plug. What he was still looking for was a song strong enough to match the impact of the first single. Elvis's first two songs remained his most popular numbers. "Blue Moon Of Kentucky" was stronger on country stations than either of the more country-flavored tunes on the second and third records, "I Don't Care If The Sun Don't Shine" and "You're A Heartbreaker." The two rhythm and blues numbers, "Good Rockin' Tonight" and "Milkcow Blues Boogie," were decent follow-ups, but they lacked the light, breezy, melodic quality that made "That's All Right" such a surprising and successful record.

9. Studio Sessions For Sun
February (?), 1955: Sun Studio, Memphis

Producer/Engineer: Sam Phillips

Guitar: Scotty Moore
Guitar: Elvis Presley

Bass: Bill Black

I Got A Woman
Ray Charles
Trying To Get To You
McCoy/Singleton
F2WB 8046-na   **Baby Let's Play House**   Single A-side
Arthur Gunter—Excellorec Music   SUN 217/1955

RCA received, and subsequently lost, a tape from this session including two takes of "I Got A Woman," two takes (including the master) of "Baby Let's Play House," and one take of "Trying To Get To You." The recording date is generally mentioned as February 5, but given that Elvis performed at the Hayride that night, it's more likely to have been earlier that week.

A session was squeezed in over a few days in early February, and Elvis began by trying out a popular feature from his live act, Ray Charles's groundbreaking "I Got A Woman." Then they ran through another R&B number, Charles Singleton and Rose Marie McCoy's "Trying To Get To You," a current hit for the Eagles, a group out of Washington, D.C. But when they turned to "Baby Let's Play House," yet another regional R&B hit, the Arthur Gunter number clicked right from its sensational start— Elvis's unaccompanied hiccup "Oh, baby, baby, baby . . . ," its rhythm picked up immediately by the loud slapping of Bill's standup bass and Scotty's driving rhythm guitar. The recording captures the quantum leap in confidence that the group had made in the last six months. A line like "I'd rather see you dead, little girl, than to be with another man" suggested a brazenness that transcended mere posing, while the

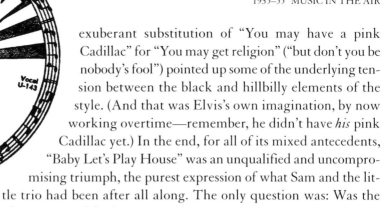

exuberant substitution of "You may have a pink Cadillac" for "You may get religion" ("but don't you be nobody's fool") pointed up some of the underlying tension between the black and hillbilly elements of the style. (And that was Elvis's own imagination, by now working overtime—remember, he didn't have *his* pink Cadillac yet.) In the end, for all of its mixed antecedents, "Baby Let's Play House" was an unqualified and uncompromising triumph, the purest expression of what Sam and the little trio had been after all along. The only question was: Was the world ready for such unrepressed fun?

Bob Neal's show at the Ellis Auditorium in downtown Memphis was headlined by Faron Young, with Martha Carson, Ferlin Husky, the Wilburn Brothers, and—bottom of the bill—Elvis Presley. Neal was hoping to get the Colonel interested in doing more for Elvis than just the occasional booking. To that end he brought Sam Phillips and Thomas A. Parker together for the first time, and it was obvious from the start that the two men didn't like each other. Each was used to having his own way, and they had widely differing agendas for Presley. Phillips, a creative, instinctual, and proud man, was hardly ready to accept the Colonel's claim that Sun, with its limited financial base and distribution, would never be able to take an artist to national success. And Parker recognized that even *with* Sam's cooperation it would take plenty of work to get the young singer onto a national label; if Sam stood in the way, it might prove impossible. In fact, Parker had already mentioned Elvis's name to RCA's country-and-western artist-and-repertoire (A&R) man, Steve Sholes. Sholes had expressed some interest, but for the time being about all Parker felt he could do for the boy was give him the chance to go on the road with the Hank Snow Jamboree.

The Hank Snow tour began in Roswell with a fire-department show and gradually traveled back toward Memphis, picking up occasional local acts along the way. In Lubbock, Texas, for example, Buddy Holly and Bob Montgomery would appear in their first significant billing: This time it was Buddy and Bob at the bottom of the bill, creeping up behind the Hillbilly Cat. Touring with a big name like Snow was great exposure for Elvis, putting him in front of big crowds who often had no clue who he was. With radio stations promoting the shows Elvis started getting more airplay, and with Bob Neal busily working away wherever he could, Elvis's popularity was slowly but surely beginning to build.

Back in Memphis, meanwhile, Sam was getting concerned. The third single had completely stalled, and he was anxious to record something to use as the B-side of "Baby Let's Play House."

10. Studio Sessions For Sun
March (?), 1955: Sun Studios, Memphis

Producer/Engineer: Sam Phillips

Guitar: Scotty Moore   Bass: Bill Black
Guitar: Elvis Presley   Drums: Jimmie Lott

F2WB 8047-05	**I'm Left, You're Right, She's Gone (slow version)**	**A Golden Celebration**
	Kesler/Taylor—Hill & Range	*CPM6 5172/1986*
F2WB 8047-06	**I'm Left, You're Right, She's Gone**	**Single B-side**
	Kesler/Taylor—Hill & Range	*SUN 217/1955*

This song's slow version, take 5, was first released on A Golden Celebration in 1984, but it is not known whether this was ever considered as a master take.

Grasping for ways to broaden Elvis's appeal, Sam turned to a young steel guitarist who had been hanging around Sun hoping to record. Stan Kesler didn't let Sam down, coming up with an original tune, "I'm Left, You're Right, She's Gone," which the group tried first as a slow blues featuring a guitar lick based on the Delmore Brothers' "Blues, Stay Away From Me." When that didn't work, Sam brought in a teenage drummer, Jimmie Lott, employing percussion for the first time on an Elvis Presley session. With this new element in place, the song was completely rearranged to emphasize its melodic country qualities; it wasn't lost on Sam that Arkansas and Texas DJs were getting more requests for the country-influenced "You're A Heartbreaker" than for the beat side, "Milkcow Blues Boogie." In an effort that proved less successful, the young drummer set a rhumba beat to Webb Pierce's "How Do You Think I Feel," but this was quickly abandoned—perhaps for the best, as the song was Hank Snow's son Jimmie Rodgers Snow's new single.

11. Live Recordings
March 19, 1955: Eagles Hall, Houston

Guitar: Scotty Moore   Bass: Bill Black
Guitar: Elvis Presley

Good Rockin' Tonight
Roy Brown
Baby Let's Play House
Arthur Gunter
Blue Moon Of Kentucky
Bill Monroe
I Got A Woman
Ray Charles

That's All Right

Arthur Crudup

Scotty Moore is not convinced that this is the correct recording location; he feels the acoustics on the tape suggest an outdoor location, possibly Magnolia Gardens, also in Houston. If Magnolia Gardens is the location the date could be up to three months later.

12. Live Recordings
April 30, 1955: Gladewater, Texas

Guitar: Scotty Moore
Guitar: Elvis Presley
Bass: Bill Black

Steel Guitar: Jimmy Day
Piano: Floyd Cramer

WPA5 2535 **Tweedle Dee**

Winfield Scott

Elvis: The First Live Recordings
PB 3601/1984

This recording may come from a tape made by KWKH, as the show was a remote broadcast of the Louisiana Hayride.

The famous Houston DJ Biff Collie recalled what he saw as a "vehement reaction" to Elvis's performances, even on the singer's first Houston show back in 1954. By March 1955 Elvis was already a substantial draw, and although the crowd's reaction to his just-recorded (and not yet released) "Baby Let's Play House" was a little hesitant, there was plenty of screaming and hollering when he did his radio hits, as well as "I Got A Woman," the new Ray Charles song he'd been trying out in the studio. "Tweedle Dee" was still in his set list, as it was with so many other touring artists. Back in January, in Lubbock, he'd told a young Waylon Jennings that "Tweedle Dee" would be his next single, but he never got around to recording it, and now a new version was suddenly happening on the R&B stations, by LaVern Baker, a definite favorite of Elvis's.

Bob Neal kept booking dates, trying to figure out how to get national exposure for the group. With help from the Colonel he did manage to get Elvis a tryout in New York City for the "Arthur Godfrey Talent Show," but the young singer was judged "not ready for the big time." Tensions were starting to rise between Neal and Parker; the Memphis DJ was getting concerned about losing his budding star to the older, more experienced ex-carny, and the Colonel was increasingly frustrated by Neal's provincialism and general lack of efficiency and professionalism. Nonetheless, the relative success of the February dates led to a second tour, this time for three weeks beginning in New Orleans on May 1. This tour featured Hank Snow, Faron Young, the Wilburn Brothers, Mother Maybelle and the Carter Sisters, the Davis Sisters (Skeeter and Georgie), Onie Wheeler, and Jimmie Rodgers Snow. As a "special added attraction,"

Elvis would be exposed to territories well beyond the reach of the Hayride and the Memphis radio stations.

In Richmond, Virginia, on May 16, two RCA representatives, regional sales manager Brad McCuen and C&W promotions manager Chick Crumpacker, arrived to check out the show and in particular to support their new RCA hopeful, Jimmie Rodgers Snow. The younger Snow had been signed specifically because of his appeal to a younger audience, and Chick Crumpacker still remembers the shock he felt when Elvis Presley hit the stage. The RCA pair's loyalty to the already-signed Snow couldn't obscure the facts: Elvis blew away not only Jimmie, but everyone else on the show. Crumpacker didn't quite believe what he was seeing: a slicked-up country-rhythm hybrid, so raw he spit out his chewing gum and tossed it into the audience. Chick could have done without that, but the music stayed with him. He bought copies of the four Sun singles the boy had made and took them back to his boss, Steve Sholes.

"The polished style of Elvis Presley came over in true fashion on an intriguing and forceful item with a solid beat." So read *Cashbox*'s verdict on the A-side of Elvis's fourth single, "I'm Left, You're Right, She's Gone," while the magazine called "Baby Let's Play House," its flip, "a real different, fast-paced piece on which Presley sparkles." The April 10 release gave Sun Records what they needed to support the three-week Hank Snow Jamboree tour as it moved around through Virginia, the Carolinas, Georgia, and Florida, and the payback was instantaneous. Because local DJs often had a financial incentive to promote a big show like the Jamboree tour (frequently they were hired on as announcers; sometimes there was a more direct payoff), they almost always pushed artists with upcoming appearances on their radio shows. That was why "Nervous" Ned Needham of WMOP in Ocala, Florida, was the first DJ after Bob Neal to add "I'm Left, You're Right, She's Gone" to his top ten plays, as recorded in the May 15 *Cashbox* charts. WMYR in Fort Myers and Red Smith in New Orleans soon followed suit. Elvis was sparking interest all over the new territory, as well as back in his core region, the mid-South.

And there was some drama to the question of which side would be the hit. Dean Evans of WXOK in Baton Rouge was the first to add "Baby Let's Play House" to his top ten, and throughout July the two sides battled it out from station to station. By mid-August "Baby Let's Play House" had taken the lead, eventually ending the year on the *Cashbox* overall country DJ chart at number twenty-two. Elvis's wild live performances were no doubt fueling the record's progress all over the South, and more than ever they accentuated his difference from anyone else on the traditional country circuit. At the same time there was no question that Sam Phillips's attempt to thread the racial needle had paid off, as "I'm Left, You're Right, She's Gone," with all the bright melodic attractiveness of "That's All Right" and none of the threat of "Baby," won huge country airplay and opened the door to many new markets.

The impact of Elvis's performances on this summer tour—and in particular a highly publicized riot in Jacksonville, Florida—wasn't lost on Colonel Parker. His talks with Bob Neal led to a deal in which the Colonel obtained exclusive booking rights while Neal stayed on as the nominal manager, an arrangement that enabled the Colonel and his assistant Tom Diskin to start pitching Elvis aggressively to promoters throughout the country. Earlier in the year they'd tried without luck to place Elvis in some northern markets; now they included him as part of their artist roster at prices ranging from five hundred dollars as a single act to one thousand dollars for a package show headlined by Elvis—a significant step up for Elvis and the Blue Moon Boys. With such bright future prospects, and a new partnership agreement in hand, Bob Neal finally felt confident enough—overconfident may have been the more appropriate word—to venture out of Memphis and see what he could do about finding Elvis a new, more powerful, record label.

13. Studio Sessions for Sun
July 11, 1955: Sun Studio, Memphis

Guitar: Scotty Moore
Guitar: Elvis Presley
Piano: Elvis Presley? (8039)

Bass: Bill Black
Drums: Johnny Bernero

F2WB 8000-na	**I Forgot To Remember To Forget**	**Single A-side**
	Stan Kesler/Charlie Feathers—E. B. Marks Music	*SUN 223/1955*
F2WB 8001-na	**Mystery Train**	**Single B-side**
	Junior Parker/Sam Phillips—Hill & Range	*SUN 223/1955*
F2WB 8039-na	**Trying To Get To You**	**Elvis Presley**
	Singleton/McCoy—Hill & Range	*LPM 1254/1956*

Elvis's acoustic guitar drops out of the mix on "Trying To Get To You," supporting the suggestion that the piano part, barely audible in the track, may be his own.

Sam Phillips, on the other hand, showed no signs of interest in selling that contract. With Elvis back in Memphis after three July 4 shows in Texas, the only thing Sam had on his mind was cutting yet another single. For material he went back to Stan Kesler, who with Sun artist Charlie Feathers came up with a second country melody with a similar play-on-words title. At first Elvis expressed doubts about "I Forgot To Remember To Forget," but at Sam's urging—and with new drummer Johnny Bernero playing around with the tempo, slowing it down as Sam directed him to—he slowly warmed up to the song. For the R&B side, Sam suggested covering a song he shared the copyright on, Junior Parker's "Mystery Train," a 1953 hit for Sun and all that was left of Parker at the label after a falling-out with Phillips. Combining the melody and lyric of "Mystery Train" with the beat from the B-side of the same Junior Parker single, "Love My Baby," Elvis, Scotty, and Bill drove the track along on their own steam, no drums necessary as the singer wailed about that train, sixteen coaches long. At the end

Elvis broke into delighted laughter, unaware that his chuckle would go down as one of rock 'n' roll's memorable moments. They'd nailed down the single, but that didn't stop Elvis: Going back to "Trying To Get To You" from the last session, this time they tried it with drums—and this time they got it. In Sam's mind, it was another definite contender for future single release.

Over the next few months Tom Parker stepped up his commitment to Elvis Presley. In August he went to Memphis with Tom Diskin to meet with Elvis, his father Vernon, and Bob Neal. The Colonel had conceived a new and far-reaching deal for Neal and the Presleys to sign, in which he would be named as special advisor to both the singer and his manager. The deal would run for one year, with two one-year options, giving him an annual fee of $2,500 plus travel, promotion, and advertising expenses. The most arresting piece of the arrangement was the one that gave the Colonel the rights to one hundred appearances at a fixed rate of $200 per show for Elvis and his band, and the exclusive rights to more than forty specifically named cities in which Elvis had proven successful. A penalty clause was included should Neal take his business elsewhere. The contract called for the Colonel to "assist in any way possible the build-up of Elvis Presley as an artist," and, significantly, entitled him to "negotiate all renewals on existing contracts." This put the Colonel in what amounted to an all-powerful position: He had the exclusive right to steer Elvis Presley's career. It took a lot of maneuvering, a lot of cajoling, a lot of selling to convince Elvis's mother and father that the new arrangement was in their son's best interest, but in the end they signed. Not long afterward, against the Colonel's specific directive, Bob Neal negotiated a renewal of Elvis's Hayride contract for another twelve months—and once again Vernon signed, no doubt feeling caught in the middle and not sure whom to trust.

14. Live Recordings
August 20, 1955: Municipal Auditorium, Shreveport

Guitar: Scotty Moore
Guitar: Elvis Presley

Bass: Bill Black

	Baby Let's Play House	**Elvis: The First Live Recordings**
	Arthur Gunter	*PB 3601/1984*
WPA5 2536	**Maybellene**	**Elvis: The First Live Recordings**
	Chuck Berry	*PB 3601/1984*
	That's All Right	**Elvis: The First Live Recordings**
	Arthur Crudup	*PB 3601/1984*

Elvis's fame in the South had grown so rapidly that he was flooded with booking requests; now he was starting to return to the sites of his earliest appearances, often accompanied by Sun's new recording artist, Johnny Cash. His band now included D. J. Fontana on drums, and frequently Jimmy Day on steel guitar and pianist Floyd Cramer. A return to Florida, where business was better than ever, was followed by another Hank Snow tour through the Southeast, with the popular religious duo Charlie and Ira Louvin and Cowboy Copas; the young star was now getting three hundred dollars per day. On August 27 Nervous Ned Needham was again the first to list the new Presley record, "I Forgot To Remember To Forget" at number ten, even as "Baby Let's Play House" hung on at number three. In Gladewater, Texas, where Elvis had just appeared with Jim Ed and Maxine Brown for a week of engagements, DJ Tom Perryman did Nervous Ned one better, entering "Mystery Train" at number two while "Baby Let's Play House" stood at number four. The two sides of the newest single battled it out for a time until, finally, "I Forgot To Remember To Forget" emerged as the winner, peaking at number seven on the *Cashbox* country charts.

Still looking for a way to break Elvis out of the South, Bob Neal booked Elvis on another Cleveland show, this one hosted by popular DJ Bill Randle. It was on this jaunt that Elvis was filmed as part of a documentary film entitled *A Day in the Life of a D.J.* Jane Scott, an area teenager, remembers, "He was a skinny nineteen-year-old kid in a red suit with white buck shoes and a bad case of acne," and from her point of view he was lost in the shadows of the day's other, bigger stars: Pat Boone, Bill Haley, and the Four Lads. The film would have given Elvis a welcome step toward national recognition, but union disputes kept it from being released, and it was eventually lost. Movement was also stalled in other areas around the country; Elvis was as strong as ever in the South, but Sun's limited distribution and promotion were hampering Neal's efforts to expand the group's horizons. In this climate the relationship between the Colonel and Bob Neal began to deteriorate dramatically, with each appealing to the artist for support and each battling to eclipse the other. The balance of power swung back and forth on a weekly basis, propelled by the Colonel's constant refrain that without a major label contract Elvis's career would never break out. Despite serious misgivings, particularly on the part of Gladys Presley, and despite Elvis's own loyalty to Sam Phillips and Neal, the Colonel gradually gained ground. He promised a lucrative record deal, national television, even a shot at the movies: after all, hadn't he taken both Eddy Arnold and Hank Snow to the top? Why couldn't he do the same for their son?

15. Studio Sessions for Sun
November, 1955: Sun Studio, Memphis

Guitar: Scotty Moore
Guitar: Elvis Presley

Bass: Bill Black
Drums: Johnny Bernero

NPA5 5826-09   **When It Rains, It Really Pours**
William Emerson—Hi-Lo Music

Elvis: A Legendary Performer Vol. 4
CPL1 4848/1983

Take 10 is not an official master, but probably the best take.

When it came time for another single, Sam Phillips and Elvis agreed that all they really needed was a B-side for "Trying To Get To You." Sam suggested Sun artist Billy "the Kid" Emerson's "When It Rains, It Really Pours," and he already had a good idea of how to arrange the song to make it more commercial. As the tape began to roll Sam warned Scotty away from his single-string picking again—"Scotty, don't make it too damn complicated," he told him, insisting on the priority of the beat. But complicated it was, and the session was never completed. Johnny Bernero, the drummer who'd played on "I Forgot To Remember," remembers, "Elvis paid me fifty dollars for a session, which was far more than scale. One night we were recording a good little while. Elvis went into the control booth and talked to Sam a good half hour. He came out and told me, 'Johnny, we're not going to be able to finish this session.' Still, he paid me the fifty dollars." What had happened was what everyone had been waiting for: Speaking with Colonel Tom Parker on the telephone, Sam had just agreed to give the Colonel an option to sell the contract to another label. Sam Phillips the creative innovator might not have wanted to sell Elvis's contract, but Sam Phillips the businessman saw it as a way out of a financial squeeze. Elvis's success had put Sun in a bind: It took a lot of cash to keep product flowing, and Phillips was getting strapped. At the same time he was in need of funds to finance the new radio station, WHER, he was just opening in the brand-new Holiday Inn downtown.

The Colonel, meanwhile, had spent the past weeks in constant talks and negotiations with both Phillips and RCA C&W head Steve Sholes, and he didn't want the release of a new single to jeopardize the deal he'd just about arranged. If Elvis cut a new Sun record that broke through on the national level, Sam's price might go

A log of the Sun tapes transferred to RCA

through the roof—and the Colonel might get cut out of the picture altogether. Sam was already asking an astronomical forty thousand dollars (thirty-five thousand plus back royalties), despite the fact that every record company Parker approached had balked at paying ten thousand to twenty-five thousand dollars for Presley. Now, against all odds, the Colonel and Bob Neal had convinced Sam to give them the option they needed. The Colonel had two weeks to come up with the money. He had already put down five thousand dollars of his own, which he'd lose if he failed to finish the deal. But he was bent on success, and suddenly everything seemed to be going his way.

On November 11, at the Country Disc Jockey Convention in Nashville, Elvis was voted the most promising country male artist of 1955. There was already talk that he'd soon be moving to RCA; when songwriter Mae Boren Axton brought Elvis a new song, "Heartbreak Hotel," he promised her he'd make it his first RCA single. The Colonel was left with three days to complete the forty-thousand-dollar deal for the young man's contract. He succeeded in getting some financial support from the Aberbach Brothers, owners of the Hill & Range song-publishing company, in exchange for a copublishing deal with the artist, and that may be what put RCA over the top. In any case, RCA finally agreed to the deal, and even threw in a promise to help set up some national TV appearances for Elvis in the early months of the following year. On November 15, just as Parker's option was about to expire, the deal was finalized; on November 21 all the parties gathered at the Sun studio to sign on the dotted line. All his maneuvering had finally paid off: Colonel Tom Parker had succeeded in placing Elvis Presley on the brink of stardom.

1956

It All Happened So Fast

*The NAME: Elvis Presley, one that will be your guarantee of
sensational plus sales in the months to come!*

John Burgess, Jr.
Manager of Sales and Promotions
Single Record Department, RCA
November 28, 1955

"Biggest C&W Record News of the Year" was the headline for the information sheet
John Burgess distributed to his staff just days after RCA Victor signed Elvis Presley on
November 21, 1955. The record Burgess was promoting, "I Forgot To Remember To
Forget"/"Mystery Train," was a new RCA re-pressing of Elvis's fifth and final Sun release, which RCA took over after it started to lose momentum on *Billboard*'s national
country charts. The thirty-five thousand dollars RCA had paid for this twenty-year-
old's contract was the largest purchase price for a pop act up to that time, and the label
was anxious to start getting its money back even before the first scheduled RCA
recording session in January 1956. Burgess's aggressive campaign included sending
out more than four thousand promo records—to every pop and C&W radio station on
the so-called A list—as well as full-page ads, run twice in both *Billboard* and *Cashbox*
with publicity stories to match. By mid-December the effort had paid off: Daily re-
orders climbed to 3,700 units, and the single started heading back up the country
charts, this time on its way to number one. A dynamic Popsie photograph of Elvis,
taken at a summer concert in Tampa, was blown up for counter and window dis-
plays—the same image that would later appear on the sleeve of Elvis Presley's first
RCA Victor album.

John Burgess's prediction that the name of Elvis Presley would "guarantee sales"
was starting to sound plausible when on December 19 the singer was signed to four appearances on Jackie Gleason's CBS-TV program "Stage Show" (starring swing-era vet-
erans Jimmy and Tommy Dorsey), starting in January, with an option for two more.
With network television locked into Elvis's upcoming schedule, Burgess was justified
in calling his new artist "the year's most publicized recording star and the brightest new
hope for 1956."

This was certainly the dream of Colonel Parker, who with the sale to RCA had effectively taken over Elvis's management from Bob Neal. "We'll do great things to-

gether," Parker confided to RCA promotion man Chick Crumpacker as they slogged with Tom Diskin through the snow after a December 4 show at the Lyric Theater in Indianapolis. And there were things to do: Elvis was much improved as a showman, the three agreed, but there was still a rough edge to his performances that would have to be hammered out before too long.

Then Elvis was back on the road, careening through the mid-South on the same frenetic touring schedule he'd sustained for the past year. When he appeared at Bob King's club just north of Swifton, Arkansas, on December 9, he entertained a full house of 250 with the customary three forty-five-minute sets, backed by Scotty and Bill and drummer D. J. Fontana, who'd joined on in August. After going through his Sun Records repertoire and a few predictable covers (Bill Haley's "Rock Around the Clock," the Platters' "Only You"), Elvis announced, "I've got this brand new song and it's gonna be my first hit," then launched into the as-yet-unrecorded "Heartbreak Hotel." During the last weeks of December and the first week of the new year he barnstormed through the small auditoriums and schoolhouses of Arkansas and Mississippi, frequently appearing with Johnny Cash and Sun's other hot new act, Carl Perkins. And he honored his contract with the Louisiana Hayride, performing his Sun hits along with cover ver-

Colonel Tom Parker, RCA artist Eddy Arnold, and Steve Sholes with their new discovery:
New York, December 1, 1955

sions of "I Got A Woman," "Shake, Rattle And Roll," "Money Honey," "Tutti Frutti," and "Sixteen Tons."

As Elvis made his way around the country, Steve Sholes, potentially the chief scapegoat for Elvis Presley's signing, was busily combing through material for the all-important recording session scheduled for the second week of January. Sholes was desperate to find hits that would justify the company's investment and, just as significantly, his own role in the signing. Just before Christmas he sent ten demonstration records with lyric sheets to Elvis's 1414 Getwell Street address in Memphis. In the accompanying letter Sholes asked the young singer, whom at this point he had barely met, to listen to the songs carefully and let him know which ones he liked.

Finally, at two o'clock in the afternoon on January 10, the waiting was over. Everything was ready—as ready as it could be, anyway—at RCA's Nashville recording facility, located in a building on McGavock Street owned by the Methodist TV, Radio and Film Commission. Steve Sholes had asked Chet Atkins, his Nashville coordinator, to set up the sessions. Scotty and Bill were both there, along with D. J. Fontana, who hadn't yet recorded with the group. Added to this nucleus was piano player Floyd Cramer, who brought his partner, steel guitar player Jimmy Day, strictly to observe. Chet Atkins was there to play rhythm guitar. Ben and Brock Speer, whose family gospel group the Speer Family had recently signed to the label, were on call to sing backup on the ballads along with Gordon Stoker of the Jordanaires, but they weren't due to be called until the second day. On hand in the control room with Steve Sholes were Tom Parker and "Heartbreak Hotel" coauthor Mae Boren Axton, who'd once been Parker's publicity aide. Axton had written the song that fall with fellow Jacksonville songwriter and performer Tommy Durden, and promised him a third of the song's copyright; now it was Elvis's turn to fulfill his promise and make it his first RCA single.

16. Studio Sessions for RCA
January 10–11, 1956: RCA Studios, Nashville

Engineer: Bob Ferris

Guitar: Scotty Moore
Guitar: Chet Atkins
Guitar: Elvis Presley
Bass: Bill Black

Drums: D. J. Fontana
Piano: Floyd Cramer
Vocals: Gordon Stoker, Ben & Brock Speer

1/10, 2–5PM

G2WB 0208-08   **I Got A Woman**   **Elvis Presley**
Ray Charles—Progressive Music   *LPM 1254/1956*

G2WB 0209-07   **Heartbreak Hotel**   **Single A-side**
Mae Boren Axton/Tommy Durden/Elvis Presley—Tree Music   *47-6420/1956*

7–10PM

G2WB 0210-sp   **Money Honey**   **Elvis Presley**
Jesse Stone—Walden Music   *LPM 1254/1956*

1/11, 4–7PM

G2WB 0211-17   **I'm Counting On You**   **Elvis Presley**
Don Robertson—Ross Jungnickel   *LPM 1254/1956*

G2WB 0218-07   **I Was The One**   **Single B-side**
Schroeder/DeMetrius/Blair/Peppers—Ross Jungnickel   *47-6420/1956*

The master of "Money Honey" (0210) is spliced from takes 5 and 6.

Any apprehension Steve Sholes or anyone else in the room might have felt was scarcely reflected in the performance of the young man at the center of everybody's attention. Without any apparent nervousness or any more than the normal effort he put into every performance, Elvis kicked off Ray Charles's "I Got A Woman," a staple of his live act and a number he'd already tried at an earlier Sun session. Once Floyd Cramer got the piano part sorted out there was no stopping them, and they had their first RCA master within an hour. Elvis may have looked to Chet Atkins or Steve Sholes for direction, but when none was forthcoming he intuitively moved ahead with his own agenda. With the warm-up of "I Got A Woman" out of the way, Elvis moved to Mae Axton's song. It would have been hard to say what genre "Heartbreak Hotel" was written in—perhaps it was more like a blues than anything else—but Elvis and his band had been doing it live for months, and they knew what to make of it. With just a few takes and a change in the lyrics ("they pray to die" became simply "they could die"), Elvis's first hit was in the can.

The entire three-hour evening session was consumed trying to capture another familiar R&B favorite, and another song familiar to anyone who'd seen them live: "Money Honey," the Drifters hit of 1953. They couldn't get a perfect take on the song, but they got two that were nearly perfect and spliced them together. The sessions came to a close late the following afternoon, with Elvis recording the two ballads he had selected from Sholes's list. Contributed by professional writers, these songs represented a breath of diversity for Elvis's repertoire; the songs he'd suggested himself were all basically R&B, but "I'm Counting On You" was more of a country ballad, while "I Was The One" had an element of doo-wop in its structure. Still, they all came out sounding like Elvis.

The ballads Sholes had brought were published by Ross Jungnickel, a subsidiary of Hill & Range, the New York— and West Coast—based country song publisher who had helped underwrite the RCA deal in exchange for a role in the recording process. In partnership with Colonel Parker and Elvis, the brothers Jean and Julian Aberbach who owned the company would set up two publishing firms for Elvis, Elvis Presley Music and Gladys Music, in which they would share fifty-fifty with the new RCA artist. When informed that his song "I'm Counting On You" was going to be cut not by a major artist but by a newcomer he'd never heard of, ace Hill & Range songwriter Don Robertson was disappointed. The band had had problems with ballad material in live performances, so Chet Atkins took a far more active role on the afternoon of January 11, not only suggesting simple arrangements but offering the solid underpinning of his own guitar work. Elvis, meanwhile, was ready with some bravura vocal tricks of his own; in later interviews he'd often recall the second ballad, "I Was The One," as one of the proudest moments of his early RCA career.

Following standard Nashville recording procedure, Steve Sholes's aim would undoubtedly have been to

From the first RCA publicity shoot

spend three hours in the studio cutting four sides, to end up as either two singles releases or one single and two album cuts. But Elvis had taken nine hours in the studio to come up with only five sides, and Sholes knew only "Heartbreak Hotel" had A-side potential. Besides that he had two covers and two ballads, and while Sholes may have known that Elvis had wanted to cut ballads since he first set foot in the Sun studio, the Nashville A&R chief was very unsure of their commercial potential. The sound on the other songs was murky, there was none of the country-flavored material that had worked so well on the last two Sun releases, and the executives in RCA's New York offices, Sholes knew, were already sharpening their knives for him. Elvis, for his part, was more than satisfied. He had fully realized "Heartbreak Hotel," a song he believed in; he had successfully recorded ballads in the quartet context he loved so well; and he had remade two favorite songs by R&B artists he fervently admired. With his twenty-first birthday only two days behind him, in his first time in the studio without Sam Phillips, he had taken control.

But back in RCA's New York headquarters the reaction to the session was as bleak as Sholes had feared. The sound Sholes had gotten, they complained, was nothing like Sam Phillips's crisp, vibrant Sun sound. Carl Perkins's "Blue Suede Shoes" was starting to heat up the airwaves, and some suggested he'd signed the wrong Sun artist. Others told him he ought to go back to Nashville and do the session all over.

Steve booked time at RCA's New York studios to work on the Nashville tapes and to come up with a plan for Elvis's Sun material. Sholes had purchased all of Sam's Elvis tapes to keep Sun from trying to piggyback off RCA's future success with future Elvis singles, but he also suspected that the Elvis tracks Phillips had rejected as singles would make fine album cuts. If indeed Elvis proved just another flash in the pan, he could forget about "Heartbreak Hotel" and just repackage some of the best Sun titles. "I Forgot To Remember to Forget"/"Mystery Train" was still selling very well, so Sholes mastered an extended play (EP) record grouping those two songs with what he considered the strongest of the other Sun items, "That's All Right" and "Baby Let's Play House," holding it while he considered his options. It was a matter of faith, and of sitting and waiting. Elvis's upcoming TV gig—four appearances in two months—was a real chance to make something happen; with the right song, there was still the chance that Elvis could go all the way. It was "Heartbreak Hotel" that Elvis himself believed in, and with an eye on the TV shows Steve Sholes decided to make that the single. But there was no reason not to take out a little insurance: He scheduled Elvis for another session on January 30, just three days after the release of "Heartbreak Hotel," this time in New York City. In his distress Sholes called Sam Phillips, unburdening all of his doubts and those of his RCA compatriots. Sam didn't like "Heartbreak Hotel" one bit, but he offered the advice that had sustained him with all his own artists, including Elvis: Just be patient. Sholes was grateful, but he also wanted something more concrete; by the end of the conversation he'd secured Phillips's blessing to let Elvis record and release his own version of Carl Perkins's Sun hit "Blue Suede Shoes"—under certain conditions, it was understood, and only as a last resort.

Elvis stayed for more than a week when he came to New York, doing promotion work and going back into the studio with Sholes as well as making his first appearance on "Stage Show." Hoping to get a fuller sound, Sholes had hired boogie-woogie piano player Shorty Long for the session, but this time there were no backup singers. On the original Sun recordings there had been no other voices, and that was, after all, the sound Sholes was aiming to reproduce.

17. Studio Sessions for RCA
January 30–31 and February 3, 1956: RCA Studios, New York

Guitar: Scotty Moore
Guitar: Elvis Presley
Bass: Bill Black

Drums: D. J. Fontana
Piano: Shorty Long
Vocal overdub: Presley, Moore, Black, Fontana (1294)

1/30, 11AM–2PM

G2WB 1230-10	**Blue Suede Shoes**	**Elvis Presley**
	Carl Perkins—Hi-Lo Music	*LPM 1254/1956*
G2WB 1231-09	**My Baby Left Me**	**Single B-side**
	Arthur Crudup—Elvis Presley Music	*47-6540/1956*

3–6PM

G2WB 1232-08	**One-Sided Love Affair**	**Elvis Presley**
	Bill Campbell—Sheldon Music	*LPM 1254/1956*
G2WB 1233-10	**So Glad You're Mine**	**Elvis**
	Arthur Crudup—Elvis Presley Music	*LPM 1382/1956*

1/31, 12–3PM

G2WB 1254-18	**I'm Gonna Sit Right Down And Cry (Over You)**	**Elvis Presley**
	Thomas/Biggs—Royal Music	*LPM 1254/1956*
G2WB 1255-10	**Tutti Frutti**	**Elvis Presley**
	Dorothy LaBostrie/Richard Penniman—Venice Music	*LPM 1254/1956*

2/3, 10:30AM–1:30PM

G2WB 1293-10	**Lawdy, Miss Clawdy**	**Elvis Presley (EP)**
	Lloyd Price—Venice Music	*EPA 830/1956*
G2WB 1294-12	**Shake, Rattle And Roll**	**Elvis Presley (EP)**
	Charles Calhoun—Progressive Music	*EPA 830/1956*

Things were more difficult as they got started in RCA's studios in New York. There was a hesitation and stiffness in Elvis's voice in the ten takes it took to produce a cover of Carl Perkins's "Blue Suede Shoes" on that first day; maybe Elvis felt uncomfortable "stealing" a former stablemate's song, or maybe he was taken aback by the unspoken, but perfectly understood, doubt in the air about his own potential. Sholes was still having a hard time figuring out how to record his singer. No matter what he did he couldn't seem to replicate the warm, condensed, natural sound Sam got in the Sun studio, despite all the technical limitations of the Memphis recording room and its equipment. That didn't make Elvis's version of "Blue Suede Shoes" a failure, though it did set it apart from what had come before; energy and toughness were starting to replace the natural swing and underplayed charm of both Presley's Sun sides and Perkins's original.

When the group launched into "My Baby Left Me," it was a different story. Like "That's All Right" it was written by blues singer Arthur Crudup, and save for the addition of drums and piano the feel was close to that of the Sun sides. Sholes stuck to what had worked in the past; with no idea of anything new to do with Elvis, it was hardly a bad strategy. Of the many songs he'd sent the young singer, only "One Sided Love Affair" passed muster with Elvis, and even that may have been a gesture of politeness from the ever-courteous young southerner. Once he'd accepted the challenge, though, Elvis and the band did their best to beef up the country song on every level. Shorty Long played serious boogie-woogie, Elvis threw in almost every vocal trick he knew, and the result was more than worthwhile. The last song of the day was another Crudup cover, closer in feel to "My Baby Left Me" than to "That's All Right." "So Glad You're Mine" fit the singer like a glove, and if Steve Sholes couldn't duplicate the Sun sound, by now at least he was getting somewhere on his own. Presley sounded totally confident, the band played better than you'd have thought they could from watching them live, and what the well-tested cover material lacked in originality, it made up in energy and urgency.

The next day brought two more favorites, and Elvis's first cover of another of his musical idols. Elvis very much admired R&B singer Roy Hamilton, especially on dramatic ballads like "Unchained Melody," "Hurt," and "You'll Never Walk Alone." On the B-side of the last Hamilton had recorded a cover of Joe Thomas's "I'm Gonna Sit Right Down And Cry (Over You)," and Elvis had sung it on the Louisiana Hayride back when he had only four songs out on record. Now he did an inspired job on the Hamilton number, putting down a take that echoed some of the bouncy swing he'd captured at Sun. His next pick, a stab at Little Richard's "Tutti Frutti," though a favorite at live performances, leaned more toward the cleaner, almost northern aggressiveness of his "Blue Suede Shoes"; where Little Richard had sounded manic, Elvis just seemed a little rushed.

Steve Sholes, who wished Elvis had liked more than one of the six songs he'd submitted, still needed to come up with a follow-up to "Heartbreak Hotel," so the group returned to the studio three days later. Demonstrating once again that he was capable of making a fresh and convincing version of an already classic recording, Elvis took on Lloyd Price's "Lawdy Miss Clawdy." There was a little nervous laughter as they got going, an indication that the real confidence Elvis often displayed in front of a microphone could be quickly shattered when he or the band made a mistake. But it was almost never Elvis who goofed; instead it became an established pattern that it took the band about ten takes to play a song without any serious mistakes. In the absence of any more original material he liked, Elvis next turned to Big Joe Turner's R&B hit "Shake, Rattle and Roll," which had taken Bill Haley to national stardom two years earlier. After a handful of takes, Sholes expressed concern at the lyric "You're wearing them dresses, the sun comes shining through," suggesting Elvis leave that verse out. (At the same time he seemed unaware of the suggestiveness of another line, "I'm like a one-eyed cat, peeping in the seafood store"; even an A&R man as well versed in R&B and country as Sholes wasn't necessarily hep to what was really going down.) When the verse went out, so did Shorty Long's piano solo, and it took Elvis an additional take to get used to the change. In the end Sholes felt the song needed backing vocals, so Elvis and the band overdubbed the part themselves, singing to a playback of the master take while the engineer mixed the two sources onto a new tape—the first and last time that ever happened.

At the end of the sessions, Sholes was still feeling the same concerns he had at the start. He wrote to Colonel Parker, "On Friday we didn't have any new material that suited Elvis so we recorded 'Lawdy Miss Clawdy' and 'Shake, Rattle and Roll.' Neither one of the two will be suitable for single release, but I know they will make good selections for the second album." (Sholes hadn't yet finished the first album, though he must have been assuming it would be comprised almost entirely of leftover Sun material.) Sholes's momentary doubts aside, the eight sides from the New York sessions were a beautiful documentation of latter-day Elvis Presley, just before his style began changing. They were recorded truly professionally; as Sholes saw, they would make excellent album material. But only "Blue Suede Shoes" would be strong enough for single release, and then only with Sam's permission. Well aware that the Colonel had Elvis tied up in a heavy schedule of touring, Sholes now had something new to worry about: When was he going to be able to get Elvis back to cut a proper single?

The TV card had been the trump in the Colonel's pitch to take over Elvis's management; he'd insisted to the Presleys and Bob Neal that television was the only way to break the boy nationally, and that only he could deliver it. Likewise, RCA's promise to secure a TV gig for Elvis was a crucial part of their offer. So when the deal with "Stage Show" had been finalized in December, it wasn't so much the $1,250 per show that was important—it was the fulfillment of a promise, and the chance to make a national impression. The show, hosted by big band leaders Jimmy and Tommy Dorsey, wasn't exactly the hottest thing on TV, but its lackluster ratings made it more flexible in its bookings, and the influence of the mighty RCA was enough to make the difference.

18. TV Soundtrack Recordings for CBS's "Stage Show" January–March 1956: CBS Studios, New York

Guitar: Scotty Moore
Guitar: Elvis Presley
Bass: Bill Black

Drums: D. J. Fontana
Vocals: n/a (2/18 only)
The Dorsey Orchestra

1/28

OPA1 4199 **Shake, Rattle And Roll/Flip, Flop And Fly**
Charles Calhoun; Charles Calhoun/Lou Willie Turner

A Golden Celebration
CPM6 5172/1984

OPA1 4200 **I Got A Woman**
Ray Charles

A Golden Celebration
CPM6 5172/1984

2/4

OPA1 4801 **Baby Let's Play House**
Arthur Gunter

A Golden Celebration
CPM6 5172/1984

OPA1 4802 **Tutti Frutti**
Dorothy LaBostrie/Richard Penniman

A Golden Celebration
CPM6 5172/1984

2/11

OPA1 4803 **Blue Suede Shoes**
Carl Perkins

A Golden Celebration
CPM6 5172/1984

OPA1 4804 **Heartbreak Hotel**
Axton/Durden/Presley

A Golden Celebration
CPM6 5172/1984

2/18

OPA1 4805 **Tutti Frutti**
Dorothy LaBostrie/Richard Penniman

A Golden Celebration
CPM6 5172/1984

OPA1 4806 **I Was The One**
Schroeder/DeMetrius/Blair/Peppers

A Golden Celebration
CPM6 5172/1984

3/17

OPA1 4807 **Blue Suede Shoes**
Carl Perkins

A Golden Celebration
CPM6 5172/1984

OPA1 4808 **Heartbreak Hotel**
Axton/Durden/Presley

A Golden Celebration
CPM6 5172/1984

3/24

OPA1 4809 **Money Honey**
Jesse Stone

A Golden Celebration
CPM6 5172/1984

OPA1 4810 **Heartbreak Hotel**
Axton/Durden/Presley

A Golden Celebration
CPM6 5172/1984

"Shake, Rattle And Roll/Flip, Flop And Fly" (OPA1 4199) and "Heartbreak Hotel" (OPA1 4808) were first released on *This Is Elvis* (CPL2 4031) with overdubbed drums; *A Golden Celebration* represents their first undubbed release. All six shows were recorded before live audiences.

Despite the poor ratings, four consecutive Saturdays of national TV exposure was nothing to sneeze at. For a young and, by New York standards, unproven artist, it was unheard of. The show did require that the songs Elvis performed be those that worked out best in rehearsal. The Colonel and RCA had timed the release of "Heartbreak Hotel" to coincide with the first TV appearance, and it would have been natural for Elvis to debut the song on that first show, but evidently his rehearsal wasn't convincing enough for the Dorseys to give it a go. So for the first two Saturdays in a row, Elvis Presley, in his first national appearances, performed nothing but the kind of rocking covers of R&B material he'd been playing around the South for two years. The performances were high-powered, almost to the point of taking off. As the band sped through their two songs a show, the nation got its first look at Elvis Presley: an awkward, wild, almost bizarre young man, who made faces straight out of a silent movie farce while shaking his legs in a manner that had more to do with Saturday-night Southern Baptist revivals than prime-time TV. The set itself was dark, the lighting dramatic, and with lyrics like "I've got so many women, I don't know which way to jump," the television audience was definitely being served its first helping of a kind of entertainment no average white American household expected its children to be exposed to.

Meanwhile the powerful RCA radio promotion department worked overtime to get Elvis on stations around the nation, insisting that not just the South but the whole country was their marketplace. The push applied to the five rereleased Sun singles eventually propelled "I

On the Dorsey Brothers'
"Stage Show"

Forgot To Remember To Forget" to number one, but only on the country charts. Then, on the third "Stage Show," Elvis was finally allowed to perform "Heartbreak Hotel," the song RCA needed him to do. The EP Steve Sholes had prepared back in January had been shelved, but in the aftermath of the New York sessions he worked up another safeguard EP, this one built around the cover of "Blue Suede Shoes," in effect fudging his agreement with Sam Phillips not to release the song as a single. The performance of this song on the third Dorsey show was a reasonable approximation of the recorded version, and it certainly came across better than the awkward debut of "Heartbreak Hotel." The fault the first time out had lain not with Elvis or the band but with the Dorsey orchestra, who tried to fill out the song with a full-band arrangement but achieved only confusion; unable to follow the singer's rhythms, they performed the entire last verse off-beat. Even Elvis himself got caught up in the mess, slipping back into the original lyric "they pray to die" instead of the more neutral "they could die" they'd decided on for the recorded version. That was the end of the fancy Dorsey arrangements.

By the time of the third show the option for two more appearances at $1,500 each had already been picked up. The Colonel knew he needed to get out of the deal with the Louisiana Hayride, and eventually chose a ten-thousand-dollar buyout over sending his boy back to Shreveport almost every week for paltry wages. With his TV performances well underway (and even before Elvis achieved national chart success at RCA) the Colonel's gaze was already moving westward, to Hollywood. During his time with Eddy Arnold, Parker had forged a long-term relationship with William Morris Agency head Abe Lastfogel, and the head of the New York office, Harry Kalcheim; Parker had first thrown the Elvis TV assignment to them for booking, but the agency was slow to take the young star seriously, and Parker had given the job instead to a young independent agent, Steve Yates. Now the Morris agents were moving fast, trying to make up for their loss of exclusivity on Presley. And there weren't just movies to consider: The Colonel also wanted Elvis to play Las Vegas, a showcase that could demonstrate once and for all to the entertainment industry that his boy had really made it.

While the Colonel schemed and plotted, Elvis was on the road every weekday between his Saturday-night TV spots, appearing in a new town every night, often doing more than one show. Meanwhile, at RCA, Sholes was still pushing the Colonel to get Elvis back into the studio to record that follow-up single and lay down some more album tracks. The first album, simply called *Elvis Presley,* was assembled using five of the Sun rejects. Sholes had four more RCA cuts available, but felt he needed to stretch the material as much as possible, insecure as he was about

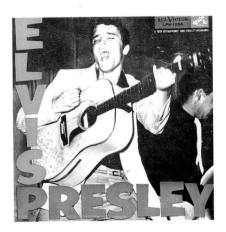

The first album

how, when, and what to record. The sales division was moving records into new terri-tories, and they needed Elvis to make personal appearances in New York, the Midwest, and Los Angeles, areas where the records had not yet proven themselves. Finally, in March, rock 'n' roll burst out of its southern radio base and flooded into mainstream pop, as both "Heartbreak Hotel" and Carl Perkins's original "Blue Suede Shoes" en-tered the *Billboard* charts, Presley's record at number sixty-eight, Perkins's at number eighty-six. The following week "Heartbreak Hotel" leapt forty places, but it was left in the dust by "Blue Suede Shoes," fast on its way to becoming the anthem of a generation as it reached number twenty-three. Once again Steve Sholes suffered a crisis of confi-dence, but both records continued to rise until March 17, with Elvis's fifth television ap-pearance, in which he delivered very convincing versions of both songs, then repeated his own single "by popular request" on the final show. The battle was ended; "Heartbreak Hotel" shot past the Perkins hit once and for all. The night before that final show, on March 23, Elvis flew directly into New York while his band, who were driving, made a brief stop at the Dover, Maryland, hospital where Carl Perkins was re-covering from a car accident in which he and his two brothers had been seriously in-jured. Perkins himself had been on his way to New York to make his debut on national TV, on the rival "Perry Como Show." Elvis sent a telegram that concluded, "If I can help in any way please call me," then substituted "Money Honey" for "Blue Suede Shoes" on the show the following night. And Tommy Dorsey made the announcement that Elvis was going straight to Hollywood for a screen test.

19. TV Soundtrack Recordings for NBC's "The Milton Berle Show" April 3, 1956: The U.S.S. *Hancock*, San Diego Naval Station

Guitar: Scotty Moore
Guitar: Elvis Presley

Bass: Bill Black
Drums: D. J. Fontana

Shake, Rattle And Roll
Charles Calhoun

OPA1 4811   **Heartbreak Hotel**
Axton/Durden/Presley

A Golden Celebration
CPM6 5172/1984

OPA1 4812   **Blue Suede Shoes**
Carl Perkins

A Golden Celebration
CPM6 5172/1984

"Blue Suede Shoes" was performed twice on the show, and both versions were released on *A Golden Celebration*, using the same matrix number.

With his first EP just out (the "Blue Suede Shoes" compilation, titled simply *Elvis Presley*), Elvis was certainly in a position to make his own song selections for the up-coming "The Milton Berle Show," and he took advantage of the opportunity with sizzling versions of "Blue Suede Shoes." His performance on the deck of the U.S.S. *Hancock* in San Diego, cheered on by an audience of appreciative sailors and their dates (and egged on by the ever-popular Uncle Miltie), provided the most efficient and direct record promotion RCA could have imagined. Elvis looked better than he had on any of the "Stage Shows"—thinner, with less grease in his hair, and sporting a big smile—and Steve Sholes finally began to relax.

At RCA suddenly everything was coming up roses. "Heartbreak Hotel" was in the top ten, the B-side, "I Was The One," in the top thirty; the album was charting; and on April 7 the EP entered the top one hundred at number eighty-eight. Now the only concern Sholes had was the next single. He was confident of "My Baby Left Me" for the rock 'n' roll side, but he felt he needed an original song for the A-side, and for that he needed the Colonel to let Elvis get back in the studio. It wasn't that Colonel Parker wanted to deny Sholes a new single, but his constant cautiousness and concern about overexposure were simply fed by the new opportunities he was being presented with every day: opportunities to make money, and to move into new fields. Elvis was scheduled to open in Las Vegas in late April. In the meantime, ongoing discussions with Hollywood and various TV companies required that the singer be available on short notice. And then there was the ever-increasing number of offers for personal appearances, which, by now, were just flooding in.

But the cancellation of the Hayride contract had freed up all the Saturdays in April, so the Colonel arranged for Elvis, Scotty, and Bill to fly to Nashville after a Friday-night show in Amarillo, giving them one day in the studio. What happened next became a story retold on the back of *Elvis' Golden Records* two years later: The chartered flight almost didn't make it. The pilot got lost in the dark after takeoff, landed, had trouble with the fuel tank, landed again, and after one or two additional mishaps left Elvis and the band in Nashville, safe and sound, but in a state of near panic.

20. Studio Sessions for RCA
April 14, 1956: RCA Studios, Nashville

Engineer: Bob Ferris

Guitar: Scotty Moore
Guitar: Chet Atkins
Guitar: Elvis Presley
Bass: Bill Black

Drums: D. J. Fontana
Piano: Marvin Hughes
Vocals: Gordon Stoker, Ben & Brock Speer

9AM–12PM

G2WB 0271-sp   **I Want You, I Need You, I Love You**   Single A-side
Maurice Mysels/Ira Kosloff—Elvis Presley Music   47-6540/1956

The master is spliced from takes 14 and 17.

When the group finally arrived at the studio, they weren't in much of a mood for recording. Steve Sholes was on hand to present Elvis with a gold record for "Heartbreak Hotel," and a *Life* magazine photographer was waiting to do a story on the phenomenal rise of the young singer. After Elvis posed for photos with the gold record the session finally got underway; Elvis stripped off his jacket and shoes to record in his stocking feet, his hands stuck deep into the back pockets of his black pants. He had come to the session with no new ideas, so he had little choice but to go with what Sholes had brought. The first suggestion was "I Want You, I Need You, I Love You," a song that under ordinary circumstances Elvis might have rejected. It was a ballad with a beat, but for whatever reason it came out sounding stiff, no matter what they did. The terrifying plane ride couldn't have helped, nor could the band's crazy schedule or the fact that they weren't used to working that early in the day. For whatever reason they made little progress from take to take, and Elvis, normally the fastest of learners, couldn't keep from messing up the words again and again. Marvin Hughes had replaced Floyd Cramer on piano for this session, but otherwise the group was the same as it had been in January, with Ben and Brock Speer and Gordon Stoker providing the backup voices. This time, though, the vocals didn't sound quite right; Gordon felt "it wasn't a real quartet," and when he told Elvis as much, the two agreed that from now on Stoker's group, the Jordanaires, would act as Elvis's backup singers. After just three hours, seventeen takes, and more than a hundred photographs, Elvis and the band flew through turbulent weather back to Memphis and a brief visit with their families before rejoining the tour in San Antonio the following day.

Sholes himself wasn't disappointed with the recording he got, but he was certainly unhappy with

Nashville, April 14, 1956

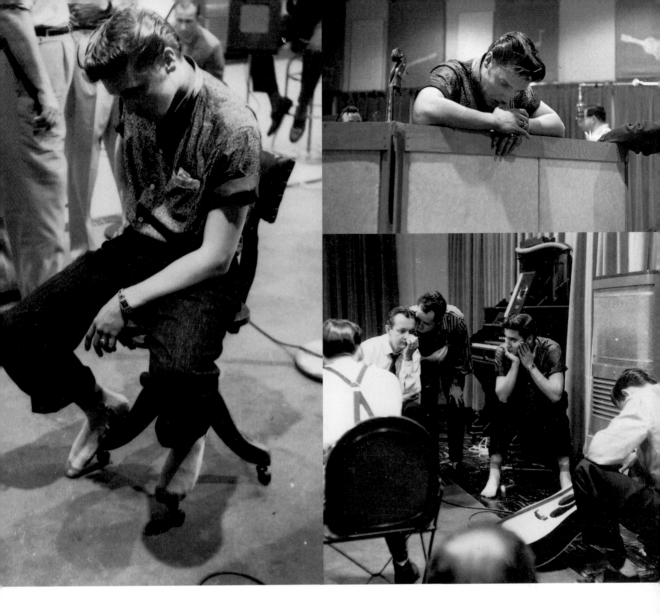

the bigger picture. He wrote the Colonel right away to complain about what a "hassle" the whole session had been, and to express his frustration that producing a second album seemed to be such a low priority to everyone but him. Elaborate arrangements had been made to fly the musicians into Nashville, and the result was just a single song, when the three-hour session should have produced four masters. In the eyes of a very professional man, this was unprofessional behavior. Steve had also noticed that Elvis and Chet Atkins didn't seem to hit it off and wondered whether that was why the record didn't sound as good as the session Steve himself had overseen in New York. Gordon Stoker remembers that Chet had referred to the young singer as just "another flash in the pan"—but then Gordon also felt it was Chet who had pushed aside his group in the first place in favor of the Speers, who were under contract to RCA.

Sholes's concerns weren't bothering anyone else at the record company, where the only problem now was how to fill the miraculously escalating orders. "Heartbreak Hotel" was a winner by every measure. Elvis earned the Triple Crown award for achieving the top spot on sales, DJ, and jukebox charts. He was number one not just in pop, but on the country and R&B charts as well. The EP featuring "Blue Suede Shoes" was now in the top-thirty singles chart, along with the B-side of the single, "I Was The One." The album, too, catapulted into the number-one position, where it remained for a solid ten weeks, giving the label its first million-dollar pop album. To add to the furor, the new coupling of "I Want You, I Need You, I Love You" and "My Baby Left Me" would be released to pre-orders of more than 300,000, the largest in the history of the label. During the month of May sales of Elvis product would rise to fifty percent of the total pop sales at RCA, already one of the biggest record companies in the United States.

21. Private Recordings
May 6, 1956: Venus Room, New Frontier Hotel, Las Vegas

Guitar: Scotty Moore
Guitar: Elvis Presley
Bass: Bill Black

Drums: D. J. Fontana
Freddy Martin's Orchestra

KPA5 9538	**Heartbreak Hotel**	**Elvis Aron Presley**
	Axton/Durden/Presley	*CPL8 3699/1980*
KPA5 9539	**Long Tall Sally**	**Elvis Aron Presley**
	Johnson/Penniman/Blackwell	*CPL8 3699/1980*
KPA5 9540	**Blue Suede Shoes**	**Elvis Aron Presley**
	Carl Perkins	*CPL8 3699/1980*
KPA5 9541	**Money Honey**	**Elvis Aron Presley**
	Jesse Stone	*CPL8 3699/1980*

The above four songs comprise Elvis's complete performance on the last day of his two-week engagement at the hotel.

Las Vegas was something of a miscalculation. The audiences weren't the young teenagers who so reliably swooned over Elvis's music, to be sure. Elvis's corny jokes, the tiny sound of his three-piece band, and his provocative style found little sympathy with the Las Vegas regulars, but Elvis and the band enjoyed themselves anyway. In fact, the time Elvis spent catching other acts on the Strip may have proved more valuable than anything else he did during those two weeks. Most significant were the performances he witnessed by Freddie Bell and the Bellboys, whose act included a takeoff on blues singer Big Mama Thornton's 1953 hit, "Hound Dog." The song had been written by the young

white writer-producer team of Jerry Leiber and Mike Stoller, with lyrics meant to be sung by a woman. But it was Freddie Bell's version that Elvis loved, and as soon as he left Las Vegas he began to include the song as the closing number of his live act.

Relaxing in Las Vegas, May 1956

22. TV Soundtrack Recordings for NBC's "The Milton Berle Show" June 5, 1956: NBC Studios, Los Angeles

Guitar: Scotty Moore
Bass: Bill Black
Drums: D. J. Fontana

Piano: n/a
Vocals: The Jordanaires

OPA1 4813 **Hound Dog**
Jerry Leiber/Mike Stoller

A Golden Celebration
CPM6 5172/1984

OPA1 4814 **I Want You, I Need You, I Love You**
Maurice Mysels/Ira Kosloff

A Golden Celebration
CPM6 5172/1984

For his second appearance on "The Milton Berle Show," Elvis performed without a guitar and seemed to explode in front of the camera, as if the instrument had somehow been holding him back. He performed his new single for a substantially larger audience than had seen his "Stage Show" appearances. But the showstopper was his burlesque-queen version of "Hound Dog," bumping and grinding into a half-speed ending that fueled an uproar in the next day's press. "Vulgar" and "obscene" were the words most favored by the media, and the spectre of "juvenile delinquency" for a moment eclipsed the communist threat on front pages across the nation as viewer reaction mushroomed. His next scheduled TV appearance, on "The Steve Allen Show," was actually thrown into jeopardy when the network demanded that he tone down his act

The second Berle show:
June 5, 1956 . . .

. . . and Steve Allen, on July 1

or miss out on the $7,500 spot. Indeed, they went even further, requiring him to dress in a tuxedo and sing the new song to a terrified basset hound in a display that was mortifying to the singer. Recovering his dignity a few days later, though, at a triumphant outdoor performance back home in Memphis, Elvis declared, "You know, those people in New York are not gonna change me none. I'm gonna show you what the real Elvis is like tonight."

23. TV Soundtrack Recordings for NBC's "Steve Allen Show"
July 1, 1956: The Hudson Theatre, New York

Guitar: Scotty Moore
Guitar: Elvis Presley
Bass: Bill Black

Drums: D. J. Fontana
Vocals: The Jordanaires

OPA1 4815	**I Want You, I Need You, I Love You**	**A Golden Celebration**
	Maurice Mysels/Ira Kosloff	*CPM6 5172/1984*
OPA1 4816	**Hound Dog**	**A Golden Celebration**
	Jerry Leiber/Mike Stoller	*CPM6 5172/1984*

Elvis also sang four lines of a specialy written song for a comedy sketch.

24. Studio Sessions for RCA
July 2, 1956: RCA Studios, New York

Engineer: Ernie Ulrich

Guitar: Scotty Moore
Guitar: Elvis Presley
Bass: Bill Black

Drums: D. J. Fontana
Piano: Shorty Long
Vocals: The Jordanaires

2–5PM, 6–9PM

G2WB 5935-31	**Hound Dog**	**Single B-side**
	Jerry Leiber/Mike Stoller—Elvis Presley Music/Lion Publishing	*47-6604/1956*
G2WB 5936-28	**Don't Be Cruel**	**Single A-side**
	Otis Blackwell/Elvis Presley—Shalimar Music/Elvis Presley Music	*47-6604/1956*
G2WB 5937-12	**Any Way You Want Me**	**Single A-side**
	Aaron Schroeder/Cliff Owens—Ross Jungnickel	*47-6643/1956*

Gordon Stoker plays piano on "Hound Dog" (5935). The Jordanaires are: Gordon Stoker (lead), Neal Matthews (tenor), Hoyt Hawkins (Baritone), Hugh Jarrett (bass).

Elvis had one more New York recording session just before going home to Memphis, immediately following his television appearance. The day before the session, between rehearsals for the show, Steve Sholes sat down with the young artist and tried to clear up some of their past problems and come to an agreement about material. Both "I Want You, I Need You, I Love You" and "Heartbreak Hotel" remained in the top ten, and RCA wanted a new single to send out before the moment passed. Sholes had decided to use "Lawdy Miss Clawdy" and "Shake, Rattle And Roll" for an EP release, leaving "So Glad You're Mine" for the next album. "Hound Dog" was the obvious choice for a single, but it took some time for Steve and the Colonel to convince Elvis that this wasn't just a novelty item for live performance—and it took some work on the part of Elvis's song publisher to obtain a cut-in on publishing royalties for an already

New York, July 2, 1956

well-known song. It was up to Hill & Range, Elvis and the Colonel's partners in Elvis Presley and Gladys Music, to make those deals if they wanted to make a profit for themselves and for Elvis. From 1956 on, it was their job to convince any songwriter they did not control, or publisher with a song Elvis wanted to record, that it was worthwhile to give up one third of the mechanical royalties in exchange for a cut by the hottest young singer in the business.

As Sholes and Elvis sifted through a huge pile of demonstration records, Elvis's attention was caught by "Any Way You Want Me (That's How I Will Be)," a ballad by Aaron Schroeder, the cowriter of "I Was The One." Schroeder had written the song with Elvis in mind after meeting the R&B songwriter Clyde Otis (who wrote as Cliff Owens) at New York's famed Brill Building; Schroeder suggested the title, and within an hour they had the finished song, which Sholes felt would be perfect for Elvis's style. In short order Elvis selected four other demos to take back with him to Memphis: "Anyplace Is Paradise," "I Ain't Studying You, Baby," "Naughty Mama," and "Too Much." They were for the future, though. His work the next day was already cut out for him.

If Sholes had been impatient during the recording of "I Want You, I Need You, I Love You," he was really in for a rude awakening now. He had hired Shorty Long for the session once again, but when another commitment made him late Gordon Stoker took over at the piano for the start of work on "Hound Dog." The Jordanaires, who were now performing with Elvis on the road, were in the studio in full force for this session, but the fact that everyone had been playing the song for more than a month on the road didn't make it any easier to put it on record. Elvis may still have had apprehensions about the song or what to do with it in the studio, but Sholes and the Colonel had both seen the effect it had on audiences everywhere, and they were determined to get it on disc. When there were screaming teenagers outside the very doors of the studio with signs reading "We want the real Elvis," who could doubt the record would be a hit?

What they needed to figure out was how to turn the live performance into a record that would have the same effect. Elvis had performed the song live with a half-time, bump-and-grind ending à la "I Got A Woman," but now that was quickly dropped in favor of a full-speed-ahead version that had more to do with energy and overall impact than anything else. Scotty's guitar sounded loud and propulsive against a churning rhythm from Bill and D. J., while the Jordanaires delivered a backdrop of clapping hands and flowing "ahhhhs." The end result was like a musical machine gun, and take after take rang through the room, growing tougher and sharper each time.

This was the session where Elvis's perfectionist streak first became apparent. From Sholes's point of view several of the earlier takes would have been just fine, and he tried to get the singer to listen to the playbacks, but it was obvious that the singer was marching to his own beat; he wouldn't rest until he had recorded the song to his own—not anyone else's—satisfaction. Finally, with thirty-one, Elvis declared himself satisfied, and the room breathed a sigh of relief.

Freddy Bienstock, an Austrian-born double first cousin of the Aberbach Brothers and a junior employee of theirs, had come to the session to meet Elvis for the first time; with him he had brought a new song, "Don't Be Cruel." To his delight Sholes played the demo during the coffee break, and Elvis, who admired the writer, a blues singer named Otis Blackwell, fell in love with it immediately. Again it took more than two dozen takes, but from Scotty's opening lick the simple shuffle swept up everyone in the room, and it was clear that Elvis and the group were onto something. Elvis turned his own guitar around, slapping its back to add a little percussion, and the rest of the track fell in with a natural grace that sounded almost effortless—and like nothing ever heard before.

In the meantime, with the air-conditioning turned off in the studio, it had become unbearably hot. After "Don't Be Cruel" there was time to do only one more song, and Elvis was excited about the ballad Sholes had played for him the day before. Sholes in turn was excited about the way his suddenly commanding young star took on "Any Way You Want Me" in such a full but intimate voice; Elvis sang far more passionately than he had on the ballads he'd cut at the Nashville sessions, and the recording engineer did a far better job capturing his performance. By the time Elvis left for Memphis, Steve Sholes had three exciting new masters, and he'd had an eye-opening glimpse into Elvis's rising determination to push himself, and everyone else, toward making perfect records. The future was looking even brighter than the already brilliant present.

Back in March Elvis's screen test had proven to producer Hal Wallis that Elvis possessed the charisma, and in particular the rebel image, that would draw young audiences in the same mass numbers his record sales (as well as the careers of Marlon Brando and the recently deceased James Dean) pointed to. But Wallis and his partner, Joe Hazen, a highly successful production team with hits from Martin and Lewis comedies to Humphrey Bogart's *Casablanca* to their credit, found

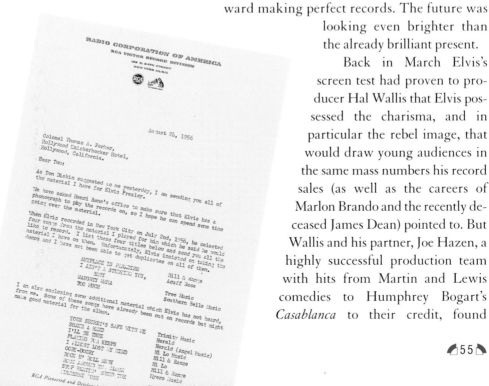

Colonel Parker a hard bargainer. The Colonel, of course, had the advantage of representing a client whose career was taking off like a rocket, but Wallis and Hazen simply weren't prepared for the ferocity of the Colonel's assault. By the time Elvis finally signed with Wallis, the producers had paid more than they planned—and even given up exclusivity—but they had secured Elvis's services for seven pictures over as many years. To everyone's surprise, his first picture wouldn't be for Wallis and Hazen; with no appropriate vehicle ready, they agreed to let him make his first picture with 20th Century–Fox. With the movie deal under his belt, the Colonel had risen with his young star to the highest levels of the entertainment industry, and he wasn't one who was easily rolled over; yet even he was bewildered at first by Wallis's hot and cold reactions to the phenomenon. One day the producer would gush to the press over his new acquisition, the next he would disappear from sight, as he did after Elvis's June appearance on the Milton Berle show. As soon as the new single of "Hound Dog"/"Don't Be Cruel" exploded on the charts, though, Wallis was back in the trade papers talking about his plans for Presley's *second* movie—before Fox had even made a first, or more to the point, before Wallis had consulted with the Colonel.

Being in the movies was Elvis's lifelong dream, and he couldn't have been more thrilled with his first script, *The Reno Brothers*—particularly because there were no plans for him to sing. But that was a decision that couldn't last forever, and when the studio decided to have Elvis record a title song, he poured out his concerns over the phone to his girlfriend, June Juanico. Elvis and June (whom he'd met a year before in Biloxi, Mississippi) were serious, and when he sang the new title song, "Love Me Tender" to her, he was relieved at how well she responded. Only when he learned that two more songs would be added to the picture—songs that had more novelty appeal than real justification in the picture—did his disappointment return.

Elvis's records were all over the charts. The new single, "Hound Dog," had sold a million before it even charted at number twenty-four the first week, followed the next week by the A-side, "Don't Be Cruel." "I Want You, I Need You, I Love You" was still peaking, and "Heartbreak Hotel" remained on its twenty-seven-week-long chart run. By the end of the month both sides of the new single were in the top ten, and RCA responded by dumping another seven singles into the market. The album, *Elvis Presley,* now gold, was cut into six little 45 rpm pieces, and the combination "Shake, Rattle And Roll"/"Lawdy Miss Clawdy" was released as well. At RCA, Steve Sholes was the man of the hour. The past few months had been like nothing ever known in the record business. The fact that "I Want You, I Need You, I Love You" had gone no further than to number three suggested only that it wasn't quite right for the singer. Presley's overall sales were too astonishing for anyone to worry about anything other than getting more and better product out into the market.

25. Soundtrack Recordings for 20th Century–Fox's *Love Me Tender*
August 24, September 4–5, October 1, 1956: Fox Stage 1, Hollywood

Producer: Lionel Newman
Arranger: Ken Darby
Engineers: Bob Mayer/Ken Runyon

Guitar: Vito Mumolo
Bass: Mike "Myer" Rubin
Drums: Richard Cornell
Banjo: Luther Rountree

Accordion: Dom Frontieri (8/24)
Accordion: Carl Fortina (9/4)
Vocals: Rad Robinson, Jon Dodson,
Charles Prescott

8/24, 1–6PM

S-sp	**We're Gonna Move**	**Love Me Tender (EP)**
G2WB 7260	*Vera Matson/Elvis Presley—Elvis Presley Music*	*EPA 4006/1956*
S-16 (take 2)	**Love Me Tender**	**Single A-side**
G2WB 4767	*Vera Matson/Elvis Presley—Elvis Presley Music*	*47-6643/1956*
S-sp	**Poor Boy**	**Love Me Tender (EP)**
G2WB 7216	*Vera Matson/Elvis Presley—Elvis Presley Music*	*EPA 4006/1956*

9/4, 9AM–12PM

S-sp	**Let Me**	**Love Me Tender (EP)**
G2WB 7261	*Vera Matson/Elvis Presley—Elvis Presley Music*	*EPA 4006/1956*

10/1, 1–4PM

	Love Me Tender (end title version)	**Essential Elvis**
SPA5 2875	*Vera Matson/Elvis Presley*	*6738-2/1986*

20th Century–Fox didn't use individual slate and take numbers, but ran them consecutively; as a result, take information is not completely clear. "We're Gonna Move" (G2WB 7260) is a splice of takes 4 and 9, with backing vocals, handclaps, and finger-snapping overdubbed separately. "Poor Boy" (G2WB 7261) consists of the original recording plus an additional third verse recorded instrumentally on September 4. Elvis overdubbed his vocal for the new verse on September 5. "Let Me" was recorded as an instrumental track on September 4, and Elvis overdubbed his vocal on September 5. Master is take 2 of instrumental track and a splice of take 3 and 4 of Elvis's vocal overdub.

In interviews from the time, Elvis confessed to having trouble sleeping, being hurt by the criticism that followed his Milton Berle appearances—in general, having problems because "everything is happening to me so fast." What to the world seemed like no more than a series of phenomenally lucky breaks had actually come as the result of his own determination, application, and hard work. Now, already haunted by personal insecurities and lack of direction from the record company, Elvis had to learn how to make movies; it was, really, like starting all over. Elvis was enormously excited about the idea of filming—he knew his own lines and everyone else's in the script by heart—

but the music issue still rankled him. 20th Century–Fox had refused to let him record with his band, but seemingly for all the wrong reasons: Their excuse was that Scotty and Bill couldn't play country, which was what the script required, and which of course would have been a surprise to Sam Phillips or any of the Starlite Wranglers.

Making matters worse, he was forced to record in the uncomfortable environment of a big soundstage, and without any say in the matter he was obliged to sing four songs dashed off by the film's musical director, Ken Darby (though the songs would be credited to Darby's wife, Vera Matson, and Elvis himself). Most of the tunes were in the public domain anyway, with the Civil War setting of the movie inspiring the use of the beautiful folk air "Aura Lee" for the title tune's melody. That, at least, was a song he liked. But when he had to sing a silly up-tempo "hillbilly" number called "Let Me" to a prerecorded track, he found himself for the moment really beginning to question his new vocation. Back in May he had told Little Rock DJ Ray Green that hillbilly music was a thing of the past; now here he was singing Hollywood hillbilly pastiche instead of something worthwhile like "Any Way You Want Me," which the Colonel had tried in vain to get included in the score.

Despite wave after wave of success, Steve Sholes was still under constant pressure to get that second album recorded. RCA had its own reasons for the push: They needed a new Elvis record for the critical fourth quarter, when record sales peaked. The Colonel was finally forced to agree to a Labor Day weekend session in a Los Angeles studio. The Jordanaires and the band would be flown out, and Sholes sent Elvis another collection of acetates to choose from. Hill & Range, too, worked overtime to come up with songs that would echo the feel of the July session material. Now that they had a better idea of what Elvis actually liked, they went back to the same writers for more. And, of course, with so little time it was inevitable that they fell back on a certain number of covers: "Rock Around The Clock," Faye Adams's "Shake A Hand," and Ivory Joe Hunter's "I Almost Lost My Mind," with which Pat Boone had just had an enormous hit, were among the songs suggested to Elvis. Two of them even came from Elvis's Sun Records breeding ground. The first was "Playing For Keeps," a new song from Stan Kesler of "I'm Left, You're Right, She's Gone" and "I Forgot To Remember To Forget," which came in an accomplished demo by Sun artist Barbara Pittman; the other was "Ooby Dooby," a song that Sam Phillips's new artist Roy Orbison had already recorded twice with little commercial success.

26. Studio Sessions for RCA
September 1–3, 1956: Radio Recorders, Hollywood

Engineer: Thorne Nogar

Guitar: Scotty Moore
Guitar, Piano: Elvis Presley
Bass: Bill Black

Drums: D. J. Fontana
Piano: Gordon Stoker
Vocals: The Jordanaires

9/1, 1–4PM, 5–8PM

G2WB 4920-sp	**Playing For Keeps**	**Single B-side**
	Stanley A. Kesler—Hill & Range Songs	*47-6800/1956*
G2WB 4921-09	**Love Me**	**Elvis**
	Jerry Leiber/Mike Stoller—Hill & Range Songs/Quintet Music	*LPM 1382/1956*
G2WB 4923-07	**How Do You Think I Feel**	**Elvis**
	Walker/Pierce—Cedarwood Music	*LPM 1382/1956*
G2WB 4924-07	**How's The World Treating You**	**Elvis**
	Chet Atkins/Boudleaux Bryant—Tannen Music	*LPM 1382/1956*

9/2, 1–4PM, 4:30–7:30PM, 8–11PM

G2WB 4925-10	**When My Blue Moon Turns To Gold Again**	**Elvis**
	Wiley Walker/Gene Sullivan—Peer Intl.	*LPM 1382/1956*
G2WB 4926-04	**Long Tall Sally**	**Elvis**
	Enotris Johnson—Elvis Presley Music/Venice Music	*LPM 1382/1956*

G2WB 4927-01	**Old Shep**	**Elvis**
	Red Foley—Westpar Music	*LPM 1382/1956*
G2WB 4922-sp	**Paralyzed**	**Elvis**
	Otis Blackwell/Elvis Presley—Travis Music/Elvis Presley Music	*LPM 1382/1956*
G2WB 4928-sp	**Too Much**	**Single A-side**
	Lee Rosenberg/Leonard Weinman—Southern Belle/Elvis Presley Music	*47-6800/1956*
G2WB 4929-22	**Anyplace Is Paradise**	**Elvis**
	Joe Thomas—Elvis Presley Music	*LPM 1382/1956*

9/3, 2–5PM, 5:30–8:30PM

G2WB 4930-12	**Ready Teddy**	**Elvis**
	Blackwell/Marascalco—Venice Music/Elvis Presley Music	*LPM 1382/1956*
G2WB 4931-27	**First In Line**	**Elvis**
	Aaron Schroeder/Ben Weisman—Ross Jungnickel	*LPM 1382/1956*
G2WB 4932-19	**Rip It Up**	**Elvis**
	Robert Blackwell/John Marascalco—Venice Music/Elvis Presley Music	*LPM 1382/1956*

The master of "Playing For Keeps" is spliced from take 7 and ending of take 18. The master of "Paralyzed" is spliced from take 12 and insert take 5. The master of "Too Much" is spliced from take 12 and insert take 2.

RCA booked Radio Recorders, a studio on Santa Monica Boulevard known to be the best recording facility in Los Angeles, not least because of engineer Thorne Nogar. A big man, Nogar conveyed a sense of calm and patient support and worked well with all kinds of artists. His experience with movie productions made him an expert on microphone placement in the large recording room at Radio Recorders called the Annex. For him the Presley group would be a piece of cake. Elvis took an instant liking to Thorne, finding in him someone whose judgment he could trust, someone who could actually help in the studio—as opposed to Steve Sholes, who just sat and offered encouragement. When Elvis arrived he was met by a guard and a "No Visitors Allowed" sign, both indications that the Colonel had done his work. Bill Bullock and Steve Sholes were on hand with the Colonel, as well as West Coast sales-and-promotion manager Robert Mosley. Sporting a beautiful tan and dressed in black pants and patterned shirt, Elvis appeared ready to put all his anxieties behind him and focus on the agenda: an album and a new single.

Sitting down at the piano, he warmed up with the band, singing whatever came to mind. The 20th Century executives hadn't thought he was good enough to play on "Love Me Tender," but here he was, serenading an enthralled crowd with his singing and playing. They started with the new Stan Kesler ballad "Playing For Keeps," with Elvis still at the piano because no keyboard player had been hired for the session. He and Gordon Stoker would split the piano work, with Elvis for the most part playing on songs he'd performed at home, some for many years. This new song presented more of

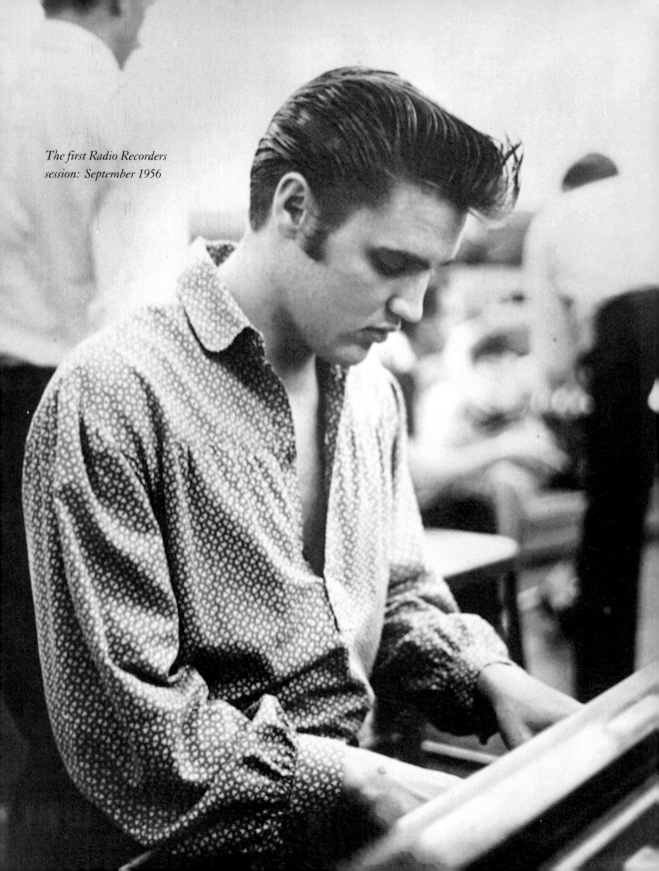

The first Radio Recorders
session: September 1956

With Thorne Nogar . . .   *. . . and the Jordanaires*

a challenge, and Elvis insisted on eighteen takes before he agreed that number seven would work if the ending from the last take was spliced on. Because of the success of "Hound Dog," Freddy Bienstock had tried desperately to get new material from writers Jerry Leiber and Mike Stoller, but all he had been able to come up with was "Love Me," which had originally been released two years earlier by Willie and Ruth, and then was covered unsuccessfully by Georgia Gibbs. Leiber and Stoller maintain that they'd written the song almost as a parody of country music, a genre the hip R&B writers cared little for; they'd later call it one of the worst songs they ever penned. But all that meant nothing to Elvis, who threw himself into the ballad with an entirely earnest reading, and achieved a satisfactory master with take number nine.

Next up was Otis Blackwell's latest, "Paralyzed," written along the same lines as "Don't Be Cruel," which was currently number four on the charts. When the band couldn't work out an arrangement properly, the number was abandoned after only one complete take. "I Almost Lost My Mind" was considered but quickly rejected, perhaps because Pat Boone's version was at the top of the charts. It may be hard to imagine today, but at the time Boone was Elvis's chief rival for the teen market; having blocked "I Want You, I Need You, I Love You" from the number-one spot, he was now vying with "Hound Dog" for the same mark. If Elvis had only remembered it, at home he was sitting on a demo for "Don't Forbid Me," which was destined to be Boone's next smash—he might have beaten Boone to the punch at this session. Instead he went on to an Ivory Joe Hunter 1950 number-one R&B hit, "I Need You So," but for all Elvis's admiration for Hunter, the song didn't really work any better than "Paralyzed."

With two aborted efforts in a row the session was starting to lose direction, but as so often when he faced a musical problem, Elvis turned back to his early days with Sam Phillips. At Sun he'd tried recording the Webb Pierce/Wayne Walker song "How Do You Think I Feel" after hearing Jimmie Rodgers Snow's version in 1955, but Sun drummer Jimmie Lott had thrown the band off by trying the song with a rhumbalike beat. Now Elvis plunged into it as he might have if Sam had really been committed to the idea, but the band still couldn't play it; poor Bill Black's bass was out of tune, and he seemed unable to follow the rhythm. The atmosphere between Elvis and Chet Atkins had been so cool on the disastrous "I Want You, I Need You, I Love You" that the singer decided to stay out of the Nashville studio altogether, but here in Hollywood Elvis had no problem laying down a cut of "How's The World Treating You," a song Chet had cowritten with and for Eddy Arnold. The day ended with Elvis back at the piano and four masters on tape.

They were almost on schedule, but somehow the question of what to record seemed to hang over the session like a cloud. The problem was simple: Elvis rejected almost all of the demos one by one, and when they ran dry all he could do was draw on old favorites. He couldn't quite remember all the lyrics to "When My Blue Moon Turns To Gold Again," a country classic from the '40s, but they made a record out of the verses he did know, just as they'd done with "Hound Dog." He had no such trouble with "Old Shep," the Red Foley tearjerker that had won him fifth place in the Tupelo talent contest, delivering a master in one take (although he kept going for another four). And in between those two he covered Little Richard's "Long Tall Sally," another number from his live show.

For lack of any other material, and also because he felt a true appreciation for both the song and its writer, he returned now to "Paralyzed." The band still found it hard to loosen up the rhythm enough to get it to work straight through, and in the end they had to splice part of an earlier take onto the best one. The same procedure was used on "Too Much," one of the few surviving numbers from Sholes's July stack of demos. It wasn't much of a song, but it did have a nice drive and the kind of rhythm that teenagers liked, and Scotty's almost totally "lost" guitar solo on this one still makes him chuckle forty years later. Splicing takes was the kind of last-resort solution Elvis could have done without, but Sholes knew Elvis had to get back to filming on September 4, so they had to do what they could. Still, any hope for efficient recording was canceled out with the twenty-two takes Elvis called for on the night's last song, the great, bluesy "Anyplace Is Paradise."

Steve Sholes could hardly have been pleased when the next day started with Elvis bringing some of his newfound Hollywood friends by the studio. Nick Adams and Natalie Wood, who had both appeared in *Rebel Without a Cause* with James Dean, were all very well for the movie magazines and gossip columns, but Elvis had work to do. Of course Sholes was happy they'd been able to record six songs the day before; he just hoped that they could match the feat on this third and final day—though he had no idea where the songs were going to come from. Elvis was all set to begin with "First In Line," another pretty ballad from Hill & Range staff writers Ben Weisman and Aaron Schroeder, which allowed Elvis to try out another side of his talent. Unfortunately, it took twenty-seven takes, which to Sholes must have seemed like forever and only compounded his fear that the singer would blow out his voice before they could get to another number. In fact, they didn't have another number to do, and about all anyone could come up with were two well-executed Little Richard covers.

Elvis returned to Fox to finish up filming and recording parts of the soundtrack for what was now definitely going to be called *Love Me Tender.* Assessing the commercial impact of the material, Steve Sholes wrote, "I don't think any of the songs from *Love Me Tender* will do much for Elvis outside of the title song, but I don't think this should worry us too much." It was a view shared by most people involved, including the artist himself. Against all odds the Colonel had arranged for Elvis to appear on TV's most popular and important variety show, Ed Sullivan's "Toast of the Town," a venue that would only cement Presley's popularity and sell countless new records. And there were other causes for celebration: "Don't Be Cruel," the other side of "Hound Dog," followed its flip to number one. By mid-September the disc was past the two million mark, and plans were being made to put out a new single, backing "Love Me Tender" with "Any Way You Want Me" from the July sessions. An EP of all the songs from the movie soundtrack was scheduled to coincide with the movie opening, and the appearance of two other EPs meant that almost every song that Elvis had recorded was now available in several formats.

27. TV Recordings for CBS's "Toast of the Town" September 9, 1956: CBS Studios, Los Angeles

Guitar: Scotty Moore
Guitar: Elvis Presley
Bass: Bill Black

Drums: D. J. Fontana
Piano: Gordon Stoker
Vocals: The Jordanaires

OPA1 4817	**Don't Be Cruel**	**A Golden Celebration**	
	Otis Blackwell/Elvis Presley	*CPM6 5172/1984*	
OPA1 4818	**Love Me Tender**	**A Golden Celebration**	
	Vera Matson/Elvis Presley	*CPM6 5172/1984*	
OPA1 4819	**Ready Teddy**	**A Golden Celebration**	
	Robert Blackwell/John Marascalco	*CPM6 5172/1984*	
OPA1 4820	**Hound Dog**	**A Golden Celebration**	
	Jerry Leiber/Mike Stoller	*CPM6 5172/1984*	

This first Ed Sullivan show was actually hosted by Charles Laughton, as Sullivan was recuperating from a car accident.

28. Private Recordings
September 26, 1956: Mississippi-Alabama Fair and Dairy Show, Tupelo

Guitar: Scotty Moore
Guitar: Elvis Presley
Bass: Bill Black

Drums: D. J. Fontana
Vocals: The Jordanaires

Afternoon show

OPA5 8178	**Heartbreak Hotel**		**A Golden Celebration**
	Axton/Durden/Presley		*CPM6 5172/1984*
OPA5 8179	**Long Tall Sally**		**A Golden Celebration**
	Enotris Johnson		*CPM6 5172/1984*
OPA5 8181	**I Was The One**		**A Golden Celebration**
	Schroeder/DeMetrius/Blair/Peppers		*CPM6 5172/1984*
OPA5 8182	**I Want You, I Need You, I Love You**		**A Golden Celebration**
	Mysels/Kosloff		*CPM6 5172/1984*
OPA5 8183	**I Got A Woman**		**A Golden Celebration**
	Ray Charles		*CPM6 5172/1984*
OPA5 8184	**Don't Be Cruel**		**A Golden Celebration**
	Otis Blackwell/Elvis Presley		*CPM6 5172/1984*
OPA5 8185	**Ready Teddy**		**A Golden Celebration**
	Robert Blackwell/John Marascalco		*CPM6 5172/1984*
OPA5 8186	**Love Me Tender**		**A Golden Celebration**
	Vera Matson/Elvis Presley		*CPM6 5172/1984*
OPA5 8187	**Hound Dog**		**A Golden Celebration**
	Jerry Leiber/Mike Stoller		*CPM6 5172/1984*

Evening Show

OPA5 8188	**Love Me Tender**		**A Golden Celebration**
	Vera Matson/Elvis Presley		*CPM6 5172/1984*
OPA5 8189	**I Was The One**		**A Golden Celebration**
	Schroeder/DeMetrius/Blair/Peppers		*CPM6 5172/1984*
OPA5 8190	**I Got A Woman**		**A Golden Celebration**
	Ray Charles		*CPM6 5172/1984*
OPA5 8191	**Don't Be Cruel**		**A Golden Celebration**
	Otis Blackwell/Elvis Presley		*CPM6 5172/1984*
OPA5 8192	**Blue Suede Shoes**		**A Golden Celebration**
	Carl Perkins		*CPM6 5172/1984*
OPA5 8193	**Baby Let's Play House**		**A Golden Celebration**
	Arthur Gunter		*CPM6 5172/1984*
OPA5 8194	**Hound Dog**		**A Golden Celebration**
	Jerry Leiber/Mike Stoller		*CPM6 5172/1984*

The sound quality of these recordings is quite poor.

The return to Tupelo: September 26, 1956

On Ed Sullivan's
"Toast of the Town"

29. TV Recordings for CBS's "Toast of the Town" October 28, 1956: CBS Studios, New York

Guitar: Scotty Moore
Guitar: Elvis Presley
Bass: Bill Black

Drums: D. J. Fontana
Vocals: The Jordanaires

OPA1 4821	**Don't Be Cruel** *Otis Blackwell/Elvis Presley*	**A Golden Celebration** *CPM6 5172/1984*
OPA1 4822	**Love Me Tender** *Vera Matson/Elvis Presley*	**A Golden Celebration** *CPM6 5172/1984*
OPA1 4823	**Love Me** *Jerry Leiber/Mike Stoller*	**A Golden Celebration** *CPM6 5172/1984*
OPA1 4824	**Hound Dog** *Jerry Leiber/Mike Stoller*	**A Golden Celebration** *CPM6 5172/1984*

At the end of September, in the wake of his first Sullivan appearance, Elvis returned to Tupelo for a riotous homeocming concert. Despite their inferior audio quality, the surviving tapes of those two shows reflect the pandemonium that had set in by the end of 1956 at Elvis shows across the country. The crowd let out one long wail from start to finish, screaming and cheering so loudly that no one—including the band—could hear a thing. All Scotty and the boys could do was keep an eye on the singer from behind: "We were the only band," he recalls, "directed by an ass."

The ratings for the October 28 Ed Sullivan show, Elvis's second appearance, reached a staggering new record of 80.6 percent of the national audience. Song selection for the appearances was dictated almost entirely by commercial considerations; Elvis plugged both sides of his biggest single, his new single, and two album tracks. Singing "Love Me Tender" on the first show, just before its release, had resulted in one million advance orders; it was another first, and it left the industry gasping. Performing the newly recorded "Love Me" and "Ready Teddy" not only promoted the second album, *Elvis,* but showcased the two potential lead tracks from EPs culled from that same album. At the time EPs were an important part of sales to teenagers—for both their price and their ability to fit inexpensive popular record players—and if there was one thing RCA didn't want to miss any corner of, it was the teenage market.

30. Jam Session
December 4, 1956: Sun Studios, Memphis

Guitar, Piano: Elvis Presley
Guitar: Carl Perkins
Guitar: J. B. Perkins
Guitar: Charlie Underwood
Bass: Clayton Perkins

Drums: W. S. Holland
Piano: Jerry Lee Lewis
Vocals: Carl Perkins
Vocals: Jerry Lee Lewis

VPA4 5298	**You Belong To My Heart** *Ray Gilbert/Augustin Lara*	**The Million Dollar Quartet** *2023-2/1990*
VPA4 5299	**When God Dips His Love In My Heart** *Traditional*	**The Million Dollar Quartet** *2023-2/1990*
VPA4 5300	**Just A Little Talk With Jesus** *Clevant Derricks*	**The Million Dollar Quartet** *2023-2/1990*
VPA4 5301	**Jesus Walked That Lonesome Valley** *Traditional*	**The Million Dollar Quartet** *2023-2/1990*
VPA4 5302	**I Shall Not Be Moved** *Traditional*	**The Million Dollar Quartet** *2023-2/1990*
VPA4 5303	**(There'll Be) Peace In the Valley (For Me)** *Thomas A. Dorsey*	**The Million Dollar Quartet** *2023-2/1990*
VPA4 5304	**Down By The Riverside** *Traditional*	**The Million Dollar Quartet** *2023-2/1990*

VPA4 5305	**I'm With A Crowd But So Alone**	**The Million Dollar Quartet**
	Ernest Tubb/Carl Story	*2023-2/1990*
VPA4 5306	**Farther Along**	**The Million Dollar Quartet**
	Traditional	*2023-2/1990*
VPA4 5307	**Blessed Jesus (Hold My Hand)**	**The Million Dollar Quartet**
	Traditional	*2023-2/1990*
VPA4 5308	**On The Jericho Road**	**The Million Dollar Quartet**
	Traditional	*2023-2/1990*
VPA4 5309	**I Just Can't Make It By Myself**	**The Million Dollar Quartet**
	Herbert Brewster	*2023-2/1990*
VPA4 5310	**Little Cabin On the Hill**	**The Million Dollar Quartet**
	Bill Monroe/Lester Flatt	*2023-2/1990*
VPA4 5311	**Summertime Is Past And Gone**	**The Million Dollar Quartet**
	Bill Monroe	*2023-2/1990*
VPA4 5312	**I Hear A Sweet Voice Calling**	**The Million Dollar Quartet**
	Bill Monroe	*2023-2/1990*
VPA4 5313	**Sweetheart You Done Me Wrong**	**The Million Dollar Quartet**
	Bill Monroe	*2023-2/1990*
VPA4 5314	**Keeper Of The Key**	**The Million Dollar Quartet**
	Beverly Stewart/Harlan Howard/Kenny Devine/Lance Guynes	*2023-2/1990*
VPA4 5315	**Crazy Arms**	**The Million Dollar Quartet**
	Ralph Mooney/Charlie Seals	*2023-2/1990*
VPA4 5316	**Don't Forbid Me**	**The Million Dollar Quartet**
	Charles Singleton	*2023-2/1990*
VPA4 5317	**Too Much Monkey Business**	**The Million Dollar Quartet**
	Chuck Berry	*2023-2/1990*
VPA4 5318	**Brown Eyed Handsome Man**	**The Million Dollar Quartet**
	Chuck Berry	*2023-2/1990*
VPA4 5319	**Out Of Sight, Out Of Mind**	**The Million Dollar Quartet**
	Ivory Joe Hunter/Clyde Otis	*2023-2/1990*
VPA4 5320	**Brown Eyed Handsome Man**	**The Million Dollar Quartet**
	Chuck Berry	*2023-2/1990*
WPA5 2537	**Reconsider Baby**	**The King Of Rock 'N' Roll**
	Lowell Fulsom	*66050-2/1992*
VPA4 5321	**Don't Be Cruel**	**The Million Dollar Quartet**
	Otis Blackwell/Elvis Presley	*2023-2/1990*
VPA4 5322	**Don't Be Cruel**	**The Million Dollar Quartet**
	Otis Blackwell/Elvis Presley	*2023-2/1990*
VPA4 5323	**Paralyzed**	**The Million Dollar Quartet**
	Otis Blackwell/Elvis Presley	*2023-2/1990*
VPA4 5324	**Don't Be Cruel**	**The Million Dollar Quartet**
	Otis Blackwell/Elvis Presley	*2023-2/1990*

VPA4 5325	There's No Place Like Home	The Million Dollar Quartet
	John Howard Payne/Henry Rowley Bishop	*2023-2/1990*
VPA4 5326	When The Saints Go Marching In	The Million Dollar Quartet
	Traditional	*2023-2/1990*
VPA4 5327	Softly And Tenderly	The Million Dollar Quartet
	Traditional	*2023-2/1990*
VPA4 5328	Is It So Strange	The Million Dollar Quartet
	Faron Young	*2023-2/1990*
VPA4 5329	That's When Your Heartaches Begin	The Million Dollar Quartet
	Hill/Fisher/Raskin	*2023-2/1990*
VPA4 5330	Brown Eyed Handsome Man	The Million Dollar Quartet
	Chuck Berry	*2023-2/1990*
VPA4 5331	Rip It Up	The Million Dollar Quartet
	Robert Blackwell/John Marascalco	*2023-2/1990*
VPA4 5332	I'm Gonna Bid My Blues Goodbye	The Million Dollar Quartet
	Hank Snow	*2023-2/1990*

In the Million Dollar Session, as it has become known, the primary singers, Elvis, Carl Perkins, and Jerry Lee Lewis, traded songs back and forth, sometimes singing only one or two lines. The jam continued with five songs sung by Jerry Lee Lewis. The above sequence is not definitive, and some have suggested that more than this was recorded. Carl Perkins's band played on only certain songs.

The Million Dollar Session: Jerry Lee Lewis, Carl Perkins, Elvis, and Johnny Cash at the Sun Studio, December 4, 1956

Elvis and Sam

At the end of the year Elvis was finally able to rest. He attended several showings of his first movie, visited Las Vegas, and finally returned to Memphis, where he saw old friends like Dewey Phillips and popped by Lansky Brothers on Beale Street and the little Sun studio down on Union, where Sam Phillips was now busier than ever with the success of Elvis's old touring partners Johnny Cash and Carl Perkins. One afternoon Carl was just finishing up a session when Elvis stopped by. Sam's latest discovery, twenty-one-year-old Jerry Lee Lewis from Louisiana, was picking up a few dollars playing piano on the session. And before long, Carl, Jerry Lee, and Elvis were gathered around the piano, singing country and gospel songs they recalled from their childhoods, trying out current hits, enjoying themselves the way they might have any Sunday afternoon at home. At Sam's instigation Johnny Cash came down to the studio for a photo opportunity, and *Press-Scimitar* reporter Bob Johnson was there to write it up. Just to get a record of the event Sam captured it all on tape; they talked about everything and nothing, and Elvis was able for a moment to enjoy the camaraderie that seemed to have disappeared with the onset of stardom. He told the assembled group how he'd lost out on "Don't Forbid Me," and now Pat Boone was getting the hit. He spoke with undisguised admiration of the singer he'd seen in Las Vegas performing with the Dominoes—this was Jackie Wilson, though he didn't know it—who had outdone him with his own version of "Don't Be Cruel." And he suggested that the right singer could really make a hit with the old Ink Spots song "That's When Your Heartaches Begin," something he himself had tried before, and would again. The ease with which Elvis shared the spotlight, happily swapping leads with Carl and Jerry, held no element of star arrogance. The mood was exactly the same as Elvis liked to establish at his recording sessions—just a bunch of pals jamming along to get in the mood for recording. Before leaving Elvis remarked, with no regret, "That's why I hate to get started in these jam sessions. I'm always the last one to leave."

But there was no need to stop: It was Christmastime, and there were plenty of friends at home. Elvis had a new home tape recorder, and over the holiday he spent time jamming with them on every kind of song he knew, from "When The Saints Go Marching In" to Pat Boone's "I'll Be Home." Many of these tapes were erased, some survive, but the music was always there.

31. Private Recordings
December 1956: Audubon Drive, Memphis

Piano: Elvis Presley

Vocals: Red West, Arthur Hooten

WPA5 2588   **When The Saints Go Marching In**
Traditional

Platinum: A Life In Music
67469-2/1997

This tape, one of those recorded at Elvis's house, also captured thirty minutes of Elvis shooting pool and watching TV—seemingly unaware that the tape recorder was still running.

1957

THE KING OF ROCK 'N' ROLL

For the Colonel, looking back on 1956, there could have been only one concern: How could he follow his own act? For Elvis, the new movie—his first for Hal Wallis—overshadowed everything else.

In 1956, four Elvis Presley singles had together accumulated sales of more than eight million copies in the United States. One of them alone, the pairing of "Don't Be Cruel" and "Hound Dog," had sold more than three million. To the sales of those four could be added another two to three million sales for the five reissued Sun singles and the seven additional singles released in August. Of the nine EPs, *Elvis Vol. 1* had reached number six on the singles charts and sold more than one million. Each of the two LPs were number one as well. The world market, too, was growing by leaps and bounds, bringing in additional royalties. And, recordings aside, Elvis had appeared on eleven television shows and in a major motion picture which, if not critically acclaimed, was certainly successful. What further dreams remained? Elvis had ten titles on *Billboard*'s Top 100 Singles Chart at the year's end, and pre-orders for the new single, "Too Much"/"Playing For Keeps," were close to half a million. With the third and last of the contracted Ed Sullivan performances set for January 6, it looked as if things were simply going to follow the same preordained pattern as the previous year. Why tamper with success? Why change a winning plan? As the year progressed, the Colonel demonstrated exactly why.

Recording Jailhouse Rock: *Spring 1957*

32. TV Soundtrack Recordings for CBS's "Toast of the Town"
January 6, 1957: CBS Studios, New York

Guitar: Scotty Moore   Drums: D. J. Fontana
Bass: Bill Black   Vocals:The Jordanaires

OPA1 4825	**Hound Dog**	**A Golden Celebration**
	Jerry Leiber/Mike Stoller	*CPM6 5172/1984*
OPA1 4826	**Love Me Tender**	**A Golden Celebration**
	Vera Matson/Elvis Presley	*CPM6 5172/1984*
OPA1 4827	**Heartbreak Hotel**	**A Golden Celebration**
	Mae Axton/Tommy Durden/Elvis Presley	*CPM6 5172/1984*
OPA1 4828	**Don't Be Cruel**	**A Golden Celebration**
	Otis Blackwell/Elvis Presley	*CPM6 5172/1984*
OPA1 4829	**Too Much**	**A Golden Celebration**
	Lee Rosenberg/Bernard Weinman	*CPM6 5172/1984*
OPA1 4830	**When My Blue Moon Turns To Gold Again**	**A Golden Celebration**
	Wiley Walker/Gene Sullivan	*CPM6 5172/1984*
OPA1 4831	**(There'll Be) Peace In The Valley (For Me)**	**A Golden Celebration**
	Thomas A. Dorsey	*CPM6 5172/1984*

For his third Sullivan show, Elvis was filmed only from the waist up in an attempt to do more subtly what Steve Allen had tried so awkwardly the previous summer: to make Elvis Presley respectable. Dressed in a flashy golden vest, he raced through some of his biggest hits, plugging both his new single and "When My Blue Moon Turns To Gold Again," available both on his second album and the *Elvis Vol. 1* gold EP. The final song of the extended appearance was a deeply felt version of Thomas A. Dorsey's "Peace In The Valley." As Sullivan closed the show, in an unexpected and apparently genuine move, he told his audience and the singer: "This is a real decent, fine boy . . . We've never had a pleasanter experience with a big name than we've had with you." Acknowledging the tribute, Elvis looked both sheepish and a little overwhelmed. In the wings the Colonel must have been beaming; this was the image he'd been working so hard to achieve. Elvis's controversial, vulgar, unprofessional performance habits had been toned down; now Hollywood would see his boy as a dependable young artist, completely controllable, no matter how rebel-minded he might appear on the surface. Tom Parker was observing the final arc of the rocketlike liftoff that that had elevated his country-boy artist into the firmament of stars. And to him the future was plain: There would be no more TV shows, much less touring, fewer records . . . but definitely more movies. The Colonel had seen how quickly overexposure could kill a career, how soon the public grew tired of what they were offered for free. He would never let that happen to his boy.

33. Studio Sessions for RCA
January 12–13, 1957: Radio Recorders, Hollywood

A&R/Producer: Steve Sholes
Engineer: Thorne Nogar

Guitar: Scotty Moore
Guitar: Elvis Presley
Bass: Bill Black

Drums: D. J. Fontana
Piano: Gordon Stoker
Vocals: The Jordanaires

1/12, 12–3PM, 4–7PM

H2WB 0253-09	**I Believe**	**Peace In The Valley (EP)**
	Drake/Graham/Shirl/Stillman—Cromwell Music	*EPA 4054/1957*
H2WB 0254-05	**Tell Me Why**	**Single A-side**
	Titus Turner—Melody Lane/Brent Music	*47-8740/1965*
H2WB 0255-09	**Got A Lot O' Livin' To Do**	**Loving You**
	Aaron Schroeder/Ben Weisman—Gladys Music	*LPM 1515/1957*
H2WB 0256-10	**All Shook Up**	**Single A-side**
	Otis Blackwell/E. Presley—Shalimar/Elvis Presley Music	*47-6870/1957*

1/13, 12–3PM, 4–7PM

H2WB 0257-14	**Mean Woman Blues**	**Loving You**
	Claude DeMetrius—Elvis Presley Music	*LPM 1515/1957*
H2WB 0258-09	**(There'll Be) Peace In The Valley (For Me)**	**Peace In The Valley (EP)**
	Thomas A. Dorsey—Hill & Range Songs	*EPA 4054/1957*
H2WB 0259-12	**I Beg Of You**	**Stereo '57**
	Rosemarie McCoy/Kelly Owens—Elvis Presley Music	*9589-1-R/1988*
H2WB 0260-sp	**That's When Your Heartaches Begin**	**Single B-side**
	Raskin/Brown/Fisher—Fred Fisher Music	*47-6870/1957*

8–11PM

H2WB 0261-14	**Take My Hand, Precious Lord**	**Peace In The Valley (EP)**
	Thomas A. Dorsey—Hill & Range	*EPA 4054/1957*

The master of "That's When Your Heartaches Begin" (0260) is spliced from takes 7 and 14.

Elvis's performance of "Peace In The Valley" on national TV may have been a conscious attempt to improve his image, but it sprang from Elvis's lifelong, fundamental love of church music. At the Hollywood recording session squeezed in just a few days after his twenty-second birthday—the weekend before the start of his new movie—Elvis got the chance to follow it up with something he very much wanted to do: cut a gospel record. The agenda was to cut four songs for a gospel EP, along with some singles. Primary among them was "I Believe," the pop inspirational tune that had been recorded by Roy Hamilton. Besides recording R&B material like "I'm Gonna Sit Right

Down And Cry," Hamilton often cut the kind of big-voiced, soulful ballads and religious songs Elvis aspired to sing, and with Gordon Stoker at the piano Elvis delivered a highly emotional and dedicated performance, showing a confidence in his ballad singing that he had developed only in the last few months. With the same sort of sincerity, in almost the same voice, he next took on Titus Turner's "Tell Me Why," a number he'd found on his own. Turner's only other claim to fame at the moment was writing "Hey Doll Baby" for one of Elvis's favorite R&B groups, the Clovers, and this new song had already been cut three times (unsuccessfully) the previous year; with Elvis at the mike, it began taking shape in a version that emphasized both spirituality and sensuality. Everything was proceeding nicely until a sudden concern arose in the control room: As Steve Sholes pointed out, the new song's melody bore a noticeable similarity to the religious standard "Just A Closer Walk With Thee." His apprehension wasn't lost on Parker and Diskin, who were worried lest Elvis's newfound respectability be subjected to charges of plagiarism. The songs' apparent similarity might have been artificially highlighted by the sound of "I Believe" still ringing in their ears, but it was enough in any case to cause the group to shelve the cut. (In a rare instance of unsolicited musical advice, though, the Colonel was so impressed by Elvis's singing that later he suggested to Elvis that he make a recording of "Just A Closer Walk With Thee.")

By the time the session got back on track, it was Otis Blackwell's voice that came blasting out of the speakers, singing another pair of songwriters' new tune on a demo Freddy Bienstock had brought in. Hill & Range, along with many pop music publishers, had offices in New York's famous Brill Building, where the staff writers, working in piano-stocked cubicles, produced songs as if they were working on an assembly line. Among the regulars in the building were Aaron Schroeder and Ben Weisman, who had written "First In Line" for the Labor Day session; Schroeder, with other partners, had gotten cuts by Presley on both "I Was The One" and "Any Way You Want Me." Professional songwriters were supposed to be able to produce material tailor-made for any artist they were assigned to, and for Freddy and Hill & Range Elvis Presley was the most important assignment there was. For the writers the reward was clear: Even after they gave up a third of their writer's royalty to Presley—a concession that couldn't have come easily—the reduced share they earned far exceeded the full share they'd have made with a recording by anyone else. Based on their own understanding of what rock 'n' roll was supposed to be, Schroeder and Weisman had come up with "Got A Lot O' Livin' To Do"—not exactly a Little Richard raver, but there was abundant energy and a carefully planned arrangement on the Blackwell demo, which made it easy to get started. After nine takes Elvis had it, and Steve Sholes was ready to move on to the next item for million-selling consideration. Blackwell was once again the demo singer on the next track, but this time he was offering his own brand-new rocker, "All Shook Up," based on a catchphrase of the day. Blackwell had actually been challenged to write a song including the line, and what he came up with was another irresistible shuffle-rhythm tune whose negligible melody was less important than its style. Otis had given away half of his writer's share on "Don't Be Cruel," agreeing to allow Presley cowriting credit. The success of that song certainly put him in no mood to fight, and "All Shook Up" got the same treatment; but it would be the last time Blackwell or any other writer suffered that indignity, as both Elvis and his song publisher partners began fearing that the arrangement would leave them vulnerable to criticism from both journalists and the public. "All Shook Up" was almost as much of a natural as "Don't Be Cruel," and Elvis knew just how to deliver it. Thorne Nogar overdubbed Elvis slapping the back of his guitar just as he had on "Don't Be Cruel," enhancing the combination of laid-back feeling and driving beat that made Blackwell's songs unique. It was as perfect a pop record as its predecessor, and Elvis put himself in the decision-making seat when he insisted that it be his next single.

By Steve Sholes's standard, productivity could still be improved, but quality could not. The problem he faced as they began a second day of recording was exactly the one he had predicted to Parker—the pressure of time. He had reserved the studio for the following weekend, but he was hoping that they wouldn't have to use it: After a week of working on the new movie soundtrack, he was afraid Elvis would simply be worn out.

Recording began at the same time on Sunday, and with the same energy and spirit. It was obvious that the young Hill & Range "song searcher" Freddy Bienstock had grasped what Presley music was all about in a way his middle-aged cousins the Aberbachs hadn't, and for this session he had commissioned a staff writer, Claude DeMetrius, to come up with a firebomb of a rock 'n' roll tune. "Mean Woman Blues" was more than just skilled pop songwriting. Its foundation was basic blues—which made it a natural for Elvis and the band. And it was just the kind of song Elvis would have picked for his live shows back in his earliest days. It took fourteen takes, but that was only Elvis worrying at it, trying to get it right. Try as they might, though, they couldn't seem to get the next song, "I Beg Of You," anywhere near right. A promising composition, it had all the pop flavor of one of the Otis Blackwell hits, but when they tried to work it the same way they just couldn't get the beat they wanted, and after twelve takes Elvis decided to move on.

The religious EP was still before them, and they started with "Peace In The Valley," but after getting it down in nine takes Elvis took up yet another agenda, whether to replenish his creative energies or simply because he got distracted. "That's When Your Heartaches Begin," the Ink Spots number, had fascinated him long before he made it half of his first acetate. "If somebody could sing it right," he had told Carl and Jerry Lee the month before, "you know, and have a guy with a real deep voice talking it off—you know, I think it'd sell." He sounded as if he were talking in the abstract, but anyone who knew him would have sensed he was itching to be that guy. It wasn't easy to get the song to live up to Elvis's vision, but Steve Sholes was able to splice two takes together so they could move on to the next song and complete the religious EP. At eleven that night they recorded a second Thomas Dorsey classic, "Take My Hand, Precious Lord"; with Elvis due at the movie studio early the next morning, though, that had to be the last song. They were still short a fourth religious number for the EP; Steve was going to need that second session the following weekend after all.

Sessions for the new Wallis-Hazen production, working title "Something for the Girls," were scheduled for the following morning at ten o'clock at the Paramount scoring stage. After all the trouble about the *Love Me Tender* music, Hal Wallis was smart enough to accommodate Elvis, bringing his band as well as the Jordanaires out to Hollywood; he even went a step further, finding bit parts in the production for the seven musicians and singers. It was a thrill, but the gesture also made the trip worthwhile for the musicians—particularly the three band members, who had no studio work in Nashville to return to.

34. Soundtrack Recordings for Paramount's *Loving You* January 15–18, 21–22: Paramount Scoring Stage and February 14, 1957: Radio Recorders, Hollywood

Engineer at Paramount: n/a
Engineer at Radio Recorders: Thorne Nogar

Guitar: Scotty Moore
Guitar: Tiny Timbrell
Bass: Bill Black
Drums: D. J. Fontana
Piano: Dudley Brooks

Piano: Gordon Stoker
Piano: Hoyt Hawkins
Harmonica: George Fields (1/21–22, 2/14)
Vocals: The Jordanaires

1/15, 10AM–12:20PM, 1:30–5:05PM

1/16, 9AM–12:15PM, 1:30–3:30PM

1/17, 9AM–12:30PM, 1:30–6PM

1/18, 9AM–2PM, 3:30–6PM, 7–11:25PM

A-07	**(Let's Have A) Party** (vocal and band)	**Essential Elvis**
SPA5 2868	*Jessie Mae Robinson—Gladys Music*	*6738-2-R/1986*
C-sp	**Lonesome Cowboy**	**Loving You**
H2WB 2194	*Sid Tepper/Roy C. Bennett—Gladys Music*	*LPM 1515/1957*
D-17	**Got A Lot O' Livin' To Do** (opening)	
	Aaron Schroeder/Ben Weisman—Gladys Music	
F-13	**(Let Me Be Your) Teddy Bear**	**Single A-side**
H2WB 2193	*Kal Mann/Bernie Lowe—Gladys Music*	*47-7000/1957*
J-16	**Loving You** (end version)	
	Jerry Leiber/Mike Stoller—Elvis Presley Music	
K-03	**Loving You** (main version)	
	Jerry Leiber/Mike Stoller—Elvis Presley Music	

	One Night (Of Sin)	**Elvis: A Legendary Performer Vol 4.**
NPA5 5820	*Bartholomew/King—Travis Music*	*CPL1 4848/1983*
	Blueberry Hill	**Platinum: A Life In Music**
WPA5 2589	*A. Lewis/L. Stock/V. Rose—Chappell & Co.*	*67469-2/1997*
Q-17	**Hot Dog**	**Loving You**
H2WB 2196	*Jerry Leiber/Mike Stoller—Elvis Presley Music*	*LPM 1515/1957*
R-13	**Got A Lot O' Livin' To Do (finale)**	**Essential Elvis**
SPA5 2871	*Aaron Schroeder/Ben Weisman—Gladys Music*	*6738-2-R/1986*

1/21, 9AM–2PM, 3:30–8PM

1/22, 8–11AM

	(Let's Have A) Party (vocal and group)	**Loving You**
A1X-11		**LPM 1515/1957**
H2WB 2195	*Jessie Mae Robinson—Gladys Music*	
BX-07	**Mean Woman Blues**	
	Claude DeMetrius—Elvis Presley Music	
HX-14	**Loving You (farm version)**	
	Jerry Leiber/Mike Stoller—Elvis Presley Music	

2/14, 9AM–12PM

	Loving You (main version)	**Essential Elvis**
KX-21		**6738-2-R/1986**
WPA5 2539	*Jerry Leiber/Mike Stoller—Elvis Presley Music*	**The King Of Rock 'N' Roll**
HZ-12	**Loving You (farm version)**	**66050-2/1992**
WPA5 2538	*Jerry Leiber/Mike Stoller—Elvis Presley Music*	

The master of "Lonesome Cowboy" (H2WB 2194) is spliced from takes 20 and 25. The exact order in which these tracks were recorded is unclear. Tracks labeled A to R were probably made between 1/15 and 1/18; some rerecordings might also have been done on those dates. "Loving You" (farm version) (HX) was recorded either on 1/21 or 1/22. Recordings made on 1/21 and 1/22 may have been made at Radio Recorders. On a tape box the recording date for "(Let Me Be Your) Teddy Bear" (H2WB 2193) and "One Night (Of Sin)" (NPA5 5820) is noted as 1/24/57; the film numbers O and P are guesses. The presence of Thorne Nogar's voice on all extant lacquers means that the mixing, splicing, and lacquer-cutting was done at Radio Recorders for all recordings. Also planned for the movie was a version of "Mean Woman Blues" in which Elvis sang solo, with orchestra following in the middle of the song. This title was intended for the finale, but was replaced by the "Got A Lot O' Livin' To Do" finale (R-13 SPA5 2871). An instrumental version of "Peter Cottontail" was recorded for the film, instead of the originally planned "Tennessee Saturday Night." The farm version of "Loving You" was originally planned to be guitar and harmonica (as HX and HZ), while the end version was supposed to have a full orchestra backing. HZ without the harmonica (binaural tape) with orchestra overdubs from 4/19 and 4/22 was used both places in the movie. The jungle of *Loving You* material can be ventured into by checking out Volumes 1 and 2 of the *Essential Elvis* series; volume 2 features mixes made from two-track (binaural) tapes. Binaural was introduced at Radio Recorders in late 1956; the binaural tracks Elvis made were cut with his lead vocal on one channel and the entire band on the other, in a strategy designed to allow greater flexibility in changing the mix after recording. At the time, the binaural tapes themselves were thought of as backup material, and were almost always recorded over when final mixing was complete.

The Colonel had negotiated with Wallis and Hazen to have Elvis's own music firms deliver all the music to be used in the film, including not only Presley's numbers but anything else that might be needed. When Hill & Range first presented its new material to the producers and then to Steve Sholes in December of 1956, it was met with enthusiastic approval. Built around a quartet of Leiber and Stoller songs—the first ones they'd written especially for Elvis—the seven-song score constituted an important part of a story that had been rewritten to portray a young singer's rise to fame. The writer-director, Hal Kanter, had flown to Memphis for dinner at the Presley home, and then traveled with Elvis to the benefit show in Shreveport that represented Elvis's final Hayride appearance, all with the idea of giving him a close-up look at the singer and his audience. The goal wasn't exactly to replicate the arc of Elvis's life, but to develop a story that suited him, to capture something of his experience, and to produce a musical score that would allow the real Elvis to shine through more fully than he could in a stock Western.

One request Wallis didn't want to grant Elvis was permission to record at the Radio Recorders studio he now favored. Before long it became obvious that Elvis resented recording on the big soundstage, whether he had sound reason to or not. He had gotten his start recording in a room that was barely twenty by thirty-five feet; the intimacy that had become part of his creative process was completely absent in the huge, hangarlike facility. The formality of the musician union's rules, designed to apply to a recording situation where music was already written out and planned to the last detail, was also destined to clash with Elvis's spontaneous music-making process. And so, despite the film's promising score, the first days of recording were discouraging and unproductive, with insecurity and frustration spreading around the stage.

The band included two new members, who were quickly absorbed into the group. Wallis had added his regular session players, Hilmer J. "Tiny" Timbrell, a heavy-set Canadian who would play Elvis's rhythm guitar part, and Dudley Brooks, an experienced black jazz pianist and studio veteran who could also help Paramount's music director Charles O'Curran work out the arrangements. The first number they tried on the soundstage was a rock 'em–sock 'em tune called "Party," done first with the band alone, then with the Jordanaires added. Hal Wallis, who'd been present at the RCA sessions the weekend before, liked "Mean Woman Blues" so much he decided he wanted it to replace Leiber and Stoller's "Without You" in the film soundtrack. But Elvis was getting disgruntled with the recording setup and the sound within the cavernous space, and trying to get him to record a song he'd already completed was an uphill struggle. Over the course of four days progress hovered between ultraslow and nonexistent: It took twenty-five takes to get "Lonesome Cowboy," which for a few days was considered the title cut, and even then it had to be spliced together by Thorne Nogar.

During a break in recording songwriter Ben Weisman introduced himself to Elvis. He had flown to California to meet his most promising client and hoped that his presence might help him get one of his songs onto the soundtrack. "I noticed Elvis sitting in a corner, ad-libbing some blues on the guitar," Ben recalls. "I wandered over to the piano next to him, sat down, and joined in. He didn't look up, kept on playing and even changed keys on me, but I followed along. Then he looked up with that smile he was famous for and asked who I was and what was I doing in the studio. I told him I was invited to the session and that I had composed one of the songs he was about to record, called 'Got A Lot O' Livin' to Do.' " Elvis had already done the song over the weekend, but Ben's presence gave him the impetus to try it again. Much like "Mean Woman Blues," though, it proved difficult to recapture; they just couldn't get it to sound as good as it had at Radio Recorders. Eventually the Colonel was summoned by Wallis to try to straighten matters out and rescue the sessions; by rearranging the schedule to give the band time to record some of the instrumental parts, he arranged to give Elvis's overworked voice a rest. And he made at least a little difference in keeping things going; now they were moving like a faster snail.

Picking up on Elvis's fondness for teddy bears, writers Kal Mann and Bernie Lowe had written a song Wallis loved: "(Let Me Be Your) Teddy Bear." The catchy, upbeat tempo made up for the silly lyrics, and it made the perfect extension of what the band had done with "Don't Be Cruel"—here was another contender for single release. But the one sure way for a writer to get an Elvis single was to write a movie title song—preferably one flexible enough that it could be worked up into various arrangements to fit different scenes throughout a film. The best candidate in this instance was Leiber and Stoller's "Loving You," but none of the three versions the band recorded in January really sounded like the blockbuster hit they wanted. The film had called for a version for the farmyard setting, a straight ballad rendition for the romantic ending, and an up-tempo version for the opening credits; but the band sounded awkward on all of them, struggling to play properly, and even Elvis sounded flat. When Hal Wallis asked for a few more songs for the movie, Elvis and the boys spent some time rehearsing cover versions of Fats Domino's current hit "Blueberry Hill" and Smiley Lewis's "One Night (Of Sin)," written by Domino's musical partner Dave Bartholomew and credited in part to Bartholomew's wife. Both of the original records were marked by the rich sound and rhythmic sophistication of classic 1950s New Orleans R&B, and though Elvis had no trouble connecting with it, the band clearly did; no final recordings were achieved. There was another Leiber and Stoller rocker, "Hot Dog," that lasted all of a minute and twelve seconds but took seventeen takes to record, followed by a third version of "Got A Lot O' Livin' To Do" that took thirteen. By the end of that Friday, a sense of impending crisis began to set in, as the musicians left the Paramount soundstage just a day before they were to report to Radio Recorders to finish the religious EP.

At the Paramount sound stage,
January 1957 . . .

. . . and back at Radio Recorders

35. Studio Sessions for RCA
January 19, 1957: Radio Recorders, Hollywood

A&R/Producer: Steve Sholes
Engineer: Thorne Nogar

Guitar: Scotty Moore
Guitar: Elvis Presley
Bass: Bill Black
Drums: D. J. Fontana

Piano: Dudley Brooks
Organ: Hoyt Hawkins
Vocals: The Jordanaires

2–5PM, 6–9PM

H2WB 0282-13	**It Is No Secret (What God Can Do)**	**Peace In The Valley (EP)**
	Stuart Hamblen—Duchess Music	*EPA 4054/1957*
H2WB 0283-09	**Blueberry Hill**	**Loving You**
	A. Lewis/L. Stock/V. Rose—Chappell & Co.	*LPM 1515/1957*
H2WB 0284-15	**Have I Told You Lately That I Love You**	**Loving You**
	Scott Wiseman—Duchess Music	*LPM 1515/1957*
H2WB 0285-12	**Is It So Strange**	**Just For You (EP)**
	Faron Young—Lancaster Music/Elvis Presley Music	*EPA 4041/1957*

Elvis and the band, with Dudley Brooks from Paramount in tow, met at Radio Recorders at 2:00 P.M. Stuart Hamblen's "It Is No Secret" was selected as the final song for the religious EP; it was another hymn, which meant the record would include none of the exciting up-tempo gospel material Elvis had loved since childhood. But "It Is No Secret" was quickly dispatched, and with the EP completed Elvis turned once again to the two New Orleans numbers that had eluded them the day before. With renewed energy Elvis tackled "Blueberry Hill," although the resulting version remains one of his least convincing covers. "One Night (Of Sin)" presented an even more complicated problem. Both the Colonel and RCA had serious reservations about the words of the song, but Elvis liked it so much that they appealed to Hill & Range to negotiate with the song's copyright holder, Lew Chudd of Imperial Records, for permission to rewrite the lyrics. Freddy was fresh out of new material, but Jean Aberbach, who had combed through the company's vast country-and-western repertoire, came up with a handful of songs for which he was able to make the appropriate financial arrangements. These included two Jimmy Wakely compositions as well as "I Love You So Much It Hurts Me" and "One Has My Name (The Other Has My Heart)," and a number of Gene Autry hits. The only one Elvis warmed to was Autry's "Have I Told You Lately That I Love You," which Elvis also knew in Red Foley's version, but the lifeless master they made that day hardly justified the fifteen takes it took to get there. Worse yet, it only highlighted the trouble Elvis's little band was prone to whenever it strayed from its limited musical foundations.

There was time for one last song, "Is It So Strange," by country singer Faron Young, who had toured on several early shows with Elvis. He had submitted the song to Elvis himself, and Elvis commented at the Sun jam session that Faron wouldn't give him any part of the writer's share. But he was determined to cut it, so Freddy was forced to work out whatever arrangement he could. The band was more at ease here, making a substantial improvement on their previous two efforts and producing a master that recalled Elvis's great early ballad "I Was The One." Sholes must have been relieved to have his religious EP done as the day ended, but those four songs represented a lot less than he had hoped for—and they suggested that the problems at the Paramount soundstage couldn't all be blamed on the setting. The week's worth of sessions at Paramount and Radio Recorders had yielded some great recordings, but they were slowed down considerably by insubstantial arrangements, musical shortcomings, and—equally important—a very tired Elvis Presley.

After a day off, Elvis and the group returned to Paramount on Monday to clean up the previous week's mess. They plowed through another eleven takes of the Jordanaires version of "Party" before they were satisfied; in seven more of "Mean Woman Blues" they still failed to beat the Radio Recorders version, and in the end Paramount had to splice the "live"-sounding opening bars of the soundstage version onto the superior earlier cut. And, after eleven hours that night and most of the following morning, they failed to come up with a usable version of "Loving You" for the farmyard scene: Elvis still sounded uncertain, his backing too sparse.

Meanwhile, over at Radio Recorders, Thorne Nogar was frantically preparing tapes, editing pieces together, and cutting lacquers. When Steve Sholes received his sample from the session he fired off a letter informing the Colonel bluntly that none of the recordings of "Loving You" (now almost certainly the movie title) was good enough for single release. After a torturous week at Paramount, Hal Wallis finally relented and booked a session to rerecord the title cut at Radio Recorders. Up against a deadline, Elvis and the band took the time to rehearse the song the day before, so they'd waste no time in the studio; even so, it took twenty-one takes to complete the up-tempo title version and another twelve to do the farmyard version, after which George Fields's harmonica part was replaced by an orchestra. But it wasn't over yet. Sholes still wasn't convinced he had the single he needed. He suggested two alternatives: overdubbing the slow farm version, or booking yet another session at Radio Recorders for February 23 and 24. In the end it was a war of sensibilities: Sholes was a record man who wanted only the best possible single; Hal Wallis, the moviemaker, was concerned only that the songs be recorded to fit the film's actual scenes. In the end the Colonel was caught in the middle, and though he worked hard to please both sides, he also learned a lesson: Forever after, RCA would be kept well away from the soundtrack sessions. Whether it was the right lesson remained to be seen.

36. Studio Sessions for RCA
February 23–24, 1957: Radio Recorders, Hollywood

A&R/Producer: Steve Sholes
Engineer: Thorne Nogar

Guitar: Scotty Moore
Guitar: Elvis Presley
Bass: Bill Black

Drums: D. J. Fontana
Piano: Dudley Brooks
Vocals: The Jordanaires

2/23, 10AM–2PM, 3–6:30PM

H2WB 0414-29	**Don't Leave Me Now**	**Loving You**
	Aaron Schroeder/Ben Weisman—Gladys Music	*LPM 1515/1957*
H2WB 0259-34	**I Beg Of You**	**Single A-side**
	Rose Marie McCoy/Kelly Owens—Elvis Presley Music	*47-7150/1958*
H2WB 0415-10	**One Night**	**Single A-side**
	Bartholomew/King—Travis Music/Elvis Presley Music	*47-7410/1958*
H2WB 0416-20	**True Love**	**Loving You**
	Cole Porter—Buxton Hill Music	*LPM 1515/1957*
H2WB 0417-08	**I Need You So**	**Loving You**
	Ivory Joe Hunter—St. Louis Music	*LPM 1515/1957*

2/24, 2–5PM

H2WB 0418-04	**Loving You**	**Single B-side**
	Jerry Leiber/Mike Stoller—Elvis Presley Music	*47-7000/1957*
H2WB 0419-08	**When It Rains, It Really Pours**	**Elvis For Everyone**
	William Robert Emerson—Hi-Lo Music	*LPM 3450/1965*

It was becoming almost a tradition to include an Aaron Schroeder song on every session, and this time he and his partner Ben Weisman had come up with "Don't Leave Me Now." But the band started having problems again almost immediately, and now there were starting to be serious doubts about whether the musicians could live up to the formal requirements of soundtrack recording—or even the demands Elvis was likely to put on them as he broadened the scope of his repertoire. It took twenty-nine takes, in any case, to complete this mid-tempo ballad, and another twenty-two to rere-cord "I Beg Of You"—twenty-two that seemed to get them nowhere. Meanwhile the new, bowdlerized lyrics for the Dave Bartholomew song had been produced as requested; "One night of sin is what I'm now paying for" became "One night with you is what I'm now praying for," and the deal they'd prayed and paid for freed them to pencil the song in for the *Loving You* album. In the end, the rewrite was a fortunate stroke. The discerning listener might have missed the more direct lyrics of the original, but Elvis's performance on the new version made up for it: Freed from worry about the song itself, he was all intensity and command. "One Night" was so good, in fact, that it was eventually dropped from the soundtrack and picked as a single with "I Beg Of You" for some indeterminate future date. (And one solution begat another problem: Hill & Range was forced to reopen negotiations with Lew Chudd to extend the publishing deal on "One Night," since at this point RCA had more singles waiting to be released than it knew what to do with.)

The *Loving You* soundtrack had just seven songs, so additional material was needed. In another eye-opening musical choice, Elvis recorded Cole Porter's "True Love" (a big hit for Bing Crosby the year before) on the first day of recording, as well as Ivory Joe Hunter's "I Need You So," which had been abandoned the previous September. The reworking of the title song was done in just four takes the following day; all that rehearsing had paid off, and finally they had a take that was singleworthy. In the remaining time Elvis blew the dust off Billy Emerson's "When It Rains, It Really Pours," the song he'd been working on at Sun when the Colonel called to tell him to knock it off. Something was still missing with the song, and Scotty was still playing those "too-damn-complicated" guitar figures Sam Phillips had always tried to steer him away from. But despite the stiff rhythm it was sung with guts and dedication, and with it Elvis had honored a pledge to his mentor Sam—the copyright holder—to remake it someday as an RCA release.

"Too Much"/"Playing For Keeps" was shipped to record dealers two days after Christmas with advance orders of close to half a million units. Elvis did the song on the third Ed Sullivan show, but the single didn't overtake Pat Boone's "Don't Forbid Me," which held the number-one spot, and eventually it peaked at number two behind Tab Hunter's "Young Love." Still, sales of nearly two million copies left RCA excited about the March release of "All Shook Up." Where "Too Much" was chosen by RCA as a single, it was Elvis himself who chose "All Shook Up," and the record was a runaway success, with eight weeks at number one and sales of 2.3 million. The Colonel lost no time pointing out to RCA that Elvis knew how to pick the hits, and all the label could do was look up from counting their money to agree. Meanwhile, *Strictly Elvis,* the third EP lifted from Elvis's second album, was a little disappointing compared to the first two, but another pair of EPs was still planned for April. A big Easter push for *Peace In The Valley* provided another surprise hit, eventually selling over half a million copies and leaving many wondering whether this artist could do no wrong.

Elvis himself returned home in the midst of all this for a few weeks of rest. He was in Memphis long enough to cause traffic jams, pull a movie-prop pistol on a Private Hershel Nixon in an incident that wound up in court, and purchase a home called Graceland for himself and his parents, before leaving on a ten-day tour of northern cities (Chicago, Detroit, Philadelphia) along with several stops in Canada. Back in Memphis he visited with Sam Phillips and picked up the newest Sun releases, including one by Rudi Richardson entitled "Fool's Hall Of Fame." He stopped by the

Holiday Towers apartments to see songwriter Charles Underwood, who'd been at the December jam; Underwood, who wrote Warren Smith's Sun hit "Ubangi Stomp," pitched his latest song, "Titles Will Tell," and Elvis liked it well enough to get his publishing company to make a deal. With Elvis about to start work on a ten-week production for a new MGM movie, Steve Sholes was anxious to get more tracks recorded for a fall album, knowing there wouldn't be enough soundtrack recordings for a complete LP. He had left nine demos with Elvis at the last session, and the young singer politely indicated that he liked two of them, although in the end they were never recorded. Aware that more often than not Elvis would run out of material at a session, Sholes resolved to come prepared this time.

The Colonel, meanwhile, had started formulating new plans. The Paramount contract allowed Elvis one outside picture per year, so he negotiated a second deal with MGM to take advantage of the clause. Always quick to learn and just as ambitious as his client, he began putting into practice what he'd learned about moviemaking during *Loving You*. First, in an effort to eliminate all the confusion that was natural when soundtrack recordings and RCA recordings overlapped, he made sure that this time all the movie recording would be done separately. Second, he dictated a new schedule that would allow Elvis plenty of room to breathe; *Loving You* had demonstrated that neither Elvis nor the band thrived when there was too much work to do in too short a period. And finally, reasonable or not, he demanded that the singer be allowed to do all his work at Radio Recorders; Elvis was a proven box-office attraction now, after all, and there was no reason he shouldn't make a demand or two. Once again, all songs for the new movie—which chronicled the rise of a young singer through hardship and imprisonment—had to be assigned to Elvis's own publishing companies, and scripts were sent to all of Hill & Range's principal writers indicating the four scenes where songs were required. On the previous film the most impressive material had come from Jerry Leiber and Mike Stoller, who delivered four tunes and saw two used. Just as with their biggest hit, "Hound Dog," the young writing duo had been more impressed by their royalty checks than they had by Elvis's performance, but Jean Aberbach wasn't going to let anyone miss out on this opportunity. Aberbach set them up in a New York room, joking that he wouldn't let them out until they had produced four new songs. Sid Tepper and Roy Bennett, whose "Lonesome Cowboy" had nearly become the title song for the last film, delivered three songs for the new movie. Aaron Schroeder, this time with Josephine Peebles, came up with a song called "That Ain't Right," and McCoy and Owens, who had done "I Beg Of You," brought in one called "Don't Be Afraid." In the established procedure, Hill & Range got approval on the songs from MGM before they were sent on to RCA. The final vote, of course, rested with Elvis and the Colonel.

By mid-April MGM had deemed three songs "completely satisfactory": Leiber and Stoller's "I Want To Be Free" and "Treat Me Nice" and a late entry, a ballad by Silver and Schroeder called "Young And Beautiful." The last song was so similar to "Love Me Tender" and "Loving You" that it worried Jean Aberbach—as far as he knew, Elvis hadn't enjoyed singing either one of those—and all he could do was stress to the Colonel how beautiful the tune was and how well it would lend itself to film treatment. For Tepper and Bennett it was back to the piano; none of their numbers got picked for Elvis to sing, although eventually they did succeed in getting "One More Day" into the script—if only as sung by Elvis's roommate in the film. (Another, "Young Heart," they gave to Jim Reeves.) Leiber and Stoller had two of their four selected, but another new one, not circled for submission in the script, was a production number called "Jailhouse Rock." Snapped up by the movie producers, it led to a whole new level of involvement for Jerry Leiber and Mike Stoller in the making of the new MGM film.

37. Soundtrack Recordings for MGM's *Jailhouse Rock*
April 30 and May 3, 1957: Radio Recorders
May 9, 1957: MGM Soundstage, Hollywood

MGM Producer: Jeff Alexander
Engineer, Radio Recorders: Thorne Nogar
Engineer, MGM Soundstage: n/a

Guitar: Scotty Moore
Guitar: Elvis Presley
Bass: Bill Black
Bass: Elvis Presley (2013)
Drums: D. J. Fontana

Piano: Dudley Brooks
Piano: Mike Stoller (2010)
Piano: Elvis Presley (2016, 2023)
Vocals: The Jordanaires

<u>4/30, 10AM–1:45PM, 2:45–6:10PM</u>

2001-06	**Jailhouse Rock**	**Single A-side**
H2WB 6779	*Jerry Leiber/Mike Stoller—Elvis Presley Music*	*47-7035/1957*
2001-06	**Jailhouse Rock (movie version)**	**Essential Elvis**
H2WB 6780	*Jerry Leiber/Mike Stoller—Elvis Presley Music*	*6738-2-R/1986*
2004-sp	**Young And Beautiful (movie end)**	**Essential Elvis**
	Abner Silver/Aaron Schroeder—Gladys Music	*6738-2-R/1986*
2004-22	**Young And Beautiful**	**Jailhouse Rock (EP)**
H2WB 6777	*Abner Silver/Aaron Schroeder—Gladys Music*	*EPA 4114/1957*
2005-03	**Young And Beautiful (jail version)**	**The King Of Rock 'N' Roll**
WPA5 2507	*Abner Silver/Aaron Schroeder—Gladys Music*	*66050-2/1992*
2006-07	**Young And Beautiful (Florita Club version)**	
	Abner Silver/Aaron Schroeder—Gladys Music	

2008-sp	**Treat Me Nice**	**Essential Elvis**
H2WB 6778	*Jerry Leiber/Mike Stoller—Elvis Presley Music*	*6738-2-R/1986*
2009-sp	**I Want To Be Free (jail version)**	**The King Of Rock 'N' Roll**
WPA5 2508	*Jerry Leiber/Mike Stoller—Elvis Presley Music*	*66050-2/1992*
2010-11	**I Want To Be Free**	**Jailhouse Rock (EP)**
H2WB 6781	*Jerry Leiber/Mike Stoller—Elvis Presley Music*	*EPA 4114/1957*
2013-16 (tr)	**(You're So Square) Baby I Don't Care**	**Jailhouse Rock (EP)**
H2WB 6782	*Jerry Leiber/Mike Stoller—Elvis Presley Music*	*EPA 4114/1957*
2016-na	**Don't Leave Me Now (movie version—not used)**	**Jailhouse Rock (EP)**
	Aaron Schroeder/Ben Weisman—Gladys Music	*67453-2/1997*
2017-21	**Don't Leave Me Now**	
	Aaron Schroeder/Ben Weisman—Gladys Music	

2022-12	**Don't Leave Me Now**	**Jailhouse Rock**
H2WB 6783	*Aaron Schroeder/Ben Weisman—Gladys Music*	*EPA 4114/1957*
2023-02	**Don't Leave Me Now**	
	Aaron Schroeder/Ben Weisman—Gladys Music	

(2007)—unsuccessful attempt at recording "I Want To Be Free". The master of "Jailhouse Rock" (2001/6780) is the same as 6779, except for overdubs made for the movie. The master of the movie end version of "Young And Beautiful" (2004) is spliced from takes 8, 12, 18, and 22. Elvis's vocal overdub on "Baby, I Don't Care" is take 6; the vocal overdub was made 5/8 at the MGM Soundstage. The master of "Treat Me Nice" is spliced from takes 10 and 13. The master of "I Want To Be Free" (2009) is spliced from takes 10, 12, and 13. No master was selected for "Don't Leave Me Now" (2017); takes 18 and 21 were pulled for possible use. On "Don't Leave Me Now" (2022 and 2023) made-up take numbers were included on the tape for later use in the movie's recording-session scene. 2022 was called number 2 take 1, and 2023 was called "number 1 take 1." These two additional recordings were done at MGM. The missing MGM numbers do not hide any unreleased Presley recordings or even finished takes, but generally cover bits and pieces recorded during the sessions, including an unsuccessful recording attempt on "Treat Me Nice" (2003).

Jerry Leiber and Mike Stoller couldn't have been less interested when Jean Aberbach suggested they get involved in the movie production. As they waited for Elvis to arrive at Radio Recorders—where Big Mama Thornton had recorded the original version of "Hound Dog"—they were feeling skeptical at best about the whole enterprise. They were sure this country kid would be musically ignorant, not to mention too spoiled to do real work. Elvis and some of his Memphis buddies—including disc jockey George Klein, his high school classmate—had arrived by train in Los Angeles the night before; when the group tumbled into the studio the impression they made only alarmed the songwriters more. But the polite southern boy, whom Mike and Jerry would later label a kind of "idiot savant," charmed them immediately. Not only was Elvis a big fan of all the important R&B acts of the past decade—Ray Charles, Wynonie Harris—but he could discuss, in minute detail, the kinds of obscure R&B records Jerry

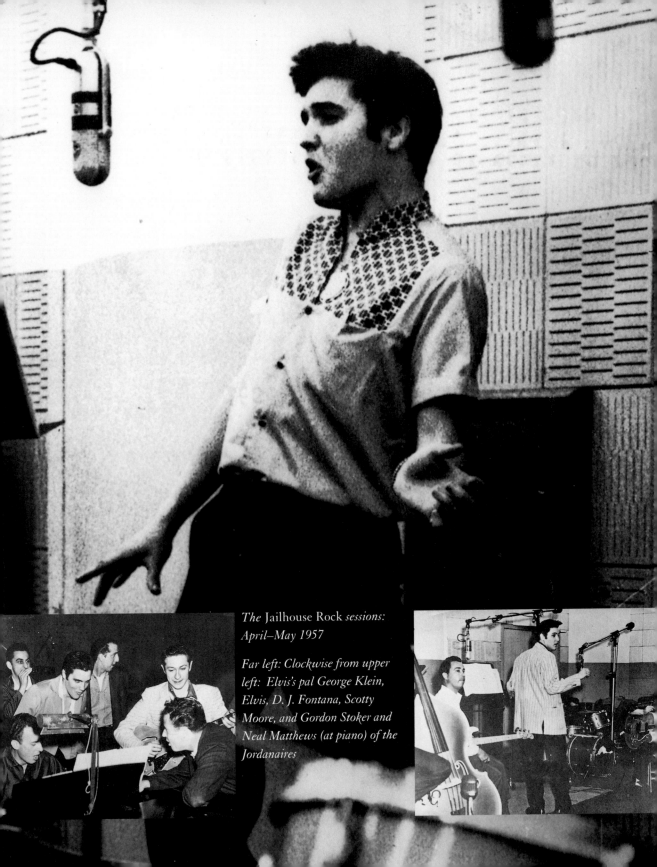

The Jailhouse Rock *sessions:*
April–May 1957

Far left: Clockwise from upper
left: Elvis's pal George Klein,
Elvis, D. J. Fontana, Scotty
Moore, and Gordon Stoker and
Neal Matthews (at piano) of the
Jordanaires

and Mike thought only *they*'d ever heard. As work began, their astonishment grew. Elvis was no lucky go-getter: He wanted to work as hard as they did, insisting on a kind of perfection that had less to do with faultlessness than it did with emotional satisfaction. In a way that rarely happens to songwriters (and would never again happen during Elvis's career), Jerry and Mike became an integral part of the recording effort—both in the control room and on the studio floor.

And their song, "Jailhouse Rock," became the centerpiece of the session. Later D. J. Fontana confessed that the intro he and Scotty came up with was copped from a '40s swing version of "The Anvil Chorus," but with Bill Black's walking bass figure (played on his new electric Fender) falling in right on its heels and Scotty and Elvis taking off in full force, this was Elvis's hardest rocker yet. Elvis's quick, sure grasp of the tune—and his instinct to sing the song with an urgency that transcended its satirical intent—rocked Jerry and Mike back on their heels. Their "Treat Me Nice" wasn't quite as easy, although Elvis raved about it and thought it could be one of his biggest hits. After a number of fruitless attempts the group shifted temporarily to "Young And Beautiful," which had to be sung in three different versions to be used in the film at three stages of the young singer's development. It proved difficult for Elvis to produce a convincing version for the character's mature stage, but he had no trouble sounding young, insecure, and flat. Maybe Jean Aberbach was right; perhaps this wasn't the kind of thing Elvis liked after all.

The next morning Leiber and Stoller stayed on to help with their song, "I Want To Be Free." Once again the film called for three versions and once again the boys got a slow start—probably because Elvis spent most of the morning singing gospel music around the piano with the Jordanaires. During the lunch break MGM's representative, Jeff Alexander, told the quartet they had to get back to work, but when Elvis figured out why everyone was edging away from him, he got so angry he simply walked out of the studio—and stayed away until Friday.

With Elvis away blowing off steam, Jerry and Mike had a chance to work out proper arrangements for both "Treat Me Nice" and "I Want To Be Free," and with those in hand the group completed the songs with little difficulty. But the limitation of Elvis's backing musicians, Steve Sholes's old bugbear, surfaced again—this time dramatically—when the singer returned. The immensely talented Jerry Leiber, now more or less in charge of production, decided to throw in "Baby I Don't Care," a song left over from their original writing session in New York. Leiber was now directing everything from the studio floor, which was just fine until Bill Black found he couldn't play the song's bubbly opening on his new electric bass. Now it was Black's turn to blow his top: Frustrated and embarrassed, Black threw the instrument down and stormed out of the room. Elvis, to everyone's amazement, picked up the bass and played the part himself, and with Jerry throwing in a scratch vocal they cut a perfect instrumental master for Elvis to sing a new vocal track over.

There was time left for just one more song, and Elvis wanted to try for a better take of "Don't Leave Me Now," which they had originally recorded in February. They spent another two or three hours on this, and then finally, after more than nine hours

Left: Elvis takes over on Fender bass for the intro of "Baby I Don't Care": May 5, 1957
Right: Overdubbing the vocal on May 8

of recording—and with takes eighteen and twenty-one as possible masters for the new song—wearily called it a day. The session had been a revelation on every level, with the team of Leiber and Stoller offering just the kind of strong musical counterpoint he thrived on—the first real studio support he'd had since leaving Sun. Jerry and Mike had guided him surely toward new musical territory, even if the actual recording had at times left him feeling unsure. He couldn't verbalize it, but he knew that both "Treat Me Nice" and the February recording of "One Night" could, and should, be improved. On the other hand, he was positive that the single from the film had to be the new title cut, "Jailhouse Rock," with "Treat Me Nice" as the B-side—a coupling that Tom Diskin, the Colonel's more music-minded right-hand man, noted as a "very similar pairing to 'Hound Dog' and 'Don't Be Cruel.'"

> *Overexposure is like a sunburn. It can hurt.*
> —Thomas A. Parker

> *It has now reached the point where we are getting consumer mail criticizing us for infrequent releases on Elvis singles and albums.*
> —Steve Sholes

A basic standoff between artist management and record label left Steve Sholes feeling frustrated and powerless. Though it was he who'd first put himself on the line to sign Elvis Presley as an unproven artist, his influence had now seriously eroded. Save for a few of the earliest cuts, Steve had had little say in what was recorded, hardly justifying his title as Elvis's A&R man. Ever since the triumphal releases of the past fall, the Colonel's priorities seemed to lie exclusively with motion pictures, soundtrack recordings, and promotion; his interest in RCA products had waned almost completely. Sholes hadn't even heard the *Jailhouse Rock* tapes by early June, a month after they were finished, and only then did the Colonel think to tell him there would be no *Jailhouse Rock* album for the Christmas season, nor any television shows to support other releases. If that wasn't enough, Elvis himself was scrapping the planned single, "One Night"/"I Beg of You," despite significant demand for the first song after he performed it several times during his March-April tour. Sholes and the Colonel had argued over, and then had to postpone, the springtime *Just For You* EP release of "Is It So Strange?" because Faron Young still hadn't agreed to relinquish any of his writer's share. Occasionally a tone actually approaching outright hostility began to creep into the communication between the two men—and in almost every instance, if peace was going to be made, it had to be made by Sholes. When Paramount suddenly moved up the opening of *Loving You* by two weeks, RCA had to scramble to coordinate the simultaneous debut of the soundtrack album and the advance release of "Teddy Bear"/"Loving You," the new single. Following that, the Colonel wouldn't even consider another new single until "Jailhouse Rock"; it hardly mattered, in any case, since the only thing Sholes had ready was "One Night," now out of commission. The Colonel's original contract with RCA stated quite clearly that "additional recordings shall be made at our [RCA's] election." But that line was worth no more than the one that read "The musical compositions to be recorded shall be mutually agreeable."

Still, there were oases of harmony between management and label. A Christmas album was traditional record company fodder for most major stars; RCA and the Colonel both wanted to cut one on Elvis, but the singer—who wasn't consulted at first—balked, remaining stubbornly uncommitted. The artist was much more excited about two demos he had received from Mike Stoller, back in June at the Beverly Wilshire. Mike had sent a note saying it was "kicks" working with Elvis on the *Jailhouse Rock* soundtrack, and included two brand-new compositions from the writing team: "Don't" and "I'm A Hog For You Baby" (recorded the following year by the Coasters). Nevertheless, by early August Hill & Range were working hard to gather titles: "Santa You've Done Me Wrong" by Sid Tepper and Roy Bennett; "Let's Play Jingle Bells," a new lyric to the old song (with the music credited to Elvis Presley); "Let It Snow, Let It Snow," "I'll Be Home For Christmas," "Blue Christmas," and "You're All I Want For Christmas." The only thing Elvis told the label was that he wouldn't record in Nashville, so a session was set for September 5–7 in Los Angeles, together with a short West Coast tour.

For the session Elvis wanted Leiber and Stoller back; he also asked for a Nashville-based soprano backup singer, Millie Kirkham, whose work on Ferlin Husky's "Gone" had impressed him. To aid in the song-selection process, he also suggested that Freddy Bienstock travel with him on the train so they could listen to demos together. By September RCA had decided the Christmas album should contain the four religious songs from the *Peace In The Valley* EP, so only eight Christmas numbers were now necessary. And Elvis was determined to redo "Treat Me Nice" and "One Night," and was so keen on Rudi Richardson's Sun single "Fool's Hall Of Fame" that when he played it in live performances he announced that it would be his next recording. There was the song Charlie Underwood had given him in Memphis in December, and a song sent by the Statesmen Quartet bass singer Jim "Big Chief" Wetherington. And Ivory Joe Hunter, one of Elvis's favorite songwriters and performers, had visited Graceland and played Elvis a new song that Elvis fell in love with—"My Wish Came True."

38. Studio Sessions for RCA
September 5–7, 1957: Radio Recorders, Hollywood

A&R/Producer: Steve Sholes
Engineer: Thorne Nogar

Guitar: Scotty Moore
Guitar: Elvis Presley
Bass: Bill Black
Drums: D. J. Fontana

Piano: Dudley Brooks
Vocals: Millie Kirkham
Vocals: The Jordanaires

9/5, 12–3PM, 4–8PM

H2PB 5523-15   **Treat Me Nice**   **Single B-side**
Jerry Leiber/Mike Stoller—Elvis Presley Music   *47-7035/1957*

H2PB 5525-03   **Blue Christmas**   **Elvis' Christmas Album**
Billy Hayes/Jay Johnson—Choice Music   *LOC 1035/1957*

9/6, 12–3:30PM, 4:30–8PM

H2PB 5524-28   **My Wish Came True**   **Single B-side**
Ivory Joe Hunter/Ivory Music   *47-7600/1959*

H2PB 5526-09   **White Christmas**   **Elvis' Christmas Album**
Irving Berlin—Irving Berlin, Inc.   *LOC 1035/1957*

H2PB 5527-02   **Here Comes Santa Claus**   **Elvis' Christmas Album**
Gene Autry/Oakley Haldeman—Western Music   *LOC 1035/1957*

H2PB 5528-09   **Silent Night**   **Elvis' Christmas Album**
Joseph Mohr/Franz Gruber—Elvis Presley Music   *LOC 1035/1957*

H2PB 5529-07   **Don't**   **Single A-side**
Jerry Leiber/Mike Stoller—Elvis Presley Music   *47-7150/1958*

9/7, 12–3PM, 4–8PM

H2PB 5530-04   **O Little Town Of Bethlehem**   **Elvis' Christmas Album**
Philips Brooks/Lewis Redner—Elvis Presley Music   *LOC 1035/1957*

H2PB 5531-09   **Santa Bring My Baby Back (To Me)**   **Elvis' Christmas Album**
Aaron Schroeder/Claude DeMetrius—Gladys Music   *LOC 1035/1957*

H2PB 5532-07   **Santa Claus Is Back In Town**   **Elvis' Christmas Album**
Jerry Leiber/Mike Stoller—Elvis Presley Music   *LOC 1035/1957*

H2PB 5533-15   **I'll Be Home For Christmas**   **Elvis' Christmas Album**
Gannon/Kent/Ram—Gannon And Kent Music   *LOC 1035/1957*

It was obvious to everyone at the session that Elvis wasn't fired up about the Christmas material; what he really wanted was to get "Treat Me Nice" fixed up for release. He'd been excited about the song from the first time he'd heard it, insisting that this was a real hit single, and no effort was spared to make sure it turned out that way. The soundtrack recording had sounded so thin that the loudest element was the Jordanaires' hand clapping. This time, with Leiber and Stoller's new arrangement and their expertise as de facto producers, a proper drum part was established, a piano intro added, and both key and tempo were lowered, creating a less exciting but sexier feel for the song. They wound it up in fifteen takes, then moved on to "My Wish Came True." Elvis was passionate about recording the song, if perhaps more out of friendship and admiration for Hunter than for anything outstanding about the song. This was where he wanted to use Millie Kirkham's soaring soprano; seven months pregnant, Millie found the young star excessively polite as he arranged a chair for her before beginning the Hunter song. Its hymnlike quality was unlike Ivory Joe's better-known R&B and pop material, and they labored mightily for several hours before giving up. Turning to "Blue Christmas," previously recorded by several artists (including Ernest Tubb, who'd had a number-two country hit with it in 1950), they found the song perfect for Elvis's slow and sexy, rock-it-up approach, very much along the lines of "One Night." When Elvis had Millie perform a wordless soprano obbligato behind his lead vocal, she worried that it might seem ridiculous—but, of course, she didn't voice her reservations to the overjoyed singer. With only two songs completed after the first night, Steve Sholes was close to despair. He put most of the blame on the band, whose inadequacy was only confirmed in his mind when it took them twenty-nine takes to get "My Wish Came True" the next day. The result wasn't even particularly outstanding—it was usable, certainly, but failed to fulfill any of Elvis's lofty ambitions for it.

Next was a version of "White Christmas" that followed closely the playful arrangement of Clyde McPhatter and the Drifters' version—and so upset Irving Berlin that he wrote to every radio station in an attempt to get the record banned. And they knocked off Gene Autry's "Here Comes Santa Claus" in a version both inoffensive and uninventive.

A beautiful version of "Silent Night" preceded what was the most important song—the one Elvis played again and again on the train ride out. "Don't," the ballad Jerry Leiber and Mike Stoller had written expressly for the young singer and sent along back in June, was the perfect fit for his style and talents; even its title perfectly fit the teenage mood. They took it at a mournful pace, with the barest of arrangements, and Elvis sang it as if it were his last stab at be-

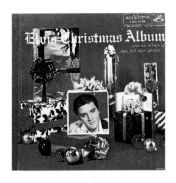

coming another Dean Martin, or a Bill Kenny, or a Roy Hamilton. He still couldn't quite control his vibrato—that would take him another few years—but the sincerity of the performance, and the beauty of the simple song, made it an obvious choice for a new single.

Four more Christmas songs were needed, and one of them was actually being written while the session was going on. Seeing Elvis's reaction to all these bland Christmas standards, Leiber and Stoller were asked to come up with something more to his taste, and thus "Christmas Blues" was born. Its tough blues approach—putting Santa in a big black Cadillac, sending him down your chimney tonight—exuded the kind of down-to-earth humor Elvis loved, and he knocked it off in seven takes before it was renamed "Santa Claus Is Back In Town." The final number of the day, "I'll Be Home For Christmas," was the third associated with Bing Crosby, and with its successful waxing the session was over. There had been no "Fool's Hall Of Fame," no rerecording of "One Night," and no lucky break for Charles Underwood. When the songwriter was arrested later that month for robbery, he claimed to the astonished police that Elvis Presley was recording one of his songs. As for Leiber and Stoller, they had again proven themselves a great addition to the team, not only delivering the all-important new single, but helping to arrange the songs and even do some writing on the spot when Elvis ran out of material. Elvis hadn't cut "I'm A Hog For You," although he would keep it in play as late as 1959, for what would become the *Elvis Is Back* sessions. Maybe the lyrics were too bold—but they were nothing compared to the boldness of Colonel Parker's reaction when he found out that Stoller had submitted two songs straight to Elvis, and not through Hill & Range as instructed. The writers were told never to do this again—underlining the Colonel's strategy of securing publishing deals for the music companies before Elvis could fall in love with a song, which always made such deals much more difficult to obtain.

In September 1957 Steve Sholes received a promotion at RCA, no doubt largely the result of his signing Elvis to the label. Yet it came just as his relationship with Elvis's manager was falling apart. The Colonel's latest scheme called for the Christmas album to be packaged in a deluxe foldout sleeve with a booklet of publicity photographs from *Jailhouse Rock*. For the first guaranteed 100,000 units Elvis and the Colonel would receive a ten-thousand-dollar fee for use of the photographs, and the special Christmas EP photographs would cost RCA another six thousand. This became the model for side deals the Colonel would institute for years thereafter—deals nearly as profitable as RCA's contractual commitments.

Now the other issue troubling Sholes came to a head: the continuing troubles with Elvis's band. Scotty and Bill had been promised recording time at the end of the Christmas session to record an instrumental album of their own (and Elvis had even promised to play piano); when they failed to get it—this wasn't the first time, they felt, that they had come up short—it was too much for the pair to take. For over a year they'd gone along with an arrangement that kept them on a low retainer for the many weeks when they weren't needed, and the work they did backing him got almost no recognition; the session would have been a way to make a little extra money and do something for their own careers for a change. Now they made their demands explicit, and when they got no response Scotty and Bill publicly announced their resignation from Elvis Presley's employ.

This gave Steve Sholes the opportunity to address directly what he had only hinted at before, and he wrote the Colonel in no uncertain terms: The "two musicians certainly hold up the Presley recording sessions a great deal. I am confident we can move faster and make better records if we didn't have to use [them]." The Colonel might not have disagreed with Sholes, but he knew better than to go on record saying so; Elvis wanted them back, and that was that. Once again Sholes lost out to Colonel Parker. The band was rehired, and from this point on the Colonel called the shots on all new releases. At year's end, despite Sholes's begging for more, there had been only the four contracted singles—but each had sold about two million copies. Elvis had also had two number-one albums and three number-one EPs, and in all had spent twenty-one weeks at the top of the singles charts, fourteen heading the album charts. The single "Jailhouse Rock" sold an instant two million copies, and the EP became Elvis's second million-seller in that category. Despite the fact that the Colonel had denied Steve Sholes a Christmas single, the album and EP both went to number one on their respective charts, so it would have been hard at this point to fault the Colonel's strategy.

But then, on December 19, Elvis received news that was devastating not just to himself but to his manager, his record company, and his film studio: his draft notice.

1958

THE END OF THE ROAD

---

39. Soundtrack Recordings for Paramount's *King Creole*
January 15–16 and 23, 1958: Radio Recorders
February 11, 1958: Paramount Soundstage, Hollywood

Paramount producers: Walter Scharf, Phil Khagan
Engineer, Radio Recorders: Thorne Nogar
Engineer, Paramount: Unknown

Guitar: Scotty Moore
Guitar: Elvis Presley
Bass: Bill Black
Bass, Tuba: Ray Siegel
Bass, Guitar: Neal Matthews
Drums: D. J. Fontana
Drums: Bernie Mattinson (1/23)
Bongos: Gordon Stoker

Cymbals: Hoyt Hawkins
Piano: Dudley Brooks
Clarinet: Mahlon Clark
Trumpet: John Ed Buckner
Sax: Justin Gordon
Trombone: Elmer Schneider (1/15–16)
Trombone: Warren Smith (1/23)
Vocals: Kitty White (3607)
Vocals: The Jordanaires

Band on 2/11: Moore, Tiny Timbrell, Fontana, Mattinson, Brooks, Black.

1/15, 9AM–1:20PM, 2:20–5:40PM

B-10	**Hard Headed Woman**	**Single A-side**
J2PB 3603	*Claude DeMetrius—Gladys Music*	*47-7280/1958*
C-05	**Trouble**	**King Creole Vol. 2 (EP)**
J2PB 3604	*Jerry Leiber/Mike Stoller—Elvis Presley Music*	*EPA 4321/1958*
D-05	**New Orleans**	**King Creole Vol. 1 (EP)**
J2PB 3605	*Sid Tepper/Roy C. Bennett—Gladys Music*	*EPA 4319/1958*
E-18	**King Creole**	**Hits Like Never Before**
J2PB 3606	*Jerry Leiber/Mike Stoller—Elvis Presley Music*	*2229-2-R/1990*
F-07	**Crawfish**	**King Creole Vol. 2 (EP)**
J2PB 3607	*Fred Wise/Ben Weisman—Gladys Music*	*EPA 4321/1958*

1/16, 9AM–5:30PM

G-14	**Dixieland Rock**	**King Creole Vol. 2 (EP)**
J2PB 3608	*Claude DeMetrius/Fred Wise—Gladys Music*	*EPA 4321/1958*
H-07	**Lover Doll**	**King Creole Vol. 1 (EP)**
J2PB 3262	*Sid Wayne/Abner Silver—Gladys Music*	*EPA 4319/1958*

J-12	**Don't Ask Me Why**		**Single B-side**
J2PB 3610	*Fred Wise/Ben Weisman—Gladys Music*		*47-7280/1958*
K-10	**As Long As I Have You**		**King Creole Vol. 1 (EP)**
J2PB 3611	*Fred Wise/Ben Weisman—Gladys Music*		*EPA 4319/1958*
M-06	**Steadfast, Loyal And True (movie version)**		**Hits Like Never Before**
	Jerry Leiber/Mike Stoller—Elvis Presley Music		*2229-2-R/1990*
N-08	**As Long As I Have You (movie version)**		**Hits Like Never Before**
WPA5 2509	*Fred Wise/Ben Weisman—Gladys Music*		*2229-2-R/1958*

<u>1/23, 8–11PM</u>

EX-13	**King Creole**		**King Creole Vol. 1 (EP)**
J2PB 3612	*Jerry Leiber/Mike Stoller—Elvis Presley Music*		*EPA 4319/1958*
Q-08	**Young Dreams**		**King Creole Vol. 2 (EP)**
J2PB 3613	*Martin Kalmanoff/Aaron Schroeder—Gladys Music*		*EPA 4321/1958*

<u>2/11, 1–5:05PM, 6:05–9:55PM</u>

U-10	**Danny**		**Elvis: A Legendary Performer Vol. 3**
WPA1 8123	*Fred Wise/Ben Weisman—Gladys Music*		*CPL1 3078/1978*
	Steadfast, Loyal And True		**King Creole**
J2PB 3261	*Jerry Leiber/Mike Stoller—Elvis Presley Music*		*LPM 1884/1958*

1/23, 11PM–12:55AM: rehearsals of "My Wish Came True" and "Doncha' Think It's Time" for upcoming RCA sessions.

The masters of "Steadfast, Loyal and True" (3261) and "Lover Doll" (3262) were overdubbed by the Jordanaires on a June 19 session in Nashville supervised by Steve Sholes. Yet "Lover Doll" was first released on the EP without the overdubs; the subsequent album release reinstated them. Most of Kitty White's vocal on "Crawfish" (3607) was edited out for record release, but kept in the movie.

The draft notice hit like a bomb. Elvis had to go back to the draft board to petition for a deferment in order to save the production of *King Creole*. And since any plans for live work and recording sessions would be derailed once he entered the army, now they would all have to work overtime to get as much done as they could before the deadline. *King Creole* gave Elvis his most challenging movie role yet. Based on the Harold Robbins novel *A Stone for Danny Fisher,* it presented an opportunity to work with the acclaimed Hungarian-born director Michael Curtiz (whose work included *Casablanca*) and placed Elvis alongside accomplished actors such as Carolyn Jones, Walter Matthau, and Dean Jagger. The music was to be an integral part of this serious and rather dark story of a young singer (in the novel he'd been a boxer) trying to make it in the nightclubs of New Orleans. Traditional New Orleans music had its own very specific African-American roots, and Elvis always pointed to New Orleans R&B (Fats Domino was probably its leading exemplar) as instrumental to his development. But Elvis hadn't gone over all that well

The Dixieland-flavored King Creole sessions: January 1958

Listening to playback

in New Orleans when he appeared there three times in 1955, and the Memphis brand of rock 'n' roll was very different from the New Orleans tradition. To help create an authentic Dixieland sound, Paramount hired some of L.A.'s best session players for the recording: a four-piece brass section augmented by bass player Ray Siegel, who doubled on tuba. Elvis's own band was supplemented again by piano player Dudley Brooks, and by a second drummer at an extra recording date later when the complexity and variety of the rhythms proved too much for Bill Black and D. J. to handle. With fourteen musicians in the band, this was by far the largest group Elvis had ever worked with in the studio, but for engineer Thorne Nogar it would be business as usual. Elvis's support team included Paramount musical director Charles O'Curran as well as Jerry Leiber and Mike Stoller, who had just signed on as producers for RCA. As Elvis's favorite writers of the moment they brought material to the session, along with other Elvis Presley Music regulars like Aaron Schroeder and Claude DeMetrius, who sent in two infectious rock 'n' roll originals. The ever-dependable Ben Weisman and his partner, Fred Wise, came up with "Danny" as a proposed title cut, along with several other new songs.

The session opened with Claude DeMetrius's "Hard Headed Woman." Driven by a catchy, horn-driven arrangement that captured the spirit of New Orleans while retaining the basic rock 'n' roll trio flavor, "Hard Headed Woman" was a sure success, but it was topped by Leiber and Stoller's own "Trouble," a Muddy Waters–style stop-time blues whose classic opening—"If you're looking for trouble, you've come to the right place"—was perfect for the rebel Danny Fisher. Leiber and Stoller were on the West Coast on other business, but they came by on the first day to help with the arrangements on their own songs, and it's more than likely that they lent a hand on some of the other tunes. "Hard Headed Woman" and "Trouble," along with "Dixieland Rock," "New Orleans," and "King Creole," became the nucleus of a unique soundtrack for Elvis. If singer and band were looking for trouble, they found it in "King Creole"; its double-time pace particularly challenged the newly returned Scotty and D. J., and

though they made it through eighteen takes no one could agree on which was best. In the end the third and final takes were transferred to the master reel, giving Elvis a chance to review them later on.

The next day they started off with the other up-tempo tune from Aaron Schroeder (and Rachel Frank, a.k.a Beverly Ross), "Dixieland Rock," then moved on to the ballads, by now as much a part of Elvis's repertoire as rock 'n' roll. Weisman and Wise had four candidates in this category: "Danny," "As Long As I Have You," "Don't Ask Me Why," and the wonderfully off-beat "Crawfish," which had been successfully recorded on the first night. True to form, the songwriters had had demos cut by Jimmy Breedlove, whose vocals clearly demonstrated how the song could work for Elvis. Freddy Bienstock was always grateful for a demo that did his work for him, and it was a strategy that paid off for the flexible, aggressive Ben Weisman: Together with Fred Wise and many other cowriters, Weisman would amass an astounding career total of fifty-seven Elvis Presley cuts. "Don't Ask Me Why" and "As Long As I Have You" gave the crew no problems; the latter was done in two versions, one for the movie session and one for potential record release, because Elvis felt it was strong enough to justify such an approach. In the end, Paramount used Elvis's version in the picture. "Lover Doll" was a charming, inoffensive acoustic recording that Steve Sholes liked so much he beefed it up with vocal overdubs with an eye to a single release. The final Weisman and Wise offering, "Danny," was ultimately set aside, for one thing because it wasn't as strong as the three previous movie title cuts, "Love Me Tender," "Loving You," and "Jailhouse Rock," every one a big hit.

Perhaps equally pertinent was Leiber and Stoller's interest in replacing it with their own "King Creole." Elvis knew well how instrumental the team had been in the successes of his last eighteen months, and at this point in his career their instincts may have been the only ones he trusted as much as his own; changing the name of a motion picture was a major decision, but Jerry and Mike knew that a good song could make it happen (as it had with each of Elvis's previous pictures). By the end of the second day the issue of the title song was still undecided; "King Creole" had given the band some problems, but "Danny" hadn't even been recorded.

Over the next few days the title debate continued between the Presley camp and the studio. Neither Paramount nor the Colonel was convinced that they'd cut a good enough "King Creole" yet, so it was decided to go back to the studio the following week and try again. This would give the group an opportunity to record an instrumental version as well—just in case the title was changed back—and to record one more needed number. Significantly, this was what gave Steve Sholes the opportunity to augment the rhythm section, bringing in Bernie Mattinson to assist D. J. Fontana on drums. Scotty and Bill had returned to the fold after the Christmas album debacle, but both Ray Siegel and Jordanaire Neal Matthews had to fill in for Bill on electric bass when the rhythms got too tough. The fact was, Elvis's original band members were young, practically amateur country players, who had no trouble charging through a straight-ahead rock 'n' roll number, but who just weren't ready to take on every new demand a Hollywood score could make of them—certainly not as ready as Elvis was proving to be.

Elvis wasn't prepared to admit he might have outgrown Scotty and Bill, though, so for the moment Steve's only resort was to send in another drummer and hope for the best. The first goal of the extra session was, of course, to rerecord "King Creole." Right away the song took on new life, its new, simplified arrangement reducing the role of the horn section and leaving it out altogether for certain passages. More for commercial than for artistic reasons, the introduction was changed to highlight the Jordanaires singing the words "King Creole" before Elvis came in. Finally, Scotty Moore came up with a finger-bleeding guitar solo, which completed the song's transformation into straight rock 'n' roll. There was still the instrumental version to do, but before Scotty got to that they worked on a pleasant if stale version of the new song, "Young Dreams." Then Elvis wanted to go over some additional songs for the upcoming singles session that RCA was planning; without his creative aides Leiber and Stoller to bounce ideas off of, though, Elvis's efforts got nowhere. Before they left for the night, Elvis made sure to instruct Tom Diskin to get hold of the two songwriters—in particular Jerry Leiber—for the next session. Tom duly typed the letter and mailed it to Steve Sholes.

40. Studio Sessions for RCA
February 1, 1958: Radio Recorders, Hollywood

A&R/Producer: Steve Sholes
Engineer: Thorne Nogar

Guitar: Scotty Moore
Guitar: Tiny Timbrell
Guitar: Elvis Presley
Bass: Bill Black

Drums: D. J. Fontana
Piano: Dudley Brooks
Vocals: The Jordanaires

10AM–7PM

J2WB 0178-nm	**My Wish Came True**	
	Ivory Joe Hunter—Southern/Elvis Presley Music	
J2WB 0179-sp	**Doncha' Think It's Time**	**Single B-side**
	Clyde Otis/Willie Dixon—Elvis Presley Music	*47-7240/1958*
J2WB 0180-10	**Your Cheatin' Heart**	**Elvis For Everyone**
	Hank Williams—Acuff/Rose	*LPM 3450/1965*
J2WB 0181-22	**Wear My Ring Around Your Neck**	**Single A-side**
	Bert Carroll/Russell Moody—Rush/Elvis Presley Music	*47-7240/1958*

The master of "Doncha' Think It's Time" (0179) is spliced from takes 40, 47, and 48. For the master of "Wear My Ring Around Your Neck" (0181), Elvis overdubbed "Guitar Back Beat" and piano background himself on the evening of February 26.

They were running out of time. The movie had to be finished before Elvis was inducted, and Steve Sholes was desperate to get Elvis back into the studio so that RCA could be assured of a steady stream of new releases available during his two-year tour of duty. Elvis's RCA contract committed him to deliver four singles per year, and still the only potential single Sholes had in the can was "One Night," which Elvis didn't want released until he had a chance to beat the record he'd made in January 1957. He was anxious to work on the two tunes he had rehearsed at the final *King Creole* session, "Doncha' Think It's Time" by Clyde Otis and Brook Benton (writing under the name of Willie Dixon) and "My Wish Came True," which he hadn't been satisfied with when they first tried it in September. But then came dismaying news: Jerry Leiber, whose innovative arranging skills Elvis was counting on for the session, was in a New York hospital with pneumonia and couldn't even consider traveling to Los Angeles. Elvis's first reaction was to postpone or even call off the session, but with his induction imminent and the RCA obligation looming overhead, he returned to the studio with no outside help and no other musicians besides Dudley Brooks and Tiny Timbrell, now semiregulars.

Without any real direction, they got nowhere with "My Wish Came True." Then they spent forty-eight takes trying to inject a little bit of swing into "Doncha' Think It's Time." Then they reached back to Hank Williams's classic, "Your Cheatin' Heart," and inflicted an awkward mid-tempo reading on it. None of it worked, and to Elvis's mind neither did the last song, probably the best recording of the evening—"Wear My Ring Around Your Neck." The only way he would allow "Ring" to be released was if the master were overdubbed with a new piano part and some guitar-slapping percussion, "Don't Be Cruel"–style; by now he'd learned it was best for him to insist on control, so rather than risk any more mistakes he overdubbed the parts himself. At the time, Elvis's word about what could and couldn't be released was firm—and "Your Cheatin' Heart" went unreleased for seven years.

It was a disheartening session, and it could only have magnified Elvis's fears about being snatched away from his burgeoning career. Steve Sholes was close to panic at the thought that his golden boy was about to leave for two years with almost no usable product in the can. It was indeed the end of an era; as things turned out, this would be the last full session between Elvis and his original band, and his final recording with Bill Black (save for a quick return to the studio ten days later to wrap up some unfinished business on the new movie). The title-song debate still hadn't been settled, and the verdict on the new version of "King Creole" was inconclusive enough that they returned to the Paramount soundstage on February 11 to try recording the alternative, "Danny"—Hal Wallis's title choice. They also needed a better version of the school song "Steadfast, Loyal And True," a purely ex-positional a cappella number Leiber and Stoller had contributed for the film. In early March "Danny" was finally rejected. (It would eventually turn up in yet another mutation as "Lonely Blue Boy" by Conway Twitty.) Still, "King Creole" wasn't considered strong enough to be the new single; the Colonel preferred combining the two ballads, "Don't Ask Me Why" and "As Long As I Have You," while Steve Sholes wanted to couple the latter with one of the rhythm songs. His selection was "Lover Doll," the only up-tempo number without the brass section; it lacked the raw aggressive dynamic of any of the other possibilities, but he still felt it could work.

Sholes's primary concern was the recordings due RCA. Although technically the *King Creole* material didn't yet belong to RCA, he called Thorne Nogar at Radio Recorders and requested a reference lacquer of everything that had been recorded. Elvis had already made up his mind to put out one single and two EPs, leaving out the school song, and the Colonel communicated his decision to Steve. The Colonel made it sound like an agreeable compromise; after all, everyone wanted a hit single, and historically EPs had done exceptionally well. Sholes, however, wanted to go all-out and release a full soundtrack album right away. Elvis was RCA's biggest money-maker, and a slowdown in sales could affect the entire company. Once again conventional record-company wisdom and the Colonel's long-term vision were clashing swords: As far as Sholes was concerned fans were a fickle lot, so better to make hay while the sun shone. Everyone knew the *King Creole* recordings were very different from Elvis's usual material, but the Colonel was philosophical in summing up the situation to Steve: "Who knows, at this time a little change may be better. No one has a crystal ball that works all the time." In the end, this round went to Steve Sholes: The single paired the hard-hitting "Hard Headed Woman" with the ballad "Don't Ask Me Why," and Parker allowed RCA to follow up with both EPs and a full-fledged album including everything recorded for the film—even "Steadfast, Loyal And True."

41. Studio Sessions for RCA
June 10, 1958: RCA's Studio B, Nashville

A&R/Producer: Steve Sholes
Engineer: RLJ

Guitar: Hank Garland
Guitar: Chet Atkins
Guitar: Elvis Presley
Bass: Bob Moore

Drums: D. J. Fontana
Piano: Floyd Cramer
Bongos: Buddy Harman
Vocals: The Jordanaires

7–10PM, 10:30PM–1:30AM

| J2WB 3253-18 | **I Need Your Love Tonight** | **Single B-side** |
| | *Sid Wayne/Bix Reichner—Gladys Music* | *47-7506/1959* |

J2WB 3254-sp	**A Big Hunk O' Love**	**Single A-side**
	Aaron Schroeder/Sid Wyche—Gladys Music	*47-7600/1959*
J2WB 3255-04	**Ain't That Loving You Baby**	**Single B-side**
	Clyde Otis/Ivory Joe Hunter—Elvis Presley Music	*47-8440/1964*
J2WB 3256-09	**(Now And Then There's) A Fool Such As I**	**Single A-side**
	Bill Trader—Bob Miller/Elvis Presley Music	*47-7506/1959*

2–5AM

J2WB 3257-24	**I Got Stung**	**Single B-side**
	Aaron Schroeder/David Hill—Gladys Music	*47-7410/1958*

The master of "A Big Hunk O' Love" (3254) is spliced from takes 3 and 4. Ray Walker replaced Hugh Jarrett as bass singer in the Jordanaires from this session on.

After finally settling on the release schedule, Steve Sholes continued to push for more sessions before Elvis shipped out to Germany in September, and the Colonel reluctantly agreed to both a recording and a photo session during a two-week furlough in June. Hit singles were the top priority, and Freddy Bienstock contacted his writers for material strong enough for single release. Clyde Otis recalls that he was down in Louisiana visiting Ivory Joe Hunter. "We'd gone duck hunting, and when we got back, there was this call from the people at Hill and Range asking us if we had anything for an upcoming Elvis session. We said, 'Yes,' but really we didn't have anything. So we sat down and wrote that song, and rushed it off to them." What they came up with was

Studio B, Nashville, June 10, 1958

"Ain't That Loving You Baby," the third of five songs recorded during the session, every one of which would eventually appear on a single.

In Nashville, at RCA's new Studio B, Chet Atkins assembled a group of session musicians—Nashville's so-called "A-team," made up of players known for their musical mix of grace, grit, and originality; they were by far the most competent band to back Elvis Presley yet. In a sense, putting together this group was RCA's first real creative contribution to an Elvis Presley recording session. The new quartet's star was undoubtedly guitarist Hank "Sugarfoot" Garland, who in addition to a recording career of his own (in which he had created a new form of music, "hillbilly jazz") had played with Eddy Arnold back when the Colonel was managing him. Hank had also played for Elvis briefly in the fall of 1957, during that strange period after Scotty and Bill had resigned. Bob Moore (no relation to Scotty) was the bass player, and Murrey "Buddy" Harmon would join D. J. Fontana, the sole holdover from the original trio, on percussion. The two drummers, possibly the unsung heroes of the sessions, would help to maintain an exciting but consistent rhythm, with Buddy providing fills while D. J. concentrated on keeping the tempo solid. The lineup was completed by Floyd Cramer, Elvis's piano player from the Hayride days, and the irreplaceable, ever-present Jordanaires. The atmosphere was decidedly more professional and less relaxed than sessions at Radio Recorders; Steve Sholes needed the boys to cut as many sides as possible, and he was more active than usual in pushing the session along, scarcely giving the band a chance to breathe between takes.

There was no trouble, though, getting hard work out of these musicians. From the moment they started, they gave Elvis not just solid back-

ing but the kind of energy that spurred him to go all out on a song like the up-tempo "I Need Your Love Tonight." The lyrics ("paw, paw," "ooh wee") may have bordered on the silly, but they were all part of the irresistibly light arrangement, and Elvis had fun playing around with them, using every trick in his book of sexy phrasings. Before the session even began Ray Walker, the new bass singer for the Jordanaires, took center stage; Gordon Stoker had been concerned that Ray wasn't as low a bass singer as Hugh Jarrett, but Elvis took to him right away, asking him to double several words and lines on this first song, leaving the other Jordanaires with a simple supporting "ooh" part. Elvis loved bass voices and had no hesitation with Ray, asking him to use the same mike he did so that he could control the blend of the voices and prevent the engineer from turning Ray's voice down in the final mix. By take number seven, Hank Garland's guitar was blasting out the solo with Buddy's drums filling the bridges, and it sounded great. It felt great too, but Elvis wasn't ready to quit until they got to take eighteen.

"A Big Hunk O' Love" proved even steamier. With lines like "I ain't greedy baby—all I want is all you've got," it echoed the spirit of some of Elvis's best movie lines ("That ain't tactics, honey, it's just the beast in me.") A tailor-made piece from Bienstock's staff of pop music fashion designers, the song was bluesier than the previous one, and the band took it at full force, with Elvis injecting an edge of sexuality almost comparable to 1955's "Baby Let's Play House." He was totally absorbed, singing and humming along during the solos from Floyd and Hank. In the end they agreed to splice the piano solo from the exuberantly wild take number four into the more controlled take three. This brought them to the tune Clyde Otis and Ivory Joe Hunter had written especially for the session, "Ain't That Loving You Baby," but for Elvis and the band it was considerably less natural than the previous cuts. Flailing about in search of a good arrangement, at first they chose a tempo that made the Jordanaires sound thoroughly extraneous; Hank Garland's guitar work, meanwhile, recalled Scotty's on "When It Rains It Really Pours" in both its bluesy orientation and its lack of swing. Take four was complete, but everyone agreed that something was still lacking, so Chet Atkins stepped in to help. "Boogie, Chet," Elvis called out, and with Bob Moore on acoustic bass Atkins worked up a walking bass figure on guitar to help stabilize the rhythm in a new speeded-up arrangement. Even then Elvis had trouble with the tempo change, and the Jordanaires were reduced to hand-claps by the time they got to take number eleven, when they finally decided to leave the song behind and move on. Both the slower and the fast version would be considered winners by most artists, but Elvis was chasing something he heard in his head; if he couldn't get it down on tape he'd just abandon the song and keep RCA from releasing it, as he did for six years with "Ain't That Loving You Baby."

The next number, "(Now And Then There's) A Fool Such As I," was familiar to all, and a special favorite of Tom Diskin's from the days when he and the Colonel had managed Hank Snow (who had the original hit with it in 1953). Neither of Elvis's companies owned any publishing on the song, which made it an unlikely single candidate, but Diskin felt it had potential and made a very uncharacteristic pitch to the Aberbachs to make a deal on the song. Chet's rhythm guitar lent real excitement to the lilting melody, giving it the kind of distinctive flavor that Elvis's treatment of "Your Cheatin' Heart" could have used back in February. After requesting a small adjustment on the echo, Elvis now leapt confidently into "I Got Stung." By this stage in the evening, both Elvis and Steve recognized there had already been a major improvement over earlier sessions, but the Colonel wasn't so sure. He felt the band was too loud, as noisy as the *King Creole* soundtrack—too noisy for people to appreciate the singing, which was, after all, why they bought the records in the first place. Then again it was hard to complain too much; this was a furlough session, and there was Elvis laughing, enjoying himself, ad-libbing a line from "When Irish Eyes Are Smiling" with the Jordanaires falling right in behind. Sporting his uniform, complete with hat, Elvis dropped bits of army jargon into conversation, calling out "at ease" between takes. Eventually the group was overcome with fatigue, and Elvis kept repeating the same mistake, complaining, "Man, you better hurry up, my brain's getting weaker every minute"—but neither he nor Steve Sholes was ready to give up on "I Got Stung." Hank Garland, carrying the solo, made some adjustments; Elvis changed the melody at the spot he'd been tripping over; the Jordanaires, who'd had some difficulties hearing the words they were supposed to sing, found their place; then, finally, they had it. "Ready on the left, ready on the right, ready on the firing line," he announced, and Private Presley led the troops to an overwhelming victory on take twenty-four.

In the early morning hours of June 11 Elvis Presley walked out of the studio, leaving the responsibility for his future recording career in the hands of Tom Parker and Steve Sholes. He'd done everything he could; now it was up to these two men to make sure he'd have a career to return to.

1958–59

GOETHESTRASSE

As the U.S.S. *Randall* left the Brooklyn army terminal on September 22, 1958, the reality of Colonel Tom Parker's new role set in: All at once he was a manager without an artist. Even though Elvis had been inducted into the armed services in March he was still very much in the public eye, and the Colonel had to deal with continual demands from the press for interviews and photographs while Elvis was stationed at Fort Hood in Texas. There was some good news—Steve Sholes's uninterrupted pressure for more recordings had led to the successful June sessions—but when Elvis's mother died on August 12 the Colonel was forced to step in and make all the arrangements to support his devastated client. "Everything I have is gone," Elvis cried hopelessly, and the Colonel was well aware that on another level he might well have been fearing that everything—his music, his career, even rock 'n' roll itself—might well be gone when he returned to civilian life in March of 1960.

As always, though, the Colonel had a plan. He'd been developing it ever since he realized the army stint was unavoidable (special services weren't an option; that would have meant Elvis giving away his talent for free). By now rock 'n' roll was well established as a market niche, but RCA could only assume that like any other trend it would be replaced soon enough by the next new thing. RCA had informed the Colonel that the total record market was down: Singles sales were dropping, and albums hadn't yet developed enough of a market to compensate for the decline. There was no doubt that Elvis Presley was still the hottest item in the recording business, but the three singles he'd put out after "Jailhouse Rock," though all million-sellers, couldn't be compared with his earlier hits. Neither *Elvis' Christmas Album* nor *Elvis' Golden Records* had approached the sales of the *Loving You* LP. There was every reason to look upon this two-year break, then, as a chance for a fresh start. And while the Colonel would never abandon his efforts to keep Elvis's name in the public eye, this breathing space gave him time to step back and work on his ambitious new project: to make Elvis a full-time movie star.

It was, from the first, Elvis's own long-standing ambition, something he'd talked about quite openly as far back as 1955 with Faron Young, then being represented himself in Hollywood by the Colonel. In the entertainment world a film career was more prestigious than that of a recording star, and the Colonel knew this was where the real money was. Elvis's success in the record business outstripped any previous performer's, but even he believed there was no way to keep such a streak going without adding a new element. His task was clear: While maintaining as high a profile as possible for the young GI, the Colonel had to set the stage for the new career Elvis would begin as soon as he returned home. Elvis's first films had depended on his teen-idol status; now Parker would have to convince Hollywood that Elvis could transcend that, could hang on to his core audience and expand it by refining his image as his audience grew older and settled into adult lives. Making a silk purse out of a sow's ear, the Colonel's first course of action was to turn Elvis's inconvenient tour of duty to his advantage: Here was a young man who was responsible, patriotic, even clean-cut, someone who didn't look for the easy way out, who, despite the tragic loss of his beloved mother, was prepared to accept the same duties as any other GI without any complaint or special treatment. This was a boy movie audiences would flock to see—the rebel transformed into something like a peacetime war hero. It took a lot of selling, but before the year was out the Colonel had negotiated a substantial improvement in Elvis's contract with Wallis and Hazen at Paramount (who would produce the first post-army picture) and with 20th Century–Fox, who had a lock on the next two. The Colonel was seeing to it that Elvis had something solid to come home to.

Meanwhile, Steve Sholes and Parker continued to bicker over the record release schedule. They had been fighting for more than two years now just over the issue of how many records a year should be released—the Colonel always coming down on the side of market scarcity, while Sholes was always pushing for the kind of heavy schedule that Parker feared would saturate the market. With so few sides in the can and no prospect of Elvis supplying any more before 1960, the Colonel seemed to have the upper hand, but Sholes was adamant that they all stick to the release schedule dictated in Elvis's contract—four singles and one album per year. RCA had little choice: With Elvis accounting for up to 40 percent of their annual sales, there was no way Sholes could give up the point. But with Elvis's proven ability to pick a hit, Sholes wasn't about to ride roughshod over his desires, and it was finally agreed that if Elvis expressed dissatisfaction with a particular recording the company wouldn't release it; only in the absence of a timely response would they put out a song as a single without his okay. When Elvis left for Germany, the record company had five songs from the June session, as well as a small backlog of unreleased material. Among the takes still unreleased were "Tomorrow Night," an unfinished master acquired from Sun Records, as well as "Tell Me Why," the song thought to be too close to "Just A Closer Walk With Thee." Elvis considered "One Night," "Your Cheatin' Heart," "Ain't That Loving You Baby," and "My Wish Came True" all only unfinished masters, and "When It Rains, It Really Pours" no more than a possible album cut. Sholes had wanted fresh material for at least five singles and not less than one album—twenty-two cuts in all. Instead he had just twelve, and few without problems.

Elvis Presley's record sales in the fall of 1958 were strong enough, led by all the new

King Creole releases, but there were some worrisome signs. There was a loyal audience of about a million who were ready to snap up each new release, but the days of two- to three-million-sellers seemed to be over. "Hard Headed Woman" peaked at number two, and each of the EPs sold over half a million, battling for number one and number two on the new EP chart. The album also went to number two, but sales were definitely slower than they had been for its predecessor, *Loving You.* The album's lackluster performance shouldn't have been much of a surprise; with the single and EPs already out, most of Elvis's teenage fans didn't need to duplicate their collections by buying the album, too. To Sholes, though, the album meant another 100,000 units of turnover.

A new single had to be chosen, and both Sholes and the Colonel were still pulling for "One Night" over Elvis's objections; the publishing company had made a deal for part of the royalties, but the deal depended upon the song's release as a single and couldn't be extended past October 31, 1958. The Colonel felt it would be foolish not to take advantage of the deal, and at last he persuaded Elvis to agree. With "I Got Stung" from the June session as the B-side, the new single caused an immediate sensation. DJs clearly preferred the A-side, but both cuts shot up the charts right away, eventually reaching number four and number eight, respectively. Split airplay may well have been what stopped "One Night" from going to number one on the charts, but the single sold several hundred thousand copies more than the last two releases, even matching "Don't"/"I Beg Of You."

In another effort to keep Elvis's profile up while generating new material for the fans (not to mention further income), the Colonel convinced Steve Sholes to put out a recording of the pre-embarkation press conference, *Elvis Sails;* without Elvis even singing a note, they sold another 100,000 EPs. For the Christmas season there was talk of releasing "Santa Claus Is Back In Town" as a single, but since it was already on an EP and LP, four other Christmas songs were pulled together as a sequel EP instead. With Elvis himself momentarily out of reach, the disagreements between Sholes and the Colonel grew more heated. Sholes, who was very proud of the June recordings, wanted to use them for new singles instead of the leftover material; the Colonel, acting out of sincere reservations but also never one to give up a good fight, kept arguing that the new masters were too noisy. They were like little boys playing he-said-she-said in the schoolyard: When Sholes dismissed the Colonel's suggestion of "My Wish Came True" as an A-side, Parker tried to play Elvis against Steve, forgetting that Elvis himself had told Sholes he was dissatisfied with the take. RCA did release "A Fool Such As I," Tom Diskin's long-time favorite, with "I Need Your Love Tonight" in March 1959, and both songs stormed up the charts, the first landing at number two, the other at number four, and the single achieving its expected million sales. The Colonel was always at the helm of Elvis's career, but in this case his assistant's judgment had triumphed over his own.

When "A Big Hunk O' Love" and "My Wish Came True" came out in July, the Colonel turned out to be even more wrong. His personal favorite, "My Wish Came True," languished at number twelve, while "A Big Hunk O' Love," the noisiest of the Nashville recordings, climbed all the way to the top of the charts. The Colonel didn't spend any time worrying about what was past, though; he had new fish to fry. The first was repackaging Elvis's older singles into a series of EPs called *A Touch Of Gold* and putting together three new albums (*For LP Fans Only, A Date With Elvis,* and *Elvis Golden Records Vol. 2*) that included a number of songs never previously released on LP. It was a holding action, to be sure, but the Colonel was perfectly content to take the money; with the movie deals in his pocket, there was no need to spend too much time sweating the small stuff.

Despite all the outward confidence, there were moments of doubt: From time to time Elvis would call from Germany, homesick, worried, generally unhappy, and more than once the Colonel gave some thought to the idea of getting him an early discharge. Most of the time, though, Parker simply worked hard to keep things going. He signed a deal with ABC-TV for Elvis to appear on Frank Sinatra's "Timex Show" in conjunction with his release from the army (and RCA's release of his first post-army single). The Colonel even toyed with the idea of getting Elvis to record an EP in Germany and encouraged him to purchase some good home recording equipment; perhaps he could sing some of the religious numbers he loved so much to his own piano or guitar accompaniment. Elvis did in fact make some very rough home recordings both by himself and with his friends Red West and Charlie Hodge, and two distorted tapes of these performances survive; they show Elvis fooling around with old material and new, trying out songs he's clearly considering for the future—the Drifters' "Such A Night," the mock-aria "There's No Tomorrow." The tapes are a fascinating window into his evolving musical thinking, but none of his home-taped efforts were mentioned to Steve Sholes, and they would never have been suitable for commercial release.

To Freddy Bienstock, on the other hand, they may well have been useful. Freddy met Elvis on leave in Paris and came to Germany in August of 1959 while Paramount was filming test background footage (later rejected) for what came to be known as *G.I. Blues*. On those visits he brought demos for Elvis's future consideration, and returned home with a list of titles Elvis was interested in recording when he got back. As the spring of 1960 approached and Freddy busied himself securing rights on Elvis's choices, the Colonel prepared to set his carefully laid plans in motion. The movie arrangements were all set. The TV show was in place, even a pair of songs for a new single had been selected. Now all he could do was await Elvis's return.

In Germany, 1959

42. Home Recordings
April 1959: Goethestrasse, Bad Nauheim, Germany

Guitar: Elvis Presley

NPA5 5821	**I'm Beginning To Forget You**	**Elvis: A Legendary Performer Vol. 4**
	Phelps	*CPL1 4848/1983*
WPA5 2591	**I Can't Help It (If I'm Still In Love With You)**	**Platinum: A Life In Music**
	Hank Williams	*67469-2/1997*
NPA5 5822	**Mona Lisa**	**Elvis: A Legendary Performer Vol. 4**
	Livingston/Evans	*CPL1 4848/1983*
OPA5 8201	**Danny Boy**	**A Golden Celebration**
	Weatherly	*CPM6 5172/1984*
	Loving You	
	Leiber/Stoller	
WPA5 2592	**I'm Beginning to Forget You (a capella)**	**Platinum: A Life In Music**
	Phelps	*67469-2/1997*

In spite of notations in the booklet to *Platinum: A Life in Music*, new information proves that these recordings are not from 1961.

43. Home Recordings
April 1959 or later: Goethestrasse, Bad Nauheim, Germany

He Knows Just What I Need
Mosie Lister
Cool Water
Bob Nolan
His Hand In Mine
Mosie Lister
Return To Me
Carmen Lombardo/Danny Di Minno
Are You Lonesome Tonight?
Roy Turk/Lou Handman
Stand By Me
Traditional
Take My Hand, Precious Lord
Thomas A. Dorsey
Oh, Lonesome Me
Don Gibson

As of this writing only the track listing for this tape has yet been located; it is uncertain whether the tape itself is lost, but the list reveals more of the material Elvis and his friends worked on during their time in Germany.

44. Home Recordings
After April 1959: Goethestrasse, Bad Nauheim, Germany

Piano: Elvis Presley

OPA5 8205	**I Asked The Lord**	**A Golden Celebration**
	Johnny Lange/Jimmy Duncan	*CPM6 5172/1984*
	Apron Strings	
	Weiss/Schroeder	
OPA5 8203	**Soldier Boy**	**A Golden Celebration**
	Jones/Williams Jr.	*CPM6 5172/1984*
OPA5 8204	**Earth Angel**	**A Golden Celebration**
	Belvin	*CPM6 5172/1984*
	I'll Take You Home Again Kathleen (fast version)	
	Thomas P. Westendorf	
	Que Sera, Sera/Hound Dog	
	Jay Livingston/Ray Evans—Jerry Leiber/Mike Stoller	
	I'll Take You Home Again Kathleen	
	Traditional	
	It's Been So Long Darling	
	Ernest Tubb	
	I Will Be True	
	Ivory Joe Hunter	
	There's No Tomorrow	
	Hoffman/Corday/Carr	
	Unidentified (possibly called "Number Eight")	
	n/a	
	Send Me Some Lovin'	
	Marascalco/Price	
OPA5 8206	**The Fool**	**A Golden Celebration**
	Naomi Ford	*CPM6 5172/1984*

"I'll Take You Home Again Kathleen," "I Will Be True," "It's Been So Long Darling," "Apron Strings," and "There's No Tomorrow" appeared together as "Bad Nauheim Medley" on 1997's *Platinum: A Life In Music* (67469-2). Some of the songs were used only in part because of distortion on the original tape. "I Asked The Lord" was released by RCA under the title "He's Only A Prayer Away."

1960

ELVIS IS BACK

I'm writing this column on the day after THE day. In other words today is March 4, and yesterday was E day, when Elvis returned to the United States after his tour of duty in Germany for the army. Believe me, it was a thrill to be on hand, even in a snowstorm, and I won't go into that, along with his manager Col. Parker and many other personal friends to welcome Elvis back. I didn't get to talk to the popular, about to be Mr. again Presley for very long, as he was being besieged with questions from reporters, and radio/TV men. By now you have no doubt heard all about the press conference at Fort Dix, New Jersey, so there's no need to cover that ground again. Elvis looked wonderful. Thinner than I've seen him, but it's most becoming, and he said that the first thing he wants to do, is go home and relax. We second that. Next on the agenda, Elvis told me he wants to record and we are hoping to set up a session at a studio near to his home, very soon. We'll keep you posted.

> —RCA A&R man Steve Sholes, in his column
> "Steve's Beat" in *D. J. Digest,* March 15, 1960

Elvis made it back to Memphis not long after Steve Sholes finished off his column, but with little time to rest. The Frank Sinatra TV special was coming right up, and the starting date for *G.I. Blues* was scheduled soon afterward. That meant the first RCA recording session would have to be squeezed in almost immediately, and it seemed to make the most sense to record in Nashville, site of the last sessions before Elvis left for Germany. The feeling of that session had been terrific, and despite the Colonel's concerns about their sound (and his client's voice getting lost in the mix), the records they'd made there had been commercial winners.

In the two-year interim Hill & Range had come up with a strong list of songs from their staff writers; a new team, Doc Pomus and Mort Shuman, had recently signed with the publisher, and Doc had spent time with Lamar Fike in England discussing the kind of thing Elvis wanted to record. Lamar was genuinely intrigued by the music business, and he may already have been eyeing for himself the role he'd take in the Presley camp three years later as Freddy Bienstock's right-hand man in Nashville. For their part, Pomus and Shuman weren't convinced the Elvis courtship would lead to anything. Earlier that year Elvis had passed on a song they'd written especially for him, "Turn Me Loose," which had ended up a hit for Fabian. Now "A Mess Of Blues" and "Doin' The Best I Can" were at the top of Freddy's pile, and Pomus and Shuman sat back to wait. Other familiar names cast their hats into the ring: Knowing how much Elvis liked "One Night," the ever-professional Ben Weisman wrote "It Feels So Right" along the same lines. With Fred Wise, Weisman also brought in a stirring ballad aptly entitled "Fame And Fortune." And Elvis, Steve Sholes, and Freddy Bienstock had already agreed on the first post-army single: "Stuck On You," a branch from the "All Shook Up" tree by Aaron Schroeder and Leslie McFarland.

Elvis's band was the question mark. From Steve Sholes's point of view, and perhaps the Colonel's too, there was no musical reason to keep the old group. Bill Black, who already had a successful solo career with his own combo, had no interest in coming back. D. J. had been playing off and on with various singers, and Scotty had been having some success with his own Fernwood label—but they were both anxious to return, and Elvis had no intention of walking away from them. Scotty had been with him since the beginning, and despite some misunderstandings he'd remained a quiet presence through the turmoil of the past six years. Loyalty was all-important to Elvis, and in the end that's how the decision was made: Both Scotty and D. J. would stay on as regular members of the studio bands for the next eight years. In the meantime, RCA booked the studio musicians who had made such outstanding contributions to the last session, soon to be joined by sax player Boots Randolph.

All the most important figures in Elvis's present career—Colonel Parker, his partner Tom Diskin, and RCA's Bill Bullock and Steve Sholes—gathered at RCA's Studio B on Sunday night at 7:00 P.M. to be there as work began. Engineer Bill Porter had arrived late in the afternoon to set up the machines; this would be the first time Elvis was recorded on a three-track machine, giving more space to each player (as well as a separate track for Elvis's voice) and making real stereo records possible. For a group of sophisticated players like this, three-track was a distinct advantage: The music they made could be reproduced in finer detail, and the option of postsession remixing allowed for useful fine-tuning if something hadn't come out quite right. Still, Porter was determined to capture Elvis and his band live, to get the mix right the first time and rely on postproduction only if an overdub was called for.

Freddy Bienstock, in charge of finding new songs, had flown to Memphis ahead of time to go over the material with Elvis and in particular to ensure that he stuck with the plan to cut "Stuck On You" as the single. Then he rode to Nashville with Elvis and his entourage in a bus chartered by the Colonel. As they pulled up to the back entrance of the studio they were greeted by the Colonel's ever-present security guards, and before getting to work Elvis unwound with his customary presession socializing. The group exchanged greetings, joked, and listened as Elvis told a few army stories. Before long they'd begun the usual vocal warm-ups, as the group gathered around the piano and ran through familiar gospel numbers. It's unlikely anyone voiced any concern, but everyone in the room must have felt the tension. It had been almost two years since any of the businessmen present—not to mention the musicians—had heard Elvis sing. Did he still have it? And would "it" still work for them?

45. Studio Sessions for RCA
March 20, 1960: RCA's Studio B, Nashville

A&R/Producers: Steve Sholes & Chet Atkins
Engineer: Bill Porter

Guitar: Scotty Moore
Guitar: Elvis Presley
Bass: Bob Moore
Electric Bass: Hank Garland

Drums: D. J. Fontana
Drums: Buddy Harman
Piano: Floyd Cramer
Vocals: The Jordanaires

8PM–12AM

L2WB 0081-19	**Make Me Know It**	**Elvis Is Back**
	Otis Blackwell—Elvis Presley Music	*LSP 2231/1960*
L2WB 0082-15	**Soldier Boy**	**Elvis Is Back**
	David Jones/Theodore Williams Jr.—E. B. Marks Music	*LSP 2231/1960*

12:30–3:30AM

L2WB 0083-03	**Stuck On You**	**Single A-side**
	Aaron Schroeder/S. Leslie McFarland—Gladys Music	*47-7740/1960*
L2WB 0084-sp	**Fame And Fortune**	**Single B-side**
	Fred Wise/Ben Weisman—Gladys Music	*47-7740/1960*

4–7AM

L2WB 0085-05	**A Mess Of Blues**	**Single B-side**
	Doc Pomus/Mort Shuman—Elvis Presley Music	*47-7777/1960*
L2WB 0086-05	**It Feels So Right**	**Elvis Is Back**
	Fred Wise/Ben Weisman—Gladys Music	*LSP 2231/1960*

The master of "Fame And Fortune" (0084) is spliced from takes 15 and 14.

Although the primary concern was the single, they began with Otis Blackwell's new tune, "Make Me Know It." Perhaps it was because of Blackwell's credentials and Elvis's confidence in his abilities—you couldn't beat "Don't Be Cruel" or "All Shook Up," after all. In any case, if Blackwell was the good-luck talisman of the moment, the strategy worked. Elvis and the band sank their teeth into the up-tempo song ("awfully wordy," Elvis joked), and from the beginning their music had drive and brilliance and swing. They might have spent fewer takes on the song if they

had rehearsed it a little longer, but everybody was eager to start recording—and by take nineteen it was terrific, the three-track process capturing the music with vivid, immediate clarity.

Bill Porter recalled, "I felt a lot of tension in the room. I really did . . . right at my elbow almost was Colonel Parker, this VP from RCA [Bill Bullock], Steve Sholes—I mean, I could reach out and touch them. When Elvis did the first tune, they didn't say anything to me, but once he got the first tune down, they all started talking about other things. So it was, apparently, the anticipation of him singing again in the studio." And "Make Me Know It" couldn't have done a better job putting them all at ease.

Elvis had spent time in Germany practicing the 1955 Four Fellows hit "Soldier Boy," and discussed recording it with Freddy Bienstock, who had immediately made a deal with the original publisher. As they went to work on it now Chet Atkins had to remind Elvis to avoid "popping" his "b"s into the mike when he hit the word "boy," but the final version, take fourteen, only confirmed the measure of depth and ease the star had added to his singing style in the two years he'd been away. They still had a single to cut, though, and after a midnight break they came back to work on "Stuck On You."

RCA had already printed generic sleeves for the new 45 with two pre-army photos and a hole in the center so record-buyers could read the label; the only legend on the cover itself read ELVIS' 1ST NEW RECORDING FOR HIS 50,000,000 FANS ALL OVER THE WORLD, just in case Elvis decided to substitute a different song at the last minute. Arrangements had been made for the master tape to be rushed directly from the studio to the pressing plant, with 1.4 million units due to be shipped directly to dealers without waiting for orders to come in. "Stuck On You" had been selected for one good reason: It sounded like an Elvis hit. What they were aiming for were the hardcore Elvis fans as RCA imagined them, now a little older and ready to make the transition from the sexy Elvis of the '50s image to a new figure, more mature but still a rocker. The sound they wanted was closer to the upbeat pop model of "Don't Be Cruel" or "Teddy Bear" than to the raunchier Elvis of "Jailhouse Rock" or "Hound Dog." The RCA press materials may have captured the Presley camp's sentiment in their description of the song: "a clever, catchy rhythm piece with exactly the kind of mild rock beat that today's kids like." Never mind that Elvis didn't really like the song himself (or so Gordon Stoker recalls); he put in a solid performance and wrapped it up in three takes.

Then it was time to throw himself into a song he really believed in: the Ben Weisman ballad "Fame And Fortune," slated for the single's

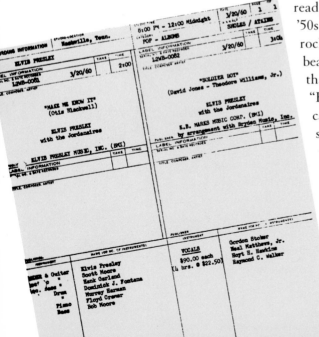

flip side. As early as his Sun days, Elvis's ambitions and insecurities had always clashed when it came to ballad singing, and his phrasing on "Fame And Fortune" still leaned a little toward the mannered. But the last two songs of the night, "A Mess Of Blues" and "It Feels So Right," were grittier, bluesy numbers Elvis felt right at home with, and along with everything else he recorded that day they went a long way toward proving the young singer's versatility and range. On both cuts the band played in full harmony with both singer and material, and overall Elvis had never sung better. With six cuts in a single night this was Elvis's most productive session ever, and the new technology made it his best-sounding. Having delivered to RCA everything the Colonel promised, the singer left for Florida to take on the next challenge in his manager's carefully planned assault.

46. TV Recordings for ABC's "The Frank Sinatra–Timex Show" March 26, 1960: Fontainebleau Hotel, Miami

Guitar: Scotty Moore
Drums: D. J. Fontana

Vocals: The Jordanaires
The Nelson Riddle Orchestra

WPA5 2559	**It's Nice To Go Trav'ling**		
	Sammy Cahn/Jimmy Van Heusen		
WPA5 2560	**Fame And Fortune**	**Platinum: A Life In Music**	
	Fred Wise/Ben Weisman	*67469-2/1997*	
WPA5 2561	**Stuck On You**	**Platinum: A Life In Music**	
	Aaron Schroeder/S. Leslie McFarland	*67469-2/1997*	
WPA5 2562	**Witchcraft/Love Me Tender**	**From Nashville To Memphis**	
	C. Coleman/C. Leigh—V. Matson/E. Presley	*66160-2/1993*	

"It's Nice To Go Trav'ling" had special lyrics written for the show; Frank Sinatra, Elvis Presley, Nancy Sinatra, Joey Bishop, and Sammy Davis, Jr., each sang a few lines. "Witchcraft"/"Love Me Tender" is a duet: Elvis sings Sinatra's "Witchcraft," while Sinatra sings "Love Me Tender." All material was performed live before an audience.

Elvis and his group traveled by train through Birmingham and Decatur, arriving in Miami in the early hours of March 22 to settle in and set up for rehearsal. Elegantly dressed in a tuxedo, with his hair brushed high, Elvis seemed to be of a different species from everyone else on "The Frank Sinatra–Timex Show." If he was nervous onstage with such pillars of American popular music as Sinatra (and his daughter Nancy), Sammy Davis, and conductor Nelson Riddle, he didn't show it. Even during the duet that featured Frank doing "Love Me Tender" while Elvis mimicked Sinatra's famous "Witchcraft," he maintained a distance that came across as boundless confidence and poise. He was in, but not of, his surroundings—altogether his own man. Of course he performed the just-released new single, and if he had any misgivings about "Stuck On You," it didn't show in his performance. (In fact, his reading of "Fame And Fortune" seemed less contrived than the version he'd recorded just days earlier.) The show's broadcast attracted 65 percent of the viewing audience, more than justifying the exorbitant fee of $125,000 that the Colonel had negotiated for his boy.

As soon as the group got back to Memphis, another Nashville session was scheduled to finish the album RCA was planning for April. RCA already had the record's gatefold sleeve completed, with photographs taken in Germany by the Colonel's photographer and a blank space ready to be filled with the song list as soon as the lineup was determined. Freddy's meetings with Elvis in Memphis (and Germany before that; he'd even chaperoned a trip to Paris) had prepared him to take care of the publishing well in advance. He provided demos for some older songs such as "Such A Night," originated by the Drifters and then recorded by Johnnie Ray in a version banned from the radio because of suggestive lyrics and a controversial performance to match. Elvis had told Freddy how much he loved Tony Martin's 1949 hit, "There's No Tomorrow"; his mother had owned a 78 of Caruso's "O Sole Mio," the turn-of-the-century Italian ballad the song was based on, and the aria's vocal challenge attracted him so much he'd already taped himself singing it while in Bad Nauheim. Under the impression that the melody was in the public domain, Freddy had Aaron Schroeder and Wally Gold compose new lyrics for it, and the new Hill & Range version became a top priority as they headed into the studio at the beginning of April.

47. Studio Sessions for RCA
April 3, 1960: RCA's Studio B, Nashville

A&R/Producers: Steve Sholes & Chet Atkins
Engineer: Bill Porter

Guitar: Scotty Moore
Guitar: Hank Garland
Guitar: Elvis Presley
Bass: Bob Moore
Drums: D. J. Fontana

Drums: Buddy Harman
Piano: Floyd Cramer
Sax: Boots Randolph
Vocals: The Jordanaires
Vocals: Charlie Hodge (harmony on 0108)

7:30PM–12AM

L2WB 0098-04	**Fever**	**Elvis Is Back**
	John Davenport/Eddie Cooley—Jay & Cee Music	*LSP 2231/1960*
L2WB 0099-06	**Like A Baby**	**Elvis Is Back**
	Jesse Stone—Bob Abbott & Elvis Presley Music	*LSP 2231/1960*
L2WB 0100-04	**It's Now Or Never**	**Single A-side**
	Aaron Schroeder/Wally Gold—Gladys Music	*47-7777/1960*

<u>12:45–3:45</u>AM

L2WB 0101-10	**The Girl Of My Best Friend**	**Elvis Is Back**
	Beverly Ross/Sam Bobrick—Elvis Presley Music	*LSP 2231/1960*
L2WB 0102-04	**Dirty, Dirty Feeling**	**Elvis Is Back**
	Jerry Leiber/Mike Stoller—Elvis Presley Music	*LSP 2231/1960*
L2WB 0103-03	**Thrill Of Your Love**	**Elvis Is Back**
	Stanley Kesler—Jack Music & Elvis Presley Music	*LSP 2231/1960*
L2WB 0104-02	**I Gotta Know**	**Single B-side**
	P. Evans/M. Williams—Gladys Music	*47-7810/1960*

<u>4–7</u>AM

L2WB 0105-05	**Such A Night**	**Elvis Is Back**
	Lincoln Chase/Raleigh Music/Elvis Presley Music	*LSP 2231/1960*
L2WB 0106-sp	**Are You Lonesome Tonight?**	**Single A-side**
	Roy Turk/Lou Handman—Bourne & Cromwell Music	*47-7810/1960*
L2WB 0107-04	**Girl Next Door Went A'Walking**	**Elvis Is Back**
	Bill Rise/Thomas Wayne—Bluff City & Elvis Presley Music	*LSP 2231/1960*
L2WB 0108-04	**I Will Be Home Again**	**Elvis Is Back**
	Benjamin/Leveen/Singer—Leeds Music	*LSP 2231/1960*
L2WB 0109-02	**Reconsider Baby**	**Elvis Is Back**
	Lowell Fulsom—Arc Music	*LSP 2231/1960*

The master of "It's Now Or Never" (0100) was overdubbed with piano and claves. The master of "Are You Lonesome Tonight?" (0106) is a splice of take 5 and the last bar from another, unidentified take.

Elvis's first post-army session had been a tremendous success, with a million-selling single and four album cuts beautifully recorded in under twelve hours. Steve Sholes attributed its success largely to the professionalism of the session musicians and the improvements in recording quality, but he also recognized Elvis's own newfound maturity. Nothing, however, could have prepared him for what came next.

Elvis returned to Studio B ready to tackle a new set of songs, pushed by an RCA deadline of April 5 for the album masters, but also hoping to get a single or two knocked off in the bargain. First up was "Fever," written by Ed Cooley and Otis Blackwell (under a pseudonym). The song had been a 1956 hit for Little Willie John, but it was Peggy Lee's arrangement Elvis followed, with Bob Moore's acoustic bass and Buddy Harman's congas as the only accompaniment. Originality wasn't what counted here; confidence carried the day, and the sultry beauty of his vocal made "Fever" a classic Presley performance. The control Elvis showed over his phrasing and tonal quality was outstanding, and it was all in service of his obviously expanding musical ambition.

In just as convincing (if more familiar) fashion, the group completed "Like A Baby," by the brilliant Atlantic songwriter Jesse Stone, in six takes. The first session two weeks before had been driven by the need for a new single, so Elvis had devoted most of his time to newly written material; now, though, with an obvious hit already in the can, things were clearly loosening up a bit. Freddy Bienstock had watched unhappily as Elvis ditched stacks of new songs he'd worked hard to get; now, with songs like "Fever" and "Like A Baby," the singer was building the session repertoire out of his own record collection. Jesse Stone often wrote for the Clovers, but they weren't the act who originated "Like A Baby"; it was first released by Vikki Nelson, but another important version had come from Tony Arden, whose version of "Padre" Elvis had once cited as his favorite record. The band gathered around him had been raised on the same mix of musical genres as Elvis, and many of them were practiced jazz musicians as well, so they had no trouble following Elvis into a persuasive R&B performance.

Yet the Clovers' influence did find its way into Elvis's work on this session; you might say it snuck in through the front door. One of the records that was definitely in the Graceland record collection was their Atlantic single "Down In The Alley"—and on its B-side, of all things, was a version of "There's No Tomorrow." So to Elvis the transition from rhythm and blues to "It's Now Or Never," the new English version Freddy had just commissioned, must have seemed almost natural. "I sing all kinds," Elvis had told Marion Keisker seven years before, and he was as good as his word: This wasn't opera, exactly, but it was the kind of Neapolitan recitation opera singers often performed before popular audiences. Aaron Schroeder, the new lyricist, was in the studio for the event, and after the first playback Elvis moaned, "I'm sorry, Aaron. I don't know if I can do this song justice. You've done a beautiful lyric, and I want to sing the notes I have in my mind." Fighting back tears, he went back into the studio and laid down a master in four takes. This was pure pop music, delivered with both superb musical command and the highest level of professionalism—and it all represented exactly Colonel Tom Parker's dreams and hopes for Elvis's new artistic direction. In a few extra minutes an extra piano figure and claves were added to the master; in just five hours Elvis had produced three perfect records.

After a quick break for his favorite Krystal burgers, he settled down next to work on "The Girl Of My Best Friend." It didn't really fit any of the singer's particular musical interests, and the band took a while to work up an arrangement, but in ten takes—the most of any song in the sessions—they had a potential hit. "Dirty, Dirty Feeling" was a Leiber and Stoller song intended for the *King Creole* soundtrack, but never recorded; business disputes with the Colonel kept the team from sending in any new material, but Elvis got this one done in four rocking takes. Next they moved on to "Thrill Of Your Love," a ballad with a gospel flavor by Stan Kesler (who'd written two of Elvis's Sun sides as well as RCA's "Playing for Keeps"). He had gotten the song into the session through Jack Clement, the former Sun engineer and producer who now worked for Chet Atkins. The band took to it instantly, and Elvis sang his heart out to complete the recording in just three takes. Freddy came up with another straight pop song, "I Gotta Know"; Elvis probably didn't know it had just been recorded by England's Cliff Richard, but he was having so much fun he might not have cared. He knocked off the slight little pop ditty in something under ten minutes.

At nearly 4:00 A.M. with no additional new material in sight, under ordinary circumstances the session would surely have ended. But they still needed more cuts for the album, and Elvis knew they had to have it finished by April 5, not just because of its scheduled release date but also because the start of work on his new Paramount picture was looming just ahead. In an atmosphere charged with creativity, then, Elvis and the group pressed on, pulling songs out of the air. The choice of "Such A Night" echoed the feel of the first two songs, "Fever" and "Like A Baby," and walked the fine line between suggestiveness and aloof humor with a newly sparkling charm. It seemed like yet another candidate for a smash single. After finishing that, they moved on to a rare musical contribution from the Colonel himself. Though it was his own oft-stated policy never to interfere with the music, the year before, when they were still talking about possibly recording in Germany, he had suggested that Elvis try a song that was a favorite of his wife, Marie. "Are You Lonesome Tonight?" had been recorded with notable success by several artists; the biggest of them was Al Jolson, who had a hit with it in 1927. Now, with the studio lights turned down, Elvis gave the sentimental song the full theatrical treatment, creating a credible drama in which the singer is seduced, deceived, and finally abandoned. It was a surprising selection, yet almost at once—and almost as surprisingly—it became an immediate contender for single release.

With that gorgeous set piece safely accomplished, Elvis fulfilled a promise to Scotty Moore, cutting a song by the Scotty's Fernwood Records act Thomas Wayne. "Girl Next Door Went A'Walking" was no great composition, but Elvis glided through it in four takes. Then, in another favor to a friend, he cut "I Will Be Home Again." Elvis had met fellow G.I. Charlie Hodge on the boat to Germany; a professional musician who'd sung with the Foggy River Boys behind artists such as Red Foley and Gene Autry, Charlie had spent a lot of time singing and harmonizing with Elvis in the past two years, and had introduced him to the song as a pop entry on a Golden Gate Quartet album. Elvis brought Charlie in to sing the song with him as a duet, their voices blending together perfectly for the first time on record.

It was seven in the morning when Elvis dug into "Reconsider Baby," a Lowell Fulsom blues he'd known since its 1954 release. The musicians were just a few hours away from their scheduled Monday morning sessions, but the opportunity to get down and blow some blues seemed to be enough to keep them going. At heart an unrehearsed jam, the track starred the newest addition to the group, Homer "Boots" Randolph—a Kentucky-born player brought up on jazz who'd been supplementing his club-gig income working Nashville sessions. His sax solo, the first on a Presley record, went straight into the book of classic rock 'n' roll moments. On that exhilarating note, an amazing night was brought to a close, and without a moment's hesitation RCA rushed the album into release.

You never heard him like this before.
—RCA Dealer Information, April 1960

Artistically, the album *Elvis Is Back* was a triumph on every level. Every one of the earlier albums had had its musical compromises. The selections on both *Loving You* and *King Creole* were dictated by the movies' requirements; the first RCA album contained five previously rejected Sun masters, and when the second, *Elvis,* came up short of material, the extra time had been taken up with not one or two but *three* Little Richard covers. The publicity boast for 1960 rang perfectly true: Elvis had never been heard like this before, except perhaps by himself in his own head. There was new depth to his voice; his interpretations were increasingly sophisticated; the group was probably the best studio band in the business; the song selection was imaginative and varied, the technical quality excellent. Most surprising of all, the new album pointed in no one musical direction. It wasn't unmistakably related to the sound of his previous recordings. There was no strong country flavor, and only a hint of gospel in the voices of either Elvis or the Jordanaires. It was as if Elvis had invented his own brand of music, broken down the barriers of genre and prejudice to express everything he heard in all the kinds of music he loved. As a document of Elvis's first comeback, *Elvis Is Back* was irresistible; the only thing missing were the separately released singles.

But now there was business to do. After just a few weeks off, by the end of April Elvis once again found himself in front of the microphones and cameras—this time to make his first post-army movie, the service story *G.I. Blues.*

The new Paramount picture had gotten a head start with the background filming done in Germany in the summer of 1959 (though that footage was later discarded). The figure at the film's center, once again, was the Colonel's New Elvis: a red-blooded American boy, a creature wholesome enough to walk right into the hearts of grown-up fans. Elvis and the Colonel both wanted to nurture that boy into a permanent movie star, and by this point the Colonel had established a set of ground rules designed to keep that image as pure—and profitable—as possible. On the music side, it meant that all Elvis songs had to be placed with either Gladys or Elvis Presley Music (or, barring that, that writers must agree to share a third of their royalty money with Elvis and Wallis and Hazen). The Colonel also retained control of the music by making sure his publishing companies worked with each movie company in song selection, with no input from RCA; after that, only the Colonel and Elvis would decide what songs the record label could release.

At the November 1959 meeting with Hill & Range, Paramount had selected four songs as *G.I. Blues* candidates, including two by Leiber and Stoller, "Tulsa's Blues" and "Dog Face"; the latter was good enough that for a while they considered changing the movie title to match the song. The two non-Leiber-and-Stoller selections were both based on European melodies, with new English lyrics: "Tonight Is So Right For Love," from a classic theme by Offenbach, and a lullaby by German band leader Bert Kaempfert. Throughout his relationship with Elvis, Freddy Bienstock always took notice of which songs caught the singer's attention, and even if they weren't chosen immediately he kept them around against the day when they might be useful. Such was the case with "Shoppin' Around" by the team of Tepper, Bennett, and Schroeder, which now went directly to Hal Wallis with Freddy's strong recommendation that it would be a smash hit and an excellent choice to close the movie. By the time they were done with their meetings, the producers were short only three songs for the film.

But before production started, there was a near-crisis that almost threw the entire publishing situation off track. Paramount had asked that Jerry Leiber and Mike Stoller help out at the recording sessions, as they had done so successfully with *Jailhouse Rock* and *King Creole*. But their request came just as tension was building again between the two writers and the Presley organization. Earlier Jerry Leiber, without saying anything to the Colonel directly, had gone to the Aberbachs and pitched the idea of Elvis starring in a film version of *A Walk On The Wild Side,* with Elia Kazan as the possible director. To Tom Parker this kind of unilateral meddling in Elvis's business affairs was tantamount to treason, and Leiber was warned in no uncertain terms that if he ever tried to intervene again it would be the end of any association with Presley. For Leiber and Stoller, that was the end of the line. They were already discouraged, even disgusted, with Parker's lack of artistic ambition and vision, and this kind of brutal rejection only steeled them against him further. "Dog Face," the song Paramount was so enthusiastic about, had actually been an unreleased leftover from a Coasters session, as the writers had no intention of writing specifically for Elvis ever again. What rankled them even further was the Colonel's insistence that Hill & Range get publishing rights to even the Leiber and Stoller songs that were *cut* from a soundtrack album (an arrangement that held for their other writers as well). Trying to keep the savvy writing team at arm's length, the manager decided to make a stand over the rejected-songs issue: "It is unfair," he wrote Jean Aberbach, "to make different deals for the same service with one party, and not give the same deal to another party giving the same service." This was a convenient business ethic to espouse in this situation, though not the kind of thing that would ever, in different circumstances, have kept the Colonel from exacting some new benefit for his boy. What Leiber and Stoller had asked, in the Colonel's mind, amounted to special financial consideration, and that was simply a deal-breaker.

Jean Aberbach, for his part, felt the whole thing could have been ironed out. But the Colonel was bent on getting these two out-of-control characters, as he saw them, completely isolated from his artist, and he succeeded in making an example of them: Eventually, neither Leiber and Stoller song appeared in the film, and needless to say the team never made it near the *G.I. Blues* sessions. With the exception of "She's Not You," they never again wrote a new song for Elvis Presley. Probably unbeknownst to Elvis himself, these two men who might have made a world of difference in his career were summarily ushered out of the picture.

During Elvis's time in the army, RCA had made a deal with the recording engineers' labor union requiring all subsequent RCA records to be recorded in RCA's own studios. Steve Sholes, now based in Los Angeles, informed the Colonel that the new rule would apply to Elvis's movie recordings, since some or all of them might someday be released by RCA. The first *G.I. Blues* session, as a result, was scheduled at the record company's studio on Sunset Boulevard. Paramount was in charge, and to ensure versatility the studio brought back Tiny Timbrell and Dudley Brooks as well as top session player Ray Siegel on bass. Since a second drummer had proved useful on *King Creole,* Frank Bode was also included, along with an accordion player. Alas, Paramount took far less care about the quality of the songs themselves; almost all were written to fit into specific scenes in the script, and among them only two might have been considered good enough to be recorded at a regular RCA session.

48. Soundtrack Recordings for Paramount's *G.I. Blues*
April 27–28, 1960: RCA Studios, Hollywood

Paramount Producers: Joseph Lilley/Hal Wallis
Engineers: n/a

Guitar: Scotty Moore
Guitar: Tiny Timbrell
Guitar: Neal Matthews
Guitar: Elvis Presley (BO only)
Bass: Ray Siegel
Drums: D. J. Fontana

Drums: Frank Bode
Piano: Dudley Brooks
Accordion: Jimmie Haskell
Tambourine: Hoyt Hawkins
Vocals: The Jordanaires

4/27, 9AM–2PM, 3–8PM

BO-11	**Shoppin' Around**		**G.I. Blues**
WPA5 2542	*Tepper/Bennett/Schroeder—Gladys Music*		*66960-2/1997*
CO-02	**Didja' Ever**		**G.I. Blues**
L2PB 3686	*Sid Wayne/Sherman Edwards—Gladys Music*		*LSP 2256/1960*
DO-13	**Doin' The Best I Can**		**G.I. Blues**
L2PB 3688	*Doc Pomus/Mort Shuman—Elvis Presley Music*		*LSP 2256/1960*
EO-sp	**G.I. Blues**		**G.I. Blues**
L2PB 3682	*Sid Tepper/Roy C. Bennett—Gladys Music*		*LSP 2256/1960*
HO-13	**Frankfort Special**		
WPA5 2543	*Sid Wayne/Sherman Edwards—Gladys Music*		
FO-11	**Tonight Is So Right For Love**		**G.I. Blues**
L2PB 3678	*Sid Wayne/Abner Silver—Gladys Music*		*LSP 2256/1960*

4/28, 12:30–6: 30PM, 7:45–11:03PM

M10-07	**Big Boots**	**Collectors Gold**
WPA5 2514	*Sid Wayne/Sherman Edwards—Gladys Music*	*3114-2-R/1991*
MO-04	**Big Boots (slow)**	**Elvis Sings For Children (And Grown Ups Too)**
L2PB 3685	*Sid Wayne/Sherman Edwards—Gladys Music*	*CPL1 2901/1978*
GO-sp	**What's She Really Like**	**G.I. Blues**
L2PB 3679	*Sid Wayne/Abner Silver—Gladys Music*	*LSP 2256/1960*
PO-01	**Blue Suede Shoes**	**G.I. Blues**
L2PB 3687	*Carl Perkins—Hill & Range Songs*	*LSP 2256/1960*
QO-04	**Wooden Heart**	**G.I. Blues**
L2PB 3681	*Wise/Weisman/Twomey—Gladys Music*	*LSP 2256/1960*
NO-28	**Pocketful Of Rainbows**	
WPA5 2544	*Fred Wise/Ben Weisman—Gladys Music*	

The master of "G.I. Blues" (3682/EO) is spliced from take 7 and take 10 (work part ending only). The master of "What's She Really Like" (3679/GO) is spliced from take 19 and take 22 (work part ending only). A movie version of the song was sung directly on camera.

The 9:00 A.M. start ensured that Elvis would be late, and before he arrived the band worked on an instrumental version of "Shoppin' Around," the song Freddy Bienstock had been plugging so enthusiastically to Hal Wallis. When Elvis did arrive, it was to a distressing scene: The RCA studios were arranged in a pattern totally unlike any other he'd ever worked in, and the sight made him immediately uneasy. Recording film soundtrack music with three-track machines would give the studio the chance to match the music to the sound of the film more accurately, but the only way to take full advantage of the system was to ensure that there was minimal leakage from one track to the next—hence the odd new positioning of the microphones. Elvis had no choice; all he could do was follow the studio requirements, but as a result "Shoppin' Around," a good '50s-style pop song, came out disturbingly flat. The problem must have come as a serious disappointment after the new standards set back in March, and it was one that would dog Elvis's soundtrack recordings for the rest of his movie career.

After the pedestrian "Didja' Ever," he started work on "Doin' The Best I Can," the only other song that might have had any potential for an Elvis RCA session. Written by Doc Pomus and Mort Shuman, who had successfully landed "A Mess Of Blues" at the Nashville sessions, it was a slow doo-wop song perfectly suited to Elvis's silky new voice. A perfectly realized master was produced in thirteen takes before the return to more of the usual movie fare. "G.I. Blues" was now definitely the all-important title song, but the master had to be pieced together from pieces of different takes. Then the group tried "Tonight Is So Right For Love," but an up-tempo rock version of Offenbach's German tune wasn't exactly what Elvis and the band had grown up on,

The ill-fated G. I. Blues session at RCA's Hollywood studios: April 27–28, 1960

and they abandoned it after seven takes. The same thing happened after five takes of "What's She Really Like" and thirteen of "Frankfort Special." The work was hard, progress slow. After one more try they did get a cut on the Offenbach tune, but in a version that left both Elvis and Paramount with strong reservations.

Starting at the more sensible hour of 12:30 the next afternoon, the band tackled some of the instrumental pieces, but there wasn't much on the agenda to excite Elvis. A throwaway version of "Blue Suede Shoes" was written into the script, and the German children's song *Muss I Denn* had been turned into "Wooden Heart" by Fred Wise and Ben Weisman. The two writers had submitted another, more ambitious number called "Pocketful Of Rainbows," with a melody that tested Elvis's range and rhythm skills, but twenty-nine takes later he clearly hadn't met the challenge. In fact it was questionable whether they had succeeded in getting even an acceptable version.

By the end of the day, on the face of it, Paramount had achieved what they had set out to do, with "acceptable" versions of each of the required cuts. But no one was very happy about the whole affair. As if anybody needed further problems, an unexpected copyright complication came up concerning "Tonight Is So Right For Love," so another session was scheduled for a little over a week later, on May 6—and this time Elvis insisted that they return to Radio Recorders, union deal or not.

49. Soundtrack Recordings for Paramount's *G.I. Blues*
May 6, 1960: Radio Recorders, Hollywood

Paramount Producers: Joseph Lilley/Hal Wallis
Engineers: Thorne Nogar

Guitar: Scotty Moore
Guitar: Tiny Timbrell
Guitar: Neal Matthews
Bass: Ray Siegel
Drums: D. J. Fontana

Drums: Bernie Mattinson
Piano: Dudley Brooks
Accordion: Jimmie Haskell
Tambourine: Hoyt Hawkins
Vocals: The Jordanaires

1–7PM, 8:15–10PM

M10-X-02	**Big Boots (fast)**	**G.I. Blues**
WPA5 2545	*Sid Wayne/Sherman Edwards—Gladys Music*	*66960-2/1997*
BO-X-07	**Shoppin' Around**	**G.I. Blues**
L2PB 3684	*Tepper/Bennett/Schroeder—Gladys Music*	*LSP 2256/1960*
NO-X-02	**Pocketful Of Rainbows**	**G.I. Blues**
L2PB 3683	*Fred Wise/Ben Weisman—Gladys Music*	*LSP 2256/1960*
HO-X-10	**Frankfort Special**	**G.I. Blues**
L2PB 3680	*Sid Wayne/Sherman Edwards—Gladys Music*	*LSP 2256/1960*
R10/R20-sp	**Tonight's All Right For Love**	**Elvis: A Legendary Performer Vol. 1**
L2PB 3975	*Wayne/Silver/Joe Lilley—Gladys Music*	*CPL1 0341/1974*

MO-X	**Big Boots**	
	Sid Wayne/Sherman Edwards—Gladys Music	
M20-X-04	**Big Boots (insert)**	
	Sid Wayne/Sherman Edwards—Gladys Music	
SO-03	**Big Boots (composite)**	**G.I. Blues**
L2PB 3685	*Sid Wayne/Sherman Edwards—Gladys Music*	*LSP 2256/1960*

No takes of the MO-X "Big Boots" were completed. The master of "Big Boots" (SO/3685) is spliced from MO take 4 and M20-X take 4. The master of "Tonight's All Right For Love" (3975) is spliced from R10 take 10 and R20 (insert) take 2. "Tonight's All Right For Love" was released on the original *G.I. Blues* album outside the U.S., replacing "Tonight Is So Right For Love."

At Radio Recorders, with Thorne Nogar engineering, Elvis was both more comfortable and more confident. First came a speeded-up version of the lullaby "Big Boots," followed by a new take on the potential hit "Shoppin' Around." Both tunes were substantial improvements over anything they had gotten on the first days. Adding a little echo, Nogar created exactly the right blend of elements to make each song sound like an Elvis Presley record; suddenly vocals that had sounded flat and dry in the RCA studio came alive. A week before, they'd struggled away at "Pocketful Of Rainbows," loping through twenty-nine takes with only an unsatisfactory master to show for it; now they got what they wanted in just two. "Frankfort Special" was brought down to a human tempo, with Scotty and D. J. basing their playing loosely on "Mystery Train." Elvis called out, "Let's go again before this train runs out of juice"; he messed up the words, but by take ten they had another master, and Elvis was ready to tackle the last two songs.

But they were still working for the movie company, and the union representative at the session demanded a contractual break of 75 minutes after their first six hours of work. Elvis was in a hurry to finish and get home, but he had no choice and took his break with everyone else. Next up was "Tonight's All Right For Love." Hill & Range had been working under the impression that the song "Tonight Is So Right For Love," based on Offenbach's "Barcarole," was in the public domain; that may have been true in the United States, but the melody was still under copyright in Europe, so they had to come up with a substitute to cover them in the European market. With the help of Hal Wallis musical director Joe Lilley, songwriters Wayne and Silver made a quick switch to the melody line of *"Geschicten auf dem Wienerwald,"* a Strauss melody that was demonstrably out of copyright; with a few changes to the lyrics and an ever-so-slightly new title—"Tonight's All Right for Love"—they were on their way. (The song's working title was "Vienna Woods Rock and Roll.")

When the first take after the break collapsed, Elvis started showing signs of strain. "We should have never broke for lunch," he griped. "I was in good spirits." He was joking—"It's almost time for a ten-minute break," he kidded a few minutes later; "these damn unions!"—but something of an adversarial relationship was developing between Elvis and the control room, and the Jordanaires started whispering among themselves that Elvis seemed to be getting a little "punchy." After a poor take ten Freddy told Elvis he thought it was "a pretty good take," to which the star snapped, "Let's do one more and make it a little better." The businessmen's concern for speed and efficiency was being challenged by the singer's concern for his craft. Elvis kept up his sniping: "They got a new law at the union. You quit at [take] ten, whether you're through or not." Almost as if on purpose he screwed up the next few tries before finally giving up after take seventeen, and accepting the "pretty good" take ten with a redone ending. Elvis was still bothered by the tempo shift in the middle of the lullaby, "Big Boots," and insisted on rerecording that section for insertion into the previous day's master. Then, finally, all their work was done: The studio had what it needed for the soundtrack, and the Colonel and Elvis retreated to decide whether they would allow RCA to release a soundtrack album.

In the meantime, the first post-army single, "Stuck On You," had spent four weeks at number one, but of the 1.4 million units that were shipped out, a disappointing half-million came back. At least Elvis hadn't been forgotten, though—and RCA breathed a sigh of relief that it hadn't given away the store during contract negotiations with the Colonel a few months earlier. Since the 1950s, RCA's marketing strategy had always been very simple—just rush the product out there, and watch it sell. But this was the '60s, and the market was already changing, whether RCA kept up with it or not. They did see fit to alert the Colonel of one adjustment: There would be no EPs of the material from *Elvis Is Back,* as the format was swiftly going out of style. But by midsummer it was obvious that *Elvis Is Back* itself was going to sell only around two hundred thousand copies, and with no supplementary EP sales Elvis's royalties were going to be substantially lower than they'd been since 1956. It all went to confirm the Colonel's fundamental belief that no one at RCA understood sales or promotion as well as he did: *Elvis Is Back* was simply going to fade away, selling to the singer's many loyal fans, but failing to reach the broader audience it deserved.

With the summer it came time to release the second single. They had all agreed on "Stuck On You" as a safe compromise for the first outing, but the next one, "It's Now Or Never," would be a radical departure for both Elvis and his fans. Before it could happen, though, Elvis's concerns about sound quality came to the fore again— this time leading to a serious dispute with RCA. Elvis ordinarily received acetates made up from the master tapes as soon as a session was over, so that he could hear on record exactly what he had heard and approved in the studio. RCA's engineers would then transfer the master tape to "production parts" from which records would be manufactured, but during this stage there was room for the record company to fine-tune the mix to achieve the sound they felt was necessary to make the record a success—to make a record, in short, that would sound good coming through even the cheapest transistor radio. But that often meant seriously compressing the sound; lead vocals were regularly lifted out in front of the rest of the music, and the whole thing run through an extra layer of reverb. The Colonel had no objection to this; as far as he was concerned it was Elvis's voice that sold records. But when Elvis received a test pressing of "It's Now Or Never," it sounded nothing like the acetate he'd taken away from the session. When he complained to his manager, the Colonel had little option but to demand that RCA recut the single to Elvis's specifications, whatever the cost or delay.

The record was held up, and everyone from Elvis to the Colonel to RCA fumed, but all's well that ends well: When "It's Now Or Never" finally came out, it took off in a big way. The trade papers had been cautious in their sales predictions, but they were wise enough to call the single "potent." It was more than that. It took five weeks to reach number one, but when it got there it stayed for another five, and sold half a million copies more than the previous record. Elvis was *now* again, not *never*.

New publishing problems kept cropping up. Before long Hill & Range learned that the melody of "It's Now Or Never" was also still under copyright in Europe, forcing RCA to release the British-penned "The Girl Of My Best Friend" in its place overseas; the silver lining came when UK sales were so strong they suggested it might make another U.S. hit as well. The Colonel was still working on making a deal to release "It's Now Or Never" internationally, and he wasn't happy about having to share publishing rights with the European copyright holder; eventually Hill & Range persuaded RCA to compensate them for the lost publishing royalties, even though it's hard to see how the record company could have been found responsible for the mixup.

But Elvis's career was hardly slowed by any such issues. While he was in Germany the Colonel had worked to line up plenty of work for his return, so two months after *G.I. Blues* he jumped right into the first of two scheduled 20th Century–Fox films, reporting on August 8 to record the soundtrack for a picture to be titled either *Black Star* or *Flaming Lance*.

50. Soundtrack Recordings for 20th Century–Fox's *Flaming Star*
August 8 and October 7, 1960: Radio Recorders, Hollywood

Fox Producer: Urban Thielmann
Engineer: Thorne Nogar

Guitar: Howard Roberts
Guitar: Tiny Timbrell
Bass: Myer Rubin
Drums: Bernie Mattinson

Piano: Dudley Brooks
Accordion: Jimmie Haskell
Vocals: The Jordanaires

8/8, 8PM–4AM

WPA5 2502-sp **Black Star**
Sid Wayne/Sherman Edwards—Gladys Music

Collectors Gold
3114-2-R/1991

WPA5 2510-06	**Black Star (end title)**	**Collectors Gold**
	Sid Wayne/Sherman Edwards—Gladys Music	*3114-2-R/1991*
M2PB 1986-20	**Summer Kisses, Winter Tears**	**Elvis By Request: Flaming Star**
	Wise/Weisman/Lloyd—Gladys Music	*LPC 128/1961*
SPA3 6744-01 (tr)	**Britches**	**Elvis: A Legendary Performer Vol. 3**
	Sid Wayne/Sherman Edwards—Gladys Music	*CPL1 3078/1978*
SPA3 6743-sp	**A Cane And A High Starched Collar**	**Elvis: A Legendary Performer Vol. 2**
	Sid Tepper/Roy C. Bennett—Gladys Music	*CPL1 1349/1976*
WPA5 2546-01 (tr)	**Summer Kisses, Winter Tears (movie version)**	**Double Features**
	Wise/Weisman/Lloyd—Gladys Music	*66557-2/1995*

10/7, 8–11PM

M2PB 1987-06	**Flaming Star**	**Elvis By Request: Flaming Star**
	Sid Wayne/Sherman Edwards—Gladys Music	*LPC 128/1961*
WPA5 2547-05	**Flaming Star (end title)**	**Double Features**
	Sid Wayne/Sherman Edwards—Gladys Music	*66557-2/1995*

The master of "Britches" (6744) has a vocal overdub spliced from take 7 and insert 1 take 1. The master of "A Cane And A High Starched Collar" (6743) is spliced from take 6 and instrumental insert take 6. The master take number of the vocal overdub on the movie version of "Summer Kisses, Winter Tears" (2546) is unknown; the drum overdub was recorded on 8/11.

The new picture cast Elvis as a halfbreed Indian, in a serious dramatic Western that bore no resemblance to the musical format employed at Paramount. Of the four songs included only the title cut had any commercial potential; the others were just there to keep the story moving. Elvis normally preferred not to sing over prerecorded instrumental tracks, but "Britches" was so silly he didn't much care. After test screenings two of the songs, "Britches" and "Summer Kisses, Winter Tears," were dropped; then, after the title track was recorded, Fox changed the movie title from *Black Star* to *Flaming Star.* Naturally they asked Elvis to rerecord the title song, but the Colonel tried to shrug them off; as far as he was concerned, all this meant was the studio would have no title song, and no tie-in record release to support their picture. In the end Fox coughed up five thousand dollars themselves to get Elvis to rerecord the tune with revised lyrics—still with no guarantee that the Colonel would allow RCA to put out a single, since he had already met his RCA quota of four singles per year.

Amid all this activity and turmoil, by late in the summer a project that everyone seemed enthusiastic about had begun taking shape. Nearly every successful country singer on RCA cut a gospel album at one time or another in his or her career, and in Elvis's case there was plenty of reason to follow up 1957's highly successful *Peace In*

The Valley EP with a full-fledged sacred album. Elvis was always eager to promote religious music, and this was an opportunity he relished; for the Colonel, it was a perfect vehicle for his new image of the mature, family-friendly Elvis Presley. While preparing to make the album, the Colonel arranged for his favorite photographer, Don Cravens, to take pictures of Elvis on August 25 during a break in the filming of *Flaming Star.* Hill & Range, meanwhile, went over material with the singer and arranged for deals on many of the songs, including "I'll Meet You In The Morning," and "If We Never Meet Again" by Albert E. Brumley; "When You Travel All Alone" and "His Hand In Mine" by Mosie Lister; "Only Believe" by Paul Rader; "Mansion On The Hilltop" and "Room At The Cross" by Ira Stamphill; "Angels In The Sky" by Dick Glasser; "Milky White Way," by Theodor R. Fry; and "Over The Moon" by V. B. Ellis. Elvis kept adding favorites of his own: "Working On The Building," "You'll Never Walk Alone," "I Believe In The Man In The Sky," "Joshua Fit The Battle," "Jezebel," "Jesus Is The One," "God's Gonna Cut You Down," and "Who At My Door Is Standing." The date of the session kept being pushed back as filming ran over schedule, and it wasn't until October 30 that Elvis and his boys, plus Scotty, D. J., and Freddy Bienstock, drove into the parking lot behind RCA's Studio B in Nashville, once again in a Greyhound bus chartered by the Colonel. Elvis wore black pants, a shiny silk shirt, and the sailor's cap he fancied at the time. He arrived with his left hand in bandages—he'd broken a finger during a game of touch football—but otherwise he was in great spirits and more than ready to record.

51. Studio Sessions for RCA
October 30, 1960: RCA's Studio B, Nashville

A&R/Producer: Steve Sholes
Engineer: Bill Porter

Guitar: Scotty Moore
Guitar: Hank Garland
Guitar: Elvis Presley
Bass: Bob Moore
Drums: D. J. Fontana
Drums: Buddy Harman

Piano: Floyd Cramer
Sax: Boots Randolph
Vocals: The Jordanaires
Vocals: Millie Kirkham
Vocals: Charlie Hodge (harmony on 0374, 0375, 0376)

6:30–9:30PM

L2WW 0373-07	**Milky White Way**	**His Hand In Mine**
	Arranged and Adapted by Elvis Presley—Elvis Presley Music	*LSP 2328/1960*
L2WW 0374-sp	**His Hand In Mine**	**His Hand In Mine**
	Mosie Lister—Bregman, Vocco & Conn	*LSP 2328/1960*
L2WW 0375-04	**I Believe In The Man In The Sky**	**His Hand In Mine**
	Richard Howard—Rosarita Music	*LSP 2328/1960*

10PM–1AM

L2WW 0376-10	**He Knows Just What I Need**	**His Hand In Mine**
	Mosie Lister—Mosie Lister Publications	*LSP 2328/1960*
L2WW 0377-sp	**Surrender**	**Single A-side**
	Doc Pomus/Mort Shuman—Elvis Presley Music	*47-7850/1960*
L2WW 0378-03	**Mansion Over The Hilltop**	**His Hand In Mine**
	Ira Stamphill—Hymntime Publishers	*LSP 2328/1960*

1:30–4:30AM

L2WW 0379-08	**In My Father's House**	**His Hand In Mine**
	Ailecne Hanks—Jimmy Davis & Elvis Presley Music	*LSP 2328/1960*
L2WW 0380-04	**Joshua Fit The Battle**	**His Hand In Mine**
	Arranged and Adapted by Elvis Presley—Elvis Presley Music	*LSP 2328/1960*
L2WW 0381-04	**Swing Down Sweet Chariot**	**His Hand In Mine**
	Arranged and Adapted by Elvis Presley—Elvis Presley Music	*LSP 2328/1960*
L2WW 0382-01	**I'm Gonna Walk Dem Golden Stairs**	**His Hand In Mine**
	Cully Holt—Ben L. Speer Music	*LSP 2328/1960*

5–8AM

L2WW 0383-01	**If We Never Meet Again**	**His Hand In Mine**
	Albert E. Brumley—Stamps Quartet Music	*LSP 2328/1960*
L2WW 0384-05	**Known Only To Him**	**His Hand In Mine**
	Stuart Hamblen—Hill & Range Songs	*LSP 2328/1960*
L2WW 0385-03	**Crying In The Chapel**	**Single A-side**
	Artie Glenn—Valley Publishers	*447-0643/1965*
L2WW 5001-05	**Working On The Building**	**His Hand In Mine**
	W. O. Hoyle/Lillian Bowles—Hill & Range Songs	*LSP 2328/1960*

The master of "His Hand In Mine" (0374) is spliced from take 5 and the ending of take 4. The master of "Surrender" (0377) is spliced from take 4 and a work part for the ending, take 8.

In front of the hired bus, with a bandaged hand, outside Studio B: October 30, 1960.

The session opened with the black gospel standard "Milky White Way," inspired by a 1947 version by the Trumpeteers. The song took on an earthy, bluesy sound, finding a slow, insistent groove. Boots Randolph followed the bass line with a deep, whispery hissing on sax, and the quartet and soprano voices blended perfectly. Their funky soulfulness redefined the genre; even the later, slightly faster takes retained the same soulful confidence. The gospel music Elvis knew and loved was made up of more than a single strand; his awareness of the black gospel tradition was nearly as extensive as his knowledge of the white. He always prided himself on his gospel repertoire, and now he was finally able to pay homage to the groups whose music had inspired him and his family throughout his childhood.

Appropriately, both the Statesmen and the Blackwood Brothers—Vernon's and Gladys's favorite group—would be well represented on this first gospel-album session. Elvis chose Statesmen songwriter and arranger Mosie Lister's "His Hand In Mine" to follow "Milky White Way," harmonizing once again with Charlie Hodge, who was as familiar as Elvis with the genre. Over the course of only five takes they developed an impressive vocal arrangement featuring both the Jordanaires and Millie Kirkham—further evidence of the familiarity of everyone on the session with the material. Scarcely any of the selections required more than an hour, and each came out a deeply felt and highly polished gem. Elvis stayed with the Statesmen for the next two songs, choosing both sides of one of the 78s that the group had put out themselves in the early '50s for sale exclusively at their concerts. Elvis had repeatedly expressed his admiration for lead singer Jake Hess, and now he made an almost perfect copy of "I Believe In The Man In The Sky," differing from the original only in the restrained and beautiful backdrop supplied by the band.

The list of songs Elvis had given Freddy Bienstock had been carefully researched, and all the appropriate publishing rights secured. But once in the studio Elvis substituted material in a constant reevaluation of his artistic goals, and it was only good luck that, when he dropped one Mosie Lister tune, "When You Travel All Alone," he was ready to substitute another, "He Knows Just What I Need." But the switch ended up presenting a problem in performance—the song was simply too spirited, starting off fast and requiring Charlie Hodge's tenor to soar so high it almost broke in the process. Eventually Charlie just wore out and Millie Kirkham covered the part, but without the same spirited effect Charlie's voice would ideally have added.

A diversion from the gospel material was unavoidable. With the release of "Are You Lonesome Tonight?" RCA had no material left for a new A-side, and since the Colonel had decided not to release the recordings from *Flaming Star*, at least one new pop song had to be squeezed into the session. The metamorphosis of "O Sole Mio" into "It's Now or Never" had worked so well that Elvis suggested applying the same procedure to another old Italian favorite, *"Torna A Sorrento."* Doc Pomus and Mort Shuman got the assignment this time and cut a demo that, Shuman says, Elvis followed closely. This melody required an even greater demonstration of vocal powers than

"Now Or Never," but Elvis was determined to rise to the challenge. During the first takes he held back, not wanting to blow out his voice before the band had nailed the arrangement. By take four the band had sorted out the song's distinctive spy-movie intro; they were ready, but Elvis wasn't, and he missed the difficult high notes. After several more blown takes, Ray Walker, the Jordanaires' bass singer, took an obviously distressed Elvis aside during a break. Retiring to the only place that afforded any privacy—the bathroom—Ray proceeded to show Elvis an exercise in breath control. Demonstrating how to use the stomach for projection (a technique that requires the singer to heave as if about to throw up) Walker gave the singer the trick he needed to clear the hurdle. Elvis practiced, then returned to the studio, and in eight tries finally produced an ending that could be spliced onto the otherwise perfect take four. (If the recording sounded a little more muffled than the usual crystal-clear studio sound, it may have been because engineer Bill Porter was spending a fair amount of time in the bathroom himself, with an upset stomach that caused him some real heaving in between mixdowns and recording.)

The next selection, "Mansion Over The Hilltop," came from the Blackwood Brothers catalog; it was first released in 1954, the year two members of the group were killed in an airplane accident just days before Elvis made his first Sun recordings. A second Blackwood number, "In My Father's House," followed, concluding Elvis's tribute to two of the quartets that had most influenced his singing style. Then a change of source material brought a new flavor to the sessions. Charlie Hodge had first introduced Elvis to the recordings of the Golden Gate Quartet, a black gospel group that went back to the '30s whose vocal blend resembled the pop stylings of the Mills Brothers. The group's repertoire was drawn from the "Jubilee" tradition, full of rousing up-tempo numbers delivered with an infectious beat. Elvis had seen the quartet perform in Paris, and had met and even sung with them backstage, joining in on one of the two songs of theirs he would perform at this session: "Swing Down Sweet Chariot." The other, "Joshua Fit The Battle," completed his salute to yet a third important strand of America's gospel tradition and Elvis's own musical upbringing.

The Jordanaires, meanwhile, were themselves an outfit with a long history in gospel (though with many personnel changes along the way); former bass singer Cully Holt had written "I'm Gonna Walk Dem Golden Stairs," which the group recorded for RCA in 1949, and almost before anyone knew what was happening Elvis joined them in delivering a master of the song in only one take. (Freddy Bienstock assumed the well-known song must have been in the public domain, but Jordanaire Gordon Stoker knew otherwise, and when he called Cully Holt to tell him they'd recorded the song, he made it clear that Cully should keep quiet about it until the record was released, to help him escape the usual copublishing gambit from Hill & Range.) Now they were on a roll: The next song, Albert Brumley's "If We Never Meet Again," was another one-take master, followed by a quick success with "Known Only To Him," a song recorded by both the Statesmen and the Blackwood Brothers.

Just as dawn began to break, Elvis hit upon another surprise: the well-known inspirational number "Crying In The Chapel." "Chapel" had been a big country hit in 1953 for country singer Darrell Glenn, whose father Artie had written the song, but it had been an equally big hit on the rhythm and blues charts for the Orioles, and any number of other individual singers and groups had hit with it over the years. Even the Statesmen had cut their own version of the song on their own 78 custom pressing. The recording log for early morning on October 31 says that no satisfactory master was completed, and ultimately the song was not released until 1965, when RCA was desperately combing the vaults for unreleased material.

Still short one gospel cut, Gordon Stoker suggested one of his own group's most popular numbers, "Working On The Building." Originally a black gospel song, it had the same kind of swing as the Golden Gate cuts. (When asked how he liked the sound of it, all Elvis could answer, shyly amused, was "I like it.") The ultimate result may have been more Jordanaires than Elvis, but it was as spirited an offering as any the whole night had produced: As the song progressed Elvis seemed to relish stepping from the solo spot to become a part of the group performance, as he had so desperately wanted to do back in 1953. And so closed a remarkable night: Elvis and those around him had completed thirteen songs in one fell swoop, a new personal record; they were all songs close to his own heart; they were selected with panache and sung with effortless grace, and the result was as musically accomplished as anything the young singer had ever done.

Packaged in a full-color sleeve with a confident, smiling Elvis on the cover, the single "Are You Lonesome Tonight?" was released in October—but only after the same kind of brouhaha that had preceded the release of "It's Now Or Never." Once again Elvis was angry when the first pressing failed to achieve the sound of the acetate. The New York engineers, with their usual taste for equalization and compression, had lifted his voice at the expense of the Jordanaires', and he insisted that the single be remastered to correct the imbalance. His self-assured look on the sleeve proved justified: In three weeks the new record was in the number-one slot, its sales approaching pre-army levels with two million copies in the United States alone. Not surprisingly, the Colonel had also given RCA the green light to put out a full soundtrack recording of *G.I. Blues* to tie in with the movie's October release. Unlike in the past, though, there would be no single release six weeks before the movie opening; clearly there was other, better material in the vaults that Elvis preferred. And the international market was continuing to grow. RCA negotiated a new arrangement with the Colonel guaranteeing him royalties for one million European sales if he would allow them to put out a single of the rewritten German song "Wooden Heart" especially for that market. Ironically, they may have missed an opportunity to do the same thing in the United States, as Joe Dowell's hit cover version the following year went on to prove.

52. Soundtrack Sessions for 20th Century–Fox's *Wild In The Country*
November 7–8, 1960: Radio Recorders, Hollywood

Fox Producer: Urban Thielmann
Engineer: Thorne Nogar

Guitar: Scotty Moore
Guitar: Tiny Timbrell
Guitar: Elvis Presley
Bass: Meyer Rubin

Drums: D. J. Fontana
Piano: Dudley Brooks
Accordion: Jimmie Haskell
Vocals: The Jordanaires

11/7, 8PM–2:30AM

L2PB 5381-13	**Lonely Man**	**Single B-side**
	Bennie Benjamin/Sol Marcus—Gladys Music	*47-7850/1961*
WPA5 2504-04	**Lonely Man (solo)**	**Collectors Gold**
	Bennie Benjamin/Sol Marcus—Gladys Music	*3114-2-R/1991*
L2PB 5384-08	**In My Way**	**Elvis For Everyone**
	Fred Wise/Ben Weisman—Gladys Music	*LSP 3450/1965*
L2PB 5383-19	**Wild In The Country**	**Single B-side**
	Peretti/Creatore/Weiss—Gladys Music	*47-7880/1961*
L2PB 5385-03	**Forget Me Never**	**Elvis For Everyone**
	Fred Wise/Ben Weisman—Gladys Music	*LSP 3450/1965*

11/8, 9–11:45AM

L2PB 5382-13	**I Slipped, I Stumbled, I Fell**	**Something For Everybody**
	Fred Wise/Ben Weisman—Gladys Music	*LSP 2370/1961*
WPA5 2548-05	**I Slipped, I Stumbled, I Fell (lower key)**	**Collectors Gold**
	Fred Wise/Ben Weisman—Gladys Music	*3114-2-R/1991*

Elvis drove straight to Los Angeles after the gospel sessions; a week later he was recording the soundtrack for his third 20th Century–Fox movie, *Wild in the Country*. Like *Flaming Star,* this was a film featuring Elvis the actor, not Elvis the singing star, and with the exception of "I Slipped, I Stumbled, I Fell," the five tunes selected for the soundtrack were a collection of pretty, understated ballads, far better suited to movie scenes than to the pop marketplace. Yet the Colonel had promised Fox to help create radio support and publicity for the picture by releasing some of the material on singles. "Lonely Man," in a specially recorded but less convincing band version, was picked to back "Surrender," and the Colonel intended for RCA to pair "I Slipped, I Stumbled, I Fell" with the title song.

Clowning around with saxman Boots Randolph on the set of Wild in the Country, *probably November 1960*

It was during the filming of *Flaming Star* that Elvis and his group were introduced to Nancy Sharpe, a young woman working for 20th Century–Fox. Though never a love interest Nancy quickly became a new friend to Elvis, and she was often invited over to the house, where she joined in on evenings of music. A technically inferior but charming tape exists from one of these nights, and it suggests what life with Elvis must have been like during this heady year of music-making and new beginnings.

53. Private Recordings
Fall 1960: Monovale Drive, Hollywood

Piano: Elvis Presley
Vocals: Red West
Vocals: Nancy Sharpe

You'll Never Walk Alone (incomplete)
Rodgers/Hammerstein
If I Loved You
Rodgers/Hammerstein
The Lord's Prayer
Traditional
I Wonder, I Wonder, I Wonder
Daryl Hutchinson
An Evening Prayer (incomplete)
Battersby/Gabriel
Make Believe
Hammerstein/Kern
She Wears My Ring
Boudleaux Bryant/Felice Bryant
Sweet Leilani
Harry Owens
Beyond the Reef (incomplete)
Pitman
When The Swallows Come Back To Capistrano
Leon Rene
He
J. Richards/R. Mullen
Hands Off
Bowman/McShann
Lawdy Miss Clawdy (incomplete)
Lloyd Price

The filming of *Wild in the Country* wasn't completed by Christmas, but Fox did give the star time to go home for the holidays. From the vantage point of Graceland he could look back, with a mixture of pride and relief, on a truly remarkable year. It wasn't simply that he hadn't been forgotten; in some ways, indeed, he had eclipsed any of his previous accomplishments. In the nine months since his discharge he had made three movies. He had recorded a staggering fifty-one sides, and enjoyed three number-one singles. *Elvis Is Back,* an artistic watershed, had gone to number two on the LP charts; now the *G.I. Blues* soundtrack was on its way to becoming his biggest-selling long-playing record ever. By broadening his musical scope he had expanded his international appeal considerably, to a point where the world was his. Sales of "It's Now Or Never" reached a staggering 100,000 in the small country of Holland alone, and a full million in England. In the United States Elvis's comeback hadn't quite matched the sales standards of his 1956–57 heyday, but his recordings represented about twenty percent of RCA's total turnover—and RCA was doing just fine.

1961

A PICTURE EMERGES

Before *G.I. Blues* started making box office and album sales history, Tom Parker and producer Hal Wallis were already plotting their next move. Both had a perfect understanding of where they wanted to take Elvis Presley the movie star, and that was toward less acting, less story, more songs, more beautiful girls, and more lush, romantic, bankable settings. It wasn't what 20th Century–Fox—or, for that matter, Elvis himself—was hoping for. But by the time filming on *Blue Hawaii* began, the relative fiasco of *Flaming Star* had been duly noted, while Wallis and Parker passed time counting the $4 million in box-office receipts from *G.I. Blues*. The second Fox picture, *Wild in the Country,* was relegated to the back burner by the Colonel, who saw no payoff in putting any promotion behind it; but his promise to issue a single to accompany the Fox picture was as much support as he felt inclined to muster.

Early in the year the Colonel compromised with Fox and agreed to a February-March EP including the only two songs from *Flaming Star* deemed worthy of release: the title cut and "Summer Kisses, Winter Tears." The other two slots would be filled with "It's Now Or Never" and "Are You Lonesome Tonight?" A picture was definitely emerging, but the Colonel was still a step or two short of grasping its implications. The phenomenal sales of the *G.I. Blues* soundtrack—over 700,000 copies —begged the question of why *Elvis Is Back,* with its good and varied repertoire, had sold only 200,000. *His Hand In Mine*, released for Christmas 1960, got no higher than number thirteen on the charts, but everyone expected it to be a catalog perennial rather than an overnight success. With a follow-up album session already in the works, the Colonel could see only one answer before him: He simply had to continue promoting Elvis Presley. To that end he set up two benefit shows, one in Memphis and one in Hawaii, that would be sure to garner widespread public attention. Meanwhile, on a Sunday in March just a year after his triumphant return to the studio, Elvis traveled to Nashville once again to record with the same studio band at RCA's Studio B.

54. Studio Sessions for RCA
March 12, 1961: RCA's Studio B, Nashville

A&R/Producer: Steve Sholes
Engineer: Bill Porter

Guitar: Elvis Presley
Guitar: Scotty Moore
Guitar: Hank Garland
Bass: Bob Moore
Drums: D. J. Fontana
Drums: Buddy Harman

Piano: Floyd Cramer
Sax: Boots Randolph
Vocals: The Jordanaires
Vocals: Millie Kirkham

<u>6–9PM</u>

M2WW 0567-07 I'm Comin' Home
Charlie Rich—Knox & Elvis Presley Music
Something For Everybody
LSP 2370/1961

M2WW 0568-05 Gently
Murray Wisell/Edward Lisbona—Porgie/Elvis Presley Music
Something For Everybody
LSP 2370/1961

M2WW 0569-02 In Your Arms
Aaron Schroeder/Wally Gold—Gladys Music
Something For Everybody
LSP 2370/1961

M2WW 0570-04 Give Me The Right
Fred Wise/Norman Blagman–Gladys Music
Something For Everybody
LSP 2370/1961

<u>9:30PM–12:30AM</u>

M2WW 0571-02 I Feel So Bad
Chuck Willis—Berkshire/Elvis Presley Music
Single A-side
47-7880/1961

M2WW 0572-04 It's A Sin
Fred Rose/Zeb Turner—Milene Music
Something For Everybody
LSP 2370/1961

M2WW 0573-02 I Want You With Me
Woody Harris—Darwood/Gladys Music
Something For Everybody
LSP 2370/1961

M2WW 0574-10 There's Always Me
Don Robertson—Gladys Music
Something For Everybody
LSP 2370/1961

<u>1:45–5:15AM</u>

M2WW 0575-03 Starting Today
Don Robertson—Gladys Music
Something For Everybody
LSP 2370/1961

M2WW 0576-02 Sentimental Me
Jimmy Cassin/Jim Morehead—Ross Jungnickel
Something For Everybody
LSP 2370/1961

M2WW 0577-08 Judy
Teddy Redell—Progressive/Elvis Presley Music
Something For Everybody
LSP 2370/1961

M2WW 0578-05 Put The Blame On Me
Twomey/Wise/Blagman—Gladys Music
Something For Everybody
LSP 2370/1961

Steve Sholes, Bill Porter, Chet Atkins, Tom Diskin, Freddy Bienstock, and a host of other guests and hangers-on watched from the control room as work began on the first song. Elvis had been listening to a new Sam Phillips–produced record called "I'm Comin' Home," written by one of Phillips's recording artists, Charlie Rich, and recorded by another, Carl Mann. Mann's record proved to be yet another unsuccessful follow-up to his hit reworking of "Mona Lisa," and because it hadn't been brought in through Elvis's publishing companies there was no sheet music at hand. "Let's start it off in the right tempo," Sholes suggested over the intercom. "I need a couple of lines, Mr. Sholes," Elvis stuttered in response; "just a second." Mann's version basically functioned as the band arrangement, and Elvis threw himself into the task of fine-tuning his vocal ideas as the band learned the song.

As usual, as soon as Chet Atkins was confident that everything was running smoothly he took off, leaving Sholes and the others to oversee a session that would progress with as much comfortable ease as the finished master of "I'm Comin' Home."

The entire experience would mirror that of the previous year, with songs drawn equally from a batch of specially written new material, from Hill & Range's vast catalog, and from Elvis's own memory. There was a finished master almost every hour, with Elvis pushing to start recording even before a full run-through was completed. The British import "Gently," with its folklike structure, gave Hank Garland a chance to demonstrate some truly delicate picking. "In Your Arms" took two takes and was over before Boots Randolph had time to think out anything more than a rudimentary solo. The bluesiness of "Give Me The Right" was toned down a little after the first take, but take four, which became the master, still came complete with a wonderfully desolate, wordless wail from soprano Millie Kirkham. Elvis's take on Chuck Willis's 1954 hit "I Feel So Bad" was effective, but the fast pace of the session resulted in an aural anomaly: Evidently Elvis walked over to cheer Boots on during his solo, and as a result the saxophone suddenly shifts from the left channel onto Elvis's center channel on the master. (Remarkably, it happened on both takes, but nobody noticed until it was too late.) Elvis actually saw Eddy Arnold (backed by the Jordanaires) perform the next song, "It's A Sin," at Ellis Auditorium in 1954—on the very occasion he'd told Gordon Stoker he wanted the quartet to back him up someday. It took a while to sort out the harmonies and speed up the arrangement to the old "heart ballad," but the second full take became the master.

The aim at any Elvis session was to balance up-tempo material with ballads, and for the most part the rock 'n' roll songs were covers while the love songs represented original material. "I Want You With Me" was such a case; the Woody Harris rocker was originally written—with an arrangement straight out of the Fats Domino New Orleans tradition—for the 1960 Bobby Darin album *For Teenagers Only*. Elvis, who had met Darin in Las Vegas not long before the session, echoed his vocal phrasing, while the band came up with its own individualized brand of rock 'n' roll.

Songwriter Don Robertson had gotten a cut on Elvis's first RCA session with "I'm Counting On You," while at the same time he was embarking on a performing career himself (in April 1956 he hit with "The Happy Whistler"). With what he later came to call the foolish indiscretion of youth, he'd then submitted a song for Elvis's second album session, only to withdraw it after his label convinced him to record it himself— thus falling out of favor with Steve Sholes, and finding himself temporarily out of the running for further Elvis commissions. Since that time, however, he'd had a string of big hits for other artists, including Hank Locklin's "Please Help Me I'm Falling"; as a Hill & Range writer with a natural affinity for the kind of ballads Elvis loved, he couldn't be blacklisted forever on the basis of one youthful transgression. Starting work on Robertson's "There's Always Me," Elvis declared, "This is my song"; he threw himself into the song's challenging ending, and when he had a master he was happy. Just days later he played it for the songwriter with obvious pride. The next Robertson ballad, "Starting Today," was just as tender but sadder and more wistful. That was followed by a cover of the Ames Brothers' 1949 hit, "Sentimental Me," set to a slow steady beat by the ever-adaptable band.

It's doubtful that one can find any real match for the effortless grace and swing, the sheer unforced mastery, of Elvis's vocal on the next song, "Judy." Playing acoustic guitar himself (gradually and deliberately buried in the mix as the takes progressed), Elvis told the band "twice in D," then led them through a cover of Teddy Redell's 1960 Atco recording. Floyd Cramer scattered his right-hand triplets like gold dust over the track, which epitomized Elvis and his Nashville band's particular brand of timeless pop. Twelve songs were needed, and the blues-tinged "Put The Blame On Me" was a good choice for the last spot on the record; by the time they had finished Elvis had an impressive new set of tracks on his hands—though there were few obvious single candidates among them.

In the session's aftermath RCA's Bill Bullock wrote Elvis an enthusiastic message: "I want to tell you how thrilled we were with the way the album came out." Intriguingly, the letter came at a time when RCA was trying to get out of a commitment it had made to finance the construction of a recording studio at Graceland. After initially promoting the idea, the label realized it would be a mistake to single one of its artists out above all others; eventually the Colonel worked out a compromise in which Elvis received, among other considerations, some up-to-date RCA stereo equipment—and RCA got to keep Nashville's Studio B as Elvis's recording home base.

Most of the Nashville band went out to California on their way to the Hawaii charity concert, making them available to play on the *Blue Hawaii* sessions. As usual, Tiny Timbrell and Dudley Brooks were on the scene, and the producers had hired Hal Blaine, a well-known studio drummer and expert on exotic percussion, to help with the Hawaiian-flavored music. A steel guitar, ukuleles, and harmonica player George Fields (who'd played on the *Loving You* soundtrack) filled out the roster.

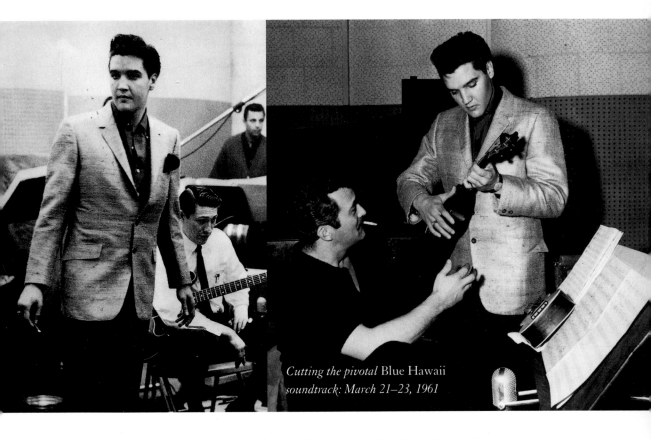

Cutting the pivotal Blue Hawaii *soundtrack: March 21–23, 1961*

55. Soundtrack Recordings for Paramount's *Blue Hawaii*
March 21–23, 1961: Radio Recorders, Hollywood

Paramount Producer: Joseph Lilley
Engineer: Thorne Nogar

Guitar: Scotty Moore
Guitar: Hank Garland
Guitar: Tiny Timbrell
Bass: Bob Moore
Drums: D. J. Fontana
Drums: Hal Blaine
Drums: Bernie Mattinson
Piano: Floyd Cramer
Piano, Celeste: Dudley Brooks

Sax: Boots Randolph
Steel Guitar: Alvino Rey
Harmonica: George Fields
Ukulele: Fred Tavares
Ukulele: Bernie Lewis
Vocals: The Jordanaires
Vocals: The Surfers
Overdubbed: Vocals: D. McCarty, V. Rees,
L. Norman, J. Allen (NO only)

3/21, 1–11:50PM

AO-sp	**Hawaiian Sunset**		**Blue Hawaii**
M2PB 2994	*Sid Tepper/Roy C. Bennett—Gladys Music*		*LSP 2426/1961*
BO-sp	**Aloha Oe**		**Blue Hawaii**
M2PB 2986	*Arranged and Adapted by Elvis Presley—Elvis Presley Music*		*LSP 2426/1961*

CO-09	Ku-U-I-Po	Blue Hawaii
M2PB 2991	*Peretti/Creatore/Weiss—Gladys Music*	*LSP 2426/1961*
DO-sp	No More	Blue Hawaii
M2PB 2987	*Don Robertson/Hal Blair—Gladys Music*	*LSP 2426/1961*
EO-19	Slicin' Sand	Blue Hawaii
M2PB 2993	*Sid Tepper/Roy. C Bennett—Gladys Music*	*LSP 2426/1961*

3/22, 1–6:55PM

FO-07	Blue Hawaii	Blue Hawaii
M2PB 2984	*Lee Robin/Ralph Rainger—Famous Music/Gladys Music*	*LSP 2426/1961*
GO-09	Ito Eats	Blue Hawaii
M2PB 2992	*Sid Tepper/Roy C. Bennett—Gladys Music*	*LDP 2426/1961*
JO-02	Hawaiian Wedding Song	Blue Hawaii
M2PB 3015	*King/Hoffman/Manning—Pickwick/Gladys Music*	*LSP 2426/1961*
KO-13	Island Of Love	Blue Hawaii
M2PB 3000	*Sid Tepper/Roy C. Bennett—Gladys Music*	*LSP 2426/1961*
LO-sp	Steppin' Out Of Line (movie version)	Blue Hawaii*
WPA5 2549	*Wise/Weisman/Fuller—Gladys Music*	*66959-2/1997*
LO-17(09)	Steppin' Out Of Line	Pot Luck
M2PB 3038	*Wise/Wiseman/Fuller—Gladys Music*	*LSP 2523/1962*

8–10:20PM

MO-08	**Almost Always True**	**Blue Hawaii**
M2PB 2985	*Fred Wise/Ben Weisman—Gladys Music*	*LSP 2426/1961*
NO-03	**Moonlight Swim**	**Blue Hawaii**
M2PB 2990	*Sylvia Dee/Ben Weisman—Gladys Music*	*LSP 2426/1961*

3/23, 1–5:22PM

RO-23	**Can't Help Falling In Love (movie version)**	**Blue Hawaii***
WPA5 2550	*Peretti/Creatore/Weiss—Gladys Music*	*66959-2/1997*
RO-29(06)	**Can't Help Falling In Love**	**Blue Hawaii**
M2PB 2988	*Peretti/Creatore/Weiss—Gladys Music*	*LSP 2426/1961*
SO-02	**Beach Boy Blues**	**Blue Hawaii**
M2PB 2995	*Sid Tepper/Roy C. Bennett—Gladys Music*	*LSP 2426/1961*
SO-03(01)	**Beach Boy Blues (movie version)**	**Blue Hawaii***
WPA5 2585	*Sid Tepper/Roy C. Bennett—Gladys Music*	*66959-2/1997*
TO-05	**Rock-A-Hula Baby**	**Blue Hawaii**
M2PB 2989	*Wise/Weisman/Fuller—Gladys Music*	*LSP 2426/1961*

The master of "Hawaiian Sunset" (2994) is spliced from takes 4 and 7. The master of "Aloha Oe" (2986) is spliced from section 1 take 4, and section 2 takes 7 and 5. The master of "No More" (2987) is spliced from take 13 and ending of take 16. Master of the movie version of "Steppin' Out Of Line" (LO) is spliced from takes 8 and 19(2) (ending). Paramount didn't start over with their slate numbers when recording alternate versions; in this case the first number is the official slate and the number in brackets is the master take of this particular version of the song. Instrumental parts for "Aloha Oe," and other instrumental pieces for the movie, were cut on 3/23, from 9AM–12PM. The Surfers: Patrick Sylva, Bernard Ching, Clayton Naluai, Alan Naluai. *RCA released an updated *Blue Hawaii* soundtrack in 1997, including these previously unreleased titles.

Freddy Bienstock had come up with a number of new songs for the occasion, but the new movie would also include such Hawaiian pop classics as "Blue Hawaii" and "Hawaiian Wedding Song," as well as the old island chant "Aloha Oe." At Freddy's instigation Don Robertson had already written English lyrics to the classic melody of "La Paloma," calling the new song "No More"; it was an obvious choice, as were several other songs from some of the regular teams. The songwriters knew how difficult it was to predict which songs would be chosen, but it was worth the effort, because an Elvis cut was still a gold mine. At this point Sid Tepper and Roy Bennett were leading the pack as Elvis songwriters: To their five *G.I. Blues* songs, they now added another five on *Blue Hawaii*. Elvis invited Don Robertson to the first day of recording, and, eager to impress the writer with his seriousness, pushed the band through take after take of "No More" and its demanding ending. After thirteen tries Thorne Nogar recommended cutting a separate ending, which Elvis briefly rejected before moving on to a faux rock 'n' roll number, "Slicin' Sand." The song obviously inspired a streak of silliness in Elvis; singing its nonsense reprise over and over, he threw in a line from Jimmy

Pearl Harbor, March 25, 1961

Swan's 1953 country record "I Had A Dream," before launching into a new take on "There's Always Me": "When the evening shadows fall, and you're wondering who to ball. . . ." Only later did Don Robertson realize this was the singer's tongue-in-cheek way of letting the writer know he'd cut the song back in Nashville.

In general it took the band longer to work out arrangements than it had the week before in another setting; still, the session moved along smoothly. The ambition and concentration he put into a marathon twenty-nine takes of "Can't Help Falling In Love" on the final day suggested how seriously he took the beautiful, intimate ballad; when he finished, he seemed already aware that he'd created a classic. The group sped through "Beach Boy Blues" before ending the session in an all-out frenzy with "Rock-A-Hula Baby." Thorne pushed the record button before everyone was set, and Elvis shouted not to roll tape—"no one knows it yet," another cried. Wondering what song they were doing, Elvis launched into a line from "I Went To Your Wedding," and the room exploded with laughter and energy. On the third take the group went crazy, like a bunch of kids about to go on summer vacation, barely able to control themselves. The fifth, slightly less manic take was a master, and everyone took off for Hawaii and the benefit show that would be Elvis's last live performance for eight years.

56. Live Recordings
March 25, 1961: Bloch Arena, Pearl Harbor

Guitar: Scotty Moore
Guitar: Hank Garland
Bass: Bob Moore
Drums: D. J. Fontana

Piano: Floyd Cramer
Sax: Boots Randolph
Vocals: The Jordanaires

<u>8:30PM</u>

KPA5 9543	**Heartbreak Hotel**	**Elvis Aron Presley**	
	Axton/Durden/Presley	*CPL8 3699/1980*	
KPA5 9544	**All Shook Up**	**Elvis Aron Presley**	
	Blackwell/Presley	*CPL8 3699/1980*	
KPA5 9545	**(Now And Then There's) A Fool Such As I**	**Elvis Aron Presley**	
	Bill Trader/Bob Miller	*CPL8 3699/1980*	
KPA5 9546	**I Got A Woman**	**Elvis Aron Presley**	
	Ray Charles	*CPL8 3699/1980*	
KPA5 9547	**Love Me**	**Elvis Aron Presley**	
	Jerry Leiber/Mike Stoller	*CPL8 3699/1980*	
KPA5 9549	**Such A Night**	**Elvis Aron Presley**	
	Lincoln Chase	*CPL8 3699/1980*	
KPA5 9550	**Reconsider Baby**	**Elvis Aron Presley**	
	Lowell Fulsom	*CPL8 3699/1980*	
KPA5 9551	**I Need Your Love Tonight**	**Elvis Aron Presley**	
	Sid Wayne/Bix Reichner	*CPL8 3699/1980*	
KPA5 9552	**That's All Right**	**Elvis Aron Presley**	
	Arthur Crudup	*CPL8 3699/1980*	
KPA5 9553	**Don't Be Cruel**	**Elvis Aron Presley**	
	Blackwell/Presley	*CPL8 3699/1980*	
KPA5 9554	**One Night**	**Elvis Aron Presley**	
	Bartholomew/King	*CPL8 3699/1980*	
KPA5 9555	**Are You Lonesome Tonight?**	**Elvis Aron Presley**	
	Roy Turk/Lou Handman	*CPL8 3699/1980*	
KPA5 9556	**It's Now Or Never**	**Elvis Aron Presley**	
	Aaron Schroeder/Wally Gold	*CPL8 3699/1980*	
KPA5 9557	**Swing Down Sweet Chariot**	**Elvis Aron Presley**	
	Traditional/Arranged by Elvis Presley	*CPL8 3699/1980*	
KPA5 9558	**Hound Dog**	**Elvis Aron Presley**	
	Jerry Leiber/Mike Stoller	*CPL8 3699/1980*	

A technically troubled tape serves as the only evidence left of what an artist Elvis could have been had he spent the '60s performing live instead of wasting his talent on an endless string of silly movies. What he had to offer, judging from this recording, was a great band, an imaginative repertoire selection—and a voice that was growing better with every year.

All the material from the Nashville session was put out on an album called *Something For Everybody,* with the exception of a single song. The Colonel had promised 20th Century–Fox that Elvis's next single would plug *Wild in the Country*. He thought the title song would be well paired with a special version of "I Slipped, I Stumbled, I Fell," but RCA wanted to back "Wild in the Country" with a nonmovie song, and Elvis selected "I Feel So Bad" from the Nashville sessions to accommodate them. His choice went to number five while the title song dragged at number twenty-six; when the album was released in May, "I Slipped, I Stumbled, I Fell" had replaced "I Feel So Bad."

When Tom Diskin asked Freddy Bienstock to check out some songs written by Elvis's friend Red West, Freddy dismissed the request as another tiresome instance of Elvis's friends (and acquaintances, and fast-talking hustlers) taking advantage of his good graces. As Freddy would soon learn, though, Red was a legitimate writer who'd already had a song cut by Pat Boone, and over the years he would contribute a number of impressive songs to Elvis's repertoire. His initial submissions were "Ain't Nobody Gonna Take My Place," a number that will remain lost to history, and an early version of a number called "You'll Be Gone," which would reappear the following year. The Colonel's one goal for the upcoming session was to record material for the new single; determined to prevent what had happened at the March Nashville session, he announced he wanted no covers, no public-domain knockoffs, only "fresh new material, strong rock 'n' roll songs to select the two songs from." Freddy turned to his newest writing team, Pomus and Shuman, temporarily holed up in Los Angeles writing for Bobby Vee and Bobby Darin. Neither Bobby, however, had been able to come up with a satisfactory cut on either of their best new songs, "Little Sister" and "His Latest Flame," so they were sent to Elvis for consideration along with another song, "Kiss Me Quick." The June sessions, to be held just before the start of the Mirisch Brothers picture that came to be called *Follow That Dream,* were originally booked at Radio Recorders; when the picture's location was switched to Florida, the session was moved back to Nashville.

57. Studio Sessions for RCA
June 25, 1961: RCA's Studio B, Nashville

A&R/Producer: Steve Sholes
Engineer: Bill Porter

Guitar: Scotty Moore
Guitar: Hank Garland
Guitar: Neal Matthews
Bass: Bob Moore
Drums: D. J. Fontana
Drums: Buddy Harman

Piano, Organ: Floyd Cramer
Piano: Gordon Stoker
Claves: Boots Randolph
Vocals: The Jordanaires
Vocals: Millie Kirkham

6–9PM, 9:30PM–12:30AM

M2WW 0857-12	**Kiss Me Quick**	**Pot Luck**
	Doc Pomus/Mort Shuman—Elvis Presley Music	*LSP 2323/1962*
M2WW 0858-08	**That's Someone You Never Forget**	**Pot Luck**
	Red West/Elvis Presley—Elvis Presley Music	*LSP 2523/1962*

1–4AM, 4:30–7:30AM

M2WW 0859-sp	**I'm Yours**	**Pot Luck**
	Don Robertson—Gladys Music	*LSP 2523/1962*
M2WW 0860-08	**(Marie's The Name Of) His Latest Flame**	**Single A-side**
	Doc Pomus/Mort Shuman—Elvis Presley Music	*47-7908/1961*
M2WW 0861-04	**Little Sister**	**Single B-side**
	Doc Pomus/Mort Shuman—Elvis Presley Music	*47-7908/1961*

The master of "I'm Yours" (0859) is spliced from take 6 and work part 1 take 2 (ending). Elvis's harmony vocal and spoken part is spliced from overdub take 6 and 5 (spoken part). RCA later released the master without the overdubs, presumably by mistake.

Perhaps it was knowing they only had to come up with two songs for a single that put Elvis and the band in such an unhurried mood as they began the session. They started with "Kiss Me Quick," an up-tempo pop song with a distinctive European feel that even included a mandolin part to be replicated by Scotty on guitar. Like Pomus and Shuman's Drifters hit "Save The Last Dance For Me," the song's melody line swings in Latin fashion, its language echoing every twist in the rhythm. "I like this tune," Elvis announced after one failed take, and though he and the band had to run through eleven more before they mastered its tricky meter, he never gave up on it. Next came Red West's first moment in the sun. Elvis had been persistent with Freddy about Red's songwriting—enough so that Bienstock had encouraged him about one song, "This Is My Only Prayer"—but Elvis wanted to record another song Red had written, this one based on a line suggested by Elvis himself. "That's Someone You'll Never Forget" would make a good title, Elvis told his friend, and during these years it's hard not to wonder whether it was his own mother he had in mind. Red crafted a pretty melody around the line, expanding the lyric while leaving it open to the broadest interpretation; at one point during the session Elvis asked, "How do you like the arrangement, Red?" and Red couldn't have been more thrilled. The recording was built around an acoustic guitar, supported by Bob Moore's understated bass and Buddy Harman's brushes on the cymbals; with slip-note touches from Floyd Cramer and a bit of coloring from the Jordanaires, the record had a simple, intimate sound. Determined to do justice to the song, Elvis worked hard on his own phrasing and added Hank Garland's softly played electric guitar to the second take; the fifth try could have been the master, but they patiently tried twice more before Elvis was satisfied. "That's Someone You Never Forget" was hardly a commercial project, but its sincerity gave it a timeless quality that some of Elvis's recent work had lacked.

Don Robertson's "I'm Yours" had been among the songs considered and rejected for *Blue Hawaii;* the Colonel wanted it saved for the upcoming picture, but Elvis had become so fond of the songwriter's ballads that he couldn't wait. Responding to its wedding-song flavor, Floyd took up the organ for the occasion, while Gordon Stoker took over on piano. Elvis decided to sing his own two-part harmony, and he wanted to give the song the kind of spoken interlude he'd tried as early as "I Love You Because" and finally mastered on "Are You Lonesome Tonight?" They would build the recording in two parts: After one basic run-through, Elvis added the harmony line and spoken bridge in a second pass, and while the technique was unfamiliar to Elvis, everything came off flawlessly (until the RCA production department, on a later re-release, inadvertently released the undubbed master).

The recording of "(Marie's The Name Of) His Latest Flame" was like a party. "It's a good song. I like it," Elvis ventured, "even if it takes us thirty-two hours." Taping started with what was still a rehearsal, an almost acoustic rundown with Buddy on congas and Boots on shakers chugging out the Bo Diddley beat Mort Shuman had given the song. Take three added the sound of a shoebox, and Elvis's voice melted every lyrical line into pure vocal delight. Slowly the sound grew more forceful as they continued: On take four Hank Garland shifted to tic-tac bass, while Jordanaire Neal Matthews took over on guitar and Buddy Harman left the congas to return to the drums. "I need to hear it the whole way through," he said when Elvis said he had skipped a beat, "to get the [drum] pattern." Every variation was tried: Floyd Cramer took a stab at the organ, Hank Garland toned down the tic-tac. In the middle of the night they stopped and put in a call to Mort Shuman: How had he gotten the piano sound on the demo? Each take brought the song from a charming campfire singalong closer and closer to a fully realized pop record. When Shuman heard the finished product, he noticed not only the different piano sound but the curious intro—just three bars long, one shorter than any conventional arrangement would have suggested. The same thing had occurred on "Surrender"; whether it was intentional cleverness or just Elvis's impatience, it gave the song a fresh, surprising kickoff.

"When I wrote 'Little Sister,' " Mort Shuman recalled years later, "I played it in a totally different way. It had a different rhythm. Elvis cut the tempo in half and slowed it down." The song had a tough edge to it, and as he had with "His Latest Flame" Scotty strapped on the acoustic guitar while Hank Garland took the electric lead. "I remember when they cut 'Little Sister,' " guitarist Harold Bradley recalled, "Hank had to borrow my Fender [Jazz Master] guitar. Hank was contracted to Gibson, but he felt he needed a different sound for that particular record. . . . He didn't think the guitars he used were funky enough or had enough throttle." Funky it was, and Floyd Cramer's organ only underlined the feeling. Before the first take Bill Porter announced "It's got a classic in there"; Elvis was on the same wavelength—"Burn!" he said simply when take three took off. Take four was a master—and with that they'd filled the Colonel's demand for a new single—but Elvis and the group were all so excited they played the song over and over until 7:30 in the morning.

58. Soundtrack Recordings for Mirisch Company's *Follow That Dream*
July 2, 1961: RCA's Studio B, Nashville

Mirisch Producer: Hans Salter
Engineer: Bill Porter

Guitar: Scotty Moore
Guitar: Hank Garland
Guitar: Neal Matthews
Bass: Bob Moore
Drums: D. J. Fontana

Drums: Buddy Harman
Piano: Floyd Cramer
Sax: Boots Randolph
Vocals: The Jordanaires
Vocals: Millie Kirkham

7–10PM

M2WW 0873-07	**Angel**	**Follow That Dream (EP)**
	Sid Tepper/Roy C. Bennett—Gladys Music	*EPA 4368/1962*
M2WW 0874-06	**Follow That Dream**	**Follow That Dream (EP)**
	Fred Wise/Ben Weisman—Gladys Music	*EPA 4368/1962*
M2WW 0875-07	**What A Wonderful Life**	**Follow That Dream (EP)**
	Sid Wayne/Jerry Livingston—Gladys Music	*EPA 4368/1962*
M2WW 0876-08	**I'm Not The Marrying Kind**	**Follow That Dream (EP)**
	Mack David/Sherman Edwards—Gladys Music	*EPA 4368/1962*
M2WW 0877-04	**A Whistling Tune**	**Collectors Gold**
	Sherman Edwards/Hal David—Gladys Music	*3114-2-R/1991*
M2WW 0878-06	**Sound Advice**	**Elvis For Everyone**
	Giant/Baum/Kaye—Elvis Presley Music	*LSP 3450/1965*

The master of "A Whistling Tune" (0877) features an overdub of Ray Walker whistling, but since the master has been lost, the version released on *Collectors Gold* is the same take without the whistling overdub.

The two-picture Mirisch deal had been made before the astonishing success of *G.I. Blues* and *Blue Hawaii,* and the Colonel would never forget that at one point the company had tried to back out of the deal. The first picture, *Follow That Dream,* was a lighthearted comedy, and once again, except for two songs—the title cut and "Angel"—the material was decidedly below par. When the soundtrack EP was released Elvis insisted that the worst song, "Sound Advice," be omitted, even though that meant the record couldn't really be considered a true soundtrack—and, with only four songs, wasn't exactly a bargain for his fans.

Directing Elvis's career was like trying to lasso three horses at once, and the Colonel—always intent on making as much money as efficiently as he could—monitored every moment of perceived failure and success. When *Something for Everybody,* the new studio album, hit number one, it was with sales of only 100,000 copies—not even as strong as *Elvis Is Back,* which everyone had considered a relative commercial failure. The Colonel wrote to RCA vice president Bill Bullock hoping for an explanation, but Bullock, a canny businessman, was never really able to formulate much of an answer. It was true that there wasn't much rock 'n' roll on either album, but then there wasn't much on the *G.I. Blues* soundtrack either—nor, for that matter, on his biggest recent singles, "It's Now Or Never" or "Are You Lonesome Tonight?" Simply arguing that soundtracks sold better ignored the success of the singles charts, where Elvis had had four consecutive number-one singles (and even the last-resort single "I Feel So Bad"/"Wild In The Country" registered at number five). The one sure thing was that the two so-called "serious" pictures for Fox had flopped dramatically compared to the Paramount musicals. These were the factors that the Colonel had to take into account, as he poked about for answers. The new single, "His Latest Flame"/"Little Sister," had disappointing sales, especially given how excited everyone was about the record itself. Both songs were naturals for airplay—and the A- and B-sides reached numbers four and five respectively—but the sides were each so strong they competed with each other for airplay, and sales hovered just under a million.

One thing seemed certain to the Colonel: It made sense to go into the studio for another singles-only session. The June 25 session proved that Elvis and his band could focus their attention better when they were all trying to cut a hit single; increasingly, too, scheduling was becoming a problem, and between the two Mirisch pictures there would only be time to arrange a short session. Once Freddy understood the Colonel's goal, he knew exactly where to turn for hit material—to his hot new team, Pomus and Shuman. Having gotten three cuts on the last session was more than enough motivation to propel the songwriters into action. Mort Shuman had a simple formula for writing hits—"Chorus, break, and gimmick"—and the two had noticed that Elvis was drawn to first-person songs; in no time, then, they came up with a stranger's tale, a gimmick, and a Phil Spector–produced demo. The song, "Night Rider," was just the kind of rocker Freddy was looking for, and he sent it off to Elvis along with two Tepper and Bennett compositions, "Just For Old Time Sake" and "For The Millionth And The Last Time," as well as two others ("Ecstasy" and "You Never Talked to Me") and the promise of "a couple of real strong songs in the next few days."

59. Studio Sessions for RCA
October 15, 1961: RCA's Studio B, Nashville

A&R/Producer: Steve Sholes
Engineer: Bill Porter

Guitar: Scotty Moore
Guitar: Jerry Kennedy
Bass: Bob Moore
Drums: D. J. Fontana
Drums: Buddy Harman

Piano: Floyd Cramer
Sax & Clarinet: Boots Randolph
Accordion: Gordon Stoker (1002)
Vocals: The Jordanaires
Vocals: Millie Kirkham

6–9PM, 9:30PM–12:30AM

M2WW 1002-12	**For The Millionth And The Last Time**	**Elvis For Everyone**
	Roy C. Bennett/Sid Tepper—Gladys Music	*LSP 3450/1965*
M2WW 1003-04	**Good Luck Charm**	**Single A-side**
	Aaron Schroeder/Wally Gold—Gladys Music	*47-7992/1962*
M2WW 1004-10	**Anything That's Part Of You**	**Single B-side**
	Don Robertson—Gladys Music	*47-7992/1962*

1–4AM

M2WW 1005-18	**I Met Her Today**	**Elvis For Everyone**
	Don Robertson/Hal Blair—Gladys Music	*LSP 3450/1965*
M2WW 1006-03	**Night Rider**	**Pot Luck**
	Doc Pomus/Mort Shuman—Elvis Presley Music	*LSP 2325/1962*

"For The Millionth And The Last Time," the first Tepper-Bennett song Elvis had taken on for a nonmovie session, opened the proceedings on October 15. Perhaps it was the Latin dance feel that slowed things down, or the fact that the song seemed a little stale; maybe it was the change in band personnel. Guitarist Hank Garland, who'd lent such fire and authority to Elvis's sound since the June '58 session, had suffered serious brain damage in an automobile accident; he was replaced by the less versatile Jerry Kennedy, leaving Scotty Moore back in charge for the first time since Elvis had returned from the army. Elvis wasn't very impressed with the results on "For The Millionth," but he got his kicks watching Gordon Stoker sweating it out on accordion. "Damn, Gordon," he joked, "quit breathing so heavy." Aaron Schroeder and Wally Gold's "Good Luck Charm" was a straight-ahead pop song, and Elvis was all business: "If we goof up," he told the band, "just keep going." He knew his players—Scotty's rhythm comping did cause a little trouble—but by take four they had it down, and the new single was on tape.

The "real strong songs" Freddy had mentioned in his note were two brand-new Don Robertson ballads. Elvis's careful phrasing suggests that he'd done serious preparation on the first, "Anything That's Part Of You," but that didn't stop him from working hard on it, running through six takes as Floyd Cramer worked to duplicate the slip-note fills Robertson had played on the demo. Years later Elvis would tell audiences that "I'm So Lonesome I Could Cry" was "probably the saddest song I've ever heard," but he never portrayed abandonment more convincingly than on this cut. Among Elvis's recorded ballads perhaps the only competition comes from some of the other Robertson songs recorded in 1961 and '62. The second of his contributions, "I Met Her Today," told a more hopeful story, but it proved harder to get right. After a promising first take Elvis paused to correct some problems with the song's challenging octave-and-a-half leaps, but as soon as he'd mastered that, band mistakes began to multiply. After twenty takes the group's concentration had worn thin, and they agreed to stop, leaving take eighteen as the master. But the recording lay unused for four years until RCA resurrected it for *Elvis For Everyone*.

They didn't have much better luck with "Night Rider," the Pomus and Shuman song that was Freddy's golden hope. By now they were tired, and no one could come up with a decent groove for the song; they ended up just taking it at a breakneck pace, and though take three was accepted as a master, everyone knew they could have done better.

But if anyone was disappointed it wasn't RCA. True to the agenda, Elvis had delivered sterling cuts on "Good Luck Charm" and "Anything That's Part Of You"—and together they'd make as strong a single as the label could wish for.

60. Soundtrack Recordings for Mirisch Company's *Kid Galahad* October 26–27, 1961: Radio Recorders, Hollywood

Mirisch Producer: Jeff Alexander
Engineer: Thorne Nogar

Guitar: Scotty Moore
Guitar: Tiny Timbrell
Guitar: Neal Matthews
Bass: Bob Moore
Drums: D. J. Fontana

Drums: Buddy Harman
Piano: Dudley Brooks
Sax: Boots Randolph
Vocals: The Jordanaires

10/26, 6PM–12AM, 1–4:25AM

M1-31	**King Of The Whole Wide World**	
WPA5 2551	*Ruth Batchelor/Bob Roberts—Elvis Presley Music*	
M2-sp	**A Whistling Tune**	**Kid Galahad (EP)**
N2PB 3136	*Sherman Edwards/Hal David—Gladys Music*	*EPA 4371/1962*
M3-21	**Home Is Where The Heart Is**	**Kid Galahad (EP)**
N2PB 3134	*Sherman Edwards/Hal David—Gladys Music*	*EPA 4371/1962*
M4-09	**Riding The Rainbow**	
	Ben Weisman/Fred Wise—Gladys Music	
MX4-sp	**Riding The Rainbow**	**Kid Galahad (EP)**
N2PB 3133	*Ben Weisman/Fred Wise—Gladys Music*	*EPA 4371/1962*

10/27, 4–8PM

M5-06	**I Got Lucky**	
	Fuller/Weisman/Wise—Gladys Music	
MX5-02	**I Got Lucky**	**Kid Galahad (EP)**
N2PB 3135	*Fuller/Weisman/Wise—Gladys Music*	*EPA 4371/1962*
M6-10	**This Is Living**	**Kid Galahad (EP)**
N2PB 3132	*Ben Weisman/ Fred Wise—Gladys Music*	*EPA 4371/1962*
M7-04	**King Of The Whole Wide World**	**Kid Galahad (EP)**
N2PB 3131	*Ruth Batchelor/Bob Roberts—Elvis Presley Music*	*EPA 4371/1962*

The master of "A Whistling Tune" (3136) is spliced from take 1 (opening) and take 8. The master of "Riding The Rainbow" (3133) is spliced from MX4 take 7 and last bars of M4 take 9. Both "Riding The Rainbow" and "I Got Lucky" were tried in two slightly different arrangements. In each case, the latter version was used for the record. Masters of "King Of The Whole Wide World," "Home Is Where The Heart Is," "I Got Lucky," and "A Whistling Tune" were shortened for original release.

Yet another Elvis movie project, and Freddy Bienstock and his writers were reeling under the never-ending demand for more songs. Freddy knew he needed at least one strong song for each film, to be used as either title cut or potential radio hit—or both. With so many films, the demand for Elvis material had increased to forty-eight songs this year, and competition among the writers only added to the stress. As Ruth Batchelor, who with Bob Roberts made up a new Hill & Range writing team, remembers, "We only got three or four weeks' notice to write songs for a film." In that time the writers had to produce a lyric, a melody, and a well-produced demo for each submission. "More than 300 demos [were] submitted to one film by ten or twelve writers," Bachelor continues, "so the odds against you [were] very high." Ruth got her chance with "King Of The Whole Wide World," a fiery up-tempo number with all the ingredients of a major hit. Not all her songs were accepted, of course, but the ongoing need for material meant that songs rejected for one film had a chance to be accepted later for another. Giant, Baum, and Kaye, who had broken into Elvis movies with "Sound Advice," were discouraged when Elvis cut it from the soundtrack EP—and even more so when their *Kid Galahad* candidate "I Don't Wanna Be Tied" failed to get recorded at all. What a surprise, then, when the song turned up some five months later on the *Girls! Girls! Girls!* sessions, just as easily dropped into one storyline as it had been into the other. Such was the life of an Elvis songwriter.

The relative failure of the movie songs of this period was no reflection of Elvis's performances, or those of the Nashville players. Just as much time and musicianship was spent on this soundtrack as on the RCA albums. The group worked hard on the *Kid Galahad* sessions at Radio Recorders, and especially on "King Of The Whole Wide World." They went through thirty-one takes on the first day before settling on a master, then came back the next day and tried it again, finally cutting the kind of freewheeling record they wanted after two days and thirty-five takes. The problem had nothing to do with seriousness or commitment; the problem was with the material. One great song out of six was definitely a descending hit ratio for the world's top recording artist.

As they had a year earlier, Elvis's (and the Colonel's) triumphs came in the last few months of the year—this time with the release of the movie and soundtrack of *Blue Hawaii.* But the celebration came on the heels of grumbling and argument between the Colonel and the record company. First RCA wanted to charge extra for the album because it contained fourteen cuts, something the Colonel wouldn't even consider. Then, at the last minute, the label asked to put out a single of "Can't Help Falling In Love" during the film's release. The Colonel's policy had always been clear: Movie singles must precede the movie and album release by six weeks, and in his estimation any single taken from an already-released album (i.e., using songs the fans already owned) would die on the vine. Besides, he worried, releasing a single from the film while "His Latest Flame"/"Little Sister" was still on the charts would only cut into that record's sales. Parker had "Good Luck Charm" ready to go as the required fourth single of the year, and that's how he wanted things to stay. Yet

RCA had tremendous hopes for the coupling of "Can't Help Falling In Love" and "Rock-A-Hula Baby," and they were afraid of being scooped by a cover again, the way they'd been when Joe Dowell had covered Elvis's "Wooden Heart" from *G.I. Blues.* In the end, they agreed to guarantee royalties on a million units, and their faith proved well placed: Released in November, the single sold a million in the United States alone. The album stayed an incredible twenty weeks at number one, outselling the previous record-setter, *G.I. Blues,* by two to one and eventually climbing to an unheard-of two million

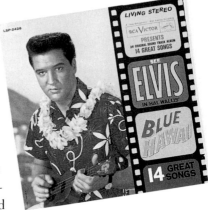

units. No record—no picture—had ever made Elvis and the Colonel so much money, and it can be argued that nothing in his highly eventful future would ever have as much impact on the course of Elvis Presley's musical career.

1962-63

The Formula

Manage (man'-aj) v.t. to oversee and make decisions

The Colonel was in an enviable position. There was no question of whether his artist's projects would be successful; it was only a matter of how successful. Even Elvis Presley's lesser achievements would have satisfied anyone else in entertainment. The musical climate of 1960 and 1961 had been stable—there had been no major new trends, no competition to speak of—and now the Colonel had what looked like a foolproof prescription for future prosperity.

It was the gigantic success of *Blue Hawaii* that had done it. *G.I. Blues* had shown the way, while *Flaming Star* and *Wild in the Country* confirmed the Colonel's suspicion that artistically ambitious movies meant only disappointment at the box office—and in record sales, because they featured very little music. *Blue Hawaii,* on the other hand, had fourteen songs, beautiful scenery, pretty girls, and a plot as transparent as the water on the beach of Kauai—and it was an enormous success. In just twelve months the album sold an astonishing two million copies worldwide, propelled by the dynamic "Can't Help Falling In Love" single. It didn't take any sophisticated market research to decide on the next move. Before *Blue Hawaii* had hit the theaters Elvis had already made two movies for the Mirisch Company, *Follow That Dream* and *Kid Galahad;* with four and six songs respectively, they hardly fit the new model, and by the time they were completed it was clear that there was no point in wasting too much time on their promotion.

The nonmovie singles continued to do well; the February release of "Good Luck Charm," the only obvious single remaining in the vault, went to number one. On the other hand, *Something For Everybody,* the regular RCA album for 1961, hadn't performed nearly as well as *Blue Hawaii.* That might have confused the Colonel, but he went ahead and put the 1960–61 strategy into gear once again: An RCA recording session was set for Nashville on March 18, 1962, to be followed a week later by soundtrack sessions for the new Paramount movie.

The sheer volume of recording activity continued to be a major challenge for Elvis's music-publishing companies, forcing Freddy Bienstock to be on the lookout constantly for new writers and material. The previous year he had succeeded in bringing Don Robertson back into the fold with four songs, and Doc Pomus and Mort Shuman had delivered an impressive pairing with "Little Sister"/"His Latest Flame."

RCA had six unreleased songs to fill out a new album, but still they needed another ten, and Freddy's problems grew as he cast around trying to find songs for thirteen scenes in the new Hal Wallis production, *Girls! Girls! Girls!*

Surprisingly enough, Elvis and his pals had spent some time the previous year trying to help out with the problem themselves. Along with Charlie Hodge and Red West, Elvis had been planning to rework some old public-domain songs for which Freddy would have little trouble obtaining new copyrights. Then Elvis, Charlie, and Red took a notion to write a new lyric for a popular classic—no less than Cole Porter's "Begin The Beguine." Freddy soon discovered that Porter had no intention of granting his consent to such an idea, and the frustrated trio was stuck until Charlie, with the simplest of chord substitutions, created an entirely new tune they could claim as their own. 1961 had gone by without the song making it onto a recording session, but it was not forgotten.

61. Studio Sessions for RCA
March 18–19, 1962: RCA's Studio B, Nashville

A&R/Producer: Steve Sholes
Engineer: Bill Porter

Guitar: Scotty Moore
Guitar: Harold Bradley
Guitar, Vibes: Grady Martin
Bass: Bob Moore
Drums: D. J. Fontana

Drums: Buddy Harman
Piano: Floyd Cramer
Sax, Vibes: Boots Randolph
Vocals: The Jordanaires
Vocals: Millie Kirkham

3/18, 7:30–10:30PM, 11PM–2AM, 2:30–6:30AM

N2WW 0685-07	**Something Blue**	**Pot Luck**
	Paul Evans/Al Byron—Gladys Music	*LSP 2523/1962*
N2WW 0686-07	**Gonna Get Back Home Somehow**	**Pot Luck**
	Doc Pomus/Mort Shuman—Elvis Presley Music	*LSP 2523/1962*
N2WW 0687-05	**(Such An) Easy Question**	**Pot Luck**
	Otis Blackwell/Winfield Scott—Elvis Presley Music	*LSP 2523/1962*
N2WW 0688-10	**Fountain Of Love**	**Pot Luck**
	Bill Giant/Jeff Lewis—Elvis Presley Music	*LSP 2523/1962*
N2WW 0689-05	**Just For Old Time Sake**	**Pot Luck**
	Sid Tepper/Roy C. Bennett—Gladys Music	*LSP 2523/1962*
N2WW 0690-nm	**Night Rider**	
	Doc Pomus/Mort Shuman—Elvis Presley Music	
N2WW 0691-03	**You'll Be Gone**	**Single B-side**
	Red West/E. Presley/Charlie Hodge—Elvis Presley Music	*47-8500/1965*

3/19, 7:30–10:30PM, 11PM–2AM

N2WW 0692-05	I Feel That I've Known You Forever	Pot Luck
	Doc Pomus/Alan Jeffreys—Elvis Presley Music	*LSP 2523/1962*
N2WW 0693-06	Just Tell Her Jim Said Hello	Single B-side
	Mike Stoller/Jerry Leiber—Elvis Presley Music	*47-8041/1962*
N2WW 0694-sp	Suspicion	Pot Luck
	Doc Pomus/Mort Shuman—Elvis Presley Music	*LSP 2523/1962*
N2WW 0695-sp	She's Not You	Single A-side
	Doc Pomus/Mike Stoller/Jerry Leiber—Elvis Presley Music	*47-8041/1962*

The master of "Suspicion" is spliced from take 5 and take 3 of a work part. The master of "She's Not You" is spliced from take 3 and a work part take 5 (ending).

The group that gathered once more in RCA's Studio B in Nashville on a March Sunday was in many ways a carbon copy of the group Elvis had been working with for two years. Chet Atkins and Steve Sholes were still formally in charge, but as usual Elvis ran the show. Bill Porter was the engineer, and almost all the usual musicians checked in. The gap left by Hank Garland's incapacitating accident had been partially glossed over by Jerry Kennedy during the "Good Luck Charm" sessions, but Chet Atkins knew they would need to do something more to fill Hank's shoes in the long term. No greater tribute to Garland's genius could be paid than the fact that it took two of Nashville's most celebrated guitarists, Harold Bradley and Grady Martin, to fill the bill.

Paul Evans, who had contributed "I Gotta Know" in 1960, sent in a pretty ballad he had written with Al Byron called "Something Blue." A gentle riff spun off the old wedding ritual "something old, something new, something borrowed, something blue," the song was submitted on a demo that used part of "The Wedding March" in the introduction. The idea didn't really work—Elvis's group tried it briefly before dropping it—but fortunately everything else did. There was nothing eye-opening about the record, but the musicians (most of whom were major contributors to the renowned Nashville sound of the 1960s) performed at a standard of musicianship that most recording artists would only dream of. Doc Pomus and Mort Shuman's past successes put them at the top of the most-wanted-songwriters list, and the next song Elvis tackled was one of five titles Pomus contributed, and one of three with Shuman. "Gonna Get Back Home Somehow," a moody rocker, the band attacked with the same natural grace that

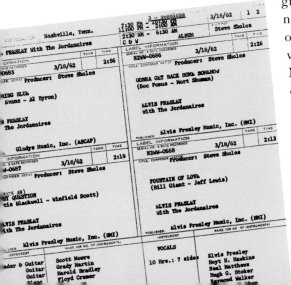

had worked on the earlier ballad. Harold Bradley played tic-tac, doubling the notes of Bob Moore's acoustic bass, but one octave higher. Grady Martin played both lead and rhythm, spontaneously trading duties with Scotty Moore throughout the sessions.

A new song from Otis Blackwell was always welcome; only Leiber and Stoller rivaled him among Elvis hit-writers, so there was every reason to expect something outstanding from him and his current cowriter, Winfield Scott. "(Such An) Easy Question" was exactly that: a medium-tempo pop song with just the right kind of bluesy phrasings. Elvis playfully sexed it up, and again the controlled, carefully worked-out arrangement of instruments and vocals created a perfect pop record—a real single candidate. The only new team that succeeded in getting anything included was Bill Giant and Jeff Lewis, with their Latin-flavored "Fountain Of Love." The song itself wasn't quite up to standard—nothing bad, just less accomplished than the musicians deserved—but Elvis's voice, on this and everything he sang that night, never sounded better. He took command of the almost operatic song, sliding up and down his extended range with an ease few popular singers could have approached. Grady Martin added some Spanish-influenced guitar picking (à la his work on Marty Robbins's "El Paso"), while Harold Bradley shifted from tic-tac back to guitar; saxman Boots Randolph filled in on shakers and vibes, demonstrating the value of using versatile musicians.

Another pretty ballad, "Just For Old Time Sake" by regular writers Sid Tepper and Roy Bennett, offered no surprises or originality, but gave Elvis a chance to apply some of the Dean Martin vocal techniques he'd studied so intensely. Next Elvis wanted to give another shot to "Night Rider," the Pomus and Shuman song he had recorded the previous October, but he gave up after an hour of struggling, as nobody seemed to be able to see beyond the typically overwhelming arrangement on the Phil Spector–produced demo. Then, in the early morning hours, Elvis finally brought out the song inspired by "Begin The Beguine." "You'll Be Gone" suggested deep undercurrents of passion, and Elvis threw himself into its atmosphere, offering a dramatic delivery on top of the Latinate arrangement. The fact that the song was shelved for three years suggests that Elvis wasn't convinced of its success, but it's remarkable as the only song in which Elvis was ever seriously involved as a writer.

The following day began with a Doc Pomus and Alan Jeffreys ballad, "I Feel That I've Known You Forever"—a lovely thought, and a great vocal challenge, but not sufficiently developed to be a single. On the next number, "Just Tell Her Jim Said Hello," Freddy thought he had a potential hit. The song represented a return to Leiber and Stoller material, the first since the conflict over *G.I. Blues*. Now, with such an overwhelming need for strong new songs, Freddy used every capable writer he could get. The song had already been recorded with little commercial success, but the melody was memorable and the lyric had a nice twist to it, so it made sense to put some effort into the arranging and recording. Elvis and his band tried the song at all kinds of tempos, several significantly faster than the take that became the master. It was on take six that the band came up with the unusually structured mid-tempo arrangement they eventually settled on, but an annoyingly loud triangle disturbed the otherwise well-balanced mix.

One of the last songs of the session, "Suspicion," was another rhythmic departure—but this time it had *hit* written all over it. Elvis had saved the best for last; the song seemed built to showcase every little vocal trick in his bag, without ever devolving into parody. The final number was a joint venture by Leiber and Stoller and Doc Pomus, a team that could be expected to produce a dynamite song, and they did—with the infectious "She's Not You." Elvis would never sound as honey-sweet on anything else, gliding through an effortless recording that's a model of unaffected intimacy. Freddy Bienstock's enthusiasm for the material he had collected proved contagious, and as the sessions came to a close, lacquers of a single backing "Just Tell Her Jim Said Hello" with "You'll Be Gone" were ordered by Elvis, the Colonel, and Freddy himself.

62. Soundtrack Recordings for Paramount's *Girls! Girls! Girls!* March 26–28, 1962: Radio Recorders, Hollywood

Musical Director for Paramount: Joseph Lilley
Engineer: Thorne Nogar

Guitar: Scotty Moore
Guitar: Tiny Timbrell
Guitar: Barney Kessel
Guitar: Robert Bain (AAO)
Guitar: Alton Hendrickson (AAO)
Bass: Ray Siegel
Drums: D. J. Fontana
Drums: Hal Blaine

Drums: Bernie Mattinson
Organ: Harold Brown (CO)
Piano: Dudley Brooks
Sax, Clarinet: Boots Randolph
Vocals: The Jordanaires
Vocals: The Amigos (AAO)
Vocals: Ginny & Elisabeth Tui (NO)

3/26, 11AM–4:30PM, 6PM–12:10AM

AO-03	**I Don't Want To**	**Girls! Girls! Girls!**
N2PB 3275	*Janice Tarre/Fred Spielman—Gladys Music*	*LSP 2621/1962*
BO-06	**We're Comin' In Loaded**	**Girls! Girls! Girls!**
N2PB 3288	*Otis Blackwell/Winfield Scott—Elvis Presley Music*	*LSP 2621/1962*
CO-05	**Thanks To The Rolling Sea**	**Girls! Girls! Girls!**
N2PB 3281	*Ruth Batchelor/Bob Roberts—Elvis Presley Music*	*LSP 2621/1962*

3/27, 1–5:50PM

DO-14	**Where Do You Come From**	**Single B-side**
N2PB 3274	*Ruth Batchelor/Bob Roberts—Elvis Presley Music*	*47-8100/1962*
EO-03	**Girls! Girls! Girls!**	**Girls! Girls! Girls!**
N2PB 3272	*J. Leiber/M. Stoller—Progressive/Elvis Presley Music*	*LSP 2621/1962*

FO-02	**Return To Sender**	**Single A-side**
N2PB 3279	*Otis Blackwell/Winfield Scott—Elvis Presley Music*	*47-8100/1962*
GO-06	**Because Of Love**	**Girls! Girls! Girls!**
N2PB 3280	*Ruth Batchelor/Bob Roberts—Elvis Presley Music*	*LSP 2621/1962*

<u>3/27, 6:45PM–12:30AM</u>

HO-12	**The Walls Have Ears**	**Girls! Girls! Girls!**
N2PN 3283	*Roy C. Bennett/Bob Roberts—Elvis Presley Music*	*LSP 2621/1962*
JO-06	**Song Of The Shrimp**	**Girls! Girls! Girls!**
N2PB 3282	*Roy C. Bennett/Sid Tepper—Gladys Music*	*LSP 2621/1962*
KO-05	**A Boy Like Me, A Girl Like You**	**Girls! Girls! Girls!**
N2PB 3277	*Sid Tepper/Roy C. Bennett—Gladys Music*	*LSP 2621/1962*

<u>3/28, 1–5:45PM</u>

LO-10	**Mama**	**Double Features**
WPA1 8121	*Charles O'Curran/Dudley Brooks—Gladys Music*	*66130-2/1993*
MO-09	**Earth Boy**	**Girls! Girls! Girls!**
N2PB 3278	*Sid Tepper/Roy C. Bennett—Gladys Music*	*LSP 2621/1962*
NO-sp	**Earth Boy (movie version)**	
	Sid Tepper/Roy C. Bennett—Gladys Music	

<u>3/28, 7:15–1:40AM</u>

PO-06	**Dainty Little Moonbeams**	**Double Features**
WPA5 2505	*Unknown*	*66130-2/1993*
PO1-15	**Girls! Girls! Girls! (finale)**	**Double Features**
WPA5 2506	*J. Leiber/M. Stoller—Progressive/Elvis Presley Music*	*66130-2/1993*
QO-08	**I Don't Wanna Be Tied**	**Girls! Girls! Girls!**
N2PB 3273	*Giant/Baum/Kaye—Elvis Presley Music*	*LSP 2621/1962*
RO-sp	**Plantation Rock**	**Double Features**
NPA5 5824	*Giant/Baum/Kaye—Elvis Presley Music*	*66130-2/1993*

<u>Unknown</u>

AAO-11	**We'll Be Together**	**Girls! Girls! Girls!**
N2PB 3276	*Charles O'Curran/Dudley Brooks—Gladys Music*	*LSP 2621/1962*

The *Let's Be Friends* album release (CAS 2408/1970) of "Mama" (WPA1 8122) is spliced from LO take 10 and film version sung by the Amigos. "Earth Boy" (movie version) is spliced from takes 2 and 4, with female voices overdubbed. "Plantation Rock" (RO) is spliced from take 17 and unknown take. The original release on *Elvis: A Legendary Performer Volume 4* (CPL1 4848) is incorrectly edited. The release on the *Double Features* CD (66130-2) is spliced to match the original lacquer. The Amigos: Jose Vadis, Pedro Berrios, Miguel Alcaide, Felix Melendes.

Otis Blackwell and his partner, Winfield Scott, had been working on songs for Paramount's new picture, *Girls! Girls! Girls!* but could only come up with two numbers that fit the score: "We're Comin' In Loaded" and a stab at a title song. Otis always got the attention of the Presley organization, and the song he'd written with Winfield Scott, "(Such An) Easy Question," had been a standout at the Nashville session earlier that month. At a meeting with the Colonel in Hill & Range's New York offices, Blackwell reported that he'd written only two songs for the new script, but then mentioned another number called "Return To Sender." The Colonel wasn't normally involved in song-pitching, but he was well aware of the constant need for material, and he asked Blackwell to play it for him. "Don't worry," Parker told him after hearing it, "that will go into the movie. I can tell you that, 'cause it's a great song." Of course not every song could be a masterpiece, and Blackwell and Scott's own take on "Girls! Girls! Girls!" was found wanting compared to the song of the same name Leiber and Stoller had written for the Coasters in 1960, and it was Jerry and Mike's version that became the title song of the new Elvis movie.

Just as with the *Blue Hawaii* sessions, there were at least fifteen different songs available when soundtrack recording started: several very mediocre songs from the Tepper and Bennett team, two from the new Giant, Baum, and Kaye group, and two very nice ballads from the pens of Ruth Batchelor and Bob Roberts, who had had their first cuts on *Kid Galahad*. When a birthday song was needed to fit the story, musical director Charles O'Curran sat down with his longtime studio pianist, Dudley Brooks, and wrote a tune called "Mama." It wasn't right, so after the session they tried again and immediately recorded a backing track for "We'll Be Together," on which Elvis would later overdub a vocal. Elvis, as usual, wanted some of his own musicians with him on the Coast, so the studio flew out Scotty, D. J., Boots, and the Jordanaires a few days ahead of Elvis, who still preferred to drive himself. The studio band differed only slightly from that of the *Blue Hawaii* sessions. When Bob Moore couldn't make the date he was replaced by Ray Siegel, who had played with the group before. The other addition was well-known jazz guitarist Barney Kessel, a frequent session player, who had been working recently with up-and-coming producer Phil Spector; with so many guitarists on hand, though, he was reduced to strumming along—a humble gig for a musician who'd played with the likes of Charlie Parker and Art Tatum. Charles O'Curran directed a series of rehearsals before Elvis arrived, leaving the singer little chance for any substantial musical interaction with his band. Boots Randolph's extended sax solo on the title song is the only real evidence of improvisation on the sessions; as with "King Of The Whole Wide World," the extra time Elvis allowed Boots only confirmed how much Elvis thought of his playing.

Bunny Lewis, the English composer who'd cowritten "The Girl Of My Best Friend" (under a pseudonym), arrived as a guest on the third day of the session. Elvis "knows the sound he wants," Lewis reported to the magazine *The Reveille,* "although [he is] not always coherent enough to get his message through." Elvis sounded as good as he had on the *Blue Hawaii* album, but on the whole the *Girls! Girls! Girls!* soundtrack lacked the romantic feeling that seemed to emanate from the exotic Hawaiian location.

And Elvis's track record, in terms of both record sales and chart performance, was beginning to slip. The four-track EP *Follow That Dream*—a collection of unspectacular music in a dying format—only reached number fifteen on the singles chart. Four months later the release of the *Kid Galahad* EP, featuring six tunes, never got above number thirty. The real follow-up to the number-one "Good Luck Charm," everyone expected, would come from the March Nashville sessions. As the excitement from the sessions wore off, so did Elvis's initial confidence in "You'll Be Gone," the song he had written with Red and Charlie. The material for *Pot Luck* had already been selected and included "For The Millionth And The Last Time," as well as two songs initially considered for single release—"(Such An) Easy Question" and "Suspicion"—Afterward, Elvis determined that "She's Not You" and Freddy's favorite, "Just Tell Her Jim Said Hello," should be coupled as the next single. ("You'll Be Gone" was relegated to the shelves of RCA's New York vault.) When the single came out, "She's Not You" got almost all of the radio attention, which proved Freddy wrong—but when the record stopped at a disappointing number five, it seemed as if Elvis's ability to pick a hit had failed him, too. The *Pot Luck* album went to number four but never captured the expected top position, which only went to reaffirm that studio album sales seemed to level out at about 200,000.

After the disappointing showing of *Flaming Star* and *Wild in the Country,* meanwhile, 20th Century–Fox declined to pursue its relationship with Elvis further—and around the same time the Mirisch deal turned into two pictures instead of four. Suddenly it was incumbent upon the Colonel to come up with something big. The deal with Paramount allowed Elvis to make one movie a year with another studio, so the Colonel went back to MGM, the company that had produced *Jailhouse Rock*. Whatever reservations had prompted MGM not to secure a follow-up picture in 1957 had long since been erased by the phenomenal success of *Blue Hawaii,* and the Colonel was able to parlay that into a four-year, four-picture MGM deal. At first there was talk of a movie based on the life of country singer Hank Williams, to be called *Your Cheatin' Heart.* But Elvis and the Colonel dismissed the idea soon enough; not only did it strain credulity to imagine Elvis playing another performer, but any such project would naturally be limited to Hank Williams material, which offered none of the financial pay-off that recording songs from his own publishing companies did. They were left with just two pictures for 1962—the just-completed *Girls! Girls! Girls!* and the first MGM production.

Originally titled *Take Me to the Fair,* the new film was conceived along familiar (and successful) lines—a lightweight story wrapped around a family theme, filled with plenty of songs. This cut down on the number of scantily clad young women offered in the Paramount pictures, true, but it had the potential of substantially expanding the audience.

The songs were the showpieces anyway, just as they'd been with *Blue Hawaii* and *Girls! Girls! Girls!*—all of which meant that Freddy Bienstock would have to keep pushing his writers as hard as he could, trying always to balance the burden among those who were creative, those who wrote in volume, and those who needed a break. Leiber and Stoller seemed to be permanently estranged from writing for Elvis; all Freddy could get from them were songs already written for someone else. Perhaps even more distressing, his golden team—Doc Pomus and Mort Shuman—was showing signs of drying up. Freddy knew Elvis had gone overboard on the four Don Robertson songs he had recorded the year before, and now Robertson submitted an impressive new ballad, "They Remind Me Too Much Of You." It hadn't been written for the new movie, but Freddy loved it so much he set out to persuade producer Ted Richmond to write the song into the story. Elvis went through all the material, including ten Robertson songs. There were three different submissions for the title song, from which he chose Wise and Weisman's "Take Me To The Fair" as the winner. But when Ted Richmond, the film's producer, reviewed the demos himself, he preferred the Tepper and Bennett candidate to Elvis's choice, and, dissatisfied with both the songs and Elvis's selection, requested still more demos from Freddy.

63. Soundtrack Recordings for MGM's *It Happened At The World's Fair*
August 30 and September 22, 1962: Radio Recorders, Hollywood

Musical Director MGM: Leith Stevens
Engineer: Dave Weichman

Guitar: Scotty Moore
Guitar: Billy Strange
Guitar: Tiny Timbrell
Bass: Ray Siegel
Drums: D. J. Fontana
Drums: Frank Carlson

Piano, Organ: Dudley Brooks
Piano, Organ: Don Robertson
Sax: Clifford Scott
Vocals: The Jordanaires (8/30)
Vocals: The Mello Men (9/22)

8/30, 7–11:45PM

WPA5 2552-na	**Take Me To The Fair**		
	Sid Tepper/Roy C. Bennett—Gladys Music		
PPA3 2717-08	**Happy Ending**	**It Happened At The World's Fair**	
	Ben Weisman/Sid Wayne—Gladys Music	*LSP 2697/1963*	
PPA3 2717-09	**Happy Ending (movie version)**		
	Ben Weisman/Sid Wayne—Gladys Music		
PPA3 2726-13	**Relax**	**It Happened At The World's Fair**	
	Sid Tepper/Roy C. Bennett—Gladys Music	*LSP 2697/1963*	

9/22, 11:30AM–4:30PM, 5:30–11PM

PPA3 2719-08	**I'm Falling In Love Tonight**	**It Happened At The World's Fair**
	Don Robertson—Gladys Music	*LSP 2697/1963*
PPA3 2725-09	**They Remind Me Too Much Of You**	**Single B-side**
	Don Robertson—Gladys Music	*47-8134/1963*
PPA3 2720-05	**Cotton Candy Land**	**It Happened At The World's Fair**
	Ruth Batchelor/Bob Roberts—Elvis Presley Music	*LSP 2697/1963*
PPA3 2721-01	**A World Of Our Own**	**It Happened At The World's Fair**
	Giant/Baum/Kaye—Elvis Presley Music	*LSP 2697/1963*
PPA3 2722-06	**How Would You Like To Be**	**It Happened At The World's Fair**
	Ben Raleigh/Mark Barkan—Elvis Presley Music	*LSP 2697/1963*
WPA5 2512-01	**One Broken Heart For Sale (movie version)**	**Collectors Gold**
	Otis Blackwell/Winfield Scott—Elvis Presley Music	*3114-2/1991*
PPA3 2724-05	**One Broken Heart For Sale**	**Single A-side**
	Otis Blackwell/Winfield Scott—Elvis Presley Music	*47-8134/1963*
PPA3 2723-04	**Beyond The Bend**	**It Happened At The World's Fair**
	Ben Weisman/Fred Wise/Dee Fuller—Gladys Music	*LSP 2697/1963*
PPA3 2718-08	**Take Me To The Fair**	**It Happened At The World's Fair**
	Sid Tepper/Roy C. Bennett—Gladys Music	*LSP 2697/1963*

The Mello Men: Thurl Ravenscroft, Bill Lee, Bill Cole, Max Smith.

The soundtrack sessions were booked for August 28 and 29; mostly likely to cut costs, only the Jordanaires, Scotty, and D. J. were flown to the coast. Rarely were songwriters invited to a session, but in a surprising decision based on Elvis's personal friendship and Robertson's impressive contribution, Don Robertson was asked to participate as a session musician, alternating with Dudley Brooks on organ and piano. Robertson was no stranger to the recording studio—it was he who had invented the "slip-note" piano style that Floyd Cramer had made into his trademark—and his presence would prove lucky for both himself and Elvis. And Robertson wasn't the only writer there for the sessions. Ben Weisman, the only experienced Hill & Range staff writer connected to Elvis, lived in Los Angeles and had delivered some of the faster numbers MGM continued to request; called in at the last minute to help come up with a new song for the finale, he worked against deadline and came up with "Happy Ending"—only to discover that Elvis had arrived in L.A. with a cold and the session would be postponed for two days.

When they finally got around to recording, Elvis still wasn't feeling well. There was time to do only three numbers: the finale, which Ben arranged on the spot, along with Tepper and Bennett's "Relax," and an unsuccessful attempt at "Take Me To The Fair." Then, because of the shooting schedule, the rest of the soundtrack recording was put off until late September. By the time Elvis returned on September 22 the Jordanaires were unavailable, so a local group, the Mello Men, took their place. The first task was to rerecord "Take Me To The Fair," but all their work on Ted Richmond's preferred "title song" proved wasted when the picture was renamed to highlight the Seattle World's Fair location, and the song lost its title status (though it stayed in the picture).

Engineering on the MGM soundtrack sessions was a far cry from that of Elvis's other recordings. The Nashville recordings were graced with a natural room ambience and enhanced by tape echo to create a certain brilliance of sound. On the Paramount pictures Hal Wallis had cooperated with the Colonel (after the arguments over *Loving You*), allowing Elvis to record at Radio Recorders to ensure good sound for his RCA releases. MGM, on the other hand, had a policy of recording their movie music very "dry"—in other words, without echo. And for the picture mix they insisted on radical sound separation, with Elvis on one track, all the instruments on a second, and backing vocals alone on the third. Echo could be added later wherever needed, but that kind of after-the-fact treatment could never reproduce the same full-bodied sound they normally achieved in Nashville or Radio Recorders. This was in principle a mono recording process; when stereo records were made from the tapes, the result came out sounding dull and one-dimensional— a steep step down from Elvis's recent recordings.

There was no doubt that at this time Don Robertson was Elvis's favorite writer, and the morning session began with two of his ballads. The movie songs needed to fit the demands of the plot, so such material came out sounding forced, even inarticulate; Robertson's contributions, on the other hand, were two love songs that stood on their own. Elvis took his time, striving to create the proper feeling for each song, and worked through eight takes of "I'm Falling In Love Tonight" and nine of "They Remind Me Too Much Of You" before he was satisfied. Robertson's presence put him in an enviable position to promote and support his own material. As Elvis started work on "They Remind Me Too Much Of You," he remembers, "someone in the control room thought that the melody was too close to 'Chapel In The Moonlight,' " Don remembers. "So I thought 'God, what can I do here?' so I fiddled around on the piano a little bit. . . . I went over to Elvis, who was standing in front of the vocal mike, and while the people in the booth were arguing about it, sang him this little phrase I had figured out. . . . [The song] was within a millimeter of being thrown out! I'm certain that if I hadn't been there, it would have been"—and Elvis would have been deprived of one of his classiest movie ballads.

Elvis progressed at a reasonable speed through the next three numbers, which can only be described as mediocre-to-bland movie fare. Sounding relaxed, he lit up a cigarillo and laughed dismissively at the absurdly arranged "How Would You Like To Be." The catchiest of the up-tempo numbers came from Otis Blackwell and Winfield Scott, whose "Return To Sender" was about to be released as a single from the *Girls! Girls! Girls!* album. "One Broken Heart For Sale" seemed destined for the same recognition, as the group breezed through it. Yet there's something marginally less ambitious about their work on this track, in which Elvis and the musicians relied on a trick-bag full of familiar vocal and instrumental routines. Imitating Jackie Wilson, falling into a growl as each line trailed off, and closing the song with a fade-out might all have been decent musical strategies, but taken together they suggested a lack of imagination—or dedication. "Beyond The Bend" followed, and on its heels the remake of "Take Me To The Fair." With factory efficiency, they had wrapped up eight songs in just twelve hours.

64. Soundtrack Sessions for Paramount's *Fun In Acapulco*
January 22–23, 1963; Radio Recorders, Hollywood

Musical Director for Paramount: Joseph Lilley
Engineer: Dave Weichman

Guitar: Scotty Moore
Guitar, Mandolin: Tiny Timbrell
Guitar: Barney Kessel
Bass: Ray Siegel
Drums: D. J. Fontana
Drums: Hal Blaine

Percussion: Emil Radocchia
Piano: Dudley Brooks
Trumpet: Anthony Terran
Trumpet: Rudolph Loera
Vocals: The Jordanaires
Vocals: The Amigos

1/22, 1–7PM, 8PM–1:15AM

AO-11   **Bossa Nova Baby** — Single A-side
PPA3 4431   *Jerry Leiber/Mike Stoller—Elvis Presley Music* — *47-8243/1963*

BO-sp   **I Think I'm Gonna Like It Here** — **Fun In Acapulco**
PPA3 4430   *Don Robertson/Hal Blair—Gladys Music* — *LSP 2756/1963*

CO-05   **Mexico** — **Fun in Acapulco**
PPA3 4425   *Sid Tepper/Roy C. Bennett—Gladys Music* — *LSP 2756/1963*

DO-sp   **The Bullfighter Was A Lady** — **Fun In Acapulco**
PPA3 4428   *Sid Tepper/Roy C. Bennett—Gladys Music* — *LSP 2756/1963*

EO-08   **Marguerita** — **Fun In Acapulco**
PPA3 4427   *Don Robertson—Gladys Music* — *LSP 2756/1963*

FO-05   **Vino, Dinero Y Amor** — **Fun In Acapulco**
PPA3 4424   *Sid Tepper/Roy C. Bennett—Gladys Music* — *LSP 2756/1963*

1/23, 1–5:25PM, 6:45–11:50PM, 12:20–3:50AM

JO-01   **(There's) No Room To Rhumba In A Sports Car** — **Fun In Acapulco**
PPA3 4429   *Fred Wise/Dick Manning—Gladys Music* — *LSP 2756/1963*

KO-01   **Fun In Acapulco** — **Fun In Acapulco**
PPA3 4423   *Ben Weisman/Sid Wayne* — *LSP 2756/1963*

LO-sp   **El Toro** — **Fun In Acapulco**
PPA3 4426   *Giant/Baum/Kaye—Elvis Presley Music* — *LSP 2756/1963*

BO-sp   **I Think I'm Gonna Like It Here (remake)**
WPA5 2540   *Don Robertson/Hal Blair*

DO-17   **The Bullfighter Was A Lady (remake)**
WPA5 2541   *Sid Tepper/Roy C. Bennett—Gladys Music*

NO-05   **You Can't Say No In Acapulco** — **Fun In Acapulco**
PPA3 4432   *S. Feller/D. Fuller/L. Morris—Elvis Presley Music* — *LSP 2756/1963*

PO-sp(tr)   **Guadalajara** — **Fun In Acapulco**
PPA3 4433   *Pepe Guisar* — *LSP 2756/1963*

"I Think I'm Gonna Like It Here" (BO-PPA3 4430) is spliced from take 10 and last line of take 7. "The Bullfighter Was A Lady" (DO-PPA3 4428) is spliced from takes 9 and 7. "El Toro" (LO) is spliced from take 2 and a few seconds of take 1. "I Think I'm Gonna Like It Here" (remake) (BO-WPA5 2540) is spliced from take 18 and the start of take 19. "Guadalajara" (PO) is spliced from takes 1 and 7 and vocal overdubs take 6 and 2. Elvis overdubbed his vocal on February 27.

Any suspicion that the flat sound of *It Happened At The World's Fair* had anything to do with engineer Thorne Nogar being replaced by Dave Weichman would vanish like tequila beneath the Acapulco moon as the new recording sessions began on January 22. From the energetic opening cut of "Bossa Nova Baby," through the intoxicating Tijuana sweetness of the horn players on "Marguerita," to the Spanish flavor on cuts like "Guadalajara" and "The Bullfighter Was A Lady," the recordings are a triumph of sound and atmosphere. Elvis was motivated. He sang brilliantly, with wholehearted enjoyment. And even though some of the songs merely served the plot, for once there was also some outstanding material.

Don Robertson and his partner, Hal Blair, went out of their way to increase the chances of having their songs accepted for *Fun In Acapulco,* visiting a Spanish nightclub and studying the music for inspiration. The result was a pair of up-tempo numbers that fit the Mexican setting—not to mention gesturing to the current popularity of Herb Alpert and his Tijuana Brass. Don had been impressed by the other songwriters' demos on the last session, so this time around he abandoned his usual piano-and-vocal demo style. Hiring a band that even included some of Elvis's own studio musicians, he created full performances made for Elvis and his group to copy exactly. The strategy worked: Both "I Think I'm Gonna Like It Here" and "Marguerita" were reproduced almost note for note. Freddy Bienstock had to dig into the Leiber and Stoller songbook to come up with "Bossa Nova Baby," a flop the previous year by Tippy and the Clovers. The bossa nova was actually a Brazilian phenomenon, but that was just a technicality; the song fit right into the film, and it gave Elvis a peppy, commercial new single feeding right into the happy world of the early '60s.

Meanwhile, as RCA was preparing to release the soundtrack album to *It Happened At The World's Fair,* the Colonel began agitating for a deluxe gatefold cover for the album, with a full photo spread. To cover the cost the label wanted to move the album into a deluxe series, which would have allowed them to charge more. The increased price would have benefited both RCA and Elvis, but the Colonel backpedaled instantly at the notion of an extra dollar at the retail level: His habitual concern that the fans get their money's worth was matched by his realistic sense that a ten-track album that ran barely twenty minutes was hardly the place to start charging more. Then, despite the fact that a normal-length version was available, RCA released "One Broken Heart For Sale" as a truncated one-minute-thirty-four second single. Perhaps its length, combined with the flat sound, explained why it was the first regular Elvis Presley single to fail to reach the top five; in fact, it fell one place short of the top ten. The album did get to number four, but it sold 200,000 fewer copies than *Girls! Girls! Girls!*

65. Studio Sessions for RCA
May 26–27, 1963: RCA's Studio B, Nashville

A&R: Steve Sholes
Engineer: Bill Porter

Guitar: Scotty Moore
Guitar: Grady Martin
Guitar: Jerry Kennedy (5/27)
Guitar: Harold Bradley
Bass: Bob Moore
Drums: D. J. Fontana

Drums: Buddy Harman
Piano: Floyd Cramer
Sax, Vibes, Shakers: Boots Randolph
Vocals: The Jordanaires
Vocals: Joe Babcock (as member of the Jordanaires)
Vocals: Millie Kirkham

<u>5/26, 6:30PM–5:30AM</u>

PPA4 0290-10   **Echoes Of Love**   **Kissin' Cousins**
Bob Roberts/Paddy McMains—Elvis Presley Music   *LSP 2894/1964*

PPA4 0291-06   **Please Don't Drag That String Around**   **Single B-side**
Otis Blackwell/Winfield Scott—Elvis Presley Music   *47-8188/1963*

PPA4 0292-06   **(You're The) Devil In Disguise**   **Single A-side**
Giant/Baum/Kaye—Elvis Presley Music   *47-8188/1963*

PPA4 0293-03   **Never Ending**   **Single B-side**
Buddy Kaye/Phil Springer—Gladys Music   *47-8400/1964*

PPA4 0294-01   **What Now, What Next, Where To**   **Double Trouble**
Don Robertson/Hal Blair—Gladys Music   *.LSP 3787/1967*

PPA4 0295-03   **Witchcraft**   **Single B-side**
Dave Bartholomew/P. King—Travis Music   *47-8243/1963*

PPA4 0296-03   **Finders Keepers, Losers Weepers**   **Elvis For Everyone**
Dory Jones/Ollie Jones—Elvis Presley Music   *LSP 3450/1965*

PPA4 0297-08   **Love Me Tonight**   **Fun In Acapulco**
Don Robertson—Elvis Presley Music   *LSP 2756/1963*

<u>5/27, 7PM–4AM</u>

PPA4 0302-02   **Memphis Tennessee**   **Collectors Gold**
Chuck Berry—Arc Music   *3114-2/1991*

PPA4 0303-02   **(It's A) Long Lonely Highway**   **Kissin' Cousins**
Doc Pomus/Mort Shuman—Elvis Presley Music   *LSP 2894/1964*

PPA4 0304-02   **Ask Me**   **Collectors Gold**
Modugno/Giant/Baum/Kaye—Elvis Presley Music   *3114-2/1991*

PPA4 0305-04   **Western Union**   **Speedway**
Sid Tepper/Roy C. Bennett—Gladys Music   *LSP 3989/1968*

PPA4 0306-05   **Slowly But Surely**   **Fun In Acapulco**
Sid Wayne/Ben Weisman—Gladys Music   *LSP 2756/1963*

PPA4 0307-02   **Blue River**   **Single B-side**
Paul Evans/Fred Tobias—Gladys Music   *47-8740/1965*

Joe Babcock replaced Hoyt Hawkins of the Jordanaires on these sessions. Jerry Kennedy replaced Grady Martin on guitar at 10PM on May 27. "Blue River" was extended for release, with the last part repeated to achieve an acceptable playing time. New numbers were assigned on two occasions: SPA4 6768 and SPKM 7357.

By 1963 Elvis's spring recording session for RCA had become almost obligatory, and the only surprise left was who would be playing guitar. The easiest solution was to continue to include everybody, so Scotty Moore, Harold Bradley, and Grady Martin all played on the first night, with Jerry Kennedy sitting in for Martin at ten o'clock the following evening. The repertoire came almost exclusively from Freddy Bienstock's sky-high pile of demonstration records, with an occasional Elvis favorite thrown in. The usual standbys—Leiber and Stoller, Pomus and Shuman, and to some extent even Don Robertson—seemed to have come up short, and the material provided by a number of new writers lacked the melodic richness and rhythmic subtlety Elvis thrived on. The first song, "Echoes Of Love," by Bob Roberts and Paddy McMains, was built around a set of endlessly repeated figures from Floyd Cramer; offering Elvis little vocal challenge, its predictable cadences became grating about halfway through. The band seemed at a loss with this brand of blatantly pop material, which lacked even a shred of country, blues, or gospel feeling. Otis Blackwell and Winfield Scott at least managed to deliver a song, "Please Don't Drag That String Around," but while it was professional, it seemed mainly to duplicate its predecessors "Return To Sender" and "One Broken Heart For Sale." The same was true of most of the other writing teams. The one outstanding title of the day came from Giant, Baum, and Kaye, who thus far had had only one song in each of the last three pictures. "(You're The) Devil In Disguise" was a perfect mix of predictable Presley pop and surprising rhythm structure. Lulling listeners in with a soft-and-slow opening, it hardly wasted a beat before jumping into full-blast rock 'n' roll; it was a trick Elvis had enjoyed since the days of "Milkcow Blues Boogie" and "I'll Never Let You Go," but this time he kept the stop-and-start approach going for the rest of the song. With Grady Martin's blistering guitar work, the band swung loose at the end, and the whole thing faded away with the sense that there was more where that came from.

The same model was used for "Witchcraft," an R&B hit for the New Orleans group the Spiders—and one of many Elvis covers originally recorded in that heady summer of 1955. The hold-back-cut-loose trick fell short of what they'd pulled off in "Devil In Disguise," but Boots Randolph's sax solo offered further proof that the band could have blown up a storm if given the chance—or, more to the point, the right material. Songs like "Never Ending," "Finders Keepers, Losers Weepers," and the two new Don Robertson songs, "What Now, What Next, Where To" (originally submitted to Johnny Cash—and rejected) and "Love Me Tonight," were all passable, and their flawless, pleasant sound made them records Elvis fans could enjoy. But the entire session showed nary a sign of artistic progression. "Love Me Tonight" may have been the most ambitious song of the batch—Elvis injected true passion into his performance—but the song was out of touch with the musical trends of the time, and it was destined for commercial limbo.

Another 1955 hit, "Maybellene," had impressed Elvis so much back in that formative year that he had immediately put it into his live repertoire, and he continued to be drawn to Chuck Berry's songwriting. Chuck's great 1959 record "Memphis Tennessee" was almost an inevitable choice: The novelty of Elvis singing about his own hometown made it a potential smash. As the evening of May 27 started Elvis got it down in only two takes, exactly as many as it took to record the next song, the Pomus and Shuman submission "(It's A) Long Lonely Highway."

Freddy Bienstock was always on the lookout for European, particularly Italian, pop songs. "It's Now Or Never" had proven that commercial potential walked hand in hand with Elvis's own musical fascination with artists such as Mario Lanza and Dean Martin. Dominico Modugno's huge 1958 hit "Volare" was another role model for such a repertoire transition, and now Freddy sent Modugno's new record, "Io," to the Giant, Baum, and Kaye team. Changing the title to "Ask Me," they produced a medium-paced ballad that forced Elvis to sing at the very top of his range. "This song will kill me," he uttered between the two takes he managed before putting the song aside.

The next song was a joke, though the songwriters couldn't have meant it as one. Sid Tepper and Roy Bennett's "Western Union," a bald rehash of "Return To Sender," summed up the problem created by Bienstock's endless demand for more material. Even the most gifted songwriters fell into the trap of writing songs the way they thought Elvis and the publishers might want to hear them—ideally, similar enough to past hits to be accepted, different enough to stand on their own. Clearly, "Western Union" fell embarrassingly short of freshness, yet somehow that didn't stop Elvis from recording it. Next followed another result of the process Don Robertson had earlier discovered—submitting a song on a fully produced demo using a singer who could ape Elvis's voice and style. A band that included players such as Hal Blaine on drums, Carol Kaye on bass, Leon Russell on piano, and guitarists from James Burton and Tommy Tedesco to Glen Campbell could spark real fire even on an acetate, and the demo of "Slowly But Surely" was no exception. A new song by Sid Wayne and Ben Weisman, who had more Elvis cuts than any other team, it was sung on the demo by P. J. Proby, a Weisman discovery who seemed determined to outsing Elvis—and, in this case, succeeded. Elvis's version of "Slowly But Surely," driven by Jerry Kennedy's fuzz guitar figure, had more life than many of the best songs on the session, but it failed to recapture the freshness and energy of Proby's cut. Toward the end of the night a half-finished recording of a half-written song called "Blue River" was given one shot, yielding a brief take that was eventually extended in the cutting room for release. And before the night was over the group returned to the Italian cover, "Ask Me"; the sixth take was deemed a master, but Elvis left the sessions unconvinced of its success.

Following the unwritten rule that Elvis chose his own singles—he'd long been the best judge of the commercial potential of his work—"(You're The) Devil In Disguise" was rush-released the following month; the record reversed the failure of "One Broken Heart For Sale," going to number three on the charts. It went on to become a huge international hit, even spending an astounding thirteen weeks at number one in faraway Denmark.

66. Soundtrack Recordings for MGM's *Viva Las Vegas*
July 9–11 and August 30, 1963: Radio Recorders, Hollywood

Musical Director for MGM: George Stoll
Engineer: Dave Weichman

Guitar: Scotty Moore
Guitar: Tiny Timbrell
Guitar: Billy Strange
Bass: Bob Moore
Drums: D. J. Fontana
Drums: Buddy Harman
Drums: Frank Carlson (7/10–11)
Percussion: (7/10 see notes)
Piano: Floyd Cramer
Piano: Dudley Brooks
Piano: Calvin Jackson (7/10)
Organ: Calvin Jackson (7/11)
Sax: Boots Randolph
Sax: William Green (7/10)
Trumpet: Oliver Mitchell (7/9)
Trumpet: James Zito (7/10)
Trombone: Herb Taylor (7/10)
Trombone: Randall Miller (7/10)

Vocals: The Jordanaires
Vocals: The Jubilee Four (8/30)
Vocals: Ann-Margret (duet on 2010, 2011, 2012)

Musicians on 8/30:
Guitar: Billy Strange
Guitar: Alton Hendrickson
Guitar: Glen Campbell
Bass: Ray Siegel
Drums: Frank Carlson
Percussion: Roy Hart
Piano: Artie Cane
Sax: Steve Douglas

Overdubbed:
Guitar: Al Caiola (2007)
Accordion: Dominic Cortese (2007)
Vocals: The Carol Lombard Quartet (2580)

<u>7/9, 7PM–12AM, 1–4:15AM</u>

2001-14	**Night Life**	**Flaming Star***
WPA1 8023	*Giant/Baum/Kaye—Elvis Presley Music*	*PRS 279/1968*
2002-05	**C'mon Everybody**	**Viva Las Vegas (EP)**
RPA3 0389	*Joy Byers—Elvis Presley Music*	*EPA 4382/1964*
2003-13	**If You Think I Don't Need You**	**Viva Las Vegas (EP)**
RPA3 0387	*Red West/Joe Cooper—Elvis Presley Music*	*EPA 4382/1964*

<u>7/10, 7–11PM, 12–3:30AM</u>

2004-na	**Viva Las Vegas**	**Single B-side**
RPA3 0234	*Doc Pomus/Mort Shuman—Elvis Presley Music*	*47-8360/1964*
2005-20	**I Need Somebody To Lean On**	**Viva Las Vegas (EP)**
RPA3 0386	*Doc Pomus/Mort Shuman—Elvis Presley Music*	*EPA 4382/1964*
2006-07	**Do The Vega**	**Flaming Star***
WPA1 8025	*Giant/Baum/Kaye—Elvis Presley Music*	*PRS 279/1968*
2007-03	**Santa Lucia**	**Elvis For Everyone**
SPA1 6898	*Arranged by Elvis Presley—Elvis Presley Music*	*LSP 3450/1965*
2009-09	**Yellow Rose Of Texas/The Eyes Of Texas**	**Flaming Star***
WPA1 8024	*Wise/Starr—Gladys Music & Sinclair—Paxwin Music*	*PRS 279/1968*
2002-07	**C'mon Everybody (movie version)**	
	Joy Byers—Elvis Presley Music	

7/11, 3–5:45PM, 7PM–12:40AM

2010-10	**The Lady Loves Me**	**Elvis: A Legendary Performer Vol. 4**
NPA5 5825	*Sid Tepper/Roy C. Bennett—Gladys Music*	*CPL1 4848/1983*
2011-16	**You're The Boss**	**Elvis Sings Leiber & Stoller**
WPA5 2511	*Jerry Leiber/Mike Stoller—Elvis Presley Music*	*3026-2/1991*
2012-06	**Today, Tomorrow And Forever (duet)**	
	Giant/Baum/Kaye—Elvis Presley Music	
2013-04	**Today, Tomorrow And Forever**	**Viva Las Vegas (EP)**
RPA3 0388	*Giant/Baum/Kaye—Elvis Presley Music*	*EPA 4382/1964*

8/30, Hours unknown

2580-04	**What'd I Say**	**Single A-side**
RPA3 0235	*Ray Charles—Progressive Music*	*47-8360/1964*

Two different endings for "You're The Boss" (2011) have been released. The version on *Elvis Sings Leiber & Stoller* (3026-2-R) and *Collectors Gold* (4114-2) consists of take 16 plus take 3 (ending); the *Double Features* (66129-2) release is the complete, undoctored take 16. "Today, Tomorrow And Forever" (2012) is a duet between Elvis and Ann-Margret. The Jubilee Four: Bill Johnson, George McFadden, Jimmy Adams, Ted Brooks. The Carol Lombard Quartet: Carol Lombard, Gwen Johnson, Jackie Ward, Marjorie Cranford. On 7/10 the following percussionists played: Hal Rees, Roy Hart, Larry Bunker, Frank Flynn, Michael Sylva. *The full title of PRS 279 is *Singer Presents Elvis Singing Flaming Star and Others*.

The Nashville session, and the album that should have come from it, were soon set aside and focus turned to Hollywood again. In the Colonel's moviemaking model, what mattered weren't strong scripts or good songs but rather a glamorous location—and Las Vegas fit the bill perfectly. For all the hype and all the money, though, MGM's *Viva Las Vegas* soundtrack would be recorded as sloppily as their last effort, *It Happened At The World's Fair*. Perhaps the shoddy quality was inevitable, given how quickly the soundtrack was thrown together: Just six weeks after the Nashville sessions wrapped, Freddy presented a dozen more new songs for the new picture. There was the usual Leiber and Stoller cover, in this case "You're The Boss," a 1961 LaVern Baker–Jimmy Ricks duet for Elvis to sing with his costar Ann-Margret. (The actress was soon to become his love interest not only on-screen but off, and both singers put in wonderfully seductive performances, but for some reason the record was left out of the finished film.) Red West, writing with Joe Cooper of the *Shindig* TV series, came up with an R&B number called "If You Think I Don't Need You." "We tried to get a Ray Charles feel," Red remembers—certainly a better idea than writing for an "Elvis feel." It was even suggested that English lyrics be put to the surprise hit of the year, "Sukiyaki" by Japanese recording artist Kyu Sakamoto, but the original version shot to number one with such speed that the idea of doing a cover soon seemed pointless.

The songs were a miserable lot, with few exceptions; Elvis's pell-mell filming schedule was making it virtually impossible for his publishing companies to live up to their obligations. Freddy was being asked each year not just to come up with forty good new songs, but to deliver forty songs tailor-made for a movie script on which the writers would accept substandard royalties. One of the few exceptions with *Viva Las Vegas* was Doc Pomus and Mort Shuman's title cut, a shimmering appraisal of the neon-lit city, as infectious as a quick stroll down the Strip. The density of the band performance and the seemingly limitless excitement of Elvis's own delivery matched the brilliant pop song, which curiously only became a classic decades after its original release.

The team of Giant, Baum, and Kaye had just delivered a much-needed hit with "(You're The) Devil In Disguise," but that didn't prevent their two songs from being cut out of this movie along with the Leiber and Stoller duet. At the end of August MGM decided that a strong up-tempo number was needed to complete the film, and summoned Elvis to record one additional song. There was so little good material available that Elvis just took the occasion to cut a version of another old favorite, Ray Charles's R&B classic "What'd I Say." Strangely, though, neither that nor Red West's Charles pastiche "If You Think I Don't Need You" added up to anything more than watered-down R&B. Elvis had delivered a far more authentic performance for Pomus and Shuman's portrait of late-night desolation, "I Need Somebody To Lean On"; perhaps the Hollywood surroundings lent themselves better to Sinatra-style balladry than to gutsy jump blues.

As far back as January 1963 the Colonel had informed a very disappointed Bill Bullock at RCA that there might not be a soundtrack album for *Fun In Acapulco*. Bullock accepted the Colonel's decision, but never resigned himself to the broader scheme Parker had in mind, which included two new albums—one drawn from the May 1963 sessions, the other a new installment of the *Golden Records* saga. There were certainly more than enough hits for that, even excluding hit movie singles like "Can't Help Falling In Love" and "Return To Sender," and the *Golden Records* album looked like a sure winner—another step in the boy's transformation from rock 'n' roll singer to adult entertainer. But somehow the Colonel changed his mind, and the *Fun In Acapulco* soundtrack he had dismissed was soon back on the boards. In keeping with the Colonel's value-for-money philosophy, it contained all eleven songs from *Fun In Acapulco* plus two "bonus songs," "Love Me Tonight" and "Slowly But Surely"; in the Colonel's eyes, that compensated for the scheme perpetrated on Elvis's public by the skimpy ten-cut *It Happened At The World's Fair* album. And "Bossa Nova Baby" was slated for single release, backed with "Memphis Tennessee" in what everyone thought to be a dynamite pairing.

67. Soundtrack Recordings for MGM's *Kissin' Cousins*
September 29–30, 1963: RCA's Studio B, Nashville
October 10, 1963: MGM, Studios, Culver City

Musical Directors for MGM: Gene Nelson & Fred Karger
Engineer/Nashville: Bill Porter
Engineer/Hollywood: n/a

Guitar: Scotty Moore
Guitar: Grady Martin
Guitar: Jerry Kennedy
Guitar: Harold Bradley
Bass: Bob Moore
Drums: D. J. Fontana
Drums: Buddy Harman
Banjo: Jerry Kennedy (0224)
      Harold Bradley (0220)
Jug: Boots Randolph (0220)

Piano: Floyd Cramer
Sax: Boots Randolph
Sax: Bill Justis
Fiddle: Cecil Brower
Vocals: The Jordanaires
Vocals: Winnifred Brest, Millie
Kirkham, Dolores Edgin

9/29–30, 7PM–2AM

2002-03(tr)	**There's Gold In The Mountains**	**Kissin' Cousins**
RPA3 0226	*Giant/Baum/Kaye—Elvis Presley Music*	*LSP 2894/1964*
2003-05(tr)	**One Boy, Two Little Girls**	**Kissin' Cousins**
RPA3 0223	*Giant/Baum/Kaye—Elvis Presley Music*	*LSP 2894/1964*
2004-03(tr)	**Once Is Enough**	**Kissin' Cousins**
RPA3 0222	*Sid Tepper/Roy C. Bennett—Gladys Music*	*LSP 2894/1964*
2005-02(tr)	**Tender Feeling**	**Kissin' Cousins**
RPA3 0225	*Giant/Baum/Kaye—Elvis Presley Music*	*LSP 2894/1964*
2006-02(tr)	**Kissin' Cousins No. 2**	**Kissin' Cousins**
RPA3 0218	*Giant/Baum/Kaye—Elvis Presley Music*	*LSP 2894/1964*

9/30–31, 7PM–3:30AM

2007-04(tr)	**Smokey Mountain Boy**	**Kissin' Cousins**
RPA3 0224	*Rosenblatt/Millrose—Elvis Presley Music*	*LSP 2894/1964*
2008-04(tr)	**Catchin' On Fast**	**Kissin' Cousins**
RPA3 0221	*Giant/Baum/Kaye—Elvis Presley Music*	*LSP 2894/1964*
2009-07(tr)	**Barefoot Ballad**	**Kissin' Cousins**
RPA3 0220	*Dolores Fuller/Lee Morris—Gladys Music*	*LSP 2894/1964*
2010-05(tr)	**Anyone (Could Fall In Love With You)**	**Kissin' Cousins**
RPA3 0227	*Benjamin/Marcus/DeJesus—Elvis Presley Music*	*LSP 2894/1964*
2011-02(tr)	**Kissin' Cousins**	**Single A-side**
RPA3 0219	*Fred Wise/Randy Starr—Gladys Music*	*47-8307/1964*

Elvis overdubbed all vocals at MGM's Soundstage, Hollywood, on October 10 (and possibly 11). Elvis vocal overdubs:
"There's Gold In The Mountains" (2019 take 3), "One Boy, Two Little Girls" (2020 take 2), "Once Is Enough" (2014 take 7),

"Tender Feeling" (2026 take 1), "Kissin' Cousins" No. 2 (2025 take 4), "Smokey Mountain Boy" (2017 take 3), "Catchin' On Fast" (2015 take 7), "Barefoot Ballad" (splice of 2023 take 2 and 2024 take 4), "Anyone" (2016 take 3), "Kissin' Cousins" (splice of 2021 take 2 [regular vocal] and take 1 [hillbilly vocal]). The numbers in brackets were assigned for Elvis's vocals, and reflect the order in which he recorded them. "Kissin' Cousins No. 2" (RPA3 0218) and "Catchin' On Fast" (RPA3 0221) were shortened for record release.

In his business diary the Colonel wrote, "It was decided for the sake of economy and efficiency that the recording sessions for *Kissin' Cousins* should be held at the RCA Victor studios in Nashville." From MGM's point of view Nashville might have sounded like an apt choice to cut some "hillbilly" songs, but the real reasons for the switch from Hollywood back to Nashville were obvious to all. Both the filming and the recording sessions for *Viva Las Vegas* had gone way over budget; more musicians than ever before had been hired for the dates, and many sat idle while others played. Since Elvis and the Colonel shared in the actual profits from the movie, these extra expenses cut into their share, and the Colonel made it clear that they wouldn't make the same mistake with *Kissin' Cousins*. In fact, his concern for "economy and efficiency" probably contributed to *Kissin' Cousins*'s status as the first true "low-budget" Elvis movie, with filming lasting only four weeks. The demand for songs was now so great that Freddy Bienstock was able to collect no more than a bare minimum of material for the *Kissin' Cousins* session, and half of the ten songs had a Giant/Baum/Kaye credit. To make matters worse Elvis came down with another cold come session time, so the musicians ended up recording backing tracks for Elvis to overdub later in Los Angeles. The film had Elvis playing two roles—a soldier and a hillbilly—and the title song was conceived as a duet between the two, obliging Elvis to record two sets of vocals, one in his normal voice, the other with a mock-Tennessee twang. (It was left to an engineer to splice the two versions into the required duet.) The sound was arguably better than on the previous MGM recordings, yet still nothing really sparkled.

Fun In Acapulco and its soundtrack album were in line for release in November 1963, so following the usual schedule the "Bossa Nova Baby" single hit the streets in October. Elvis felt he could have done a better job on "Memphis Tennessee," so for the B-side the rousing version of "Witchcraft" from the same sessions was chosen instead. "Bossa Nova Baby" got to number eight, with "Witchcraft" reaching number thirty-two—the kind of strong showing that ironically hurt more than it helped, and suggested that once again the B-side may have cut into the A-side's chart success. The album went to number three, but sold about the same number as *It Happened At The World's Fair*, only about half of the 600,000 units that *Elvis' Golden Records Vol. 3* would rack up.

If "to manage" means to oversee and make decisions, Colonel Tom Parker was now charged with managing a situation that seemed to call for several different and potentially conflicting decisions. Only recently he'd concluded that the best strategy for record releases was a repeating pattern of soundtrack albums and independent studio recordings, each accompanied by their own singles. But the studio albums were struggling in the stores, and the constant demand for material was breaking the back of his publishing companies. The one strategy that seemed foolproof was putting a lot of hits together in an attractive package, along the *Golden Records* model. But how to get the hits? That was the one thing the Colonel couldn't do for himself. That was where management stopped and artistic and commercial vision had to take over. That was where Elvis Presley had to show the way.

1964-65

Lost in Hollywood

On Sunday night, January 12, 1964, about an hour after a new round of sessions was scheduled to begin, Elvis roared into the parking lot at RCA's studios on his motorcycle. His mission: to rerecord the two songs from the previous May he'd been dissatisfied with—the ballad "Ask Me" and "Memphis Tennessee," which Elvis had in mind for his next single.

At first, as he strode into the control room of Studio B, it seemed as though his priorities had shifted. Announcing he was hungry, he had food ordered in, and recording was delayed for almost three hours while they got dinner out of the way. Then, just as abruptly as they'd halted, the proceedings started up again. With virtually no rehearsal time, drummers Buddy Harman and D. J. Fontana exploded into the opening bars of "Memphis Tennessee," in a much more confident rumble than they'd managed back in May. At the console, first-time Elvis engineer Ron Steele was scrambling to get proper recording levels on the double-drum-kit intro when the three guitar players, bass, and piano all jumped in as well, flooding the tape with busy rhythmic patterns. It was obvious that Elvis wanted a more exciting, up-to-date feel from his rhythm section than he'd had on the previous version. For Ron Steele it was a rocky baptism. Chet Atkins offered little help as the new engineer struggled along; Steele was so beleaguered trying to control the balance and keep down the distortion crowding in from several channels—just trying to find space for each of the instruments to breathe—that he could barely make it through each new slate announcement (*you* try saying "RPA four-one-oh-oh-four, take three," three times fast). Take one was complete. Takes two and three were false starts, and there was no take four at all because Steele got lost in his count. On take five (the second complete run-through) Steele was still shifting instruments from one side to the other and then into the middle, but by take six Elvis had what he wanted, and except for a few minor glitches Ron Steele got there too.

Elvis radiated pure concentration: There was no fooling around, no joking as they turned to the next item on the agenda. With a new, very slick pop arrangement, and with Elvis singing far better than he had eight months before, they quickly polished off "Ask Me"; after that they made it through a new song, "It Hurts Me"—cowritten by Charlie Daniels of later Charlie Daniels Band fame—in just fifteen minutes. They might have worked on the number longer, but take five had everything they were looking for: a strong, unclichéd melody, a mature lyric, an arrangement that was both simple and forceful, and a vocal performance so passion-filled that it must rank among the absolute best of Elvis's pre-1968 efforts.

68. Studio Sessions for RCA
January 12, 1964: RCA's Studio B, Nashville

A&R: Chet Atkins
Engineer: Ron Steele

Guitar: Scotty Moore
Guitar: Grady Martin
Guitar: Harold Bradley
Bass: Bob Moore
Drums: D. J. Fontana

Drums: Buddy Harman
Piano, Organ: Floyd Cramer
Sax, Vibes: Boots Randolph
Vocals: The Jordanaires
Vocals: Millie Kirkham

6:30–9:30PM, 9:30–11:30PM

RPA4 1004-06	**Memphis Tennessee**	**Elvis For Everyone**
	Chuck Berry—Arc Music	*LSP 3450/1965*
RPA4 1005-11	**Ask Me**	**Single A-side**
	Modugno/Giant/Baum/Kaye—Elvis Presley Music	*47-8440/1964*
RPA4 1006-05	**It Hurts Me**	**Single B-side**
	Joy Byers/Charles E. Daniels—Elvis Presley Music	*47-8307/1964*

When Elvis left RCA's studios at midnight, he left more than just the three likely singles he'd cut—for the moment, at least, he'd left his RCA studio recording career behind. It would be twenty-eight months before he would do another regular, non-movie recording session, and he would never again record under the supervision of Chet Atkins or Steve Sholes. The sound, the style, and the repertoire that had worked so well for him in the early '60s were all abandoned.

On the day he made them, all three new sides must have seemed ripe with commercial possibilities; if the session hadn't been prolific, at least it was focused. Unfortunately, two of the three lost their potential almost immediately. Elvis relegated the marvelous "It Hurts Me" to the B-side of "Kissin' Cousins," and although the A-side managed to climb into the top twenty at number twelve, selling a respectable 750,000 records, its flip never attained the classic stature promised by the song and the performance. "Memphis Tennessee"—originally slated for the "Kissin' Cousins" B-side before "It

Hurts Me" replaced it—suffered a second blow just weeks after it was recorded, when Lonnie Mack scored a top-five hit with an instrumental version. And the natural coupling of "Memphis" with "Ask Me" as a single received its death knell in May 1964, after Johnny Rivers heard the unreleased version on a visit to Elvis's house; Rivers recorded his own version of "Memphis Tennessee" taking the song to the top of the charts for the second time in twelve months and knocking it out of the running as an Elvis single.

No one examining Elvis's record sales between 1961 and 1964 could fail to see how soundly his soundtrack albums were outselling his studio albums—by margins of two, three, even four to one. And since the 1961 *Blue Hawaii* single "Can't Help Falling In Love," the situation with singles had been virtually the same. Elvis Presley's record-buying audience simply didn't support the artistic brilliance of an *Elvis Is Back* album as strongly as a throwaway movie product like *It Happened At The World's Fair*. And none of this was lost on the Colonel, who always kept his eye on the hits.

Even during the early '60s Elvis's record output was managed far differently from that of most other artists, who would release an album of songs recorded in a brief series of one or two sessions, including—*featuring*—the hit singles from those sessions. Not so with Elvis. At the Colonel's insistence, Elvis's hits were assembled on special collections such as the *Golden Records* series, about to enter its third installment. The rest of the session material, *minus* the hits, was released on albums like *Elvis Is Back* or the aptly named *Something For Everybody* (1961) and *Pot Luck* (1962); random collections with no movie exposure, they met with little radio support and received paltry attention considering that they were the work of such a major recording star. Any other artist would have highlighted his new album with cuts like "Stuck On You," "It's Now Or Never," and "Are You Lonesome Tonight?"—hits that surely would have put *Elvis Is Back* at the top of the charts for a long time. Similarly, "Surrender," "I Feel So Bad," "Little Sister," and "His Latest Flame" would have given *Something For Everybody* an incalculable boost, just as *Pot Luck* could have benefited from the inclusion of "Good Luck Charm" and "She's Not You." What other artist would have failed to name an album after one of these hit singles?

The bottom line was the income generated by the movies. At the start of each new picture, Elvis and the Colonel collected up to a million dollars—to which they could add up to fifty percent of the film's profits. The income from just one picture amounted to substantially more than all the RCA royalties they received in any given year. And the soundtrack program was filled with extra benefits: From each one they collected both recording royalties and publishing income through Elvis's two publishing companies, while fulfilling contractual obligations to RCA at the same time.

One obvious result of the Colonel's short-term thinking was the fate of the recordings Elvis made at his May 1963 RCA sessions. Two of the standouts, "Devil In Disguise" and "Please Don't Drag That String Around," were immediately released as a single, while the rest of the tracks were slated to be the basis of a new studio album.

But in August the album slot was filled by *Elvis Golden Records Vol. 3*, under the prevailing logic that greatest-hits records would sell better than untested studio material. So the studio album was shelved; it remained on the release schedule, but when the *Fun In Acapulco* soundtrack and the *Viva Las Vegas* and *Kissin' Cousins* projects began piling up, the logical illogical conclusion was to use the 1963 studio cuts for album filler and single B-sides. By January 1964 *Elvis Golden Records Vol. 3* had already passed the half-million mark, and *Fun In Acapulco* had no trouble matching *Pot Luck* in sales. Not until 1990 was the original 1963 album finally released, as *The Lost Album /For The Asking*. If you ignored artistic aspirations and aesthetic judgments, it all made perfect sense.

So now it was off to Hollywood, full-time.

69. Soundtrack Sessions for Paramount's *Roustabout*
March 2–3, April 29, and May 14, 1964: Radio Recorders, Hollywood

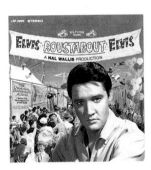

Paramount Producer: Joseph Lilley
Engineer: Dave Weichman

Guitar: Scotty Moore
Guitar: Tiny Timbrell
Guitar: Billy Strange
Guitar: Barney Kessel (3/2 only)
Bass: Bob Moore
Bass: Ray Siegel (4/29 only)
Drums: D. J. Fontana
Drums: Hal Blaine

Drums: Buddy Harman
Drums: Bernie Mattinson (4/29 only)
Piano: Floyd Cramer
Piano: Dudley Brooks (4/29 only)
Sax: Boots Randolph
Vocals: The Jordanaires
Vocals: The Mello Men (5273 only)

3/2, 1–6:40PM, 8–11:35PM

AO-15	**Little Egypt**	**Roustabout**
RPA3 5270	*Leiber/Stoller—E. Presley, Progressive & Trio Music*	*LSP 2999/1964*
BO-07	**Poison Ivy League**	**Roustabout**
RPA3 5272	*Giant/Baum/Kaye—Elvis Presley Music*	*LSP 2999/1964*
CO-11	**Hard Knocks**	**Roustabout**
RPA3 5267	*Joy Byers—Elvis Presley Music*	*LSP 2999/1964*
DO-13	**It's A Wonderful World**	**Roustabout**
RPA3 5268	*Sid Tepper/Roy C. Bennett—Gladys Music*	*LSP 2999/1964*

3/3, 12:30–5:50PM, 7:10PM–12AM

EO-17	**Big Love Big Heartache**	**Roustabout**
RPA3 5265	*Dee Fuller/Les Morris/Sonny Hendix—Gladys Music*	*LSP 2999/1964*
FO-05	**One Track Heart**	**Roustabout**
RPA3 5271	*Giant/Baum/Kaye—Elvis Presley Music*	*LSP 2999/1964*
GO-na	**Roustabout**	
	Otis Blackwell/Winfield Scott	

HO-02(tr)	It's Carnival Time	Roustabout
RPA3 5269	*Ben Weisman/Sid Wayne—Gladys Music*	*LSP 2999/1964*
JO-09	Carny Town	Roustabout
RPA3 5266	*Fred Wise/Randy Starr—Gladys Music*	*LSP 2999/1964*
KO-05	There's A Brand New Day On The Horizon	Roustabout
RPA3 5274	*Joy Byers—Elvis Presley Music*	*LSP 2999/1964*
LO-07	Wheels On My Heels	Roustabout
RPA3 5275	*Sid Tepper/Roy C. Bennett—Gladys Music*	*LSP 2999/1964*

4/29, 7–9:50PM

NO-11(tr)	Roustabout	Roustabout
RPA3 5273	*Giant/Baum/Kaye—Elvis Presley Music*	*LSP 2999/1964*

Elvis overdubbed his vocal (take 9) to "It's Carnival Time," probably just after the track was laid down. He overdubbed his vocal (take 17) to "Roustabout" on May 14, over the backing track recorded on April 29.

70. Soundtrack Sessions for MGM's *Girl Happy*
June 10–12 and 15, 1964: Radio Recorders, Hollywood

Musical Director: George Stoll
Engineer: Dave Weichman

Guitar: Scotty Moore
Guitar: Tiny Timbrell
Guitar: Tommy Tedesco
Bass: Bob Moore
Drums: D. J. Fontana
Drums: Buddy Harman

Drums: Frank Carlson
Piano: Floyd Cramer
Sax: Boots Randolph
Vocals: The Jordanaires
Vocals: The Jubilee Four (2010-2011)
Vocals: The Carole Lombard Trio (2010)

6/10, 7–11:40PM, 12:40–3:00AM

2001-11	Puppet On A String	Girl Happy
SPA3 2010	*Sid Tepper/Roy C. Bennett—Gladys Music*	*LSP 3338/1965*
2002-13	The Meanest Girl In Town	Girl Happy
SPA3 2008	*Joy Byers—Elvis Presley Music*	*LSP 3338/1965*
2003-sp	Girl Happy	Girl Happy
SPA3 2001	*Doc Pomus/Norman Meadse—Elvis Presley Music*	*LSP 3338/1965*

6/11, 7–11:45PM, 12:45–5AM

2004-sp	Cross My Heart And Hope To Die	Girl Happy
SPA3 2007	*Sid Wayne/Ben Weisman—Gladys Music*	*LSP 3338/1965*
2005-24	Spring Fever	Girl Happy
SPA3 2002	*Giant/Baum/Kaye—Elvis Presley Music*	*LSP 3338/1965*
2006-36	Do Not Disturb	Girl Happy
SPA3 2006	*Giant/Baum/Kaye—Elvis Presley Music*	*LSP 3338/1965*

2007-02(tr)	**I've Got To Find My Baby**	**Girl Happy**
SPA3 2011	*Joy Byers—Elvis Presley Music*	*LSP 3338/1965*
2008-07(tr)	**Fort Lauderdale Chamber Of Commerce**	**Girl Happy**
SPA3 2003	*Sid Tepper/Roy C. Bennett—Gladys Music*	*LSP 3338/1965*

<u>6/12, 7–10:40PM</u>

2009-03(tr)	**Startin' Tonight**	**Girl Happy**
SPA3 2004	*L. Rosenblatt/V. Williams—Elvis Presley Music*	*LSP 3338/1965*
2010-05(tr)	**Do The Clam**	**Single A-side**
SPA3 2009	*S. Wayne/B. Weisman/D. Fuller—Gladys Music*	*47-8500/1965*
2011-sp(tr)	**Wolf Call**	**Girl Happy**
SPA3 2005	*Giant/Baum/Kaye—Elvis Presley Music*	*LSP 3338/1965*

<u>6/15, 2–6PM Elvis vocal overdubs on 2007–2011</u>

The master of "Girl Happy" (2003) is spliced from take 13 and insert 1 take 4 (ending) with new intro, and was sped up approximately 8 percent for release. The master of "Cross My Heart And Hope To Die" (2004) is spliced from takes 9 and 11 with overdubbed piano intro. Masters of "I've Got To Find My Baby" (2007) and "Fort Lauderdale Chamber Of Commerce" (2008) were shortened for release.

With Marty Lacker and a fan at the time of the Harum Scarum *sessions, February 1965*

71. Soundtrack Sessions for MGM's *Harum Scarum*
February 24–26, 1965: RCA's Studio B, Nashville

MGM Producer: Fred Karger & Gene Nelson
Engineer: n/a

Guitar: Scotty Moore
Guitar: Grady Martin
Guitar: Charlie McCoy
Bass: Henry Strzelecki
Drums: D. J. Fontana
Drums: Kenneth Buttrey

Tambourine: Hoyt Hawkins
Piano: Floyd Cramer
Congas: Gene Nelson
Flute: Rufus Long
Oboe: Ralph Strobel
Vocals: The Jordanaires

2/24, 11:30PM–3:30AM

SPA3 6752-sp	**Shake That Tambourine**	**Harum Scarum**
	Giant/Baum/Kaye—Elvis Presley Music	*LSP 3468/1965*

2/25, 10:15PM–3:30AM

SPA3 6754-sp	**So Close, Yet So Far (From Paradise)**	**Harum Scarum**
	Joy Byers—Elvis Presley Music	*LSP 3468/1965*
SPA3 6761-12	**My Desert Serenade**	**Harum Scarum**
	Stanley Gelber—Gladys Music	*LSP 3468/1965*
SPA3 6760-05	**Wisdom Of The Ages**	**Harum Scarum**
	Giant/Baum/Kaye—Elvis Presley Music	*LSP 3468/1965*
SPA3 6758-05	**Kismet**	**Harum Scarum**
	Sid Tepper/Roy C. Bennett—Gladys Music	*LSP 3468/1965*
SPA3 6759-05	**Hey Little Girl**	**Harum Scarum**
	Joy Byers—Elvis Presley Music	*LSP 3468/1965*

2/26, Session hours unknown

SPA3 6753-sp	**Golden Coins**	**Harum Scarum**
	Giant/Baum/Kaye—Elvis Presley Music	*LSP 3468/1965*
SPA3 6757-06	**Animal Instinct**	**Harum Scarum**
	Giant/Baum/Kaye—Elvis Presley Music	*LSP 3468/1965*
SPA3 6755-02 (tr)	**Harem Holiday**	**Harum Scarum**
	P. Andreoli/V. Poncia, Jr./J. Crane—Elvis Presley Music	*LSP 3468/1965*
SPA3 6751-03 (tr)	**Go East, Young Man**	**Harum Scarum**
	Giant/Baum/Kaye—Elvis Presley Music	*LSP 3468/1965*
SPA3 6756-05 (tr)	**Mirage**	**Harum Scarum**
	Giant/Baum/Kaye—Elvis Presley Music	*LSP 3468/1965*

Master of "Shake That Tambourine" (6752) is spliced from takes 24 and 38. Master of "So Close, Yet So Far (From Paradise)" (6754) is spliced from takes 3 and 4. Master of "Golden Coins" (6753) is spliced from takes 16 and 11. Elvis's vocal master on "Harem Holiday" (6755) is spliced from takes 7 and 6. Elvis's vocal master on "Go East, Young Man" (6751) is spliced from takes 7 and 8. Elvis's vocal master on "Mirage" (6756) is spliced from takes 4 and 3. Elvis's vocal on "Harem Holiday" (6755) on 2/26 was repaired, and on this and the last two Elvis overdubbed his vocal on March 9.

72. Soundtrack Sessions for United Artists' *Frankie and Johnny*
May 12–14, 1965: Radio Recorders, Hollywood

Producer: Fred Karger
Engineer: Dave Weichman

Guitar: Scotty Moore
Guitar: Tiny Timbrell
Guitar, Harmonica: Charlie McCoy
Bass: Bob Moore
Drums: D. J. Fontana
Drums: Buddy Harman
Piano: Larry Muhoberac
Trumpet: George Worth

Trombone: Richard Noel
Sax:Gus Bivona
Tuba: John Johnson
?: Robert Corwin
Vocals: The Jordanaires
Vocals: Ray Walker (duet on 7379)
Vocals: Eileen Wilson

5/12, 7–12PM, 1–4AM

SPA3 7374-06 (tr) Come Along   **Frankie And Johnny**
  David Hess—Gladys Music   *LSP 3553/1966*
SPA3 7380-05 (tr) Beginner's Luck   **Frankie And Johnny**
  Sid Tepper/Roy C. Bennett—Gladys Music   *LSP 3553/1966*
SPA3 7381-07 (tr) Down By The Riverside/When The Saints Go Marching In   **Frankie And Johnny**
  Giant/Baum/Kaye—Elvis Presley Music   *LSP 3553/1966*

5/13, Session hours unknown. Elvis vocal overdub on 7374, 7380, 7381

5/13, 5–10PM, 11PM–4AM

SPA3 7384-19   Please Don't Stop Loving Me   **Single B-side**
  Joy Byers—Elvis Presley Music   *47-8780/1966*
SPA3 7382-07   Shout It Out   **Frankie And Johnny**
  Giant/Baum/Kaye—Elvis Presley Music   *LSP 3553/1966*
TPA3 3997-sp (tr) Frankie And Johnny (movie version)
  A. Gottlieb/F. Karger/B. Weisman—Gladys Music
SPA3 7377-06 (tr) What Every Woman Lives For   **Frankie And Johnny**
  Doc Pomus/Mort Shuman—Elvis Presley Music   *LSP 3553/1966*
SPA3 7383-05 (tr) Hard Luck   **Frankie And Johnny**
  Ben Weisman/Sid Wayne—Gladys Music   *LSP 3553/1966*

5/14, 5–7:30PM Elvis vocal overdub on 3997, 7375, 7377

5/14, 8PM–12AM, 1–4:30AM

SPA3 7375-06   Petunia, The Gardener's Daughter   **Frankie And Johnny**
  Sid Tepper/Roy C. Bennett—Gladys Music   *LSP 3553/1966*
SPA3 7379-12   Look Out, Broadway   **Frankie And Johnny**
  Fred Wise/Randy Starr—Gladys Music   *LSP 3553/1966*
SPA3 7385-15   Everybody Come Aboard   **Frankie And Johnny**
  Giant/Baum/Kaye—Elvis Presley Music   *LSP 3553/1966*
SPA3 7376-07   Chesay   **Frankie And Johnny**
  Fred Karger/Ben Weisman/Sid Wayne—Gladys Music   *LSP 3553/1966*

SPA3 7378-06	**Frankie And Johnny**	**Single A-side**
	A. Gottlieb/F. Karger/B. Weisman—Gladys Music	*47-8780/1966*

The vocal overdubs on "Hard Luck" (7383) the following week (possibly on May 19) at Goldwyn Studios. All music tracks and Elvis vocals recorded at Radio Recorders.

73. Soundtrack Sessions for Paramount's *Paradise, Hawaiian Style*
July 26–27 and August 2–4: Radio Recorders, Hollywood

Engineers: Thorne Nogar & Dave Weichman

Guitar: Scotty Moore
Guitar: Barney Kessel
Guitar: Charlie McCoy
Guitar: Howard Roberts (3839)
Guitar: Alton Hendrickson (3839)
Bass: Ray Siegel
Bass: Keith Mitchell
Drums: D. J. Fontana

Drums: Hal Blaine
Drums: Milton Holland
Drums: Victor Feldman
Piano: Larry Muhoberac
Steel Guitar: Bernal Lewis
Vocals: The Jordanaires (3835, 37, 38, 42) (7/26–27)
Vocals: The Mello Men (3837, 39, 40, 41, 42) (8/2–4)

<u>7/26, Session hours unknown</u>

AO-02(tr)	**Drums Of The Islands**	**Paradise, Hawaiian Style**
TPA3 3837	*Polynesian Culture Center/Tepper/Bennett—Gladys Music*	*LSP 3643/1966*
BO-02(tr)	**Datin'**	**Paradise, Hawaiian Style**
TPA3 3843	*Fred Wise/Randy Starr—Gladys Music*	*LSP 3643/1966*
CO-04(tr)	**Scratch My Back**	**Paradise, Hawaiian Style**
TPA3 3840	*Giant/Baum/Kaye—Elvis Presley Music*	*LSP 3643/1966*

<u>7/27, Session hours unknown</u>

DO-09(tr)	**Stop Where You Are**	**Paradise, Hawaiian Style**
TPA3 3841	*Giant/Baum/Kaye—Elvis Presley Music*	*LSP 3643/1966*
EO-05(tr)	**A Dog's Life**	**Paradise, Hawaiian Style**
TPA3 3836	*Sid Wayne/Ben Weisman—Gladys Music*	*LSP 3643/1966*
FO-05(tr)	**This Is My Heaven**	**Paradise, Hawaiian Style**
TPA3 3838	*Giant/Baum/Kaye—Elvis Presley Music*	*LSP 3643/1966*
GO-03(tr)	**Paradise, Hawaiian Style**	**Paradise, Hawaiian Style**
TPA3 3835	*Giant/Baum/Kaye—Elvis Presley Music*	*LSP 3643/1966*
HO-07(tr)	**House Of Sand**	**Paradise, Hawaiian Style**
TPA3 3842	*Giant/Baum/Kaye—Elvis Presley Music*	*LSP 3643/1966*
JO-03(tr)	**Queenie Wahine's Papaya**	**Paradise, Hawaiian Style**
TPA3 3834	*Giant/Baum/Kaye—Elvis Presley Music*	*LSP 3643/1966*

<u>8/2, 2–10:30PM</u>

KO-10	**Sand Castles**	**Paradise, Hawaiian Style**
TPA3 3839	*Herb Goldberg/David Hess—Gladys Music*	*LSP 3643/1966*

Live recording of "Sand Castles" (KO) and vocal overdubs by Elvis and the Mello Men on "Drums Of The Islands" (AO) and "This Is My Heaven" (FO) were done on 8/2. Overdubs on all other tracks by Elvis Presley and the Mello Men were done 8/3 (3–10PM) and 8/4 (7PM–12:30AM). Elvis vocal masters: "Drums Of The Islands" (AOV take 6), "Datin' " (BOV take 14), "Scratch My Back" (COV take 2), "Stop Where You Are" (spliced from DOV take 3 and D10V [ending] takes 9 plus 6), "A Dog's Life" (EOV take 9), "This Is My Heaven" (spliced from FOV takes 8 plus 6), "Paradise, Hawaiian Style" (spliced from GOV takes 4 plus 3), "House Of Sand" (HOV take 1), "Queenie Wahine's Papaya" (spliced from J1V take 2 [first 2 lines] and JOV take 6), "Sand Castles" (KOV take 1). Miscellaneous: The Jordanaires: Gordon Stoker, Neal Matthews, Hoyt Hawkins, Ray Walker. The Mello Men: Bill Lee, Max Smith, Bill Cole, Gene Merlino.

74. Soundtrack Recordings for MGM's *Spinout*
February 16–17, 1966: Radio Recorders, Hollywood

Producer: George Stoll
Engineer: Dave Weichman

Guitar: Scotty Moore
Guitar: Tommy Tedesco
Guitar: Tiny Timbrell
Bass: Bob Moore
Drums: D. J. Fontana

Drums: Buddy Harman
Piano: Floyd Cramer
Piano: Charlie Hodge (5310)
Sax: Boots Randolph
Vocals: The Jordanaires

2/16, 3–5PM, 7PM–12AM

2004-07	**Smorgasbord**	**Spinout**
TPA3 5312	*Sid Tepper/Roy C. Bennett—Gladys Music*	*LSP 3702/1966*
2005-sp	**Stop, Look And Listen**	**Spinout**
TPA3 5305	*Joy Byers—Elvis Presley Music*	*LSP 3702/1966*
2006-07	**Am I Ready**	**Spinout**
TPA3 5309	*Sid Tepper/Roy C. Bennett—Gladys Music*	LSP 3702/1966
2007-04	**Beach Shack**	**Spinout**
TPA3 5310	*Giant/Baum/Kaye—Elvis Presley Music*	*LSP 3702/1966*

2/17, 7PM–12AM

2008-06	**Never Say Yes**	**Spinout**
TPA3 5308	*Doc Pomus/Mort Shuman—Elvis Presley Music*	*LSP 3702/1966*
2009-05	**Spinout**	**Single B-side**
TPA3 5311	*Sid Wayne/Ben Weisman/Dee Fuller—Gladys Music*	*47-8941/1966*
2010-05	**All That I Am**	**Single A-side**
TPA3 5307	*Sid Tepper/Roy C. Bennett—Gladys Music*	*47-8941/1966*
2011-20	**Adam And Evil**	**Spinout**
TPA3 5306	*Fred Wise/Randy Starr—Gladys Music*	*LSP 3702/1966*
2012-01	**I'll Be Back**	**Spinout**
TPA3 5313	*Sid Wayne/Ben Weisman—Gladys Music*	*LSP 3702/1966*

Master of "Stop, Look And Listen" (2005) is spliced from first four bars of take 6 and take 7. Master of "Never Say Yes" (2008) has drum ending of take 5 added to take 6.

The Colonel remained busier than ever. Each time a new movie came out, the promotion machine developed a few years earlier kicked into gear along with it. With three movies a year, he couldn't have asked for more merchandise to promote. The publishing companies printed sheet music for the new songs, while both RCA and the various movie companies, under the Colonel's very specific and particular supervision, led worldwide promotional campaigns that kept Elvis's name, if not in the headlines, on everyone's lips.

For the movie companies business was good—and it was simple. With the exception of Elvis's payment ($225,000 to $1,000,000 per picture, with a 50 percent profit share on top), production budgets for the movies were minimal. They were filmed in a matter of weeks, sometimes fewer than three; interior scenes were shot on back lots using inexpensive, often reused sets. The scoring, including Elvis's soundtrack sessions, was completed in less than two weeks. RCA Records, overseen and virtually controlled by the Colonel in these matters, was an ideal partner in publicity and promotion. For a total investment of less than two million dollars, an Elvis Presley movie could easily gross four million in the United States alone, before the lucrative foreign markets were even factored in.

By January 1964, though, the movies and their soundtracks were piling up. Over the next twenty-four months the movie companies would manufacture another seven installments of that marketing man's dream, the Elvis Presley movie. "It's fun, it's girls, it's song, it's color," announced a flyer for Allied Artists' *Tickle Me*. Each new picture came complete with its own radio commercials in the form of new Elvis Presley singles, and its own promotion angle (movie stills, merchandising, stories in the press linking Elvis with his latest costar to feed the audience's appetite for star gossip). Best of all, there was always another one coming just a few months down the line—the repetition alone was its own best motivation. As a former MGM employee remarked, "They don't need titles. They could be numbered. They would still sell."

It's true, the movies could just as easily have been filled with great new and older songs; after all, their plots were insubstantial enough that virtually any song could have been squeezed into their story lines. But that would have cut into the Hill & Range profits, and Freddy Bienstock worked vigilantly to guarantee that *all* songs were controlled by either Elvis Presley Music or Gladys Music—a strategy that accounted for an additional $400,000 of income for Elvis in 1965 alone. Successful commercial and creative songwriters like Doc Pomus and Mort Shuman, Jerry Leiber and Mike Stoller, Don Robertson, and Otis Blackwell eventually lost interest in writing for Elvis; not only were they required to give up a third of their normal songwriter's royalties, but often as not they found their efforts rejected as movie title after movie title was discarded. Otis Blackwell gamely wrote a title song for *Roustabout,* only to find it replaced by a Giant, Baum, and Kaye effort under the same title. It wasn't that the Giant, Baum, and Kaye team couldn't write a hit—after all, they had delivered the hugely successful "Devil In Disguise"—but how could anyone deliver twenty-two soundtrack songs in two years (34 percent of the entire soundtrack repertoire from the period), and sustain substance and integrity? Ben Weisman was saddled writing songs like "A Dog's Life" for *Paradise, Hawaiian Style*. "What do you do if they insist on a song about a dog?" he asks. "You either do it, or somebody else will."

When the regular studio sessions were abandoned, RCA was left without any A&R influence over its biggest star's career. The movie companies, controlled and guided by the Colonel's office, sent RCA a complete package for each new album—from master tapes to promo photos to a full marketing plan, gossipy stories and all. The record label had only to coordinate each new release with its corresponding movie opening, ship the product, follow the Colonel's instructions, and collect the checks.

RCA enjoyed growing sales overall for its Elvis catalog, as his records dominated the international market. At home, though, the new singles from these years saw a significant drop in unit sales—from almost four million copies in 1960 to approximately two million in 1963. Total album sales returned to the two-million level of 1960 and 1961, mainly on the strength of *Elvis Golden Records Vol. 3*. But soundtrack albums showed a sharp decline, a matter of greater concern perhaps to RCA than to the Colonel, who made money on the movies as well as the records.

RCA's solution to slumping singles sales was unique. If you can't get to number one anymore—for that matter, if you can't even get into the top ten—then what better way to get unit sales up than to release twice as many records? So in 1964 they released six singles. The first, "Kissin' Cousins," climbed to a respectable sales level of 700–800,000 units, but the May release of "What'd I Say"/"Viva Las Vegas" dropped below the half-million mark, failing even to reach the *Billboard* top twenty. Elvis product was flooding the market so thoroughly that it began competing not only with other artists' records but with itself. Rushing to catch up with Terry Stafford's top-five cover, RCA brought out the original version of "Suspicion" from the *Pot Luck* album in May—but too late to move more than a few hundred thousand units. By now the die was cast, and with so few new studio cuts in the can, RCA was forced to reach back to *Elvis Is Back* for "Such A Night," but unit sales were so poor they couldn't push the single past number sixteen. "Ask Me" proved a considerably better choice, with sales figures hovering around the three-quarters-of-a-million mark. But the holiday season saw a reissue of "Blue Christmas," from all the way back in 1957—a purely commercial gesture that hardly dented the charts. And the picture wasn't much better on the album front. In 1964 RCA released only two new Elvis albums, plus a disastrous *Viva Las Vegas* EP, and while *Roustabout* made it all the way to number one, it was a feat that had little to do with its mediocre sales: RCA ended up with a total of fewer than a million Elvis albums sold that year.

The only thing that might have improved sales in 1965 would have been a serious new set of recordings. But Elvis and the Colonel delivered three soundtrack albums only, along with a *Tickle Me* EP and pair of singles that recycled nine previously released studio recordings. The first single for '65, "Do The Clam," failed miserably, and justifiably. For Easter RCA got lucky when they dug up "Crying In The Chapel" from the 1960 *His Hand In Mine* sessions; the record raced up the charts, reaching number three in the United States and number one in the United Kingdom, selling a million copies in the United States alone. Even more distressing, the illogical releases were beginning to be matched by illogical sales patterns: The next two singles, "Easy Question" and "I'm Yours"—pulled from the three-year-old *Pot Luck* album, like most of the *Tickle Me* soundtrack—both reached number eleven. By the end of the year RCA was reduced to resurrecting the 1957 cut on "Tell Me Why," whose religious melody had originally scared Steve Sholes off. The record's vintage sound was hardly the kind that was burning up pop radio by 1965, and it went nowhere.

With only moderate success for 1965's two movie soundtrack LPs, *Girl Happy* and *Harum Scarum,* RCA invented an *Anniversary Album* to celebrate Elvis's ten years on the label. Executives were given the task of combing the vaults for anything still unreleased by Presley, and an album (eventually retitled *Elvis For Everyone*) was pieced together from leftover movie and studio cuts, some dating back to the '50s. There was no hypocrisy about the album cover: Rather than the customary romantic image, it featured Elvis with a cash register on the front, and reproductions of all of Elvis's album covers with their cash sales listed on the back. The press release for the album proudly proclaimed that this was the first new nonsoundtrack album since *Pot Luck,* failing to men-

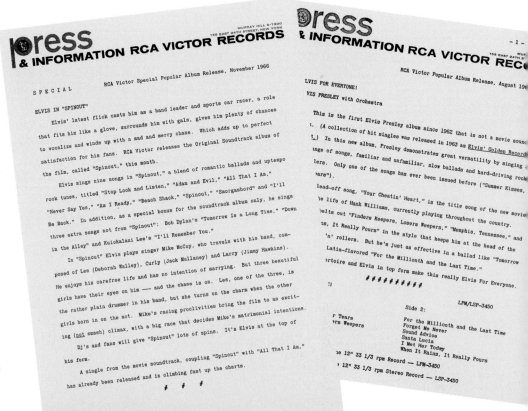

tion that its contents had been assembled from tapes with "scrap" and "rejects" written all over them. This would be the first '60s album to sell fewer than 300,000 units.

Elvis accepted the situation with as much grace as he could muster. Although he complained about the material, left sessions halfway through, sometimes failed to turn up for the first night of recording, never rehearsed, lost his concentration during the recording process, and openly ridiculed the very songs he was trying to record, he *always* came back to finish the job. He tried to keep the atmosphere lighthearted, made jokes at his own expense, kept the boredom away by singing lines at random from whatever songs happened to cross his mind.

As Gordon Stoker remembers, sometimes "he backed up so far from the microphone that the engineer would put the mike he was recording on as close to the wall as possible, and he [Elvis] would lean against the wall. How many times have I seen him sit as far from the microphone as possible? They put a soundboard around him to pick him up. . . . The material was so bad that he felt like he couldn't sing it." The session tapes that survive from these soundtrack sessions reveal an Elvis frequently angry and embarrassed; after twenty-four takes of a song called "Do Not Disturb," he chattered like a machine gun: "This is undoubtedly the weirdest goddamn chord change I ever tangled with in my life, man. I'll beat the hell out of it, if it takes me ninety-four years. Come back at the end of the picture and record it for hours."

The artistic direction of Elvis Presley's recording career had fallen into the hands of the movie companies and the Hill & Range staff writers; Elvis had become a kind of hired hand, farming out his services through RCA and the Colonel to the highest bidder with the least amount of effort. Occasionally a decent song slipped through, barely noticed, and every once in a while the studios made passing efforts to give their soundtracks an element of musical identity. But this was nothing like making real

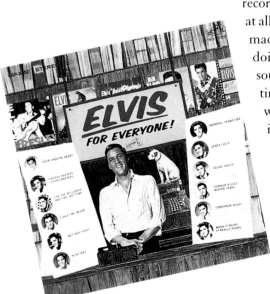

records; sometimes it hardly seemed like making music at all. By the mid-'60s good music was something Elvis made only at home. Despite everything, he kept doing his job, showing up for movie shoots and soundtrack sessions, hitting his marks. On his own time he dated his costars in Hollywood, spent time with Priscilla Beaulieu and his family and friends in Memphis, played games and watched movies with his entourage, and indulged an almost obsessive interest with current spiritual fashions. RCA continued to send him test pressings of each new release—a sky-high stack of acetates filled with movie songs he had grudgingly recorded and tunes he had rejected outright back when he really cared.

Meanwhile, from his offices at MGM, the Colonel exercised greater control than ever before. Its vaults depleted of any usable material, RCA could only wait for the Colonel to schedule each new film and soundtrack. And from this position, despite all the danger signs, the Colonel was able to renegotiate Elvis's recording contract, securing bigger advance payments, recoupable bonuses, and a host of special "favors" for himself and his boy.

1966

How Great Thou Art

In January of 1966 Elvis received a birthday telegram from RCA, signed by more than twenty staffers. President Frank Folsom's name was followed by those of Chet Atkins and Steve Sholes, along with George Parkhill and Harry Jenkins. It was a routine gesture, but also the signal of a new agenda: the revitalization of a career, a feat that would require a changing of the guard and a shift in tactics without breaking stride. RCA, in a rare move, sent out a press release boasting that 1965 had been the best year yet for Elvis, suggesting that with extra effort 1966 would be the next Best Year Yet.

Harry Jenkins had taken over from Bill Bullock as the Colonel's new partner in charge of "merchandise," the term the Colonel used for everything sellable, whether it was an Elvis lipstick or a new album. Jenkins, echoing the RCA logo, listened faithfully to his master the Colonel, but at the same time he gingerly began raising his company's concerns over Elvis's diminishing career. Fortunately Jenkins and the Colonel agreed on one major point: They could no longer continue to couple together soundtrack recordings and session leftovers and expect Elvis's records to perform as strongly as they once had. Soundtrack sales were plunging, and the artist's former sovereign status had been not only challenged but actually supplanted in many respects by a younger generation of artists. The changes to come were natural, and the Colonel was ready to listen to new ideas; he was already considering new "merchandise" proposals that fit right into the Parker mold—"Promotions Proven Profitable."

The first order of business was the recording of the *Spinout* soundtrack, which would follow the established model of production, promotion, publicity, and sales. But after that, Elvis would report to the RCA studio to record a brand-new religious album—a long-awaited follow-up to *His Hand In Mine,* which had grown from commercial insignificance to catalog item extraordinaire, selling solidly for five years. Two pop singles were needed, and the Colonel wanted to make one of them a new Christmas record, given the success of the original 1957 Christmas album, another catalog mainstay. Moreover, the Colonel knew that the seasonal radio market was the kind of sure thing that would help Elvis get around the constant competition of new artists. No matter who was on the charts during the rest of the year, at Christmastime radio stations played Christmas songs, and at Easter religious music. If radio's top-ten format was moving in other directions, at least the Colonel was still able to make an Elvis niche record bigger than most artists' mainstream efforts.

The "new merchandise," as usual, demanded careful preparation. A new recording session couldn't be scheduled until it was clear when Elvis would finish with movie production. But Freddy Bienstock was already at work in March, following up on a song Elvis had expressed interest in recording: a French melody entitled *"Et Maintenant,"* currently on the charts in an instrumental version by Herb Alpert and the Tijuana Brass and in an English-language vocal called "What Now My Love" by Sonny and Cher. Freddy checked the publishing in hopes of finding it in the public domain, but when he made the disappointing discovery that it was a copyrighted composition, he suggested to Tom Diskin, who was coordinating for the upcoming session, that they drop it altogether. In the meantime, Freddy submitted a number of new efforts by the same staff writers who had been churning out mediocre songs for all the soundtracks. Over the next few weeks some new Fred Wise and Randy Starr material was forwarded to Diskin, as well as numbers by the Giant, Baum, and Kaye team, including "Power Of My Love" (which Elvis would return to a few years later). In addition, Mort Shuman contributed a number of songs, and Freddy dug up whatever Christmas material he had on hand, including "The Wonderful World Of Christmas" and "Merry Christmas Baby," which would also surface again much later on.

Singing and playing music with friends had always been a part of Elvis's home life, but lately it had taken a new turn. Red West had bought two semiprofessional tape recorders for Elvis to use in producing demos, and Charlie Hodge had stopped touring with country music veteran Jimmy Wakely and moved into Red's Hollywood apartment to go to work for Elvis again full-time. Red was writing a lot of songs, and Charlie sometimes helped in overdubbing the demos he was putting together. They got Glen Campbell, then working as a session musician, and paid him twenty dollars to play guitar on some of the demos. Sometimes Red and Charlie would take the tape recorders over to Elvis at Rocca Place and the trio would lay down tracks, alone or with whoever else was around. Not surprisingly they turned often to their favorite gospel numbers—"Show Me Thy Ways," "He," "Hide Thou Me," "Oh, How I Love Jesus," or "I, John," another song Elvis would eventually record. Other times they simply tried anything that caught their fancy, from old standards like "Fools Rush In" and "It's A Sin To Tell A Lie" to more contemporary material—"Blowin' In The Wind," "What Now My Love," and "500 Miles." Often they dug into old country standards, and sometimes they even got Elvis to sing along on Red's new tunes. In the intense yet comfortable atmosphere of collaboration with friends, Elvis had found an alternative to the endlessly tedious soundtrack recording process; at home he could work away at the music he loved, and that in its own rough way made a truer musical statement than anything he was likely to do under the employ of a Hollywood movie factory.

75. Home Recordings
February 1966–early 1967: Rocca Place, Hollywood

Engineer: Red West

Guitar, Piano: Elvis Presley
Guitar, Piano, Vocals: Charlie Hodge

Vocals: Red West and others

Except for the last five listed, which were discovered on an acetate and released in part during the 1980s, all of the recordings below were part of a selection of tapes discovered at Graceland in 1996. They all appear to have been made on Red West's tape recorder; as far as can be determined they are all circa 1966, although West remembers recording them over a longer period of time. It is also impossible to be sure about which songs were recorded together; the listings below are based in part on aural evidence.

CPA5 5154	**After Loving You**	**Platinum: A Life In Music**
	E. Miller/J. Lantz	*67469-2/1997*
	If I Loved You	
	Oscar Hammerstein/Richard Rodgers	

The above two recordings feature Elvis singing and playing piano.

	Beyond the Reef	
	J. Pitman	
	Show Me Thy Ways, O Lord	
	Hazel Shade	
	Tumblin' Tumbleweeds	
	Bob Nolan	
	Hide Thou Me	
	Lowry/Crosby	
	It's No Fun Being Lonely	
	Red West	
	San Antonio Rose	
	Bob Wills	
CPA5 5152	**Tennessee Waltz**	**Platinum: A Life In Music**
	Redd Stewart/Pee Wee King	*67469-2/1997*
	Mary Lou Brown	
	Red West	
	Moonlight Sonata	
	Beethoven	
CPA5 5151	**Oh How I Love Jesus**	**Platinum: A Life In Music**
	Traditional	*67469-2/1997*
	I, John (incomplete)	
	William Gaither	
	Suppose	
	S. Dee/G. Goehring	

The above recordings feature Elvis, Charlie, and Red singing and playing. On several tracks other friends join in. On several of the performances Elvis sings bass, and Charlie Hodge does the lead vocal. "Moonlight Sonata" features Elvis, Charlie, and Red singing tones without words, to a piano track. Red West remembers that Elvis had wanted to have lyrics written for the piece, for possible future recording. "Suppose" was later overdubbed at a March 20, 1967 session in Nashville.

Fools Rush In
R. Bloom/J. Mercer
It's A Sin To Tell A Lie
Billy Mayhew
What Now My Love
Sigman/Becaud
500 Miles
West

CPA5 5153   **Blowin' In the Wind**   **Platinum: A Life In Music**
Dylan   *67469-2/1997*

The above five recordings feature Elvis and friends singing along to instrumental records.

Be My Love
Sammy Cahn/Nicholas Brodszky
Baby What You Want Me To Do
Jimmy Reed

CPA5 8217   **Write To Me From Naples**   **A Golden Celebration**
A. Alstone/J. Kennedy   *CPM6 5172/1984*

CPA5 8212   **My Heart Cries For You**   **A Golden Celebration**
P. Faith/C. Sigman   *CPM6 5172/1984*

CPA5 8213   **Dark Moon**   **A Golden Celebration**
N. Miller   *CPM6 5172/1984*

The above five recordings all come from an acetate, and feature Elvis, Charlie, and Red singing harmony.

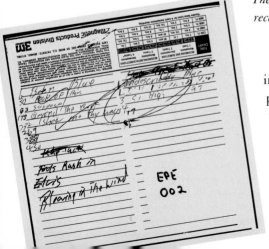

The "Blowin' In The Wind" tape found recently at Graceland

By the end of April Elvis was back at Graceland and starting to make noises about recording again. Tom Diskin reported to Freddy Bienstock that he was interested in cutting the Clovers' old hit "Down In The Alley," and "I'll Remember You" by the recently deceased Hawaiian songwriter, Kui Lee. "My Special Prayer," a Ben E. King–type soul ballad, was another possibility, and Freddy was able to arrange a publishing deal on that right away. By early May the Colonel, still at his MGM Studio office, informed Harry Jenkins that the session was scheduled for 7 P.M. on May 25 at RCA's Studio B in Nashville, and that Elvis was now sifting through and rehearsing material with Charlie and Red. By May 9, the line of communication from Elvis through Red to Tom and on to Freddy had produced a list of more than twenty songs that Elvis was considering.

Selecting religious songs was relatively easy, although many of the selections on this round never made it onto an Elvis record. More than half of the material Elvis had approved were favorites from his own collection of LPs, including "Lord, I Need You Again Today" by the Statesmen, "Room At The Cross" by the Blackwood Brothers, Stuart Hamblen's "Wasted Years," Roy Hamilton's "He" (Elvis had the Pat Boone EP too), "Don't Knock" by the Staple Singers, and two similar songs by the the Golden Gate Quartet: "You Better Run" and "Run On." Elvis told Red to get Tom Diskin to find bass singer Jimmy Jones of the Harmonizing Four to see if he was available to join the session. Red's two songs, the gospel number "He Lifted Me" and a Christmas song, "If Every Day Was Like Christmas," were possibilities, but Elvis felt the new pop material being submitted by Freddy "just wasn't strong enough." The kinds of things attracting his attention at this point were classic ballads like "Danny Boy" and "Greensleeves," both candidates for that old Freddy Bienstock trick—commission a new set of lyrics to an old tune, and voilà! A new copyright for Elvis's publishing companies.

Charlie and Red now had a serious working collaboration with Elvis—Freddy was starting to call them the Imperial Council—and their listening sessions at Graceland produced plenty of other suggestions. "Fools Rush In," Ivory Joe Hunter's "I Will Be True," "Love Is A Many Splendored Thing," and another favorite inspired by a Jackie Wilson performance, "Rags To Riches," were all suggested, and when Freddy reacted by sending more Giant, Baum, and Kaye material, all he got were negative responses. The list of gospel material was expanding every day, though: "How Great Thou Art," "Walk That Lonesome Valley," "Where No One Stands Alone," "By And By," and Thomas A. Dorsey's "I'll Tell It Where I Go." But if there was an embarrassment of gospel riches, the pop singles were another story. One secular song came from another longtime member of Elvis's staff, Lamar Fike; now working in the Nashville office of Hill & Range, who represented regular Elvis writers such as Joy Byers and Gerald Nelson, he came up with "Indescribably Blue." The song was by Darrell Glenn, who had had a huge hit with his father Artie Glenn's "Crying In The Chapel" in 1953, twelve years before Elvis's own version became an even bigger hit. But now hit songs were looking scarce on the ground.

As the session grew near, Tom Diskin kept busy making all the practical arrangements for the sessions while acting as a go-between for all the parties involved. It was decided to book three nights, just in case Elvis felt like recording more than they were planning for. As always there were complications: The Jordanaires and Floyd Cramer would have to miss the first three hours of the second night due to previous commitments, and neither Diskin nor RCA could track down Jimmy Jones, the gospel bass singer Elvis had been listening to almost obsessively at Graceland. Chet Atkins's secretary, Mary Lynch, suggested a local white gospel group called the Imperials Quartet, led by former Statesmen lead singer Jake Hess. RCA had used the quartet recently on several albums of religious and Christmas material, and Mary had become friendly with Jake, whose office was in RCA's Nashville building. The Statesmen had always been Elvis's and Vernon's favorite quartet, and of course Jake remembered Elvis when he was just a "bright-eyed kid," a fan of the group as far back as the Tupelo years.

76. Studio Sessions for RCA
May 25–28, 1966: RCA's Studio B, Nashville

A&R/Producer: Felton Jarvis
Engineer: Jim Malloy (5/25, 26, 27)
Engineer: Al Pachucki (5/28)

Guitar: Scotty Moore
Guitar: Chip Young
Bass: Bob Moore (5/25, 26, 27)
Bass: Henry Strzelecki (5/28)
Bass, Harmonica, Guitar: Charlie McCoy (5/25, 27, 28)
Drums, Tympani: Buddy Harman
Drums: D. J. Fontana
Piano: Floyd Cramer
Piano, Organ: Henry Slaughter (5/25, 26, 27)

Piano, Organ: David Briggs (5/26)
Steel Guitar: Pete Drake
Sax: Rufus Long
Sax: Boots Randolph
Trumpet: Ray Stevens (5/28)
Vocals: The Jordanaires
Vocals: The Imperials (not 5/28)
Vocals: Millie Kirkham, June Page,
Dolores Edgin

5/25, 6:30–9:30PM. No recordings finished.

10PM–1AM

TPA4 0908-07	**Run On**	**How Great Thou Art**
	Arranged by Elvis Presley—Elvis Presley Music	*LSP 3758/1967*
TPA4 0909-04	**How Great Thou Art**	**How Great Thou Art**
	Stuart K. Hine—Manna Music	*LSP 3758/1967*

1–4AM

TPA4 0910-11	**Stand By Me**	**How Great Thou Art**
	Arranged by Elvis Presley—Elvis Presley Music	*LSP 3758/1957*
TPA4 0911-sp	**Where No One Stands Alone**	**How Great Thou Art**
	Mosie Lister—Mosie Lister Pub.	*LSP 3758/1967*

4–7AM

TPA4 0912-09	**Down In The Alley**	**Spinout**
	Jesse Stone and the Clovers—Progressive Music	*LSP 3702/1966*
TPA4 0913-03	**Tomorrow Is A Long Time**	**Spinout**
	Bob Dylan—M. Witmark & Sons	*LSP 3702/1966*

5/26, 6:30–9:30PM. No recordings finished.

10PM–1AM

TPA4 0914-09 **Love Letters**
E. Heyman/V. Young—Gladys Music/Famous Music

Single A-Side
47-8870/1966

1–4AM

TPA4 0915-04 **So High**
Arranged by Elvis Presley—Elvis Presley Music

How Great Thou Art
LSP 3758/1967

TPA4 0916-03 **Farther Along**
Arranged by Elvis Presley—Elvis Presley Music

How Great Thou Art
LSP 3758/1967

4–7AM

TPA4 0917-10 **By And By**
Arranged by Elvis Presley—Elvis Presley Music

How Great Thou Art
LSP 3758/1967

TPA4 0918-03 **In The Garden**
C. A. Miles—Robbins Music

How Great Thou Art
LSP 3758/1967

TPA4 0919-02 **Beyond The Reef**
J. Pitman—Herald Square Music

From Nashville To Memphis*
66160-2/1993

5/27, 7–10PM

TPA4 0920-16 **Somebody Bigger Than You And I**
J. Lange/H. Heath/S. Burke—Bulls Eye Music

How Great Thou Art
LSP 3758/1967

10PM–1AM

TPA4 0921-12 **Without Him**
Mylon LeFevre—LeFevre Sing Music Co.

How Great Thou Art
LSP 3758/1967

1–5AM

TPA4 0922-05 **If The Lord Wasn't Walking By My Side**
Henry Slaughter—Imperial Pub./Elvis Presley Music

How Great Thou Art
LSP 3758/1967

TPA4 0923-02 **Where Could I Go But To The Lord**
J. B. Coats—Stamps Baxter Music/Affiliated Music Ent.

How Great Thou Art
LSP 3758/1967

5/28, 7–10PM

TPA4 0924-08 **Come What May**
Tableporter—Tiger Music

Single B-side
47-8870/1966

TPA4 0925-05 **Fools Fall In Love**
J. Leiber/M. Stoller—Tiger Music

Single B-side
47-9056/1967

10PM–1AM. No recordings.

The master of "Where No One Stands Alone" (0911) is spliced from take 4 and work part take 7 (second half of song). The master of "Somebody Bigger Than You And I" (0920) is spliced from take 16 and work part of take 6 (ending). "Beyond The Reef" (0919) was first released on *Elvis Aron Presley* in a version overdubbed by Felton Jarvis on August 9, 1968, with further instrumentation as follows: Guitar: Ray Edenton; Bass: Norbert Putnam; Drums: Buddy Harman; Steel guitar: Jerry Byrd; Vocals: Priscilla Hubbard, Dorothy Dillard, William Wright, Lois Nunley. *From Nashville to Memphis* (66160) marked the first release of the undubbed recording featuring the singing of Red West, Charlie Hodge, and Elvis Presley, who plays the piano. The Imperials: Jake Hess, Sherrill Nielsen, Gary McSpadden, Armond Morales, Henry Slaughter (who sang on the songs for which he didn't play piano). *Full title: *Elvis: From Nashville to Memphis: The Essential 60's Masters, Vol. 1.*

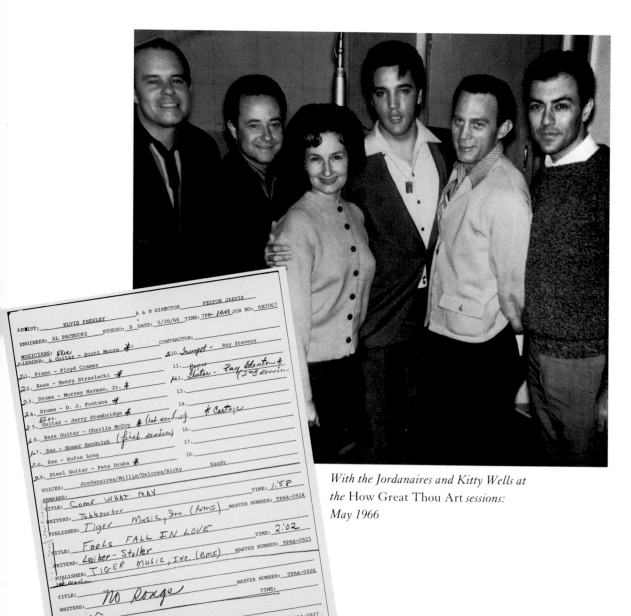

With the Jordanaires and Kitty Wells at the How Great Thou Art *sessions: May 1966*

When Elvis walked into the studio on the first night, he was greeted by a new producer: Charles Felton Jarvis, who would take over—and surpass—the role Steve Sholes had played in Elvis's career. Elvis didn't know it then, but their paths had crossed once before. Felton had been born in Atlanta, Georgia, in 1935, the same year as Elvis. He had fallen in love with rock 'n' roll as early as 1955, when he witnessed a virtually unknown Elvis Presley blow Hank Snow off the stage at the Norfolk City Auditorium. He had started his career in the recording business as an Elvis imitator, and through promotion work for ABC Records had become a producer. His continued fascination with Elvis brought him a regional hit when he produced a carbon copy of "Such A Night" with a singer whom he dubbed Vince Everett, after the character Elvis portrayed in *Jailhouse Rock*. He had made his name, though, with the Tommy Roe million-seller "Sheila," and by 1963 he was ABC's man in Nashville. In 1965 Chet Atkins was looking for some help producing the many artists signed to RCA's Nashville division, and he was more than ready to relinquish oversight of the singer's lengthy all-night sessions to this young Elvis admirer. John D. Loudermilk was Chet's candidate for the job, but neither his new engineer, Jim Malloy, nor his assistant, Mary Lynch, were keen on the idea. Jim had become friendly with Felton and, knowing there were plans afoot at ABC to let Felton go, recommended him to Chet. Mary, on the other hand, had reservations; Felton had a reputation as a womanizer and practical joker, whose idea of fun was to keep his pet boa constrictor in his office and watch people's faces when the snake began to move in its sack. But Felton was a good old boy, and in the end Chet hired Felton and immediately put him to work. When he found out he was going to be producing a session with Elvis Felton could hardly contain himself.

Because this was such a crucial session, the studio was buzzing with expectation; there were enough music business types to make any free-spirited rock 'n' roll producer sweat, let alone an enthusiastic neophyte like Felton. Freddy Bienstock and Lamar Fike were there representing Hill & Range, Tom Diskin had the Colonel's authority to voice management interests, and Harry Jenkins was RCA's man from New York, there to make sure that the "new merchandise" would be delivered. Felton's friend, engineer Jim Malloy, was new to Elvis sessions, too, but like Felton, Jim had met Elvis before. In late 1956 he had been hired by Radio Recorders in Los Angeles as technical engineer at the same time that Bones Howe joined as

Attention: Felton Jarvis

Dear Felton,
    Please convey how much I deeply appreciate the cooperation and consideration shown to me and my associates during my last two trips to Nashville.
    I would like to thank you, the engineers, musicians, singers and everyone connected with the sessions.
    Please see that every one of them know my feelings. And as General McCarther once said, "I Shall Return."

Greatfully
Elvis Presley

RECEIVED
JUN 16 1966

assistant engineer. Elvis recorded at the studio often, and Jim had met him in the building, occasionally even sitting in on sessions with chief engineer Thorne Nogar. When RCA's Steve Sholes moved to LA in 1960, he hired Malloy for RCA's studios on Sunset, and there he worked for five years recording dozens of artists, including Duane Eddy and Henry Mancini. In 1965 he had been persuaded by Chet Atkins to come to Nashville as chief engineer. For Jim the Elvis sessions didn't offer quite the same thrill they did for Felton, but there was an undeniable air of anticipation in seeing Elvis again.

There were other new faces. Scotty Moore brought in a Memphis protégé, Chip Young, as rhythm guitarist for the band. Then, too, the regular lineup would be augmented for the first time by Nashville's steel-guitar ace, Pete Drake, sax player Rufus Long, and session singers June Page and Dolores Edgin. Jake Hess and the Imperials were just the icing on the cake.

As always, Elvis warmed up by singing some gospel numbers with the whole group, joking and trading stories, seemingly oblivious to the passage of time. This time, though, several hours of unwinding led directly into a rehearsal of the first song, the Golden Gate Quartet's classic "Run On," an up-tempo number in the jubilee tradition. They began softly with Floyd Cramer's piano run, picked up by the vocal group's low "hmmm." Elvis missed his lead-in the first time around, but the second take was full of energy, with the full electric band and eleven singers making a very joyful noise. It was a remarkable updating of traditional gospel music—tough, powerful, even threatening—different from any religious music Elvis had ever recorded. Before they leapt into the final take, Felton made his presence felt, encouraging them to "swing." And swing they did.

The next song, which would become the signature piece of the sessions—and a real high point in Elvis's recording career—suggested that those endless hours of singing at home may well have been the most in-depth rehearsals he had ever undertaken. Charlie had played Elvis a version of "How Great Thou Art" by the Sons of the Pioneers, a group Charlie knew from his stint with the Foggy River Boys. Elvis also knew the Statesmen's 1964 recording of the same song, done after Jake Hess had left the group; Elvis borrowed from both. (Charlie had avoided playing the best-known version of the song, a rather formal rendering by George Beverly Shea that he knew wouldn't have excited Elvis.) In the studio it became clear that Elvis's months of practice at home had paid off: He knew the song inside and out, instructing the singers on the powerful lead-in during a brief, fifteen-minute rehearsal before the final take. Elvis sang with sincerity and dedication, in a slower tempo than the Statesmen's version that accentuated the spirituality of the material and allowed him to build the song into a powerful anthem. He had crafted for himself an ad-hoc arrangement in which he took every part of the four-part vocal, from Big Chief's bass intro to the soaring heights of the song's operatic climax. In an extraordinary fulfillment of his vocal ambitions, he had become a kind of one-man quartet, making the song both a personal challenge and a tribute to the singing style he'd always loved.

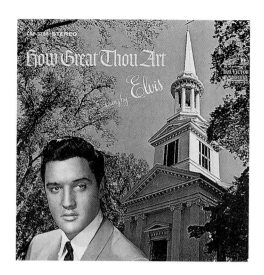

"How Great Thou Art" was originally a traditional gospel number from Sweden, translated into English by missionary Stuart K. Hine. For the next number he drew on another tradition. "Stand By Me" was written by the legendary black gospel composer Charles Tindley, and Elvis asked that the lights in the studio be turned down to create a more intimate feeling. Because the song was newer to him, though, he found himself unable to read the lyric sheet in the dark, and started saying they ought to "do another type of song." Sensing that they might miss a wonderful opportunity, though, Felton stepped in to encourage Elvis, and the singer quickly regained confidence and finished the song. The next number was going to be demanding on his voice, and he started off by warning Felton and the engineers that he wanted more power from the backing vocalists. "Where No One Stands Alone" had been a hit for the Ink Spots in 1951 as well as the B-side of the Statesmen's version of "Crying In The Chapel," and it built to a grand finale, which was here repeated for added effect. "It sounded great, Elvis. God, I was scared to death," Felton called out, and with Charlie's help Elvis was able to complete the last part of the song in a separate take to save his voice for the remaining cuts.

It was four in the morning when Felton, by now directing the session with relaxed, supportive comments from the control room, announced a shift from Sunday morning to Saturday night: " 'Down In The Alley'—funksville, take one." This was a genuine rocker, the kind of thing Felton could really sink his teeth into, and Elvis was just as excited, ready to unwind. As a teenager he'd loved the Clovers; he had sung their songs on the road in the early years, and in 1960 he'd done a passionate job with "Like A Baby," written by their frequent arranger and director Jesse Stone. Elvis himself had requested Stone's "Down In The Alley" for this session, and now he looked to the original members of his band, Scotty and D. J., to get it started. The backup singers were on less familiar ground, so Charlie Hodge came up front on vocals, helping to relieve the tension by gladly acting the fool and throwing Elvis and everyone else into paroxysms of laughter. This was a chance to let go and have a good time, and by take six they had. Felton pushed for one more try, parts were adjusted, changed, added, subtracted; after take nine Felton suggested, "Let's listen to that" and an R&B master was ready for the master reel.

After a full night's work the Imperials went home, leaving Elvis and the musicians to probe a little deeper into Elvis's constantly surprising musical interests. In the months before the session Charlie had been playing the *Odetta Sings Dylan* album, and Elvis had become taken with "Tomorrow Is A Long Time," a Bob Dylan original that had been recorded by several other artists, though Dylan himself had never released a version. Charlie McCoy had been among the Nashville players on Dylan's *Blonde On Blonde* sessions; now, nine months later, here he was watching Elvis give Dylan a try. True to the song's folk origins this was a guitar piece, so Scotty, Chip, and Charlie McCoy grabbed their acoustics while Bob Moore shifted to the electric bass. With only a tambourine added to the arrangement, they delved into another world, a place where Elvis had never ventured before. By take three they had completed a gorgeous—and, for Elvis, extraordinarily long—five-minute master. That made six masters in one long night, including one number Bob Dylan would later list as one of his favorite versions of his own material.

This was the first Elvis session for David Briggs, a young piano player from Muscle Shoals, Alabama, who was already working a good many sessions in Nashville. He had been called to sit in for the first three hours of the second evening until Floyd Cramer arrived. He later told writer Peter Guralnick how nervous he was coming in for the session: "Normally Elvis didn't come in until late, but as it turned out, he came in early that night, ready to go to work." Elvis began the evening by sneaking up behind Briggs at the piano; then he gathered everyone around the piano for the customary gospel sing before getting down to work. "The first song he wanted to do was 'Love Letters,' which is all piano," Briggs recalls. "So I had to play on it. I had just met him, and five minutes later I was sitting on a stool beside him at the piano." Engineer Jim Malloy was watching Briggs from the control room; like Felton he was impressed with the young man's playing and was delighted he was on the session. Jim noticed how anxious Briggs was—he had red blushes all over the back of his neck—but the new keyboard player had no trouble with gospel, having recorded with the Statesmen just weeks earlier. By the time they got to "Love Letters" David was in full swing.

"Then pretty soon he moved to the back of the room, he had the piano moved to the back of the room, and we turned out all the lights and he had a candle on the piano. It was a tense situation! At this point Floyd walks in, and I say 'Great, man, come over here and play this thing.' I was relieved to get out of the pressure seat, Floyd sat down and played a little bit, and I went over and got on the organ, but then Elvis said, 'Where's that boy? I kind of got used to the way he played.' And I thought, 'Oh shit, now I'm not only playing with Elvis, I'm playing in front of Floyd!' " There were only the female voices backing up Elvis, and Millie, Dolores, and June had some trouble working out their parts. Elvis sensed the song was dragging, so they all went back to listen to the original recording to get it straight. After nine takes David was finally off the hook, but he was invited to stay all night, moving over to play the organ. "When we got done, he must have listened back to it fifty times."

It was past midnight by the time they got back to the gospel album. Over the past months the artist Elvis had returned to most often was bass singer Jimmy Jones of the Harmonizing Four, and he was disappointed that Tom Diskin hadn't been able to find him for the session. "So High" was the number of his that Elvis most wanted to perform, and he was happy to go along with Jones's jubilee arrangement, so reminiscent of the Golden Gate Quartet's classic recordings. Once again everybody knew exactly what to do. Buddy Harman's brushes drove the piece as if it were straight rockabilly. D. J. worked the tambourine to add to the frenzy, but it was the immaculate interaction between the singers and Elvis, right down to their true-to-the-spirit hand-clapping, that made the moment. On the last chorus Buddy Harman cut loose on the overhead cymbal to bring the song to a rousing conclusion.

The Harmonizing Four's version of the standard "Farther Along" was another of Elvis's favorite Jimmy Jones records. Underlined by a metallic-sounding guitar drone, it had a country feel that was brought out even more by the richness of the voices and Floyd's hallmark piano style. Mixing things up a little, they returned to the up-tempo jubilee sound next with "By And By." On each of the faster numbers Felton and Jim put the drums and tambourine way up in the recording mix, but it took a while to achieve just the right arrangement. "Try that fuzz again, Pete," Felton told Pete Drake, the steel player. "Fuzz?" Elvis asked. "Fuzz tone, that he has on his steel," Felton explained. They tried it with and without, but in the end kept Drake's fuzz-steel in, giving the song a loud, almost angry feel. It might not have been the rock 'n' roll that Felton loved, but truth be told it rocked harder than many of the "rock" records of 1966—and it was miles beyond almost anyone else's version of gospel. By now they had found the sound they were after, and the mournful church traditional "In The Garden" came off beautifully in one take.

It was now 6 A.M. and time to go home, but not before Elvis, Red, and Charlie unwound by harmonizing on one of the songs they'd worked on around Red's home tape recorder, "Beyond The Reef." With Elvis on piano, Bob Moore on bass, and Pete Drake on steel, they concluded the second night by committing the perfectly studied vocal piece to tape, this time in a real recording studio rather than Red's uncontrolled home-taping environment. Most likely this was considered an informal take rather than a true candidate for release, but Elvis must have been curious to hear how the trio would sound in a studio environment.

The third night began by returning again to a Jimmy Jones album, this time for the song "Somebody Bigger Than You And I." Elvis knew several influential versions of the song, including one by the Ink Spots and another by the Statesmen, but Jones's basso profundo version enthralled him. Ever ambitious, Elvis tried recording it in Jones's key, but as they started recording Elvis couldn't quite control his low notes, and they raised the key. Felton asked D. J. to lighten up a hair, much to Elvis's amusement. In fact, the session was shaping up into such a rewarding experience that Elvis himself was filled with congeniality—enough to carry them all through sixteen takes of the song. The singers mixed up their vocal parts on the last few bars of the final take, but Felton suggested that they could graft a "work-part" retake on for the ending. Now they began to stray from the planned playlist. Elvis tried and rejected several of his own choices as well as several songs Freddy had made deals on, including Joe & Eddy's "To Be Myself" and "Room For Everybody." Gordon Stoker remembers singing Hank Williams's "I Saw The Light," but that wasn't recorded either. Finally Elvis asked if anyone else had any good songs. Gordon Stoker threw in some suggestions, and Jake Hess agreed to walk over to his office to get some material. He returned with Mylon LeFevre's "Without Him," which the Statesmen had recorded on an album that also included "Show Me Thy Ways," another number Elvis had rehearsed with Charlie and Red. "Without Him" was highly dramatic (and a real vocal challenge), and though he didn't know it well Elvis gave it his undivided attention—until he noticed an odd squeaking noise coming through on the tape. "That's my shoe sole!" he laughed. "That's the wrong soul, man." He apologized for not knowing the song better, but they eventually arrived at a solid version on take fourteen. "If The Lord Wasn't Walking By My Side," by the Imperials' piano player, Henry Slaughter, provided the opportunity to feature all of the vocalists in yet another revival-style number, and Elvis insisted, to Jake Hess's embarrassment, that Jake's voice be featured high in the mix. At 4 A.M. Elvis reached back to "Where Could I Go But To The Lord," a song he and his father Vernon sang often at home. It was in the Statesmen's repertoire, and Jimmy Jones had done a version on the same 1957 session when he'd recorded another Elvis favorite, "Sometimes I Feel Like A Motherless Child." They took "Where Could I Go" at a slow, bluesy pace, the female voices weaving wonderfully with the quartets, all sprinkled with jazzy piano and cool finger-popping. It was more explicitly soulful than any of the other material, and after a brief rehearsal they got it in two. "My Special Prayer" was next, but it was 5:00 A.M. and Elvis was finally ready to call it a night—thereby canceling out one of Freddy's deals and his own cut on the publishing.

But they still needed one more night in the studio to hammer out some more pop tunes and the Christmas single. RCA had booked just three nights, and of course some of the participants had other commitments. Al Pachucki took over for engineer Jim Malloy, the Imperials hit the road, and Henry Strzelecki replaced Bob Moore on bass. Ray Stevens, singer of the top-five hit "Ahab The Arab," sat in on trumpet. They started with "Come What May," a song by Frank Tableporter originally recorded by Clyde McPhatter in 1958, in an attempt to get a B-side for "Love Letters." Jerry Lee Lewis had recorded the song in an unreleased solo version at Sun just after the McPhatter record came out, and in fact Elvis had jammed on it with him at Graceland. As the tape started to roll there was a great deal of noise in the room—everybody seemed to be rehearsing at once, and Elvis was fooling around, changing the lyrics and generally sounding pleased with himself. They worked on getting the feel and adjusting the Jordanaires' part before arriving at a master on the eighth take, though compared to the more soulful feeling of the previous day's work there was something a little shallow-sounding about the whole affair.

The fact that the session hadn't been properly scheduled continued to cause disruption throughout the evening. They were able to rush through a Drifters song,

"Fools Fall In Love," before Charlie McCoy and Boots Randolph had to leave, but thereafter Ray Edenton had to pick up the slack on rhythm guitar for Charlie. Sandy Posey (who would have three top-twenty hits over the next twelve months—two more than Elvis) came in to replace one of the female singers. But in the end, neither Sandy nor Ray did any recording that night. Elvis was tired before they got to the Christmas song; another session would have to be scheduled to finish what they'd started, but before leaving Elvis asked Al Pachucki to have Jim Malloy cut lacquers of "Love Letters" and "Come What May," the two songs he wanted for his next release.

Recording eighteen sides was a major step toward reestablishing a normal relationship between Elvis Presley and RCA Records. But a closer inspection would reveal problems with what Elvis actually recorded. Freddy Bienstock couldn't have been entirely happy; Red's warning that the new material submitted for the sessions "just wasn't strong enough" was brought home by the results. Not one new pop original was recorded. Freddy was able to claim many of the "public domain" religious songs for Elvis's publishing companies and most of the rock 'n' roll oldies were under his publishing control, but he had failed utterly at his most important assignment: to deliver a new pop single and a Christmas song. "Love Letters" was a beautiful song, and a stunning performance, which made it Elvis's choice for a single; but there was no way a subdued Elvis cover of a decade-old ballad (already revived three years earlier by Kitty Lester) was going to make it on 1966 popular radio, so it wasn't much of a choice at all.

But it was the Christmas single that was the key merchandising element both the Colonel and RCA's Harry Jenkins felt they needed—and that hadn't even been attempted. It was essential, then, that Elvis return to the studio in June before beginning work on his new movie, *Double Trouble*. Once again, there were new lists of songs; once again, Elvis and the boys listened diligently in Memphis. But what they were really thinking about were songs from the past: Bob Wills's country classic "Faded Love," Faye Adams's "Shake A Hand," LaVern Baker's version of the Leiber and Stoller number "Saved." Elvis had a steady stream of R&B coming off the record player at Graceland, with Jimmy Reed, Percy Mayfield, and Della Reese's version of "After Loving You" in heavy rotation. Brook Benton's "A Million Miles From Nowhere," Sanford Clark's "The Fool," and Ray Peterson's "The Wonder Of You" were favorites too. To RCA and Freddy Bienstock it was all old material, but to Elvis it was just great music—and all they could do was stand by painfully as he dismissed one new song after another submitted by his own publishing organization.

77. Studio Sessions for RCA
June 10–12, 1966: RCA's Studio B, Nashville

A&R/Producer: Felton Jarvis
Engineer: Jim Malloy

Guitar: Scotty Moore
Guitar: Chip Young
Guitar: Harold Bradley
Bass: Bob Moore
Drums: D. J. Fontana
Drums, Tympani: Buddy Harman
Piano: David Briggs

Organ: Henry Slaughter
Steel Guitar: Pete Drake
Sax: Rufus Long
Vocals: The Jordanaires
Vocals: The Imperials
Vocals: Millie Kirkham, June Page,
Dolores Edgin

<u>6/10, 7–10PM</u>

TPA4 0982-na (tr) Indescribably Blue   **Single A-side**

Darrell Glenn—Elvis Presley Music   *47-9056/1967*

<u>10PM–2AM</u>

TPA4 0983-na (tr) I'll Remember You   **Spinout**

Kuiokalani Lee—Herb Montei Music   *LSP 3702/1966*

TPA4 0984-na (tr) If Every Day Was Like Christmas   **Single A-side**

Red West—Atlantic Music Corp.   *47-8950/1966*

The above recording dates represent sessions at which Elvis's band recorded backing tracks and guide vocals only. Elvis over-dubbed his vocals on June 12. Vocal master takes are: "Indescribably Blue," take 2; "I'll Remember You," splice of takes 3 and 1; "If Every Day Was Like Christmas," take 2. A celeste was overdubbed onto the intro of "If Every Day Was Like Christmas" (0984) on June 20. "I'll Remember You" (0983) was shortened in its original release. As Elvis was, officially, unable to attend sessions due to a throat infection, Red West sang guide vocals for all three songs during the sessions. The Imperials: Jake Hess, Jim Murray, Gary McSpadden, Armond Morales.

The scene in RCA's Studio B in Nashville wasn't quite what Felton Jarvis had hoped for. The session was about to start, but the guy in front of the microphone was *not* Elvis Presley but his friend, bodyguard, and songwriter, Red West. Back at the hotel Elvis had told Red and Charlie Hodge to go to the studio and fill in for him while the musicians laid down tracks. He had a cold, he said; he wasn't in any mood for recording. The musicians took it well, and the music they recorded was a perfect extension of the interests Elvis had been showing at home. Red showcased a full and pleasant baritone on "Indescribably Blue," the song Lamar Fike had brought in for the last session. Over the next few hours Red sang "I'll Remember You," following the Don Ho record they'd first heard in Hawaii. It wasn't until midnight that they finally got to the mandatory Christmas single—and a moment of high triumph for Red himself, as he recorded his own "If Every Day Was Like Christmas."

At two in the morning Red, Charlie, and Lamar headed back to the hotel to report their success to Elvis. The three songs they'd recorded were all ballads, all potential hit singles; the arrangements Felton and the musicians had worked out featured state-of-the-art recording technique and beautiful acoustic gut-string guitar playing from Chip Young and Harold Bradley. The tracks were a definite stylistic departure for Elvis; they sounded *contemporary,* and it'd been a long time since anyone had said that of an Elvis record. The next morning acetates were delivered to the hotel to help Elvis prepare for his vocal overdubs; Felton was even hoping they might get some more recording done that night. But after waiting in vain Felton was forced to send everyone home; once again Elvis didn't feel like doing anything. Maybe his throat was sore; perhaps he resented being forced into the studio again. There was no way to be sure.

It wasn't until the following night that he finally delivered on the Colonel's promise to RCA to finish up the three songs. Felton and Jim Malloy watched as he breezed through them in just seven takes, spending little more than thirty minutes of actual recording time on the process. Was this going to become Elvis's new approach to recording? If it did, there didn't seem to be any real cause for complaint. The performances were sincere and beautifully sung; they would make good records. When he returned to Memphis, with the acetates of the new recordings on his turntable, Elvis himself sent a rare written thank-you note to Felton Jarvis:

> Dear Felton,
>   Please convey how much I deeply appreciate the cooperation and consideration shown to me and my associates during my last two trips to Nashville. I would like to thank you, the engineers, musicians, singers and everyone connected with the sessions. Please see that every one of them know my feelings. And as General McArthur once said, "I shall return."

Felton Jarvis had every reason to feel good about the session. With his great good humor, real talent for encouraging his artist, and natural ability to get the best out of everyone, he had easily overcome Elvis's habitual shyness with new faces; even more, he'd established a real rapport with the singer. If he hadn't yet become Elvis's new Jerry Leiber, at least he was no Chet Atkins.

As difficult as they'd become by the end, this series of sessions would be a turning point in Elvis's recording career—not because of any great commercial rewards, but perhaps for exactly the opposite reason: Elvis was finally channeling his artistic ambitions, his appetite to develop as a singer and recording artist, into his studio work. In the two and a half years since his last RCA session, Elvis had retreated and regrouped— and had begun, in the comfortable atmosphere of his own home, with his friends gathered around him, to revive his musical instincts. Far from just duplicating the successful *His Hand In Mine,* the new gospel album he'd cut suggested new horizons for recorded religious music. With the sophisticated "Love Letters" Elvis was taking a chance with his new single, abandoning the out-of-the-box hit formula he'd stuck to since coming out of the army in favor of a message of growing maturity as a singer. He was taking an interest again, taking some chances—taking control.

1966–67

DOUBLE TROUBLE

78. Soundtrack Sessions for MGM's *Double Trouble*
June 28–30, 1966: Radio Recorders
and MGM Studios Recording Stage, Hollywood

MGM Producer: Jeff Alexander
Engineer: Dave Weichman (Radio Recorders)
            Unknown (MGM Studios Recording Stage)

Guitar: Scotty Moore
Guitar: Tiny Timbrell
Guitar, Harmonica: Charlie McCoy
Bass: Bob Moore
Drums: D. J. Fontana
Drums: Buddy Harman
Piano: Floyd Cramer
Steel Guitar: Pete Drake
Sax: Boots Randolph

Trombone: Richard Noel
Vocals: The Jordanaires

Overdubbed later:
Guitar: Mike Deasy
Bass: Jerry Scheff
Drums: Toxey Sewell
Sax: Michael Henderson
Sax: Butch Parker

6/28, 7PM–12AM, 1–2:45AM. Radio Recorders

2001-03(tr)	**City By Night**	**Double Trouble**
UPA3 3938	*Giant/Baum/Kaye—Elvis Presley Music*	*LSP 3787/1967*
2002-06	**Could I Fall In Love**	**Double Trouble**
UPA3 3936	*Randy Starr—Gladys Music*	*LSP 3787/1967*
2003-10	**There's So Much World To See**	
	Sid Tepper/Ben Weisman—Gladys Music	
2004-01	**There's So Much World To See**	**Double Trouble**
UPA3 3941	*Sid Tepper/Ben Weisman—Gladys Music*	*LSP 3787/1967*
2005-06 (tr)	**Long Legged Girl (With The Short Dress On)**	
	J. L. McFarland/W. Scott—Elvis Presley Music	

6/29, 7PM–12AM, 1–3AM. MGM Studios Recording Stage

2006-04	**Double Trouble**	**Double Trouble**
UPA3 3934	*Doc Pomus/Mort Shuman—Elvis Presley Music*	*LSP 3787/1967*
2007-05	**Baby, If You'll Give Me All Of Your Love**	**Double Trouble**
UPA3 3935	*Joy Byers—Elvis Presley Music*	*LSP 3787/1967*

2008-02	**I Love Only One Girl**	**Double Trouble**
UPA3 3940	*Sid Tepper/Roy C. Bennett—Gladys Music*	*LSP 3787/1967*
2009-na	**It Won't Be Long**	**Double Trouble**
UPA3 3942	*Sid Wayne/Ben Weisman—Gladys Music*	*LSP 3787/1967*
2010-07(tr)	**Old MacDonald**	**Double Trouble**
UPA3 3939	*Randy Starr—Gladys Music*	*LSP 3787/1967*
2011-05	**Long Legged Girl (With The Short Dress On)**	**Double Trouble**
UPA3 3937	*J. L. MacFarland/W. Scott—Elvis Presley Music*	*47-9115/1967*

6/30, 7PM–12AM. Elvis vocal overdubs. MGM Studios Recording Stage

Elvis overdubbed vocals as follows: "City By Night" (2001), take 5; "Could I Fall In Love" (2002), take 4 (harmony vocal); "Old McDonald" (2010), take 2 (beginning only). On July 14, instrumental overdubs were done on "City By Night" (2001) and "Baby, If You'll Give Me All Of Your Love" (2007) at the MGM Studios Recording Stage.

Ever since the frustrating exercise of making the music for his first two movies, *Love Me Tender* and *Loving You,* Elvis had insisted on doing his soundtrack recording in a regular studio setting, not on a large, impersonal soundstage where he felt he couldn't perform at his best. Disgusted with yet another round of lackluster material provided by his own publishing companies, Elvis showed up late at Radio Recorders for the *Double Trouble* sessions; but this time the result was that MGM studio executives moved the next night's sessions to their own soundstage, saving money for themselves and for the film's eventual bottom line (in which Elvis and the Colonel too had a share). Elvis had long since learned from Colonel Tom to be mindful of his obligations, and he raised no explicit objections—but he could not have been pleased when he heard the sound of the recordings they were making. The soundstage had all the presence of a giant tin can. Poor miking and generally sloppy engineering produced a sound that might have worked for mono cinema playback, but scarcely for the work of a major recording artist. There was so much leakage into the vocal mike that it was impossible to mix the tapes properly, and the overdubbing of Elvis's vocal harmony on "Could I Fall In Love" created so much hiss it drowned out any detail achieved on the instrumental track recorded the night before at Radio Recorders. Being forced to record "Old MacDonald" was only the final indignity, and Elvis left, forcing the movie company to use an incomplete, seventh take as the master. The session concluded with the rerecording of a single with a title as long as the song was short—"Long Legged Girl (With A Short Dress On)," which ran, mercifully, for one minute, twenty-seven seconds.

The timing of record releases was now dictated by the movie release date, which meant that recording often preceded album or single issue by many months. In June 1966, as he began work on *Double Trouble,* his film *Frankie and Johnny,* whose soundtrack Elvis had recorded more than a year earlier, was only just hitting theaters. He had two more, *Paradise, Hawaiian Style* and *Spinout,* backed up behind it, which only confirmed the distance that had grown up between Elvis and his fans. The difference between the clean, classic, and well-crafted gospel album and the dated, pedestrian, poorly recorded soundtrack albums was like day and night. Elvis was thrilled about the recordings he'd done in Nashville, but where once his latest recordings would have hit the street practically the following day, now they would have to wait nine months, taking their place amid a procession of lackluster soundtrack efforts. And it was hardly surprising that those efforts were meeting with dwindling sales themselves. The failure of both the single and the album from *Frankie and Johnny* prompted a June release of "Love Letters" b/w "Come What May" from the May 1966 session; to save face, it was billed as a "vacation special," but at number nineteen it did little better than "Frankie And Johnny," with neither selling even half a million copies. The albums from the two films fared just as badly, turning up in the top twenty but selling under 300,000. When *Paradise, Hawaiian Style* was released in June, it met with sales of less than a quarter of a million copies, establishing a new low.

It was in this climate that Freddy Bienstock tried to organize material for yet another soundtrack session, *Easy Come, Easy Go,* in September. They were still following standard soundtrack wisdom: Each song was meant to fit a specific scene, rendering most previously commissioned work irrelevant. The first twelve songs Freddy submitted failed to impress even the Colonel, who was sensitive enough to Elvis's disillusionment that he was starting to take an interest himself. Normally the Colonel stayed out of decisions regarding music selection, but he was concerned over slumping sales, and he thought repertoire may have had something to do with it. Ever the determined plugger, Ben Weisman complained to the Colonel that he couldn't get the go-ahead (i.e., payment) from Freddy Bienstock to produce demos for the songs he'd written with Sid Wayne. Seizing the opportunity to raise the broader issue, Parker told Freddy that Elvis needed more material to choose from, and pushed him to have the demo sessions set up. Knowing that *Easy Come, Easy Go* featured scenes set in both a nightclub and a soul-saving revival, Bienstock took the precaution of pushing two well-known songs Hill & Range already controlled: Ray Charles's "Leave My Woman Alone" and Leiber and Stoller's "Saved," made famous by LaVern Baker. A backing track for "Leave My Woman Alone" was done, though for reasons unknown Elvis never recorded a vocal. Nor did he cut "Saved" during the *Easy Come* sessions— though he would return to the song again before too long, in a far more promising setting.

79. Soundtrack Sessions for Paramount's *Easy Come, Easy Go*
September 28–29, 1966: Paramount Studio Recording Stage, Hollywood

Paramount Producer: Joseph J. Lilley
Engineer: James Wright

Guitar: Scotty Moore
Guitar: Tiny Timbrell
Guitar, Organ, Harmonica: Charlie McCoy
Bass: Bob Moore
Drums: D. J. Fontana
Drums: Buddy Harman
Drums: Hal Blaine (A-E)
Drums: Curry Tjader (C,D,F,G)
Drums: Larry Bunker (E)

Percussion: Emil Radocchia (A, B)
Harpsichord: Michel Rubini
Trumpet: Mike Henderson (A-E)
Trumpet: Anthony Terran (D, F-H)
Trombone: Butch Parker (A-E)
Sax: Jerry Scheff (A-E)
Sax: Meredith Flory (D, F-H)
Sax: William Hood (D, F-H)
Vocals: The Jordanaires

9/28, 10–11:45AM, 1–6:15PM
AOVC-09 **Easy Come, Easy Go**
UPA3 3805 *Ben Weisman/Sid Wayne—Gladys Music*
BOVC-sp **I'll Take Love**
UPA3 3810 *Dolores Fuller/Mark Barkan—Elvis Presley Music*

Easy Come, Easy Go (EP)
EPA 4387/1967
Easy Come, Easy Go (EP)
EPA 4387/1967

7:30PM–12:45AM
COVC-22 **Sing You Children**
UPA3 3809 *Gerald Nelson/Fred Burch—Elvis Presley Music*

Easy Come, Easy Go (EP)
EPA 4387/1967

9/29, 1–3:30PM, 3:30–6:15PM
EOVC-13 **She's A Machine (movie version)**
Joy Byers—Elvis Presley Music
EOVC-15 **She's A Machine**
WPA1 8027 *Joy Byers—Elvis Presley Music*

Double Features
66558-2/1995
Flaming Star
PRS 279/1969

6:15–7:45PM
DOVC-12 **The Love Machine**
UPA3 3806 *G. Nelson/F. Burch/C. Taylor—Elvis Presley Music*

Easy Come, Easy Go (EP)
EPA 4387/1967

9PM–2:05AM
FOVC-12 **Yoga Is As Yoga Does**
UPA3 3807 *Gerald Nelson/Fred Burch—Elvis Presley Music*
GOC-05 (tr) **You Gotta Stop**
UPA3 3808 *Giant/Baum/Kaye—Elvis Presley Music*

Easy Come, Easy Go (EP)
EPA 4387/1967
Easy Come, Easy Go (EP)
EPA 4387/1967

The master of "I'll Take Love" (BOVC) is spliced from takes 4 and 8, with a pickup take 3.

Bad news travels fast in Hollywood. When Hal Wallis heard Elvis had given in to MGM and recorded on their soundstage, he saw no reason not to demand the same on his own picture, *Easy Come, Easy Go*. He even managed to set up daytime recording sessions, something Elvis would never choose to do himself. The number of songs by now was reduced from seven to six, and the two R&B numbers had been ditched in favor of some late arrivals from the songwriting staff. Only one of the Wayne and Weisman demos had gotten any spark from Elvis—a stab at the title song, which had last been submitted for *Double Trouble* with different lyrics. The only other thing that appealed to Elvis was a pretty hymn, "We Call On Him," which he loved but ultimately rejected because it did not have the revival spirit called for by the script. None of the material inspired either Elvis or the musicians, and they all had their difficulties both singing and playing. By the second day it was obvious Elvis detested "She's A Machine," so after he left the session players cut tracks for two possible replacements, resurrecting "Leave My Woman Alone" and a Giant, Baum, and Kaye reject, "Stop, You're Wrong." Eventually Elvis selected the latter, had Red West adjust the lyrics, and the song went into the soundtrack as "You Gotta Stop."

History would bear it out: The *Easy Come, Easy Go* material represented the newest all-time low for Elvis's recording career. Up until then virtually any Elvis release was guaranteed a certain level of success at least among his many loyal fans, but in the United States the six-song EP *Easy Come, Easy Go* never even made the charts and ultimately sold little more than thirty-thousand units—the surest testimony to the inevitable collapse of the soundtrack program. This would be the last movie Elvis made for Hal Wallis and Paramount, and the last extended-play release of his career.

There was more discouraging news when the "Spinout" single, which coupled "All That I Am" with the title song, climbed no higher than number forty. Sales of the *Spinout* album, even with "Tomorrow Is A Long Time," "Down In The Alley," and "I'll Remember You" thrown in as added bonuses, fared only a little better, and did nothing to salve everyone's disappointment. On top of all that, Red West's Christmas song never made it into the top 100.

At the start of the new year, on January 2, 1967, a new business arrangement between Elvis and the Colonel went into effect. Between falling record sales and movies whose grosses were

- 2 -

PARAMOUNT PICTURES CORPORATION

RECORDING INFORMATION

RECORDING DIVISION

MUSIC DEPARTMENT

PRODUCTION: "EASY COME, EASY GO" (CONT.)   DATE:

SCORER OR MUS. ADV.:

PERMANENT	TEMP.	REMARKS: Title of musical number, tracks used in temp, dubbed units, tracks intercut and point of splice, etc.
		"SHE'S A MACHINE"
		(This song was not used in picture)
EOVC-13		Elvis, Orch. and Jordanaires
	ETDX10-1)	
	ETDX11-1) Playback records with new lyrics (Not used)
		"YOGA IS AS YOGA DOES"
		Elvis, Orch. and Jordanaires
FOVC-12	PTD-1	Playback record NOT used
	FTDX-1	Playback record used (Shortened version)
		"YOU GOTTA STOP" - A.K.A. "STOP YOU'RE WRONG AGAIN"
		Orch. and Jordanaires
GOC-5	GTD-1	Playback record used (With Elvis' voice added)
		"LEAVE MY WOMAN ALONE"
		ng was not used in picture)

too low for the "profit-sharing" agreements to kick in, the Presley organization had witnessed a dramatic drop in revenue over the past few years. The Colonel's new arrangement preserved the original split of 75 percent to Elvis, 25 percent to the Colonel on all contractually guaranteed record royalty and movie income, but it regarded everything beyond the guarantee as a "joint venture" on which Parker would receive a fifty-fifty split. In other words, the Colonel got half of everything defined as "profits." The new deal gave the Colonel new incentive to seek out extra merchandising opportunities, for which he'd thereafter receive half the income. On the other hand, it diminished his interest in negotiating guarantees from RCA or the movie companies; the lower the guarantees, after all, the earlier his own profits would kick in. By the end of 1966 it was clear that Elvis had fallen from the artistic and commercial heights of his first ten years in show business, and the Colonel argued forcefully that it would take an even greater promotional effort on his part to maintain, let alone improve, their income. Elvis had no choice but to accept; the Colonel, on his side, understood that his new strengthened position was to be used—not abused.

80. Soundtrack Recordings for United Artists' *Clambake*
February 21–23, 1967: RCA's Studio B, Nashville

Movie Company Producer: Jeff Alexander
A&R/Producer: Felton Jarvis
Engineer: Jim Malloy

Guitar: Scotty Moore
Guitar: Chip Young
Guitar, Harmonica: Charlie McCoy
Bass: Bob Moore
Drums: D. J. Fontana
Drums: Buddy Harman
Piano: Floyd Cramer
Piano: Hoyt Hawkins
Steel Guitar: Pete Drake

Sax: Norm Ray
Vocals: The Jordanaires
Vocals: Millie Kirkham

Overdubbed:
Vocals: Ray Walker (duet on 8444)
Vocals: June Page, Priscilla Hubbard, Dolores Edgin, Millie Kirkham (2753)

2/21, 6PM–6AM

UPA3 8447-09	**The Girl I Never Loved** *Randy Starr—Gladys Music*	**Clambake** *LSP 3893/1967*
UPA3 8448-06	**How Can You Lose What You Never Had** *Ben Weisman/Sid Wayne—Gladys Music*	**Clambake** *LSP 3893/1967*
WPA1 2501-20	**You Don't Know Me** *Walker/Arnold—Bresmer Music*	**Double Features** *66362-2/1994*
UPA3 8445-08	**A House That Has Everything** *Sid Tepper/Roy C. Bennett—Gladys Music*	**Clambake** *LSP 3893/1967*

UPA3 8444-na (tr) Who Needs Money?   **Clambake**
  Randy Starr—Gladys Music   *LSP 3893/1967*
UPA4 2753-na (tr) Confidence   **Clambake**
  Sid Tepper/Roy C. Bennett—Gladys Music   *LSP 3893/1967*
UPA3 8446-na (tr) Hey, Hey, Hey   **Clambake**
  Joy Byers—Elvis Presley Music   *LSP 3893/1967*
UPA3 8443-na (tr) Clambake   **Clambake**
  Ben Weisman/Sid Wayne—Gladys Music   *LSP 3893/1967*

2/23. Session hours unknown

WPA5 2554-04   Clambake (reprise)   **Double Features**
  Ben Weisman/Sid Wayne—Gladys Music   *66362-2/1994*

Sequencing from T. Rolf - 9/11/67 -
via phone

1. CLAMBAKE (Sparse vocal behind credits)
2. WHO NEEDS MONEY
3. HOUSE WITH EVERYTHING
4. CONFIDENCE
5. CLAMBAKE (Reprise)
6. YOU DON'T KNOW ME
7. HEY, HEY, HEY (same as SANDPAPER SONG)
8. THE GIRL I NEVER LOVED

*HOW CAN YOU LOSE (WHAT YOU NEVER HAD)

*Not used in picture - couldn't find a
spot for it - Mr. Rolf thinks it is
the best song of the lot and would like
to see it included in the album!

On 2/23 Elvis also overdubbed "Hey, Hey, Hey" (8446), take 13; "Clambake" (8443), take 10; "Who Needs Money?" (8444), cue overdub; "Confidence" (8450, number changed to UPA4 2753 at overdubbing session); Ray Walker overdubbed his part of the duet on "Who Needs Money?" (8444) on the same day. On 3/6 Elvis rerecorded the first verse of "Confidence" (8450/2753) and an insert vocal on "Who Needs Money?" (8444) at Annex Studios (formerly Radio Recorders) in Hollywood.

Whatever the next soundtrack might turn out to be, Elvis had lost interest in it before he even started. In early February his attention had turned to the Circle G, a farm he had just purchased in north Mississippi, where he and the guys had begun spending almost all their time. In his enthusiasm Elvis spent the better part of $100,000 purchasing farm equipment, televisions, pickup trucks, housetrailers, televisions for the housetrailers, more pickup trucks, and more housetrailers. Entertaining the thought of settling there with friends and family, he momentarily turned his back on Hollywood and the obligations the Colonel kept badgering him about, sending word that he had a "sore behind" from too much horseback riding. After a week's postponement he finally reported to RCA's building in Nashville, on February 21 at 5:30 P.M. for the obligatory medical examination at the start of the new picture, *Clambake*. Thirty minutes later he attended the music meeting and finalized song selection before walking over to the studio to begin recording. Felton Jarvis was present that night along with the usual Nashville musicians, but interest and energy had gone AWOL. Even a proven classic like Eddy Arnold's "You Don't Know Me" eluded Elvis and the band through twenty takes. Elvis went home and stayed home the next night while the band laid down tracks for him to overdub on the third and final evening.

81. Studio Sessions for RCA
March 20, 1967: RCA's Studio B, Nashville

A&R Producer: Felton Jarvis
Engineer: Jim Malloy

Guitar: Scotty Moore
Guitar: Chip Young
Guitar: Grady Martin
Bass: Bob Moore
Drums: D. J. Fontana
Drums: Buddy Harman

Piano: David Briggs
Steel Guitar: Pete Drake
Harmonica: Charlie McCoy
Vocals: The Jordanaires
Vocals: Millie Kirkham

10AM–1PM

UPA4 2263-na **Suppose**
Sylvia Dee/George Goehring—Gladys Music

From Nashville To Memphis*
66160/1993

The above session was called to overdub background for a piano-and-vocal home recording made by Elvis and Charlie Hodge.
*The full title of this set is *Elvis: From Nashville to Memphis: The Essential '60s Masters, Volume I.*

At home, surrounded by his friends, Elvis still thrived on music. He practiced away on his new electric bass, listened to records, even sent the guys out to the record store to pick up the entire top 100. When they weren't working on a film or riding horses down on the ranch they often sang all night, returning again and again to old favorites while working up new material. "Suppose," a submission from Dee and Goehring for *Easy Come, Easy Go,* had caught Elvis's attention, and Charlie Hodge learned the piano part. Together they had taped a vocal-and-piano rendition on Red's semiprofessional equipment, and Elvis was encouraged enough by the results to send the tape to Felton Jarvis. Felton, definitely disheartened by all the recent failures, obediently booked musicians and studio for a three-hour session to overdub a new background. The result wasn't far different from the sound of "Indescribably Blue," but it met with little enthusiasm, and the whole idea was soon abandoned.

Elvis's disaffection with moviemaking presented the Colonel with new problems. The start of *Clambake* had to be postponed when Elvis claimed to have hurt himself tripping over a cord; he finally arrived so overweight that all the costumes needed to be let out. If this kind of unprofessional behavior was troubling in and of itself, though, even more alarming was its possible cause: Elvis's growing dependency on prescription medication. The Colonel knew he had to effect whatever changes he could, and with his new partnership role in place he moved in and insisted on a shake-up within Elvis's circle of friends. And there were other time bombs ticking away: Elvis's ongoing relationship with Priscilla Beaulieu, who had been living at Graceland for the past five years, could have exploded at any moment into a scandal. Once a May 1 wedding date was set the Colonel was left to get back to his regular business—that of shoring up Elvis's cash flow enough to support the singer, his growing retinue, and his extravagant spending habits.

He wasn't getting much help from record sales. "Indescribably Blue" reached number thirty-three, while "Long Legged Girl" sank at number sixty-three. The gospel album, *How Great Thou Art* joined the twelve new songs with the 1965 hit "Crying In The Chapel"; "It's great," *Billboard* raved, but it peaked at number eighteen, no better than *Spinout* and a little lower than *His Hand In Mine* had done on its first release. Nevertheless, it was worth noting that the album's sales had been achieved without a new movie or even a supporting single. While record company support and the Colonel's promotion undoubtedly helped, *How Great Thou Art* was succeeding almost entirely on word-of-mouth—and the dedication Elvis had put into it.

The Paramount movie deal was over, but Elvis's contract with MGM was still in effect; there were more movies to churn out, more lousy soundtracks to record, more hours of tedium to swallow. The new film, *Speedway,* was as predictable as ever; the only moment of musical interest for Elvis was a chance to rerecord "Suppose." He and Charlie made two different versions, but in the end the song—the only one he cared about—was cut from the film (although it stayed on the album). The remaining numbers were a bust; "There Ain't Nothing Like A Song" was a reject from *Spinout*. There wasn't enough material for a *Speedway* album, and none of the songs were strong enough to stand as a single. In retrospect, perhaps the high point of the session was meeting the billionaire politician Nelson Rockefeller, who had come into the studio to record an album of patriotic recitations.

Meeting Nelson Rockefeller at the Speedway *session, June 20, 1967*

82. Soundtrack Recordings for MGM's *Speedway*
June 20–21, 1967: MGM Studios, Hollywood

MGM Producer: Jeff Alexander
Engineer: n/a

Guitar: Chip Young
Guitar: Tiny Timbrell (1022–1028)
Guitar: Tommy Tedesco (1029–1030)
Bass: Bob Moore
Drums: Buddy Harman
Drums: D. J. Fontana
Piano: Larry Muhoberac

Piano: Charlie Hodge (1027–1028)
Steel Guitar: Pete Drake
Sax: Boots Randolph
Trumpet: Charlie McCoy
Vocals: The Jordanaires

Overdubbed:
Vocals: Nancy Sinatra (1022)

6/20, 7PM–12AM, 1–4AM

2001-06	**There Ain't Nothing Like A Song**	**Speedway**
WPA1 1022	*Joy Byers/Bob Johnston—Elvis Presley Music*	*LSP 3989/1968*
2003-01	**Your Time Hasn't Come Yet Baby (movie version)**	
WPA5 2555	*Hirschhorn/Kasha—Elvis Presley Music*	
2004-06	**Your Time Hasn't Come Yet Baby**	**Single B-side**
WPA1 1023	*Hirschhorn/Kasha—Elvis Presley Music*	*47-9547/1968*
2005-03	**Five Sleepy Heads**	**Speedway**
WPA1 1024	*Sid Tepper/Roy C. Bennett—Gladys Music*	*LSP 3989/1968*
2006-06	**Who Are You?**	**Speedway**
WPA1 1025	*Sid Wayne/Ben Weisman—Gladys Music*	*LSP 3989/1968*
2007-04	**Speedway**	**Speedway**
WPA1 1026	*Glazer/Schlaks—Gladys Music*	*LSP 3989/1968*
2008-01	**Suppose (long version)**	**Double Features**
WPA1 1027	*Sylvia Dee/George Goehring—Gladys Music*	*66558-2/1995*
2009-07	**Suppose (short version)**	**Speedway**
WPA1 1028	*Sylvia Dee/George Goehring—Gladys Music*	*LSP 3989/1968*

6/21, 7–11PM

2010-sp	**Let Yourself Go**	**Single A-side**
WPA1 1029	*Joy Byers—Elvis Presley Music*	*47-9547/1968*
2011-07	**He's Your Uncle Not Your Dad**	**Speedway**
WPA1 1030	*Sid Wayne/Ben Weisman—Gladys Music*	*LSP 3989/1968*

More than a year had now passed since Elvis had made any real music—since he'd taken control of a session. In the interim four soundtracks had been recorded. He didn't care for them, and as time passed, he hardly cared *about* them anymore—a feeling increasingly shared by the record-buying public. As 1966 came to a close, bizarrely, that was the one way in which he and the audience were completely in sync.

*With Felton Jarvis (above)
and steel guitar wizard
Pete Drake (left) at the
"Guitar Man" sessions:
September 1967*

1967-68

TRYING TIMES

Back on the MGM lot, the Colonel was in the midst of his customary flurry of exploitations. Without losing any momentum he had to deal with *Speedway,* Elvis's ninth film for MGM, set up promotions for the upcoming release of *Clambake,* and get the finishing touches for the *Clambake* soundtrack album taken care of. The *Clambake* sessions had been something of a fiasco; they had yielded only eight songs, and two of them had already been edited out of the film, including the best of the lot, "How Can You Lose What You Never Had." Elvis still had to resing parts of "Confidence," and he was so dissatisfied with his performance on Eddy Arnold's "You Don't Know Me" that he wanted to rerecord it. If pressed he might have admitted he was unhappy with the lot of them, but at least this was a song of some substance, and he hated to give it short shrift.

There would be no movie soundtrack EP this time; the failure of the *Easy Come, Easy Go* EP had proven that the format was no longer viable. They needed new recordings to fill out a long-playing album, but when would they be able to get Elvis back into the studio? MGM was already pushing to start recording sessions for the next picture, *Stay Away, Joe,* as soon as filming on *Speedway* was completed—possibly as early as August 4. Elvis was busy working on the *Speedway* soundtrack, and the Colonel knew no good could come from forcing him into the recording studio on weekends.

Still the principal problem was material. There were plenty of songs to pick from, but Elvis rejected most of them out of hand, and Freddy Bienstock didn't seem able to come up with any good new sources. The fact was, with slumping record sales, writing for an Elvis movie was no longer as attractive as it had once been—especially when there was no guarantee a song would even be used.

The idea of a new RCA studio session, on the other hand, seemed more promising. The Colonel had spoken with Elvis, and Tom Diskin had advised Freddy that Elvis had already chosen a number of songs he wanted to cut. The material he had in mind was a combination of recent hits and older standbys, many of which Elvis had suggested before; left to his own devices, Elvis still chose his repertoire the same way he had since the Sun Records days—drawing on a lifetime of listening to everything in the air around him. Many of the songs came from records he'd loved for years: Della Reese's version of "After Loving You," Ray Peterson's "The Wonder Of You," "The Fool," "Hello, Josephine," "Pledging My Love," and Roy Hamilton's "Don't Let Go."

There were country songs, too: "Just Call Me Lonesome," "Ramblin' Rose," "From A Jack To A King." A few of these were already in Freddy's publishing catalog, but it was still his job to try to make deals for as many of the rest as he could before Elvis actually cut the songs. Of Freddy's new titles only Ben Weisman's religious number, "We Call On Him," had inspired Elvis, but Lamar Fike of Hill & Range's Nashville office had come up with a number of songs by two new songwriters, A. L. "Doodle" Owens and Eddie Rabbitt, including Owens's "Singing Tree" and Rabbitt's "Inherit The Wind."

When the filming of *Speedway* was delayed and the recording session for *Stay Away, Joe* was pushed back, the Colonel saw his opening and scheduled the new non-soundtrack session for the nights of August 22 and 23, getting Harry Jenkins to book RCA's Studio A in Hollywood. Felton Jarvis and engineer Jim Malloy would fly in, while former LA session guitarist Billy Strange put together the band and wrote arrangements for the chosen songs. Elvis kept adding to his list of suggestions, including Chuck Berry's "Brown Eyed Handsome Man" and "Too Much Monkey Business," Jimmy Reed's "Baby What You Want Me To Do," Clyde McPhatter's "Without Love," and a pop-gospel number called "I Was Born About Ten Thousand Years Ago," for which Freddy could find neither publisher nor proper lyric sheets. Then, as the date approached, Elvis got excited by a new song he'd heard on the radio—"Guitar Man" by the guitar whiz Jerry Reed, another RCA artist. Hill & Range was asked to make a deal on it, but the request arrived while Freddy was on vacation—a piece of bad timing that would resurface as events progressed.

Just days before the session, Billy Strange had in hand what he hoped would be the final list of songs. To avoid musical chaos and help ensure he'd be able to record the band, the backup singers, and the brass section all at the same time, he wanted to make sure that they had arrangements written out for each player. The list was down to eleven songs: "We Call On Him," "Here Comes Tomorrow," "Ramblin' Rose," "From A Jack To A King," "After Loving You," "Guitar Man," "And I Tell The Sea," "Brown Eyed Handsome Man," "I'll Never Find Another You," "Tonight I Won't Be There," and "Baby What You Want Me To Do." But the selections kept changing, almost on a daily basis—or perhaps it was just that different people were working with different lists. In any event, on the day before the sessions were to begin Tom Diskin was informed for the first time that Elvis's music companies couldn't make deals on five of the songs on the so-called final list. In the end, none of it would matter.

83. Studio Sessions for RCA—Canceled
August 22–23, 1967: RCA's Studio A, Hollywood

A&R/Producer: Felton Jarvis
Arranger: Billy Strange
Engineer: Jim Malloy

Guitar: Al Casey
Guitar: Dennis Budimir
Guitar: Jerry Cole
Bass: Chuck Berghofer
Bass: Carol Kaye
Drums: Hal Blaine
Piano: Larry Knechtal
Vibes, Tambourine: Gary Coleman

Trumpet: Roy Caton
Trumpet: Ollie Mitchell
Trombone: Dick Hyde
Trombone: Lou McCreary
Vocals: B. J. Baker, Gwen Johnson, Banji
Carmichael, Ron Hickland, Bob Tiboe,
Thurl Ravenscroft, Gene Merlino

The sessions were booked to start each day at 7PM; because they were canceled at such short notice, all musicians were paid for three hours each night.

On the afternoon of August 22 engineer Jim Malloy arrived at RCA's Hollywood studio from a vacation at his parents' home in Des Moines; Felton followed, from Nashville, shortly thereafter. Before they even had a chance to get settled though, Harry Jenkins joined them in the studio with the astonishing news that the sessions had been canceled. Richard Davis, one of Elvis's men, had accidentally killed a pedestrian, a Japanese gardener, while driving one of Elvis's cars. Always determined to keep his boy away from bad publicity or legal trouble, the Colonel had put Elvis on a plane to Vegas immediately, putting him safely out of state—and throwing cold water over RCA's recording plans.

With Elvis and his party settled into their rooms at the Aladdin, the Colonel was left with the same problem he had begun the summer with: how to get enough additional material to fill out the *Clambake* album. During the last few months sales and chart placement for the *Double Trouble* soundtrack had been dismal, stalling out at number forty-seven on the album charts. With nothing else to release they'd been reduced to putting out two 1961 recordings as the new single release—"There's Always Me" and "Judy"—but that 45 had done no better than "Long Legged Girl" on the singles charts. It didn't take sophisticated analysis to see that quality was the key: By way of contrast, the 1966 gospel album *How Great Thou Art* had charted well and continued to sell strongly. The signs were clear: Elvis simply needed to get back into the studio with strong new material. There were still soundtrack obligations to get worked out, not to mention coming up with religious material for an Easter release. But the number-one priority was to get Elvis back on the right musical track.

From Las Vegas Elvis continued home to Memphis, making it logical to reschedule the recording session for Nashville. Felton Jarvis was pleased to be back on home territory, and to be back in charge. He had struggled through the *Clambake* sessions, and now by a stroke of fate had escaped having his position challenged by Billy Strange. He intended to make the most of his opportunity; all he needed now, after the success of the gospel album, was "the real big hit single" that had escaped him with "Love Letters" (number nineteen) and "Indescribably Blue" (number thirty-three).

84. Studio Sessions for RCA
September 10–11, 1967: RCA's Studio B, Nashville

A&R/Producer: Felton Jarvis
Engineer: Jim Malloy

Guitar: Scotty Moore
Guitar: Jerry Reed (2765–2766)
Guitar: Harold Bradley
Guitar: Chip Young
Bass: Bob Moore
Drums: D. J. Fontana
Drums: Buddy Harman
Piano: Elvis Presley (2773)

Piano: Floyd Cramer
Organ: Hoyt Hawkins (2767–2769)
Organ, Guitar, Harmonica: Charlie McCoy
Sax: Boots Randolph
Steel Guitar: Pete Drake
Vocals: The Jordanaires
Vocals: Millie Kirkham

9/10, 6PM–12AM

UPA4 2765-12	**Guitar Man**	**Clambake**
	Jerry Reed—Vector Music	*LSP 3893/1967*
UPA4 2766-11	**Big Boss Man**	**Single A-side**
	Smith/Dixon—Conrad Publ. Co.	*47-9341/1967*

1–5:30AM

UPA4 2767-21	**Mine**	**Speedway**
	Sid Tepper/Roy C. Bennett—Gladys Music	*LSP 3989/1968*
UPA4 2768-13	**Singing Tree**	
	A. L. Owens/Solberg—Elvis Presley Music	
UPA4 2769-01	**Just Call Me Lonesome**	**Clambake**
	Griffin—Valley Pub. Inc.	*LSP 3893/1967*

9/11, 6–9PM, 9:30PM–12:30AM

UPA4 2770-07	**Hi-Heel Sneakers**	**Single B-side**
	Higginbotham—Medal Music	*47-9425/1968*
UPA4 2771-01	**You Don't Know Me**	**Single B-side**
	Walker/Arnold—Bresmer Music	*47-9341/1967*
UPA4 2772-09	**We Call On Him**	**Single B-side**
	Fred Karger/Ben Weisman/Sid Wayne—Gladys Music	*47-9600/1968*
UPA4 2773-sp	**You'll Never Walk Alone**	**Single A-side**
	Rodgers/Hammerstein—Williamson Music	*47-9600/1968*

1–3:30AM

UPA4 2774-05   **Singing Tree**   **Clambake**

A. L. Owens/Solberg—Elvis Presley Music   *LSP 3893/1967*

The master take of "Guitar Man" (2765) included a fade-out jam on "What'd I Say," first released on the 1993 set *From Nashville To Memphis.* The master of "Hi-Heel Sneakers" (2770) was edited from five minutes down to 2:44 for its original record release. The master of "You'll Never Walk Alone" (2773) is spliced from takes 8 and 1. The master of "Singing Tree" (2774) features an overdubbed Elvis harmony vocal.

For "Guitar Man," the song Elvis had picked up on the radio in LA, Felton Jarvis told Elvis that if he wanted that distinctive guitar sound he loved so much on the record they'd have to get Jerry Reed himself for the session. By the time they were able to track Reed down on a fishing trip on the Cumberland River outside of Nashville, he barely had time to pick up his equipment before driving straight to the studio, unshaven and in clothes that made him look like an Alabama wildman. There were no dress codes at Elvis sessions, though; Reed just had to take a little kidding from a T-shirted Felton and a trim-looking Elvis, who was wearing a casual black suit and a bright shirt with the top buttons opened. "We're rolling. 'Guitar Man,' take one," Felton called out as an obviously flustered Jerry Reed ran through guitar licks trying to get his fingers up to speed. "Phew, I haven't played all weekend," he excused himself, talking to everybody and nobody in particular. "Your house is a mess," Felton joked, and Elvis laughed along. Elvis seemed as fascinated by the man as by the music, yielding center stage as Jerry explained that there was no way to do all the guitar parts from his own original record at one time. "It's going to sound like a room full of spastics— or something." They adjusted the tempo and length of the intro; Jerry asked Bob Moore to count it off, then did it himself, made a number of mistakes, and concluded: "I may wander off into the parking lot. Stay with me, or I'll get with you—sometime tonight." By take five, though, the song began to come together. Directing along with Felton, Jerry suggested they end the record with a fade, and Felton prodded his singer on: "Sing the living stuff out of it, El." Elvis relaxed, started cutting up himself, and by take ten the whole band was cooking. Everyone seemed caught up in the moment as the song drifted into a jam, the band taking on power as Elvis started singing "What'd I Say." By take twelve they had an energetic, gutsy country record; Jerry added his second guitar part, and Felton pushed on.

"Big Boss Man" was probably an even better Jimmy Reed selection than the original choice, "Baby What You Want Me To Do." Jerry Reed remained on guitar, Charlie's harp and Boots's sax added a bluesy flavor to the proceedings, and right away they hit a groove. Any tension that may have carried over from early in the evening was gone by now, and Felton's enthusiasm was infectious. "Starting to feel real good. Let it all hang out," he cheered. "That's a gas, man. Go apeshit!" Between takes the room buzzed with energy, and by midnight they had a second song in the can. The sound was different from anything Elvis had ever done before, and worlds away from most anything coming out of Nashville at the time. The recordings had an acoustic, guitar-driven sound that was crisp and vibrant, but also an R&B funkiness unknown to country. The engineering was immaculate; what could have sounded like a cacophonic blast of jamming came off instead with an intricate, fiery precision.

Jerry Reed had stayed on for "Big Boss Man," but with a change in the material he got ready to leave. At Freddy's request, Lamar approached Jerry to make the usual publishing arrangements—but this time, he found, they'd put the cart before the horse. Reed just wouldn't give up any of his writer's share, and with such a terrific take already in the can, he had little incentive to give in. With Elvis himself unwilling to intervene Freddy was stuck, his oversight painfully apparent to Tom Diskin, the Colonel's representative in the control room.

After a roaring start to the evening, the session took a more familiar turn with "Mine," an average contribution from two of Freddy's staff writers, Sid Tepper and Roy C. Bennett. The song had been rattling around for years, having been a long-standing candidate for 1965's *Paradise, Hawaiian Style* before it was dropped in favor of "This Is My Heaven." Freddy had resubmitted it for this session along with other offerings from the same team, a handful of tunes by Wayne and Weisman, seven Giant/Baum/Kaye numbers, and two numbers Elvis had requested, "Power Of My Love" and "Greensleeves"—now transformed into "Evergreen," but still four months away from being recorded as "Stay Away." After four hapless attempts at "Mine" Elvis uncharacteristically asked Felton for a backing track, but by take eight he was back singing with the band. Felton urged "togetherness," but with no rhythmic frame to cling to everyone struggled separately through twenty-one attempts, emerging with an insubstantial performance—pretty enough, but slight.

Lamar Fike of Hill & Range was still looking for his first big hit with Elvis. "Indescribably Blue," cut the year before, hadn't done as well as he'd expected. This time he brought material from his two new writers, Eddie Rabbitt's "That's How You Want Me To Be" and "Inherit The Wind," and Doodle Owens's "Singing Tree." It took thirteen takes before they gave up on "Singing Tree," unable to work out an arrangement. The rhythm track dragged, and even with the dependable Jordanaires (a trio now, with Hoyt Hawkins sitting out to take the organ) adding their vocal wash to the record, they were forced to move on. "Just Call Me Lonesome," one of the few survivors from the aborted August session, was an old country standard that everyone in the room must have known. Elvis suggested a change of drum figure for D. J. at the outset, and take one flowed effortlessly, as Elvis soared over a straightforward country track, flavored by Pete Drake's steel. Although clearly they had a master, Felton wanted to continue on. "Hit those first [notes] like you're mean, or scared of them," he urged. Drake knew just what to do, but after a few tries they settled on the first good take, and brought the night to a close at 5:30 A.M.

It was Chip Young, or maybe Harold Bradley, who suggested "Hi-Heel Sneakers" as a good lead-in to the second night. No one intended to go behind Freddy's back in making the recommendation; it just seemed like a good idea. The song was no more than a jam, really, and even with Felton encouraging them to pick up the tempo, it ran on for five minutes, at least two minutes longer than a single. The record's hard-romping beat harked back to 1960's "Reconsider Baby" and "Down In The Alley" from Felton's first session with Elvis; it had a raunchy barroom sound, with Charlie McCoy's harp wailing high over Boots's sax. Best of all, Elvis was clearly enjoying himself, throwing in ad-libs and calling for the band to "do the mess around" before the first solo. On the next verse they all cut loose, with Charlie's bluesy fills, Harold Bradley's unusual electrified sitar sound, and Floyd's piano completing the audio picture. Even when he'd run out of lyrics Elvis scatted right along with the horn riff Boots and Charlie were playing; then he came back for another verse, with Buddy Harman hammering the offbeat on the cymbal, before wrapping it up: "All right, take it home, baby, take it home."

The tension over publishing was coming out into the open. Loud enough for Freddy to hear, Bob Moore playfully remarked that he'd heard Lamar Fike had missed a chance to pick up the rights on Bobbie Gentry's enormous hit, "Ode To Billy Joe." Pressing the point, Harold Bradley hit the opening lick of Gentry's song, and Elvis chimed in with his best Bobbie Gentry voice: "Well I was out choppin' cotton, and my brother was baling hay," before cheerfully launching into what became the master of "Hi-Heel Sneakers." No sooner had they finished than Freddy's voice came through the door of the little office where he was sitting: "Lamar?" The room roared with laughter.

Next Elvis turned back to "You Don't Know Me," the Eddy Arnold and Ray Charles cover he'd tried at the *Clambake* session. Elvis focused in on it during a brief rehearsal, with Felton cheering him on: "Go home with it," the producer said. "God almighty, it's fine." As with "Just Call Me Lonesome," the first take, with its safe arrangement, eventually became the master; they tried it again, but before too long it was clear that they'd already done the job.

The Easter religious single was still a must, and Karger, Wayne, and Weisman's "We Call On Him" seemed a graceful extension of the spirit of the previous song. The soft piano and bass intro was traced over with the faint sound of a mandolin, while the Jordanaires's full quartet sound, a cellolike steel guitar, and Millie Kirkham's soaring soprano gave the song a delicate coloration that bore witness to the controlled mastery of the players. Elvis's voice, too, had that note of graceful sincerity that made his early '60s recordings so moving, even when the material was not up to par. "We Call On Him" was simple but memorable, as much a pop ballad as a hymn, and it was a worthy choice for the next year's Easter release.

As the evening progressed, Elvis continued to sprinkle spontaneous suggestions in with the preplanned material—a welcome change from the locked-in soundtrack sessions. "You'll Never Walk Alone," in versions by Roy Hamilton and others, was a song Elvis loved and sang frequently at home; now, as he did so often, Elvis sat down at the piano and dived into the song in full voice, hammering away at the keys in his staccato style. Elvis was lost in the music, in a private moment, and Jim Malloy knew he'd have to live with the loud piano leaking into the vocal microphone if he wanted to capture the performance. The band fell in wherever they could, and as fast as they could, working out parts in their heads as they played along. Felton knew enough not to disturb his artist, and sat back to see where it all would go.

It went just where Elvis wanted it to, as the singer began transforming his sudden inspiration into a delicate group performance. He asked for an introductory figure on acoustic guitar, which Harold Bradley provided. Bob Moore contributed a stabilizing beat on the double bass, and an organ was added for underlying color. The Jordanaires, of course, knew where to fit in. After finishing the first run-through Elvis started from the top again without the slightest break, improving the drama of the song, accepting the challenge of its range and the previous achievements of some of his greatest heroes. The actual moment may have been improvised, but its foundations were in Elvis's endless hours of gospel singing with friends at home and in the studio. The second take was another extended version, with Elvis throwing himself into the ending, trying to define both the vocal and piano conclusion to the song. They kept going. Millie tried out a part, the drummers came up with percussion ideas, Harold Bradley redefined the guitar runs, and they slowly moved from a jam into a regular recording process. On take eight Elvis's voice cracked on one of the high notes, but Felton knew they already had the elements of a magnificent performance on tape.

With Buddy and Harold still practicing and Elvis listening in the control room, they agreed to go on to the remake of "Singing Tree" before the night was through—much to Lamar's relief. Now that the song had been properly arranged, with a faster tempo and four guitar parts, there was a noticeable improvement; Elvis did the harmony vocal himself, and in less than an hour—by 3:30 A.M.—they were all on their way home.

Mission accomplished. Elvis had delivered exactly what the Colonel had promised RCA, and almost everyone left the session feeling pleased. With "Hi-Heel Sneakers," "Big Boss Man," and "Guitar Man," Felton had started recording the kind of rock 'n' roll he thought Elvis should have been doing all along. "Singing Tree" gave Lamar his break as a song publisher for Hill & Range's Nashville office. Only Freddy could have had misgivings: It was becoming clear that he was losing his ability to control what Elvis recorded, or even to supply songs worthy of the honor.

The Colonel was still holding to his policy that singles needed to be out at least four weeks prior to the album, so RCA quickly combined the rerecording of "You Don't Know Me" with the exciting new version of "Big Boss Man" and rushed it into the stores.

85. Soundtrack Recordings for MGM's *Stay Away, Joe*
October 1, 1967: RCA's Studio B, Nashville

MGM Producer: Jeff Alexander
A&R/Producer: Felton Jarvis
Engineer: Al Pachucki

Guitar: Scotty Moore
Guitar: Chip Young
Bass: Bob Moore
Drums: D. J. Fontana
Drums: Buddy Harman

Piano: Floyd Cramer
Harmonica: Charlie McCoy
Fiddle: Gordon Terry
Vocals: The Jordanaires

Session hours not available

U3KM 2246-sp (tr) Stay Away, Joe
Ben Weisman/Sid Wayne—Gladys Music

U3KM 2247-03 (tr) All I Needed Was The Rain
Sid Wayne/Ben Weisman—Gladys Music

U3KM 2248-05 Dominick
Sid Wayne/Ben Weisman—Gladys Music

Let's Be Friends
CAS 2408/1970
Flaming Star
PRS 279/1969
Double Features
66362/1994

The master of "Stay Away, Joe" (2246) is a splice of take 2 of an instrumental backing track with an added intro, and a vocal overdubbed later that day or the following day (exact times unknown). Before the backing-track recording began, though, Elvis sang nineteen takes with the band with no success. RCA accidentally released the live take 17 on the 1970 budget release *Almost In Love* (CAS 2440). The original demos of "Stay Away, Joe," and "All I Needed Was The Rain" were performed by Glen Campbell.

The next movie, *Stay Away, Joe,* cast Elvis in a Western comedy that called for only three songs. None of the usual going back and forth with demos had taken place, and Elvis arrived in the studio in Nashville, on October 1, faced with the fact that the film's producer, Jeff Alexander, had already chosen the numbers—all written by the tireless team of Ben Weisman and Sid Wayne. Elvis had already recorded about fifty of Weisman's songs, most of them for the soundtracks. More often than not it was Ben who came up with the truly peculiar movie songs ("A Dog's Life"), and this time he had managed to write "Dominick," a song written for Elvis to sing to a bull. Elvis hated the song—no surprise—and made Felton, who was in complete agreement, promise it would never appear on a record. He went through with it dutifully, but he was barely able to keep a straight face for the minute and forty-two seconds it took to complete a master. Neither of the other songs had any more commercial potential: The title cut was a nice-enough hoedown chant, and the bluesy "All I Needed Was The Rain" was pleasant but slight. For the first time in Elvis's film career it was looking as though there would be no soundtrack of any kind released along with the film, and the Colonel and MGM agreed they should get Elvis to record an additional song that could be played over the opening credits and released as a single. It took three months before he finally did.

As the year came to an end, despite the musical strides Elvis had made, there was only discouraging news in the charts. The latest single, pairing "Big Boss Man" and "You Don't Know Me," had sold a respectable 350,000 units, but split airplay held the two sides down to number thirty-eight and number forty-four, respectively. The *Clambake* album had been improved with five cuts from the September sessions, but it continued the downward trend; with sales of less than 200,000, it fared even more poorly than its miserable predecessor *Double Trouble*. Something drastic needed to be done, and the new year saw Elvis and the Colonel digging in to take care of business. What the Colonel had in mind amounted to going back to square one, where it had all begun: television. It was TV that had launched Elvis nationally in 1956, and welcomed him back in 1960 with the Sinatra special. Now, needing to pull another rabbit out of the hat, Parker began negotiations with NBC's Tom Sarnoff. His careful policy of underexposure had put him in the perfect position: Presley's first TV appearance in eight years would be a coup by anybody's estimation, so the Colonel felt comfortable demanding a sum far greater than his record sales alone would seem to warrant. What Parker and Sarnoff agreed to was a Christmas 1968 special, featuring all seasonal material; the inclusion of a new Elvis film as part of the deal brought the price to over one million dollars for his client.

Elvis, for his part, was thinking about music. He'd chosen "Guitar Man" as his new single, and he began the year by informing RCA that he wanted them to master his new single as loudly as they could—to get the maximum loudness in the groove of the record without sacrificing the bass, so it would come off as forcefully as possible on the radio. The second single off the *Clambake* album, it would be paired with another one of the nonmovie selections, an abbreviated version of the five-minute "Hi-Heel Sneakers" jam. And on January 15 he was scheduled to record material for the *Stay Away, Joe* single, which had once more sent Freddy scurrying for material. Again he turned to the old "Greensleeves" melody he knew Elvis liked, commissioning Tepper and Bennett for yet another set of new lyrics; this time they came up with a lyric called "Stay Away." Meanwhile Joy Byers had come up with a decent offering called "Goin' Home," which fit the spot lyrically; with these in hand the usual group assembled in Nashville.

86. Soundtrack Recordings for MGM's *Stay Away, Joe*
Studio Sessions for RCA
January 15–16, 1968: RCA's Studio B, Nashville

A&R/Producer: Felton Jarvis
Engineers: Al Pachucki (1/15), Bill Vandevort (1/16)

Guitar: Scotty Moore
Guitar: Jerry Reed
Guitar: Chip Young
Bass: Bob Moore
Drums: D. J. Fontana

Drums: Buddy Harman
Piano: Floyd Cramer
Steel Guitar: Pete Drake
Harmonica: Charlie McCoy
Vocals: The Jordanaires

1/15, 7PM–12AM
WPA4 1800-na **Too Much Monkey Business**
Chuck Berry—Arc Music

Flaming Star
PRS 279/1969

1–5AM
WPA1 1001-30 **Goin' Home**
Joy Byers—Elvis Presley Music

Speedway
LSP 3989/1968

1/16, 10PM–2AM
WPA1 1002-15 **Stay Away**
Sid Tepper/Roy C. Bennett

Single B-side
47-9465/1968

2AM–5AM
WPA4 1807-12 **U.S. Male**
Jerry Reed—Vector Music

Single A-side
47-9465/1968

Ever since the *How Great Thou Art* sessions in 1966, much of the material under consideration for each new session had been suggested by Elvis himself, but among his selections only a handful had actually been recorded. At the start of this session they turned to a Chuck Berry tune to get things going. With Jerry Reed on hand, replacing Grady Martin (who demurred on all-night sessions), they took "Too Much Monkey Business" at full speed, led by Jerry's aggressive, acoustic gut-string picking and supported by Buddy Harman's dry-sounding snare and Bob Moore's double bass way up front in the mix. It was the same feel they'd pulled off on "Guitar Man" and "Big Boss Man," just the kind of rocking country blues Elvis had always loved.

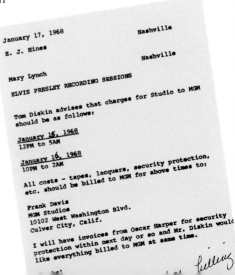

January 17, 1968   Nashville
E. J. Hines   Nashville

Mary Lynch
ELVIS PRESLEY RECORDING SESSIONS

Tom Diskin advises that charges for Studio to MGM should be as follows:

January 15, 1968
12PM to 5AM

January 16, 1968
10PM to 2AM

All costs - tapes, lacquers, security protection, etc. should be billed to MGM for above times to:

Frank Davis
MGM Studios
10102 West Washington Blvd.
Culver City, Calif.

I will have invoices from Oscar Harper for security protection within next day or so and Mr. Diskin would like everything billed to MGM at same time.

MGM's agenda had to be dealt with, so next up was Joy Byers's "Goin' Home." It was after midnight, concentration was slipping, and as the tape machine started Elvis and the guys were feeling loose and high-spirited. Over and over they failed to even get through the first verse without Elvis falling into fits of giggles, which were taken up by all. "I just don't know what I can do to improve this," he quipped, "except go home." The band plugged along, but now he was playing around, stringing them along through the song's intro before breaking into the first line of "Heartbreak Hotel." Snatches of other songs ran through his head: "Papa-oom-maw-maw," he sang; "I got a woman . . ." He faked them out every time. It took thirty tries to get a decent take of the song they were actually there for; by then it was 5:00 A.M. and there was no reason to go on.

Elvis had never been held accountable for the studio time he used, and by now he was used to wasting it: He lost his concentration, excused a poor performance with a wisecrack, or just broke into uncontrollable laughter with the close friends who were always nearby. If he failed to get a lot of work done one night, he usually made up for it the next. But this time it would be different. Right from the first take of "Stay Away," the new version of "Greensleeves," they had trouble staying on track. When one of the guitarists played some off chords, Elvis jumped in with well-meaning sarcasm: "Everybody's entitled to one stupid-ass mistake." The slow to medium tempo on the demo, with its halting rhythmic structure, was finally abandoned in favor of a decidedly up-tempo arrangement; Jerry Reed and Chip Young contributed some fine fingerpicking in the style they'd first developed touring as a duo earlier in the '60s. Still Elvis was distracted, edgy, throwing out inappropriate lines and swearing more than ever. Felton finally called a halt in his usual careful way—"That's a gas, El"—before wrapping it up with one last guitar part overdubbed on the spot by Jerry Reed.

Felton had begun the evening with optimism, with half a dozen matrix numbers ready, but they had gotten off to a late (10:00 P.M.) start and by two o'clock in the morning had only one song completed. According to Jerry Schilling, one of the friends who was there that evening, Elvis started getting frustrated and angry when he couldn't find anything suitable to record, and it wasn't until Chip Young asked Jerry Reed to play Elvis his talking blues, "U.S. Male," that they were able to get back to work. Freddy was never happy about song pitching in the hallways, but they needed a new single desperately; there was nothing he could do. For whatever reason—too many words to learn, too much guitar picking to get right—the song fell apart after the first take. Instead, they went right into "The Prisoner's Song," an old country weeper, but Elvis was in no mood for serious work and substituted lyrics that guaranteed the record could never see the light of day. "If you do two more," Felton broke in from the control room, "we'll have a whole party album." Somehow they were able to get back on track, giving "U.S. Male" a country feel with an upfront bass and some hot licks from Jerry. The two nights of work had produced only four songs, and certainly no decision was made then, but as it turned out this would be the last session with this particular band—and the last time Elvis would record in Nashville for at least thirty months.

87. Soundtrack Sessions for MGM's *Live A Little, Love A Little*
March 7, 1968: Western Recorders, Hollywood

Musical Conductor: Billy Strange
Engineer: Chuck Britz

Guitar: Joseph Gibbons
Guitar: Neil Levang
Guitar: Charles Britz
Guitar: Alvin Casey
Bass: Larry Knechtal
Bass: Charles Berghofer

Drums: Hal Blaine
Drums: Gary Coleman
Piano: Don Randi
Vocals: B. J. Baker, Sally Stevens,
Bob Tebow, John Bahler
Strings and Horns

7PM–3AM

2001-17	**Wonderful World**	**Flaming Star**
WPA1 5768	*Fletcher/Flett—Elvis Presley Music*	*PRS 279/1969*
2003-08	**Edge Of Reality**	**Single B-side**
WPA1 5769	*Giant/Baum/Kaye—Elvis Presley Music*	*47-9670/1968*
2004-16	**A Little Less Conversation**	**Single A-side**
WPA1 5767	*Billy Strange/Mac Davis—Gladys Music*	*47-9610/1968*
2006-04(tr)	**Almost In Love**	**Single B-side**
WPA1 6766	*Bonfa/Starr—Gladys Music*	*47-9610/1968*

Elvis's vocal overdub on "Almost In Love" (2012), take 3, was presumably recorded on 3/11. On the released version the intro was shortened.

Speedway was the last of the typical, formulaic Elvis films, and MGM was looking for a more successful format for their next contracted release. *Stay Away, Joe* was seen as a lighthearted western comedy, but the press was offended by the film's "quaint and patronizing view of American Indians as brawling, balling, boozing children." *Live A Little, Love A Little,* based on the novel *Kiss My Firm But Pliant Lips,* offered a more contemporary story with just as little music. To record the four new titles Billy Strange was selected as the arranger and producer. Strange, who'd spent some time hanging out with Elvis in LA, had played guitar on other soundtrack sessions; he'd also been responsible for organizing the aborted August '67 sessions. Not exactly a hot producer with a string of hit records, he was still more alert to pop music of the day than most Nashville record folks. Strange liked recording with an orchestra in the studio, and for these sessions he brought with him not only a new group of musicians (except for Hal Blaine), but a totally different approach to recording. With written-out arrangements for the musicians, he treated each song individually, in a way that was foreign to Elvis's informal style. "Almost In Love," a bossa-nova-style song by Luis Bonfa, was arranged like a sleepy nightclub piece. The waltz "Wonderful World," from Freddy Bienstock's new U.K. songwriting team of Flett and Fletcher, maintained its European pop feel.

With producer Billy Strange (left) and backup singers (right) at the
Live A Little, Love A Little *sessions: March 7, 1968*

And "Edge Of Reality" stayed true to its title, matching its bizarre cryptopsychedelic imagery with an overblown, '60s-LA production. The one funky oasis came from Strange's new discovery, Mac Davis, who brought in "A Little Less Conversation," a good attempt at combining Elvis's basic rock 'n' roll music with contemporary lyrics and a timely arrangement. The soundtrack was musically a step in the right direction, but as time would show, of no commercial consequence.

Despite Elvis's hopes and everyone else's expectations for the "Guitar Man" single, it peaked at number forty-three and fell flat, with sales of almost 100,000 less than "Big Boss Man." The new fourth volume of *Elvis' Golden Records,* which traditionally guaranteed significant sales, stopped at number thirty-three with less than 400,000 units sold. Its predecessor had reached number three and had gone well beyond gold, but then that was 1963. The failure of "Guitar Man" prompted RCA to release "U.S. Male"/"Stay Away" only six weeks later, and as "U.S. Male" crept up into the top thirty there seemed to be a slim hope that the peppy little single might give Elvis another chance at the top of the charts. But the Colonel's Easter single, "You'll Never Walk Alone"/"We Call On Him," and the single from the *Speedway* soundtrack both bombed instantly. All they had left was the upcoming TV special. And did anyone really believe a Christmas show was going to turn things around?

1968

The Comeback

While Elvis was busy filming *Live A Little, Love A Little,* the Colonel was devoting himself full-time to the NBC TV special. By March of 1968 a suitable sponsor, the Singer Sewing Machine Company, had been found, which led to immediate discussions of an actual air date. By the end of the month the network had recommended a promising young team, Steve Binder and Bones Howe, to handle the production.

Bones had met Elvis early in his career, when he first went to work as an engineer at Radio Recorders in Hollywood. "You and Elvis would really hit it off," he told his partner when NBC first approached them. "You should meet this guy." Steve Binder, just twenty-three years old, was the producer of "Hullabaloo," next to "Shindig!" the most successful pop music show on TV; he had also produced and directed *The T.A.M.I. Show,* a feature film showcasing the Rolling Stones and numerous other pop acts and introducing James Brown to white America. A recent Petula Clark TV special he'd produced had received high ratings and critical acclaim; it also created controversy when Binder included a shot of guest star Harry Belafonte kissing Petula in what amounted to an interracial first for prime-time TV.

From the first, Steve Binder and Bones Howe brought to the nascent Elvis project the kind of independent thinking that had long since gone missing from Presley's own organization. With the Elvis show they challenged the conventional wisdom that dictated that TV specials must be jam-packed with as many stars, major and minor, as possible. Before 1968, Binder recalls, "I don't think there was a one-man show in commercial TV *ever*." The Colonel, of course, loved the idea. Elvis had done a Christmas radio show the previous fall—just a narrator, some Elvis records, and a taped greeting from the star—and the Colonel sent Binder a tape of the show thinking that somehow the NBC team could translate it onto the small screen. In fact, the ever-efficient Colonel already had Tom Diskin busy gathering Christmas material and making the usual publishing arrangements. Hill & Range sent along a list of recommendations including "Jingle Bell Rock," "Little Stranger (In A Manger)," and "The Voice In The Choir." They were hip enough to point to Elvis's previous success with blues numbers like "Reconsider Baby" and "Down In The Alley," and recommended "Merry Christmas Baby." Steve Binder wasn't thrilled about the idea of being restricted to Christmas songs, but he got put off by the Colonel every time he tried to make any other suggestion. He would simply have to wait until he could meet face to face with his sheltered star.

When they finally did meet in the Binder and Howe offices on Sunset Boulevard, Steve and Elvis hit it off just as Bones had predicted. During the meeting Steve raised his concern over the limitations of a seasonal theme—and was delighted to find Elvis agreeing with him. He complained that his mandate from NBC and the Colonel was pretty much written in stone, but Elvis brushed his worries aside: "Hey, we're doing whatever we want to do. Don't worry about it." It was a promise that, much to Binder's delight, would come to define the approach of the whole show. They agreed that a script would be developed during May, so there would be something concrete to discuss when Elvis returned from a suntanning holiday in Hawaii.

Binder had his work cut out for him. He'd hired a production team to put the special together—writers Alan Blye and Chris Beard went to work drafting a script, and at Elvis's suggestion Billy Strange was signed as musical director—but plenty of questions remained. Elvis said he was looking for a new direction, a new sound, but would he still want to use his usual Nashville band and the Jordanaires? Though he would harbor doubts right up until the moment of taping, Binder was convinced that Elvis still had the magic to captivate a TV audience with his music alone, given the right setting. But the Colonel's deal with NBC and Singer was based on the idea of a Christmas show; could they all be persuaded to abandon the idea for a fresher approach? In the end, everything rested on the star's own pledge: Elvis might have believed he was going to get to do whatever he wanted, but if things came to a head could he be counted on to stand up to the Colonel?

As it happened, he didn't have to. In the end, it was Singer executive Alfred DiScipio who talked the Colonel into accepting Binder's new idea: A "semidocumentary" that would showcase Presley as the innovator he really was. The script Blye and Beard were evolving was a kind of loose musical docudrama, stringing together Presley classics and standout songs from his recent output to tell the story of a young singer's rise to fame—like his early movie *Loving You,* autobiographical but in only the broadest of terms. "A Little Less Conversation," the funky Billy Strange–Mac Davis single from *Live A Little, Love A Little,* was first chosen for the linking theme. There would be a gospel segment, a fight scene, production numbers with a modern-dance look, even straight-ahead concert sequences. Bones Howe, who would be supervising the actual recordings, brought in some of LA's best session players—among them drummer Hal Blaine, guitarist Tommy Tedesco, and pianist Larry Muhoberac—to help create a new, contemporary sound for Elvis. One song from the original conception, "I'll Be Home For Christmas," made the cut temporarily, but everything else had changed. And when Elvis returned from Hawaii and read the script, he fell in love with it.

By early June they were all having daily meetings followed by rehearsals, held first at Binder and Howe's offices and later at NBC. At first Steve was surprised at how easily the Colonel accepted the new plan, but soon obstacles began to appear at almost every turn, and for a while things grew tense. Among them was the question of credit: Bones Howe naturally felt he was entitled to producer credits and royalties on the record that would come out of the special, but naturally he was denied such credit just as surely as every other Elvis producer had ever been. Worse yet, he was unable even to requisition the proper equipment, having to make do with single-channel (mono) sound off the video cameras for recording purposes. Steve Binder, for his part, soon found he didn't get along with musical director and arranger Billy Strange; he eventually pushed him out for not delivering arrangements on time and replaced him with his own man, Billy Goldenberg—who at first wasn't convinced that he and Elvis had anything in common.

Further adjustments were made as they went along. "They would unwind after rehearsal," Binder remembers, "and start improvising all of these blues songs and just rock 'n' roll. It was just a way of unwinding, and that's when I really got the idea: Wouldn't it be great if I had a camera in here and they didn't know I was here?" A true cinema-verité setup wouldn't have been practical, of course, but it was only a small leap from that to the "boxing ring" stage of the final special, where an Elvis surrounded by fans could put together an almost improvisational set of his old hits. The original contract with NBC stipulated that under no circumstances were there to be any live audiences involved in the show, so Binder first had to persuade Elvis that he could let himself go on a live stage just the way he did in the dressing room—and then play Elvis against the Colonel to get

Elvis with producer Steve Binder, who helped transform Elvis's 1968 Christmas TV special into an epochal comeback

final approval. Cautious at first, clearly nervous about appearing before an audience for the first time in seven years, Elvis finally agreed to give it a shot. When Binder suggested that he tell stories about his early years, Elvis hesitated—"I'm not sure it's gonna be a good idea for me to go out and do this." Even once he'd conceded the point he couldn't help musing, "What if I can't think of anything to say?"

There were so many last-minute script changes that the song selection wasn't finalized until the moment they all entered Western Recorders to begin recording. To make room for the new live sequences in their one-hour time slot, Binder needed to cut songs, and one he wanted to remove was "A Little Less Conversation." The Colonel had wanted the song included, not as a favor to the exiled Billy Strange but simply as a promotion for the upcoming picture. In another assault on the Colonel's power, Binder and Goldenberg urged songwriter W. Earl Brown to write a message song to replace "I'll Be Home For Christmas" as the grand finale. It was too late for the Colonel to object—especially after Elvis heard the Brown song, "If I Can Dream." Echoing the song's idealistic message, he remarked loud enough for everybody to hear: "Steve, I'm never going to sing another song I don't believe in. I'm never going to make another picture I don't believe in."

Binder may have won the fight, but the Colonel hadn't really lost either: Despite all the changes from his original idea, even he began to see that the newly reimagined special was shaping up a winner. Parker commanded Freddy Bienstock to make sure no one interfered with song selection once recording started, and Bienstock had his assistant Lamar Fike on hand during the sessions to make deals on anything he could. Most important, though, the Colonel's boy was once again dedicated to his work: Elvis was excited, and Parker knew that his new sense of involvement would pay off for everyone.

88. Studio Recordings for NBC's "Elvis"
June 20–23, 1968: Western Recorders, Burbank

Producer: Bones Howe
Engineer: Bones Howe

Guitar: Tommy Tedesco
Guitar: Mike Deasy
Guitar: Al Casey
Bass, Keyboards: Larry Knechtal
Bass: Charles Berghofer
Piano: Don Randi
Drums: Hal Blaine

Percussion: John Cyr
Percussion: Elliot Franks
Bongos: Frank DeVito
Harmonica: Tommy Morgan
Vocals: The Blossoms
Orchestra Conducted by Billy Goldenberg

6/20
WPA1 8045-10 **Nothingville**
Strange/Davis—Gladys Music

Elvis TV Special
LPM 4088/1968

WPA1 8112-sp	**Let Yourself Go**	**Elvis: A Legendary Performer Vol. 3**
	Joy Byers—Elvis Presley Music	*CPL1 3078/1978*
WPA1 8046-03	**Big Boss Man**	**Elvis TV Special**
	Smith/Dixon—Ludix Publ. & Conrad Music	*LPM 4088/1968*
WPA1 8113-sp	**It Hurts Me**	**Elvis: A Legendary Performer Vol. 3**
	Joy Byers/Charlie E. Daniels—Elvis Presley Music	*CPL1 3078/1978*

6/21

WPA1 8047-sp	**Guitar Man (evil/live)**	**Elvis TV Special**
	Jerry Hubbard—Vector Music Corp.	*LPM 4088/1968*
WPA1 8048-na	**Little Egypt**	**Elvis TV Special**
	Jerry Leiber/Mike Stoller—Elvis Presley Music/Trio Music Co./	*LPM 4088/1968*
	Progressive Music Co.	
WPA1 8030-na	**Trouble (after karate/live)**	**Elvis TV Special**
	Jerry Leiber/Mike Stoller—Elvis Presley Music	*LPM 4088/1968*
WPA1 8039-07	**Where Could I Go But To The Lord**	**Elvis TV Special**
	J. B. Coats—Affiliated Music Enterprises Inc.	*LPM 4088/1968*

6/22

WPA1 8040-13	**Up Above My Head**	**Elvis TV Special**
	W. Earl Brown—Gladys Music	*LPM 4088/1968*
WPA1 8041-sp	**Saved**	**Elvis TV Special**
	Jerry Leiber/Mike Stoller—Progressive Music/Trio Music	*LPM 4088/1968*
WPA1 8030-21	**Trouble (opening)**	**Elvis TV Special**
	Jerry Leiber/Mike Stoller—Elvis Presley Music	*LPM 4088/1968*
WPA1 8047-sp	**Guitar Man (opening)**	**Elvis TV Special**
	Jerry Hubbard—Vector Music Co.	*LPM 4088/1968*

6/23

WPA1 8029-05	**If I Can Dream**	**Single A-side**
	W. Earl Brown—Gladys Music	*47-9670/1968*
WPA1 8044-04 (tr)	**Memories**	**Elvis TV Special**
	Strange/Davis—Gladys Music	*LPM 4088/1968*
	A Little Less Conversation	
	Billy Strange/Mac Davis—Gladys Music	

"Let Yourself Go" (8112) is spliced from take 7 of first part and take 7 of second part. "It Hurts Me" (8113) is spliced from take 7 of first part and take 11 of second part. "Saved" (8041) is splice of takes 6 and 5 (end), and was short-ened for release. "Guitar Man" (opening) (8047) is splice of takes 32 and 19 (end). Although they are separate recordings, all versions of "Guitar Man" and "Trouble" were assigned the same matrix numbers by RCA: 8047 and 8030 respectively. The vocals on "Memories" and "A Little Less Conversation" may have been done on June 24. The Blossoms: Jean King, Darlene Love, Fanita James.

By the time the musicians gathered at Western Recorders to record the songs that would form the backbone of the show's musical story line, Billy Strange and Mac Davis had three songs left in the revised script for the show. The first was "A Little Less Conversation," and the film backing track was used to record a new vocal—a sure sign that the number had very low priority with the show's producers, who would have started from scratch if they were serious about using the song. Binder retained the other two numbers, "Nothingville" and the beautiful ballad "Memories." The latter appealed to Elvis so much that the song would be featured in a full performance, while most of the other material would be used in the medley accompanying the story of the young singer's rise to fame. This format, of course, permitted the use of many songs chosen from the wealth of material Presley had recorded over the years.

As he so often had in the past, Elvis worked harder when there were new people to impress, and the result was a focused and surprisingly flexible performance. Throughout his career he had always preferred recording a song in a single complete take, but Bones's insistence on working in bits and pieces didn't throw him at all—nor did the relatively new experience of working with a big group including horns and strings. His genuine enthusiasm even extended to putting the blame on himself for every new mistake that came along. The gospel medley, which featured a dance ensemble in the show, reunited Elvis with a music that had inspired some of his most committed performances, and the new, desperate roughness of his voice—sometimes he was almost screaming—recalled the singing of his early career. If there was a single highlight of the sessions it was the rousing extended version of LaVern Baker's "Saved," the song Freddy Bienstock had originally suggested for *Easy Come, Easy Go.* As a Leiber and Stoller song it was as much rock 'n' roll as gospel—almost a takeoff on gospel, in fact—but once again Elvis, with backing from the black vocal group the Blossoms, obliterated the songwriters' irony with the sheer passion of his performance. In his hands it was a pure gospel rave-up, and there were no complaints about doing an extra take.

As they carried on, the lesser songs disappeared from the script. They'd been thinking of showcasing Elvis's movie period by choosing "Cotton Candy Land" and "How Would You Like To Be"

```
6/11/68
RUNDOWN                               "ELVIS"
                          STARRING ELVIS PRESLEY    TAPE: 6/27-29/68
1.  Disclaimer                  ( 1)                 AIR:  12/3/68
2.  Peacock                     ( 2)
3.  "GUITAR MAN" Opening        ( 3)
    Elvis, 59 Boys
4.  Opening Commercial
    Billboard                   ( 8)
5.      FIRST COMMERCIAL        ( 9)
6.  Arena Segment
    a.  "LITTLE LESS
        CONVERSATION"           (10)
        Elvis
    b.  Arena Talk
        Elvis                   (14)
7.  Arena Medley
    Elvis
    a.  "JAILHOUSE ROCK"        (15)
    b.  "HEARTBREAK HOTEL"      (16)
    c.  "DON'T BE CRUEL,"       (18)
    d.  "FALLING IN LOVE
        WITH YOU"               (19)
    e.  "HOUND DOG"             (20)
    f.  "BLUE SUEDE SHOES"      (22)
    g.  "LOVE ME TENDER"        (24)
    h.  "ALL SHOOK UP"          (25)
    i.  "U.S. MALE"             (27)
8.  "LITTLE LESS CONVERSA-
    TION" REPRISE               (31)
    Elvis
9.      SECOND COMMERCIAL       (33)
10. Informal Segment
    Talk & Songs                (34)
    Elvis
11.     THIRD COMMERCIAL        (44)
12. Gospel Medley               (45)
    Elvis, Singers, Dancers
```

from *It Happened At The World's Fair,* but in the face of what they were achieving that must have looked ridiculous, and they scrapped the idea. "U.S. Male" was thrown out, too; it hadn't been the comeback single they'd hoped for, but probably more important, it just wasn't easy to capture the charm of the record without guitarist Jerry Reed. But the two other singles from the Reed sessions, "Big Boss Man" and "Guitar Man," remained as features in the medley sequence.

The climax of the evening came with W. Earl Brown's new number, "If I Can Dream." From the beginning Elvis sang as if he were pleading for his very life, and only little mistakes by the band prevented take one from becoming the master. Afterward in the studio he called for endless playbacks of the chosen take, immersing himself in the experience—reveling in how far the journey had taken him, and how well it had all turned out.

Bones Howe spent the following day mixing the material. Some additional mixes were made without Elvis's voice so that he could sing them live during the actual taping of the show, when everyone hoped the excitement of the event would fuel even better performances. That night, after rehearsing at NBC with newly arrived band members Scotty Moore and D. J. Fontana, Elvis returned to the studio to listen to "If I Can Dream" again and again.

89. Informal Rehearsals
June 24–25: Dressing Room at NBC, Burbank

Acoustic, Electric Guitar: Elvis Presley
Acoustic, Electric Guitar: Scotty Moore
Acoustic Guitar: Charlie Hodge

Percussion: D. J. Fontana, Alan Fortas
Tambourine: Lance Legault

6/24, 4PM

CPA5 5128   **I Got A Woman**   **Platinum: A Life In Music**
Ray Charles   *67469-2/1997*
Blue Moon/Young Love/Happy Day
Rodgers/Hart—Carol Joyner/Ric Cartey—unknown
When It Rains It Really Pours
B. Emerson
Blue Christmas
Hayes/Johnson
Are You Lonesome Tonight?/That's My Desire
Roy Turk/Lou Handman—Carroll Loveday/Helmy Kresa
That's When Your Heartaches Begin
Raskin/Brown/Fisher
Love Me
Jerry Leiber/Mike Stoller

When My Blue Moon Turns To Gold Again
Walker/Sullivan
Blue Christmas/Santa Claus Is Back In Town
Hayes/Johnson—Jerry Leiber/Mike Stoller

6/25, 10AM–12PM

Danny Boy
Weatherly
Baby What You Want Me To Do
J. Reed
Love Me
Jerry Leiber/Mike Stoller

CPA5 5120 **Tiger Man**
S. Burns/J. H. Louis
Santa Claus Is Back In Town
Jerry Leiber/Mike Stoller
Lawdy, Miss Clawdy
Lloyd Price
One Night
Bartholomew/King
Blue Christmas
Hayes/Johnson
Baby What You Want Me To Do
J. Reed
When My Blue Moon Turns To Gold Again
Walker/Sullivan
Blue Moon Of Kentucky
Bill Monroe

Platinum: A Life In Music
67469-2/1997

The above rehearsals were recorded by Joe Esposito on Elvis's own tape recorder.

Steve Binder, expanding on the live-performance portion of the show, had arranged to bring in Scotty and D. J., the two surviving members of Elvis's original trio, to tape an informal jam session in the "boxing ring" format. Determined to re-create the casual "rehearsals" Elvis held in his own dressing room—and hoping to combat Elvis's nerves—Binder added Elvis pals Charlie Hodge and Alan Fortas, along with Elvis's movie stand-in, Lance Legault; together, Binder hoped, they would act as a kind of buffer for Elvis as well as prompting him with subjects to talk about. Elvis, Scotty, and Charlie Hodge would play guitars, D. J. would use a guitar case for a drum, and Alan Fortas and Lance Legault would add guitar back-slapping and tambourine to the ensemble. Steve's idea of capturing Elvis at his most basic was becoming central to his vision of the special, but two days away from taping he was still fighting to include the se-

On the TV special soundstage

quence. With all the other elements of the show firmly in place, he was afraid Elvis might back out at the last minute.

In the final rehearsal the day before the actual taping, the group ran through a likely repertoire, focusing on the old material Scotty and D. J. knew best. Playing "Danny Boy" on guitar served as a kind of introduction before they got into the down-and-dirty feeling of "Baby What You Want Me To Do." Binder and his writers, Alan Blye and Chris Beard, took it as their job to add a sense of order, ever so cautiously, to the "staged informality" of the upcoming segment. Always attentive to Elvis's re-actions, they made suggestions designed at once to make him comfortable and to expand his vision of how the session might come off. "The idea of this segment to me," Alan Blye began, "is [that] the songs and everything are secondary to the fact that we hear Elvis talking." After a long pause Elvis agreed. Knowing that this was a crucial time, Binder and the writers kept reaffirming his free-dom to do anything he wanted to do. They offered to write out cues to remind him of stories. They said he could play anything he felt like, and greeted his version of "Are You Lonesome Tonight?" warmly. If only they could show the world the real Elvis, the team believed, the world would be as fascinated with him as they were themselves. Elvis himself did get a little jittery about the whole thing as they went along: "Well, you see I find myself in a situation right now of *trying* to come up with something [to say]," he declared, "which is no good for me. It's no good for the spot." Binder and Blye fell over them-selves trying to take the pressure off: Just talk, don't worry about the stories, they counseled, and Elvis's friends chimed in with their own support. Finally, with the last rehearsal over, all that was left were the shows themselves: June 27, two shows only, Elvis Presley's first performance before an audience in seven years.

90. Live Recordings for NBC—Informal Segment
June 27, 1968: NBC Studios, Burbank

Producer/Engineer: Bones Howe

Acoustic, Electric Guitar: Elvis Presley
Acoustic, Electric Guitar: Scotty Moore
Acoustic Guitar, Vocal: Charlie Hodge

Percussion: D. J. Fontana, Alan Fortas
Tambourine: Lance Legault

6PM

	That's All Right	
	Crudup	
	Heartbreak Hotel	
	Axton/Durden/Presley	
	Love Me	
	Leiber/Stoller	
	Baby What You Want Me To Do	
	J. Reed	
LPA5 5817	**Blue Suede Shoes**	**This Is Elvis**
	Carl Perkins	*CPL2 4031/1981*
WPA1 8032	**Baby What You Want Me To Do**	**Elvis TV Special**
	J. Reed	*LPM 4088/1968*
	Lawdy, Miss Clawdy	
	Lloyd Price	
	Are You Lonesome Tonight?	
	Roy Turk/Lou Handman	
CPA5 5138	**When My Blue Moon Turns To Gold Again**	**Platinum: A Life In Music**
	Walker/Sullivan	*67469-2/1997*
	Blue Christmas	
	Johnson/Hayes	
CPA5 5139	**Trying To Get To You**	**Platinum: A Life In Music**
	McCoy/Singleton	*67469-2/1997*
	One Night	
	Bartholomew/King	
WPA1 8120	**Baby What You Want Me To Do**	**Elvis: A Legendary Performer Vol. 2**
	J. Reed	*CPL1 1349/1976*
WPA1 8043	**One Night**	**Elvis TV Special**
	Bartholomew/King	*LPM 4088/1968*
	Memories	
	Strange/Davis	

The master of "Blue Suede Shoes" (LPA5 5817) released on *Elvis TV Special* is a splice of the performances on 6/27 (6PM show) and 6/29 (6PM show). Elvis sang "Memories" to a prerecorded backing track on both shows. These "live" versions are shorter than the released version.

	Heartbreak Hotel	
	Axton/Durden/Presley	
	Baby What You Want Me To Do	
	J. Reed	
WPA1 8115	**That's All Right**	**Elvis: A Legendary Performer Vol. 4**
	Crudup	*CPL1 4848/1983*
WPA1 8116	**Are You Lonesome Tonight?**	**Elvis: A Legendary Performer Vol. 1**
	Roy Turk/Lou Handman	*CPL1 0341/1974*
	Baby What You Want Me To Do	
	J. Reed	
WPA1 8117	**Blue Suede Shoes**	**Elvis: A Legendary Performer Vol. 2**
	Carl Perkins	*CPL1 1349/1976*
	One Night	
	Bartholomew/King	
WPA1 8118	**Love Me**	**Elvis: A Legendary Performer Vol. 1**
	Jerry Leiber/Mike Stoller	*CPL1 0341/1974*
WPA1 8119	**Trying To Get To You**	**Elvis: A Legendary Performer Vol. 1**
	McCoy/Singleton	*CPL1 0341/1974*
WPA1 8031	**Lawdy, Miss Clawdy**	**Elvis TV Special**
	Lloyd Price	*LPM 4088/1968*
	Santa Claus Is Back In Town	
	Jerry Leiber/Mike Stoller	
WPA1 8042	**Blue Christmas**	**Elvis TV Special**
	Johnson/Hayes	*LPM 4088/1968*
WPA1 8028	**Tiger Man**	**Flaming Star**
	Burns/Louis	*PRS 279/1969*
	When My Blue Moon Turns To Gold Again	
	Walker/Sullivan	
	Memories	
	Strange/Davis	

On the night of the taping Elvis paced the dressing room in the tight black leather outfit that had been made for him by the show's costume designer, Bill Belew. To Binder he seemed genuinely terrified. Afraid he might walk out at any moment, the producer tried everything he could think of to reassure him. When it became evident that it was the talking in the informal segment that worried him most, Binder insisted it didn't matter, that he could pull it off. Finally Elvis simply asked, "What if nobody likes me?"

But once he got onstage, surrounded by his friends, he began to relax, and his native charm took over. "Good night," he told the audience as he arrived, and Charlie

Hodge chimed in with his best W. C. Fields: "It's been a long show." Ice thus broken, he launched right into "That's All Right," beating away at his acoustic guitar like he was back on Union Avenue in Memphis. The group messed up "Heartbreak Hotel," but he kept going without missing a beat; they followed with a loose version of "Love Me" before Elvis took over electric-guitar duties from Scotty and brought everything under control with a commanding rave-up on "Baby What You Want Me To Do." He made jokes off the typed-out cues the writers had supplied him with, and with his self-mocking ad-libs he won over the audience in a heartbeat. During the preshow discussions the Colonel had suggested that a group of pretty women be grouped around Elvis, and in the closing segment Binder got Elvis to sit on the edge of the stage to sing "Memories" directly to them. After the first show had wrapped a new audience was led in while Elvis grabbed a shower backstage; he'd worked up such a sweat that Bill Belew had to get his leather suit cleaned and pressed in the hour-long break between shows. When Elvis reappeared it was with renewed confidence, singing more freely, taking chances with his phrasing, then going wild on "Tiger Man" and "Trying To Get To You." His look was driven, almost evil, and his voice had taken on a rough exuberance it hadn't seen since the 1957 recording of "Jailhouse Rock."

The informal jam session with Scotty, D. J., and the boys: June 27, 1968

91. Live Recordings for NBC—Arena Segment
June 29, 1968; 6 and 8pm Shows: NBC Studios, Burbank

Producer/Engineer: Bones Howe

Guitar: Tommy Tedesco
Guitar: Mike Deasy
Guitar: Al Casey
Bass & Keyboards: Larry Knechtal
Bass: Charles Berghofer
Piano: Don Randi
Drums: Hal Blaine

Percussion: John Cyr
Percussion: Elliot Franks
Bongos: Frank DeVito
Harmonica: Tommy Morgan
Vocals: The Blossoms
Orchestra Conducted by Billy Goldenberg

6PM Show

	Heartbreak Hotel	
	Axton/Durden/Presley	
	One Night	
	Bartholomew/King	
WPA1 8033	**Heartbreak Hotel**	**Elvis TV Special**
	Axton/Durden/Presley	*LPM 4088/1968*
WPA1 8034	**Hound Dog**	**Elvis TV Special**
	Jerry Leiber/Mike Stoller	*LPM 4088/1968*
WPA1 8035	**All Shook Up**	**Elvis TV Special**
	Blackwell/Presley	*LPM 4088/1968*
WPA1 8036	**Can't Help Falling In Love**	**Elvis TV Special**
	Peretti/Creatore/Weiss	*LPM 4088/1968*
	Jailhouse Rock	
	Jerry Leiber/Mike Stoller	
	Don't Be Cruel	
	Blackwell/Presley	
LPA5 5817	**Blue Suede Shoes**	**This Is Elvis**
	Carl Perkins	*CPL2 4031/1981*
	Love Me Tender	
	Presley/Matson	
	Trouble/Guitar Man	
	Jerry Leiber/Mike Stoller/Jerry Hubbard	
	Baby What You Want Me To Do	
	J. Reed	

8PM Show

	Heartbreak Hotel
	Axton/Durden/Presley
	Hound Dog
	Leiber/Stoller

	All Shook Up	
	Blackwell/Presley	
	Can't Help Falling In Love	
	Peretti/Creatore/Weiss	
WPA1 8037	**Jailhouse Rock**	**Elvis TV Special**
	Jerry Leiber/Mike Stoller	*LPM 4088/1968*
WPA1 8114	**Don't Be Cruel**	**NBC TV Special**
	Blackwell/Presley	*61021-2/1991*
	Blue Suede Shoes	
	Carl Perkins	
WPA1 8038	**Love Me Tender**	**Elvis TV Special**
	Presley/Matson	*LPM 4088/1968*
	Trouble	
	Jerry Leiber/Mike Stoller	
	Trouble/Guitar Man	
	Jerry Leiber/Mike Stoller-Jerry Hubbard	

For note on the spliced master of "Blue Suede Shoes," see 6/27, 8PM show. "Trouble/Guitar Man" was sung to the original June 23 session master. "If I Can Dream" was also lip-synched by Elvis on both shows. On the first show Elvis plays electric guitar on "Baby What You Want Me To Do."

The next recording in front of an audience would be the arena segment that placed Elvis on the same "boxing ring" stage, this time all alone, with a full orchestra off to one side behind part of the crowd. Though there would be later vocal overdubs, both Elvis and the musicians would be recorded live during the segment. Elvis seemed not only comfortable but confident on the tiny stage that provided so little room to move, remaining calm and in control even when technical problems delayed the taping, and his performances were charged with the same kind of animal energy of the informal segment just two days before.

After the shooting one additional day had been scheduled to make video recordings and vocal repairs; Elvis resung various parts of the show altogether, including the version of "If I Can Dream" that would be used on the broadcast. (A different version was released on the record.) By the time they were through, everyone associated with the show knew they had a winner on their hands. At the outset of the long, agonizing process, Elvis had told executive producer Bob Finkel, "I want everyone to know what I can really do." He had accomplished just that.

*Floor plan
for the NBC Special*

92. Soundtrack recordings for National General's *Charro*
October 15, 1968: Samuel Goldwyn Studio, Hollywood

Musical Conductor: Hugo Montenegro
Engineer: Kevin Cleary

Guitar: Tommy Tedesco
Guitar: Ralph Grasso
Guitar: Howard Roberts
Bass: Raymond Brown
Bass: Max Bennett
Drums: Carl O'Brian
Percussion: Emil Radocchia

Piano: Don Randi

Overdubbed:

Sue Allen, Allan Capps, Loren Faber,
Ronald Hicklin, Ian Freebairn Smith,
Sally Stevens, Robert Zwirn
Strings
Horns

7PM–12AM		
M10-02(tr)	**Let's Forget About The Stars**	**Let's Be Friends**
ZPA4 1055	*A. L. Owens—Elvis Presley Music*	*CAS 2408/1970*
M11-05(tr)	**Charro**	**Single B-side**
WPA1 8091	*Mac Davis/Billy Strange—Gladys Music*	*47-9731/1969*

Rhythm group repairs and a full orchestra backing were recorded on November 25–27; Elvis probably overdubbed his vocal at the rhythm group sessions. The vocal master of "Let's Forget About The Stars" (1055) is take 5, and the vocal master of "Charro" (8091) is a splice of takes 5 and 9.

With no more than a week of rest, Elvis reported to work on his next motion picture: *Charro,* a serious Western with no musical interludes, which would offer Elvis a chance to concentrate on acting. The studio eventually hired arranger-producer Hugo Montenegro to produce two songs in conjunction with the film, although only one, the title cut, actually made it to the screen.

93. Soundtrack Recordings for MGM's *The Trouble with Girls*
October 23, 1968: United Artist Recorders, Hollywood

Musical Conductor: Billy Strange
Engineer: Eddie Brackett

Guitar: Jerry McGee
Guitar: Morton Marker
Guitar: Robert Gibbons
Bass: Max Bennett
Drums: Frank Carlson
Drums: John Guerin
Piano: Don Randi
Clarinet: Buddy Colette (2004)
Trumpet: Roy Caton (2004)

Trombone: Lew McCreary (2004)
Vocals: The Mello Men (2003–2004)
Vocals: Jack Halloran (2004, 2006)
Vocals: Ronald Hicklin (2004, 2006)
Vocals: Marilyn Mason (2004)

Overdubbed:
Vocals: The Blossoms (2002)
Horns (2002, 2003, 2005)
Strings (2005)

7–11:45PM, 12:15–3:15AM

2002-06	**Clean Up Your Own Back Yard**	**Single A-side**
XPA1 3976	*Mac Davis/Billy Strange—Gladys Music*	*4-9747/1969*
2003-10	**Swing Down Sweet Chariot**	**Elvis: A Legendary Performer Vol. 4**
XPA1 3977	*Arranged by Elvis Presley—Elvis Presley Music*	*CPL1 4848/1983*
2004-09	**Signs Of The Zodiac**	**Double Features**
WPA5 2568	*B. Kaye/B. Weisman—Gladys Music*	*66559-2/1995*
2005-31	**Almost**	**Let's Be Friends**
XPA1 3978	*B. Kaye/B. Weisman—Gladys Music*	*CAS 2408/1970*
2006-03	**The Whiffenpoof Song**	**Double Features**
WPA5 2556	*Galloway/Minnigerode/Pomeroy—Unknown*	*66559-2/1995*
2006-03	**Violet**	**Double Features**
WPA5 2557	*Dueker/P. Lohstroh—Unknown*	*66559-2/1995*

Strings and horns were overdubbed at American Sound on May 7 and 8, 1969, by Felton Jarvis. The Blossoms were over-dubbed at an unknown date. "College Medley" (2006) consists of six short segments of which Elvis sings on only two: "The Whiffenpoof Song" (2556) and "Violet" (2557). The Mello Men: Thurl Ravenscroft, Bill Cole, Bill Lee, Gene Merlino. The Blossoms: Darlene Love, Jean King, Fanita James.

After *Charro* Elvis completed his final picture on the MGM deal, *The Trouble with Girls (And How to Get Into It)*. The film contained a handful of insignificant songs, the only exception being another Billy Strange and Mac Davis collaboration, "Clean Up Your Own Back Yard." Billy Strange produced the session, but Felton Jarvis was thereafter given the task of beefing up the masters in an attempt to improve their commercial potential. Having produced almost nothing successful or artistically significant, Billy Strange's relationship with Elvis Presley ended with these recordings.

The next three single releases succeeded only in erasing the memory of the promise, artistic and commercial, of the three before. "You'll Never Walk Alone" peaked at number ninety, "Your Time Hasn't Come Yet Baby" reached number seventy-one, and "A Little Less Conversation" only sixty-nine. The *Speedway* album landed at a dismal number eighty-two on the album charts, suggesting that by the summer of 1968, Elvis Presley was left with virtually no recording career.

But Elvis himself wasn't about to dwell on that kind of bleak notion. The TV special, simply entitled "Elvis," was scheduled for December 3, and it held out a bright hope that would carry him through the end of the year. "If I Can Dream," the climactic finale into which Elvis had poured all of his emotions, was scheduled to be released in October. As it happened, the song was right for the times: In the wake of the tragic assassinations of Martin Luther King and Bobby Kennedy that summer (King, of course, had been killed in Elvis's hometown), its plea for brotherhood and understanding was relevant, sensitive, and serious in a way Elvis had never been before. The single was slow to start, first appearing at number ninety-nine, just a week before the show aired. RCA's Harry Jenkins had to push frantically to get the album into stores after Elvis himself forced the label to remake its masters at the last minute: Concerned once again about the quality of his records, he asked for the opening of "Trouble" and "Guitar Man" to be edited together as one piece, demanded that more bass be added to the gospel medley, and called for the level to be raised on "Little Egypt." He also insisted on keeping Bones Howe's mono mixes on "Memories" and "If I Can Dream"; he'd always preferred mono, and may have felt they had more power than the more transparent stereo versions. The RCA engineers worked overtime, lacquers were rushed to Elvis for final approval, and the records were shipped to the stores just in time.

The show aired at 9:00 P.M. Eastern Standard Time on December 3, and it was received around the world with a mixture of surprise and awestruck acclaim. *The New York Times,* who once had panned Elvis as vulgar, now called him "charismatic." Others used words such as "fresh," "virile," "humorous," and "magical" to describe what critics and the viewing public recognized as the musical surprise of the year. The show might have been even better; cutting it down from ninety to sixty minutes meant that two of the wildest performances of the informal section, "Tiger Man" and "Trying To Get To You," were out—along with a few bits too racy for the sponsor. Phil Spector complained that the cuts had ruined the show, but what he missed everyone else saw: Against all odds, it was Elvis's greatest comeback yet.

The payoff came instantly. Both the single and the album soared to the top of the charts, and the following day Tom Diskin, on behalf of the Colonel, was feeling expansive enough that he went on record in *The New York Times* with the news that profits from Elvis's motion pictures had fallen off so dramatically that the reclusive star was now considering a return to live performing. Just twelve months earlier, a vaguely defined plan for a Christmas special was all there had been on the horizon. Transformed by Elvis and his producers, the program that emerged now virtually guaranteed Elvis's resurrection. Once again the Colonel had turned to television to jump-start his boy's career. And once again Elvis had made good, spinning talent, charm, and sheer desire into a whole new career in a dazzling fifty minutes.

1969

From Elvis in Memphis

In 1968, just as it always had before, television exposure had focused national attention on Elvis Presley and given him a new beginning. "Elvis," the TV special, only gave Elvis's record sales a modest boost at first, but its real effect was much broader and deeper: It reestablished his place as a dominant force in American music and culture, reminding the audience of who he was, what he'd done, and how well he was still capable of doing it. Before the new year had even turned, Colonel Parker knew they couldn't afford to lose an inch of the ground they'd gained: Elvis needed to follow up swiftly and surely, and not just with new recordings but with the right kind of recordings.

Only weeks after the TV show, Elvis made another crucial decision: He chose not to return to Nashville for his next scheduled round of recording sessions. Felton Jarvis was at Graceland to discuss the sessions, as were members of Elvis's inner circle, and many of them happened to be connected to a new music scene that was burgeoning right under their noses, in Presley's own Memphis. Lamar Fike held a position with Hill & Range publishing in Nashville, and now Marty Lacker, George Klein, and Red West all had song-plugging or songwriting arrangements with Chips Moman, the head of Memphis's American Studio. When Moman had opened the studio he had his eye on a rising trend in rhythm and blues that combined elements of both black and white traditions—the trend that became known as soul. Within a few years he had produced more than a hundred hit singles, including records like "The Letter" by the studio's own creation the Box Tops as well as others by countless R&B acts and name artists like Neil Diamond and Dusty Springfield. With Stax, Hi, and other independent labels thriving off a sound that synthesized most of the elements Elvis had always responded to in his own music, it was evident that Memphis had overtaken Nashville as the creative hub for recording. At any other time Marty's suggestion that they forget about Nashville and move to Chips's little studio at Chelsea and Thomas would almost certainly have been dismissed in Elvis's usual "someday" fashion, but on this winter night Elvis and Felton withdrew from the dining room to confer, reemerging shortly to announce that they would change the session if arrangements could be made between Chips and RCA.

94. Studio Sessions for RCA
January 13–16 and 20–23, 1969: American Studios, Memphis

A&R/Producers: Chips Moman & Felton Jarvis
Engineer: Al Pachucki

Guitar, Sitar: Reggie Young
Guitar: Elvis Presley
Bass: Tommy Cogbill (not 1/22)
Bass: Mike Leech
Drums: Gene Chrisman
Piano: Bobby Wood
Piano: Elvis Presley (1160)
Organ: Bobby Emmons
Steel Guitar: John Hughey (1154, 56, 58)
Harmonica: Ed Kollis (1149)

Overdubbed:
Guitar: Reggie Young (1147, 42, 55)
Bass: Tommy Cogbill (1155)
Drums: Gene Chrisman (1147)
Piano: Bobby Wood (1142)
Piano: Ronnie Milsap (1155)
Organ: Bobby Emmons (1147–1155)
Harmonica: Ed Kollis (1155)
Vocals: Charlie Hodge (1148)
Horns: Trumpet: A. Vasquez,
N. Prentice, B. Shew; Trombone:
A. Le Cogue, J. Boicie; Bass

Overdubbed:
Trombone: K. Adkins (Las Vegas overdub on 1227)
Trumpet: R. F. Taylor
Trumpet: Wayne Jackson
Trumpet: Dick Steff
Sax, Trombone: Jackie Thomas
Sax: Andrew Lowe
Sax:Glen Spreen
Sax: J. P. Luper
Trombone: Ed Logan
Trombone: Jack Hale
Trombone: Gerald Richardson
French Horn: Tony Cason
French Horn: Joe D'Gerolamo
Vocals: Mary Green, Donna Thatcher,
Susan Pilkington, Mary Holladay
Vocals: Dolores Edgin, June Page,
Hurschel Wiginton, Joe Babcock,
Ginger Holladay, Millie Kirkham,
Mary Holladay, Mary Green.
Sandy Posey (1152)

1/13, 7–10PM
XPA5 1142-09　　**Long Black Limousine**

Vern Stovall/Bobby George—American Music

From Elvis In Memphis
LSP 4155/1969

10PM–1AM
XPA5 1143-02　　**This Is The Story**

Arnold/Morrow/Martin—Elvis Presley Music

From Memphis To Vegas
LSP 6020/1969

1–5AM
XPA5 1145-15　　**Wearin' That Loved On Look**

Dallas Frazier/A. L. Owens—Blue Crest & Elvis Presley Music

From Elvis In Memphis
LSP 4155/1969

1/14, 7–10PM
XPA5 1146-23　　**You'll Think Of Me**

Mort Shuman—Elvis Presley Music

Single B-side
47-9764/1969

10PM–1AM
XPA5 1148-03　　**A Little Bit Of Green**

Arnold/Morrow/Martin—Elvis Presley Music

From Memphis To Vegas
LSP 6020/1969

<u>2–5AM, 5:30–8:30AM</u>

XPA5 1147-01	**I'm Movin' On**	**From Elvis In Memphis**
	Clarence E. Snow—Hill & Range Songs	*LSP 4155/1969*
XPA5 1155-na	**Gentle On My Mind**	**From Elvis In Memphis**
	John Hartford—Glaser Publications	*LSP 4155/1969*

<u>1/15, 7–10PM</u>

XPA5 1149-na (tr)	**Don't Cry Daddy**	**Single A-side**
	Mac Davis—B-n-B & Elvis Presley Music	*47-9768/1969*

<u>2–5AM</u>

XPA5 1151-na (tr)	**Inherit The Wind**	**From Memphis To Vegas**
	Eddie Rabbitt—S-P-R & Noma Music	*LSP 6020/1969*
XPA5 1152-na (tr)	**Mama Liked The Roses**	**Single B-side**
	John Christopher—Press Music	*47-9835/1970*

<u>1/16, 7–10PM</u>

XPA5 1153-na	**My Little Friend**	**Single B-side**
	Shirl Milete—Last Straw & Elvis Presley Music	*47-9791/1970*

<u>1/20–21, 9PM–12AM, 1–4AM</u>

XPA5 1154-23	**In The Ghetto**	**Single A-side**
	Mac Davis—B-n-B & Gladys Music	*47-9741/1969*
XPA5 1156-02	**Rubberneckin'**	**Single B-side**
	Dory Jones/Bunny Warren—Elvis Presley Music	*47-9768/1969*
	Gentle On My Mind—*(vocal overdub)*	

<u>1/21, 8–11PM</u>

XPA5 1157-07	**Hey Jude**	**Elvis Now**
	John Lennon/Paul McCartney—Maclen Music	*LSP 4671/1972*

<u>1–4AM</u>

XPA5 1158-05	**From A Jack To A King**	**From Memphis To Vegas**
	Ned Miller—Jamie Music	*LSP 6020/1969*

Vocal overdubs only: "My Little Friend," "Inherit The Wind," "Mama Liked The Roses," "I'm Movin' On" (parts), "Long Black Limousine" (parts), "Don't Cry Daddy," and "Poor Man's Gold" (not completed)

<u>1/22(23) 12:30–3:30AM</u>

XPA5 1159-05	**Without Love**	**From Memphis To Vegas**
	Danny Small—Progressive & Suffolk Music	*LSP 6020/1969*
XPA5 1160-01	**I'll Hold You In My Heart**	**From Elvis In Memphis**
	Dilback/Horton/Arnold—Adams Vee & Abbott Inc.	*LSP 4155/1969*

<u>4–7</u>AM

XPA5 1161-03	**I'll Be There**	**Let's Be Friends**
	Bobby Darin—Hudson Bay Music	*CAS 2408/1970*
XPA5 1227-08	**Suspicious Minds**	**Single A-side**
	Mark James—Press Music Co.	*47-9764/1969*

Backing tracks for two songs, "Come Out, Come Out" by Don Thomas and Mike Millius (1144) and "Poor Man's Gold" by Mac Davis (1150), were also recorded; Elvis is not known to have recorded a vocal for "Come Out," and only the first line of the song is known to have survived. The rest has been erased. The ending of "Suspicious Minds" (1227) was spliced on for longer playing time.

January 13, 1969, was a Monday. To accommodate Elvis Chips Moman had to re-arrange a number of scheduled sessions, including one with Neil Diamond; legend has it that Diamond agreed to a postponement in return for a promise that Elvis would record one of his songs. Elvis, whose sessions were booked in the evenings, was thrilled to discover that his boyhood idol Roy Hamilton would be working at the same studio during the day: It was the perfect omen. Bobby Wood, the piano player, has described how Elvis, with some fanfare, walked in the back door of 827 Thomas Street that evening. "He was in his prime." Bobby remembers. "He looked better than most women I've seen." What Elvis saw could only be described as a dump, and the neigh-

With Chips Moman (left) and Felton Jarvis (right) at American Studios, Memphis, January 1969

borhood wasn't much better; on the other hand, the room seemed to vibrate soulfulness. "There were rats up there in the rafters, chirping," recalled guitarist Reggie Young. The sound produced at American had little to do with high-tech equipment and everything to do with its stable of musicians, who had developed a heavily R&B-influenced style that far transcended any bluesy edges the Nashville players might have boasted. Tommy Cogbill, bass player and producer at American, was a brilliant jazz musician whose rhythmic suppleness propelled the music while retaining a melodic quality that made his elaborate bass parts seem like simple commercial hooklines. Guitarist Reggie Young played with an understated but eloquent spareness, always seeking the individuality and coloring of each song. The rest of the band consisted of drummer Gene Chrisman, Bobby Wood on piano, Bobby Emmons on organ, and Mike Leech doubling with Cogbill on bass (but also available for percussion extras). John Hughey would be called in for any steel guitar parts, and Chips's assistant, Ed Kollis, filled in on harmonica when needed. All southerners, all close to Elvis's age, they shared a musical heritage that blended country, gospel, and rhythm and blues.

To the musicians Chips Moman was a godfather-like figure in the studio, who would tolerate nothing less than total commitment. As far as he was concerned the musicians had no life outside recording and could be called to appear at any hour. But their hard work as a session band had paid off, giving them a reputation equaled only by the house bands at Motown, Muscle Shoals, and across town at Stax. They cut records as sharp and funky as their local rivals at Stax, but they also knew how to give them a genuinely "white" commercial gloss, essential for the making of mainstream pop records.

Though now the head of a mini-empire, including Press Music Publishing and the newly formed AGP label, Chips was still a hands-on producer. He could be a patient listener, waiting, offering suggestions, corrections, or encouragement while the musicians worked together to find the essence of each song. Like many producers Chips preferred to record vocal tracks separately, which prevented leakage from other instruments and produced a track that was easier to mix. With the kind of eight-track board American had, all live recording was done on four tracks, leaving four more open for overdubs. The vocalist could sing along with the band as an arrangement developed, but it was with the understanding that this was a scratch vocal only, to be replaced later by a more perfect rerecording. Maintaining this degree of control allowed Chips to assemble every element himself, creating the individual sound that was the hallmark of the studio. And he had no reason to take any different approach with Elvis Presley; after all, wasn't Elvis drawn to the studio for the same reasons that any other performer came to American—for its unique sound and Chips Moman's unique ability to produce hit records?

As always, Freddy Bienstock came to the American sessions prepared with a combination of Elvis's requests and new songs from his staff writers, as well as titles they hadn't gotten around to at previous sessions. On Elvis's list were many of the old diehards he hadn't yet gotten out of his system: "From A Jack To A King," "Without Love," "Rags To Riches," Ivory Joe Hunter's "I Will Be True," Bobby Darin's "I'll Be There," Dusty Springfield's "You Don't Have To Say You Love Me," and finally Hank Snow's "I'm Moving On." Otis Blackwell, Billy Strange, and the Giant, Baum, and Kaye team all delivered new songs; Ben Weisman submitted "Rubberneckin'," and Mort Shuman came up with two: "You'll Think Of Me" and "Over My Head." Among the repeat demos was Tepper and Bennett's "Can You Find It In Your Heart," which had almost made it into the TV show. Newly signed British writers Guy Flett and Doug Fletcher sent material, and Freddy had three promising cuts by the team of Arnold, Martin, and Morrow: "This Is The Story," "A Little Bit Of Green," and "Sweet Angeline." Lamar Fike brought in "My Little Friend" from a new writer of his, Shirl Milete, as well as "Wearin' That Loved On Look" from Doodle Owens, and the Eddie Rabbitt song "Inherit The Wind," which he had submitted at literally every session since August of 1967.

Around this time the Elvis music companies had acquired half ownership of another publisher, American Music (no relation to the studio); the first song from this new cata-

With the American studio band: (left to right) Bobby Wood, Mike Leech, Tommy Cogbill, Gene Chrisman, Elvis, Bobby Emmons, Reggie Young, Ed Kollis, and Dan Penn

log was "Long Black Limousine," at the time a minor country hit for Jody Miller. Written in highly melodramatic form, it tells the grim tale of a country girl who leaves everything behind in search of big-city success only to be returned home in a hearse, and when Elvis selected it as his first number at the session, he brought to it a sense of loss and desolation, a kind of anger that seemed driven by an almost personal identification with the subject of the song. Whatever the source of the feeling, the passion in his voice has few counterparts in his recorded work; perhaps only in "It Hurts Me" and "If I Can Dream," and in the fervor of his 1966 gospel recordings, does he give himself over so completely to anguish. The band played with simple effectiveness, leaving space for the singer to explore, and the story of the song emerges almost like a movie, brought to life by the detailed additions of the overdubbed arrangement. When they recorded the song, Chips left the middle eight bars open; it was a strategy that would have been unusual to Elvis, who was used to his players soloing live as he cheered them on, but for Chips the break was simply a setting for the horn and vocal overdubs he already had in his head.

"This Is The Story," from the newly signed English team of Arnold, Morrow, and Martin, got a big push from Freddy, who had just concluded arrangements to have all music from his London-based company, Carlin Music, go through Elvis's companies in the United States. This slow ballad was brought to life once again by the simplicity of the musical setting, particularly by Tommy Cogbill's fluid bass lines and Chips's later overdubs, which added strings and a female vocal that blended perfectly with Elvis's, giving the song even greater richness. There was a rough, almost hoarse tone to Elvis's voice in this performance—a coloring that recalled the passion of the NBC special, but also a sign that he was developing a cold. He took a break as the band cut a backing track for one of RCA's submissions, Don Thomas and Mike Millius's "Come Out, Come Out," but though they tried it in two different tempos Elvis never laid down a vocal.

At three in the morning Elvis was back at the microphone, ready to tackle "Wearing That Loved On Look," a song written in a funky, soulful genre that was both contemporary and well suited to Elvis. Altering the lyrics, laughing as his voice cracked, throwing in the first two lines of "A Little Less Conversation," Elvis was relaxed and energetic as they ran through a series of incomplete takes, finally making it to the end at take ten. The rhythm track was still a mess, Elvis's voice was wearing thin, and Chips had to make some adjustments to the reverb to compensate. "If we get a good one on the first part," Elvis suggested, "we better keep it." Chips agreed, and chose take fifteen as the master with a plan to have Elvis repair the ragged lines the following week. Things were definitely looking up as everyone left the studio that morning. Elvis was in good spirits, the publishing setup had delivered recordable material, and the tracks sounded more in step with the times than anything Elvis had released since the '50s.

That spirit carried over to the opening song on the second night, with Reggie Young's electric sitar setting the innovative tone. Echoing the sound he'd gotten on the Box Tops hit "Cry Like A Baby" the previous summer, Reggie worked out an introduction to "You'll Think Of Me." Songwriter Mort Shuman had written some of

Elvis's biggest '60s hits with Doc Pomus, but as the sole writer here he was looking for his first cut since 1966. After a handful of false starts, one of the group called out "That's a Top Ten already!" and Felton agreed. Chips pushed them on to more than twenty takes until he finally had what he wanted, knowing all along he'd have to redo Elvis's vocal track once his voice had recovered. They limped through "A Little Bit Of Green," another Arnold, Morrow, and Martin song with little commercial potential, before it was time to eat. At 2:00 A.M. they began jamming on Hank Snow's classic "I'm Moving On," Elvis singing what lyrics he could remember with what little voice he had left. The night ended with John Hartford's "Gentle On My Mind," a hit for Glen Campbell (Felton Jarvis had recorded Hartford's original version back in 1967). With its sophisticated, intricate lyrics, the song ripped apart whatever was left of Elvis's larynx, and they called it quits.

The next day Elvis was grounded with full-blown laryngitis. But the building-block approach meant that for the moment they could go on without him, so the group worked on a song that had reached the session through Billy Strange's intervention. Encouraged by the cuts he and cowriter Mac Davis had landed on both the TV special and two movie soundtracks, he had invited Elvis to meet Mac. According to Marty Lacker they had gotten together in an apartment in Los Angeles, where Mac sat in the corner playing guitar and singing his songs. From a tape he was later sent Elvis selected several numbers, and on the third night of the recording session the band laid down tracks for two of them, "Don't Cry Daddy" and "Poor Man's Gold." Chips's goal, as always, was simplicity; getting the correct key and tempo with bass and drums was all he needed. As with "Come Out, Come Out," they cut the second song in two different tempos, with Bobby Wood providing a guiding vocal.

Lamar's song, "Inherit The Wind," was next, and then Chips worked in a sentimental tune from his own Press Publishing, Johnny Christopher's "Mama Liked The Roses," a song that Elvis had really fallen for. The next evening, with Elvis still laid up at Graceland, Freddy and Lamar came up with a string of songs, "My Little Friend," "Send Out Love," "Sweet Angeline," "Salt," and "Rubberneckin'," that sounded more like standard Nashville fare, and only a backing track for "My Little Friend" was recorded. It wasn't the kind of innovative material that had so energized Elvis the first days of the session, but everyone took off in hopes that Elvis would be well enough to record the following Monday. Over the weekend Reggie Young, Gene Chrisman, and Bobby Emmons were back in the studio to repair and build

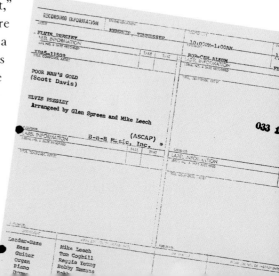

further parts onto the new arrangement of "I'm Moving On" with the Memphis Horns, whose funky stylings were an important ingredient in Chips's sound.

When he returned on Monday evening, Elvis took yet another step in his development as a serious contemporary artist. He had always avoided making any sort of political statement, but during the '60s the folk movement had engendered a change in the lyric content of pop music, and even Elvis (who by this point was as close to a rock 'n' roll "establishment" figure as there was) had begun recording lyrically challenging songs like "Clean Up Your Own Back Yard" and "If I Can Dream." Now, Chips was making no bones about it: If Elvis didn't record Mac Davis's "In The Ghetto"—an inner-city morality tale that pointed a finger at social (and, by extension, racial) injustices—he would put out the record on one of his own artists. Elvis didn't really need to be convinced. He loved the song, was convinced of the sincerity of its message, and felt strongly about the issue. And his feelings were echoed in his performance: For once devoid of any of his characteristic vocal tricks or mannerisms, it relied instead on the astonishing clarity and sensitivity of his voice. He simply told the story, and the drama came through in the quiet dignity of the telling, underlined by a steady, ominously foreshadowing drum roll. After take four the musicians stopped and listened to a playback, then decided to go for a higher key. Chips knew they almost had it, but he kept on pushing, making suggestions after each new run-through. After take eleven, when they reconstructed the middle eight bars, the group's concentration began to waver: "It's falling all to pieces," Chips warned, bringing them back on course. Take twenty was "great," but Elvis needed to watch his "p"s to avoid mike pops. Twenty-one was better still. Chips pushed through two more takes until he was fully satisfied with the band tracks, but he wanted more from Elvis, and as the musicians put down their instruments Chips got the singer to dub a new vocal performance on top of the completed background. It wasn't the way Elvis was used to working, and it might not even have been the way he preferred to work. But the circumstances hardly held him back, and he delivered an exquisitely committed performance. Elvis was singing so strongly that for the next entry Al Pachucki, the Nashville engineer that RCA had sent, cued up the backing tracks for "Gentle On My Mind," the song Elvis had given up on the week before. Elvis's flawless delivery would make the number one of the highlights of the first album to come from the sessions (after the band, in turn, redid its own parts). Ed Kollis added harmonica in the overdub, and Ronnie Milsap, a local favorite since moving to Memphis, sat in on keyboards as well as singing along on a few lines. The evening concluded on a more ordinary note with "Rubberneckin'," a song Ben Weisman had submitted in his wife's name; this was the kind of song that even a year before might have made passing movie fodder, but at American, in just two takes, Elvis and the band pounded it into solid rock 'n' roll. (And yet, inevitably, it *did* end up as a movie song—on the soundtrack of Elvis's last narrative film, *Change of Habit*.)

Nearly everyone had arrived at these sessions full of anxiety and concern about the future. Felton Jarvis, Elvis's de facto A&R man and producer, had yet to produce a full-scale hit on his friend. He'd been on the sidelines for the success of the TV special and the "If I Can Dream" single it spawned, and he had no intention of being swept aside again. If getting hit records meant sharing the producer's duties with Chips Moman—or even abandoning them for a simple A&R role—he wouldn't argue as long as he could still be a player. And on Elvis's part there was an apparent urgency in his eagerness to please, to deliver the very best he could at Chips's prodding. As the sessions went on he grew confident that they were on the right track; he knew he was being challenged, and was challenging himself, in a way he hadn't since perhaps the days with Sam Phillips. Later he would say that he never worked as hard as he did at American in the beginning of 1969.

There was a feeling of experiment in the air, and on Tuesday evening that second week of recording it seemed like a natural choice to try a Beatles song. Elvis knew only a few lines of John Lennon and Paul McCartney's "Hey Jude," and he would be unable to complete the song that evening without the lyric sheets, but what they could do vibrated with the same feeling as the night before. Elvis abandoned the idea after the takes they got that first night, leaving what they all must have considered an incomplete recording (but one that was eventually released, scratchy vocals and all, three years later, as RCA went looking for material to flesh out an album). They'd built up a backlog of songs that needed repairs, including "I'm Moving On" and "Long Black Limousine," and now he turned to his vocal-overdubbing obligations. He recorded complete vocal tracks for "My Little Friend," "Inherit The Wind," "Mama Liked The Roses," and "Don't Cry Daddy." But he only got a couple of lines into "Poor Man's Gold" before the sound of a fire engine passing outside sent him into a fit of giggles, and with that they left the RCA submission "Come Out, Come Out" behind.

To get rid of some of his excess energy he started fooling around with the old country hit "From A Jack To A King" on his guitar. It was one of his father's favorite songs, and with the sessions being held so close to Graceland his father had stopped by that night. Elvis had certainly considered cutting the song seriously, but that wasn't what he had in mind now; nonetheless, the mocking edge in his voice took nothing away from a performance that shone with pure spontaneous enjoyment. He was having a ball.

The following evening Elvis came in early to meet Roy Hamilton, who was working with producer Tommy Cogbill on an album for Chips's AGP label. In a burst of characteristic generosity, Elvis suggested that "Angelica," a Barry Mann–Cynthia Weill composition he was planning to record, would be perfect for Roy, and gave the older singer the song. "Angelica" turned out to be the single released from Hamilton's session, but the session would be his last; by that summer, Elvis's idol had succumbed to a stroke.

Excited by his meeting with a longtime role model, Elvis threw himself whole-heartedly into the next song, "Without Love," a gospel-tinged ballad originally recorded by Clyde McPhatter. This wasn't work, just an intense, go-for-broke performance caught on the third full take. In the same spirit as "You'll Never Walk Alone" from back in 1967, "Without Love" joined the simplicity of a country lyric with the passion of a great soul ballad, and his gospel-flavored treatment took it to a level of spirituality rarely matched in his career. Without a break Elvis hit the piano keys again, starting in on Eddy Arnold's "I'll Hold You In My Heart ('Till I Can Hold You In My Arms)," taking a simple country song and transforming it into a four-and-a-half-minute ecstatic, soulful plea. He lost himself in the emotion of the song, which he knew well from Eddy's version but remembered better from the more recent 1963 version by the Sons of the Pioneers. They weren't the new hits Chips and Felton were looking for, but "Without Love" and "I'll Hold You In My Heart" were pure Elvis: the kind of material he'd been suggesting since his May and June 1966 sessions, and that might have made up the bulk of the repertoire for his aborted Hollywood sessions the following year. By the time he kicked off "I'll Be There" he was just blowing off steam again; more of a spiritual partner to "From A Jack To A King," it was the kind of upbeat ballad Elvis found himself busking through in odd moments—not to be taken too seriously, but still a part of the musical universe inside Elvis's head.

The sessions were coming to an end. This was to be Elvis's last night, though Chips still had plenty of overdubbing work to do with the Memphis Horns and the girl singers. Just after midnight Chips urged Elvis to try his hand at "Suspicious Minds," a song that had gone nowhere when Chips had recorded it by its young writer, Mark James. Marty Lacker, George Klein, and Elvis's foreman Joe Esposito all recognized the song as a potential smash and encouraged Elvis to give it a shot. Working from the original arrangement, the band faltered after the first take, but Chips steered them toward the right groove; at the same time Elvis worked at getting the lyrics down, even asking Bobby Wood to sing along to help prevent Elvis from repeating mistakes. It felt good from the first take, and Elvis was relaxed enough to practice karate exercises between takes. "Save the last take for me," he sang jokingly as they neared the finish line; by the time they left that evening, they knew they'd saved one of the best for last.

The only cloud on the horizon was Chips Moman's refusal to give up any piece of "Suspicious Minds" or "Mama Liked The Roses." Freddy Bienstock, Tom Diskin, and Chips Moman were all headstrong men, and it took RCA representative Harry Jenkins, always the diplomat, to prevent publishing disputes from derailing Elvis's most significant new work in years. In a rare gesture of interference in the business side of his own career, Elvis declared that he wouldn't let a publishing dispute stop him from recording and releasing a song he liked. His enthusiasm carried into a rare, early-morning interview, when Elvis, clad in white shirt and trousers, raved to a reporter from the Memphis *Commercial Appeal*: "It all started right here in Memphis for me, man." With a gracious Chips Moman by his side, he celebrated his new surroundings. "It feels so good working in this studio," he said, and Chips returned the compliment: "He is one of the hardest-working artists I have ever been associated with. . . . What energy and enthusiasm he has while working." "We've done some hits, haven't we, Chips?" Elvis asked. "Maybe some of your biggest," was the modest response.

There was every reason to think they could keep it going at American, so before Elvis and Priscilla left to go skiing in Aspen the studio was booked for a week in February. Charlie Hodge set to work right away letting Tom Diskin know what Elvis had in mind for these new sessions. "Angelica" remained on the list, but most of the songs were old favorites, and among others included Percy Mayfield's "Stranger In My Own Home Town," Della Reese's "After Loving You," Ivory Joe Hunter's "I Will Be True," and Marty Robbins's "You Gave Me A Mountain." Freddy Bienstock was unable to make publishing deals for "When The Snow Is On The Roses," a 1957 hit for Ed Ames, or for a handful of others: "Rags To Riches," a 1953 recording by Billy Ward and the Dominoes; "Chills And Fever," Ronnie Love's 1961 hit; Dusty Springfield's "You Don't Have To Say You Love Me;" and the Five Keys' "Let There Be You," from 1957. He was trying to clear Ray Peterson's hit "The Wonder of You," but was at a loss for publishing information on the jailbreak story-song "I Washed My Hands In Muddy Water." The only song of Freddy's that Elvis had put on his list was Giant, Baum, and Kaye's "Power Of My Love," and this would be the only song from Freddy's original list that would make it into the second session at American. Elvis was always going to be prone to throwing in songs he loved, regardless of their source, but clearly they couldn't keep arguing about this kind of thing in the studio; as a result, absolutely no songs that hadn't been cleared were brought to the February sessions.

95. Studio Sessions for RCA
February 17–22, 1969: American Studios, Memphis

A&R/Producer: Chips Moman & Felton Jarvis
Engineer: Al Pachucki

Guitar: Reggie Young
Bass: Tommy Cogbill
Drums: Gene Chrisman
Piano: Bobby Wood
Piano: Elvis Presley (1269 outtakes)
Organ: Bobby Emmons
Harmonica: Ed Kollis (1265, 66, 68)

Overdubbed:
Vocals: Sonja Montgomery, Millie Kirkham, Dolores Edgin, Hurshel Wiginton, Joe Babcock
Vocals: Ronnie Milsap (1271)
Strings

Overdubbed:
The Memphis Horns:
Trumpet: R. F. Taylor
Trumpet: Wayne Jackson
Trumpet: Dick Steff (1266–67)
Sax: Glen Spreen
Sax: J. P. Luper (1266–67)
Trombone: Jackie Thomas
Trombone: Jack Hale
Trombone: Gerald Richardson (1266–67)
French Horn: Tony Cason
French Horn: Joe D'Gerolamo
Vocals: Mary Greene, Donna Thatcher, Mary Holladay, Susan Pilkinton (1266–67)

2/17, 8–11PM

WPA5 2513-01 **It's My Way/This Time/I Can't Stop Loving You**
Pierce/Walker—Chips Moman/Don Gibson

Walk A Mile In My Shoes
66160-2/1993

XPA5 1265-na	**True Love Travels On A Gravel Road**	**From Elvis In Memphis**
	A. L. Owens/Dallas Frazier—Blue Crest & Elvis Presley Music	*LSP 4155/1969*
XPA5 1266-01	**Stranger In My Own Home Town**	**From Vegas To Memphis**
	Percy Mayfield—Tangerine Music	*LSP 6020/1969*

1–4AM

XPA5 1267-06	**And The Grass Won't Pay No Mind**	**From Memphis To Vegas**
	Neil Diamond—Stonebridge Music	*LSP 6020/1969*

2/18, 7:30–10:30PM

XPA5 1268-07	**Power Of My Love**	**From Elvis In Memphis**
	Giant/Baum/Kaye—Elvis Presley Music	*LSP 4155/1969*

11PM–2AM

XPA5 1269-04	**After Loving You**	**From Elvis In Memphis**
	E. Miller/J. Lantz—Red River Songs	*LSP 4155/1969*

2:30–5:30AM

XPA5 1270-07	**Do You Know Who I Am**	**From Memphis To Vegas**
	Bobby Russell—Russell-Cason Music	*LSP 6020/1969*

2/19, 7:30–10:30PM, 11PM–2AM

XPA5 1271-10	**Kentucky Rain**	**Single A-side**
	E. Rabbitt—D. Heard/S-P-R & Elvis Presley Music	*47-9791/1970*

2:30–5:30AM

XPA5 1272-29	**Only The Strong Survive**	**From Elvis In Memphis**
	Gamble/Huff/Butler—Parabut/Double Diamond/Downstairs	*LSP 4155/1969*

2/20, 9:30PM–12:30AM

XPA5 1273-03	**It Keeps Right On A-Hurtin'**	**From Elvis In Memphis**
	Johnny Tillotson—Ridge Music	*LSP 4155/1969*

1–4AM

XPA5 1274-06	**Any Day Now**	**Single B-side**
	Bob Hilliard/Burt Bacharach—Plan Two Music	*47-9741/1969*

4:30–7:30AM

XPA5 1275-09	**If I'm A Fool (For Loving You)**	**Let's Be Friends**
	Stan Kesler—Drury Lane/Beckie Music	*CAS 2408/1970*

2/21, 7:30–10:30PM

XPA5 1276-na	**The Fair Is Moving On**	**Single B-side**
	Fletcher/Flett—Elvis Presley Music	*47-9747/1969*

2/22, 9PM–12AM

XPA5 1278-na	**Who Am I?**	**Elvis' Christmas Album (budget album)**
	Charles Rusty Goodman—Journey Music	*CAL 2472/1970*

1277 is an instrumental track for the Dallas Frazier/A. L. Owens song "Memory Revival."

It was an American Studio tradition: paying tribute to the chief with a rendition of "This Time," a Chips Moman–penned hit for Troy Shondell in 1961. Elvis had heard about the rite, and he serenaded his producer at the start of the February session with the few lines that he knew, segueing into Don Gibson's "It's My Way," a song he had asked Freddy to check out the year before. Plunking along on his acoustic guitar, laughing at his own mistakes but singing his heart out, he drew the band into another Don Gibson number, "I Can't Stop Loving You," which he would transform into a dramatic show-stopper six month later in Las Vegas. Then it was time to turn to the real agenda—Dallas Frazier and Doodle Owens's "True Love Travels On A Gravel Road." He'd delivered a successful version of the duo's "Wearin' That Loved On Look" at the January sessions, and now Lamar had returned with this soul ballad and another Frazier and Owens song, "Memory Revival." Elvis was in great high spirits, cussing when he messed up, obviously feeling comfortable and energetic. Chips listened for a while before gently interjecting, "I think it needs some arranging," then suggesting to Reggie Young that he run his guitar through his Leslie amplifier. "True Love Travels On A Gravel Road" was a ballad in need of a beat; the challenge was to find the right tempo. Elvis was still working out on acoustic guitar after one beautiful but too-slow take, when Reggie suggested politely, "Keep playing if it helps you, but that one time in the middle is a little weird, really." When was the last time anyone criticized Elvis at a recording session? There was an awkward moment of silence followed by scattered, nervous laughter, but the tension passed quickly as they struggled on together through a number of takes, before finally getting a master.

The next tune up was a blues, "Stranger In My Own Home Town"—a perfect choice, surprising only because Elvis rarely recorded straight blues. This was a selection from that brief period of intensive listening and home recording in 1966, when Elvis had begun rediscovering his own musical foundations. The song's lyrics could be read as a gloss on either his life in Memphis or his place in the rock world circa 1969 ("My home town won't accept me/Just don't feel welcome 'round here no more"), and while Chips had little interest in an old number by a philosophical blues singer (Percy Mayfield was known as "The Poet of the Blues"), Elvis couldn't be stopped from sinking his teeth into the number. Once the beat was turned around, the group produced four minutes of groove blues in a spirit that even a later coating of half-hearted overdubs couldn't dampen.

They ate a lot of chicken in the studio that week, and after one such feast Chips brought up "And The Grass Won't Pay No Mind," the song he'd promised Neil Diamond in return for rescheduling his own session. "You scared the shit out of me," Elvis complained when Gene Chrisman hit the cymbal as they were getting started, and it took a while to reset the echo and find the right tempo. Chips was determined to get this right, stopping take two before they really got into it. "The playing was all in pieces anyway," he scolded the group; "the rhythm was off." It was a night full of such interruption from Chips, and before the evening drew to a close at 4:00 A.M. a nearly spent Elvis was still able to joke. "Listen easy, you can hear," he crooned the opening line, then paused to reconsider: "You can hear Chips calling."

The writing team of Giant, Baum, and Kaye were stalwarts of Elvis's publishing stable, having followed up 1963's number-three hit "Devil In Disguise" with a string of weaker tunes for the movies. Their new submission, "Power Of My Love," was an older song Freddy had been bringing up for years, but this time he got Elvis's undivided attention. The song lent itself perfectly to the tough, soulful approach that was coming out of these sessions, and Elvis threw himself into it without shame, leering obviously over the song's clever innuendoes, transforming it into a steaming, potent blues tour de force. The upfront sexuality of the cut was underscored by the sharp horn arrangement, Ed Kollis's wailing harmonica, and a set of orgasmic countervocals from the girl singers. This was the only submission by Freddy Bienstock to make it onto tape, and it may be no accident that it's Felton, not Chips, whose encouraging voice survives on the session tapes.

That same spirited chorus of support—this time from Elvis's little circle of friends—responded to his announcement: "I'll tell you what. I'm gonna play piano," at the beginning of the next cut. To an outside observer the song Elvis had in mind, "After Loving You," might have seemed like an off-the-cuff choice, but Elvis had been practicing Eddy Arnold's 1962 hit for years and had informed Freddy that he planned to record it. Playing in his familiar staccato style, Elvis sang the song with the same passion he'd brought to "One Night," pushing it as hard as he could. As accomplished as it may have been, this kind of tossed-off performance was directly counter to the way Chips liked to work—which became clear as Moman took over once again for the next song, the lachrymose "Do You Know Who I Am." Here Chips could bring all the careful craftsmanship that was his stock in trade, while Elvis did his best with his bluesy phrasings to breathe some life into the song's folk-country melody. There were problems with one vocal modulation, and the strain was beginning to show in Elvis's voice, but these were problems that could be repaired later; for Chips the main thing was to get the rhythm track right, and once he'd asked Gene Chrisman to use brushes instead of tambourine and Tommy Cogbill to play less busily, he got the sound he wanted.

Everyone worked hard the following day as well, and Elvis's longtime comrade Lamar Fike must have been beaming. Two of his tunes, "My Little Friend" and "Inherit The Wind," had been recorded in January, and another, "Memory Revival," was slated to be cut before the end of these sessions. Newly encouraged, he had gone back to his star songwriter, Eddie Rabbitt, and persuaded him to give up his best new song, a contemporary country ballad called "Kentucky Rain." So he must have been thrilled when at 7:30 on the evening of February 19 Elvis started work on the new number, putting Lamar one song ahead of his boss Freddy Bienstock. "I like that tempo," Chips began, "but one thing is wrong. It needs to feel a little brighter. The tempo is about right, but it needs just to have a little edge to it, you know. . . . I think it'll come naturally, just count it off at the same tempo." It wasn't an easy song for the musicians to grasp, and it took hours to work out the difficulties and arrive at a truly accomplished rendition—but it was worth it. This song, everyone agreed, was a potential single. Chips and Felton were united, Chips as producer shouting instructions, Felton as cheerleader offering the kind of support Elvis relied on to spur him onward.

If "Kentucky Rain" was the best of contemporary country, Jerry Butler's "Only The Strong Survive" was its soul brother on the rhythm-and-blues side. Written by Butler with the Gamble and Huff writing team, the song was a recent soul and pop hit, and a perfect vehicle for updating Elvis's musical profile. A strange hum on the tape brought the proceedings to a halt until they discovered the source: "Somebody's got a car running out back." It wasn't easy to compete with Jerry Butler's beautifully modulated vocal performance, and in the course of twenty-nine takes Elvis berated himself repeatedly—"That's one of the worst jobs of singing I have ever heard in my life"—but he never gave up on the song. Even Freddy was impressed; even though it wasn't his song, he was impelled to rave about it to Bob Dylan several days later when he ran into him on the plane back to New York. They detoured to oldies territory again with "It Keeps Right On A'Hurtin'," Johnny Tillotson's big hit from 1962, then undertook a cover of Chuck Jackson's soul hit of the same year, "Any Day Now" by Burt Bacharach, as popular a songwriter as you could find in 1969. Here Felton was at ease, so Chips kept a lower profile; the two had found a way to work together, while that Elvis himself took care of the music.

By 4:30 the next morning they were tired—and they'd pretty much exhausted the song list they'd come in with. Elvis and piano player Bobby Wood were sitting quietly on the piano bench talking about religion and music. Bobby had had a minor hit as a recording artist with "Searchin' " and had recorded Sun writer Stan Kesler's "If I'm A Fool (For Loving You)." Elvis introduced Bobby to his father, and when Vernon said that "If I'm A Fool" was one of his favorites, Elvis decided to give it a try. Maybe it was just too late in the day to introduce a new song, but even with Bobby's help the master they produced elicited only one word from Elvis: "Rotten." It's a measure of how high Elvis's standards had risen by this point: The master of "If I'm A Fool" may have been one of the lesser cuts Elvis made at American, but measured against the years of Hollywood soundtrack crap that came before, it was still a giant leap of musicality. The next night they tried only two new songs: "The Fair's Moving On" from Freddy Bienstock's English team Flett and Fletcher, and Frazier and Owens's "Memory Revival," which came by way of Lamar Fike. Elvis threw himself into the former but didn't participate at all in the latter, never actually doing a vocal track for it. On the 22nd Elvis returned to do repairs and to try another song Bobby Wood had recorded, the religious "Who Am I"; it was a fine last-minute addition to what had been a truly epochal session.

Change of Habit would be the thirty-first and last of the Elvis Presley fiction films, and except for the up-front money Elvis and the Colonel received for it, it was an obvious commercial misfire. The script placed Elvis as an inner-city doctor against Mary Tyler Moore as a nun, but the TV special (and recordings like "In The Ghetto") had already put Elvis into the contemporary world in a far more convincing way. As a cost-

cutting measure the original plans called for the film to use a few old Nashville masters—
"Just For Old Time Sake" (1962) and "Mine" (1967)—but in the end Ben Weisman was
awarded the entire soundtrack, save for one Arnold, Morrow, and Martin song, "Let's Be
Friends," which was ultimately dropped from the film. The title song may have had
some lyrical significance, but entries like "Have A Happy" were good (read *bad*) exam-
ples of just what had gone wrong with the Elvis-musical concept. One of the Weisman
demos was sung by Ray Peterson, whose smash hit "The Wonder Of You" Elvis had only
a few weeks before considered recording in Memphis, but that was as close as the *Change
of Habit* soundtrack got to the level of achievement Elvis had managed just a few weeks
before in his hometown. Even with Billy Goldenberg from the NBC special directing the
session, Elvis must have wondered what he was doing there.

96. Soundtrack Recordings for Universal's *Change of Habit*
March 5–6, 1969: Decca Universal Studio, Hollywood

Musical Director: Billy Goldenberg
Engineers: Mel Metcalf, Phil Yen

Guitar: Dennis Budimir
Guitar: Mike Deasy
Guitar: Howard Roberts
Guitar: Robert Bain (3/6)
Bass: Joe Mondragon
Fender: Lyle Ritz
Fender: Max Bennett (3/6)

Drums: Carl O'Brian
Piano: Roger Kellaway

Overdubbed:
Vocals: B. J. Baker, Sally Stevens, Jackie Ward
Vocals: The Blossoms (1957)

3/5, 7PM–2AM. 3/6, 7PM–2AM

MB2-06	**Change Of Habit**	**Let's Be Friends**
ZPA4 1058	*Buddy Kaye/Ben Weisman—Gladys Music*	*CAS 2408/1970*
MB3-sp	**Let's Be Friends**	**Let's Be Friends**
ZPA4 1057	*Arnold/Morrow/Martin—Elvis Presley Music*	*CAS 2408/1979*
MB5-08	**Let Us Pray**	**You'll Never Walk Alone**
ZPA4 1957	*Buddy Kaye/Ben Weisman—Gladys Music*	*CAL 2472/1971*
MV6-07	**Have A Happy**	**Let's Be Friends**
ZPA4 1056	*Weisman/Fuller/Kaye—Gladys Music*	*CAS 2408/1970*

The master of "Let's Be Friends" (1057) consists of take 3 and a work-part ending. The Blossoms: Darlene Love, Jean King,
Fanita James. Elvis recorded a new vocal to "Let Us Pray," probably in September in Nashville.

Elvis's last film role might have been less than inspiring, but his record sales were
definitely on the rise. "If I Can Dream," from the TV special, peaked in early February
at number twelve, higher than any record since "I'm Yours" back in 1965. The new single sold close to three quarters of a million copies, and the TV special album put Elvis back
in the gold for the first time since *Elvis Golden Records Vol. 3* in 1963. The one other com-

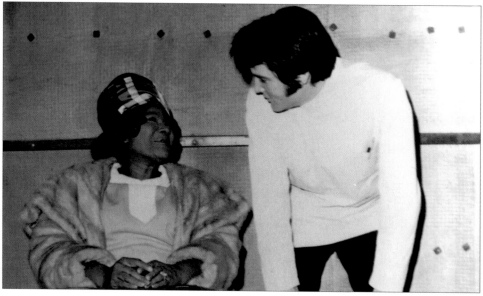

Meeting an idol: Elvis with Mahalia Jackson on the Change of Habit *set, early 1969*

mercially viable song from the special, "Memories," was released as a single with the title song from *Charro* as the B-side, a gesture from the Colonel to National General Pictures.

The Colonel's business maneuvers were always based on the perceived bargaining powers of the participants; he had always been able to make deals for Elvis when the present was bright, and the future appeared unlimited. The move to American had come at a time when the future was uncertain, and in Chips Moman they had picked a musical director who wasn't going to fall into line without a fight. In short, they had needed Chips, and now Chips was continuing to hold his ground, refusing to give up any share of the publishing on "Suspicious Minds." From the moment Elvis recorded it there was no question that "In The Ghetto" would be the first single from the sessions, and when it came time to select album cuts Chips chose twelve of the sessions' most contemporary songs. Perhaps only coincidentally, he eliminated every one of Freddy Bienstock's original songs, as well as many of Elvis's own spontaneous choices during the sessions. "Suspicious Minds," "Kentucky Rain," and "Don't Cry Daddy" were all saved for future single release, leaving room for a select quartet of Elvis favorites: "I'll Hold You in My Heart," "After Loving You," "It Keeps Right On A'Hurtin', " and "I'm Movin' On." "Mama Liked The Roses" made Chips's cut, but the air between the producer and Elvis's management was getting heady with tension, and the song was dropped from the album in favor of Giant, Baum, and Kaye's "Power Of My Love." Freddy made cut-in arrangements for "In The Ghetto" and "Don't Cry Daddy," so they didn't suffer the same stigma as Chips's songs; the same was true of "Poor Man's Gold," though Elvis would never return to cut a vocal track for the song.

Meanwhile, American was like a train station at rush hour. Mike Leech and Glen Spreen, the regular studio arrangers, were assigned to work out sweetening tracks for the Memphis Horns to lay over the single and the ten album cuts. It was also their job to finish "Rubberneckin' " for inclusion in *Change of Habit*. Working frenetically, Felton and Chips added the final elements while communicating with Elvis by special delivery and telephone calls to Los Angeles, where he was working on the movie. Elvis originally had serious doubts about the female voices on "In The Ghetto" and asked Felton to remove them, but he changed his mind again before it could be done; in the end he liked the soulful "black" sound the four white singers delivered. At this point, with most of the work done on the prime batch of songs, the tapes were shipped to Nashville for Felton to supervise his own overdubbing sessions with his own arranger, Don Tweedy, and a top-notch group of Nashville musicians.

Chips and Felton had each entered into this arrangement with good will and high hopes, and the success they'd achieved was beyond anyone's expectations. And yet now they found themselves at loggerheads over the same issues that had come up, if less dramatically, at every Nashville studio session over the last three years, including the NBC special: publishing, and production credit. Felton had long since accepted the Colonel's edict that no credits be listed on an Elvis album, but Chips Moman found this impossible to swallow. Chips Moman and American Studios had been chosen to bring their own distinctive sound to Elvis's recordings; to be told he wouldn't be listed as the album's producer, and then not to receive any producer royalties—from Chip's point of view this was both insult and injury. At some point during the selection and mixing of the titles for the album—allegedly when he was being pushed yet again to give up part of the publishing on "Suspicious Minds"—Chips told them all they could take a flying leap, that they should just consider the whole business "a very expensive demo session." In fact, maybe he wouldn't even charge them. "But don't ever come back to this studio again," he exploded. They didn't.

Felton finished overdubbing just days before the chart debut of "In The Ghetto," but without touching "Suspicious Minds." From number seventy-nine to forty-one, all the way up to number three in six weeks, "In The Ghetto" proved beyond any shadow of doubt that Elvis Presley wasn't just a temporarily resurrected former star, but once again a vital contemporary artist. Released in June, the amended album, *From Elvis In Memphis,* used a picture from the NBC show on the front and a conventional movie publicity still on the back— but what was inside was a revelation. Once again it was ELVIS LIKE YOU'VE NEVER HEARD HIM BEFORE, and the reception from the press and the fans equaled the reception that had greeted his return from the army in 1960. Now the stage was set for the consummation of his comeback—a stage that was already taking physical shape in the Nevada desert.

You're Wearing That Loved On Look
Only The Strong Survive
I'll Hold You In My Heart
Long Black Limousine
It Keeps On Hurting
Moving On

SIDE 2
Power of My Love (Single)
Any Day Now
Gentle On My Mind
After Loving You
True Love Travels On A Gravel Road
~~Mama Liked The Roses~~ (Out)
The Ghetto (Single)

1969

ALIVE AGAIN

In 1969 Elvis's career soared at a rate far exceeding that of its previous decline. Each new success initiated another, in an escalating tumble of events aided by wise decisions by both the Colonel and Elvis himself. The American Studios sessions had been highlighted by superb song selection, and the rewards were apparent by July, with rave reviews for both "In The Ghetto" and *From Elvis In Memphis*, culminating in gold records for each.

In the aftermath of the NBC special, the Colonel had instantly been approached by the management of the International Hotel, a venue scheduled to open imminently in Las Vegas featuring a two-thousand-seat showroom that was being billed as the city's largest. Elvis and his manager knew that a return to live performance was going to have to be the next step in the comeback campaign, and the Colonel took the bait. Parker proposed a two- or four-week engagement, with two shows on Fridays and Saturdays, and Mondays off. The price for four weeks would be $500,000. In the end Elvis got the money, but he had to play two shows every night except for the opening night—with no days off at all.

In many ways it was an unlikely step. Elvis's 1956 stint at the New Frontier had found him playing to deaf ears, and by the late '60s the town was firmly established as the home turf of artists like Frank Sinatra and Dean Martin, who'd originally taken great pride in distancing themselves from Elvis Presley and his kind. But Elvis had started making his peace with the Rat Pack as early as his 1960 Sinatra special, and though Sin City was a far cry from the singer's Bible Belt background, there were other considerations that made the difference. By relaunching his live career in Las Vegas, Elvis secured himself a guaranteed audience and fee for his first set of engagements— as opposed to going out on tour around the country, where his drawing power would be far less certain. The Colonel, who hadn't arranged a concert tour in twelve years (the two shows in 1961 were one-shot exceptions), was a little rusty in this line of work; almost everything had changed since Elvis's touring heyday, and many of his old connections weren't around anymore. He knew security would be a problem—it always was—and setting up in a new place every night would have demanded an organization that the Colonel hadn't had time to put together. Perhaps most important, Elvis's audience was no longer teenaged. But the Colonel felt confident that, as young adults and newlyweds like Elvis himself (who was thirty-four as he began preparing for the shows), they were more than likely to travel to Vegas for the combination of a glitzy vacation and a glimpse of their old idol.

To Elvis, though, Vegas meant something else. It was a chance to set the record straight—to wash off one of the few fiascoes of his career, to get back and get even. He had said that he'd "missed the closeness of a live audience," but just as likely he had his sights set on beating Sinatra and his gang at their own game. He talked a lot with his pals about the challenge, and he and Charlie Hodge spent a lot of time figuring out what it would take to project the small-scale TV-show setup onto a much larger Las Vegas stage. The black leather suit would be too hot to wear under the lights every day, so Elvis came up with the idea of having karate-style outfits made of a lighter fabric, which would leave him a lot of room for moving around. They talked about musicians, repertoire, and most important, how to pace an hour-long performance without driving Elvis and the band to exhaustion.

As the final arrangements were being made for Elvis to follow Barbra Streisand into the newly opened International, his various recent triumphs had already improved his status dramatically. The show would follow the basic concept of the TV special, highlighting Elvis's past achievements while featuring a smattering of new songs. Elvis's original backing group would be supplemented by the inevitable Vegas orchestra—or at least that was the plan. But Scotty Moore, D. J. Fontana, and the Jordanaires all declined the offer to come along, reluctant to give up the high-paying session work they were doing in Nashville even for a month for fear that it would no longer be there when they returned. Disappointed and hurt by what he took as a personal rejection (although it wasn't), Elvis was forced to put together a new group. He began by approaching James Burton, the mainstay of Ricky Nelson's original band and the guitarist who as a seventeen-year-old had played the famous lick that had defined Dale Hawkins's "Susie Q." Burton had spent the last ten years as one of the most in-demand session players in Hollywood, playing behind even Frank Sinatra himself; as Elvis's new group leader he brought with him fellow session standout Jerry Scheff on bass, who in turn recommended drummer Ronnie Tutt. Piano player Larry Muhoberac had played on Elvis sessions and even on Elvis's 1961 Memphis charity show, while RCA recording artist John Wilkinson rounded out this very contemporary band on rhythm guitar. Elvis compensated for the loss of the Jordanaires by hiring not one but two quartets. The Imperials returned to the fold after their stellar performance on the *How Great Thou Art* album, and while lead singers Jake Hess and Sherrill Nielsen were no longer with the group, it remained an outstanding gospel quartet. And, in a nod to the flavor of the NBC special, Elvis brought in the black gospel voices of the Sweet Inspirations, who had not only sung backup on all of Aretha Franklin's greatest hits but had a chart-topper with their own record "Sweet Inspiration." In a supreme compliment, Elvis gave them a warm-up segment of their own to introduce Elvis's one-hour performance.

Before assembling in Las Vegas for rehearsals, Elvis and Charlie Hodge worked overtime trying to settle on the best songs for the show. Although he had no official title, Charlie would be Elvis's right-hand man onstage for the rest of his live performances, singing harmony, holding sheet music should Elvis get lost, cueing the band members, later passing Elvis the scarves the star gave away to the audience. He was essentially a stage manager, and though Elvis's customary introduction ("the guy who gives me my water and my scarves") may have had a belittling edge to it, that kind of billing masked Charlie's important role in other aspects of the show. In putting together their set lists Elvis and Charlie knew they had to devote much of their time to a mix of past hits, recent singles, and the songs recorded in Memphis. But they were still eager to try new things, and among the unrecorded material they considered were numbers like the Beatles' Larry Williams cover "Slow Down" and their own "Yesterday" and "Hey Jude," country numbers like "Green, Green Grass Of Home," "Yellow Roses," "You're The Reason I'm Living," and "Release Me," even a lesser-known rockabilly classic like Carl Perkins's "Matchbox" (another Beatles cover, and one of the songs Perkins was fooling around with back when Elvis dropped into the Sun studios in December of 1956). Most of the unrecorded material was weeded out during rehearsals, as were lesser-known songs like "I Need You So," "Memphis Tennessee," and "Judy." More surprisingly, most of the Memphis material also got cut; Elvis concentrated on the current hit, "In The Ghetto," and developed a magnificent six-minute-plus version of the upcoming single, "Suspicious Minds." During the Las Vegas run Felton Jarvis mixed the final master of the latter, recording horns in former RCA engineer Bill Porter's Las Vegas studio, and adding an extended tail-fade to mimic the effect Elvis aimed at in the stage version.

Once the playlist was pared down, the group could focus on pacing the show. Naturally they would always open with a rocker, and during rehearsals they alternated between "All Shook Up," "I Got A Woman," and "Blue Suede Shoes," settling on the last when they opened. Although they'd all taken note of the unanimous praise Elvis's stripped-down TV special had received eight months earlier, Elvis and Charlie both felt that some of the new material would need a grander presentation—after all, this was Las Vegas, where the audiences were used to the kinds of elaborate and sophisticated big-band arrangements that supported the work of singers like Sinatra and Sammy Davis, Jr. For Elvis's purposes the big-band sound would be modified considerably, but he reserved the right to draw on the power of an orchestra to satisfy his own passion for drama. Don Gibson's "I Can't Stop Loving You" was worked up in a new, in-your-face arrangement, hammered out with piano triplets, bulldozing right over both its country origins and the seductively smooth Ray Charles version. In the Sweet Inspirations Elvis had a vocal group that could pour soulfulness and gospel flavor over anything he wanted just by opening their mouths, and on "I Can't Stop Loving You" he used them to add intensity throughout, before going out on a limb himself for an extended vocal workout at the end. Both of the vocal groups worked full-time, too, on the Bee Gees' sentimental ballad "Words," featuring a full choral ending. Elvis had also hired on his favorite soprano singer, Millie Kirkham, as the only musician from his Nashville band to join him in Las Vegas, and for her he came up with a high, wordless countervocal for "Are You Lonesome Tonight?," her voice soaring high above Elvis's own like a tormented soul crying out an unbearable loneliness. For the ending they debated among three candidates—"Hound Dog," with which they had usually closed in the '50s, "Such A Night," or "What'd I Say"—but in the end went with the more romantic "Can't Help Falling In Love," the perfect vehicle for a grand orchestral climax. There would be no encores.

97. Live Recordings for RCA
August 21–26, 1969: The International Hotel, Las Vegas

A&R/Producer: Felton Jarvis
Engineer: Al Pachucki

Guitar: James Burton
Guitar: John Wilkinson
Guitar & Vocals: Charlie Hodge
Bass: Jerry Scheff
Drums: Ronnie Tutt
Piano & Organ: Larry Muhoberac
Vocals: The Sweet Inspirations
Vocals: Millie Kirkham
Vocals: The Imperials

Bobby Morris & His Orchestra

Overdubbed (2315 and 2318 only):
Vocals: Jeannie Green, Mary Holladay,
Ginger Holladay, Sandy Posey,
Hurschel Wiginton, Millie Kirkham,
June Page, Joe Babcock,
Dolores Edgin

8/23, Midnight Show

WPA5 2529	**Reconsider Baby**	**Collectors Gold**
	Lowell Fulsom—Arc Music	*3114-2-R/1991*

8/24, Dinner Show

XPA5 2317	**Jailhouse Rock (not master)/Don't Be Cruel**	
	Leiber/Stoller—Elvis Presley Music—Otis Blackwell/Elvis Presley/Travis Music	

8/24, Midnight Show

XPA5 2309	**I Got A Woman**	
	Ray Charles—Progressive Music	
XPA5 2314	**Johnny B. Goode**	**From Memphis To Vegas**
	Chuck Berry—Arc Music	*LSP 6020/1969*
XPA5 2316	**Are You Lonesome Tonight?**	**From Memphis To Vegas**
	Roy Turk/Lou Handman—Bourne Co./Cromwell Music	*LSP 6020/1969*

8/25, Dinner Show

XPA5 2385	**Baby What You Want Me To Do**	
	Jimmy Reed—Conrad Pub.	

XPA5 2382	**Funny How Time Slips Away**	**Collectors Gold**
	Willie Nelson—Pamper Music	*3114-2-R/1991*
XPA5 2315	**Runaway**	**On Stage**
	Crook/Del Shannon—Vicki Music/Noma Music	*LSP 4362/1970*
XPA5 2318	**Yesterday/Hey Jude**	**On Stage/Unreleased**
	McCartney/Lennon—Maclen Music	*LSP 4362/Unreleased*
XPA5 2374	**In The Ghetto**	**From Memphis To Vegas**
	Scott Davis—B-n-B Music/Elvis Presley Music	*LSP 6020/1969*

8/25, Midnight Show

XPA5 2383	**Blue Suede Shoes**	**From Memphis To Vegas**
	Carl Perkins—Hi-Lo Music/Hill & Range	*LSP 6020/1969*
XPA5 2310	**All Shook Up**	**From Memphis To Vegas**
	Otis Blackwell/Elvis Presley—Elvis Presley Music/Travis Music	*LSP 6020/1969*
XPA5 2380	**Heartbreak Hotel**	
	Axton/Durden/Presley—Tree Pub.	
XPA5 2384	**Hound Dog**	**From Memphis To Vegas**
	Jerry Leiber/Mike Stoller—Elvis Presley Music/Lion Pub.	*LSP 6020/1969*
XPA5 2320	**I Can't Stop Loving You**	**From Memphis To Vegas**
	Don Gibson—Acuff Rose	*LSP 6020/1969*
XPA5 2381	**My Babe**	**From Memphis To Vegas**
	W. Dixon—Arc Music	*LSP 6020/1969*
XPA5 2386	**Mystery Train/Tiger Man**	**From Memphis To Vegas**
	J. H. Louis/S. Burns—Hi-Lo Music & Lewis Burns/Hi-Lo Music	*LSP 6020/1969*
XPA5 2313	**Words**	**From Memphis To Vegas**
	R. B. & M. Gibb—Nemperor Music	*LSP 6020/1969*
XPA5 2375	**What'd I Say**	
	Ray Charles—Progressive Music	

8/26, Dinner Show

XPA5 2311	**Love Me Tender**	
	E. Presley/V. Matson—Elvis Presley Music	
XPA5 2317	**Jailhouse Rock/Don't Be Cruel (not master)**	
	Leiber/Stoller—Elvis Presley Music & Otis Blackwell/Elvis Presley—Travis Music	
XPA5 2376	**Inherit The Wind**	**Collectors Gold**
	Eddie Rabbitt—S-P-R Music	*3114-2-R/1991*
XPA5 2312	**Suspicious Minds**	**From Memphis To Vegas**
	Mark James—Press Music	*LSP 6020/1969*
XPA5 2379	**Can't Help Falling In Love**	**From Memphis To Vegas**
	Peretti/Creatore/Weiss—Gladys Music	*LSP 6020/1969*

8/26, Midnight Show

| KPA5 9569 | **Are You Lonesome Tonight? (laughing version)** | **Elvis Aron Presley** |

	Roy Turk/Lou Handman—Bourne/Cromwell Music	*CPL8 3699/1980*
XPA5 2377	**Rubberneckin'**	**Collectors Gold**
	Dory Jones/Bunny Warren—Elvis Presley Music	*3114-2-R/1991*
XPA5 2378	**This Is The Story**	**Collectors Gold**
	Arnold/Morrow/Martin—Elvis Presley Music	*3114-2-R/1991*

8/21–26, Specifics Unknown

XPA5 2319   Memories

Billy Strange/Mac Davis—Gladys Music

The master of the "Jailhouse Rock/Don't Be Cruel" medley is a splice of the "Don't Be Cruel" part from the August 24 dinner show and the "Jailhouse Rock" part of the August 26 dinner show. The above list contains the masters as originally selected from these shows, with the addition of "Are You Lonesome Tonight?" (laughing version) which has become a legend in its own right. All other cuts released from this engagement are considered regular outtakes.

The reviews of the Las Vegas opening were nothing less than sensational. *Rolling Stone,* just emerging from underground to above-ground status as the country's leading music journal, had recently aimed its spotlight on rock's original heroes; now it raved, "Elvis was supernatural, his own resurrection." Clad in black karate-style outfits for most of the shows, often banging away at an electric guitar, the slim, suntanned singer worked so hard that many of the spectators wondered when he would collapse. He never did. The selection of material for the show remained much as he and Charlie had planned it. A medley of "Yesterday" and "Hey Jude" made a bow to contemporary music, as did the Bee Gees' "Words." Old favorites like "I Can't Stop Loving You," Del Shannon's "Runaway," Chuck Berry's "Johnny B. Goode," Willie Nelson's "Funny How Time Slips Away," and the R&B standard "My Babe" added variety to the shows. When the Colonel and RCA decided to record an album of the event, Felton rigged up an eight-track mobile unit, and for six nights beginning on August 21 recorded every show in its entirety. Elvis used the occasion to try out some of his recently recorded material, including "Inherit The Wind," "This Is The Story," and "Rubberneckin,'" though it was difficult to get the results to match the performance in the studio. But no matter: The entire engagement was a sellout and an overwhelming success. The only concern raised by the hotel was the content of Elvis's long monologues about his life and career. In the army, he told his audience, "those guys get awful lonely, saying *mother* all the time, and that's only half of it." When talking about his movies he'd display a disarming element of self-mockery: "I did *Loving You, Loving Her,* loving as many as I could get my hands on at the time." Just as in the early days, when the whip came down on some of Bill Black's crude country humor and off-color remarks, the Colonel reminded Elvis that this wasn't any ordinary venue; there might even be children present at the dinner shows. There was no stopping the momentum, though: The Colonel had no

The return to live performance: opening night at the International Hotel, Las Vegas, July 31, 1969.

trouble negotiating a five-year deal with the International Hotel, as well as a prestigious $150,000 six-show engagement at the Houston Livestock Show the following spring.

There was a temporary slip when "In The Ghetto," a top-three hit, was followed by a return to movie fare. The new single, "Clean Up Your Own Back Yard," was timed to the release of *The Trouble with Girls (And How to Get Into It)*, the film from which it was taken, after Felton tried to "modernize" Billy Strange's spare production with overdubs. But in spite of his efforts (and the Colonel's well-observed contention that the lyrics might appeal to a younger generation), the single never made it past number thirty-five. Elvis, though, had already moved on. The song everyone thought was the strongest from the Memphis sessions, "Suspicious Minds," proved equally successful in Las Vegas, and its late-August single release only confirmed its power. After a modest start at number seventy-seven, the song jumped more than forty places the following week, and after eight weeks became Elvis's first single since "Good Luck Charm" to reach number one. More than a million sales couldn't be wrong. By November RCA was ready with another new single, and, for the first time, an Elvis Presley double album. Mac Davis landed his second A-side single with "Don't Cry Daddy," which reached number six but sold almost as well as "Suspicious Minds." *From Memphis To Vegas—From Vegas To Memphis* (rereleased the following year as two single albums, *In Person* and *Back In Memphis*) joined the live album recorded in August with a second of ten songs from the Memphis session—including the two B-sides from the singles, "The Fair's Moving On" and "You'll Think Of Me," each published by Elvis's music companies. Perhaps in deference to the old philosophy that reserved hit singles exclusively for *Golden Records* anthologies, neither "Don't Cry Daddy" nor the single version of "Suspicious Minds" was included, although the live album did include Elvis's blazing seven-minute version of the latter, one of his most spectacular live performances ever.

Incorporating the two successful elements of the new Elvis—the Memphis sessions and the Las Vegas success—the double album wasn't as spectacular musically as *From Elvis In Memphis,* but it appealed to the record-buying public, climbing one step higher than the earlier album to number twelve on the charts. "We weren't the greatest rhythm section in the world," Larry Muhoberac recalled about the Vegas show band; "we'd speed up and down at times." But the live album had energy, and as the TV-special soundtrack album had demonstrated, there was a big audience out there for both nostalgia and souvenirs. The studio half of the set drew from what remained of the Memphis recordings, and without the singles RCA was left with what were essentially leftovers. Still Elvis's commitment shone through on many of the cuts, and the Percy Mayfield blues "Stranger In My Own Home Town" on its own was worth the price of admission.

Measured on both commercial and artistic scales, the '60s ended with Elvis's best year since the decade's first, and with the Colonel just itching to break new ground—to once again make the impossible possible. Against all logic, on January 26, 1970—just four months after his record-breaking opening—Elvis was back in Las Vegas. Booking his boy into the deadest season of what the contemporary rock press called "the graveyard of the stars" was the Colonel's way of announcing that Elvis stood ready to beat not only his own records but those of any other superstars in the sky. And the Colonel was once again proven right.

Opening night was sold out; the entire four-week January stint was sold out. The International was jammed with guests seeking the preferred-ticket status that came with registration at the hotel. The International was a small city unto itself, complete with shops, six restaurants, and a casino; a far cry from a rock venue like the Fillmore or even New York's Madison Square Garden, its theater boasted a golden curtain, chandeliers, and what Elvis called "funky angels" hanging from the ceiling. This was a setting designed for barely dressed showgirls and cabaret performers, and there may have been no more apt setting to throw into relief the abiding contradictions of Elvis Presley's career. When this young white boy with the black sound had hit the airwaves in 1954, he was a long-haired, sharp-dressed tornado amid the old-school country performers in cowboy outfits on the Louisiana Hayride. He was the tuxedo-clad rock 'n' roll singer on the "Steve Allen Show." He was the unsophisticated, barely trained amateur who became the highest-paid star in Hollywood. In 1967 he won a Grammy for Best Sacred Performance, and in 1968, at the height of flower power, he became a black-leather-clad rebel on TV. Now, as Elvis entered the 1970s, he brought all those paradoxes and more back to his second engagement at the International Hotel.

98. Live Recordings for RCA
February 15–19, 1970: The International Hotel, Las Vegas

A&R/Producer: Felton Jarvis
Engineer: Al Pachucki

Guitar: James Burton
Guitar: John Wilkinson
Guitar, Vocals: Charlie Hodge
Bass: Jerry Scheff
Drums: Bob Lanning
Piano: Glen D. Hardin
Vocals: The Sweet Inspirations
Vocals: Millie Kirkham
Vocals: The Imperials

Bobby Morris & His Orchestra

Vocals overdubbed later:
Mary Holladay, Mary Green,
Jim Glaser, Dolores Edgin
Ginger Holladay, Sandy Posey,
Hurshel Wiginton, Millie Kirkham,
June Page, Joe Babcock

2/16, Dinner Show

ZPA5 1289	**Proud Mary**	**On Stage**
	John Fogerty—Jondora Music	*LSP 4362/1970*
ZPA5 1293	**Sweet Caroline**	**On Stage**
	Neil Diamond—Stone Bridge Music	*LSP 4362/1970*

2/17, Midnight Show

ZPA5 1292	**Don't Cry Daddy**	
	Mac Davis—Elvis Presley Music/B-n-B Music	
ZPA5 1295	**Kentucky Rain**	
	E. Rabbitt/D. Heard—Elvis Presley Music/S-P-R Music	

ZPA5 1291 **Let It Be Me**   **On Stage**
    Mann Curtis/Pierre Delanoe/Gilbert Becaud—MCA Music   *LSP 4362/1970*

2/18, Dinner Show
ZPA5 1300 **The Wonder Of You**   **Single A-side**
    Baker Knight—Duchess Music   *47-9835/1970*

2/18, Midnight Show
ZPA5 1294 **Release Me**   **On Stage**
    Miller/Yount/Williams—4 Star Music   *LSP 4362/1970*
ZPA5 1290 **See See Rider**   **On Stage**
    Traditional, arranged by Elvis Presley—Elvis Presley Music   *LSP 4362/1970*
ZPA5 1298 **Polk Salad Annie**   **On Stage**
    Tony Joe White—Combine Music   *LSP 4362/1970*

2/19, Midnight Show
ZPA5 1297 **Walk A Mile In My Shoes**   **On Stage**
    Joe South—Lowery Music   *LSP 4362/1970*
ZPA5 1299 **I Can't Stop Loving You**
    Don Gibson—Acuff Rose

2/15–19, Specifics unknown
ZPA5-1286 **All Shook Up**
    Otis Blackwell/Elvis Presley—Elvis Presley Music/Travis Music
ZPA5 1287 **In The Ghetto**
    Scott Davis—B-n-B Music/Elvis Presley Music
ZPA5 1288 **Suspicious Minds**
    Mark James—Press Music
    I Got A Woman
    Ray Charles—Progressive Music
    Hound Dog
    Jerry Leiber/Mike Stoller—Elvis Presley Music/Lion Pub.
ZPA5 1296 **Long Tall Sally**
    Richard Penniman/Robert Blackwell
    Love Me Tender
    E. Presley/V. Matson—Elvis Presley Music
    Can't Help Falling In Love
    Peretti/Creatore/Weiss—Gladys Music

99. Rehearsals for RCA
February 18, 1970: The International Hotel, Las Vegas

A&R/Producer: Felton Jarvis
Engineer: Al Pachucki

Guitar: James Burton
Guitar: John Wilkinson
Guitar, Vocals: Charlie Hodge
Bass: Jerry Scheff
Drums: Bob Lanning

Piano: Glen D. Hardin
Vocals: The Sweet Inspirations
Vocals: Millie Kirkham
Vocals: The Imperials
Bobby Morris & His Orchestra

2–5PM

WPA5 2596-04	**The Wonder Of You**	**Platinum: A Life In Music**
	Baker Knight—Duchess Music	*67469-2/1997*
WPA5 2598-01	**Release Me**	**Platinum: A Life In Music**
	Miller/Yount/Williams—4 Star Music	*67469-2/1997*
WPA5 1297-01	**See See Rider**	**Platinum: A Life In Music**
	Traditional, arranged by Elvis Presley—Elvis Presley Music	*67469-2/1997*

These rehearsals were held in the showroom in preparation for live recordings on February 18 and 19.

After the Sweet Inspirations and comedian Sammy Shore had warmed up the audience, Elvis burst onto the stage and into "All Shook Up." Gone were opening-night nerves, replaced by confidence and poise. The wild performance of four months earlier was toned down into a more controlled intensity, and at the request of the hotel Elvis did his best to cut his monologues back far enough to keep his performance to one hour—giving patrons time to return to the casino. The repertoire was adjusted to showcase Elvis's current run of chart-topping singles, including "In The Ghetto," "Suspicious Minds," and the most recent hits, "Don't Cry Daddy" and "Kentucky Rain." A number of the old favorites remained as crowd pleasers, but his new hits and a handful of well-chosen covers demonstrated Elvis's knowledge and appreciation of the best contemporary songwriting. Joe South's wonderful "Walk A Mile In My Shoes" was the kind of song he must have been aching to do when he told Steve Binder "I'm never going to sing another song I don't believe in." He delivered John Fogerty's "Proud Mary" in a heavy gospel-tinged arrangement, and Neil Diamond's "Sweet Caroline" was even more persuasive than the original. But the showstopper was Tony Joe White's swamp-rock anthem "Polk Salad Annie." Launched on the back of Jerry Scheff's thundering, thumping bass line, pumped up by Elvis's ultracool spoken opening section, then pushed to a mesmerizing crescendo five minutes later in a flurry of karate kicks by Elvis (who'd been studying the sport for years), the performance set a new standard—even for the King of Rock 'n' Roll.

The Colonel and RCA took advantage of the opportunity to record another live album, and new sixteen-track recording equipment was brought in for Felton Jarvis and engineer Al Pachucki to work with. When they began recording at the midnight show on Sunday, February 15, a cold-ridden Elvis coughed during several songs; more worrisome, it soon became apparent that they were going to have a hard time coming up with enough new material for an album. At the early rehearsals before the Vegas run there had been talk of all sorts of material, from the gospel standard "I Was Born Ten Thousand Years Ago" to Joe Cocker's recent hit "Delta Lady" to Pat Boone's 1957 ballad "Love Letters In The Sand." Glen D. Hardin had written an arrangement for Neil Diamond's "Holly Holy" and several others. But these and other songs had been dropped by opening night, and as the week began they were left with few songs they hadn't recorded before. A rehearsal was called for Wednesday, and the group began by tightening up "See See Rider," then worked on the country standard "Release Me," which had also been a number one R&B hit for Esther Phillips in 1962, and "The Wonder Of You," originally written for Perry Como in 1959 by Baker Knight and eventually given to Ray Peterson. A master of "The Wonder Of You" was taped live during the first performance that very evening, and the other two songs were captured at the midnight show.

Al Pachucki returned to Nashville with the tapes after one more night, leaving it up to him and Felton to mix the tracks and complete the lineup for the new album. Still short on material, Felton turned back to the '69 concert tapes to supplement the set with Del Shannon's "Runaway" and the first half of the "Yesterday"/"Hey Jude" medley. After executing a series of repairs—particularly on the single, "The Wonder Of You," for which the Sweet Inspirations were replaced by a group of Nashville singers—Felton sent the whole thing off for mastering and release.

Two days after Elvis closed the show on February 23, he flew to Houston to meet the Colonel, who had just set up his command center in preparation for his appearance at the Houston Livestock Show to be held in the Houston Astrodome. On Friday, February 26, a relaxed and charming Elvis appeared at a press conference to promote the show, where he expressed his views on a number of subjects, including his musical background. When asked about the rising interest in country music he responded, "I think it's fantastic. You see, country music was always a part of the influence on my type of music anyway. It's a combination of country music, gospel, and rhythm and blues—all combined. As a child I was influenced by all of that."

When one reporter asked him: "Do you consider yourself basically a country music singer?" Elvis responded with characteristic consideration: "I would hate to say strictly country, because of the fact that I liked all types of different music when I was a child. The Grand Ole Opry was the first thing I ever heard, probably, but I liked the blues and the gospel music, the gospel quartets and all that." And another question spoke to just how far he'd come in the past fifteen years: Asked "Do you ever put on any of the old records from the Sun label and listen to them?" Elvis laughed: "They sound

Showing off his gold records: backstage in Houston, February 1970

funny, boy. They got a lot of echo on them, I'll tell you. But that's what I mean. I think the overall sound has improved."

The sound at the gigantic Astrodome, on the other hand, was no improvement at all; in fact, it was a tremendous problem. "The Astrodome was a pretty crummy gig," says ex-Crickets piano player Glen D. Hardin, who had replaced Larry Muhoberac in January when the latter decided to pursue his own career. Hardin, who would stay with Elvis until just before the end, told biographer Jerry Hopkins that after a few minutes of rehearsals Elvis reassured his players, "This is going to be rather atrocious, so don't fight it. Just go ahead and play." It wasn't that Elvis didn't care—in fact he flew in engineers from Las Vegas and Los Angeles to improve the sound—it was just, as Hardin put it, that the Astrodome "was not made for any serious giggin' inside." Even so, the selection of East Texas for Elvis's first live performance after Las Vegas had a certain grace. It was here that his career had first taken off, in the roadhouses, school-houses, oilfield camps, and jamborees of his first year on the road. When Elvis drove into the giant arena in a pickup truck, it was a sweet reminder of that summer day in 1955 when another pickup had carried Floyd Cramer's piano into an almost empty ballpark in nearby Gladewater. The three-day, six-show event guaranteed enormous press coverage, and once again the Colonel was able to pull off another "first": More than 250,000 people attended the shows, with an all-time record audience of 43,614 on Saturday evening. The Colonel's bigger-is-better strategy left the music business in awe, and Elvis with a reported $1,200,000 in his pocket. Setting ever-higher goals, the master manager closed a deal with MGM in May to film Presley's next Las Vegas engagement. After toying with the idea of a closed-circuit TV show, he settled instead on Denis Sanders, a seriously regarded director, to film the entire process of mounting the Elvis Presley show, from early rehearsals through the shows themselves.

RCA, meanwhile, continued to churn out Elvis product. It was a strategy aimed at the worldwide market, but the proliferation of ill-considered releases that began at this point tended to undercut not only the Colonel's commercial strategy but Elvis's own artistic vision. In February the company released "Kentucky Rain," the fourth single to be taken from the Memphis sessions; the single reached number sixteen, a little lower than its predecessors but a substantial hit by any standard—and another solid record. Before the next legitimate new album could come out, though, RCA issued *Let's Be Friends,* a haphazardly assembled budget album pulling together mostly unreleased movie songs for the hardcore fans. The album was a joke compared to the newest work of the now-revitalized Elvis, and in the past even the Colonel might have objected to the kind of market saturation it represented. But now it was "money first": The contract with RCA called for extra money for budget albums outside of the formal yearly requirements, and he and Elvis were happy to accept the cash.

If the *On Stage* album from the February Vegas recordings was a relative failure, it was only as measured against the extraordinary promise of the Memphis sessions. In fact, it went to number twelve on the LP charts, sold about the same as the previous three albums, and spawned a Top-Ten single (number one in England), "The Wonder Of You." The international market was growing even more responsive to Elvis's output than his native land, and when "Polk Salad Annie" was lifted off the album it became a huge and well-deserved hit for Elvis outside the United States. The very direct—some would say bland, if aurally overpowering—arrangements of the Las Vegas recordings contrasted with the subdued soulfulness of the Memphis sessions, though critics saw this as deference to the Vegas audience and accepted the record as an unavoidable intermission before the next "real" album. But the Colonel and RCA recognized two fundamental facts: Recording Elvis onstage was a convenient way to meet the three-album-per-year requirement; and the big, bold pop ballad, as exemplified by "The Wonder Of You," was unquestionably the road to worldwide commercial success.

1970

NASHVILLE REVISITED

Felton Jarvis was in the midst of preparing for a new series of Elvis sessions in Nashville when he officially resigned from his position with the RCA label. In the four years they'd been working together Elvis had grown comfortable with Felton's producing style and judgment, and when Elvis offered to hire him on as his personal producer, Jarvis jumped at the chance. His first order of business was to make arrangements to cut the eighteen sides (one album and two singles) the singer was required to deliver in 1970. In addition to putting him in exclusive charge of Elvis's recording career, the new position would also give Felton a central role in the artist's escalating concert schedule. The offer to Felton may have been a "spur-of-the-moment" decision on Elvis's part, but he'd made the same offer to Thorne Nogar and Jim Malloy in years past; unlike Felton, though, the two engineers were unwilling to give up their regular jobs for what must have looked in the 1960s like a very uncertain future.

Felton's new employment started with a session scheduled for the night of June 4, 1970. Two and a half years had passed since Elvis had last recorded at RCA's Studio B in Nashville; fed up with a system that was going nowhere, Elvis had given up Music City for Chips Moman's Memphis, but their uncomfortable parting meant that returning to American was out of the question this time around. And perhaps there were other reasons Elvis might have been happy to look elsewhere: Working with Moman, whose preference for strong, contemporary songs—rehearsed, played, and arranged to meet his own vision and standards—collided sharply with the freewheeling, try-anything approach to recording that Elvis had followed since the Sun days. Nor was Felton without his own feelings in the matter: *He* didn't want to be overlooked in the credit process either, and he felt he was just as responsible as Chips for some of the best of the Memphis recordings—not to mention five hit singles and the Grammy-winning *How Great Thou Art* album before Chips was even in the picture. He was more than ready to be back in the driver's seat—on his own—and he couldn't wait to get started.

New sessions, new material—and this time the principal supplier was once again Freddy Bienstock, but now almost entirely from the catalogue of Carlin, the British company he'd just bought from his cousins (and former Hill & Range employers), Jean and Julian Aberbach. The Aberbachs continued to be involved with the Elvis repertoire themselves, but in a competitive role; Julian himself had commissioned a new song, "Stranger In The Crowd," from staff writer Winfield Scott, and Lamar Fike, Elvis's former employee, continued in his role as their principal song-plugger working out at Hill & Range's Nashville office.

One other result of the thirty-month absence from Nashville—and a favorable one from Felton's point of view—was the opportunity to put together a newer, hipper studio band. Throughout the '60s Elvis had stuck by his original recording unit, which joined Scotty, D. J., and the Jordanaires, with Nashville A-teamers Floyd Cramer, Bob Moore, Boots Randolph, and Buddy Harman. The new band—James Burton (guitar), David Briggs (piano), Norbert Putnam (bass), Chip Young (rhythm guitar), Charlie McCoy (harmonica, bass, and organ), and Jerry Carrigan (drums)—all (except for Burton) had longstanding connections with Felton, and their versatile, fluid, rootsy playing made them Nashville's new starting lineup.

100. Studio Sessions for RCA
June 4–8, 1970: RCA's Studio B, Nashville

A&R/Producer: Felton Jarvis
Engineer: Al Pachucki

Guitar: James Burton
Guitar: Chip Young
Acoustic Guitar: Elvis Presley
Bass: Norbert Putnam
Drums: Jerry Carrigan
Piano: David Briggs
Organ, Harmonica: Charlie McCoy
Vocals: Charlie Hodge (1610, 1614)

Overdubbed later:
Guitar: James Burton
Percussion: Jerry Carrigan
Percussion & Vibes: Farrell Morris
Organ: David Briggs
Steel Guitar: Weldon Myrick
Banjo: Bobby Thompson (1598)
Fiddle: Buddy Spicher (1598)
Vocals: The Imperials
Vocals: The Jordanaires
Vocals: Millie Kirkham, Mary Greene,
Mary & Ginger Holladay, Temple Riser, June
Page, Sonja Montgomery, Dolores Edgin,
Joe Babcock (1607)
Strings & Horns: See below

6/4, 6–9PM, 10PM–1AM, 1:30–4:30AM

ZPA4 1593-09	**Twenty Days And Twenty Nights**	**That's The Way It Is**
	Weisman/Westlake—Gladys Music	*LSP 4445/1970*
ZPA4 1594-07	**I've Lost You**	**Single A-Side**
	Howard/Blaikley—Gladys Music	*47-9873/1970*
ZPA4 1595-01	**I Was Born About Ten Thousand Years Ago**	**Elvis Now**
	Adapted by Elvis Presley—Elvis Presley Music	*LSP 4671/1972*
ZPA4 1596-11	**The Sound Of Your Cry**	**Single B-side**
	Giant/Baum/Kaye—Elvis Presley Music	*48-1017/1971*
ZPA4 1597-02	**The Fool**	**Elvis Country**
	Naomi Ford—Malapi Music & Desert Palms Publishing	*LSP 4460/1971*

WPA5 2569-sp	**A Hundred Years From Now**	**Walk A Mile In My Shoes**
	Lester Flatt/Earl Scruggs—unknown	*66670-2/1995*
ZPA4 1598-02	**Little Cabin On The Hill**	**Elvis Country**
	Bill Monroe/Lester Flatt—Peer International	*LSP 4460/1971*
ZPA4 1599-03	**Cindy, Cindy**	**Love Letters From Elvis**
	Kaye/Weisman/Fuller—Gladys Music	*LSP 4560/1971*

<u>6/5, 6–9PM, 10PM–1AM, 1:30–4:30AM</u>

ZPA4 1600-08	**Bridge Over Troubled Water**	**That's The Way It Is**
	Paul Simon—Charing Cross Music	*LSP 4445/1970*
ZPA4 1601-01	**Got My Mojo Working/Keep Your Hands Off Of It**	**Love Letters From Elvis**
	Foster—Arc & Dare Music/Adap. E. Presley—E. Presley Music	*LSP 4530/1971*
ZPA4 1602-03	**How The Web Was Woven**	**That's The Way It Is**
	C. Westlake/M. Most—Elvis Presley Music	*LSP 4445/1970*
ZPA4 1603-05	**It's Your Baby, You Rock It**	**Elvis Country**
	Milete/Fowler—Elvis Presley & Last Straw Music	*LSP 4460/1971*
ZPA4 1604-09	**Stranger In The Crowd**	**That's The Way It Is**
	Winfield Scott—Elvis Presley Music	*LSP 4445/1970*
ZPA4 1605-07	**I'll Never Know**	**Love Letters From Elvis**
	Karger/Wayne/Weisman—Gladys Music	*LSP 4530/1971*
ZPA4 1606-05	**Mary In The Morning**	**That's The Way It Is**
	Cymbal/Rashkow—Pamco Music	*LSP 4445/1970*

<u>6/6, 6–9PM, 10PM–1AM, 1:30–4: 30AM</u>

WPA5 2583-01	**I Didn't Make It On Playing Guitar**	**A Hundred Years From Now**
	Elvis Presley—H&R Music	*66866-2/1996*
ZPA4 1607-09	**It Ain't No Big Thing (But It's Growing)**	**Love Letters From Elvis**
	Merritt/Joy/Hall—Central Songs	*LSP 4530/1971*
ZPA4 1608-03	**You Don't Have To Say You Love Me**	**Single A-side**
	Wickham/Napier—Bell/Donaggio/Pallavicine—Miller Music Corp	*47-9916/1970*
ZPA4 1609-03	**Just Pretend**	**That's The Way It Is**
	D. Flett/G. Fletcher—Gladys Music	*LSP 4445/1970*
ZPA4 1610-11	**This Is Our Dance**	**Love Letters From Elvis**
	Les Reed/Geoff Stephens—Gladys Music	*LSP 4530/1971*
ZPA4 1613-20	**Life**	**Single A-side**
	Shirl Milete—Elvis Presley Music	*47-9985/1971*
ZPA4 1614-sp	**Heart Of Rome**	**Love Letters From Elvis**
	Stephens/Blaikley/Howard—Gladys Music	*LSP 4530/1971*

<u>6/7, 6–9PM, 10PM–1AM, 1:30–4:30AM</u>

ZPA4 1615-na	**When I'm Over You**	**Love Letters From Elvis**
	Shirl Milete—Elvis Presley & Last Straw Music	*LSP 4530/1971*
ZPA4 1616-na	**I Really Don't Want To Know**	**Single A-side**
	Barnes/Robertson—Hill & Range Songs	*47-9960/1970*

ZPA4 1617-01	**Faded Love**	**Elvis Country**
	B. Wills/J. Wills—Hill & Range Songs	*LSP 4460/1971*
ZPA4 1618-sp	**Tomorrow Never Comes**	**Elvis Country**
	E. Tubb/Bond—Noma Music	*LSP 4460/1971*
ZPA4 1619-11	**The Next Step Is Love**	**Single B-side**
	Evans/Parnes—Gladys Music	*47-9873/1970*
ZPA4 1620-sp	**Make The World Go Away**	**Elvis Country**
	Hank Cochran—Tree Publishing	*LSP 4460/1971*
ZPA4 1621-01	**Funny How Time Slips Away**	**Elvis Country**
	Willie Nelson—Tree Publishing	*LSP 4460/1971*
ZPA4 1622-01	**I Washed My Hands In Muddy Water**	**Elvis Country**
	Joe Babcock—Maricana Music	*LSP 4460/1971*
ZPA4 1623-05	**Love Letters**	**Love Letters From Elvis**
	E. Heymann/V. Young—Famous Music	*LSP 4530/1971*

6/8, 6–9PM, 10PM–1AM, 1:30–4:30AM

ZPA4 1624-03	**There Goes My Everything**	**Single B-side**
	Dallas Frazier—Blue Crest Music	*47-9960/1970*
ZPA4 1625-09	**If I Were You**	**Love Letters From Elvis**
	G. Nelson—Elvis Presley/Coach & Four Music	*LSP 4530/1971*
ZPA4 1626-04	**Only Believe**	**Single B-side**
	Paul Rader—Roadheaver Co.	*47-99851/1971*
ZPA4 1627-08	**Sylvia**	**Elvis Now**
	Geoff Stephens/Les Reed—Gladys Music	*LSP 4671/1972*
ZPA4 1628-08	**Patch It Up**	**Single B-side**
	E. Rabbitt/R. Burke—Elvis Presley Music/S-P-R Music	*47-9916/1970*

Elvis overdubbed a new lead vocal to "Bridge Over Troubled Water" (1600) at the 6/5 session. The master of "A Hundred Years From Now" (2569) is spliced from takes 1 and 2. The master of "Heart Of Rome" (1614) is spliced from take 3 and a work part (take 1) of the ending. The master of "Tomorrow Never Comes" (1618) is spliced from take 13 and a work part (take 1) of the ending. The master of "Make The World Go Away" (1620) is spliced from take 3 and a work part (take 1) of the ending. "I Didn't Make It On Playing Guitar" is a jam; the vocal consists of Elvis singing the title line off-mike, picked up only through the microphone of his acoustic guitar. "I Was Born About Ten Thousand Years Ago" was first released as a series of linking excerpts on *Elvis Country*. The Jordanaires: Gordon Stoker, Neal Matthews, Hoyt Hawkins, Ray Walker. The Imperials: Terry Blackwood, Roger Wiles, Winnifred Brest, Jim Murray, Armond Morales. Horns: Charlie McCoy (trumpet), George Tidwell (trumpet), Don Sheffield (trumpet), Glenn Baxter (trumpet), Wayne Butler (sax), Norman Ray (sax), Skip Lane (flute, sax, and clarinet), Gene Mullins (trombone), William Puett (flute and saxophone). Several master takes were shortened for their original release. Session hours are official union timings; Elvis normally arrived later than 6PM and several of the musicians remember staying to 7 or 8 o'clock in the morning on some days.

Studio B, Nashville, June 1970. Top (left to right): David Briggs, Norbert Putnam, Elvis, Al Pachucki, Jerry Carrigan; bottom: Felton, Chip Young, Charlie McCoy, James Burton

June 4, 1970. At 6:00 P.M. engineer Al Pachucki began setting the levels for each of the musicians on the sixteen-track machine that had replaced the old four-track that had been in service for Elvis's last Nashville sessions. Elvis took his position in the center of the recording studio as James Burton led the group from a basic rehearsal riff into "Mystery Train." Shouts of encouragement from Elvis helped the band loosen up, and by the time they got to the "Tiger Man" part of the medley that had been created for the Las Vegas show, Elvis could be heard singing enthusiastically off-mike. After adjusting the final recording levels on Elvis's vocal, Pachucki gave the signal: time to begin.

Freddy Bienstock's first offering was "Twenty Days And Twenty Nights," a big dramatic ballad by veteran Hill & Range writer Ben Weisman and British lyricist Clive Westlake. Free of the restraints of silly movie plots, this time Weisman had contributed a solid, contemporary love song; after several false starts and one take that a laughing Elvis concluded by launching into "I Got A Woman," the song was completed in fairly short order. Next up was another new Carlin composition, Ken Howard and Alan Blaikley's "I've Lost You," recorded just months before in England by Ian Matthews's

Southern Comfort. An ambitious, swellingly melodic ballad about the breakup of a marriage and its emotional consequences, it was the first in a breed of such songs that would find their way into Elvis's songbook as the '70s rolled along. "There are so many words, you can't look away from that SOB for a minute, man," he complained, but he threw himself into the song unconditionally, working hard through seven takes until he'd gotten what he wanted. Then, as if to break the serious mood, Elvis launched into one of the old favorites he could simply bang out in a couple of takes for the pure pleasure of it. On this occasion the song was the country gospel standard "I Was Born About Ten Thousand Years Ago," and he romped through it in exactly one high-spirited take. With the recording of "The Sound Of Your Cry," yet another ballad from the Carlin stack of demos, Freddy Bienstock knew they were off to a fine start, and as the musicians broke for a midnight meal Felton too must have been relieved: Elvis had polished off four masters in the first half of the evening. He was in fine spirits, in good voice, and ready to keep going.

Although the studio setup looked the same as it had in Memphis—just Elvis with a rhythm group—the sound and the feel of this new Nashville approach were worlds apart from the Chips Moman model. In Memphis the band had laid down the basic rhythm arrangement on three tracks, leaving complicated repairs and overdubs for later. The mike setup at American, combined with the sound characteristics of the studio and Moman's distinctive use of reverb, gave even the more pedestrian songs a rich funkiness. The equipment in Nashville's Studio B, on the other hand, made ten tracks available for the initial recording, leaving six open for overdubs and far greater potential for separation of instruments and vocals. With this new sixteen-track technology came both benefits and debits: Room ambience and immediacy were necessarily minimized, but engineers had new flexibility in adding (or subtracting) effects after the fact, and there was little need to spend as much time placing the mikes to achieve just the right blend on the spot.

The Nashville rhythm section might in many respects have been interchangeable with the American group: Both were "white soul" bands, and the nucleus of the Nashville band was the famous Muscle Shoals rhythm section, who had played on an impressive string of country hits during the same years the American players were racking up their string of hits. Both had a strong grounding in country, and while there were unquestionable distinctions—particularly in their bass and drum sounds—what made them each perfect for Elvis was their instant adaptability, their ability to replicate, on demand, the sounds he heard in his head. True, the Memphis band's playing was generally more austere than that of the Nashville group, in large part because Chips Moman inevitably overlaid their work with so many layers of later overdubs. The virtuoso electric bass work of American bandleader Tommy Cogbill was also more subtle, more rhythmically sinuous, than the more straightforward underpinning of the Nashville band. Reggie Young's guitar playing was tuned in to soul music's demand for rhythmic emphasis, whereas James Burton's blistering solos came straight from rock 'n' roll. In Memphis the band was supported by dueling keyboards (Bobby Wood playing piano, Bobby Emmons on organ); in Nashville they doubled up on guitars, with Burton sparring with Scotty's old protégé Chip Young. If there was one defining distinction in the final products, though, it was in the overall sound: Where the Memphis masters were moody, rich, and elaborately arranged, the Nashville recordings sounded bright, full of snare drums and strummed acoustic guitars—and undeniably *live*.

After the break Elvis launched into yet another number from his youth, Bob Wills's western-swing standard "Faded Love." "We got the words to that, Lamar?" Elvis called out, already caught up in the feel of the song. When the answer came back in the negative, Elvis suggested: "While we wait, let's do 'The Fool.'" Chip Young and James Burton immediately picked up the delta-blues guitar riff of Sanford Clark's infectious 1956 hit, and everyone else fell into the swing of it, wrapping up a master in two takes. Next Elvis grabbed an acoustic guitar himself and broke into bluegrass territory with Flatt and Scruggs's "A Hundred Years From Now" and Bill Monroe's "Little Cabin On The Hill." By now the session had become a kind of free-for-all, but with the wonderful looseness Elvis often achieved at just the moment when he was trying to avoid buckling down to work. He was rapidly running out of tape, but Al Pachucki turned the reel around and recorded Elvis's bluegrass workouts on the free six tracks while struggling to keep everyone on mike. By night's end Felton was finally able to steer Elvis back to the business at hand, and they concluded with a new Hill & Range reworking of another song Elvis may have heard when he was growing up: "Cindy, Cindy," a public-domain number Ben Weisman had adapted and demoed for just such a purpose.

June 5. As long as Elvis felt he had something to add to a song he had no compunction about challenging an existing version—that was how he'd got his start, after all—and Paul Simon's "Bridge Over Troubled Water" offered just the kind of vocal challenge he found hard to resist. David Briggs, the young pianist who'd debuted with Elvis on "Love Letters" back in '66, led the way on the piano as Elvis delivered a powerful rendition that was both faithful to the original and deeply personal. Elvis maintained the same exemplary vocal control on the next cut, "How The Web Was Woven," running through three trouble-free takes of the Clive Westlake composition, originally recorded by Jackie Lomax for the Beatles' Apple label. Of course there was no way Elvis was going to stay on track all through the session, and during rehearsals for "It's Your Baby, You Rock It" the band jumped serendipitously, and for no apparent reason, into "Got My Mojo Working." Felton was quick to make sure Al Pachucki got the tape rolling before the band lost its groove, and the jam went on for more than six minutes—but not before Elvis interpolated "Keep Your Hands Off Of It," another half-remembered song from adolescence, into the middle of the mix. "We grew up on this mediocre shit, man," Elvis declared enthusiastically. "It's the type of material that's not good or bad—it's just mediocre shit, you know." But it was "mediocre shit" with which he was totally comfortable, for which he had great respect, and that he would always love. And with that out of the way, he was finally able to conclude "It's Your Baby, You Rock It," the new song by Shirl Milete. By the end of the night Felton had another three masters in the can—the two sincere and beautiful ballads "I'll Never Know" and "Mary In The Morning," as well as a Spanish-flavored version of "Stranger In The Crowd," the song that Hill & Range boss Julian Aberbach had submitted himself.

June 6. The third night began with Elvis taking everyone by surprise by picking up an acoustic guitar and playing the introduction to the familiar mid-'60s country hit "It Ain't No Big Thing." Caught off guard, Felton called for a new start, and Elvis abashedly asked Chip Young to take over. The group fell in effortlessly on the mid-tempo number, but by take six Elvis was banging away again on the acoustic guitar, shouting "I didn't make it on playing guitar" over the jam that had instantly developed. The take broke down, but even as Felton was trying to steer Elvis back to the song his singer was off again. This time it was a line from Ernie K-Doe's "Mother In Law" that prompted Briggs and McCoy to leap in, to Elvis's amusement: "Don't take much to spark you guys off, man. Couple of words and you're off and running." Finally they returned to the business at hand, and after one more false start the second full take of "It Ain't No Big Thing" became the master.

For the first time that evening Elvis's attention was truly focused as they began work on the Italian-derived "You Don't Have To Say You Love Me," a major 1966 hit for Dusty Springfield and the kind of big dramatic ballad that was dominating Elvis's imagination more and more. On the final rehearsal of the song, Felton gave Elvis a rousing endorsement—"Bravo, that's a gas, man"—though by this point Elvis was clearly motivated himself, and wouldn't quit even when Felton suggested that take two was good enough for a master. When he was this much into a song Elvis couldn't even be led astray by James Burton playing the opening chords of "Susie Q"; he stayed valiantly with "You Don't Have To Say You Love Me," coming up with a strong vocal performance on the third and final take. The British team of Flett and Fletcher was behind the next song, "Just Pretend," though in this gospel-inspired arrangement it sounded as if it must have come from somewhere down below the Mason-Dixon; in Elvis's hands it came off as sincere, powerful, a reprise of his triumphant "Without Love" at the Memphis sessions. Perhaps if there had been more of this kind of material the session might have moved along more surely, but as the evening wore on the old problem of inadequate material began surfacing, until finally we hear an impatient Elvis calling out, "Okay, Charlie, we gotta hurry, we gotta eat." After two miserable breakdowns on "This Is Our Dance," even the musicians had had it. "This isn't Lamar's song, is it?" demanded James Burton sarcastically. "If it is, I'm gonna kill him." "Definitely not," said Elvis, defending Lamar rather than the song. In the control room, Freddy Bienstock offered no comment.

Now they were clearly struggling, and on the tapes you can hear Elvis's frustration as he tries yet another Shirl Milete number from Lamar, this one called "Life." The lyrics were as pretentious as the title suggests, aiming for a kind of '60s-style philosophical spirituality but ultimately just plain failing to make much sense. But if Elvis was perplexed by the words he certainly saw no mystery in the melody: It wasn't long before he noticed "Life" was similar to a song of Milete's he'd cut the year before in Memphis, "My Little Friend." Mockingly, he sang the lyric of the old song to the tune of the new before complaining "The goddamn thing is as long as life itself!" But Lamar had fallen well behind Freddy in the publishing sweepstakes by now, and as a favor Elvis eventually gave in and finished the song. The last entry of the evening, "Heart Of Rome," was an up-tempo dramatic ballad in the operatic vein of "It's Now Or Never" or "Surrender"; it may have had a little more irony going for it than the earlier cuts, but by the end it had Elvis straining for the high notes—and the band struggling to keep awake.

Still, for all the problems, after only three nights in the studio they now had twenty masters—two more than the RCA contract called for—with another night of recording still ahead of them. (Back in 1968 it had taken Elvis two nights to cut four sides.) Felton was elated: He had returned Elvis to Nashville triumphantly, had taken control of the sessions, had recorded a year's worth of material in a few easygoing nights. Yet with the next night he knew they were going to start running into the same old problems. The best of the new songs—coming from Freddy—were European, with lyrics, rhythms, and chord progressions literally worlds apart from the country, R&B, and gospel Elvis and the musicians preferred when left to their own devices. Even when Elvis was engaged, this kind of material took more preparation than a simple three-chord tune. Music and musicians were clashing; Felton knew they couldn't expect the Nashville crowd to work up their usual ad-hoc arrangements for Bienstock's increasingly demanding material. Something had to give.

June 7. After an unpromising start with one more forgettable Shirl Milete song, a new idea began taking shape. The original plan to cut just eighteen songs could not have included any thought of a second album, but on the fourth night, all of a sudden, a country album began to emerge. They'd already cut a handful of solid country tunes; now they began the project in earnest with a cover of Eddy Arnold's 1954 hit "I Really Don't Want To Know," cowritten by frequent Elvis balladeer Don Robertson. All at once Elvis seemed inspired, singing with a passion and soulfulness that recalled Memphis. The band fell in with equal feeling, their confidence and expressiveness growing along with his. Both singer and band were performing out of genre, improvising their own rhythms and phrasing on the spot, challenging each other. Then with scarcely a pause Elvis returned to "Faded Love," the song he'd forgotten the words to the other night—and, as it happened, a Hill & Range number. This time Elvis and the band developed an oddly aggressive arrangement, more rock than country, and wholly their own. They achieved another transformation with Ernest Tubb's "Tomorrow Never Comes," reaching back to another of Elvis's influences. The song's ascending arrangement was guaranteed to tax Elvis's vocal range, so Felton started the tape as the musicians rehearsed to capture as much as he could. After a second pass Elvis asked if they were recording; "I snuck up on you," Felton admitted. The going wasn't easy, and Elvis, annoyed with himself for forgetting the lyrics, sang the opening line of Roy Orbison's "Running Scared" instead, and announced "I'm starting to hate this song." Elvis always claimed you couldn't improve an Orbison recording, and he never covered any of the singer's records, but it was definitely Roy's semioperatic approach he was aping on this country standard. Felton kept pushing him for one more take: "It's gonna be a gas, Elvis, really. Just hold on." "If it ain't, I'm gonna take some," Elvis snapped back, but once they had take thirteen (and a retake on the ending) down, they had something to be proud of.

"The Next Step Is Love" stepped out of the strict country agenda, matching a well-crafted tune with a curiously overreaching lyric ("We've yet to taste the icing on the cake that we've been baking with the past"); with its Beatlesque production (in the midst of a batch of American roots music!) it was the most un-Presleyan cut on the sessions. But the pendulum swung back to country for the next three songs, each of which was a master almost before they knew it. A pompous but effective version of another Eddy Arnold hit, "Make The World Go Away," was followed by a truly brilliant "Funny How Time Slips Away," a Willie Nelson standard with much the same feel as "I Really Don't Want To Know."

Finally the group launched a powerful version of "I Washed My Hands In Muddy Water," an even more hard-driving jam than "I Was Born About Ten Thousand Years Ago" and "Got My Mojo Working." Elvis put himself in the center of the bad-boy story-song, the singer paying the price for not following his father's advice. "With a peculiar combination of hypertension and soul," as Peter Guralnick wrote in *Rolling Stone,* Elvis insisted on taking the performance far beyond the end of the story, cracking the whip on the boys for a full minute longer than Felton's eventual fadeout on *Elvis Country* suggested. The night ended with a rerecording of "Love Letters" prompted by pianist David Briggs's desire to improve on his performance on the original 1966 master. David may have felt better about his new performance, but Elvis wasn't into it, and the new version lacked all the understated charm of the first.

June 8. What became the final night of the sessions began with Elvis agreeing that Dallas Frazier's "There Goes My Everything" "doesn't have to be straight country" and turning it into another fervent modern ballad. With the next three songs, "If I Were You," the inspirational "Only Believe," and "Sylvia," they all knew they'd reached the bottom of the demo pile. They were all still performing at their peak, but the material was unimaginative, and so were the arrangements. When Elvis closed the sessions with Eddie Rabbitt and Rory Bourke's frenetic rocker "Patch It Up," he brought the four days of sessions to a blazing conclusion; if the material had only been there, it seemed he could have gone on all week.

Felton Jarvis, by June 9, must have been in the grip of elation and relief. In just five nights, Elvis had recorded a staggering total of thirty-four songs. By and large they were published by Elvis, which would keep Freddy and the Colonel happy. Most important, Elvis—now Felton's personal big boss man—had clearly enjoyed himself. The material might not have been all that Felton would have wished; his own musical taste ran more to rock than country or pop. But as of that day he had more than enough for two singles and two full albums. And if they wanted to make a straightforward country album, they only needed a few additional sides, which Felton could schedule for a September session.

Now Felton had plenty of work lined up for himself finishing the masters they had, overdubbing strings, horns, and backing vocals to complete the aural picture just as Chips had done in Memphis. With sixteen tracks the opportunities were almost limitless, and the producers hired Nashville arrangers Bergen White, Cam Mullins, and Don Tweedy, along with musicians David Briggs and Norbert Putnam, to go to town. In the '60s and early '70s a large part of the engineer's art was creating a trademark sound, dropping in layers of overdubbed texture while preserving the distinctive feel of the studio itself. Nowhere was this kind of magic pulled off more successfully during these years than at southern studios like American and RCA's Studio B; as the '70s moved on and overdubbing began taking over the process, this kind of engineering became a lost art.

But for now it was Felton's own art, and he set to it, crafting string and horn arrangements to frame and complement the work of his artist. And Elvis himself? For him it was time for a few weeks off. With an unbelievably productive session behind him—and a prestigious MGM concert documentary just over the horizon—his star was still ascending.

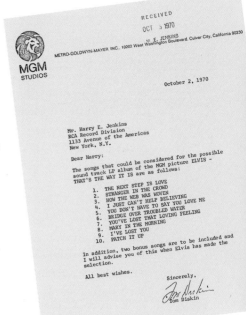

1970

SITTING ON TOP OF THE WORLD

101. Rehearsals for MGM's *That's The Way It Is*
July 15, 29, 1970: MGM's Soundstage, Hollywood
July 24, 1970: RCA Studios, Hollywood
August 4 and 7, 1970: The International Hotel, Las Vegas

A&R/Producer: Felton Jarvis
Engineer: Al Pachucki

Guitar: James Burton
Guitar: John Wilkinson
Guitar, Vocals: Charlie Hodge
Bass: Jerry Scheff
Drums: Ronnie Tutt

Piano: Glen D. Hardin
Vocals: The Imperials 8/4, 7 only
Vocals: The Sweet Inspirations 8/4, 7 only
Vocals: Millie Kirkham 8/4, 7 only
Joe Guercio & His Orchestra 8/4, 7 only

Specific dates unknown

Stagger Lee
Traditional
Got My Mojo Working
McKinley/Morganfield/Bowman/McShann
I've Lost You
Howard/Blaikley
Stranger In The Crowd
Winfield Scott
The Next Step Is Love
Evans/Parnes
You Don't Have To Say You Love Me
Wickham/Napier—Bell/Donaggio/Pallavicine

KPA5 9567 **Sweet Caroline**
Neil Diamond
Yesterday
Lennon/McCartney
Hey Jude
Lennon/McCartney
I Can't Stop Loving You
Don Gibson
Twenty Days And Twenty Nights
Clive Westlake/Ben Weisman

Elvis Aron Presley
CPL8 3699/1980

Love Me
Jerry Leiber/Mike Stoller

WPA5 2581 **Alla En Al Rancho Grande**
Silvano Ramos/E. D. Urange/J. D. Del Moral

That's All Right
Arthur Crudup

Patch It Up
Eddie Rabbitt/Rory Bourke

Cottonfields
Huddie Ledbetter

How The Web Was Woven
Clive Westlake/Mickey Most

I Got A Woman
Ray Charles

The Wonder Of You
Baker Knight

KPA5 9566 **You've Lost That Lovin' Feelin'**
Barry Mann/Cynthia Weil

Something
George Harrison

Don't Cry Daddy
Mac Davis

Polk Salad Annie
Tony Joe White

Bridge Over Troubled Water
Paul Simon

Just Pretend
G. Fletcher/D. Flett

Don't It Make You Wanna Go Home (4 lines only)
Joe South

Love Me Tender
Vera Matson/Elvis Presley

Words
R. B. & M. Gibb

Suspicious Minds
Mark James

I Just Can't Help Believin'
Cynthia Weil/Barry Mann

Tomorrow Never Comes
Ernest Tubb

Mary In The Morning
Cymbal/Rashkow

Heart Of Rome
Stephens/Blaikley/Howard

Walk A Mile In My Shoes
66670-2/1995

Elvis Aron Presley
CPL8 3699/1980

August 1970: Rehearsing at the International

Rehearsing for That's The Way It Is,
July-August 1970

Last-minute onstage rehearsals:
Las Vegas, August 1970

Memories
Billy Strange/Mac Davis
Johnny B. Goode
Chuck Berry
Make The World Go Away
Hank Cochran

WPA5 2558	**Stranger In My Own Home Town**	**Walk A Mile In My Shoes**
	Percy Mayfield	*66670-2/1995*
CPA5 5181	**I Washed My Hands In Muddy Water**	**Platinum: A Life In Music**
	Joe Babcock	*67469-2/1997*

Little Sister/Get Back
Pomus/Shuman—Lennon/McCartney

CPA5 5182	**I Was The One**	**Platinum: A Life in Music**
	Schroeder/DeMetrius/Blair/Pepper	*67469-2/1997*
CPA5 5183	**Cattle Call**	**Platinum: A Life In Music**
	Tex Owens	*67469-2/1997*
CPA5 5184	**Baby Let's Play House**	**Platinum: A Life in Music**
	Arthur Gunter	*67469-2/1997*
CPA5 5185	**Don't**	**Platinum: A Life In Music**
	Jerry Leiber/Mike Stoller	*67469-2/1997*
CPA5 5186	**Money Honey**	**Platinum: A Life In Music**
	Jesse Stone	*67469-2/1997*

(Now And Then There's) A Fool Such As I
Bill Trader

WPA5 2582	**Froggy Went A-Courtin'**	**Walk A Mile In My Shoes**
	Peretti/Creatore/Jimmie Rodgers	*66670-2/1995*

Such A Night
Lincoln Chase
It's Now Or Never
Schroeder/Gold

CPA5 5187	**What'd I Say**	**Platinum: A Life In Music**
	Ray Charles	*67469-2/1997*

The Lord's Prayer
Traditional
Hava Nagila
Traditional
My Baby Left Me
Arthur Crudup

The above list includes only songs known to exist on tape as of 1998; many more are known to have been recorded. The following have been excluded: one-liners, irreparably damaged recordings, and songs where Elvis's voice can be heard only in the background. Naturally many songs were rehearsed repeatedly, and consequently recorded several times during these weeks.

After a month's rest, Elvis and his rhythm section began more than three weeks of rehearsals for the Las Vegas opening, and the commencement of the documentary film that would go along with it. They started at RCA's studio on Sunset Boulevard, then moved to the MGM Studios in Culver City to accommodate the documentary film crews. In all, whether in earnest, in fun, or just for the cameras, Elvis and the band ran through more than sixty songs. More than twenty were from the June sessions: Some were dismissed after a few bars, some after several run-throughs, but a dozen were worked on extensively. Numbers like "I Washed My Hands In Muddy Water," "Got My Mojo Working," "Cottonfields," "Alla En El Rancho Grande," "Froggy Went A-Courtin'," "Stagger Lee," and "Stranger In My Own Home Town" served mainly as diversion, a chance to unwind in the midst of more serious work. As the days went by, the music grew more focused; once the distraction of the film crews was out of the way, Elvis and the band worked hard on those songs that had a real chance of being included in the show and subsequently in the film. Drummer Ron Tutt had rejoined the group after being temporarily replaced by Bob Lanning in February, and he needed to familiarize himself with the songs that had been added while he was gone. Piano man Glen D. Hardin worked out new arrangements of some of the old songs, proving himself once again a valuable addition to the group. Vocally demanding numbers like "Heart Of Rome" and "Tomorrow Never Comes" were most often dropped as too exhausting, but contemporary songs like George Harrison's Beatles song "Something," the B. J. Thomas hit "I Just Can't Help Believin'," and the Righteous Brothers' smash (and producer Phil Spector's masterpiece) "You've Lost That Lovin' Feelin'" added significant new dimensions to Elvis's concert repertoire.

102. Live Recordings for RCA and MGM's *That's The Way It Is* August 10–13, 1970: The International Hotel, Las Vegas

A&R/Producer: Felton Jarvis
Engineer: Al Pachucki

Guitar: James Burton
Guitar: John Wilkinson
Guitar, Vocals: Charlie Hodge
Bass: Jerry Scheff
Drums: Ronnie Tutt

Piano: Glen D. Hardin
Vocals: The Imperials
Vocals: The Sweet Inspirations
Vocals: Millie Kirkham
Joe Guercio & His Orchestra

8/10, Opening Night Show

The Next Step Is Love
Evans/Parnes

8/11, Dinner Show

ZPA5 1865   **I've Lost You**   **That's The Way It Is**
Howard/Blaikley—Gladys Music   *LSP 4445/1970*

ZPA4 1862   **I Just Can't Help Believin'**   **That's The Way It Is**
Cynthia Weil/Barry Mann—Screen Gems/Columbia   *LSP 4445/1970*

ZPA5 1866	**Bridge Over Troubled Water**	**Platinum: A Life In Music**
	Paul Simon	*67469-2/1997*

8/11, Midnight Show

WPA5 2577	**Something**	**Walk A Mile In My Shoes**
	George Harrison	*66670-2/1995*
WPA5 2576	**Men With Broken Hearts**	**Walk A Mile In My Shoes**
	Hank Williams	*66670-2/1995*
WPA5 2580	**One Night**	**Walk A Mile In My Shoes**
	Bartholomew/King	*66670-2/1995*
	Don't Be Cruel	
	Otis Blackwell/Elvis Presley	
WPA5 2578	**Heartbreak Hotel**	**Walk A Mile In My Shoes**
	Axton/Durden/Presley	*66670-2/1995*

8/12, Dinner Show

ZPA5 1863	**Patch It Up**	**That's The Way It Is**
	Eddie Rabbitt/Rory Bourke—Elvis Presley Music/S-P-R Music	*LSP 4445/1970*
	Twenty Days And Twenty Nights	
	Clive Westlake/Ben Weisman	

8/13, Dinner Show

	Don't Cry Daddy	
	Mac Davis	
	In The Ghetto	
	Mac Davis	
	Stranger In The Crowd	
	Winfield Scott	
	Make The World Go Away	
	Hank Cochran	
KPA5 9565	**Polk Salad Annie**	**Elvis Aron Presley**
	Tony Joe White	*CPL8 3699/1980*
	The Wonder Of You	
	Baker Knight	

8/13, Midnight Show

ZPA4 1864	**You've Lost That Lovin' Feelin'**	**That's The Way It Is**
	Cynthia Weil/Barry Mann—Screen Gems/Columbia	*LSP 4445/1970*
KPA5 9573	**Little Sister/Get Back**	**Elvis Aron Presley**
	Pomus/Shuman—Lennon/McCartney	*CPL8 3699/1980*
WPA5 2579	**I Was The One**	**Walk A Mile In My Shoes**
	Schroeder/DeMetrius/Blair/Pepper	*66670-2/1995*
	Are You Lonesome Tonight?	
	Roy Turk/Lou Handman	

8/10–13, Various Shows

That's All Right

Arthur Crudup

Mystery Train/Tiger Man

Junior Parker/Sam Phillips—Joe Hill Louis/Sam Burns

I Can't Stop Loving You

Don Gibson

Love Me Tender

Vera Matson/Elvis Presley

Words

B. M. & R. Gibb

Sweet Caroline

Neil Diamond

You Don't Have To Say You Love Me

Wickham Napier—Bell/Donaggio/Pallavicine

Can't Help Falling In Love

Peretti/Creatore/Weiss

I Got A Woman

Ray Charles

Hound Dog

Jerry Leiber/Mike Stoller

Suspicious Minds

Mark James

There Goes My Everything

Dallas Frazier

Just Pretend

Flett/Fletcher

Walk A Mile In My Shoes

Joe South

Love Me

Jerry Leiber/Mike Stoller

Blue Suede Shoes

Carl Perkins

All Shook Up

Otis Blackwell/Elvis Presley

RCA recorded eight complete shows in preparation for the documentary and soundtrack album. Songs that have since been released are listed in the released versions only, though other versions may have been recorded. Songs recorded only once, or in only one acceptable version recorded, are listed by the date of such recordings. Songs not released but recorded several times are listed in the final section above. Publishing information is only available on songs released on *That's The Way It Is* (LPM 4445).

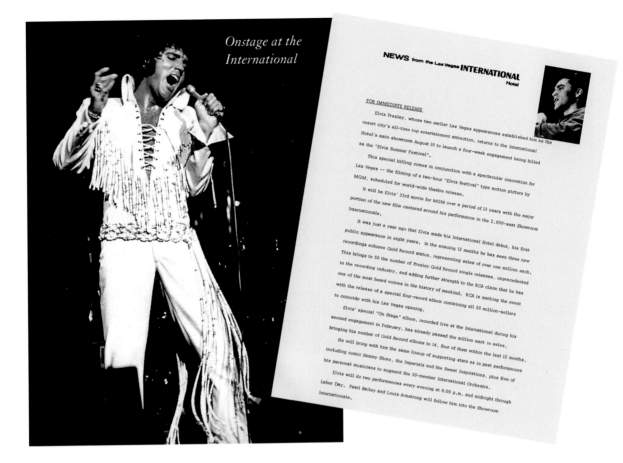

Onstage at the International

NEWS from the Las Vegas **INTERNATIONAL** Hotel

FOR IMMEDIATE RELEASE

Elvis Presley, whose two earlier Las Vegas appearances established him as the resort city's all-time top entertainment attraction, returns to the International Hotel's main showroom August 10 to launch a four-week engagement being billed as the "Elvis Summer Festival".

This special billing comes in conjunction with a spectacular innovation for Las Vegas -- the filming of a two-hour "Elvis festival" type motion picture by MGM, scheduled for world-wide theatre release.

It will be Elvis' 33rd movie for MGM over a period of 13 years with the major portion of the new film centered around his performance in the 2,000-seat Showroom Internationale.

It was just a year ago that Elvis made his International Hotel debut, his first public appearance in eight years. In the ensuing 12 months he has seen three new recordings achieve Gold Record status, representing sales of over one million each. This brings to 50 the number of Presley Gold Record single releases, unprecedented in the recording industry, and adding further strength to the RCA claim that he has one of the most heard voices in the history of mankind. RCA is marking the event with the release of a special four-record album containing all 50 million-sellers to coincide with his Las Vegas opening.

Elvis' special "On Stage" album, recorded live at the International during his second engagement in February, has already passed the million mark in sales, bringing his number of Gold Record albums to 14, four of them within the last 12 months.

He will bring with him the same lineup of supporting stars as in past performances including comic Sammy Shore, the Imperials and the Sweet Inspirations, plus five of his personal musicians to augment the 30-member International Orchestra.

Elvis will do two performances every evening at 8:00 p.m. and midnight through Labor Day. Pearl Bailey and Louis Armstrong will follow him into the Showroom Internationale.

One hour before his third Vegas opening, Elvis, sitting in his dressing room reading congratulatory telegrams, confessed to a movie camera: "This is the nitty-gritty time for getting nervous—opening night." They had continued rehearsals for one week at the hotel prior to the opening, first with the vocal groups, then onstage with the whole orchestra. The repertoire was finally settled: "Mary In The Morning" was abandoned at the last minute, and the religious vocal piece "Oh, Happy Day" considered as an alternative. As he stood in the wings, flanked by his singers and waiting to go on, Elvis worried about forgetting the words to "I Just Can't Help Believin' " and told Charlie Hodge to make sure the lyric sheet was ready onstage if he needed it. "If the songs don't go over, we can do a medley of the costumes," he joked, just seconds before striding to center stage in white boots, rings flashing, high-collared white one-piece suit dangling fringes almost to the floor. The hard work of rehearsing and a stringent diet had lost Elvis a great deal of weight, and with his deep tan and black-dyed hair he projected an image of not-quite-real superiority. RCA recorded while MGM filmed over the course of four consecutive nights, capturing an Elvis as trained and ready as an Olympic athlete. It was, in a way, the ultimate Elvis performance, bringing together virtually every type of music he had ever sung, drawing power from all the sources of his inspiration. He had yet to figure out how to incorporate the gospel songs, but there was a real spirituality to his delivery of "Bridge Over Troubled Water"—as near as rock music had come to a sacred song. Back on November 6, 1955, as a young man just signed to the Louisiana Hayride, Elvis had burst onstage to sing a song called "Sitting On The Top Of The World"; now, in August 1970, he'd reached the top once again. His comeback was rooted in a glorious past, but its exciting present held the promise of an even brighter future. Could he even have imagined a greater pinnacle?

The engagement, of course, was a complete sellout. Once MGM had finished filming, Elvis dropped the newer Nashville songs in favor of surprises like Johnny Cash's "I Walk The Line" and "Folsom Prison Blues." He threw in "Oh, Happy Day" and, on one occasion, "When The Snow Is On The Roses." And he told the crowd he'd have two new albums out that winter—the documentary soundtrack and a country LP.

Upon his return to live performing Elvis had been criticized for choosing to appear in Las Vegas—generally thought of as a playground for middle-aged gamblers, not the ordinary folks who were Elvis's fans. For his part, the Colonel had been wary of whether there would be enough demand to justify nationwide touring. But the dimensions of his Vegas success—and the record-breaking crowds in Houston—were enough to change his thinking. To meet the challenge of mounting Elvis's first full-fledged tour, the Colonel hooked up with fledgling entrepreneur Jerry Weintraub and his partner, the veteran promoter Tom Hulett, of Management III. Together they planned a six-day, eight-show tour through proven Presley territory: Phoenix, St. Louis, Detroit, Miami, Tampa, and Mobile. Elvis entertained more than 100,000 people that September; as critics raved, audiences went wild, and profits grew, all of America—and maybe the whole world—once again seemed like open territory.

103. Studio Session for RCA
September 22, 1970: RCA's Studio B, Nashville

Producer/A&R: Felton Jarvis
Engineer: Al Pachucki

Guitar: Eddie Hinton
Guitar: Chip Young
Bass: Norbert Putnam
Drums: Jerry Carrigan
Piano: David Briggs (1800)
Organ, Harmonica: Charlie McCoy
Vocals: The Jordanaires
Vocals: Millie Kirkham, Mary Green, Mary Holladay, Ginger Holladay

Harmony: Elvis Presley (1797)

Overdubbed later:
Vocals: The Imperials
Vocals: Millie Kirkham, Dolores Edgin,
Sonja Montgomery, June Page
Guitar: Harold Bradley (1797)
Piano: David Briggs
Percussion: Farrell Morris

ZPA4 1797-06	**Snowbird**	**Elvis Country**
	Gene MacLellan—Beechwood Music	*LSP 4460/1971*
ZPA4 1798-06	**Where Did They Go, Lord**	**Single A-side**
	Dallas Frazier/A. L. Owens—E. Presley & Blue Crest Music	*47-9980/1971*
ZPA4 1799-02	**Whole Lotta Shakin' Goin' On**	**Elvis Country**
	Dave Williams/Sunny David—Anne Rachel & Pic Music	*LSP 4460/1971*
ZPA4 1800-sp	**Rags To Riches**	**Single B-side**
	Richard Adler/Jerry Ross—Saunders Publications	*47-9980/1971*

The master of "Rags To Riches" (1800) is spliced from take 4 and one line of take 3. A horn arrangement for "Whole Lotta Shakin' Goin' On" (1799) was recorded, but never used. The full take, which runs 1:35 minutes longer than the edit originally released on *Elvis Country*, was released in 1997 on *A Hundred Years From Now: Essential Elvis Vol. 4*.

Elvis was due back in RCA's Nashville studios on September 21 to deliver two last cuts for the country album. But the day came and went, and when he finally did arrive, twenty-four hours later, he seemed so irritated and out-of-sorts that several of those present began to wonder what was wrong. Priscilla was with him that day and to one of the musicians she intimated, without being too specific, that there were *reasons*—a comment he took to have something to do with drugs.

From the start Elvis was badgering Felton to speed it up—he needed to fly back to LA that night. Work began with a cover of Anne Murray's "Snowbird"; it was a pretty song, but tossed off with no attempt at an original arrangement, and its guitar part was eventually replaced by Harold Bradley. The session guitarist was a very nervous Eddie Hinton, filling in for James Burton while he fulfilled a previous engagement. Elvis loved the next tune, a new Dallas Frazier–Doodle Owens ballad, "Where Did They Go, Lord?" With its single potential in mind, he belted it out at full throttle. "Whole Lotta Shakin' Goin' On" had been written in 1954 by Dave "Curly" Williams and Roy Hall (country star Webb Pierce's onetime piano player), and recorded a year later by Big Maybelle with Quincy Jones fronting the studio band; several other versions came and went before Jerry Lee Lewis put his own stamp on it forever with his 1957 Sun single. Now Elvis put it through a wild rehearsal, but he was still anxious to wind it up; he even started complaining that his guys weren't getting him enough water, and the group's forced laughter on the session tapes makes Elvis's irritation evident. He couldn't wait to get this over with, and he barreled through "Shakin' " in one take—it was almost manic, but still a fascinating performance, and a great addition to the country album. Before they were done Elvis finally attempted a song he'd been thinking about for years: "Rags To Riches," originally a hit for Tony Bennett in 1953, but more significantly an R&B cover the following year by Billy Ward and the Dominoes. Elvis gave it the powerful, crescendo-laden approach that had worked so well with

"The Wonder Of You" and "You Don't Have To Say You Love Me," and in his singing there was an appropriate air of desperation. But where in the past Elvis had always taken such songs as personal vocal challenges, working through endless takes until he'd jumped the hurdle, now he couldn't even be bothered to stay long enough to complete a master before he was gone, flying back to LA. Felton managed to repair the best take with an insert from another to create a usable version, but everyone was left nonplussed by Elvis's behavior. Priscilla's comment confirmed his own suspicion: His regimen of medications had begun coloring every aspect of their lives.

The Colonel's careful planning had driven Elvis on a Sherman march from Las Vegas to Houston, back to Nashville to record, back to Vegas for the documentary, and then back on tour for two months late in the year. RCA, on the other hand, seemed to be wandering in the wilderness. Their haphazard record-release policy left Elvis's extraordinary year in a dustcloud of five new singles, two new albums, two budget albums full of leftovers, a budget rerelease of the Christmas album, and a four-album *Worldwide Gold Award Hits* package. The two years from December 1968 through December 1970 were a high-water mark in Elvis's career, yet their very quality was diluted by RCA's strategy, which not only went against contemporary industry practice but must surely have confused his audience. Elvis was recording his best music in ten years or more, but much of the "new" Elvis product reaching the market during the same period was substandard; at a time when most artists exercised complete creative control, Elvis's fans must have wondered just who was running the show.

If you could get beyond the trappings, though, the actual content of Elvis's 1970 releases went a long way toward revealing his rapidly maturing talent. The two new albums arrived, just six weeks apart, not long after Elvis announced them to the Las Vegas audience in August. If *Elvis Country* represented a return to roots, *That's The Way It Is,* the soundtrack from the eagerly awaited documentary, pointed to the future with its mix of eight more contemporary tracks from the June sessions and four live tracks from the film. Each album made the top twenty, and each went gold, as expected. Yet right away the accompanying singles failed to match their success. The first, "I've Lost You," may have been too ambitious for its audience; it went no higher than number thirty-two on the charts, and although it sold nearly 750,000 copies it didn't do as well as "The Wonder Of You." The follow-up, "You Don't Have To Say You Love Me," carried the opposite lesson: This time, with a familiar, proven song and a kitschy Las Vegas arrangement that obliterated the delicacy of the original, RCA sold a million and got their record to number eleven. If "I've Lost You" had ambition, "You Don't Have To Say You Love Me" had only success—and it was this overblown sound that even today many people associate with Elvis Presley. *That's The Way It Is* was a graceful, well-crafted album, weaving together powerful cuts like "Just Pretend" and "Stranger In The Crowd," the delicate and contemporary arrangements of "The Next Step Is Love" and "Mary In The Morning," and a strong version of B. J. Thomas's international hit "I Just Can't Help Believin'." At the end of the day, though, it is the singles that people remember—the songs that were on the radio. And by that measure, to many listeners, Elvis was working the same ground as Tom Jones or Engelbert Humperdinck—an imitation, in other words, of his own imitators.

Rolling Stone's Peter Guralnick, in his review of *Elvis Country,* wrote that "Elvis Presley has come out with a record that gives us some of the very finest music since he first recorded for Sun almost seventeen years ago." His praise was echoed in reviews around the country— praise that was conspicuously lacking from most assessments of *That's The Way It Is,* despite the fact that both albums were recorded at the same June sessions. With its rootsy (if erratic) repertoire, the crackling contributions of the band, and Elvis's own personal commitment to the material, the country album was perceived as an authentic statement. *Elvis Country* took the informal jam-session spirit Chips Moman had found so distracting during the Memphis sessions and turned it to Elvis's advantage. Chips's carefully crafted arrangements had yielded a series of powerful and

hugely successful singles; Felton Jarvis's maiden voyage as Elvis's personal producer resulted in something different, but just as impressive—a fresh and revelatory album, his most coherent and lively since *Elvis Is Back.*

Although Elvis's behavior at the September session pointed to trouble ahead, at the end of the year most of the signs were wildly positive. The live engagements piled triumph upon triumph; if the film *That's The Way It Is* wasn't the critical success Elvis might have been hoping for, it certainly served the Colonel's pur-

poses. "Now don't you go winning no Oscar with this picture," Parker had joked with producer-director Denis Sanders in July, "because we don't have no tuxedos to wear to the celebration." As far as the Colonel was concerned, the film was a fine piece of product he could sell to anyone not fortunate enough to be able to attend an Elvis show in person.

At the end of their first year, then, the 1970s were shaping up to be the most productive and rewarding years of Elvis's career. How quickly things would change.

1971

Impossible Dreams

When I was a child, ladies and gentlemen, I was a dreamer. I read comic books, and I was the hero in the movie. So every dream that I ever dreamed has come true a hundred times. I learned very early in life that "without a song, the day would never end; without a song, a man ain't got a friend; without a song, the road would never bend—without a song." So I keep singing a song.

—Elvis Presley, accepting the Jaycees' "Ten Outstanding Young Men of the Nation" Award, January 16, 1971

The night of January 16, 1971, at the Municipal Auditorium in Memphis, was a proud one for Elvis, who had been selected by the national organization of Jaycees as one of "Ten Most Outstanding Young Men of the Nation." Each of the ten had reached the highest level of success and achievement in his chosen field. Elvis attended the ceremony with Priscilla at his side, and to the world it did indeed look as if his "every dream had come true." His new albums were high in the charts; his upcoming Las Vegas engagement was another sellout. Family photographs taken two weeks later, on Lisa Marie's third birthday, radiated the kind of genuine happiness that any good-looking, successful young millionaire would present to the world.

Come the Vegas gig, though, and Elvis had the flu. Despite his local doctor's advice he honored his two-shows-a-night commitment to the International Hotel, but there were nights when he stayed onstage no longer than thirty minutes, and his singing was often uninspired. He'd begun closing the show with "The Impossible Dream," but otherwise it was the same show he'd given in Las Vegas the previous August. And the moodiness he'd shown at the September recording session was returning. Onstage Elvis seemed churlish, dismissing the hotel management ("To hell with them") and making the kind of unprofessional remarks you wouldn't have expected from the confident, world-beating Elvis Presley of the past two years. Any astute observer would have noticed that something was wrong—and Colonel Tom Parker noticed everything.

While Elvis finished up in Las Vegas and retreated to Los Angeles and Palm Springs for a rest, the Colonel and RCA were busy planning the year's releases and recording sessions. There were still enough masters left over from the Nashville sessions to put together a new single and album; hoping to keep his recording streak going, though, they wanted Elvis to return to the studio for a host of new projects: a new religious album, a second Christmas album, and a pop album, along with several more singles. Elvis's 1957 Christmas album had been selling well in a Camden budget rerelease, but the Colonel and RCA talked a reluctant Elvis into a new Christmas session on the logic that a new one would do even better. Freddy Bienstock, still acting as Hill & Range's liaison to Elvis, was increasingly eager to push songs from his own English company, Carlin, and submitted more than thirty tunes for the session. At the same time Julian Aberbach was promoting some of the older songs in their vast catalog for the purpose; as always he managed to include songs Elvis had already rejected—and even a few like "Known Only To Him" that he'd actually recorded, an awkward sign of how distant the Aberbachs had grown from their star client since Freddy had started his own firm. In the end Elvis would record only a few songs submitted by Hill & Range, but among them were two older numbers that were particularly close to Elvis's heart: "You Gave Me A Mountain," from the Marty Robbins catalog acquired in 1967, which was passed over for the sessions but entered his live act the following year; and "Padre," a song Elvis had first mentioned as a favorite at his 1958 press conference.

But Elvis kept picking up songs on his own, and that made publishing matters trickier. It wasn't that Elvis would never cut a song his publishing companies couldn't get a deal on—those days were long gone—but naturally his organization would make every effort to get a piece of the action when they could. As the session approached Elvis's pop list included two Kris Kristofferson songs, "Help Me Make It Through The Night" and "Sunday Morning Coming Down," as well as "My Way," "The First Time Ever I Saw Your Face" and his new Vegas closer, "The Impossible Dream"—a song he felt could be his next single. Tom Diskin knew that Elvis was likely to bring up more and more titles as a session drew near; past sessions had found Hill & Range negotiating for rights while Elvis was actually in the midst of cutting the song—or even after he'd cut a master. (As the "Guitar Man" fiasco demonstrated, it was a lot harder to convince a writer to give up a cut of his royalties once he knew Elvis had already cut his song.) The one place where there'd be no problem in coming up with material was for the religious album; before the session began Elvis readily approved "Lead Me, Guide Me" and "Just A Closer Walk With Thee" from the Hill & Range catalog. Other songs, such as "An Evening Prayer," were in the public domain, making it possible for the Aberbachs to give Elvis a lucrative arranger's credit and the royalties that went with it.

The twin successes of Memphis '69 and Nashville '70 led both Elvis's management and his record company to believe it might be possible to record everything they needed for the next year in just one string of consecutive sessions—in this case, more than forty songs. It was the first time they had tried to dictate the size of the project before recording dates were set up, but in their optimism a handful of factors—a dearth of adequate material, and the singer's own motivation and even health—went unconsidered.

104. Studio Session for RCA
March 15, 1971: RCA's Studio B, Nashville

A&R/Producer: Felton Jarvis
Engineer: Al Pachucki

Guitar: James Burton
Guitar: Chip Young
Acoustic Guitar: Charlie Hodge
Bass: Norbert Putnam
Drums: Jerry Carrigan
Piano: David Briggs
Harmonica: Charlie McCoy
Vocals: The Nashville Edition
Vocals: Mary & Ginger Holladay,
Millie Kirkham

Overdubbed later:
Vocals: The Imperials (1255)
Vocals: Elvis Presley (1255)
Vocals: The Nashville Edition (1256)
Vocals: Mary & Ginger Holladay (1256)
Vocals: Temple Riser (unused duet 1255)
Vocals: Millie Kirkham
Vibes: na (1255–57)
Horns

<u>3/15, 6–9PM, 10PM–1:30AM</u>

APA4 1255-12	**The First Time Ever I Saw Your Face**	**Single B-side**
	Ewan McColl—Storm King Music	*74-0672/1972*
APA4 1256-05	**Amazing Grace**	**He Touched Me**
	Arranged by Elvis Presley—E. Presley Music	*LSP 4690/1972*
APA4 1257-na	**Early Morning Rain**	**Elvis Now**
	Gordon Lightfoot—Warner Bros. Music	*LSP 4671/1972*
APA4 1258-12	**(That's What You Get) For Lovin' Me**	**Elvis (Fool)**
	Gordon Lightfoot—Warner Bros. Music	*APL1 0283/1973*

The master of "Early Morning Rain" (1257) is probably a splice of takes 10 and 12. "The First Time Ever I Saw Your Face" (1255) was originally recorded as a duet between Elvis and Ginger Holladay; Elvis tried rerecording it with Temple Riser on June 21, when Elvis redid his vocal. Further vocal repairs and additions were made on June 9 by Elvis and the Imperials. The Nashville Edition: Dolores Edgin, June Page, Hurshel Wiginton, Joe Babcock. The Imperials: Joe Moscheo, Greg Gordon, Terry Blackwood, Jim Murray, Armond Morales.

With a three-album agenda before him, Elvis arrived on the first day of the sessions with a runny nose and aching eyes. Yet he was determined to go ahead, and his enthusiasm seemed inspired by an unlikely source: contemporary folk music. The spate of home taping he'd done during the soundtrack years reveals that Elvis had been tuned in to the folk boom since the mid-'60s, and it was through the sweet harmonies of Peter, Paul and Mary that he was introduced to songwriters like Bob Dylan and Gordon Lightfoot. With Charlie and Red he'd harmonized for hours on songs like "Blowin' In The Wind" and "500 Miles"; now Elvis had been listening to Peter, Paul and Mary's interpretations of songs like "The First Time Ever I Saw Your Face," "Early Morning Rain," "(That's What You Get) For Lovin' Me," and Dylan's "Don't

Think Twice, It's All Right" and "I Shall Be Released." Eager to work with similar textures himself, Elvis picked up on a suggestion from Charlie Hodge and brought in a male-female quartet, the Nashville Edition, to help on the sessions.

His first attempt at blending his voice with another's would come with Evan McColl's "The First Time Ever I Saw Your Face," which he wanted to try as a duet. Except for brief contributions from Ann-Margret in *Viva Las Vegas* and Nancy Sinatra in *Speedway,* Elvis had rarely shared the spotlight with female singers; now he tried the song in tandem with Ginger Holladay, one of his regular backup singers, but when it didn't come off the way Elvis wanted, Felton Jarvis shelved the backing track for a later solo overdub. In much the same mood they went on to "Amazing Grace," a recent hit in a startling a cappella version by folk singer Judy Collins. For this voice piece the rhythm section set a slow, solid, unobtrusive beat, while Chip Young added some bluesy acoustic slide guitar and David Briggs contributed flashy piano runs straight out of the showy gospel music tradition. Elvis and the singers joined in, but after the second take Felton counseled them to soften the bluesy edges ("Don't play that funky stuff, Chip"), and the take selected as a master was more conservative, less arresting, than it might have been. The rest of the evening was devoted to Peter, Paul and Mary's two Gordon Lightfoot numbers, "Early Morning Rain" and "For Lovin' Me," both grounded in the same sound: Restrained brushes from Jerry Carrigan's drums, blended with a simple, effective bass line from Norbert Putnam. "Are you gonna play something with me?" James Burton prodded Chip Young, initiating a friendly duel between the two on acoustic guitar licks. Charlie McCoy ("the fastest harp in the West," as one of his later solo albums dubbed him) took the solos. Each of the songs was true to its genre, but they lacked the feel the singer brought to any song when he was at his best. Elvis was having trouble. "Give me a Kleenex or some-

thing," he asked Charlie, snorting in every pause, struggling to keep his nose clear and his voice open. After the evening sessions he checked into a Nashville hospital for treatment of what turned out to be secondary glaucoma.

Elvis had been having problems with his eyes for the last few years, and no one who watched him record that night was surprised at his hospitalization. But for the moment his absence seemed only a minor inconvenience. Felton used some of the prebooked studio time to get some mixing and overdubbing for the up-

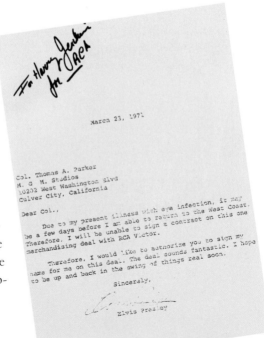

coming album out of the way, while James Burton took the opportunity to cut an instrumental album for A&M Records. RCA already had "Life" and "Only Believe" scheduled as an Easter single, and the album planned for June would mine the rest of the 1970 tapes. Elvis's hospital stay did motivate them to remove from the album two big ballads, "The Sound Of Your Cry" and "Sylvia" (on both of which they had 100 percent copyright control), for possible single release. Then in early April the album title was changed from *Festival* to *Love Letters From Elvis* after the 1970 rerecording of "Love Letters" was added. The Colonel suggested adding a live version of "Something" from the August Las Vegas tapes, but Felton knew they had a studio take of "Hey Jude" left over from Memphis, which he thought might be better. The only voice missing from the debate was that of Elvis himself; given that he'd already rejected all of these cuts in putting together his previous two albums, the whole discussion might have discouraged him anyway. Eventually the Colonel and Felton agreed with RCA to add the Easter single to the package, bringing it up to eleven cuts—a complete album in quantity, if not in quality.

105. Studio Session for RCA
May 15–21, 1971: RCA's Studio B, Nashville

A&R/Producer: Felton Jarvis
Engineer: Al Pachucki

Electric Guitar: James Burton
Guitar: Chip Young
Acoustic Guitar: Charlie Hodge
Bass: Norbert Putnam
Drums, Percussion: Jerry Carrigan (5/15, 17)
Drums: Kenneth Buttrey (5/16–21)
Piano: David Briggs
Piano: Joe Moscheo (1276–81)
Piano: Elvis Presley (1282–84)
Organ: Glen Spreen (1266–72)
Organ, Percussion, Harmonica: Charlie McCoy
Vocals: The Imperials (1273–81, 85–87)
Vocals: June Page, Kirkham, Riser (1288)
Vocals: Kirkham, G. Holladay, Riser (1273–81; 85–87)

Overdubbed later:
The Imperials: (5/19: 1259), (5/24: 1260, 61, 63, 65, 67, 71, 72)
Vocals: Millie Kirkham, Ginger Holladay, Temple Riser (5/19: 1259)
Vocals: Kirkham, Page, Riser (5/21: 1287)
Vocals: Kirkham (5/24 as Imperial)
Guitar: James Burton (1264)
Drums: Larry Londin (1266)
Percussion: Larry Londin (1263, 67, 70, 88)
Organ: na (1288)
Horns: (1259, 61, 62, 70, 87)
Vocals: (1270, 71)

5/15, 6–9PM, 9PM–12AM, 1–4AM

APA4 1259-04	**Miracle Of The Rosary**	**Elvis Now**
	Lee Denson—Acuff/Rose Music	*LSP 4671/1972*
APA4 1260-07	**It Won't Seem Like Christmas**	**Elvis Sings The Wonderful World Of Christmas**
	J. A. Balthrop—Elvis Presley Music & Pope Res Music	*LSP 4579/1971*
APA4 1261-08	**If I Get Home On Christmas Day**	**Elvis Sings The Wonderful World Of Christmas**
	Tony McCaulay—Gladys Music	*LSP 4579/1971*
APA4 1262-12	**Padre**	**Elvis (Fool)**
	LaRue/Hebster/Romans—Anne Rachel Music	*APL1 0283/1973*

APA4 1263-10	**Holly Leaves And Christmas Trees**	**Elvis Sings The Wonderful World Of Christmas**
	Red West/Glen Spreen—Elvis Presley Music	*LSP 4579/1971*
APA4 1264-01	**Merry Christmas Baby**	**Elvis Sings The Wonderful World Of Christmas**
	L. Baxter/J. Moore—Hill & Range	*LSP 4579/1971*
APA4 1265-02	**Silver Bells**	**Elvis Sings The Wonderful World Of Christmas**
	R. Evans/J. Livingston—Paramount Music	*LSP 4579/1971*

5/16, 6–9PM, 9PM–12AM, 1–4AM

WPA5 2571-01	**The Lord's Prayer**	**A Hundred Years From Now**
	Arranged by Elvis Presley	*66866-2/1996*
APA4 1266-08	**I'll Be Home On Christmas Day**	**Elvis Sings The Wonderful World Of Christmas**
	Michael Jarrett—Elvis Presley & Oten Music	*LSP 4579/1971*
APA4 1267-na	**On A Snowy Christmas Night**	**Elvis Sings The Wonderful World Of Christmas**
	S. Gelber—Gladys Music & United Artists Music	*LSP 4579/1971*
APA4 1268-10	**Winter Wonderland**	**Elvis Sings The Wonderful World Of Christmas**
	D. Smith/F. Bernard—Bregman, Vocco & Conn	*LSP 4579/1971*
APA4 1269-01	**Don't Think Twice, It's All Right**	**Elvis (Fool)**
	Bob Dylan—Warner Bros. Music	*APL1 0283/1973*
APA4 1270-01	**O Come, All Ye Faithful**	**Elvis Sings The Wonderful World Of Christmas**
	Arranged by Elvis Presley—Elvis Presley Music	*LSP 4579/1971*
APA4 1271-na	**The First Noel**	**Elvis Sings The Wonderful World Of Christmas**
	Arranged by Elvis Presley—Elvis Presley Music	*LSP 4579/1971*
APA4 1272-na	**The Wonderful World Of Christmas**	**Elvis Sings The Wonderful World Of Christmas**
	Tobias/Frisch—Gladys Music & Hampshire House	*LSP 4579/1971*

5/17, 6–9PM, 9PM–12AM, 1–4AM

APA4 1273-sp	**Help Me Make It Through The Night**	**Elvis Now**
	Kris Kristofferson—Combine Music	*LSP 4671/1972*
APA4 1274-08	**Until It's Time For You To Go**	**Single A-side**
	Buffy Sainte-Marie—Gypsy Boy Music	*74-0619/1972*
WPA5 2572-01	**Lady Madonna**	**Walk A Mile In My Shoes**
	John Lennon/Paul McCartney—Northern Songs	*66670-2/1995*
APA4 1275-06	**Lead Me, Guide Me**	**He Touched Me**
	D. Akers—Hill & Range	*LSP 4690/1972*

5/18, 6–9PM, 10PM–1AM, 1:30–4:30AM

APA4 1276-24	**Fools Rush In**	**Elvis Now**
	R. Bloom/J. Mercer—Bregman, Vocco/Conn & Commander Pub.	*LSP 4671/1972*
APA4 1277-04	**He Touched Me**	**Single A-side**
	W. Gaither—Elvis Presley Music & Gaither Music	*74-0651/1972*
APA4 1278-02	**I've Got Confidence**	**He Touched Me**
	A. Crouch—Libris Music	*LSP 4690/1972*

APA4 1279-na **An Evening Prayer** **He Touched Me**
Battersby/Gabriel—The Rodeheaver Co. *LSP 4690/1972*

<u>5/19, 6–9PM, 9PM–12AM, 1–2AM</u>

APA4 1280-14 **Seeing Is Believing** **He Touched Me**
Red West/Glen Spreen—Elvis Presley Music *LSP 4690/1972*

APA4 1281-09 **A Thing Called Love** **He Touched Me**
Jerry Reed—Vector Music *LSP 4690/1972*

<u>5/19, 2–4AM</u>

APA4 1282-05 **It's Still Here** **Elvis (Fool)**
Ivory Joe Hunter—Gladys Music *APL1 0283/1973*

APA4 1283-na **I'll Take You Home Again Kathleen** **Elvis (Fool)**
Arranged by Elvis Presley—Elvis Presley Music *APL1 0283/1973*

APA4 1284-03 **I Will Be True** **Elvis (Fool)**
Ivory Joe Hunter—Hill & Range *APL1 0283/1973*

<u>5/20, 6–9 PM, 9PM–12AM, 1–4AM</u>

APA4 1285-na **I'm Leavin'** **Single A-side**
Michael Jarrett/Sonny Charles—Elvis Presley & Oten Music *47-9998/1971*

APA4 1286-na **We Can Make The Morning** **Single B-side**
Jay Ramsey—Elvis Presley Music/Surety Songs *74-0619/1972*

WPA5 2573-01 **I Shall Be Released (2 verses only)** **Walk A Mile In My Shoes**
Bob Dylan—Warner Bros. Music *66670-2/1995*

APA4 1287-10 **It's Only Love** **Single A-side**
Mark James/Steve Tyrell—Press Music *48-1017/1971*

<u>5/21, 6–9PM, 9PM–12AM, 1–4AM</u>

APA4 1288-12 **Love Me, Love The Life I Lead** **Elvis (Fool)**
Tony Macaulay/Roger Greenaway—Gladys Music/Yellow Dog Music *APL1 0283/1973*

Elvis overdubbed a harmony vocal for "Miracle Of The Rosary" (1259) on May 19. The master of "Padre" (1262) is probably take 12 or a splice of takes 8 and 12. The master of "Help Me Make It Through The Night" (1273) is a splice of take 11 and ending of take 16. The original master of "Merry Christmas Baby" (1264) was edited and had a guitar overdub mixed directly with the two-track mixdown. The unedited master was first released in 1982 on *Memories Of Christmas* (CPL1 4395), at which point it was issued a new master serial number (MWA5 9086). The complete recording of "Don't Think Twice, It's All Right" runs 11 minutes, 25 seconds; it was edited to 2:45 for its initial release. An 8:35 version was released in 1979 on *Our Memories of Elvis—Vol. 2* (AQL1 3448), and *Walk A Mile In My Shoes: The Essential 70's Masters* included a 4:00 edit. The complete recording of "It's Still Here" runs 4:40, including a breakdown in the middle of the take; it was edited down to 2:05 for the initial master. A 3:53 edit was released in 1980 on *Elvis Aron Presley* (CPL8 3699), and a 3:29 edit in 1995 on *Walk A Mile In My Shoes*. The Imperials: Joe Moscheo, Greg Gordon, Terry Blackwood, Armond Morales, and Jim Murray (Murray not present on May 17).

On the night of May 15 RCA's Studio B had been decorated for an early Christmas. A tree with beautifully wrapped empty boxes stood in the center of the room, but Elvis brought real gifts for the musicians and his own associates—gold bracelets engraved "Elvis '71." All the players from the June 1970 sessions were back, and again there were no backup singers present. With no personnel changes and as few distractions as possible, Felton expected to be able to get all of Elvis's recording done in short order and save all the sweetening for later. As the group was getting started the old question of material came up, and there was some talk about the mysterious process new songs had to go through to make it to an Elvis session. But Elvis rendered the debate moot by choosing the first song himself: "Miracle Of The Rosary." Writer Lee Denson was an old Lauderdale Courts compatriot, and he'd brought the song directly to Elvis, who put it at the top of his agenda. As soon as they'd worked out an introduction on the organ the first take flowed beautifully, and Elvis led the musicians confidently through the four takes it took to complete the song.

With one religious song out of the way Elvis playfully launched into the first line of "Merry Christmas Baby," a song that would become the highlight of the evening's proceedings a few hours later. Then they were knee-deep in Yuletide music again, as David Briggs's celeste led the way into a brand-new song, "It Won't Seem Like Christmas." Chip Young explained the chord progressions to the group while Elvis grumbled to Charlie Hodge; his lyrics weren't written out, and he was having trouble with his voice, clearing his throat repeatedly, chewing on ice cubes from the glasses of water supplied by his entourage. A second new Christmas number Freddy had brought from England, "If I Get Home On Christmas Day," brought back the versatile Charlie McCoy on his favorite instrument, the harmonica. Elvis was straining at the bit during these numbers, just itching to cut loose, but Felton pushed the band to move along without stopping between takes. Then, coming upon a song he really wanted to do right by, the singer himself seemed to take charge. "Padre" was one of the dramatic ballads with which Elvis continued to challenge himself, and this time he found he wasn't quite up to it. After missing a few high notes he apologized ("I wasn't singing that well"), and then proceeded to curse his own performance through twelve difficult takes. Longtime friend Red West had returned to the fold (he'd left in a huff four years earlier when he wasn't invited to Elvis's wedding); he'd been involved with the music at Elvis's sessions before, and this time he brought "Holly Leaves And Christmas Trees," a pretty, undemanding song the group polished off in five takes. Felton pushed them for one more, but with only marginal improvement, and little commitment on Elvis's part.

It was after midnight when they finally got the chance to unwind and head back to their common turf—the blues. "Merry Christmas Baby" had been a 1949 hit for vocalist Charles Brown of Johnny Moore's Three Blazers, and Elvis's success with another classic blues, "Reconsider Baby," had inspired Hill & Range to suggest the Brown song for the 1968 TV special. "Just run through it a couple of times," Elvis told the rhythm section; "I'll come in somewhere." And almost before they got going, he was ready. Pushing everyone else to eke as much emotion out of the song as he was ("Dig in, James," he cajoled; "Wake up, Putt"), he cruised through more than six minutes on the first take. There was ease and menace and delight in Elvis's after-hours performance, and the result has led more than one observer to lament that it wasn't a blues album rather than a Christmas album that had brought them together that night.

This brief interlude was followed by rehearsals of the 1956 Bing Crosby hit "Silver Bells." Elvis asked Charlie Hodge to sing harmony with him, but an uncomfortable impasse followed: As engineer Al Pachucki went about setting up for the duet, Elvis cut in to correct him—he didn't want both voices on the record, he just wanted to be able to hear Charlie singing along. The gaffe had sapped any remaining energy out of the room, but Felton was determined to go for one more ("a real quickie"), and despite his exasperation Elvis agreed to do it again. "It's gonna be real nice," Felton assured him. But there was only silence following the call for third take, until Chip Young, eyeing the singer, murmured to himself, "Uh, uh, I don't think so." Elvis just couldn't bring himself to try it again. "I can't get into it," Elvis admitted a moment later. "I'm sorry. We better go back to what we had."

As the evening ended, though, Felton had seven masters on tape—and every hope that on the following night they'd be able to finish the Christmas album with ease.

The next day a visitor, English songwriter Chris Arnold, stood in the control room; after all, "You just don't *not* turn up on an Elvis session" when you get hired. As part of the Arnold, Morrow, and Martin songwriting team he'd received a rare invitation from Freddy to attend—which gave him ringside seats for the uproar created when drummer Jerry Carrigan failed to show up at the session. Carrigan had stayed up all night after the previous night's session; exhausted, he had finally fallen asleep in the late afternoon with the kettle on, only to awaken and find the house filled with smoke. Felton Jarvis, Tom Diskin, and RCA representative Harry Jenkins were unmoved by his muttered apologies when he finally called in; they'd already replaced him with Kenneth Buttrey, a top session player who'd contributed to Bob Dylan's *Blonde On Blonde* sessions (and subbed on Elvis's *Harum Scarum* soundtrack). At 7:30 P.M. Elvis arrived, accompanied by a small entourage, and clad in a black, wide-shouldered, V-necked, high-collared jacket trimmed with gold—a kind of evening-wear translation of his stage outfits. Spotting the slender new drummer, Elvis joked he'd been telling Jerry Carrigan to lose weight, "but this is ridiculous!" Chris Arnold was impressed with how good the band was and how quickly the musicians learned the new songs. Felton's role, in his observation, was more as mixer than as producer; it was Elvis who made the key decisions himself. When Felton suggested they needed a sandpaper effect on the rhythm track on one song Elvis closed him down: "He wants to do his fingernails! Do that shit on your own time, Felton. You can get a manicure tomorrow—hell!" The room laughed along with him, as they always did.

The good-natured joking continued as they worked to pare down Michael Jarrett's new song "I'll Be Home On Christmas Day" (originally titled "It Happens Every Year") from eight to six verses, finally achieving a wonderful bluesy tone. Felton's sandpaper was discarded, but he continued to cheer Elvis along, pausing after they achieved a breathtaking ending on take number four. As the group chatted, Elvis began a leisurely wander through "The Lord's Prayer," and the ever-alert control room let the tape run; what they captured may have been an overly dramatic rendition of the Mahalia Jackson song, but Elvis's phrasing on the word "heaven" midprayer was worthy of Jackson herself. He had trouble on the high notes at the ending: "Didn't think I could do it, did you?" he joked when he finally did. After two more takes of "I'll Be Home On Christmas Day," they went on to cut "On A Snowy Christmas Night" and "Winter Wonderland." Now, though, Chris Arnold witnessed how quickly things could change. Elvis had lost interest, repeatedly breaking into old favorites; finally he said flat out that he hated "Winter Wonderland" and proceeded to prove it with a lifeless rendition. A further distraction came with a call from Priscilla in Los Angeles. The power had gone off at home, and she wondered where the flashlight was.

The English songwriter perceived that there was untapped energy in the air as they cast about for what to do next, and it took only one guitar lick from James Burton to start Elvis off on an impromptu version of Bob Dylan's "Don't Think Twice, It's All Right." Al Pachucki was busy cutting the master take of the last Christmas song from the tape reel when Felton shouted, "Get the tape on." The group jammed for eleven minutes, doing the same verses over and over, adding new licks and phrasings. This was one more from the collection of folk material Elvis had brought along on March 15, and evidently it had stayed on his mind. The song wasn't meant to be taken at such a fast tempo, but no one gave too much thought to that because the feeling was there. After listening to a playback of Dylan's song Elvis had no interest in returning to work on the Christmas material, so the band recorded tracks for the three remaining songs, and Elvis overdubbed his vocals a few nights later.

Finally done with the Christmas assignment, on the third night Elvis got started on what he really wanted to do: cut a version of Kris Kristofferson's "Help Me Make It Through The Night." The song wasn't supposed to be recorded; Freddy already knew that Felton's friend Bob Beckham of Combine Music had no intention of making a deal. Kristofferson's song catalog was one of hottest of the early '70s, and Elvis's record sales just weren't big enough anymore to persuade a writer of his stature to give up royalties. But Felton wasn't troubled by the situation; thwarted himself from introducing songs to Elvis sessions, he was only too happy to see Beckham profit at Hill & Range's expense. Ever since he started working with Elvis, Felton had been hoping to break the repertoire monopoly levied through Hill & Range by the mighty Colonel. Now, with a song he really wanted to do, Elvis knocked another hole in the wall himself. He took full command of the recording, working out the arrangement both with the players and with the singers that Felton had brought back: the Imperials and a trio of female singers that included Millie Kirkham. In the end they did sixteen takes of the Kristofferson song, homed in on numbers ten, eleven, and sixteen as the best, and grafted the ending from sixteen onto take eleven to create a master.

Buffy Sainte-Marie's "Until It's Time For You To Go" was the next folk number to which Elvis gave his full attention. This kind of material might have been suitable for a pop album, less so for a single release—but Elvis was throwing himself into his performances with abandon now, and all anyone could do was stand back and watch. The atmosphere had loosened up, and between takes Elvis threw in snippets of any song that came to mind, whether "Johnny B. Goode" or a half-remembered lyric to the Beatles' "Lady Madonna." Felton was sensitive to Elvis's temper, and he was always prepared to work around his temper to get what he needed. Chip Young remembers very well the mood of the evening: "It was the first night the Imperials worked with him [since *How Great Thou Art* in 1966]. . . . He was into all that karate stuff. Well, Terry Blackwood, one of the Imperials, said 'If a man drew a pistol on you, how would you get it out of his hand?' So Elvis said, 'Red, come over here.' Red came over and took a gun out of his jacket. They unloaded it, thank God! Elvis said 'Hold that pistol on me.' Then Red held the gun on Elvis, and I'm looking over at all these guitars leaning against the drum booth. James Burton's guitars were there. I started to say, 'Let me move these g—,' but before I could get anything out of my mouth Elvis had hit Red's hand, and the gun went flying across the studio and stuck in the back of my guitar, barrel first. It was a gut-string guitar. Elvis offered to replace it."

The evening ended with a beautiful version of the new gospel song from Dorothy Akers, "Lead Me, Guide Me." The next day Elvis started with one of his choices, "Fools Rush In," an old swing-era number he'd often sung at home to a prerecorded orchestral backing. Jerry Carrigan had finally been forgiven, so now they had two drummers, but there was no real swing to the arrangement they came up with. Thereafter, with the Imperials present, Elvis turned back to the religious material. The Imperials of 1971, who backed Elvis in Vegas, were a very different group from the edition Elvis had worked with in 1966. Elvis's favorite, Jake Hess, had long since left the quartet he'd founded, as had the very impressive tenor Shaun Nielsen. The quartet's piano and organ player, Henry Slaughter, had been replaced by Joe Moscheo, who started out as the business manager of the group. But they were a tight harmony group with many gospel awards to their credit; Elvis admired their singing, and he had little trouble completing their reverent signature song, "He Touched Me," in four short takes. Turning on a dime, Elvis addressed the next religious number from an entirely different angle. "I've Got Confidence," by contemporary black gospel artist Andrae Crouch, inspired a confident treatment of its own, and Elvis gave it a rocking, almost sexy swagger that stretched the bounds of the strictly sacred. Then, as if to keep everyone guessing, he bounced back with a beautiful, and very sacred, version of Mahalia Jackson's "An Evening Prayer." Elvis seemed intent on making an album that reflected both the traditional gospel music he was raised on and the newer trends in Christian music, mixing his repertoire in just the way he had on most of his pop albums.

During the day Elvis slept, but for most of the members of the band it was business as usual—sessions all morning and afternoon. When they came back to work nights with Elvis, Felton had an unwritten rule prohibiting anyone from yawning in the studio—for fear that it might "bring down" his star—and he insisted that the musicians take their breaks in the parking lot. And even Elvis made a trip to their "outdoor lounge" when he became bogged down in "Seeing Is Believing," a new tune Red West had just frantically completed. Otherwise, though, he kept focused throughout the evening, actively directing the band, patiently discussing the backing parts with the female singers. Jerry Reed's "A Thing Called Love" was completed with an elaborate vocal arrangement that featured bass singer Armond Morales in a unison part with Elvis throughout the song. References to the previous evening's gunplay were flying, and after a while Elvis noticed how upset the Imperials became whenever he struck a karate pose. It was another night of good-humored ad-libbing. "He left the splendor of RCA—of Victor," he sang self-referentially after one verse of "Listen To The Bells"; "went back to Sun Records. . . . " The next take of "A Thing Called Love" collapsed, and Felton as always deflected blame from Elvis onto the newcomer, Joe Moscheo. But Elvis, ever-gracious when he was in good spirits, just changed the opening line of the song from "Six foot six, he stood on the ground" to "Three foot four . . . " and dedicated the song to Charlie Hodge.

After the meal break the atmosphere changed. Determined to capture the mood he achieved while performing at home, Elvis sat down at the piano for an impassioned yet unassuming solo set. Two of the three songs he chose had been favorites as far back as his days in Germany: "I'll Take You Home Again Kathleen" and Ivory Joe Hunter's "I Will Be True," both of which he'd recorded on his home equipment in Bad Nauheim. This old material was hardly what Felton or RCA were looking for in an Elvis session, but Al Pachucki was ready with the tapes rolling just the same. The most moving of the three was another Ivory Joe Hunter song, "It's Still Here," but later Felton excitedly reported to the Colonel that with overdubs they all would make "great tunes," keen to convince both Elvis and his manager of their commercial potential.

Felton was determined to get back to contemporary material, though—material that could give them that much-needed hit. Michael Jarrett and Sonny Charles's "I'm Leaving" seemed to offer Elvis the challenge he craved. "Phew, man, it's tough," he declared after one disorganized run-through. "But the thing is worth working on." Elvis saw his confidence in the song echoed by the Imperials and pianist David Briggs, who thought it was a hit for sure. Hill & Range provided two other single candidates, but "We Can Make The Morning" and "It's Only Love" lacked any of the elements—country, blues, rock 'n' roll, or gospel—that were essential to Presley's best music; rather, they were calculated stabs at pop music that set off no sparks. While Elvis struggled to remember the melody to "It's Only Love," he threw in a verse from Bob Dylan's

"I Shall Be Released," and sang it with the kind of feeling that indicated that this song should have been the record.

"Love Me, Love The Life I Lead," on the other hand, was a distinctly average song from Freddy's English firm, and it was recorded on the eighth and last night to nothing but ill will from Elvis. "Don't want to hear that goddamn demo," he complained. "I'm not sure whether that beginning is worth a damn." As the night wore on he became increasingly irritable: "These guys would hold up the Second Coming for a cigarette," he sniped during a break. It was frustration more than anything, but when one of the female backup singers asked "Are the girls balanced?" he showed he hadn't lost his sense of humor: "You should never ask that, dear." The sessions were running out of steam, and Elvis out of voice, but he ran through twelve takes, with Felton counting on getting Elvis to recut his vocal later if they wanted to release it. Elvis never did, but the record still came out.

More pressing to Felton at the moment, though, were the outstanding elements on the Christmas record. They spent the rest of the night doing vocal overdubs for that, as well as giving Temple Riser a shot at the duet vocal for "The First Time Ever I Saw Your Face." By then it was obvious that everyone needed a break, and new sessions were scheduled to complete the original agenda.

106. Studio Sessions for RCA
June 8–10, 1971: RCA's Studio B, Nashville

A&R/Producer: Felton Jarvis
Engineer: Al Pachucki

Electric Guitar: James Burton
Guitar: Chip Young
Acoustic Guitar: Charlie Hodge
Bass: Norbert Putnam
Drums: Jerry Carrigan
Drums: Kenneth Buttrey
Piano: David Briggs
Piano: Joe Moscheo (1291?)
Organ: Charlie McCoy
Organ: Glen Spreen (1289)

Vocals: The Imperials
Vocals: Millie Kirkham
Vocals: Sonja Montgomery
Vocals: June Page

Overdubbed later:
Vocals: Millie Kirkham, Dolores Edgin,
June Page (2/8/72: 1294)
Vocals: Millie Kirkham, June Page,
Sonja Montgomery (2/21/72: 1294)

6/8, 6–9PM, 10PM–2AM

APA4 1289-10	**Until It's Time For You To Go (remake)** *Buffy Sainte-Marie—Gypsy Boy Music*	**A Hundred Years From Now** *66866-2/1996*
APA4 1290-02	**Put Your Hand In The Hand** *Gene Maclellan—Beechwood Music*	**Elvis Now** *LSP 4671/1972*
APA4 1291-10	**Reach Out To Jesus** *Ralph Carmichael—Lexicon Music*	**He Touched Me** *LSP 4690/1972*

APA4 1292-05	**He Is My Everything**	**He Touched Me**
	Dallas Frazier—Blue Crest Music	*LSP 4690/1972*
APA4 1293-05	**There Is No God But God**	**He Touched Me**
	Bill Kenny—Sun Vine Music	*LSP 4690/1972*
APA4 1294-02	**I, John**	**He Touched Me**
	Johnson/McFadden/Brooks—Blackhawk Music	*LSP 4690/1970*
APA4 1295-06	**Bosom Of Abraham**	**Single B-side**
	Johnson/McFadden/Brooks—Blackhawk Music	*47-0651/1972*

APA4 1296-na	**My Way**	**Walk A Mile In My Shoes**
	Anka/Reveaux/Francois	*66670-2/1995*
APA4 1297-na	**I'll Be Home On Christmas Day (remake)**	**Memories Of Christmas**
	Michael Jarrett—Elvis Presley Music/Oten Music	*CPL1 4395/1982*

The Imperials: Joe Moscheo, Greg Gordon, Terry Blackwood, Armond Morales, Jim Murray.

This third set of spring 1971 sessions was born out of the necessity to complete the planned religious album. Continuing to add material of a more contemporary flavor than his past two gospel albums, Elvis was still saddled with an inadequate selection of good material. They started out copying a recent hit by the group Ocean, "Put Your Hand In The Hand," and in two takes had a perfunctory version in hand. But Elvis still wanted to redo "Until It's Time For You To Go"; he took it in a faster tempo this time, but the difference was minimal, and it was the earlier version that made it to vinyl. The evening concluded with a new song called "Reach Out To Jesus," proving that the right circumstances could still evoke from him a commanding gospel performance.

On the second night Elvis arrived late, and the good spirits from the day before had faded. He had always pushed himself to great work when covering performances by his heroes, so "There Is No God But God," originally recorded by Bill Kenny of the Ink Spots, provided a much-needed challenge. Yet for all of that Elvis's version sounded like a throwaway; it is an example of the kind of pedestrian arrangement that some of his musicians considered the main problem with the Elvis sessions of these years. With little time for the studio band to come up with ideas, Elvis and Felton were often all too happy to mimic whatever arrangement the demos suggested, leaving any creative embellishment to be written out later for overdubbing sessions, where the band had no input.

There was more gospel to be done, but no new material to do it with, so Elvis retreated to the jubilee of old with "Bosom Of Abraham" and "I, John." Quartet-based performances like these required very little from the sophisticated backing musicians, and Elvis made it clear that from his point of view the only important things were the harmonies he worked out with the other singers. "You're the rhythm section," one of the singers told the band only half-jokingly. "You're supposed to get it right. We're the singers." The end of the night saw further retrenchment, as Elvis finally dropped the duet approach to "The First Time Ever I Saw Your Face" and simply made a few necessary repairs to make it a conventional solo vocal.

This was to have been the second and last night of recording, but Elvis had a thing or two left on his agenda, so the band returned for one more all-nighter. First off, he wanted to try the Michael Jarrett song "I'll Be Home On Christmas Day" again, giving it a more solid beat. Then he set his sights on a project he'd been talking about since at least the beginning of the year: making his own recording of "My Way," which had only recently become Frank Sinatra's signature tune. The band provided a powerful, Las Vegas–type arrangement that built to a highly dramatic ending; the singers follow Elvis closely on the climactic notes, but the blended voices fail to mask the fact that Elvis himself was tired and no longer totally committed to the song. The master was shelved; Elvis may already have known that he could only get what he wanted with the inspiration of a live audience before him.

One of the remarkable aspects of this session had been the atypical presence of three female backup singers, and the trio was the subject of a running commentary throughout the week. Elvis had insisted on having the singers there during this session, even though Felton knew it would be quicker and more efficient to overdub their parts later, as he'd done with the Christmas songs recorded in May. And, though some of it was just good-natured ribbing, Elvis and the band seemed thrown off by the "girl singers" as the session wore on. During the first part of the week the Imperials had been featured almost exclusively on the gospel numbers, songs any vocal group could easily work out. On the pop material, though, the women were forced to work out more complicated arrangements on the spot, and their constant chatter and rehearsing in between takes had an unsettling effect on Elvis. "They just go on," he whined at one point. "They couldn't care less. They just go on." By the end of "My Way," as Elvis screamed his way toward the top of his register, he was seething with frustration—and when the singers couldn't get their vocals down fast enough he exploded: "I've run this damn song fifty times, and you still don't know your parts." With that he threw his headphones to the floor and stormed out. His entourage followed, and Felton was forced to shut down the proceedings altogether. Felton Jarvis had seen Elvis discontented before, but only while recording movie soundtracks. Now it was starting to infringe on Elvis's regular RCA recording sessions, and it worried him.

In June, as scheduled, RCA released *Love Letters From Elvis,* an album Jon Landau in *Rolling Stone* called "the most discouraging event in the last three years of Presley's career." It was dismissed by others as "a bunch of leftovers," and in fact that was what it was. For the Colonel and RCA this was business as usual, but the poor sales were just what RCA should have expected for a hodgepodge product that violated Elvis's own judgment of his material. The fact that Elvis had approved none of the songs on the album for previous release should have been indication enough of their quality, but apparently the Colonel and RCA had begun to lose focus on just what had turned Elvis's career around: not the haphazard creation of new product, but, on a very basic level, the quality of the work he was releasing.

"Life," a song for which Elvis had little tolerance, was chosen as the single from the album; it flopped too, peaking at number fifty-three—twenty places below the previous disappointment, "Rags To Riches." Hoping to make up lost ground, RCA rushed "I'm Leavin' " from the recent May sessions into release (backed with "Heart Of Rome" from the album), but the haunting if uncommercial ballad peaked at number thirty-six. Sales on all of Elvis's 1971 releases were poor, in fact, but that didn't stop RCA from flooding the market with far more product than Elvis was contracted to produce. Within this year alone there were three more budget albums, along with a second four-album box, *Elvis Worldwide Gold Award Hits, Vol. 2: The Other Sides*. Once again the Colonel's special contractual provisions reaped him great rewards on all this supplementary material—all in the form of additional advances.

Record sales may not have been skyrocketing, but the fans remained faithful, and Elvis broke all attendance records during his two weeks at the Sahara Tahoe and the following four weeks in Vegas. But the critics found his shows as uninspired as his troubled appearances in January, and the only meaningful additions to the material were the new single, "I'm Leavin'," and the permanent installment of "Can't Help Falling In Love" as the closing number. The press was beginning to make comments about Elvis's weight, but even that seemed to have little impact on fan loyalty, or upon the impact of his live performances.

On August 28 Elvis was honored by the National Academy of Recording Arts and Sciences with the Bing Crosby Award for Lifetime Achievement, a meaningful gesture from an organization that since its inception in 1958 had presented him with but a single Grammy—for the gospel album *How Great Thou Art*. The November tour proved more exciting than the Vegas stand, but record sales continued to lag. If "I'm

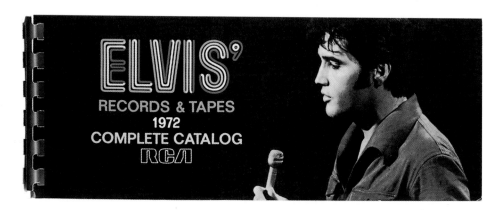

Leavin' " was the greatest hope from the 1971 sessions, it came as no surprise that the less convincing "It's Only Love" fared even more poorly on the charts. Neither the Christmas album, which the Colonel and RCA had fought so hard to get, nor the single ("Merry Christmas Baby"/"O Come, All Ye Faithful") charted at all. Far more significant, though, were the regular reports Tom Parker was receiving about Elvis's erratic behavior. Only with constant surveillance and even emergency action were those surrounding Elvis able to keep the press from learning the truth: that he was slipping out of control.

1972

Separate Ways

My woman got tired of the heartache
Tired of the grief and the strife
So tired of working for nothing
Just tired of being my wife

—"You Gave Me A Mountain," Marty Robbins

As 1971 became 1972, and Elvis's problems were compounded by the disintegration of his marriage, he seemed to be trying to sing his way through his own pain and heartache. At Christmas Priscilla announced that she was planning to leave Elvis for good—a development that was no surprise to those around Elvis, but clearly came as an emotional shock to him. As he started rehearsals for his next set of Las Vegas dates, Priscilla was moving out of the house on Monovale in Beverly Hills and into an apartment of her own. And his pain showed in his song selection: To a growing list of grief-stricken ballads including "It's Impossible," "It's Over," "Help Me Make It Through The Night," and "Until It's Time For You To Go," Elvis now added Marty Robbins's "You Gave Me A Mountain"—the first candidate from the Robbins catalog to make the cut since Bienstock and the Aberbachs had acquired it in 1967, and finally a tangible reward for their constant efforts.

107. Live Recordings for RCA
February 14–17, 1972: The Hilton, Las Vegas

A&R/Producer: Felton Jarvis
Engineer: Al Pachucki

Guitar: James Burton
Guitar: John Wilkinson
Guitar: Charlie Hodge
Bass: Jerry Scheff
Drums: Ronnie Tutt

Piano: Glen D. Hardin
Vocals: Kathy Westmoreland
Vocals: The Sweet Inspirations
Vocals: J. D. Sumner & The Stamps
Joe Guercio & His Orchestra

2/14, Midnight Show
Little Sister/Get Back
Pomus/Shuman—Lennon/McCartney

See See Rider

Traditional; arranged by Elvis Presley

Proud Mary

J. Fogerty

BPA5 1142	**Never Been To Spain**	**Walk A Mile In My Shoes**
	Hoyt Axton—Lady Jane Music	*66670-2/1996*
BPA5 1143	**You Gave Me A Mountain**	**Walk A Mile In My Shoes**
	Marty Robbins—Noma Music/Mojave Music/Elvis Presley Music	*66670-2/1996*
BPA5 1144	**A Big Hunk O' Love**	**Walk A Mile In My Shoes**
	Aaron Schroeder/Sid Wyche—Elvis Presley Music	*66670-2/1996*
BPA5 1145	**It's Impossible**	**Elvis (Fool)**
	Sid Wayne/A. Manzanero—Sunbury Music	*APL1 0283/1973*
BPA5 1146	**The Impossible Dream**	**He Walks Beside Me**
	Mitch Leigh/Joe Darion—Helena Music/Andrew Scott Inc./Sam Fox Co.	*AFL1 2772/1978*
BPA5 1147	**An American Trilogy**	**Single A-side**
	Mickey Newbury—Acuff/Rose Publ.	*74-0672/1972*

BPA5 1148	**It's Over**	**Walk A Mile In My Shoes**
	Jimmie Rodgers—Honeycomb Music	*66670-2/1996*

Love Me

Jerry Leiber/Mike Stoller

All Shook Up

Otis Blackwell/Elvis Presley

Teddy Bear/Don't Be Cruel

Kal Mann/Bernie Lowe—Otis Blackwell/Elvis Presley

Hound Dog

Jerry Leiber/Mike Stoller

Can't Help Falling In Love

Peretti/Creatore/Weiss

Elvis's February appearance in Las Vegas gave Felton Jarvis the chance to make another set of live recordings with an eye toward yet another live album, and Elvis was planning to use the venue to introduce some of the new material he'd been anxious to record. Freddy and Hill & Range had failed to provide any commercially strong new pop songs, or even fresh religious or Christmas material, for the 1971 sessions, and their poor show-ing had frustrated both Elvis and Felton. Now they were proving unable to make the customary publishing deals on the new breed of folkish songs Elvis was champing to record—Gordon Lightfoot's "The Last Time I Saw Her Face," "Sunday Morning Coming Down" by Kris Kristofferson, "The Sun Ain't Gonna Shine Anymore" by the Walker Brothers, as well as James Taylor's "Steamroller Blues," "Summer Days," and "Brown Eyes"—and Elvis's patience was wearing thin. It was becoming clear that Elvis's publishing companies were losing touch with his own tastes; when Elvis sent word that he wanted to cover Don and Dewey's "I'm Leavin' It All Up To You," a hit in 1963 for Dale and Grace, Freddy reported that they'd found the song, but it couldn't be the one Elvis was interested in. But it was, and the incident only confirmed how little they understood Elvis, even after so many years working together.

By the time live recording finally commenced on February 14, there were only six new songs chosen for taping—and half of those later proved to be unavailable for publishing deals. Since they knew from the start that the Kristofferson material was off limits to Hill & Range, not only was "Sunday Morning Coming Down" cut from the set lists, the tape machine was actually turned off every time Elvis sang "Help Me Make It Through The Night." Only "An American Trilogy" remained in the mix in spite of its publishing situ-ation, and then only because nothing could discourage Elvis from recording the Mickey Newbury composition, a medley of "Dixie," "All My Trials," and "Battle Hymn Of The Republic" that boasted an arrangement as good as any Elvis had ever gotten. With its mix-ture of patriotic fervor, vocal challenge, high drama, and emotional overload, it repre-sented a kind of catharsis for the Elvis Presley who had visited the White House and gotten his federal narcotics badge the year before, and its performance in Vegas that sea-son was always stirring and always drove the audience to a thundering response.

All of the difficulties with business and recording had begun taking their toll on Felton, who was seriously ill with kidney disease, and just as surely on his star. Elvis's onstage demeanor had changed completely since his last Vegas appearance, and hardly for the better. In August he'd taken criticism for talking and fooling around too much between songs. Now he hardly communicated with the audience at all; the only thing holding his attention seemed to be the songs he chose to sing, and his singing itself. After four days of recording in Las Vegas, it was decided that they could finish the album in Knoxville during the April tour, in hopes that the intervening months would turn up enough new material to round out a new live album.

Elvis's most recent single was his reworking of Buffy Sainte-Marie's "Until It's Time For You To Go" backed with "We Can Make The Morning," and it reached a dismal number forty on the charts. February brought a new album, *Elvis Now,* but the title was a hapless attempt to mask the facts: Seven of its cuts were nine months old, and three more were from 1969 and 1970. The total of just ten songs was a reflection of the new industry standard, and it meant that if you'd already bought the single you got only eight new cuts. RCA did offer twelve cuts on the religious album, and its Easter release (along with the requisite single, "He Touched Me"/"Bosom Of Abraham") reflected the Colonel's continuing enthusiasm for the seasonal market. Yet another new single was scheduled for April; Elvis had been announcing that "The Impossible Dream" would be his next single since December 1970, and now they finally had a live version in the can. RCA had other ideas—they were well on their way to pairing "The First Time Ever I Saw Your Face" with "Help Me Make It Through the Night"—but then Elvis announced an entirely new plan: Listening to playbacks from the Vegas recordings, he became convinced that "An American Trilogy" had to be his next single. RCA objected—the song had just been a top-forty hit for its author, Mickey Newbury—but Elvis stood his ground, and in April it became his second live single (after 1970's "The Wonder Of You").

The objectors were right. When the single did appear it reached only number sixty-six, substantially worse than Newbury's record, and it merely added to Elvis's growing list of failed releases. The album *He Touched Me* didn't do much to reverse the trend, though it was favorably received and, like each of the religious releases, would eventually become a perennial seller. But it was beginning to seem, once again, as if there might be no more out-of-the-box smashes.

108. Studio Sessions for RCA
March 27–29, 1972: RCA's Studio C, Hollywood

A&R/Producer: Felton Jarvis
Engineers: Al Pachucki, Rick Ruggieri

Guitar: James Burton
Guitar: John Wilkinson
Guitar: Charlie Hodge
Bass: Emory Gordy
Drums: Ronnie Tutt
Organ: n/a
Piano: Glen D. Hardin

Vocals: J. D. Sumner & The Stamps

Overdubbed:
Percussion: Jerry Carrigan
Guitar: Dennis Linde
Steel Guitar: na
Harpsichord: na
Strings & Horns

3/27, 7PM–3AM

BPA3 1149-21	**Separate Ways**	**Single A-side**
	Red West/Richard Mainegra—Press Music	*74-0815/1972*
BPA3 1150-04	**For The Good Times**	**Walk A Mile In My Shoes**
	Kris Kristofferson—Buckhorn Music	*66670-2/1996*
BPA3 1151-08	**Where Do I Go From Here**	**Elvis (Fool)**
	Paul Williams—Gladys Music	*APL1 0283/1973*

3/28, 7PM–4AM

BPA3 1257-06	**Burning Love**	**Single A-side**
	Dennis Linde—Combine Music	*74-0769/1972*
BPA3 1258-02	**Fool**	**Single B-side**
	Carl Sigman/James Last—Intersong Music/Gladys Music	*74-0910/1973*

<u>3/29, 7PM–1AM</u>

BPA3 1259-01	**Always On My Mind**	**Single B-side**
	Wayne Carson/Mark James/Johnny Christopher—Press Music/Rose Bridge Music	*74-0815/1972*
BPA3 1260-05	**It's A Matter Of Time**	**Single B-side**
	Clive Westlake—Gladys Music	*74-0769/1972*

The Stamps: Bill Baize, Donnie Sumner, Ed Enoch, Richard Sterban.

"When I went into those recording sessions there was a lot of exuberance, a lot of energy. I thought that was one of the best things I had ever done, and we did some great tunes and there was a lot of hashing over the tunes to get them just exactly the right way. And, everybody was there. It was very professional and at the same time the energy level was high," said Emory Gordy.

Sitting in for Jerry Scheff, bass player Emory Gordy was playing with Elvis for the first time at Elvis's first session since he had stormed out of the Nashville studio the year before. Everyone was hoping that moving to RCA's Hollywood studios—where he hadn't recorded since *G.I. Blues* in April of 1960—and recording with his touring band for the first time ever might be just the artistic and commercial shot in the arm he needed. Hill & Range's continuing disappointment gave Red West another opening; he arrived in California with a new song, "Separate Ways," that he hoped would become another of the "love gone wrong" songs Elvis was featuring almost exclusively now in Vegas. Through his connections with other Memphis writers, Red also brought out a new song cowritten by Johnny Christopher, author of "Mama Liked The Roses," and Mark James of "Suspicious Minds" fame. "Always On My Mind" was the kind of beautifully articulated ballad Elvis was always drawn to, full of the same regrets that seemed to fill his own heart: "Maybe I didn't treat you/Quite as good as I should have. . . ." Kris Kristofferson's work extended the mood, but this time, instead of "Sunday Morning Coming Down," a recent Johnny Cash hit, the winner was "For The Good Times," just covered by another favorite, Ray Price. Freddy Bienstock's offerings included two uninspiring songs from his European affiliates—"It's A Matter of Time" and "Fool"—but Felton's friend Bob Beckham from Combine Music contributed a real rocker, "Burning Love." The song had gone nowhere in a version by R&B singer Arthur Alexander, but everyone was convinced it could be a perfect vehicle for Elvis.

Elvis always pushed himself to excel whenever he was recording with new players, and despite the fact that he'd played countless live shows with them it was a whole different ball game working with his road band in the studio. Emory Gordy, the only newcomer, noted that Elvis's "intent and . . . concentration" were all there; "he was in very good shape at that time," he remembers. The others (with the exception of piano man Glen D. Hardin, who'd come in six months late) had all been working together for almost three years now, but here was an opportunity to create something more permanent together, and everyone was taking pride in the process. Glen D.'s arrangements made run-throughs more productive, and there was little of the usual fooling around between takes. Focusing in on each number carefully, they worked on no more than two or three songs each night, but each of the songs got everyone's full attention. The very first, Red's "Separate Ways," went through twenty-five takes the first night, while "For The Good Times" got four and Paul Williams's "Where Do I Go From Here," a Bienstock contribution, took eight tries. But when they started up again the following evening, it took almost everyone in the room to persuade Elvis to commit himself to "Burning Love." Felton, Joe Esposito, Jerry Schilling, and Red West were all convinced it was a hit, and Charlie Hodge dutifully hammered away on his acoustic guitar trying to get Elvis interested. Yet Elvis himself remained unconvinced, and though he eventually cut it, three months later he told reporters in New York that the reason he didn't record more rock 'n' roll was, simply, that a good rock song was "hard to find." He seemed to have no idea that the one he'd just completed would become a classic.

The night after the recording session proper ended, a film crew moved in. Their purpose was to film a mock "session" for a new MGM feature, a sequel to *That's The Way It Is* going under the working title "Standing Room Only." The filmmakers stuck around as Elvis and the band continued to rehearse for the upcoming tour. Normally they didn't need much rehearsal—their upcoming shows would simply mirror the Vegas show from February—but Elvis had a lot on his mind. Not only would he be performing for the documentary cameras on four of the April dates, but two months later he had an even more daunting prospect before him: a set of shows at Madison Square Garden. Almost two decades after he first came to New York to record in 1956, this would be Elvis's New York City concert debut, and he was unmistakably—perhaps surprisingly—agitated about it. He even expressed his anxiety to Tom Jones, a friend who frequently dropped by

March 1972

when Elvis was playing in Las Vegas. To Jones's amazement, Elvis confessed profound doubt about the wisdom of Colonel Parker's decision to book him into the Garden. It was the New York press that had given him his harshest rebukes after his national television debut back in '56, and even all these years later he was wary about throwing himself to the wolves again. Jones, a confident man himself, found himself in the odd position of having to remind an insecure superstar of who he was.

109. Rehearsals for MGM's *Elvis on Tour*
March 30–31, 1972: RCA's Studio C, Hollywood
April 5, 1972: Memorial Auditorium, Buffalo

A&R/Producer: Felton Jarvis
Engineer: Al Pachucki

Guitar: James Burton
Guitar: John Wilkinson
Bass: Emory Gordy (Hollywood)
Bass: Jerry Scheff (Buffalo)
Drums: Ronnie Tutt

Piano: Glen D. Hardin
Vocals: The Sweet Inspirations (Buffalo only)
Vocals: J. D. Sumner & The Stamps
Joe Guercio & His Orchestra (Buffalo only)

Burning Love
Dennis Linde
For The Good Times
Kris Kristofferson
Johnny B. Goode
Chuck Berry
A Big Hunk O'Love
Aaron Schroeder/Sid Wyche
Always On My Mind
Wayne Carson/Johnny Christopher/Mark James
Separate Ways
Red West/Richard Mainegra
See See Rider
Traditional/arranged by Elvis Presley
Never Been To Spain
Hoyt Axton
Help Me Make It Through The Night
Kris Kristofferson
Proud Mary
John Fogerty
You Gave Me A Mountain
Marty Robbins
Until It's Time For You To Go
Buffy Sainte-Marie
Polk Salad Annie
Tony Joe White
Love Me
Jerry Leiber/Mike Stoller
All Shook Up
Otis Blackwell/Elvis Presley
Heartbreak Hotel
Mae Boren Axton/Tommy Durden/Elvis Presley

(Let Me Be Your) Teddy Bear/Don't Be Cruel

Kal Mann/Bernie Lowe/Otis Blackwell/Elvis Presley

The First Time Ever I Saw Your Face

Ewan McColl

Hound Dog

Jerry Leiber/Mike Stoller

Release Me

Miller/Stevenson

Lawdy, Miss Clawdy

Lloyd Price

Funny How Time Slips Away

Willie Nelson

WPA5-2564	**I, John**		**Amazing Grace**
	William Gaither		*66421-2/1994*
WPA5-2563	**Bosom Of Abraham**		**Amazing Grace**
	Johnson/McFadden/Brooks		*66421-2/1994*
WPA5-2565	**You Better Run**		**Amazing Grace**
	Traditional/arranged by Elvis Presley		*66421-2/1994*
WPA5-2566	**Lead Me, Guide Me**		**Amazing Grace**
	Doris Akers		*66421-2/1994*
WPA5-2567	**Turn Your Eyes Upon Jesus/Nearer My God To Thee**		**Amazing Grace**
	Lemmel/Clarke—Fuller/Adams/Mason		*66421-2/1994*

Bridge Over Troubled Water

Paul Simon

I'll Remember You

Kuiokalani Lee

Can't Help Falling In Love

Peretti/Creatore/Weiss

Young And Beautiful

Silver/Schroeder

110. Live Recordings for RCA and MGM
April 9, 1972: Coliseum, Hampton Roads, Virginia
April 10, 1972: Coliseum, Richmond, Virginia
April 14, 1972: Coliseum, Greensboro, North Carolina
April 18, 1972: Convention Center, San Antonio, Texas

A&R/Producer: Felton Jarvis
Engineer: Al Pachucki

Guitar: James Burton
Guitar: John Wilkinson
Guitar: Charlie Hodge
Bass: Jerry Scheff
Drums: Ronnie Tutt

Piano: Glen D. Hardin
Vocals: Kathy Westmoreland
Vocals: The Sweet Inspirations
Vocals: J. D. Sumner & The Stamps
Joe Guercio & His Orchestra

In rehearsal . . .

and on tour, April 1972

See See Rider

Traditional; arranged by Elvis Presley

I Got A Woman/Amen

Ray Charles/Traditional; arranged by Elvis Presley

Proud Mary

John Fogerty

Never Been To Spain

Hoyt Axton

You Gave Me A Mountain

Marty Robbins

Until It's Time For You To Go

Buffy Sainte-Marie

Polk Salad Annie

Tony Joe White

Love Me

Jerry Leiber/Mike Stoller

All Shook Up

Otis Blackwell/Elvis Presley

Heartbreak Hotel

Mae Boren Axton/Tommy Durden/Elvis Presley

(Let Me Be Your) Teddy Bear/Don't Be Cruel

Kal Mann/Bernie Lowe—Otis Blackwell/Elvis Presley

Are You Lonesome Tonight?

Roy Turk/Lou Handman

Hound Dog

Jerry Leiber/Mike Stoller

Bridge Over Troubled Water

Paul Simon

It's Over

Jimmie Rodgers

Love Me Tender

Matson/Presley

I Can't Stop Loving You

Don Gibson

Suspicious Minds

Mark James

For The Good Times

Kris Kristofferson

LPA5 5822   **An American Trilogy**

Mickey Newbury

How Great Thou Art

Stuart K. Hine

This Is Elvis
CPL2 4031/1981

Burning Love
Dennis Linde
A Big Hunk O' Love
Aaron Schroeder/Sid Wyche
Release Me
Miller/Stevenson
Lawdy, Miss Clawdy
Lloyd Price
Funny How Time Slips Away
Willie Nelson—Tree Publishing
Bridge Over Troubled Water
Paul Simon
Can't Help Falling In Love
Peretti/Creatore/Weiss

The released version of "An American Trilogy" is from the April 9 show in Hampton.

With the rehearsals over—and several further nights of live recording completed—it was on to Manhattan. Elvis's entourage arrived at the New York Hilton three days before the Friday, June 9, opening of the show. It was obvious to all that these four shows were not being treated like they were in the other cities on the tour, where Joe Guercio was trusted to prepare the local horn and string sections without any need to involve Elvis. Elvis wanted to work on songs they'd never played or had tried only rarely, so a rehearsal space was set up at the hotel to accommodate the band. Together they developed an extensive repertoire, including new songs like "Burning Love," "It's A Matter Of Time," "Fool," and "For The Good Times." There were several songs they'd already cut during the spate of live recording in February: "You Gave Me A Mountain," "Never Been To Spain," "The Impossible Dream," "It's Over," and the new show-stopper, "An American Trilogy." And as always Elvis reconsidered some of his older material, from "Fever" to "I'll Remember You" and "Any Day Now," as well as country material like "I Washed My Hands In Muddy Water," "Funny How Time Slips Away," "Faded Love," and "I Really Don't Want To Know." Only when they got closer to showtime did his ambitions fade in the glare of the imminent spotlight, leaving only a fraction of the new material remaining on the set list.

111. Live Recordings for RCA
June 10, 1972: Madison Square Garden, New York

A&R/Producer: Harry Jenkins/Joan Deary
Engineers: Al Pachucki/Dick Baxter

Guitar: James Burton
Guitar: John Wilkinson
Guitar, Vocals: Charlie Hodge
Bass: Jerry Scheff
Drums: Ronnie Tutt

Piano: Glen D. Hardin
Vocals: Kathy Westmoreland
Vocals: The Sweet Inspirations
Vocals: J. D. Sumner & The Stamps
Joe Guercio Conducting The Joe Malin Orchestra

6/10, 2:30PM Show

BPA5 6381	**That's All Right**	**An Afternoon In The Garden**
	Arthur Crudup—Hill & Range	*67457-2/1997*
BPA5 6382	**Proud Mary**	**An Afternoon In The Garden**
	John Fogerty—Jondora Music	*67457-2/1997*
BPA5 6383	**Never Been To Spain**	**An Afternoon In The Garden**
	Hoyt Axton—Lady Jane Music	*67457-2/1997*
BPA5 6384	**You Don't Have To Say You Love Me**	**An Afternoon In The Garden**
	Wickham/Napier—Bell/Donaggio/Pallavicini	*67457-2/1997*
BPA5 6796	**Until It's Time For You To Go**	**An Afternoon In The Garden**
	Buffy Sainte-Marie/Gypsy Boy Music	*67457-2/1997*
BPA5 6385	**You've Lost That Lovin' Feelin'**	**An Afternoon In The Garden**
	Barry Mann/Cynthia Weil—Screen Gems, Columbia/Elvis Presley Music	*67457-2/1997*
BPA5 6386	**Polk Salad Annie**	**An Afternoon In The Garden**
	Tony Joe White/Combine Music	*67457-2/1997*
BPA5 6387	**Love Me**	**An Afternoon In The Garden**
	Jerry Leiber/Mike Stoller—Hill & Range/Quintet Music	*67457-2/1997*
BPA5 6388	**All Shook Up**	**An Afternoon In The Garden**
	Otis Blackwell/Elvis Presley—Elvis Presley Music/Travis Music	*67457-2/1997*
BPA5 6389	**Heartbreak Hotel**	**An Afternoon In The Garden**
	Mae Boren Axton/Tommy Durden/Elvis Presley—Tree Publishing	*67457-2/1997*
BPA5 6390	**(Let Me Be Your) Teddy Bear/Don't Be Cruel**	**An Afternoon In The Garden**
	Kal Mann/Bernie Lowe—Gladys Music/	*67457-2/1997*
	Otis Blackwell—Elvis Presley Music/Travis Music	
BPA5 6391	**Love Me Tender**	**An Afternoon In The Garden**
	Elvis Presley/Vera Matson—Elvis Presley Music	*67457-2/1997*
BPA5 6795	**Blue Suede Shoes**	**An Afternoon In The Garden**
	Carl Perkins—Hi-Lo Music/Hill & Range	*67457-2/1997*
BPA5 6392	**Reconsider Baby**	**Elvis: A Legendary Performer Vol. 4**
	Lowell Fulsom—Arc Music	*CPL1 4848/1983*
BPA5 6393	**Hound Dog**	**An Afternoon In The Garden**
	Jerry Leiber/Mike Stoller—Elvis Presley Music-Lion Publishing	*67457-2/1997*

BPA3 6793	I'll Remember You	Elvis: A Legendary Performer Vol. 4
	K. Lee—Herb Montei Music	*CPL1 4848/1983*
BPA3 6394	Suspicious Minds	An Afternoon In The Garden
	Mark James—Press Music	*67457-2/1997*
BPA3 6396	For The Good Times	An Afternoon In The Garden
	Kris Kristofferson—Buckhorn Music	*67457-2/1997*
BPA3 6397	An American Trilogy	An Afternoon In The Garden
	Mickey Newbury—Acuff/Rose	*67457-2/1997*
BPA3 6398	Funny How Time Slips Away	An Afternoon In The Garden
	Willie Nelson—Tree Publishing	*67457-2/1997*
BPA3 6399	I Can't Stop Loving You	Welcome To My World
	Don Gibson—Acuff/Rose	*APL1 2274/1977*
BPA3 6400	Can't Help Falling In Love	An Afternoon In The Garden
	Peretti/Creatore/Weiss—Gladys Music	*67457-2/1997*

6/10, 8PM Show

BPA5 6774	That's All Right	Recorded At Madison Square Garden
	Arthur Crudup—Hill & Range	*LSP 4776/1972*
BPA5 6775	Proud Mary	Recorded At Madison Square Garden
	John Fogerty—Jondora Music	*LSP 4776/1972*
BPA5 6776	Never Been To Spain	Recorded At Madison Square Garden
	Hoyt Axton—Lady Jane Music	*LSP 4776/1972*
BPA5 6777	You Don't Have To Say You Love Me	Recorded At Madison Square Garden
	Wickham/Napier—Bell/Donaggio/Pallavicini—Miller Music/S.D.R.M.	*LSP 4776/1972*
BPA5 6778	You've Lost That Lovin' Feelin'	Recorded At Madison Square Garden
	Barry Mann/Cynthia Weil—Screen Gems, Columbia/Elvis Presley Music	*LSP 4776/1972*
BPA5 6779	Polk Salad Annie	Recorded At Madison Square Garden
	Tony Joe White—Combine Music	*LSP 4776/1972*
BPA5 6780	Love Me	Recorded At Madison Square Garden
	Jerry Leiber/Mike Stoller—Hill & Range/Quintet Music	*LSP 4776/1972*
BPA5 6781	All Shook Up	Recorded At Madison Square Garden
	Otis Blackwell/Elvis Presley—Elvis Presley Music/Travis Music	*LSP 4776/1972*
BPA5 6782	Heartbreak Hotel	Recorded At Madison Square Garden
	Mae Boren Axton/Tommy Durden/Elvis Presley—Tree Publishing	*LSP 4776/1972*
BPA5 6783	(Let Me Be Your) Teddy Bear/Don't Be Cruel	Recorded At Madison Square Garden
	Kal Mann/Bernie Lowe—Gladys Music –Otis Blackwell–Elvis Presley—	*LSP 4776/1972*
	Elvis Presley Music/Travis Music	
BPA5 6784	Love Me Tender	Recorded At Madison Square Garden
	Elvis Presley/Vera Matson—Elvis Presley Music	*LSP 4776/1972*
BPA5 6785	The Impossible Dream (The Quest)	Recorded At Madison Square Garden
	Mitch Leigh/Joe Darion—Sam Fox Publishing	*LSP 4776/1972*
BPA5 6786	Hound Dog	Recorded At Madison Square Garden
	Jerry Leiber/Mike Stoller—Elvis Presley Music/Lion Pub.	*LSP 4776/1972*

BPA5 6787	**Suspicious Minds**	Recorded At Madison Square Garden
	Mark James—Press Music	*LSP 4776/1972*
BPA5 6788	**For The Good Times**	Recorded At Madison Square Garden
	Kris Kristofferson—Buckhorn Music	*LSP 4776/1972*
BPA5 6789	**An American Trilogy**	Recorded At Madison Square Garden
	Mickey Newbury—Acuff Rose	*LSP 4776/1972*
BPA5 6790	**Funny How Time Slips Away**	Recorded At Madison Square Garden
	Willie Nelson—Tree Publishing	*LSP 4776/1972*
BPA5 6791	**I Can't Stop Loving You**	Recorded At Madison Square Garden
	Don Gibson—Acuff Rose	*LSP 4776/1972*
BPA5 6792	**Can't Help Falling In Love**	Recorded At Madison Square Garden
	Peretti/Creatore/Weiss—Gladys Music	*LSP 4776/1972*

The full title of LSP 4776 is *Elvis As Recorded At Madison Square Garden.*

The Madison Square Garden press conference, June 1972

On Friday afternoon, before the first show, the Colonel staged a rare press conference—a setting in which Elvis could disarm and win over the New York media who had sneered at him in the 1950s. The event would promote the Garden shows in particular, but more important, it was designed to call attention to the fact that his client could still sell out one of America's premiere concert venues—lackluster chart performance and record sales be damned. He deflected the question about hard rock by saying that good rock songs were hard to come by—and by declaring that he had no plans to do a rock 'n' roll show. Instead, as he had since 1970, he would continue to present his vision of the entire musical spectrum.

As it turned out, there was little to fear in New York City. All four shows were sellouts, with an amazing eighty-thousand tickets sold—and the very visibility of the event caused RCA to change its plans for its next scheduled album. The soundtrack to the "Standing Room Only" documentary had been penciled in and a catalog number assigned; now that album was put on indefinite hold, and RCA decided to record two of the Madison Square Garden shows for release within days after the concerts. With Felton Jarvis now seriously ill and on kidney dialysis, RCA's A&R coordinator Joan Deary handled the project, and it was with great pride that she was able to announce the release of *Elvis As Recorded At Madison Square Garden*—a faithful transcription of the June 10 evening show—only eight days after the actual event. From a musical point of view the Madison Square Garden shows may not have been the best of the period,

Conquering New York: June 1972

but the sheer intensity of the performance was staggering, and its every volt was captured in the succession of twenty songs Elvis packed into one breathless hour. Elvis might have told Tom Jones he was afraid of "nobody coming," but in retrospect that must have amounted to his way of steeling himself for the challenge. "Like a Prince from Another Planet," read one headline, and while most of the critics agreed that this show might not have been exactly what they would have prescribed for the singer, Elvis himself had nevertheless transcended every known measure of popularity and success that had ever been afforded a popular singer.

The album that resulted is a perfect souvenir of a major event; like the TV special in 1968 and the first Las Vegas opening, it constituted a tour de force of the past, this time smoother than ever. Little effort was wasted on new directions or risky adventures; *Madison Square Garden* established, in no uncertain terms, that his audience was happy with the Elvis they knew. RCA was able to rush the album out by taking the front sleeve of the planned movie album and simply replacing the title. There wasn't even time to add a picture from the New York shows, so they used one from the April tour; the track listings appeared only on the back of the sleeve. The album sped into the top ten in the wake of the shows' highly visible success, achieving a peak position of number eight and going gold within weeks. For Elvis Presley it was another summit scaled. And for Colonel Parker it provided yet another lesson in merchandising, and a model to refine, adjust, and apply again, far into the future.

In August RCA released "Burning Love," enhanced by a wonderful guitar overdub by its writer, Dennis Linde. Prompted by the success of the live album, radio stations began taking notice—*a new rock 'n' roll record from Elvis Presley!*—and the single made a slow climb to number three on the *Billboard* charts, reaching a million sales just after the album went gold. The unforeseen had actually happened. Suddenly Elvis's recording career was back in full swing. And the Colonel was already prepared with a plan to top the Madison Square Garden event with a new first in the music business: A one-hour show to be transmitted live by satellite around the globe. In 1967 the Beatles had premiered their single "All You Need Is Love" on an international satellite broadcast, and Parker may have been

inspired by their success. But what the Colonel had in mind, not surprisingly, would be on a much larger scale. He'd arranged to have an entire Elvis concert broadcast around the world; it would originate in Hawaii, his favorite location, and be followed by yet another live album to commemorate the event. Initially scheduled for November, just before record sales began picking up for the holidays, the show was ultimately pushed back to January 14 to avoid stealing any thunder away from the release of the MGM documentary, now retitled *Elvis On Tour*.

It had been a year of significant successes, not least on a commercial level, but they came at a time when serious strain was being put on Elvis's finances by his divorce from Priscilla. Grasping around for a source of cash, the Colonel finally registered that Elvis Presley Music and Gladys Music had outlived their usefulness; with the Aberbachs also deciding to get out of the business, the Colonel liquidated both of Elvis's languishing publishing firms.

Elvis's continued success also gave the Colonel the opportunity to propose a partnership with RCA to manage Elvis's live performances. The record company would provide logistical support as well as the advance funds needed to pursue their demanding concert schedules—and, more important, give Elvis and the Colonel up-front show guarantees. This new setup would include the Hawaiian show, which brought the Colonel and Elvis almost a million dollars of profit. In the end, the pressure to generate cash was so great that the Colonel would venture even further in his discussions with the record label, leading to a dramatic (and later controversial) renegotiation of the whole relationship.

When *Elvis As Recorded At Madison Square Garden* and "Burning Love" both passed the one-million mark, the Colonel and RCA moved to solidify their commercial successes. The follow-up they chose joined two "broken-hearted" ballads from the March Hollywood sessions. The A-side, "Separate Ways," reached only number twenty, though the B-side, "Always On My Mind," became a substantial international hit. Later that fall the erstwhile "Standing Room Only" album was finally scrapped; much of its repertoire had been preempted on *Madison Square Garden,* and with a double album scheduled in connection with the Hawaii concert in January there was hardly room for another live Elvis album on the schedule.

Too much Elvis product: it was a growing problem. Camden, RCA's budget label, had been issuing hodge-podge Elvis albums since the turn of the decade—which provided Elvis and the Colonel with lucrative extra advances—but now stores were starting to return them unsold in huge quantities. To help boost Camden sales, "Burning Love" and "It's A Matter Of Time" were collected with some older recordings on an album anomalously titled *Burning Love And Hits From His Movies,* packaged complete with a "Special Bonus Photo of Elvis." The album marked several dubious industry firsts; most significantly, it was the first time a current hit single had been included on a budget-label album. It charted higher than any previous Camden release, and seemed to confirm the notion that a picture of Elvis and a hit song could sell just about anything. There was no

need to bother trying to make a real album, although that could have easily been accomplished by combining songs from the March session with the best of the Las Vegas February recordings. The resulting album might have shown the artist as a contemporary force to be taken seriously. But as far as the Colonel was concerned, it wouldn't have sold any more records.

During the August shows in Las Vegas Elvis introduced additional material in anticipation of the January satellite show. Older songs like "Fever" and "I'll Remember You" were revived, and others added: "Steamroller Blues," "Something," "It's Over," and "What Now My Love." The Las Vegas arrangements were slowly engulfing everything around them. During a November engagement in Honolulu Elvis and the crew checked out the arena and made plans for January. Appearing with Elvis at a Las Vegas news conference, RCA's president, Rocco Laginestra, gestured to a huge board showing all the countries to which the show would be broadcast. All Elvis could think to say was, "It's hard to comprehend."

1973

ALOHA FROM HAWAII

By the end of 1972 Elvis was definitely overweight, hardly the image of a star about to be the focus of the first worldwide satellite transmission of an entertainment spectacular. Fortunately (for the special), a regiment of diet pills, exercise, and tanning managed to improve his appearance considerably. Perhaps even more important, he gave his repertoire a comparable overhaul, so the Hawaii show would offer something more than just a duplication of the Madison Square Garden set. Once again with this satellite broadcast an album of the show would be rushed into stores, with the sleeve printed in advance and the song listings added later to the disc label and a sticker for the sleeve.

The summer season in Las Vegas had seen the addition of a new raft of high-showbiz ballads, and of course no Elvis Presley show would be complete without songs like "Hound Dog," "Suspicious Minds," "An American Trilogy," and "Can't Help Falling In Love." Still, they needed more material. As much as he hated the song, Elvis would definitely be expected to do his current hit, "Burning Love," while a number of relatively recent show favorites like "Something," "You Gave Me A Mountain," "A Big Hunk O' Love," and "It's Over" could certainly be incorporated. There were additional candidates from past and present repertoire, but among them only "The Twelfth Of Never" and "Hello, Josephine" had not been previously recorded. In the end, effi-

ciency carried the day: It was quickest and easiest to add simple country songs that were well known to musicians and singers alike, eliminating the need for working out complicated new arrangements. "Welcome To My World" by Jim Reeves, "I'm So Lonesome I Could Cry" by Hank Williams, and the familiar "I Can't Stop Loving You" were rehearsed and incorporated into the show. As a final fail-safe measure, it was decided that the show would be recorded in two identical presentations, to ensure that material for an album would be available if anything went wrong on the actual live transmission.

112. Live Recordings for RCA
January 12 and 14, 1973: H.I.C. Arena, Honolulu

A&R: Joan Deary
Engineers: Al Pachucki/Dick Baxter

Guitar: James Burton
Guitar: John Wilkinson
Guitar, Vocals: Charlie Hodge
Bass: Jerry Scheff
Drums: Ronnie Tutt

Piano: Glen D. Hardin
Vocals: J. D. Sumner & The Stamps
Vocals: The Sweet Inspirations
Vocals: Kathy Westmoreland
Joe Guercio & His Orchestra

1/12, 7:45PM Show

CPA5 4702	**See See Rider**		**The Alternate Aloha**
	Arranged by Elvis Presley—Elvis Presley Music		*6985-2-R/1988*
CPA5 4703	**Burning Love**		**The Alternate Aloha**
	Dennis Linde—Combine Music		*6985-2-R/1988*
CPA5 4704	**Something**		**The Alternate Aloha**
	George Harrison—Harrisongs Music		*6985-2-R/1988*
CPA5 4705	**You Gave Me A Mountain**		**The Alternate Aloha**
	Marty Robbins—Noma Music/Mojave Music		*6985-2-R/1988*
CPA5 4706	**Steamroller Blues**		**The Alternate Aloha**
	James Taylor—Blackwood Music/Country Road Music		*6985-2-R/1988*
CPA5 4707	**My Way**		**The Alternate Aloha**
	Paul Anka/J. Reveaux/C. Francois—S.D.R.M./Spanka Music		*6985-2-R/1988*
CPA5 4708	**Love Me**		**The Alternate Aloha**
	Jerry Leiber/Mike Stoller—Hill & Range/Quintet Music		*6985-2-R/1988*
CPA5 4709	**It's Over**		**The Alternate Aloha**
	Jimmie Rodgers—Honeycomb Music		*6985-2-R/1988*
CPA5 4710	**Blue Suede Shoes**		**The Alternate Aloha**
	Carl Perkins—Hill & Range		*6985-2-R/1988*
CPA5 4711	**I'm So Lonesome I Could Cry**		**The Alternate Aloha**
	Hank Williams—Fred Rose Music		*6985-2-R/1988*
CPA5 4712	**Hound Dog**		**The Alternate Aloha**
	Jerry Leiber/Mike Stoller—Elvis Presley Music/Lion Music		*6985-2-R/1988*
CPA5 4713	**What Now My Love**		**The Alternate Aloha**
	C. Sigman/G. Becaud—Remick Music		*6985-2-R/1988*
CPA5 4714	**Fever**		**The Alternate Aloha**
	Davenport/Cooley—Fort Knox Music		*6985-2-R/1988*
CPA5 4715	**Welcome To My World**		**The Alternate Aloha**
	R. Winkler/J. Hathcock—Tuckahoe Music/Neillrae Music		*6985-2-R/1988*
CPA5 4716	**Suspicious Minds**		**The Alternate Aloha**
	Mark James—Press Music		*6985-2-R/1988*
CPA5 4718	**I'll Remember You**		**The Alternate Aloha**
	Kuiokalaani Lee—Herb Montei Music/Konakai Pub.		*6985-2-R/1988*

CPA5 4719	**An American Trilogy**	**The Alternate Aloha**
	Mickey Newbury—Acuff Rose	*6985-2-R/1988*
CPA5 4720	**A Big Hunk O' Love**	**The Alternate Aloha**
	Schroeder/Wyche—Elvis Presley Music	*6985-2-R/1988*
CPA5 4721	**Can't Help Falling In Love**	**The Alternate Aloha**
	Peretti/Creatore/Weiss—Gladys Music	*6985-2-R/1988*

<u>1/14, 12:30AM Show</u>

CPA5 4724	**See See Rider**	**Aloha From Hawaii**
	Arranged by Elvis Presley—Elvis Presley Music	*VPSX 6089/1973*
CPA5 4725	**Burning Love**	**Aloha From Hawaii**
	Dennis Linde—Combine Music	*VPSC 6089/1973*
CPA5 4726	**Something**	**Aloha From Hawaii**
	George Harrison—Harrisongs Music	*VPSX 6089/1973*
CPA5 4727	**You Gave Me A Mountain**	**Aloha From Hawaii**
	Marty Robbins—Noma Music/Mojave Music	*VPSX 6089/1973*
CPA5 4728	**Steamroller Blues**	**Aloha From Hawaii**
	James Taylor—Blackwood Music/Country Road Music	*VPSX 6089/1973*
CPA5 4729	**My Way**	**Aloha From Hawaii**
	Paul Anka/J. Reveaux/C. Francois—S.D.R.M./Spanka Music	*VPSX 6089/1973*
CPA5 4730	**Love Me**	**Aloha From Hawaii**
	Jerry Leiber/Mike Stoller—Hill & Range/Quintet Music	*VPSX 6089/1973*
CPA5 4731	**Johnny B. Goode**	**Aloha From Hawaii**
	Chuck Berry—Arc Music	*VPSX 6089/1973*
CPA5 4732	**It's Over**	**Aloha From Hawaii**
	Jimmie Rodgers—Honeycomb Music	*VPSX 6089/1973*
CPA5 4733	**Blue Suede Shoes**	**Aloha From Hawaii**
	Carl Perkins—Hill & Range	*VPSX 6089/1973*
CPA5 4734	**I'm So Lonesome I Could Cry**	**Aloha From Hawaii**
	Hank Williams—Fred Rose Music	*VPSX 6089/1973*
CPA5 4735	**I Can't Stop Loving You**	**Aloha From Hawaii**
	Don Gibson—Acuff Rose	*VPSX 6089/1973*
CPA5 4736	**Hound Dog**	**Aloha From Hawaii**
	Jerry Leiber/Mike Stoller—Elvis Presley Music/Lion Music	*VPSX 6089/1973*
CPA5 4737	**What Now My Love**	**Aloha From Hawaii**
	C. Sigman/G. Becaud—Remick Music	*VPSX 6089/1973*
CPA5 4738	**Fever**	**Aloha From Hawaii**
	Davenport/Cooley—Fort Knox Music	*VPSX 6089/1973*
CPA5 4739	**Welcome To My World**	**Aloha From Hawaii**
	R. Winkler/J. Hathcock—Tuckahoe Music/Neillrae Music	*VPSX 6089/1973*
CPA5 4740	**Suspicious Minds**	**Aloha From Hawaii**
	Mark James—Press Music	*VPSX 6089/1973*

CPA5 4742	**I'll Remember You**	**Aloha From Hawaii**
	Kuiokalaani Lee—Herb Montei Music/Konakai Pub.	*VPSX 6089/1973*
CPA5 4743	**Long Tall Sally/Whole Lotta Shakin' Goin' On**	**Aloha From Hawaii**
	E. Johnson—Venice Mus./E. Presley Mus. & D. Williams/S. David—	
	Anne Rachel Mus./Pic Mus.	*VPSX 6089/1973*
CPA5 4744	**An American Trilogy**	**Aloha From Hawaii**
	Mickey Newbury—Acuff Rose	*VPSX 6089/1973*
CPA5 4745	**A Big Hunk O' Love**	**Aloha From Hawaii**
	Schroeder/Wyche—Elvis Presley Music	*VPSX 6089/1973*
CPA5 4746	**Can't Help Falling In Love**	**Aloha From Hawaii**
	Peretti/Creatore/Weiss—Gladys Music	*VPSX 6089/1973*

Full title of VPSX is *Aloha From Hawaii Via Satellite.*

<u>1/14, After 12:30 Show</u>

CPA5 4756-02	**Blue Hawaii**	**Elvis: A Legendary Performer Vol. 2**
	Leo Robin/Ralph Rainger—Gladys Music/Famous Music	*CPL1 1349/1976*
CPA5 4757-04	**Ku-U-I-Po**	**Mahalo From Elvis**
	Peretti/Creatore/Weiss—Gladys Music	*ACL 7064/1978*
CPA5 4758-04	**No More**	**Mahalo From Elvis**
	Don Robertson/Hal Blair—Gladys Music	*ACL 7064/1978*
CPA5 4759-02	**Hawaiian Wedding Song**	**Mahalo From Elvis**
	King/Hoffman/Manning—MCA Music/Gladys Music	*ACL 7064/1978*
CPA5 4760-02	**Early Morning Rain**	**Mahalo From Elvis**
	Gordon Lightfoot—Warner Bros. Music	*ACL 7064/1978*

Setting up in Honolulu

The show was broadcast live to the Far East, then to Europe on the following night, yet in the end the United States broadcast of this "live" satellite event was postponed until April 4 to avoid conflict with the theatrical release of *Elvis On Tour.* The "Aloha from Hawaii" show seen on American television was filled out to ninety minutes with five additional songs and a lot of scenic-landscape footage. The "bonus" selections were recorded late at night following the hour-long live show on January 14 with no audience present and featured generally uninspired performances of "Early Morning Rain" and selections from the movie *Blue Hawaii,* thus taking away some of the pace and drive of the actual concert. In fact, at times music seemed secondary to the entire Hawaii event; the audience was carried along by the excitement of the occasion, and the worldwide enthusiasm was strong enough to propel the single from *Aloha,* "Steamroller Blues," into the United States top ten.

The immense pressure of being beamed live to one billion people didn't seem to faze Elvis a great deal; showing little evidence of nerves, he was highly focused, and he executed a flawless set that sparkled with all the flash of his image. The unparalleled media attention and size of the audience, not to mention the worldwide number-one album that followed, were perhaps the most effective statement ever engineered of one artist's worldwide power.

Yet to the astute observer there was something strangely distant about the performer at the center of the storm. Watching "Aloha from Hawaii" was almost like watching Elvis Presley through a stained-glass window or a badly focused pair of binoculars. The sparkle in his eyes, the natural grace of his movements, and the joy that were all so visible back in 1970—they all seemed to be missing. During the show itself he betrayed occasional signs of impatience; when an audience member called out a request, he countered, "What? Okay, I'll do it. All four hundred and twenty-nine of 'em." After the show, when they settled down to record the extra songs for the United States broadcast, his temper flared. "Isn't this fun," he mocked; "At three o'clock in the morning, this is my favorite thing. Are you rolling? Can I record? Can we do this? Is this right?" He snapped at Glen D. Hardin for making a mistake: "Can't you follow a damn thing, Glen? I swear to God. Get with me somewhere in there." Of course he was tired, but the combination of diet medication, and whatever other pharmaceuticals were coursing their way through his system by the beginning of 1973, couldn't have helped.

During the planning for the satellite show, while arrangements were being made for RCA Record Tours to help set up the upcoming tour schedule, the record company had first learned that the Colonel and Elvis might consider selling their rights to future royalties on all Elvis's past recordings—if the price were right and a new revised contract with more favorable conditions could be arranged. Whatever the Colonel's own needs might have been, it soon became apparent that Elvis, too, could use the cash, if only to finance the burdens of his upcoming divorce settlement. Eventually a purchase price of $5.4 million was agreed upon for outright transfer of Elvis's complete back catalog, and a deal was settled that many revisionist historians would ridicule as the worst management decision ever made (a charge that had also been leveled at Sam Phillips for selling Elvis to RCA in 1956 for thirty-five thousand dollars). In retrospect, it could certainly be argued that the twin successes of "Burning Love" and *Aloha From Hawaii* should have put Elvis and the Colonel in a better bargaining position, but closer scrutiny reveals a different picture: Elvis's back catalog wasn't doing much business by 1973, and his greatest income by far came from personal appearances. What he and the Colonel wanted was a new influx of cash, and RCA was certainly happy to oblige. Both sides welcomed a fresh start.

The Colonel next turned his attention to creating a new arrangement for song publishing. After the liquidation of Elvis Presley Music and Gladys Music, plans were made to set up two new music publishing companies, eventually called Elvis Music and Whitehaven Music, with the Colonel's old ally Freddy Bienstock in charge. Hoping to avoid outside interference, the Colonel explained to Elvis the importance of keeping their plans secret until all deals had been properly set up. Furthermore, he ordered, no recording sessions could be scheduled until the new firms were ready to make deals with songwriters, to prevent anyone from the outside from unduly influencing Elvis's song selection.

RCA had tentative plans to follow up *Aloha From Hawaii* with a new album in June, but with negotiations for the new publishing contract still unresolved all they had to work with were leftover recordings. Joan Deary of RCA's New York office, who had stepped in to supervise both the *Madison Square Garden* and *Aloha* albums when Felton Jarvis fell ill, set about assembling the new collection. The album she envisioned would be named *Fool,* after the current single; along with the title cut she planned to use the five extra Hawaiian-interest songs recorded for the American "Aloha" broadcast, "Where Do I Go From Here," and an overdubbed "I'll Take You Home Again Kathleen." Also up for consideration were a few unused live performances: "It's

Impossible" from the '72 Vegas recordings, and three songs from the Madison Square Garden afternoon show—"Until It's Time For You To Go," "Blue Suede Shoes," and "Reconsider Baby," erroneously listed by RCA as "A Blues Jam" in the evident belief that it was "a new Elvis song." By the time she'd finished her recommended sequence, though, it had become clear that "Steamroller Blues" was overtaking "Fool" on the charts as the single's more powerful side—and suddenly the whole notion of a *Fool* album began to seem ill-conceived.

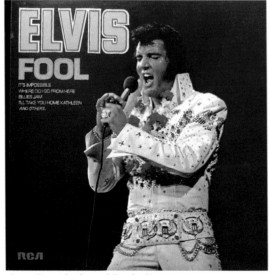

Joan Deary's aborted Fool *album*

Then, with the return of Felton Jarvis, any hopes Joan Deary had of salvaging her vision for the album were dashed altogether. Taking a completely different tack, Felton fought to eliminate all the live material Joan had overseen in favor of studio cuts *he* had produced. Some time before he had boasted proudly to the Colonel about the 1971 recordings he had made of Elvis alone at the piano; now he insisted on including not just "I'll Take You Home Again Kathleen" but the two Ivory Joe Hunter songs Elvis had recorded the same night—"I Will Be True" and "It's Still Here." To these he added the charming twelve-minute "Don't Think Twice, It's All Right" jam, though much of its freewheeling spirit was lost when it was edited down to two minutes forty-five seconds. Finally, he replaced Joan Deary's selection of six live performances with "(That's What You Get) for Lovin' Me," "Padre," and "Love Me, Love The Life I Lead," despite knowing that Elvis needed to redo the vocals on the latter cut. Except for the studio recordings of "For The Good Times" and "My Way," Felton had used everything he had for his selection, which became the released album, and it represented something of a Pyrrhic victory when the album (retitled *Elvis* midway through the process) flopped in the stores. RCA executives did not fail to notice who was responsible.

Elvis's four weeks in Las Vegas following the Hawaii special were marred by a bad case of laryngitis; once again he appeared against doctor's orders, and once again he missed several performances. A ten-day tour in April was followed by two weeks at the Sahara Tahoe and a devastating write-up in *Variety*. "Elvis is neither looking or sounding good. Some thirty pounds overweight he's puffy, white-faced and blinking against the light. The voice sounds weak, delivery is flabby with occasional dynamic great effort and no enthusiasm." The final ten days of the engagement were canceled, allegedly due to the flu and a chest infection. His demanding schedule wrapped up with a two-week tour beginning in Mobile, Alabama, on June 19, and finally ending on July 3 when he flew home to Graceland.

Awaiting him was a letter from his record company, setting out RCA's expectations for the future in no uncertain terms. Though the buyout deal would eventually prove to be a brilliant business decision on their part, at this moment all the label knew was that they'd made an enormous investment with no certainty of when they would get their money back—and so far all they had to show for themselves was another flop in the form of the *Fool* album. In a most unusual move, RCA vice president George Parkhill wrote directly to the star: "We are planning a recording session in the middle of July," he informed Elvis, at the same time demanding more control over the recording process. There was no question of whether Elvis wanted to record, or when; he was allowed to choose the studio he wanted, as long as he showed up when RCA dictated. Felton Jarvis was required to fill out paperwork exactly as Joan Deary requested, and was expected to produce a total of twenty-four masters of songs not previously recorded by Elvis. His first assignment was to produce a new pop album of ten songs, two new single records (four sides), and ten cuts for a new religious album.

Tired from being on the road, distressed by the divorce proceedings, and expecting Lisa Marie for a month-long visit, Elvis could not have faced the prospect of a string of recording sessions happily. The most practical arrangement was to stay in Memphis, and Marty Lacker suggested making the five-minute drive to the Stax studio on McLemore Avenue, which in the last ten years had virtually invented the genre of southern soul and become the kind of creative force that Sun Records once was in Memphis. There really wasn't all that much choice. American's Chips Moman had long since left town, and Marty, who had been instrumental in bringing Elvis to American, had moved over to work for Stax. While most of the American musicians now lived in Nashville, they were glad enough of the opportunity to come home for a good-paying gig, and RCA was perfectly happy with the arrangement. Marty booked the session for late July.

113. Studio Sessions for RCA
July 20–25 1973: Stax Studios, Memphis

A&R/Producer: Felton Jarvis
Engineer: Al Pachucki

Musicians (7/21–23)
Guitar: James Burton
Guitar: Reggie Young
Bass: Tommy Cogbill
Drums: Ronnie Tutt

(7/24–25)
Guitar: Bobby Manual
Acoustic Guitar: Johnny Christopher
Bass: Donald Dunn
Drums: Al Jackson

(7/21–25 only)
Acoustic Guitar: Charlie Hodge
Drums: Jerry Carrigan
Piano: Bobby Wood
Organ: Bobby Emmons
Vocals: J. D. Sumner & The Stamps
Vocals: Kathy Westmoreland, Mary Greene
Mary & Ginger Holladay

Overdubbed:
Guitar: James Burton (4772)
Acoustic Guitar: Charlie Hodge (4772)
Guitar: Dennis Linde (4763, 65, 69)
Vocals: Voice (4772)
Strings (4763, 65, 69, 72)

<u>7/20, 8PM–4AM. No Recordings</u>

<u>7/21, 9PM–3AM</u>

CPA5 4761-09	**If You Don't Come Back**		**Raised On Rock**
	Jerry Leiber/Mike Stoller—Elvis Music		*APL1 0388/1973*
WPA5 2574-na	**It's Diff'rent Now**		**Walk A Mile In My Shoes**
	Clive Westlake—Whitehaven Music		*66670-2/1996*
CPA5 4762-15	**Three Corn Patches**		**Raised On Rock**
	Jerry Leiber/Mike Stoller—Whitehaven Music		*APL1 0388/1973*
CPA5 4763-06	**Take Good Care Of Her**		**Single B-side**
	Ed Warren/Arthur Kent—George Paxton Corp.		*APBO-0196/1974*

CPA5 4764-09	**Find Out What's Happening**	**Raised On Rock**
	Jerry Crutchfield—Champion Music	APL1 0388/1973
CPA5 4765-15	**I've Got A Thing About You Baby**	**Single A-side**
	Tony Joe White—Tennessee Swamp Fox/Whitehaven Music	APBO/0196/1974
CPA5 4766-02	**Just A Little Bit**	**Raised On Rock**
	Thornton/Brown/Bass/Washington—Elvis Music	APL1 0388/1973

CPA5 4767-na	**Raised On Rock**	**Single A-side**
	Mark James—Screen Gems/Columbia	APBO 0088/1973
CPA5 4768-08	**For Ol' Times Sake**	**Single B-side**
	Tony Joe White—Tennessee Swamp Box/Whitehaven Music	APBO 0088/1973

CPA5 4769-11	**Girl Of Mine**	**Raised On Rock**
	Les Reed/Barry Mason—Whitehaven Music	APL1 0388/1973

CPA5 4772-15 (tr) Sweet Angeline		**Raised On Rock**
Arnold/Martin/Morrow—Whitehaven Music		APL1 0388/1973

Backing tracks were also recorded on 7/24 for "Good, Bad, But Beautiful" (Clive Westlake) and on 7/25 for "Color My Rainbow" (Mark James) and "The Wonders You Perform" (Jerry Chesnut), but Elvis never recorded vocal tracks to complete the songs. Overdubs for "Sweet Angeline," including Elvis's lead vocal, were recorded at Elvis's Palm Springs home on 9/22. The Stamps: Ed Enoch, Bill Baize, Dave Rowland, Donnie Sumner. Voice: Donnie Sumner, Tim Baty, Sherrill Nielsen.

It was obvious from the start that something was very wrong with Elvis Presley. Despite the studio's proximity to Graceland, Elvis failed to show up for the 8 P.M. scheduled start on July 20. When he finally arrived at eleven o'clock, dressed in a cape, piano player Bobby Wood recalls that "he had gained weight. His eyes were yellow. His complexion was yellow. . . . I couldn't believe it was the same guy. He looked totally different and acted totally different, too. He had a Korean or Japanese guy with him— Kang Rhee, his karate teacher. They were doing a movie or something together, and they were clowning around in the studio with guns and stuff. That made me real nervous." Wood was joined by guitar player Reggie Young, bassist Tommy Cogbill, and Bobby Emmons on organ, the nucleus of the Memphis studio band from 1969. To that group were added Elvis's guitarist, James Burton, along with two drummers, Ronnie Tutt and Jerry Carrigan, to replace American's Gene Chrisman. In sharp contrast to the American sessions, Elvis continued his practice of having a roomful of singers there to record with him: J. D. Sumner and the Stamps, Kathy Westmoreland, Mary

"Jeannie" Green, and the Holladay sisters, a strong vocal lineup who could provide the requisite gospel-flavored backing for any occasion.

RCA engineer Al Pachucki was astonished by the level of security when he arrived at the studio. There were several six-foot-six guards patroling the area and inspecting the name tags required for all the participants. Once inside it quickly became apparent that the recording facility itself was second-rate, at least by Pachucki's estimation. At Stax, records had always been made using the same method Chips Moman used at American, recording layer after layer and building each master piece by piece. Elvis, on the other hand, had always preferred to record "live," with everyone playing and singing together at the same time, and the Stax studio simply wasn't properly equipped for such an approach. Live multitrack recording, with everyone playing at once, requires that each participant wear headphones, and ideally each musician needs to have the sound tailored in his phones to allow him to hear what everyone (and he himself) is playing. The monitoring system at Stax didn't offer such amenities, and the band and singers were left unable to hear themselves or the band properly as they recorded.

On that first night Elvis left the studio after four hours, having recorded absolutely nothing. He arrived late again on the following night, his speech so slurred that he seemed scarcely awake. The sound of his voice on the session tapes makes it painfully evident that he had little interest in recording at all. Freddy Bienstock began by presenting a Leiber and Stoller number, "If You Don't Come Back," which he had secured under the new publishing arrangement, and Elvis barely managed to drag himself through five indistinguishable takes before Felton called him in to listen to the results. In the end the ninth take became the sorry-sounding master, devoid of anything like fire or enthusiasm.

Next was a rehearsal of "It's Diff'rent Now," by Freddy's writer Clive Westlaker, which was soon abandoned (one incomplete take was taped) in favor of a second selection by Leiber and Stoller called "Three Corn Patches," possibly the worst song the veteran partnership had ever written. The band worked hard but they got nowhere. "You can't kick this motherfucker," Elvis concluded. Finally waking up, he apologized first to Felton for a microphone pop ("I did 36 pictures and never learned to get around that 'p' ") and then to the group ("Pardon my language. I normally don't curse around the Stamps. I curse *with* them."). But even Elvis's renewed attention couldn't rescue the song, which was laid to rest with a fifteenth unexciting take.

"Take Good Care Of Her," a 1961 R&B-pop hit by Adam Wade, finally offered something to engage Elvis's attention. Bobby Wood, whom Elvis called "the most commercial piano player in the world," took the intro, and sailing straight into the chorus the band was in full control. The Stax control room, however, was a different story. Listening to a playback of take number three, Al Pachucki heard a buzz on the organ track, and the recording process had to be suspended. "What you're hearing," the Stax engineer insisted, "is just distortion in the monitoring system." "I'm hearing distortion," Pachucki replied, "but how do I know it's not on the tape?" While the technicians worked, Elvis entertained the Stamps with stories, and Tommy Cogbill practiced on the bass. Eventually they were able to complete a decent master, but they called it quits before they'd regained their momentum.

A more enthusiastic Elvis arrived on the following night, though once again at eleven. He started with "Find Out What's Happening" by up-and-coming Nashville writer Jerry Crutchfield, a Bobby Bare record from 1968 that they'd started rehearsing as the previous night was coming to a close. Straight off Elvis asked to have the volume of his earphones turned up, and as they worked out a funky groove shouted out, "It's good, girls, whatever you're doing." "I want to find the writer," he joked when he couldn't read the lyrics, "and crush his fingers, break his pens." By the ninth take they had it reasonably under control and turned their attention to "I've Got A Thing About You Baby," a tune by Tony Joe White, the author of "Polk Salad Annie." In earlier days White, a writer with a real flair for southern vernacular, might have made a great "house writer" for Elvis. But these were different times and White had his own recording career, so Elvis was obliged to cherry-pick selections from White's own records. "I've Got A Thing About You Baby" came from White's critically acclaimed 1972 album *The Train I'm On,* and it was coming along fine as they rehearsed it—maybe a little too fast, but with real swing. After one take Elvis kidded himself: "I screwed up the first part. I was singing 'Heartbreak Hotel.' . . . Hang on to it. We'll do the tail end later. Mail it in." This kind of chatter was a sure sign that Elvis was feeling good, that he was being patient, if not with himself then at least with his fellow musicians. On the other hand, he had little patience with the technical problems of the studio. "They're just slow here in Memphis," he complained; Lisa Marie was visiting the studio that evening, and he had to tell her to look away when he lost his temper. "Big idiot boards," he sniped, and as the Stamps provided harmony he sang three lines of Stuart Hamblen's religious song, "Wasted years, wasted years, oh how foolish. . . ." They completed a flawless version of the Tony Joe White tune with the fifteenth take, and followed up with a cover of Rosco Gordon's "Just A Little Bit," which they polished off in one.

Work on July 23 again began at eleven o'clock with "Raised On Rock," a brand-new Mark James tune. It might have been a relief to be trying on a rocker at this point, but the lyrics to "Raised On Rock" (which had Elvis growing up on the music he himself had helped create) were downright silly. Of greater substance was another Tony Joe White song, "For Ol' Times Sake," which came from his great 1973 album, *Homemade Ice Cream.* Perhaps because it was so close to the way he actually felt, Elvis conveyed an immense sadness with this song, achieving a far more convincing tone than he was able to with much of the dramatic Vegas "love gone wrong" material. He began almost in a daze, as if he were half-asleep, but soon he had warmed up to the song, and if the end result was uncommercial it was at least a beautiful way to end the night's recording.

• • •

When he arrived to set up for the fourth night, Al Pachucki discovered that Elvis's special lightweight hand-held microphone had been stolen. The effect of the theft was further compounded when the studio could offer only what Al considered to be "some cheap mike" as a replacement. Previous engagements had prevented the American Studio musicians from staying any longer, so Stax house band stalwarts Duck Dunn (on bass) and drummer Al Jackson filled in, along with guitarist Bobby Manuel and songwriter Johnny Christopher on rhythm guitar. The familiar touchstones were slipping away, and things were about to get worse.

The first song of the evening, "Girl Of Mine," was a not-very-appealing Tom Jones imitation; Elvis's voice sounded nasal and flat, far worse than it had on any of the previous nights. There were further engineering problems: This time there was no question that there was a "hum" on the tape itself, not—as the Stax engineer had promised—in the monitoring system. As they ended the take that would become the master, Elvis shouted, "*Hold* it, Pachuck. Man, I sound funny in the headphones." Hitting the talk-back button, Pachucki let out some frustrations of his own: "You don't *just* sound funny in the headphones. You sound funny, period." Elvis, of course, demanded an explanation, and when Al told him about the stolen microphone, Elvis simply got up and left. Tom Diskin, who had been sitting in the control room, immediately called the Colonel, who called RCA, who in turn laid the blame back on the engineer. Though Al Pachucki saw the session through, and Elvis let him know that he in no way held him at fault, this was the last time the engineer would ever work with Elvis.

With no idea whether Elvis would return, all Felton could do was mark time recording backing tracks. But now, with no input from Elvis, he found himself in the middle of a power game between the song pitchers. Determined to get at least one cut for Clive Westlake, Freddy Bienstock pushed for a song called "Good, Bad, But Beautiful," then insisted that Felton lay down a track for "Sweet Angeline," by his British team, Arnold, Morrow, and Martin. Tracks for Mark James's "Color My Rainbow" and Jerry Chestnut's "The Wonders You Perform" were recorded as well, leaving Felton with instrumental and background vocal tracks for four undistinguished songs.

Back home in Franklin, Tennessee, Felton knew he was in trouble. Elvis had recorded only nine of the twenty-four songs expected by RCA. In a session marred by technical problems, Felton's favorite engineer, Al Pachucki, had fallen from grace. The new publishing arrangements were bringing in no more worthwhile material than the old. The RCA schedule had called for a new single in September and a new album the following month, but after the battle he had fought (and won) with Joan Deary over the material on the last album, he had nothing left in the can—there was no backlog to draw on. And for the moment there was little he could do about it: Elvis would be unavailable for any more recording until he had completed his Las Vegas engagement in September.

There was pressure on Elvis from other directions as well. His health was still slipping, and while divorce proceedings continued Priscilla had begun to grant interviews, allowing disturbing stories about his private life to appear in the press for the very first time. In Las Vegas he began rehearsals on July 31, working on new songs like "Portrait Of My Love" and "The Twelfth Of Never," along with older Presley hits like "I Feel So Bad," "Such A Night," and "She's Not You." By the time of the actual show the only new material remaining was "Trouble" (from *King Creole*) and a cover of Richard Harris's "My Boy," the kind of sentimental cry-in-your beer divorce number he could no longer resist.

While in Las Vegas Elvis had the opportunity to help out his friend Tom Jones, who was facing the possibility of having to replace his vocal group the Blossoms on his current show. When Elvis heard about his predicament, he thought he might do Jones a favor by presenting him with a substitute group. One of the members of his entourage, Kenny Hicks, knew that former Statesmen Sherrill Nielsen and Tim Baty and J. D. Summer's nephew Donnie had formed a new Nashville vocal group called Voice. Elvis knew all of them well; he had worked with Sherrill in 1966 on *How Great Thou Art,* and once introduced him to an indifferent Las Vegas audience as "the greatest tenor in gospel music." Why not fly their new group out to Las Vegas to help Jones out? Transported by private jet, the nervous trio arrived at Elvis's suite, only to be put on the spot to sing for Elvis, Tom Jones, and country singer Bobbie Gentry. Jones was impressed with the group, and he was touched by the offer—but as it turned out, he told Elvis, he had an unbreakable contract with the Blossoms. It may have been the opening Elvis was looking for all along: After giving the group the bad news, with a flourish he produced a piece of paper for them to sign—a year-long contract, he explained, guaranteeing them $100,000 to serve as his backup group and sing with him in private whenever he felt like hearing them, while signing them to his new publishing company. They couldn't help being shocked, but they gratefully accepted. Before the group left the suite Elvis called his father to announce the news; Vernon, though, was less than enthusiastic to learn of his son's latest whim, which only supported his constant fear that his son's indulgences would someday leave them all bankrupt.

On the recording front, meanwhile, the Colonel was caught in a bind. RCA needed to feel he was on their side, and indeed it was anathema to the Colonel not to live up to a contract. But nothing he had heard from Diskin about the Stax sessions, nor anything he'd seen in Las Vegas, left much room for optimism. Elvis had even called to insist that "I've Got A Thing About You Baby" and "Take Good Care Of Her" be taken off the album for future single release, leaving only seven songs—which even under the new rules did not constitute a full album. Elvis resisted a good deal of pressure to go into the studio again, but as a compromise he agreed to cut vocal tracks for the four numbers Felton had cut without him at the last Stax session. He would make the recordings at his Palm Springs home, using RCA's mobile recording truck. And now that he had the new group to sing with, he brought them along and asked James Burton and Charlie Hodge to fill out the lineup.

114. Sessions for RCA
September 22–23, 1973: Elvis's Home In Palm Springs

Producer: Elvis Presley
Engineer: Rick Ruggieri

Guitar: James Burton
Acoustic Guitar: Charlie Hodge
Bass: Thomas Hensley

Piano: Donnie Sumner
Vocals: Voice

9/23, 7–9:20PM, 1:15–3: 15AM

CPA5 4774-15	**I Miss You**	**Raised On Rock**
	Donnie Sumner—Elvis Music	*APL1 0388/1973*
CPA5 4775-04	**Are You Sincere**	**Raised On Rock**
	Wayne Walker—Cedarwood Publishing	*APL1 0388/1973*

On the night of September 22, Elvis overdubbed his vocal for "Sweet Angeline." On September 23, 24, and 29 Voice recorded six demos, paid for by Elvis Presley. The first two nights were at Elvis's house, the last at RCA Studios in Hollywood.

RCA dispatched the mobile-recording truck, along with a tape of the four instrumental tracks from the Stax sessions, to Palm Springs. Microphones were set up in the middle of Elvis's Palm Springs living room, but without any monitor speakers it was difficult for the singers to hear what they were doing. To add to the drama, one of the singers, at Elvis's instigation, had had a hair transplant operation performed right at the house, and his bandaged head continued to bleed throughout the session. Elvis insisted on giving over much of the time to Voice to cut demos on some of their own compositions for his fledgling publishing operation, an exercise RCA made sure their star paid for himself. Of the four tracks supplied by RCA, Elvis finished only one, "Sweet

Angeline"; the rest would never be completed. Instead he decided to sing Donnie Sumner's "I Miss You," assuring the writer that he would take care of the publishing business himself. Then Sherrill Nielsen sat down at the piano to play a song he'd performed as a child at a talent contest (which, like Elvis, he didn't win). An Andy Williams hit, "Are You Sincere," it became the final cut for the album. When the basic tracks had been completed, the Colonel told Elvis firmly that no further overdubs could be added; the tracks would have to be left as is. And then, in a further move to control the project, he suggested strongly to RCA that Felton Jarvis have nothing further to do with the album.

"Raised On Rock"/"For Ol' Times Sake" was released in September of 1973, the album *Raised On Rock* a month later. When both album and single proved commercial failures, RCA took it as yet another sign that they had to get rid of Felton entirely. But when they tried to set up a meeting with their star, they learned how seriously they had misjudged the situation. Elvis had gone more than fifteen years without taking direction of any kind from the label, and he wasn't about to start now—there would be no firing. Now there was a further complication on the boards: Joan Deary had scheduled another album, a deluxe package made up of old masters and previously unreleased material (now owned entirely by RCA under the new contract), to come out at almost exactly the same time as *Raised On Rock*. The Colonel was furious—this wasn't how he had expected the contract to work out—and he did everything he could to derail *Elvis: A Legendary Performer, Vol. 1* from appearing at this time. In the end he succeeded in delaying the release date until January. *Legendary Performer* was a major success, selling 700,000 copies, and in the face of *Raised On Rock*'s failure it was a brutal reminder that Elvis's past glories continued to outshine his contemporary efforts.

On October 9, 1973, Priscilla and Elvis walked out of a Santa Monica courthouse together, their divorce final. Newspaper photographs depicted the couple as composed and friendly, but just days later Elvis was rushed from Graceland to the hospital with breathing and congestion problems—and, it was reported later, to dry out. Shortly after his release eighteen days later, on a visit to his new girlfriend Linda Thompson's parents' home, Elvis was recorded singing a handful of old favorites by Linda's brother Sam.

115. Private Recordings
November 1973: The Thompson Home, Memphis

Guitar: Elvis Presley

See See Rider
Arranged by Elvis Presley
That's All Right
Arthur Crudup
Baby What You Want Me To Do
Jimmy Reed
Spanish Eyes
Kaempfert/Singleton/Snyder
I'm So Lonesome I Could Cry
Hank Williams

Having tried and failed to get rid of Felton Jarvis, all RCA could do now was to try to gain some control over the technical aspects of the upcoming December sessions. Simply in order to stay close to home, Elvis insisted on returning to Stax; RCA's studio manager, Larry Schnapf, recommended his most skilled New York engineer, Mike Moran, not least because by "personality and temperament" he would make a good replacement for Al Pachucki. Moran had joined RCA in 1959, straight out of the U.S. Army unit that had been replaced by Elvis's in Germany. His work included the Youngbloods' "Get Together" and a series of Broadway cast albums and classical recordings from which he had learned the complicated skills required for live recording. To augment the dated Stax equipment, RCA's red recording truck would bring down two sixteen-track tape machines, to be manned by engineers Ron Olson and Tom Brown, while another engineer, Dick Baxter, would work inside the studio to assure that the headphones and monitoring system worked properly.

116. Studio Sessions for RCA
December 10–16, 1973: Stax Studios, Memphis

A&R/Producer: Felton Jarvis
Session Engineers: Mike Moran, Dick Baxter
Overdub Engineers: Mickey Crofford (Hollywood), Al Pachucki (Nashville)

Guitar: James Burton
Guitar: Johnny Christopher
Acoustic Guitar: Charlie Hodge
Bass: Norbert Putnam
Drums: Ronnie Tutt
Piano, Organ: David Briggs
Piano, Organ: Per-Erik Hallin
Vocals: J. D. Sumner & The Stamps
Vocals: Voice
Vocals: Kathy Westmoreland, Mary Greene,
Mary Holladay, Susan Pilkington

Harmony Vocals: Elvis Presley (1618, 1629)

Overdubbed:
Guitar: Dennis Linde
Guitar: Alan Rush
Percussion: Rob Galbraith
Piano: Bobby Ogdin
Organ: Randy Cullers
Vocals: Ginger Holladay, Mary Holladay, Mary Cain
Strings and Horns

12/10, 9PM–4:30AM

CPA5 1617-03	**I Got A Feeling In My Body**	**Good Times**
	Dennis Linde—Combine Music	*CPL1 0475/1974*
CPA5 1618-19	**It's Midnight**	**Single B-side**
	Billy Edd Wheeler/Jerry Chesnut—Imagination/Elvis Music	*PB 10074/1975*

12/11, 9PM–2AM

CPA5 1619-06	**You Asked Me To**	**Promised Land**
	Waylon Jennings/Billy Joe Shaver—Baron Music	*APL1 0873/1975*
CPA5 1620-09	**If You Talk In Your Sleep**	**Single A-side**
	Red West/Johnny Christopher—Easy Mine/Elvis Music	*APBO 0280/1974*

12/12, 9PM–12AM, 1–5AM

CPA5 1621-06	**Mr. Songman**	**Promised Land**
	Donnie Sumner—Elvis Music	*APL1 0873/1975*
CPA5 1622-08	**Thinking About You**	**Promised Land**
	Tim Baty—Elvis Music	*APL1 0873/1975*
CPA5 1623-08	**Love Song Of The Year**	**Promised Land**
	Chris Christian—Kinchell Music/Elvis Music	*APL1 0873/1975*
CPA5 1624-01	**Help Me**	**Single B-side**
	Larry Gatlin—First Generation Music	*APBO 0280/1974*

12/13, 9PM–12AM, 1–4AM

CPA5 1625-03	**My Boy**	**Good Times**
	B. Martin/P. Coulter—Col Music	*CPL1 0475/1974*
CPA5 1626-03	**Loving Arms**	**Good Times**
	Tom Jans—Almo Music/Chandos Music	*CPL1 0475/1974*

| CPA5 1627-09 | **Good Time Charlie's Got The Blues** | **Good Times** |
| | *Danny O'Keefe—Cotillion Music* | *CPL1 0475/1974* |

12/14, 9PM–12AM, 1–3AM

| CPA5 1628-04 | **Talk About The Good Times** | **Good Times** |
| | *Jerry Reed—Vector Music* | *CPL1 0475/1974* |

12/15, 9PM–12AM, 1–6AM

CPA5 1629-06	**Promised Land**	**Single A-side**
	Chuck Berry—Arc Music	*PB 10074/1975*
CPA5 1630-09	**Your Love's Been A Long Time Coming**	**Promised Land**
	Rory Bourke—Chappell & Co.	*APL1 0873/1975*
CPA5 1631-08	**There's A Honky Tonk Angel**	**Promised Land**
	Troy Seals/Danny Rice—Danor Music	*APL1 0873/1975*

12/16, 9PM–12AM, 1–5AM

CPA5 1632-04	**If That Isn't Love**	**Good Times**
	Dottie Rambo—Heartwarming Music	*CPL1 0475/1974*
CPA5 1633-04	**Spanish Eyes**	**Good Times**
	B. Kaempfert/C. Singleton/E. Snyder—Screen Gems/Columbia Music	*CPL1 0475/1974*
CPA5 1634-10	**She Wears My Ring**	**Good Times**
	Boudleaux/Felice Bryant—House Of Bryant	*CPL1 0475/1974*

Overdubbing sessions on 1/2 and 1/15, 1974, in Nashville. Strings were overdubbed in Hollywood on 1/10–11, 1974. The master of "Thinking About You" was shortened by 1:40 for release. The master of "Love Song Of The Year" was shortened by :30 for release. The master of "My Boy" was lengthened by splicing on a repeat of the last section. The master of "Good Time Charlie's Got The Blues" was shortened by 1:15 for release. The master of "Talk About The Good Times" was shortened by :30 for release. The master of "Your Love's Been A Long Time Coming" was shortened by 1:00 for release. The Stamps: Ed Enoch, Bill Baize, Dave Rowland. Voice: Donnie Sumner, Sherrill Nielsen, Tim Baty.

With the divorce settlement behind him and no live engagements in the near future, RCA's demand for new material caught Elvis at a much better time than it had back in July. The hospitalization in October had given him a much-needed rest as well as a strong motivation to clean up his lifestyle. And with Linda Thompson at his side, Elvis seemed to be looking to the future with both confidence and determination. Supported by Felton, the Colonel, and RCA, the new recording sessions were set up in an orderly and timely fashion, again at Stax Studios, but this time with every technical and musical precaution in place.

Elvis was always cautious of strangers, and the addition of four engineers from New York might have seemed like an invasion. Some of Elvis's guys even insinuated that Elvis would have a problem with the presence of Tom Brown, a six-foot-plus, heavily built African-American engineer with impeccable credentials. If there was a problem, though, it wasn't coming from Elvis, who proved typically friendly and respectful toward all the engineers when he visited the truck to listen to the first round of playbacks. Still, he didn't hesitate to test the northeners after hearing the cuts. "This sounds like a typical New York mix," he warned after listening to one tape, but after Mike Moran quickly spotted a disconnected speaker wire it was smooth sailing.

The failure of the new publishing setup, so apparent at the first Stax sessions, was confronted straight on, and now songs flowed from all sources, including Felton's Nashville connections. None was more important than his relationship with Bob Beckham, part-owner of the successful independent Combine Music. It was Combine that had supplied "Burning Love," and now the same writer, Dennis Linde, had come up with "I Got A Feeling In My Body," a funkily rhythmic contemporary religious number. It was a great kickoff for the sessions—and for Elvis, who, though still thirty pounds overweight and looking pretty peculiar in the cape he insisted on wearing throughout each evening, was plainly excited to be back in the studio. The group had been pared down to the basics: James Burton and Ron Tutt from the stage band joined Nashville players David Briggs (on piano) and Norbert Putnam, whom Felton had to pull away from a busy producing schedule to fill in on bass. The Memphis musicians were all gone, and the ever-efficient Ronnie Tutt made the idea of using two drummers redundant. Songwriter Johnny Christopher would help out on rhythm guitar, as would Per-Erik "Pete" Hallin, Voice's Swedish piano player. Hallin had recently been discovered on a Scandinavian tour by Tony Brown, the Oak Ridge Boys' pianist; he must have been amazed to find himself playing lead electric piano on the very first cut of an Elvis Presley recording session. The crowd of backup singers had grown to eleven: the three members of Voice and four women plus J. D. Sumner and the Stamps. The lyrics of "I Got A Feeling In My Body" might have been spiritual, but the playing cooked, and Elvis was totally caught up in the excitement. After a few tempo adjustments and several good takes, Elvis's voice began to wear thin on the seventh try. The playback confirmed that they already had everything they were looking for on take three, so it was transferred to the master reel.

It was still the Colonel's policy to try to get Elvis Music at least a slice of every song Elvis recorded, and hot Nashville writer Jerry Chesnut, who

Internal Correspondence

Date 6/1/73

9'

Location

Telephone 5093

To   J. Maher   5

From J. Deary

Subject: ELVIS PRESLEY — PROBABLE JULY SPECIAL — VICTOR ALBUM RELEASE

Following is a rundown of the pertinent information on the above album:

I. Repertoire
    a. Contains 9 previously unreleased performances plus the current hit single Fool. They are Where
    b. 4 of the songs have never been released, A Blues Jam (I'm
       Do I Go From Here, It's Impossible, and I'll Take You Home
       still checking the correct title), and I'll Take You Home
       Again Kathleen.
    c. The remaining 5 selections are new performances of previously released songs which were recorded in Hawaii in January '73. They were used as part of the TV show, but were not in the Satellite album. These songs are as follows:
       Blue Hawaii   (original versions of
       Ku-U-I-Po   these songs were included
       No More   in the soundtrack of "Blue
       Hawaiian Wedding Song   Hawaii" released in 1961.)
       Early Mornin' Rain   (original version included
                                in the "Now" album released
                                in early '72.)

II.   Cover - Same picture as used on the Fool single sleeve.
III. Liner - Will contain cuts of the Madison Square Garden and Satellite albums along with the sequence.
IV.   Further Info - Elvis has a new tour scheduled between June 20th and July 3rd and will go into Vegas again in August.

If you need any further information, let me know.

Thanks,

had agreed to share publishing on "Find Out What's Happening" back in July, had a new ballad, "It's Midnight," that was a natural to attract Elvis. A powerhouse of desolate, dark feeling, it described the late-night loneliness of the abandoned singer: "It's midnight, and I miss you." It was virtually a page from Elvis's own diary, and he worked on the song for hours, becoming despondent whenever he made a mistake. By take nineteen every bit of emotion had been loaded onto the tape. When Felton reassured him with his usual encouragement ("It's a gas"), Elvis rejected him: "I don't believe you." But after listening to the playback he accepted the verdict, and at 4:00 A.M. drove the short distance home to Graceland.

Clowning around and cussing, picking on Charlie Hodge, singing "On Top Of Old Smokey," Elvis couldn't be still the next evening, and for the first time that year he seemed to be enjoying it all. The night began with "You Asked Me To," a Waylon Jennings song that had been one of several recent hits for the Texas singer-songwriter. As a teenager Jennings had watched the young Hillbilly Cat perform in his hometown of Lubbock, Texas, and he (like Buddy Holly, also from Lubbock) was impressed with what he saw. Now Elvis was following Jennings's recording closely, and completed a lively take on the second try. For once, though, Elvis was satisfied before Felton; the producer wanted to get something more from his singer, but when the hopped-up Elvis messed up on the next attempt, he started taking out his frustration on Felton. With the overwhelming criticism of the previous sessions, Felton felt compelled to push, encourage, and direct his artist, in an effort to make sure he gave the very best he could. Settling for take two just wasn't good enough for what Felton was looking for, and though they had to fight through a few more mistake-ridden takes to get there, by take six he knew he'd done the right thing.

Red West, who'd contributed "Separate Ways" in 1972, knew he could always capture Elvis's attention with lyrics that reflected his employer's life. This time the theme of infidelity inspired him to craft a smoky soul number called "If You Talk In Your Sleep," and the group set about creating a propulsive bass-and-drum-heavy arrangement topped with funky guitars and David Briggs punching away at the bottom end of his electric piano. As Norbert Putnam reworked his part, Elvis serenaded the group with lines from "Find Out What's Happening" before they finally cut the master, furthering the sound they'd gotten on "I Got A Feeling In My Body" the night before. When Elvis discovered there was no food available, though, the session came to an early end; apologizing to the group, he canceled the rest of the night and left in a huff.

The group Voice was becoming a permanent fixture on the Elvis scene. Their deal with the singer included a publishing arrangement, and accordingly they brought songs—their own and those of their friends—to the session. Lamar Fike, watching his territory being encroached upon by the newcomers, was irked. "Who wrote this piece of shit?" Lamar gasped while Elvis was recording a Donnie Sumner tune, "Mr. Songman," as unadventurous in its way as anything from Freddy Bienstock's stable of English writers. But Elvis stuck with his new friends (and to the Colonel's design to increase publishing income), even going to the length of releasing "Mr. Songman" as the B-side of a single. Tim Baty's very first attempt at writing produced a more original number, "Thinking About You," though it hardly came from any musical form familiar to the band; it too wound up on a single B-side. In fact the number of

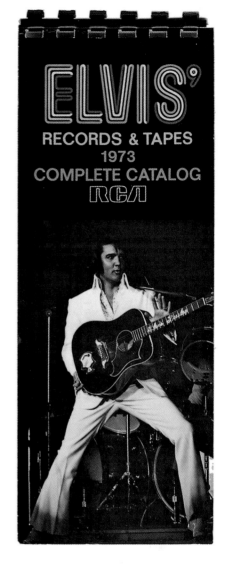

demos introduced by Voice at the session was staggering, but there were important contributions among them—including "Bringin' It Back" by Greg Gordon, which would turn up on a later session (and, eventually, as an A-side), and "Help Me" by rising star Larry Gatlin, which became a great favorite of Elvis's in live performance. "Help Me" was the last song recorded on December 12, and they got it in one take; in his book *Elvis: The Final Years,* Jerry Hopkins reports that Elvis dropped to his knees to sing it.

The next night Elvis began with a song from his live repertoire, "My Boy," which had been included in the August Las Vegas show. The song told the traumatic tale of losing a child through divorce, but Elvis wanted to be done with it fast. When Felton pushed for a third take, he exploded: "I told you to get this goddamn thing in two takes. I can't sing it no more." Take three was actually better; it lacked the long fade-out Felton wanted, but he knew better than to ask for another, confident that he could loop it in mixing to get the effect he wanted.

The next number, Tom Jans's "Loving Arms," was perfectly suited to Elvis's voice. The powerful but touching folk-country ballad instantly sparked the musicians to new heights of fresh, sophisticated playing. The song was as demanding on them as "My Boy" had been on Elvis's voice, and when Felton cautiously asked for a third take, he was relieved to watch it yield a perfect master. "Good Time Charlie's Got The Blues," another folkish ballad, had been its writer Danny O'Keefe's only hit, and now it presented Elvis at his best, identifying with the material and sure in his interpretation. Elvis's version, tellingly, left out a verse including the lyric "I take the pills to ease the pain/Can't find the thing to ease my brain," but the final take remains stunning and brought the night to a successful close.

The gospel album they'd been slated to make in July nearly materialized the following night, when they began the evening with Jerry Reed's rousing "Talk About The Good Times." Hallin and Briggs chased each other up and down the keyboards while the guitars kept up the frenetic pace. David Briggs had something more at stake on the next cut, as he had the publishing on another recent Waylon Jennings hit (and another marriage-breakup tune), "We Had It All." The rest of the evening was spent trying and failing to get the right feeling for the song, before they finally agreed to pick it up again the following night. Postponing a song often meant Elvis had lost interest; in this case he was anxious to begin again on the following day, only to resign himself to failure: "I just don't know how to improve this."

Unwinding with Chuck Berry's "Promised Land," Elvis, now completely in control, heard a wrong note from rhythm guitarist Johnny Christopher and gently pointed it out after the band had romped through the song. David Briggs's clavinet and James Burton's guitar had a near-duel, but no one enjoyed himself as much as the star, who stormed through four takes before slipping into a fragment of "Columbus Stockade Blues." This was the gesture that delighted his cousin Billy Smith, who was in the room for the session ("I did that when I was three years old," Elvis told Billy), but before long Briggs's pounding piano catapulted him back into the present, and an even more fiery final take of the Chuck Berry song.

"Your Love's Been A Long Time Coming," by Rory Bourke, who'd written "Patch It Up" with Eddie Rabbitt, was another welcome challenge. It was a medium-tempo pop song, a little predictable but still very melodic—and it mesmerized Elvis. By 4:30 A.M. they had worked later than on the previous nights, but Elvis sat listening to the playback over and over, as in days of old, while musicians and singers drifted out to the parking lot waiting to be dismissed for the night. But with his father visiting Elvis was feeling too good to stop, summoning everyone back to work on Conway Twitty's "There's A Honky Tonk Angel." "Norbert, straighten up now. You too, David," he directed, knowing it was up to him to keep everyone awake. This was Elvis as a true session leader: Joking with his band, gently scolding them all while making each player feel noticed, he even snored loudly through the intro, giving them all the motivation they needed to perk it up. For a moment he was once again the young upstart who had impressed Jerry Leiber and Mike Stoller at the *Jailhouse Rock* sessions, insisting on getting things right, following his nose and leading everyone along with him. By 6:00 A.M. he had achieved what he'd set out to do, and the crew went home tired but happy.

On the final night Elvis's voice sounded stronger and clearer than it had at the beginning, as if the sessions themselves had been a kind of healing process. Accompanied by exceptional playing from Pete Hallin, Elvis sang with passion and conviction on Dottie Rambo's spiritual number "If That Isn't Love" before moving to "Spanish Eyes." The latter was a song from the November tape he had made at Linda Thompson's parents' home, and probably more appropriate to that situation, but Elvis wanted to do it differently. Driven by his redoubled energy, they recorded it in the lighthearted way that characterized many of his best performances. By the time the second Stax sessions concluded late that night, Elvis was eighteen takes into Ray Price's 1968 hit "She Wears My Ring," a comfortable old favorite he'd sung at home for years.

Elvis Presley's career had never seen a year of greater highs or lows than 1973. From the triumph of *Aloha From Hawaii* Elvis had gone into a tailspin of failure on all fronts: plunging record sales, divorce, problems with his health and his weight. Now, just days before Christmas, at the conclusion of a set of sessions forced on him by his record company, there once again was reason for hope. Felton Jarvis had recorded eighteen new songs in a week, and Elvis, Tom Parker, and RCA could have been forgiven for believing that another turnaround was still within reach.

1974–75

T-R-O-U-B-L-E

Nineteen seventy-four, in many ways, was the calm after the storm. There were no major events, no studio recording sessions, and only modest record sales. Elvis spent much of the year on the road in his busiest touring schedule since the '50s, supplementing his customary two seasons at Las Vegas with two engagements at Lake Tahoe and four tours. The reason was simple: Live performance was where the money was.

The recordings Elvis had made at Stax in December would yield one good album, but with touring taking up most of his time in 1974, the Colonel needed to find a way to bring about a second. The answer was to cut another live record, this time from his "homecoming" concert in Memphis on March 20. Elvis hadn't performed in his hometown since the 1961 charity show, making the appearance something of an event; beyond a little extra time spent on the recording setup, though, no special effort was made to distinguish this show from the long procession that had come before. RCA's recording truck pulled up to the Mid-South Coliseum before the show; there was no rehearsal, just a cursory sound-check, and no backup plan should anything go wrong at the single performance. The

Memphis, Tennessee, March 1974: with Charlie Hodge and bassist Duke Bardwell

show itself featured just three numbers that hadn't been previously released: A cover of Olivia Newton-John's "Let Me Be There," and the gospel numbers "Why Me Lord" and "Help Me." The most impressive moment was probably Elvis's thundering version of "How Great Thou Art," which won him his third and final Grammy—once again for Best Sacred Recording, the only category in which he ever triumphed.

117. Live Recordings for RCA
March 20, 1974: Mid-South Coliseum, Memphis

A&R/Producer: Felton Jarvis
Engineers: Mike Moran/Gus Mossler/Ronnie Olson

Guitar: James Burton
Guitar: John Wilkinson
Guitar & Vocals: Charlie Hodge
Bass: Duke Bardwell
Drums: Ronnie Tutt
Piano: Glen Hardin

Vocals: Kathy Westmoreland
Vocals: The Sweet Inspirations
Vocals: J. D. Sumner & The Stamps
Vocals: Voice
Joe Guercio & His Orchestra

DPA5 0903	**See See Rider**	**Recorded Live On Stage In Memphis**
	Traditional/arranged by Elvis Presley—Elvis Presley Music	*CPL1 0606/1974*
DPA5 0904	**I Got A Woman/Amen**	**Recorded Live On Stage In Memphis**
	Ray Charles/J. Hairston—Hill & Range Songs/Schumann Music	*CPL1 0606/1974*
DPA5 0905	**Love Me**	**Recorded Live On Stage In Memphis**
	Jerry Leiber/Mike Stoller—Hill & Range Songs/Quintet Music	*CPL1 0606/1974*
DPA5 0906	**Trying To Get To You**	**Recorded Live On Stage In Memphis**
	Rose Marie McCoy/Charles Singleton—Motion Music Company	*CPL1 0606/1974*
DPA5 0907	**All Shook Up**	
	Otis Blackwell/Elvis Presley	
DPA5 0908	**Steamroller Blues**	**Platinum: A Life In Music**
	James Taylor—none listed	*67469-2/1997*
DPA5 0909	**Teddy Bear/Don't Be Cruel**	
	Kal Mann/Bernie Lowe—Otis Blackwell/Elvis Presley	
DPA5 0910	**Love Me Tender**	
	Vera Matson/Elvis Presley	
DPA5 0911	**Long Tall Sally/Whole Lotta Shakin' Goin' On/Mama Don't Dance/Flip, Flop And Fly/Jailhouse Rock/Hound Dog**	**Recorded Live On Stage In Memphis** *CPL1 0606/1974*
	Johnson/Penniman/Blackwell—Venice Music; Dave Williams/ Sunny David—Anne Rachel Music/Pic Music; Ken Loggins/Jim Messina— Jasperilla/Wingate Music; Joe Turner—Hill & Range Songs; Jerry Leiber/Mike Stoller— Elvis Presley Music; Jerry Leiber/Mike Stoller—Elvis Presley Music/Lion Publishing	
DPA5 0912	**Fever**	
	Davenport/Cooley—Jay & Cee Music Corporation	

DPA5 0913	**Polk Salad Annie**		
	Tony Joe White—Combine Music		
DPA5 0914	**Why Me Lord**	**Recorded Live On Stage In Memphis**	
	Kris Kristofferson—Resaca Music	*CPL1 0606/1974*	
DPA5 0915	**How Great Thou Art**	**Recorded Live On Stage In Memphis**	
	Stuart K. Hine—Manna Music	*CPL1 0606/1974*	
DPA5 0916	**Suspicious Minds**		
	Mark James		
DPA5 0918	**Blueberry Hill/I Can't Stop Loving You**	**Recorded Live On Stage In Memphis**	
	Lewis/Stock/Rose—Don Gibson—Chappell & Co./Acuff/Rose	*CPL1 0606/1974*	
DPA5 0919	**Help Me**	**Recorded Live On Stage In Memphis**	
	Larry Gatlin—First Generation Music	*CPL1 0606/1974*	
DPA5 0920	**An American Trilogy**	**Recorded Live On Stage In Memphis**	
	Mickey Newbury—Acuff/Rose Publ.	*CPL1 0606/1974*	
DPA5 0921	**Let Me Be There**	**Recorded Live On Stage In Memphis**	
	John Rostill—Al Gallico Music	*CPL1 0606/1974*	
DPA5 0926	**My Baby Left Me**	**Recorded Live On Stage In Memphis**	
	Arthur Crudup—Elvis Presley Music	*CPL1 0606/1974*	
DPA5 0927	**Lawdy, Miss Clawdy**	**Recorded Live On Stage In Memphis**	
	Lloyd Price—Venice Music	*CPL1 0606/1974*	
DPA5 0928	**Funny How Time Slips Away**		
	Willie Nelson		
DPA5 0929	**Can't Help Falling In Love**	**Recorded Live On Stage In Memphis**	
	Peretti/Creatore/Weiss	*CPL1 0606/1974*	

The full title of the album is *Elvis As Recorded Live On Stage In Memphis.*

The Memphis show was neither good nor bad, but, like everything else that year, it was a pale imitation of what had gone before. Elvis's record sales fluctuated slightly, but even the successes were only moderate. In January the new single, "I've Got A Thing About You Baby," sold almost half a million, substantially better than its predecessor "Raised On Rock." But it did no better in the charts, peaking at number thirty-nine. The next single, Red West's "If You Talk In Your Sleep," got better radio promotion and charted in the lower part of the top twenty, but with fewer sales. *Good Times,* the album drawn from the December Stax sessions, never rose higher than number ninety, despite featuring great cuts like "Loving Arms," "Good Time Charlie's Got The Blues," and "Talk About The Good Times." *Elvis As Recorded Live On Stage In Memphis,* featuring beautiful pictures of Graceland but none of the artist himself, sold significantly better. Only a diminishing group of diehard fans seemed to be supporting Elvis as a recording artist, while Elvis the legend was selling out concert halls across America.

RCA's Joan Deary could point with pride to the fact that the one compilation album she had produced, *Elvis: A Legendary Performer, Vol. 1,* had sold better than all three of Felton Jarvis's albums (*Elvis [Fool], Raised On Rock,* and *Good Times*) put together. What had started as a minor quibble over the tracks on the *Fool* album had grown into a full-fledged war between Deary and Felton the previous fall. As secretary for Steve Sholes, and later as administrator of Elvis releases for the label, twenty-year RCA veteran Deary had a longstanding relationship with the Colonel. With the constant changes in RCA's senior management, the label relied increasingly on her guidance in dealing with Presley and Parker, and she normally knew just how to tackle any situation. With the new recording deal from 1973 in hand, the label had wanted strong commercial records, and when their first year of efforts went unrewarded, Joan suggested that the failure lay with Elvis's producer. Elvis had refused to let Felton go at the time, and the December sessions brought great improvement in terms of both technical and performance quality. Yet the end result was still the same—no big singles, no album sales to speak of. Deary may have been right in her judgment of Felton, but in the end she and RCA lost the battle over his future. She had miscalculated her bargaining position with the Presley camp when she went after Felton, and all she got for her troubles was a defensive star who, instead of pushing himself in any new artistic direction, withdrew into a comfort zone of familiar faces and encroaching boredom.

118. Studio Rehearsals
August 16, 1974: RCA Studios, Hollywood

Guitar: James Burton
Guitar: John Wilkinson
Bass: Duke Bardwell
Drums: Ronnie Tutt

Piano: Glen D. Hardin
Vocals: Voice
Vocals: Charlie Hodge

Session hours unknown

CPA5 5109	Softly As I Leave You	Walk A Mile In My Shoes
	A. de Vita/H. Shaper	*66670-2/1995*
CPA5 5114	The Twelfth Of Never	Walk A Mile In My Shoes
	Jerry Livingston/Paul Francis Webster	*66670-2/1995*

The above performances were recorded directly from the mixing console onto a substandard-quality cassette tape.

For the August Las Vegas engagement Elvis rehearsed a substantial amount of new material, including the current single "If You Talk In Your Sleep," the upcoming single "Promised Land," as well as "It's Midnight," "Your Love's Been A Long Time Coming," and the haunting "Good Time Charlie's Got The Blues." Working harder than he usually did at the rehearsals, he concentrated on two personal favorites, "I'm Leaving" and "The First Time Ever I Saw Your Face," despite the fact they had been commercial failures when they were released. He added two unrecorded numbers, "The Twelfth Of Never" and "Softly As I Leave You," and enthused over Olivia Newton-John's "If You Love Me (Let Me Go)" ("I like it. It's such a happy song"), sticking with his own instincts in the face of concern that it might be considered bland. Yet after a good deal of preparation much of the new material was abandoned, because the show seemed to lack the excitement it had achieved in the past.

Throughout the year, reports of Elvis's increasingly eccentric behavior—sneaking into the Las Vegas Hilton showroom with the guys after hours, for example, to spray-paint the room's decorative white angels black—began circulating among the fans, along with persistent rumors of drug addiction. Increasingly the singer did appear out of control in public, even as he offered explicit denials from the stage. On September 2, the closing night of the Vegas engagement, a month of erratic behavior reached a new low. After just one song Elvis went into one of the prolonged monologues the hotel management had worked so hard to discourage. After "You Gave Me A Mountain" he introduced Priscilla, Lisa Marie, and then his girlfriend; he denied that the song was "personal," and went on about the "friendly divorce," but then went into a truly embarrassing piece about the financial settlement and the gifts he and Priscilla had exchanged. It was as if he couldn't stop himself. His band introductions went on forever, and were followed by three songs from Voice. The show wasn't bad as such, but Elvis's constant and lengthy interruptions grew increasingly bizarre as the show progressed. He introduced Bill Cosby from the stage, though he wasn't actually there. That led him into a long rap about the liver biopsy he'd been through the year before. John O'Grady, the former head of the narcotics squad in Los Angeles, was introduced next, and Elvis recommended his new book, proudly pointing to two whole pages about their friendship. He told the audience that for five years he himself had been a member of an antidrug organization. After commenting on a paternity-suit "hoax" O'Grady had investigated for him, he rambled on, in slurring words, about the stories of his hospitalization, and what caused it. Finally he seemed to have gotten around to what was really preoccupying him: The rumors that he was "strung out." Excusing his language, but insisting on his point, he declared: "By God, I'll tell you something, friend. I have never been 'strung out' in my life, except on music. . . . If I find, or hear, the individual who has said that about me, I'm gonna break your goddamn neck, you son-of-a-bitch. That [rumor] is dangerous, that is damaging to myself, to my little daughter, to my father, to my friends, my doctor, to my relationship with you up here onstage . . . *I'll pull your goddamn tongue out by the roots!*" After five minutes it was over. "Let me get out this mood," he said, and introduced, of all things, the "Hawaiian Wedding Song." By the time the show was over the audience had listened to more than thirty minutes of talk from Elvis—a desperate attempt to explain away his divorce, his health problems, and ultimately his drug problem. To those who knew him it was an astonishing whitewash; to many in the audience it must have seemed like a train wreck.

Yet somehow Colonel Tom Parker saw a silver lining in even all this. That fall, Parker launched his own record label, Boxcar Records, for the purpose of releasing an album entitled *Having Fun With Elvis On Stage*. Piecing together some of Elvis's more innocuous banter from the Las Vegas shows, with no music at all, it sold about as well as any of the regular albums. There was some hope on the music front, too; the September single, "Promised Land," showed some promise, sparking hope at RCA for the album that would follow. But at Graceland the mood was less optimistic. Elvis looked pale and bloated, and he seemed to lack the self-control needed to concentrate on any work. By December it had become obvious that he was in no physical condition to honor his contract with the Hilton for a January 1975 show, and the hotel announced a postponement.

At the end of January, a few weeks after his fortieth birthday, Elvis reentered Baptist Memorial Hospital in Memphis for the treatment of undisclosed problems. One of these was an enlarged colon; another was Elvis's recurring eye trouble. Underlying all this, though, was the hospital's renewed attempt to detoxify the artist—an attempt that was only partly successful, as certain members of Elvis's own circle kept supplying him drugs on the sly. Only a few days later, Vernon Presley was admitted to the same hospital after suffering a serious heart attack. Following a month of recuperation in Memphis, Elvis flew to Los Angeles to prepare for a truncated two-week appearance in Las Vegas. To accommodate Elvis and accomplish as much as possible at one time, a combined rehearsal and recording session was scheduled to begin on March 10 at the RCA Studio on 6363 Sunset Boulevard.

119. Studio Sessions for RCA
March 10–12, 1975: RCA's Studio C, Hollywood

A&R/Producer: Felton Jarvis
Engineers: Rick Ruggieri

Guitar: James Burton
Guitar: John Wilkinson
Guitar, Vocals: Charlie Hodge
Bass: Duke Bardwell (all erased except 1599)
Drums: Ronnie Tutt
Piano: Glen D. Hardin
Piano: Tony Brown (1602)
Clavinet: David Briggs
Clavinet: Greg Gordon (1602)
Vocals: Voice

Overdubbed:
Guitar: Chip Young
Bass: Mike Leech (except 1599)
Fiddle: Buddy Spicher
Steel Guitar: Weldon Myrick
Guitar: Johnny Christopher
Bass: Norbert Putnam
Vocals: The Holladays
Percussion: Farrell Morris
Strings and Horns

3/10, 9PM–12AM

EPA3 1594-03	**Fairytale**	**Today**
	Anita Pointer/Bonnie Pointer—Polo Grounds Music/Para Thumb Music	*APL1 1039/1975*

12:30–3:30AM

EPA3 1595-05	**Green, Green Grass Of Home**	**Today**
	Claude Putnam, Jr.—Tree Publishing	*APL1 1039/1975*
EPA3 1596-02	**I Can Help**	**Today**
	Billy Swan—Combine Music	*APL1 1039/1975*

4–7AM

EPA3 1597-05	**And I Love You So**	**Today**
	Don McLean—Mayday Music/Yahweh Tunes	*APL1 1039/1975*

3/11, 9PM–12AM

EPA3 1598-06	**Susan When She Tried**	**Today**
	Don Reid—American Cowboy Music	*APL1 1039/1975*

12:30–3:30AM

EPA3 1599-04	**T-R-O-U-B-L-E**	**Single A-side**
	Jerry Chesnut—Jerry Chesnut Music	*PB 10278/1975*
WPA5 2575-01	**Tiger Man**	**Walk A Mile In My Shoes**
	J. H. Louis/S. Burns—Hi-Lo Music	*66670-2/1996*

4–7AM

EPA3 1600-01	**Woman Without Love**	**Today**
	Jerry Chesnut—Passkey Music	*APL1 1039/1975*
EPA3 1601-03	**Shake A Hand**	**Today**
	Joe Morris—Merrimac Music	*APL1 1039/1975*

3/12, 9PM–12AM

EPA3 1602–04 **Bringin' It Back** **Today**
G. Gordon/Silverline Music *APL1 1039/1975*

12:30–3:30AM

EPA3 1603-04 **Pieces Of My Life** **Today**
Troy Seals/Danor Music *APL1 1039/1975*

Strings were overdubbed at RCA Studios, Hollywood, on 4/14. All other overdubs were done at Quadrofonic Sound, Nashville, April 8–10. Nashville engineers: Mike Shockley and Al Pachucki. The Holladays: Ginger Holladay, Mary Holladay, Lea J. Beranati, Millie Kirkham.

Maybe the decision to book the new recording sessions in Hollywood was a small concession to RCA. It was business as usual for Elvis and his group to do their Vegas rehearsing in Los Angeles, but just as significantly they would be recording just a few floors below Joan Deary's office in the RCA building on Sunset Boulevard. Deary might not have been invited to the sessions, but at least they would be done at RCA's studio, recorded to RCA's technical standards, and provide an opportunity for the label to have a listen to the tapes while the sessions were still under way.

Trailing fans caught a glimpse of Elvis and his not-so-official girlfriend Sheila Ryan in the backseat of his limousine, playing with Lisa Marie as he was driven from his home on Monovale Drive to the studio. Once there he was joined by the band and by the members of Voice, taking over all backup duties from the usual profusion of vocalists. First up was "Fairytale," written by the talented R&B group the Pointer Sisters; the song offered a good opportunity for blending voices, but Elvis had to struggle to control his high notes, which suggested that he might have done better in a lower key. The country flavor of the first song carried over to the next, "Green, Green Grass Of Home," which had first caught Elvis's attention when he heard Tom Jones's version on George Klein's WHBQ radio show while driving home from California for Christmas in 1966. Elvis had flipped over the record then and stopped repeatedly to have Joe Esposito call from Arkansas to get George to play it again and again. At the time Red West was surprised to hear Elvis raving about the song, having played Jerry Lee Lewis's version for Elvis months before that to no reaction. Elvis's voice was more suited to this second number than the first, and he had it down from the start.

This session marked the first time that Elvis's own music firms brought in no new material. Felton had been successful in recent years in bringing Elvis songs from the creative environs of Nashville, but now the primary inspiration seemed to come from other artists. Felton must have been pushing Elvis to cover Billy Swan's worldwide hit "I Can Help," which had been produced by Chip Young (Elvis's guitarist from 1965 to 1971). When the producer brought the song up, Elvis promptly joked, "I'm tired of it. Billy Swan, my ass"—and then proceeded to nail it on the first complete take. Elvis had added nothing, and the playback sounded a little bare, but Felton knew that could be dealt with later. Billy Swan, a friend of Felton's and a longtime fan of Elvis, was thrilled by the recording; after the session Felton gave him the socks Elvis was wearing that day, and he still has them today.

Now it was girlfriend Sheila Ryan's moment, as Elvis called for her: "Let me sing for you, baby." He launched into "And I Love You So," a 1973 top-thirty hit for Perry Como by writer Don McLean, and gave it a careful, delicate reading. The fifth song would be the fifth cover in a row, and it took some effort on Felton's part to coerce his employer into even making the effort. The Statler Brothers' "Susan When She Tried" was a nice up-tempo number that suited Elvis well, but the first take was, in his own word, "shit." Felton raved about the take with his usual excitement and invited Elvis to listen to the playback. By now Elvis had been listening to excited producers for twenty years, and could sniff out inflated encouragement a mile away: "You don't believe that shit, really, do you?" But Felton knew he needed to push for all the recorded material he could get, and in this rare instance he pushed the envelope. After a few more takes both men left the song content with Elvis's performance.

Back at the beginning of 1974 Emory Gordy, the bass player who had replaced Jerry Scheff, had left in turn to concentrate on production work in Nashville. He had been replaced by Duke Bardwell, who got off to a bad start in Vegas when a loud hum in his amplifier annoyed Elvis on opening night. Anxious to fit in, he thought he had finally arrived when Elvis presented him with his own TCB ("Taking Care of Business") pendant after the Memphis show. In fact Elvis wasn't very impressed with his playing— their personalities didn't seem to click either—and throughout the past year had taken to picking on Duke, even onstage. Eventually Felton erased all of the bass parts Bardwell recorded at these sessions, either at Elvis's instigation or with his consent, replacing them with new recordings by Elvis's proven old friends Mike Leech and Norbert Putnam.

The next number that evening, "T-R-O-U-B-L-E," would be Duke's only surviving record master with Elvis, and then only because RCA rushed it out as a single before Felton could get to the overdubbing. It was also the first new song of the evening, a rock number by Nashville's Jerry Chesnut, and Elvis charged through it with energy and élan; as Duke observed, he "was so good at that syncopated funky stuff." But the most musically expressive moment of the night came after a break, when the band took up one of their usual warm-up routines, "Tiger Man." Elvis joined in instantly, and Rick Ruggieri pushed the RECORD button. Free from an agenda, the group fooled with the song in a way they never could on a show. With room for everyone to play, Ron Tutt and Glen D. took full advantage of the jam until it fell apart a few minutes later and the engineer announced "we got that" to the roomful of unsuspecting musicians.

They returned to business with another new Jerry Chesnut song, a ballad called "Woman Without Love"—simple, unspectacular, and recorded in just one take. Going back to songs from Elvis's teenage years was common practice, of course, so the next number, Faye Adams's 1953 "Shake A Hand," was hardly surprising. Elvis's voice and his unique ability to rethink something old had often made for refreshing cuts in the past, but by 1975 he seemed satisfied just to walk through the tune, offering little more than a strained vocal to complement the predictable arrangement.

After two nights Elvis might not have shown much creative spark, but with eight good masters in the can Felton was optimistic enough to call New York to obtain more master numbers from RCA in hopes that they might get more songs on tape. But Elvis was predictably unpredictable. On the second night, in one of his typical whims, he decided he wanted to cut a cover of Cal Smith's current hit "Country Bumpkin." Felton couldn't see Elvis singing the song, but after a long rehearsal he agreed to send his wife Mary out to buy the record and transcribe the lyrics. The next day, when Felton called for the song, Elvis's only response was to grumble, "Fuck the 'Country Bumpkin.' I'm no country bumpkin."

Another new song, "Bringin' It Back," had been among the huge stack submitted by Voice the previous December. The writer, Greg Gordon, had resigned as the group's piano player just as they went to work for Elvis, and the song they submitted for him was pleasant if not obviously commercial. Tony Brown, Voice's new piano player, had played on the demo, and he was invited to observe the session. "I was hyperventilating. It was heaven," he recalls. Someone told him that "Elvis liked the piano playing on the demo," and when David Briggs announced that Tony was in the control room, before he knew it he found himself playing on the session. As the track was being recorded, Greg Gordon got a call from Elvis's music companies asking for half ownership of the song, and claiming that if they couldn't come to terms the song wouldn't be released. That call represented the single contribution made by Elvis's publishing companies to the session.

Just one more cut was needed to complete an album, and Troy Seals's ballad "Pieces Of My Life" gave Elvis another chance to sing about his regrets—and the sincerity and determination with which he performed the song suggested that he'd had more than a few himself, "My Way" notwithstanding. Take four was a master, and

Elvis kept all the musicians waiting at full session rate while he listened to the playback over and over. Finally Felton transferred the precious master tape to cassette, and Elvis listened to the haunting tune at least thirty times.

Felton would have kept going, but early in the morning the session was interrupted when the door burst open and Beach Boy Brian Wilson forced his way in. He had been recording a solo album next door and insisted on meeting Elvis. "You know, with Elvis," Tony Brown recalls, "he only needed one distraction." Surrounded by the swirl of their personal entourages, the meeting of the two increasingly reclusive stars created an instant commotion that prevented any further recording.

The next night saw the beginning of rehearsals for the upcoming Las Vegas engagement. Five of the new songs from the sessions were selected, as well as older numbers like "Tomorrow Night" and "Wear My Ring Around Your Neck." Two Don Robertson ballads were tried but rejected. As usual there were a number of unrecorded songs that Elvis felt could work in the show but never became regular features, songs like "Susie Q," "You Can Have Her," and "You're The Reason I'm Living."

The rough mixes of the new album, made by RCA's engineer Rick Ruggieri immediately after the sessions, led to a new wave of tension between RCA and Elvis. Although the mixes were only meant to give everybody an idea of what the new material was like, Elvis was furious when he heard them and demanded that Felton remix and overdub the entire batch of material in Nashville before it could be released. As the album was already behind schedule, they reached a compromise on the single, which matched an unrepaired "T-R-O-U-B-L-E" with the recording of "Mr. Songman" from the year before. It would be the last time RCA tried to wield any control over Presley's recordings.

Despite his uneven track record and deteriorating appearance, Elvis remained a popular attraction in Las Vegas and on the road. As long as he kept singing, kept his banter to a minimum, and kept up his frenetic schedule, it seemed he'd be able to go on making money indefinitely. The feel of those shows has been posthumously documented on RCA's *Elvis Aron Presley* (The Silver Box): solid, occasionally engaged, but with little real spark.

120. Live Recordings
May 6–June 9, 1975: Various Locations

Engineer: Bill Porter

Guitar: James Burton	Vocals: Kathy Westmoreland
Guitar: John Wilkinson	Vocals: J. D. Sumner & The Stamps
Guitar, Vocals: Charlie Hodge	Vocals: The Sweet Inspirations
Bass: Jerry Scheff	Vocals: Voice
Drums: Ronnie Tutt	Joe Guercio & His Orchestra
Piano: Glen D. Hardin	

5/6, Athletic Center, Murfreesboro

KPA5 9577 **See See Rider**
Traditional/arranged by Elvis Presley
Elvis Aron Presley
CPL8 3699/1980

KPA5 9578 **I Got A Woman/Amen**
R. Charles—J. Hairston
Elvis Aron Presley
CPL8 3699/1980

6/5, Hofheinz Pavilion, Houston

KPA5 9589 **T-R-O-U-B-L-E**
Jerry Chesnut
Elvis Aron Presley
CPL8 3699/1980

6/6, Memorial Auditorium, Dallas

KPA5 9579 **Love Me**
Jerry Leiber/Mike Stoller
Elvis Aron Presley
CPL8 3699/1980

KPA5 9580 **If You Love Me (Let Me Know)**
John Rostill
Elvis Aron Presley
CPL8 3699/1980

KPA5 9581 **Love Me Tender**
Vera Matson/Elvis Presley
Elvis Aron Presley
CPL8 3699/1980

KPA5 9582 **All Shook Up**
Otis Blackwell/Elvis Presley
Elvis Aron Presley
CPL8 3699/1980

KPA5 9583 **(Let Me Be Your) Teddy Bear/Don't Be Cruel**
K. Mann/B. Lowe—Otis Blackwell/Elvis Presley
Elvis Aron Presley
CPL8 3699/1980

KPA5 9584 **Hound Dog**
Jerry Leiber/Mike Stoller
Elvis Aron Presley
CPL8 3699/1980

KPA5 9585 **The Wonder Of You**
Baker Knight
Elvis Aron Presley
CPL8 3699/1980

KPA5 9586 **Burning Love**
Dennis Linde
Elvis Aron Presley
CPL8 3699/1980

KPA5 9587 **Dialogue/Introductions/Johnny B. Goode**
Chuck Berry
Elvis Aron Presley
CPL8 3699/1980

KPA5 9588 **Introductions/Love Live Rock And Roll**
J. Colyer
Elvis Aron Presley
CPL8 3699/1980

KPA5 9591 **How Great Thou Art**
Stuart K. Hine
Elvis Aron Presley
CPL8 3699/1980

KPA5 9592 **Let Me Be There**
John Rostill
Elvis Aron Presley
CPL8 3699/1980

KPA5 9593 **An American Trilogy**
Mickey Newbury
Elvis Aron Presley
CPL8 3699/1980

6/7, Hirsch Memorial Coliseum, Shreveport

KPA5 9594 **Funny How Time Slips Away**
Willie Nelson
Elvis Aron Presley
CPL8 3699/1980

KPA5 9595 **Little Darlin'**
Maurice Williams
Elvis Aron Presley
CPL8 3699/1980

KPA5 9596	**Mystery Train/Tiger Man**	**Elvis Aron Presley**
	S. Phillips/Jr. Parker—Joe Hill Louis/Sam Burns	*CPL8 3699/1980*
KPA5 9597	**Can't Help Falling In Love**	**Elvis Aron Presley**
	Peretti/Creatore/Weiss	*CPL8 3699/1980*

6/9, Mississippi Coliseum, Jackson

KPA5 9590	**Why Me Lord**	**Elvis Aron Presley**
	Kris Kristofferson	*CPL8 3699/1980*

The above live recordings were edited together to simulate a complete live concert. The recording was done from the mixing console during the May–June 1975 tour, with no possibility of remixing or improving much on the original stereo mixes. The shows were taped only for reference purposes, and never considered for record release while Elvis was alive.

During this period Elvis seems to have gotten more enjoyment from business ventures like an unrealized karate documentary than from his live performances. Music was how he made his living, but his artistic ambitions seemed to have faded altogether. There were occasional, halfhearted attempts to update the show. One scheme had Elvis and the band taking requests from the audience, but that arrangement lasted only five performances, until the August Las Vegas engagement was canceled three days in and Elvis once again checked into the Memphis hospital.

RCA and the Colonel continued trying to package what material they had for record buyers. The album *Promised Land* featured the remainder of the 1973 Stax material; though it included two top-twenty singles, "If You Talk In Your Sleep" and the title cut, it climbed no higher than number forty-seven on the charts. The album cut in March of 1975, *Today,* was an even poorer performer. There was still a far bigger audience for Elvis's past hits, and a midprice compilation called *Pure Gold* sold extremely well for many years; only its pricing kept it off the charts. Older material was repackaged for mail-order outlets, and the Colonel schemed to put out an album called *Elvis Sings For Children (And Grown Ups Too);* not until Elvis's death, though, would the product-starved label finally agree to its release.

While recuperating at Graceland, Elvis began once again working up new material for the Las Vegas engagement, rescheduled now for December. Writing to the Colonel in October, he suggested that they plan a new album for release early in 1976 combining studio material with live recordings from the upcoming show: "This would give a much better flavor with all the new material." But after an initial burst of enthusiasm only two new songs were actually introduced into the show, "America The Beautiful" and "Softly As I Leave You," and the idea for the album was abandoned. Whatever other songs he had in mind would have to wait for the next proper recording session.

121. Live Recordings
December 13, 1975: The Hilton, Las Vegas

Engineer: Bill Porter

Guitar: James Burton
Guitar: John Wilkinson
Guitar, Vocals: Charlie Hodge
Bass: Jerry Scheff
Drums: Ronnie Tutt
Piano: Glen D. Hardin

Vocals: Kathy Westmoreland
Vocals: The Sweet Inspirations
Vocals: J. D. Sumner & The Stamps
Vocals: Sherrill Nielsen
Joe Guercio & His Orchestra

12/13, Midnight Show

HPA5 6102	**Softly As I Leave You**	**Single B-side**
	A. de Vita/H. Shaper	*PB 11212/1978*
GPA5 3809	**America The Beautiful**	**Single B-side**
	Arranged by Elvis Presley	*PB 11165/1977*

These two performances were recorded directly from the mixing console onto a cassette tape.

1976-77

ELVIS LEAVES THE BUILDING

Throughout 1976 Elvis displayed an increasing disaffection with both recording and his life in general. Sherrill Nielsen, a member of Voice, recalls Elvis confiding in him one day in Vegas: "I'm so bored." His producer Felton Jarvis heard the same thing: "I'm so tired of being Elvis Presley." Neither friend doubted the singer's sincerity, but his growing lack of interest was having serious consequences. It was becoming impossible to get Elvis even to consider going back into the studio, despite the obligation of his RCA contract. The plan to record in Las Vegas had fallen through, and the stalemate that followed was only broken when an old idea resurfaced—recording at Graceland. RCA had once promised to build Elvis a studio; now they'd simply bring their recording truck to the house and let Elvis work in his own home. The den at the back of Graceland just behind the kitchen, known to all today as the Jungle Room, was turned into a recording studio. Nashville engineer Brian Christian was sent out two weeks before the session to assess the working conditions and work out how to prepare the room to allow each musician some degree of isolation and headset communication. There were certainly problems to be overcome; all the walls had to be draped with heavy moving blankets to dampen the acoustics, but as far as electrical needs were concerned they were more than covered: Christian was amazed to discover seven hundred amps available for his purposes (the average household has two hundred), as well as a standby generator.

One hundred and fifty miles outside of Memphis the transmission on RCA's big red recording truck died, and the ten-year-old vehicle, which had seen only infrequent use, suffered the humiliation of being towed through the gates of Graceland to what was probably its most prestigious gig. The speakers chosen by New York studio manager Larry Schnapf proved far too small for the room, so Elvis's own bedroom system was dismantled and the two sets of speakers stacked up, producing less than adequate playback sound. Whatever these technical compromises might have meant to the engineers and producer, Elvis was so thrilled with the setup that he wanted to keep the room just as it was when they were finished recording. Probably more out of hope than conviction, Felton Jarvis believed he could deliver twenty new masters on the sessions—enough material for two new albums—and had submitted a budget for six nights of recording that came to $74,378.00.

122. Sessions for RCA
February 2–8, 1976: The Jungle Room, Graceland, Memphis

A&R/Producer: Felton Jarvis
Engineers: Brian Christian

0665-0675:
Guitar: James Burton
Bass: Jerry Scheff
Piano: Glen D. Hardin
Electric Piano: David Briggs (0676)
Guitar: Bill Sanford
Bass: Norbert Putnam
Piano: David Briggs
Electric Piano: Bobby Emmons

0665–0676:
Guitar: John Wilkinson
Guitar: Charlie Hodge
Drums: Ronnie Tutt

Vocals: Kathy Westmoreland
Vocals: Myrna Smith
Vocals: J. D. Sumner & The Stamps

Overdubbed:
Guitar: Chip Young (0666, 0669, 0675)
Bass: Dennis Linde (0669, 0671, 0675)
Congas & Timpani: Farrell Morris (0669, 0672, 0674)
Moog Synthesizer: Shane Keister (0669, 71, 74, 75)
Vocals: Wendellyn Suits, Dolores Edgin (0672, 74, 75, 76)
Vocals: Hurshel Wiginton (0671, 72, 74, 75, 76)
Strings and Horns

2/2, 8–11PM, 11:30PM–2:30AM, 3–6AM, 6:30–9:30AM

FWA5 0665-07	**Bitter They Are, Harder They Are**	**From Elvis Presley Boulevard***
	Larry Gatlin—First Generation Music	*APL1 1506/1976*
FWA5 0666-17	**She Thinks I Still Care**	**Single B-side**
	Dickey Lee—S. Duffy/Gladys Music	*PB 10857/1976*
FWA5 0667-sp	**The Last Farewell**	**From Elvis Presley Boulevard***
	Roger Whittaker/R. A. Webster—Croma Music	*APL1 1506/1976*

2/3, 9PM–12AM, 12:30–3:30AM, 4–7AM, 7:30–10:30AM

FWA5 0668-11	**Solitaire**	**From Elvis Presley Boulevard***
	Neil Sedaka/Phil Cody—Don Kirschner Music/ATV Music/Welbeck Music	*APL1 1506/1976*

2/4, 9PM–12AM, 12:30–3:30AM, 4–7AM, 7:30–10:30AM

FWA5 0669-10	**Moody Blue**	**Single A-side**
	Mark James—Screen Gems, EMI/Sweet Glory Music	*PB 10857/1976*
FWA5 0670-09	**I'll Never Fall In Love Again**	**From Elvis Presley Boulevard***
	Lonnie Donegan/Jimmy Currie—Hollis Music	*APL1 1506/1976*

2/5, 9PM–12AM, 12:30–3:30AM, 4–7AM, 7:30–10:30AM, 11AM–2PM

FWA5 0671-na	**For The Heart**	**Single B-side**
	Dennis Linde—Combine Music	*PB 10601/1976*
FWA5 0672-07	**Hurt**	**Single A-side**
	J. Crane/A. Jacobs—Miller Music	*PB 10601/1976*
FWA5 0673-10	**Danny Boy**	**From Elvis Presley Boulevard***
	Frederic Weatherly—Boosey & Hawkes Inc.	*APL1 1506/1976*

FWA5 0674-14   **Never Again**   **From Elvis Presley Boulevard***
Billy Edd Wheeler/Jerry Chesnut—Imagination/Geronimo Music   *APL1 1506/1976*

FWA5 0675-05   **Love Coming Down**   **From Elvis Presley Boulevard***
Jerry Chesnut—Pass Key Music   *APL1 1506/1976*

F2WB 0676-05   **Blue Eyes Crying In The Rain**   **From Elvis Presley Boulevard***
Fred Rose—Milene Music   *APL1 1506/1976*

*The complete title of APL1 is *From Elvis Presley Boulevard, Memphis, Tennessee.*

RCA's red recording van docked behind Graceland

    Elvis had recorded Larry Gatlin's "Help Me" at Stax in 1973, and had been interested in the writer-singer's second record "Bitter They Are, Harder They Fall," since the period the previous fall he'd spent considering a half-studio, half-Vegas album. This was another of those regret-filled, almost maudlin numbers that continued to speak to Elvis and his abiding despair during these years. The next number, "She Thinks I Still Care," a George Jones standard by Memphis songwriter Dickey Lee, offered more of the same. The musicians tried adding more rhythm and new vocal parts, but finally returned to the original's slow country feel. The final cut of the evening was a cover of Roger Whittaker's "The Last Farewell," an inauspicious selection, but one that allowed them to stick more or less to their schedule. Three songs on the first night was at least some sort of accomplishment—and just how much became unfortunately clear the next day, when they spent all night trying to improve an unconvincing version of Neil Sedaka's "Solitaire."

Perhaps Elvis was looking for a challenge when he turned next to the Tom Jones hit "I'll Never Fall In Love Again." The English star had sighed, moaned, purred, and belted his way through the song, in the manner that delighted his fans while turning the stomachs of nonfollowers. Elvis, though, could no longer compete. It wasn't so much power as tonality that he'd lost, and while he seemed to be trying as hard as he could, it was clear that he could neither hit the notes nor convey the feeling. Discouraged, he set the song aside for later and moved on to a new contribution from songwriter Mark James, who'd done right by him with "Suspicious Minds" and "Always On My Mind." "Moody Blue," built around a discolike Ronnie Tutt drum figure, was strong commercial songwriting, even if it didn't have much in common with anything else in Elvis's body of work. After a number of foul-ups the engineer called out "take eight," to which Elvis replied, "Yeah. Eight, that's my number." It wasn't, and neither was nine, but ten proved to be the charm. They did return to finish the Tom Jones song with a reasonable performance, whose shortcomings Felton made up for in the overdub.

Recognizing that more than thirteen hours had now been spent on just two songs, Felton was forced to rethink his figures, and abashedly sent off to RCA for an additional thirty thousand dollars. The misjudgment wasn't entirely Felton's fault, nor were the problems he was facing at the session. They had actually gotten under way five days behind schedule, and as a result Jerry Scheff, James Burton, and Glen D. had to leave after six days of recording, the latter two to join Emmylou Harris on the road. Then there was Elvis himself: Nothing Felton could do would stop Elvis from wasting hours on Morris Albert's "Feelings," or singing every Platters song he knew. Felton knew that RCA expected him to keep everything under control, but how could you control Elvis Presley?

Through his connection with Bob Beckham at Combine Music, Felton had access to good material that didn't have to be vetted through Elvis's own publishing setup, and now he brought "For The Heart," a new song by Dennis Linde of "Burning Love" fame. For the moment Elvis seemed to relax and enjoy the easy rocker, and the musicians were certainly fired up by the sly, swinging tune. There was even room for Burton to stretch out a bit, and Jerry Scheff had a field day with some sexy sliding bass notes that added a swampy funkiness to it all.

But as usual it was Elvis's own musical memory that brought about the session's high-water mark. Roy Hamilton's early sides had often gotten the best out of Elvis, and now he turned back to Hamilton's big, bravado style, seeking renewed vigor in the source of his original inspiration. Hamilton's "Hurt" had been a top-ten R&B hit in 1955, coming back on the pop charts in the early '60s in a version by Timi Yuro. It was a song with all the right elements for Elvis to make a real commitment: Draping its lyric of abandonment over a hugely demanding melody, it evoked in this troubled, exhausted singer a performance of spellbinding ambition and sincerity. "Hurt" was probably the most convincing recording of Elvis's twilight career, and the song would become the only one from these sessions to make it into Elvis's live repertoire; critic Greil Marcus, some years later, would call it "apocalyptic."

"Hurt" was followed by yet another vocal challenge, as they ended that night's work with another old favorite of his, "Danny Boy." He began with either courage or braggadocio by asking David Briggs to raise the key, but it was too much for him: When he was unable to reach the high note on the word "here," he complained, "I can't make it. I've got too much shit in me, man. I'd like to do it in C. That's where I'd like to do it better." There was none of the usual anger that had so often spurred him on when he sensed failure. In its place was resignation, an acceptance of lesser achievement, and it took a lot of hard work even in the lower key to control that same high note. Take eight was good, take nine an improvement, and take ten became the master. He had at least been able to achieve a convincing display of his full vocal power, as he hadn't the night before with the Tom Jones song. It was two in the afternoon when they stopped—after seventeen hours of recording. "Bring out the booze, Grandma," Elvis joked; his father's mother lived in a room just beyond the kitchen.

When the recording started at midnight the next evening, Elvis was the one who attempted to get the band to loosen up, but the acoustic limitations of the room got in the way: When Ronnie Tutt commented that a take had been "all drums," Elvis thought he said "drunk," remarking: "I can get drunk now, man. You goddamn bum, you don't know where you are at." It was all amicable enough, but a shortened session produced only two numbers, pleasant versions of Jerry Chesnut songs that were destined to be album cuts.

When three of the key musicians left on the following day, Felton shifted David Briggs from electric keyboard to piano, called once again on his friendship with Norbert Putnam to lure the bassist-turned-producer to one more studio session, and for guitar got Billy Sanford, a Nashville session veteran who'd never worked with Elvis before. Throughout this bicentennial year Elvis would frequently perform "America The Beautiful" in his live shows, and now he wanted to tackle the song in the studio: " 'America,' goddamn it." Whatever his intentions, his mind and speech seemed too blurry for him to explain what he wanted, and after a while he gave up. Felton evidently recorded over the performance with a cover of Willie Nelson's "Blue Eyes Crying In The Rain," an old Fred Rose number. Perhaps tired, clearly irritated, Elvis completed one take, then snapped at David Briggs: "Will you give the guitar player a break on the instrumental?" Bill Sanford, who had executed his part perfectly on the first take, messed up the introduction on the next, and Elvis just grumbled, "David, cover him up." Recording wound down by 7:00 A.M. and when the following day was canceled the sessions were over.

Felton Jarvis moved on to Chip Young's little Murfreesboro, Tennessee, studio to overdub and mix what had become a far more costly—and less productive—project than he had anticipated. Yet amid all the trials Felton found some small measure of triumph, too, in the recordings he had managed to capture at Graceland. A month later, sitting in a small restaurant in Johnson City, Tennessee, the producer shared his excitement about the recording of "Danny Boy" with this writer: It was beautiful, he reported, and David Briggs's playing had been incredible. "Hurt," the big-voiced Roy Hamilton ballad, and "For The Heart," Dennis Linde's steady-swinging rock number, were the best Elvis could deliver, but even they were only good enough to move the single up to number twenty-eight on the charts. RCA held "Moody Blue" and "She Thinks I Still Care" for a second single, but they did include the first single on the new album, *From Elvis Presley Boulevard, Memphis, Tennessee,* which featured an unflattering photo on yet another drab sleeve, once again indistinguishable from RCA budget product. There had been two other album releases in 1976: Volume 2 of Joan Deary's hit *Legendary Performer* series, including several rare early cuts, and a long-overdue *Sun Sessions* LP that received almost universal raves. Whatever the format, though, and almost regardless of critical reception, by now

Elvis's albums were almost a presold product, with a diminishing but still sizable fan following. Both the Graceland album and the Deary compilation registered in the forties on the album charts, selling in comparable numbers, while the Sun collection, containing only material that was already available elsewhere, sold half as well.

A second Graceland session was scheduled to begin as soon as Elvis completed his October 14–27 tour. The RCA truck and crew arrived before he got home, and Mike Moran, the engineer who had been so successful in getting the 1973 Stax sessions to sound good, came prepared this time, bringing good speakers and an upgraded Neumann (67) directional mike that would screen out the rumble they had experienced on the previous recordings. After only one day off Elvis and the musicians from his road show assembled at 9:00 P.M. on October 29 to begin.

123. Sessions for RCA
October 29–30, 1976: The Jungle Room, Graceland, Memphis

A&R/Producer: Felton Jarvis
Engineers: Mike Moran

Guitar: James Burton
Guitar: John Wilkinson
Guitar: Chip Young
Guitar: Charlie Hodge
Bass: Jerry Scheff
Drums: Ronnie Tutt
Electric Piano: David Briggs
Piano: Tony Brown

Vocals: Kathy Westmoreland
Vocals: Myrna Smith
Vocals: Sherrill Nielsen
Vocals: J. D. Sumner & the Stamps

Overdubbed:
Percussion: Randy Cullers (1049, 1050)
Steel Guitar: Weldon Myrick (1048, 1052)
Moog Synthesizer: Shane Kesiter (1048)

10/29, 9PM–12AM, 1–4AM, 5–8AM

FWA5 1048-02	**It's Easy For You**	**Moody Blue**
	Andrew Lloyd Webber/Tim Rice—The Hudson Bay Music Co/Elvis Music	*AFL1 2428/1977*
FWA5 1049-02	**Way Down**	**Single A-side**
	Layng Martine, Jr.—Ray Stevens Music	*PB 10998/1977*
FWA5 1050-06	**Pledging My Love**	**Single B-side**
	F. Washington/D. Robey—Lion Pub./ABC Dunhill Music/Wemar Music	*PB 10998/1977*

10/30, 9PM–12AM, 1–4AM, 5–8AM

FWA5 1052-02 (tr)	**He'll Have To Go**	**Moody Blue**
	Joe Allison/Audrey Allison—Central Songs	*AFL1 2428/1977*

Extensive overdubbing on "Way Down" and "Pledging My Love" was done by the full band at Creative Workshop in Nashville on January 22, 1977. Elvis probably overdubbed his vocal on "He'll Have To Go" on 10/31. FWA5 1051 is a backing track only of "There's A Fire Down Below," a song written by Elvis's bass player Jerry Scheff. The Stamps: Ed Enoch, Ed Hill, Larry Strickland. Buck Buckles joined the lineup when overdubs were made in January.

The lyrics to the first song, Andrew Lloyd Webber and Tim Rice's "It's Easy For You," seemed to capture Elvis's plight perfectly: that of a man forced to face the loss of his wife, his new love, even his reason for living. Linda Thompson, Elvis's steady companion since his separation four years ago, was in the process of disentangling herself from Elvis's life, convinced it was a situation she would never be able to control. For all her hope and effort she knew she couldn't live with the extremely difficult man Elvis Presley had become, and she would leave within the next few weeks. More alarming still was Elvis's alienation from some of his oldest and closest associates, in particular his longtime friend Red West. In the past it had always been Red, along with Charlie Hodge, to whom Elvis looked for musical interaction, and Red had written several of the songs that came closest to expressing Elvis's most personal feelings. But Red and his cousin Sonny had been fired in July, and while in the past such fallings-out passed in a matter of weeks or days, now the pair had decided to make the break permanent: Bitter over their firing, they were writing a book that would reveal the hidden dark side of the star's life. On that October night, with his world crumbling around him, Elvis recited a line from the Webber and Rice song: "I had a wife, and I had children. I threw them all away." Then he added, "I get carried away very easily. Emotional son of a bitch." In one rare moment of self-effacing realism, he acknowledged his attraction to all those sad songs, and the vicious circle of depression in which he had locked himself.

Nevertheless, Elvis was in good enough humor to laugh at a few false starts from the band: "We need a red light in here," he quipped, "like in a whorehouse, so these guys will be playing better." David Briggs was playing electric piano, while Tony Brown, who had permanently replaced Glen D., was on acoustic. James Burton had planned to leave when Glen D. did, but relented when Tom Diskin pleaded that Elvis needed him. For all his reluctance to do the session, and for all of his personal suffering, Elvis seemed anxious to get on with it, and their rehearsals for Layng Martine Jr.'s rocker "Way Down" sounded great. "I'm a napalm bomb," he joked, trying to light a fire under the band, and he worried out loud when he thought the tempo was slowing down. It wouldn't be until "Briggs's fingers start bleeding," he said, teasing his favorite piano player, that "we know we've got it." But it was Elvis who messed up the best take before quickly recovering; on the final master the road band sounded better than they ever had on a studio recording.

In the past it had been dangerous business for a band member to suggest a song. But now there was an almost open forum, and Chip Young, who years ago had prompted Elvis to try cutting "Hi-Heel Sneakers," now played Delbert McClinton's version of the 1954 Johnny Ace song "Pledging My Love," from the *Genuine Cowhide* album Chip had produced. Elvis sank his teeth into his own version, drawing on his knowledge of the original recording and the musical moment it came from—that moment in the mid-'50s when blues, country, and gospel were coming together for the first time. Completely caught up, he wrenched every emotion out of the simple lyric for close to five minutes while the band worked, building on a shared experience in a manner worlds apart from the usual frenetic, almost unmusical way they raced through songs onstage.

The next night the band started work without Elvis on a new up-tempo song by bass player Jerry Scheff, "There's A Fire Down Below," playing it in the same vein as "Way Down." When the singer finally arrived, he seemed receptive to the tune, but in their enthusiasm the band's concentration deteriorated in a flurry of silly jokes and dirty language, interrupted by reprimands from Elvis himself: "You guys, straighten up. This is a recording." And then, suddenly, he was gone, returning upstairs to his bedroom. Felton pressed on, laying down an instrumental track for an old Jim Reeves hit, "He'll Have To Go." It was the night before Halloween, and when Elvis and some of his friends returned later they were dressed in gangster outfits and guns that must have alarmed the newer band members. The costume party effectively put an end to the evening's work. The lead vocal for "He'll Have To Go" was probably done the next day, although engineer Mike Moran recalls that Elvis came down on that last day, apologized to everyone for not being up to recording, and excused himself, saying that he hadn't known about the session beforehand. RCA was left with only four new recordings along with the two tunes they were just releasing as the new single, "Moody Blue" and "She Thinks I Still Care"—all told, just over half an album's worth of material.

Another session was quickly scheduled for the following January, and Buzz Carson's Creative Workshop in Nashville was booked for an entire week. Songs were selected, all the musicians arrived, and Elvis got as far as Nashville—but he never made it to the studio, brooding at his motel before turning around and flying back to Memphis. All Felton could do was to use the time to add overdubs to some of the songs from the October session. In the wake of the event the Colonel wrote to RCA president Mel Ilberman to apologize for Elvis, excusing his behavior as the result of a sore throat, including a doctor's note, then going on to speak enthusiastically about the new tour coming up in February. Felton was running out of ideas, but his wife Mary recalled that for a while he traveled around with the master track of "There's A Fire Down Below," hoping somehow to trick Elvis into doing a vocal cut.

Month after month slipped by, as Felton's requests for recording sessions were ignored by Elvis and rendered impossible by the Colonel's never-ending succession of tour dates. The only remaining option was to catch something on one of the tours, where there was always a chance that Elvis might try some unusual song he hadn't previously recorded. But then the quality of the shows, too, was a major concern. Some nights Elvis was so out of it he could barely sing; at best his performances were uninspired, and there were times when they became so traumatic that everyone involved wondered how much longer the charade could continue. The rapidly declining health of Elvis Presley, for two decades one of the world's most written-about celebrities, seemed to be proceeding almost without comment. True, there were reviewers who called him overweight, bloated, tired, uninspired, but sold-out concerts and angry fan letters to the newspapers seemed to leave enough doubt that the rest of the world hardly noticed. Not since "Aloha from Hawaii" had anything really put Elvis in the headlines, and the string of unspectacular albums after 1973 left the media indifferent to the course of his career. The loyal fans could never get enough of Elvis Presley, and although the artist himself had grown tired of the game—years before, he'd complained of how hard it was to live up to an image—it was all he knew how to be, and the only way he could keep himself and everyone around him afloat.

124. Live Recordings for RCA
March–May, 1977: Various Concert Halls

A&R/Producer: Felton Jarvis
Engineers: Clair Brothers

Guitar: James Burton
Guitar: John Wilkinson
Bass: Jerry Scheff
Drums: Ronnie Tutt
Piano: Elvis Presley (2576)
Piano: Tony Brown
Electric Piano: Bobby Ogdin
Vocals: Kathy Westmoreland
Vocals: The Sweet Inspirations
Vocals: Sherrill Nielsen
Vocals: J. D. Sumner & The Stamps
Joe Guercio & His Orchestra

Overdubbed (2576, 77, 78 only):
Guitar: Alan Rush
Bass: Dennis Linde
Bass: Norbert Putnam (2576)
Drums: Randy Cullers
Percussion: Farrell Morris (2576)
Piano: Bobby Ogden
Organ: Tony Brown (2576)
Vocals: J. D. Sumner & The Stamps
Vocals: Dennis Linde, Alan Rush

3/25, 26, Norman, Oklahoma

3/27, Abilene, Texas

3/28, Austin, Texas

3/29, Alexandria, Louisiana

4/23, Toledo, Ohio

4/24, Ann Arbor, Michigan

4/25, Saginaw, Michigan

4/27, Milwaukee, Wisconsin

4/28, Green Bay, Wisconsin

4/29, Duluth, Minnesota

4/30, St. Paul, Minnesota

5/1,2 , Chicago, Illinois

5/3, Saginaw, Michigan

Love Me Tender
Elvis Presley/Vera Matson
Blue Suede Shoes
Carl Perkins
That's All Right
Arthur Crudup
Are You Lonesome Tonight?
Turk/Handman
Blue Christmas
Bill Hayes/Jay Johnson
Trying To Get To You
Rose Marie McCoy/Charles Singleton
Lawdy, Miss Clawdy
Lloyd Price

Ann Arbor, Michigan, April 24, 1977

Jailhouse Rock
Jerry Leiber/Mike Stoller
I Got A Woman/Amen
Ray Charles
Fever
John Davenport/Eddie Cooley
O Sole Mio/It's Now Or Never
Aaron Schroeder/Wally Gold
Little Sister
Doc Pomus/Mort Shuman
(Let Me Be Your) Teddy Bear/Don't Be Cruel
Mann/Lowe—Blackwell/Presley
Help Me
Larry Gatlin

4/24, Ann Arbor, Michigan

GWA5 2576	**Unchained Melody**	**Moody Blue**
	North/Zaret	*AFL1 2428/1977*
GWA5 2575	**Little Darlin'**	**Moody Blue**
	Maurice Williams	*AFL1 2428/1977*

4/24, Saginaw, Michigan

GWA5 2574	**If You Love Me (Let Me Know)**	**Moody Blue**
	John Rostill	*AFL1 2428/1977*

Heartbreak Hotel
Axton/Durden/Presley
Polk Salad Annie
Tony Joe White
Hawaiian Wedding Song
King Hoffman/Manning
Bridge Over Troubled Water
Paul Simon
Big Boss Man
Smith/Dixon—Ludix Pub.
Hound Dog
Jerry Leiber/Mike Stoller

5/2, Chicago, Illinois

WPA5 2599	**My Way**	**Platinum: A Life In Music**
	Anka/Revaux/Francois	*67469-2/1997*

Fairytale
Anita Pointer/Bonnie Pointer
Mystery Train/Tiger Man
H. Parker, Jr.—J. H. Louis/S. Burns

It was from five weeks' worth of primitive four-track recordings that Felton had to piece together a new album, and there were only three possible songs to choose from: the near-parody "Little Darlin'," the lightweight "If You Love Me (Let Me Know)," and a decent version of "Unchained Melody," yet another tribute by Elvis to the great Roy Hamilton.

Meanwhile, the Colonel, in a desperate move to set up anything that might bring in quick income, had negotiated a new television deal. The Colonel knew, as Elvis would have if he could have admitted it, that the only motivation here was money. There was no reason for the deteriorating and increasingly erratic star to attempt the challenge of attracting a new audience, or even rallying the true believers, with another televised concert. But the deal was struck, and the footage for the special was filmed at two June shows in Omaha, Nebraska, and Rapid City, South Dakota.

125. Live Recordings for CBS's "Elvis In Concert"
June 19, 1977: Civic Auditorium, Omaha
June 21, 1977: Rushmore Civic Center, Rapid City

A&R/Producer: Felton Jarvis
Engineers: Bill Harris/Doug Nielson

Guitar: James Burton
Guitar: John Wilkinson
Guitar: Charlie Hodge
Guitar: Elvis Presley
Bass: Jerry Scheff
Drums: Ronnie Tutt
Piano: Tony Brown
Electric Piano: Bobby Ogdin
Vocals: The Sweet Inspirations
Vocals: J. D. Sumner & The Stamps
Vocals: Kathy Westmoreland

Vocals: Sherrill Nielsen
Joe Guercio & His Orchestra

Overdubbed:
Vocals: Jane Fricke, Lea Jane Beranati,
Sherilyn Kramer, Yvonne Hodges
Guitar: Chip Young
Bass: Mike Leech
Drums: Ralph Gallant (aka Larry Londin)
Percussion: Randy Cullers
Piano: Bobby Ogdin

6/19, 8:30PM Show

See See Rider
Arranged by Elvis Presley—Elvis Presley Music
I Got A Woman/Amen
Ray Charles—Hill & Range & Bourne Music
That's All Right
Crudup—Duchess Music
Are You Lonesome Tonight?
Turk/Handman—Bourne Inc./Cromwell Music
Love Me
Jerry Leiber/Mike Stoller—Hill & Range

GPA5 0445 **Fairytale**
Anita Pointer/Bonnie Pointer—Polo Grounds Music/Para Thumb Music

Elvis In Concert
APL2 2587/1977

GPA5 0446	**Little Sister**	**Elvis In Concert**
	Doc Pomus/Mort Shuman—Elvis Presley Music	*APL2 2587/1977*
GPA5 0434	**(Let Me Be Your) Teddy Bear/Don't Be Cruel**	**Elvis In Concert**
	Mann/Lowe—Gladys Music & Blackwell/Presley—Travis Music/E. Presley Music	*APL2 2587/1977*
GPA5 0447	**And I Love You So**	**Elvis In Concert**
	Don McLean—Mayday Music	*APL2 2587/1977*
	Jailhouse Rock	
	Jerry Leiber/Mike Stoller—Elvis Presley Music	
GPA5 0448	**How Great Thou Art**	**Elvis In Concert**
	Stuart K. Hine—Manna Music	*APL2 2587/1977*
	Early Morning Rain	
	Gordon Lightfoot/Warner Bros. Music	
	What'd I Say	
	Ray Charles—Progressive Music	
	Johnny B. Goode	
	Chuck Berry—Arc Music	
	I Really Don't Want To Know	
	Howard Barnes/Don Robertson—Hill & Range	
	Hurt	
	Crane/Jacobs—Miller Music	
	Hound Dog	
	Jerry Leiber/Mike Stoller—Elvis Presley Music/Lion Pub.	
	O Sole Mio/It's Now Or Never	
	Aaron Schroeder/Wally Gold—Gladys Music	
GPA5 0444	**Can't Help Falling In Love**	**Elvis In Concert**
	Peretti/Creatore/Weiss—Gladys Music	*APL2 2587/1977*

6/21, 8:30PM Show

GPA5 0423	**See See Rider**	**Elvis In Concert**
	Arranged by Elvis Presley—Elvis Presley Music	*APL2 2587/1977*
GPA5 0424	**I Got A Woman/Amen**	**Elvis In Concert**
	Ray Charles—Hill & Range & Bourne Music	*APL2 2587/1977*
GPA5 0425	**That's All Right**	**Elvis In Concert**
	Duchess Music	*APL2 2587/1977*
GPA5 0426	**Are You Lonesome Tonight?**	**Elvis In Concert**
	Turk/Handman—Bourne Inc./Cromwell Music	*APL2 2587/1977*
GPA5 0427	**Love Me**	**Elvis In Concert**
	Jerry Leiber/Mike Stoller—Hill & Range	*APL2 2587/1977*
GPA5 0428	**If You Love Me (Let Me Know)**	**Elvis In Concert**
	John Rostill—Al Gallico Music	*APL2 2587/1977*
GPA5 0429	**You Gave Me A Mountain**	**Elvis In Concert**
	Marty Robbins—Elvis Presley Music/Unichappell/Mojave Music	*APL2 2587/1977*

GPA5 0430	**Jailhouse Rock**	**Elvis In Concert**
	Jerry Leiber/Mike Stoller—Elvis Presley Music	*APL2 2587/1977*
GPA5 0431	**O Sole Mio/It's Now Or Never**	**Elvis In Concert**
	Aaron Schroeder/Wally Gold—Gladys Music	*APL2 2587/1977*
GPA5 0432	**Trying To Get To You**	**Elvis In Concert**
	Rose Marie McCoy/Charles Singleton—Slow Dancing Music	*APL2 2587/1977*
GPA5 0433	**Hawaiian Wedding Song**	**Elvis In Concert**
	King/Hoffman/Manning—Pickwick Music	*APL2 2587/1977*
	(Let Me Be Your) Teddy Bear/Don't Be Cruel	
	Mann/Lowe—Gladys Music & Blackwell/Presley—Travis Music/Elvis Presley Music	
GPA5 0436	**My Way**	**Elvis In Concert**
	Anka/Revaux/Francois—S.D.R.M./Spanka Music	*APL2 2587/1977*
GPA5 0437	**Early Morning Rain**	**Elvis In Concert**
	Gordon Lightfoot—Warner Bros. Music	*APL2 2587/1977*
GPA5 0438	**What'd I Say**	**Elvis In Concert**
	Ray Charles—Progressive Music	*APL2 2587/1977*
GPA5 0439	**Johnny B. Goode**	**Elvis In Concert**
	Chuck Berry—Arc Music	*APL2 2587/1977*
GPA5 0440	**I Really Don't Want To Know**	**Elvis In Concert**
	Howard Barnes/Don Robertson—Hill & Range	*APL2 2587/1977*
GPA5 0441	**Hurt**	**Elvis In Concert**
	Crane/Jacobs—Miller Music	*APL2 2587/1977*
GPA5 0442	**Hound Dog**	**Elvis In Concert**
	Jerry Leiber/Mike Stoller—Elvis Presley Music/Lion Pub.	*APL2 2587/1977*
GPA5 0443	**Unchained Melody**	**Single A-side**
	North/Zaret—Frank Music	*PB 11212/1978*
	Can't Help Falling In Love	
	Peretti/Creatore/Weiss—Gladys Music	

Overdubs were done at Yougun' Studio, Nashville, on August 28 and 29, 1977.

The first show was a disaster. Bloated, pale, and incoherent, Elvis stumbled through it trying desperately to keep his performance together. In the wings his staff was sure he would collapse, and they anxiously tried to help by signaling cues. At one point Elvis announced the song "Are You Lonesome Tonight?", then stopped as if to reflect on the title, before continuing as if to himself: "and I am, and I was ... " The cameras and tape recorders caught it all, but CBS was certain that much of the show was virtually unusable. Their only hope hung on the second show, and it was barely good enough to justify completion of the special.

Felton Jarvis had spent the last several months traveling with the tour; endeavoring to collect material to complete the *Moody Blue* album, ultimately he would dis-

card virtually every recording he had out of fear that releasing performances this poor could only be detrimental to Elvis's career. He did finally succeed in compiling an album of ten songs, among which four had already appeared on singles and one was the previously released 1974 recording of "Let Me Be There." The new single would consist of "Way Down," which really did show some sparkle, and the passionate "Pledging My Love." Yet after rejecting dozens of live performances he had recorded months earlier, now Felton was given the unwelcome task of crafting a *Hawaii*-style double album from the TV special—an album that could only be crippling to the same image he'd been trying to protect.

The next tour was to start in Portland, Maine, on August 16. But on that very morning Elvis died, and a new tabloid life, and a new career, began. Only the Colonel seemed to foresee it: "It's just like when he went in the army," he said. Many took the comment as profound cynicism, but it simply reflected reality: Immediately following Elvis's death a global assault on record stores began, and Presley "merchandise" began selling again in numbers not seen since 1956. The almost universal gloating and tabloid derision that erupted after his death was in many ways a tragic reversal of the bright image of hope and promise with which Elvis had started out his career.

Gradually, though, the sniping faded, and in its wake came a new wave of interest in Elvis Presley the performer. Even before his death, RCA had discovered a real demand among fans for unreleased music, and in the two decades after 1977 the label released a steady stream of newly rediscovered material—underwriting the effort to restore a sense of coherence to his body of work. A systematic survey of the RCA vaults (and contributions from Graceland and elsewhere) uncovered countless new gems and insights, from the earliest acetates to a host of outtakes and private recordings. And the culmination of these programs was the release of three major box sets covering the whole of Elvis's

career in the studio, sets that for the first time put his recordings in order and in context. When the first of these, 1992's *The King Of Rock 'N' Roll: The Complete '50s Masters,* sold over half a million sets at eighty dollars apiece, it seemed as though the abiding agendas of Tom Parker, RCA Records, and Elvis Presley had finally converged. By that time, in our worldwide culture, the name Elvis Presley had become its own definition, requiring no other point of reference, embodying all the contradictions, all the anomalies, and all the beauty that his music at its best had achieved.

"We will never agree on anything as we agreed on Elvis," declared writer Lester Bangs with the baleful romanticism of a twenty-seven-year-old when he heard the news of the death. And what we agreed on most was his music.

Elvis Presley
3764 Elvis Presley Blvd. • Memphis, Tenn. 38116

Tour #6 August

	August 17	Portland, MA
Wednesday	August 18	Portland, MA
Thursday	August 19	Utica, NY
Friday	August 20	Syracuse, NY
Saturday	August 21	Syracuse, NY
Sunday	August 22	Uniondale, NY
Monday	August 23	Lexington, KY
Tuesday	August 24	Roanoke, VA
Wednesday	August 25	Fayetteville, NC
Thursday	August 26	Asheville, NC
Friday	August 27	Memphis, Tn
Saturday	August 28	Memphis, Tn
Sunday		

This is the only schedule we have at present since RCA Tours does book each tour individually and we get last minute notice. There is nothing scheduled for Tahoe nor nothing definate yet for Las Vegas.

DISCOGRAPHY 1954–1977

Singles: Until 1968, the U.S. *Billboard* singles chart featured both sides of a record, based on sales and airplay reports. Chart placings for EPs represent singles-list chartings except where noted. (From September 1957 through 1960, EPs had their own separate charts.) RIAA status as of November 1997: E: gold; P: platinum.

Cat. no.	Title	Release Date	Top US Chart Position A/B Side	RIAA Status
Sun 209	That's All Right/Blue Moon Of Kentucky	7/54		
Sun 210	Good Rockin' Tonight/I Don't Care If The Sun Don't Shine	9/54		
Sun 215	Milkcow Blues Boogie/You're A Heartbreaker	1/55		
Sun 217	Baby Let's Play House/I'm Left, You're Right, She's Gone	4/55		
Sun 223	I Forgot To Remember To Forget/Mystery Train	8/55		

The above five Sun singles were rereleased by RCA in December 1955

Cat. no.	Title	Release Date	Top US Chart Position A/B Side	RIAA Status
20/47-6420	Heartbreak Hotel/I Was The One	1/56	1/23	P
LPM 1254	**ELVIS PRESLEY (LP)**	**3/56**	**1**	**G**

Blue Suede Shoes/I'm Counting On You/I Got A Woman/One-Sided Love Affair/I Love You Because/Just Because/Tutti Frutti/Trying To Get To You/I'm Gonna Sit Right Down And Cry (Over You)/I'll Never Let You Go (Little Darlin')/Blue Moon/Money Honey

Cat. no.	Title	Release Date	Top US Chart Position A/B Side	RIAA Status
EPA 747	**ELVIS PRESLEY (EP)**	**3/56**	**24**	**G**

Blue Suede Shoes/Tutti Frutti/I Got A Woman/Just Because

Cat. no.	Title	Release Date	Top US Chart Position A/B Side	RIAA Status
EPB 1254	**ELVIS PRESLEY (double EP)**	**3/56**		

Blue Suede Shoes/I'm Counting On You/I'm Gonna Sit Right Down And Cry/I'll Never Let You Go (Little Darlin')/I Got A Woman/One-Sided Love Affair/Tutti Frutti/Trying To Get To You

Cat. no.	Title	Release Date	Top US Chart Position A/B Side	RIAA Status
20/47-6540	I Want You, I Need You, I Love You/My Baby Left Me	5/56	3/31	P
EPA 821	**HEARTBREAK HOTEL**	**5/56**	**76**	**G**

Heartbreak Hotel/I Was The One/Money Honey/I Forgot To Remember To Forget

EPA 830	**ELVIS PRESLEY**	6/56	55	G
Shake, Rattle And Roll/I Love You Because/Lawdy, Miss Clawdy/Blue Moon				
20/47-6604	Don't Be Cruel/Hound Dog	7/56	1/2	3×P
20/47-6636	Blue Suede Shoes/Tutti Frutti	8/56		
20/47-6637	I Got A Woman/I'm Counting On You	8/56		
20/47-6638	I'll Never Let You Go/I'm Gonna Sit Right Down And Cry	8/56		
20/47-6639	I Love You Because/Trying To Get To You	8/56		
20/47-6640	Just Because/Blue Moon	8/56		
20/47-6641	Money Honey/One-Sided Love Affair	8/56		
20/47-6642	Shake, Rattle And Roll/Lawdy, Miss Clawdy	8/56		
20/47-6643	Love Me Tender/Any Way You Want Me	9/56	1/27	2×P
EPA 940	**THE REAL ELVIS (EP)**	10/56		P
Don't Be Cruel/I Want You, I Need You, I Love You/Hound Dog/My Baby Left Me				
EPA 965	**ANY WAY YOU WANT ME (EP)**	10/56	74	
Any Way You Want Me/I'm Left, You're Right, She's Gone/I Don't Care If The Sun Don't Shine/Mystery Train				
LPM 1382	**ELVIS (LP)**	10/56	1	G
Rip It Up/Love Me/When My Blue Moon Turns To Gold Again/Long Tall Sally/First In Line/Paralyzed/So Glad You're Mine/Old Shep/Ready Teddy/Anyplace Is Paradise/How's The World Treating You/How Do You Think I Feel				
EPA 992	**ELVIS VOL. 1 (EP)**	10/56	6	2×P
Rip It Up/Love Me/When My Blue Moon Turns To Gold Again/Paralyzed				
EPA 4006	**LOVE ME TENDER (EP)**	11/56	35	P
Love Me Tender/Let Me/Poor Boy/We're Gonna Move				
EPA 993	**ELVIS VOL. 2 (EP)**	12/56	47	G
So Glad You're Mine/Old Shep/Ready Teddy/Anyplace Is Paradise				
20/47-6800	Too Much/Playing For Keeps	1/57	2/34	P
EPA 994	**STRICTLY ELVIS (EP)**	1/57		
Long Tall Sally/First In Line/How Do You Think I Feel/How's The World Treating You				
20/47-6870	All Shook Up/That's When Your Heartaches Begin	3/57	1/58	2×P
EPA 4054	**PEACE IN THE VALLEY (EP)**	4/57	39	P
Peace In The Valley/It Is No Secret/I Believe/Take My Hand, Precious Lord				
20/47-7000	(Let Me Be Your) Teddy Bear/Loving You	6/57	1/28	P

LPM 1515	**LOVING YOU**	**7/57**	**1**	**G**

Mean Woman Blues/Teddy Bear/Loving You/Got A Lot O' Livin' To Do/Lonesome Cowboy/Hot Dog/Party/Blueberry Hill/True Love/Don't Leave Me Now/Have I Told You Lately That I Love You/I Need You So

EPA 1 1515	**LOVING YOU (EP)**	**8/57**	**1(EP)**	**G**

Loving You/Party/Teddy Bear/True Love

EPA 2 1515	**LOVING YOU (EP)**	**8/57**	**4(EP)**	**P**

Lonesome Cowboy/Hot Dog/Mean Woman Blues/Got A Lot O' Livin' To Do

EPA 4041	**JUST FOR YOU (EP)**	**9/57**	**2(EP)**	

I Need You So/Have I Told You Lately That I Love You/Blueberry Hill/Is It So Strange

20/47-7035	Jailhouse Rock/Treat Me Nice	9/57	1/27	2×P

LOC 1035	**ELVIS' CHRISTMAS ALBUM (LP)**	**10/57**	**1**	**2×P**

Santa Claus Is Back In Town/White Christmas/Here Comes Santa Claus/I'll Be Home For Christmas/Blue Christmas/Santa Bring My Baby Back/O Little Town Of Bethlehem/Silent Night/Peace In The Valley/I Believe/Take My Hand, Precious Lord/It Is No Secret

EPA 4108	**ELVIS SINGS CHRISTMAS SONGS (EP)**	**10/57**	**1 (EP)**	**P**

Santa Bring My Baby Back/Blue Christmas/Santa Claus Is Back In Town/I'll Be Home For Christmas

EPA 4114	**JAILHOUSE ROCK (EP)**	**11/57**	**1 (EP)**	**2×P**

Jailhouse Rock/Young And Beautiful/I Want To Be Free/Don't Leave Me Now/Baby I Don't Care

20/47-7150	Don't/I Beg Of You	1/58	1/8	P

LPM 1707	**ELVIS' GOLDEN RECORDS (LP)**	**3/58**	**3**	**5×P**

Hound Dog/Loving You/All Shook Up/Heartbreak Hotel/Jailhouse Rock/Love Me/Too Much/Don't Be Cruel/That's When Your Heartaches Begin/Teddy Bear/Love Me Tender/Treat Me Nice/Any Way You Want Me/I Want You, I Need You, I Love You

20/47-7240	Wear My Ring Around Your Neck/Doncha' Think It's Time	4/58	3/21	P
20/47-7280	Hard Headed Woman/Don't Ask Me Why	6/58	2/28	P

EPA 4319	**KING CREOLE VOL. 1 (EP)**	**7/58**	**1 (EP)**	**P**

King Creole/New Orleans/As Long As I Have You/Lover Doll

EPA 4321	**KING CREOLE VOL. 2 (EP)**	**8/58**	**1 (EP)**	**P**

Trouble/Young Dreams/Crawfish/Dixieland Rock

LPM 1884   **KING CREOLE (LP)**   8/58   2

King Creole/As Long As I Have You/Hard Headed Woman/Trouble/Dixieland Rock/Don't Ask Me Why/Lover Doll (with chorus)/Young Dreams/Crawfish/Steadfast, Loyal And True/New Orleans

47-7410   One Night/I Got Stung   10/58   4/8   P

EPA 4340   **CHRISTMAS WITH ELVIS (EP)**   10/58

White Christmas/Here Comes Santa Claus/O Little Town Of Bethlehem/Silent Night

EPA 4325   **ELVIS SAILS (EP)**   12/58   2 (EP)

Press interview with Elvis Presley, September 22, 1958/Elvis Presley's Newsreel interview/Pat Hernon interviews Elvis at sailing

LPM 1990   **FOR LP FANS ONLY (LP)**   2/59   19

That's All Right/Lawdy, Miss Clawdy/Mystery Train/Playing For Keeps/Poor Boy/My Baby Left Me/I Was The One/Shake, Rattle And Roll/I'm Left, You're Right, She's Gone/You're A Heartbreaker

47-7506   A Fool Such As I/I Need Your Love Tonight   3/59   2/4   P

EPA 5088   **A TOUCH OF GOLD VOL. 1 (EP)**   4/21/59

Hard Headed Woman/Good Rockin' Tonight/Don't/I Beg Of You

47-7600   A Big Hunk O' Love/My Wish Came True   6/59   1/12   G

LPM 2011   **A DATE WITH ELVIS (LP)**   8/59   32

Blue Moon Of Kentucky/Young And Beautiful/Baby I Don't Care/Milkcow Blues Boogie/Baby Let's Play House/Good Rockin' Tonight/Is It So Strange/We're Gonna Move/I Want To Be Free/I Forgot To Remember To Forget

EPA 5101   **A TOUCH OF GOLD VOL. 2 (EP)**   9/02/59

Wear My Ring Around Your Neck/Treat Me Nice/One Night/That's All Right

LPM 2075   **ELVIS' GOLD RECORDS VOL. 2 (LP)**   12/59   31   P

I Need Your Love Tonight/Don't/Wear My Ring Around Your Neck/My Wish Came True/I Got Stung/One Night/A Big Hunk O' Love/I Beg Of You/A Fool Such As I/Doncha' Think It's Time (splice of takes 40 and 39)

EPA 5141   **A TOUCH OF GOLD VOL. 3 (EP)**   2/60

Too Much/All Shook Up/Don't Ask Me Why/Blue Moon Of Kentucky

47/61-7740   Stuck On You/Fame And Fortune   3/60   1/17   P

LSP/LPM 2231 ELVIS IS BACK (LP)   4/60   2

Make Me Know It/Fever/The Girl Of My Best Friend/I Will Be Home Again/Dirty, Dirty Feeling/Thrill Of Your Love/Soldier Boy/Such A Night/It Feels So Right/The Girl Next Door Went A'Walking/Like A Baby/Reconsider Baby

47/61-7777   It's Now Or Never/A Mess Of Blues   7/60   1/32   P

LSP/LPM G.I. BLUES (LP)   10/60   1   P

Tonight Is So Right For Love/What's She Really Like/Frankfort Special/Wooden Heart/G.I. Blues/Pocketful Of Rainbows/Shoppin' Around/Big Boots/Didja' Ever/Blue Suede Shoes/Doin' The Best I Can (outside the U.S. and Canada "Tonight's All Right For Love" replaced "Tonight Is So Right For Love")

47/61-7810   Are You Lonesome Tonight?/I Gotta Know   11/60   1/20   2×P

LSP/LPM 2328 HIS HAND IN MINE (LP)   11/60   13   P

His Hand In Mine/I'm Gonna Walk Dem Golden Stairs/In My Father's House/Milky White Way/Known Only To Him/I Believe In The Man In The Sky/Joshua Fit The Battle/He Knows Just What I Need/Swing Down Sweet Chariot/Mansion Over The Hilltop

47/61-7850   Surrender/Lonely Man   2/61   1/32   P

LPC 128 ELVIS BY REQUEST/FLAMING STAR (EP)   2/61   14

Flaming Star/Summer Kisses, Winter Tears/Are You Lonesome Tonight?/It's Now Or Never

47/61-7880   I Feel So Bad/Wild In The Country   5/61   5/26   G

LSP/LPM 2370 SOMETHING FOR EVERYBODY (LP)   6/61   1

There's Always Me/Give Me The Right/It's A Sin/Sentimental Me/Starting Today/Gently/I'm Comin' Home/In Your Arms/Put The Blame On Me/Judy/I Want You With Me/I Slipped, I Stumbled, I Fell

47-7908   His Latest Flame/Little Sister   8/61   4/5   G

LSP/LPM 2426 BLUE HAWAII (LP)   10/61   1   2×P

Blue Hawaii/Almost Always True/Aloha Oe/No More/Can't Help Falling In Love/Rock-A-Hula Baby/Moonlight Swim/Ku-U-I-Po/Ito Eats/Slicin' Sand/Hawaiian Sunset/Beach Boy Blues/Island Of Love/Hawaiian Wedding Song

47-7968   Can't Help Falling In Love/Rock-A-Hula Baby   11/61   2/23   P

47-7992   Good Luck Charm/Anything That's Part Of You   2/62   1/31   P

EPA 4368 FOLLOW THAT DREAM (EP)   4/62   15   P

Follow That Dream/Angel/What A Wonderful Life/I'm Not The Marrying Kind

LSP/LPM 2523 POT LUCK (LP) 6/62 4

Kiss Me Quick/Just For Old Time Sake/Gonna Get Back Home Somehow/Easy Question/Steppin' Out Of Line/I'm Yours/Something Blue/Suspicion/I Feel That I've Known You Forever/Night Rider/Fountain Of Love/That's Someone You Never Forget

47/8041   She's Not You/Just Tell Her Jim Said Hello   7/62   5/55   G

EPA 4371 KID GALAHAD (EP) 8/62 30 G

King Of The Whole Wide World/This Is Living/Riding The Rainbow/Home Is Where The Heart Is/I Got Lucky/A Whistling Tune

47-8100   Return To Sender/Where Do You Come From   10/62   2/99   P

LSP/LPM 2621 GIRLS! GIRLS! GIRLS! 11/62 3 G

Girls! Girls! Girls!/I Don't Wanna Be Tied/Where Do You Come From/I Don't Want To/We'll Be Together/A Boy Like Me, A Girl Like You/Earth Boy/Return To Sender/Because Of Love/Thanks To The Rolling Sea/Song Of The Shrimp/The Walls Have Ears/We're Coming In Loaded

47-8134   One Broken Heart For Sale/They Remind Me Too Much Of You   1/63   11/53   G

LSP/LPM 2697 IT HAPPENED AT THE WORLD'S FAIR (LP) 4/63 4

Beyond The Bend/Relax/Take Me To The Fair/They Remind Me Too Much Of You/One Broken Heart For Sale/I'm Falling In Love Tonight/Cotton Candy Land/A World Of Our Own/How Would You Like To Be/Happy Ending

47-8188   Devil In Disguise/Please Don't Drag That String Around   6/63   3   G

LSP/LPM 2765 ELVIS' GOLDEN RECORDS VOL. 3 (LP) 8/63 3 P

It's Now Or Never/Stuck On You/Fame And Fortune/I Gotta Know/Surrender/I Feel So Bad/Are You Lonesome Tonight?/His Latest Flame/Little Sister/Good Luck Charm/Anything That's Part Of You/She's Not You

47-8243   Bossa Nova Baby/Witchcraft   10/63   8/32   G

LSP/LPM 2756 FUN IN ACAPULCO (LP) 11/63 3

Fun In Acapulco/Vino, Dinero Y Amor/Mexico/El Toro/Marguerita/The Bullfighter Was A Lady/(There's) No Room To Rhumba In A Sports Car/I Think I'm Gonna Like It Here/Bossa Nova Baby/You Can't Say No In Acapulco/Guadalajara/Love Me Tonight/Slowly But Surely

47-8307   Kissin' Cousins/It Hurts Me   2/64   12/29   G

LSP/LPM 2894   KISSIN' COUSINS (LP)   **4/64**   **6**

Kissin' Cousins (Number 2)/Smokey Mountain Boy/There's Gold In The Mountains/One Boy Two Little Girls/Catchin' On Fast/Tender Feeling/Anyone/Barefoot Ballad/Once Is Enough/Kissin' Cousins/Echoes Of Love/Long Lonely Highway

447-0639	Kiss Me Quick/Suspicion	4/64	34	
47-8360	What'd I Say/Viva Las Vegas	4/64	21/29	G

EPA 4382   VIVA LAS VEGAS (EP)   **5/64**   **92**

If You Think I Don't Need You/I Need Somebody To Lean On/C'mon Everybody/Today, Tomorrow And Forever

47-8400	Such A Night/Never Ending	7/64	16/-	
47-8440	Ask Me/Ain't That Loving You Baby	9/64	12/16	G

LSP/LPM 2999   ROUSTABOUT (LP)   **10/64**   **1**   **G**

Roustabout/Little Egypt/Poison Ivy League/Hard Knocks/It's A Wonderful World/Big Love, Big Heartaches/One Track Heart/It's Carnival Time/Carny Town/There's A Brand New Day On The Horizon/Wheels On My Heels

447-0720	Blue Christmas/Wooden Heart	11/64	
47-8500	Do The Clam/You'll Be Gone	2/65	21/-

LSP/LPM 3338   GIRL HAPPY (LP)   **3/65**   **8**

Girl Happy/Spring Fever/Fort Lauderdale Chamber Of Commerce/Startin' Tonight/Wolf Call/Do Not Disturb/ Cross My Heart And Hope To Die/The Meanest Girl In Town/Do The Clam/Puppet On A String/I've Got To Find My Baby/ You'll Be Gone

447-0643	Crying In The Chapel/I Believe In The Man In The Sky	4/65	3/-	P
47-8585	Easy Question/It Feels So Right	6/65	11/55	

EPA 4383   TICKLE ME (EP)   **6/65**   **70**

I Feel That I've Known You Forever/Slowly But Surely/Night Rider/Put The Blame On Me/Dirty Dirty Feeling

47-8657	I'm Yours/Long Lonely Highway (take 1)	8/65	11	G

LSP/LPM 3450   ELVIS FOR EVERYONE (LP)   **8/65**   **10**

Your Cheatin' Heart/Summer Kisses, Winter Tears/Finders Keepers, Losers Weepers/In My Way/Tomorrow Night (dubbed version)/Memphis Tennessee/For The Millionth And The Last Time/Forget Me Never/Sound Advice/Santa Lucia/I Met Her Today/When It Rains, It Really Pours

447-0650	Puppet On A String/Wooden Heart	10/65	14	G
447-0647	Santa Claus Is Back In Town/Blue Christmas	10/65		G

LSP/LPM 3468   HARUM SCARUM (LP)   11/65   8

Harem Holiday/My Desert Serenade/Go East/Young Man/Mirage/Kismet/Shake That Tambourine/Hey Little Girl/Golden Coins/So Close, Yet So Far/Animal Instinct/Wisdom Of The Ages

47-8740	Tell Me Why/Blue River	12/65	33/95	G
447-0651	Joshua Fit The Battle/Known Only To Him	2/66		
447-0652	Milky White Way/Swing Down Sweet Chariot	2/66		
47-8780	Frankie And Johnny/Please Don't Stop Loving Me	3/66	25/45	G

LSP/LPM 3553   FRANKIE AND JOHNNY (LP)   3/66   20

Frankie And Johnny/Come Along/Petunia, The Gardener's Daughter/Chesay/What Every Woman Lives For/Look Out, Broadway/Beginner's Luck/Down By The Riverside—When The Saints Go Marchin' In/Shout It Out/Hard Luck/Please Don't Stop Loving Me/Everybody Come Aboard

47-8870	Love Letters/Come What May	6/66	19

LSP/LPM 3643   PARADISE, HAWAIIAN STYLE (LP)   6/66   15

Paradise, Hawaiian Style/Queenie Wahine's Papaya/Scratch My Back/Drums Of The Islands/Datin'/A Dog's Life/House Of Sand/Stop Where You Are/This Is My Heaven/Sand Castles

47-8941	Spinout/All That I Am	9/66	40/41

LSP/LPM 3702   SPINOUT (LP)   10/66   18

Stop, Look And Listen/Adam And Evil/All That I Am/Never Say Yes/Am I Ready/Beach Shack/Spinout/Smorgasbord/I'll Be Back/Tomorrow Is A Long Time/Down In The Alley/I'll Remember You

47-8950	If Every Day Was Like Christmas/ How Would You Like To Be	11/66	
47-9056	Indescribably Blue/Fools Fall In Love	1/67	33

LSP/LPM 3758   HOW GREAT THOU ART (LP)   2/67   18   2×P

How Great Thou Art/In The Garden/Somebody Bigger Than You And I/Farther Along/Stand By Me/Without Him/ So High/Where Could I Go But To The Lord/By And By/If The Lord Wasn't Walking By My Side/Run On/Where No One Stands Alone/Crying In The Chapel

EAP 4387   EASY COME, EASY GO (EP)   3/67

Easy Come, Easy Go/The Love Machine/Yoga Is As Yoga Does/You Gotta Stop/Sing You Children/I'll Take Love

47-9115	Long Legged Girl/That's Someone You Never Forget	4/67	63/92

LSP/LPM 3787   DOUBLE TROUBLE (LP)   6/67   47

Double Trouble/Baby, If You'll Give Me All Of Your Love/Could I Fall In Love/Long Legged Girl/City By Night/Old MacDonald/I Love Only One Girl/There Is So Much World To See/It Won't Be Long/Never Ending/Blue River/What Now, What Next, Where To

| 47-9287 | There's Always Me/Judy | 8/67 | 56/78 |
| 47-9341 | Big Boss Man/You Don't Know Me (47/9341) | 9/67 | 38/44 |

LSP/LPM 3893   CLAMBAKE (LP)   10/67   40

Guitar Man/Clambake/Who Needs Money?/A House That Has Everything/Confidence/Hey, Hey, Hey/You Don't Know Me/The Girl I Never Loved/How Can You Lose What You Never Had/Big Boss Man/Singing Tree

| 47-9425 | Guitar Man/Hi Heel Sneakers | 1/68 | 43 |

LSP/LPM 3921   ELVIS GOLD RECORDS VOL. 4 (LP)   1/68   33   G

Love Letters/Witchcraft/It Hurts Me/What'd I Say/Please Don't Drag That String Around/Indescribably Blue/Devil In Disguise/Lonely Man/A Mess Of Blues/Ask Me/Ain't That Loving You Baby/Just Tell Her Jim Said Hello

47-9465	U.S. Male/Stay Away	2/68	28/67
47-9600	You'll Never Walk Alone/We Call On Him	3/68	90
47-9547	Your Time Hasn't Come Yet, Baby/Let Yourself Go	5/68	71/72

LSP/LPM 3989   SPEEDWAY (LP)   5/68   82

Speedway/There Ain't Nothing Like A Song/Your Time Hasn't Come Yet, Baby/Who Are You?/He's Your Uncle Not Your Dad/Let Yourself Go/Five Sleepy Heads/Suppose/Your Groovy Self (Nancy Sinatra)/Five Sleepyheads/Western Union/Mine/Goin' Home/Suppose

| 47-9610 | A Little Less Conversation/Almost In Love | 9/68 | 69/95 |

PRS 279   SINGER PRESENTS ELVIS
**   SINGING FLAMING STAR AND OTHERS (LP)**   10/68

Flaming Star/Wonderful World/Night Life/All I Needed Was The Rain/Too Much Monkey Business/Yellow Rose Of Texas/The Eyes Of Texas/She's A Machine/Do The Vega/Tiger Man (sold only through Singer sewing machine shops)

| 47-9670 | If I Can Dream/Edge Of Reality | 11/68 | 12 | G |

LPM 4088   ELVIS NBC-TV SPECIAL (LP)   12/68   8   G

Trouble—Guitar Man/Lawdy, Miss Clawdy/Baby What You Want Me To Do/Heartbreak Hotel—Hound Dog—All Shook Up/Can't Help Falling In Love/Jailhouse Rock/Love Me Tender/Where Could I Go But To The Lord—Up Above My Head—Saved/Blue Christmas/One Night/Memories/Nothingville—Big Boss Man—Guitar Man—Little Egypt—Trouble—Guitar Man/If I Can Dream

| 47-9731 | Memories/Charro | 2/69 | 35 |
| 74-0130 | His Hand In Mine/How Great Thou Art | 3/69 | |

CAS 2304   **ELVIS SINGS FLAMING STAR (budget LP)**   **3/69**   **96**

(Content identical to PRS 279)

47-9741   In The Ghetto/Any Day Now   4/69   3   P

LSP 4155   **FROM ELVIS IN MEMPHIS (LP)**   **6/69**   **13**   **G**

Wearin' That Loved On Look/Only The Strong Survive/I'll Hold You In My Heart/Long Black Limousine/It Keeps Right On A-Hurtin'/I'm Movin' On/Power Of My Love/Gentle On My Mind/After Loving You/True Love Travels On A Gravel Road/Any Day Now/In The Ghetto

47-9747   Clean Up Your Own Back Yard/The Fair's Moving On   6/69   35   G
47-9764   Suspicious Minds/You'll Think Of Me   8/69   1   P

LSP 6020   **FROM MEMPHIS TO VEGAS/**
             FROM VEGAS TO MEMPHIS (2 LPS)   **11/69**   **12**   **G**

ELVIS IN PERSON AT THE INTERNATIONAL HOTEL: Blue Suede Shoes/Johnny B. Goode/All Shook Up/Are You Lonesome Tonight?/Hound Dog/I Can't Stop Loving You/My Babe/Mystery Train/Tiger Man/Words/In The Ghetto/Suspicious Minds/Can't Help Falling In Love
BACK IN MEMPHIS: Inherit The Wind/This Is The Story/Stranger In My Own Home Town/A Little Bit Of Green/And The Grass Won't Pay No Mind/Do You Know Who I Am?/From A Jack To A King/The Fair Is Moving On/You'll Think Of Me/Without Love

47-9678   Don't Cry Daddy/Rubberneckin'   11/69   6   P
47-9791   Kentucky Rain/My Little Friend   1/70   16   G

CAS 2408   **LET'S BE FRIENDS (Budget LP)**   **4/70**   **105**

Stay Away, Joe/If I'm A Fool (For Loving You)/Let's Be Friends/Let's Forget About The Stars/Mama/I'll Be There/Almost/Change Of Habit/Have A Happy

47-9835   The Wonder Of You/Mama Liked The Roses   4/70   9   G

LSP 4362   **ON STAGE (LP)**   **6/70**   **13**   **G**

See See Rider/Release Me/Sweet Caroline/Runaway/The Wonder Of You/Polk Salad Annie/Yesterday/Proud Mary/Walk A Mile In My Shoes/Let It Be Me

47-9873   I've Lost You/The Next Step Is Love   7/70   32   G

LPM 6401   **WORLDWIDE 50 GOLD AWARD HITS**
             VOL. 1 (4 LPS)   **8/70**   **45**   **2×P**

Heartbreak Hotel/I Was The One/I Want You, I Need You, I Love You/Don't Be Cruel/Hound Dog/Love Me Tender/Any Way You Want Me/Too Much/Playing For Keeps/All Shook Up/That's When Your Heartaches Begin/Loving You/Teddy

Bear/Jailhouse Rock/Treat Me Nice/I Beg Of You/Don't/Wear My Ring Around Your Neck/Hard Headed Woman/I Got Stung/A Fool Such As I/A Big Hunk O'Love/Stuck On You/A Mess Of Blues/It's Now Or Never/I Gotta Know/Are You Lonesome Tonight?/Surrender/I Feel So Bad/Little Sister/Can't Help Falling In Love/Rock-A-Hula Baby/Anything That's Part Of You/Good Luck Charm/She's Not You/Return To Sender/Where Do You Come From/One Broken Heart For Sale/Devil In Disguise/Bossa Nova Baby/Kissin' Cousins/Viva Las Vegas/Ain't That Loving You Baby/Wooden Heart/Crying In The Chapel/If I Can Dream/In The Ghetto/Suspicious Minds/Don't Cry Daddy/Kentucky Rain/Excerpts from Elvis Sails (interviews)

CAS 2440   **ALMOST IN LOVE (Budget LP)**   **10/70**   **65**

Almost In Love/Long Legged Girl/Edge Of Reality/My Little Friend/A Little Less Conversation/Rubberneckin'/Clean Up Your Own Back Yard/U.S. Male/Charro/Stay Away, Joe (take 17)

47-9916   You Don't Have To Say You Love Me/Patch It Up   10/70   11   **G**

LSP/4428   **ELVIS IN PERSON AT**   **11/70**
                 THE INTERNATIONAL HOTEL (LP)

(Content as LSP 6020, album #1)

LSP 4429   **BACK IN MEMPHIS (LP)**   **11/70**

(Content as LSP 6020, album #2)

CAL 2428   **ELVIS' CHRISTMAS ALBUM (Budget LP)**   **11/70**   **P**

Blue Christmas/Silent Night/White Christmas/Santa Claus Is Back In Town/I'll Be Home For Christmas/Here Comes Santa Claus/O Little Town Of Bethlehem/Santa Bring My Baby Back/Mama Liked The Roses

LSP 4445   **THAT'S THE WAY IT IS (LP)**   **11/70**   **21**   **G**

I Just Can't Help Believin'/Twenty Days And Twenty Nights/How The Web Was Woven/Patch It Up/Mary In The Morning/You Don't Have To Say You Love Me/You've Lost That Lovin' Feeling/I've Lost You/Just Pretend/Stranger In The Crowd/The Next Step Is Love/Bridge Over Troubled Water

47-9960   I Really Don't Want To Know/There Goes My Everything   11/70   21   **G**

LSP 4460   **ELVIS COUNTRY (LP)**   **1/71**   **12**   **G**

Snowbird/Tomorrow Never Comes/Little Cabin On The Hill/Whole Lotta Shakin' Goin' On/Funny How Time Slips Away/ I Really Don't Want To Know/There Goes My Everything/It's Your Baby, You Rock It/The Fool/Faded Love/I Washed My Hands In Muddy Water/Make The World Go Away/(segments of)I Was Born About Ten Thousand Years Ago

47-9980   Rags To Riches/Where Did They Go, Lord   2/71   33

CAL 2472   **YOU'LL NEVER WALK ALONE (Budget LP)**   **3/71**   **69**   **G**

You'll Never Walk Alone/Who Am I/Let Us Pray/Peace In The Valley/We Call On Him/I Believe/It Is No Secret/Sing You Children/Take My Hand, Precious Lord

47-9985   Life/Only Believe   4/71   53

LSP 4530   **LOVE LETTERS FROM ELVIS (LP)**   6/71   33

Love Letters/When I'm Over You/If I Were You/Got My Mojo Working/Keep Your Hands Off Of It/Heart Of Rome/Only Believe/This Is Our Dance/Cindy, Cindy/I'll Never Know/It Ain't No Big Thing/Life

47-9998   I'm Leavin'/Heart Of Rome   6/71   36

CAL 2518   **C'MON EVERYBODY (Budget LP)**   7/71   70

C'mon Everybody/Angel/Easy Come, Easy Go/A Whistling Tune/Follow That Dream/King Of The Whole Wide World/I'll Take Love/I'm Not The Marrying Kind/This Is Living/Today, Tomorrow And Forever

LPM 6402   **THE OTHER SIDES/ELVIS WORLDWIDE**
                 GOLD AWARD HITS VOL. 2 (4 LPS)   8/71   120

Puppet On A String/Witchcraft/Trouble/I Want To Be Free/Poor Boy/Doncha' Think It's Time/Young Dreams/The Next Step Is Love/You Don't Have To Say You Love Me/Paralyzed/My Wish Came True/When My Blue Moon Turns To Gold Again/Lonesome Cowboy/My Baby Left Me/It Hurts Me/I Need Your Love Tonight/Tell Me Why/Please Don't Drag That String Around/Young And Beautiful/Hot Dog/New Orleans/We're Gonna Move/Crawfish/King Creole/I Believe In The Man In The Sky/Dixieland Rock/The Wonder Of You/They Remind Me Too Much Of You/Mean Woman Blues/Lonely Man/Any Day Now/Don't Ask Me Why/His Latest Flame/I Really Don't Want To Know/Baby I Don't Care/I've Lost You/Let Me/Love Me/Got A Lot O' Livin' To Do/Fame And Fortune/Rip It Up/There Goes My Everything/Lover Doll/One Night/Just Tell Her Jim Said Hello/Ask Me/Patch It Up/As Long As I Have You/You'll Think Of Me/Wild In The Country

48-1017   It's Only Love/The Sound Of Your Cry   9/71   51

CAL 2533   **I GOT LUCKY (Budget LP)**   10/71   104

I Got Lucky/What A Wonderful Life/I Need Somebody To Lean On/Yoga Is As Yoga Does/Riding The Rainbow/Fools Fall In Love/The Love Machine/Home Is Where The Heart Is/You Gotta Stop/If You Think I Don't Need You

LSP 4579   **ELVIS SINGS THE WONDERFUL**
                 WORLD OF CHRISTMAS (LP)   10/71   2×P

O Come All Ye Faithfull/The First Noel/On A Snowy Christmas Night/Winter Wonderland/The Wonderful World Of Christmas/It Won't Seem Like Christmas/I'll Be Home On Christmas Day/If I Get Home On Christmas Day/Holly Leaves And Christmas Trees/Merry Christmas Baby/Silver Bells

74-0572   Merry Christmas Baby/O Come All Ye Faithful   11/71
74-0619   Until It's Time For You To Go/We Can Make The Morning   1/72   40

LSP 4671   **ELVIS NOW (LP)**   2/72   43   G

Help Me Make It Through The Night/Miracle Of The Rosary/Hey Jude/Put Your Hand In The Hand/Until It's Time For You To Go/We Can Make The Morning/Early Morning Rain/Sylvia/Fools Rush In/I Was Born About Ten Thousand Years Ago

74-0651   He Touched Me/Bosom Of Abraham   3/72

LSP 4690   **HE TOUCHED ME (LP)**   **4/72**   **79**   **G**

He Touched Me/I've Got Confidence/Amazing Grace/Seeing Is Believing/He Is My Everything/Bosom Of Abraham/
An Evening Prayer/Lead Me, Guide Me/There Is No God But God/A Thing Called Love/I John/Reach Out To Jesus

74-0672   An American Trilogy/The First Time Ever I Saw Your Face   4/72   66

CAS 2567   **ELVIS SINGS HITS FROM HIS MOVIES VOL. 1**
    (Budget LP)   **6/72**   **87**

Down By The Riverside—When The Saints Go Marchin' In/They Remind Me Too Much Of You/Confidence/
Frankie And Johnny/Guitar Man/Long Legged Girl/You Don't Know Me/How Would You Like To Be/Big Boss Man/
Old MacDonald

LSP 4776   **ELVIS AS RECORDED**
    AT MADISON SQUARE GARDEN (LP)   **6/72**   **11**   **2×P**

Also Sprach Zarathustra/That's All Right/Proud Mary/Never Been To Spain/You Don't Have To Say You Love Me/
You've Lost That Lovin' Feeling/Polk Salad Annie/Love Me/All Shook Up/Heartbreak Hotel/Teddy Bear—Don't Be
Cruel/Love Me Tender/The Impossible Dream/Introductions by Elvis/Hound Dog/Suspicious Minds/For The Good
Times/An American Trilogy/Funny How Time Slips Away/I Can't Stop Loving You/Can't Help Falling In Love

74-0769   Burning Love/It's A Matter Of Time   8/72   2   P

CAS 2595   **BURNING LOVE AND HITS**
    FROM HIS MOVIES (Budget LP)   **10/72**   **22**   **G**

Burning Love/Tender Feeling/Am I Ready/Tonight Is So Right For Love/Guadalajara/It's A Matter Of Time/No
More/Santa Lucia/We'll Be Together/I Love Only One Girl

74-0815   Separate Ways/Always On My Mind   11/72   20   G

CAS 2611   **SEPARATE WAYS (Budget LP)**   **12/72**   **46**

Separate Ways/Sentimental Me/In My Way/I Met Her Today/What Now, What Next, Where To/Always On My Mind/I
Slipped, I Stumbled, I Fell/Is It So Strange/Forget Me Never/Old Shep

VPSX 6089   **ALOHA FROM HAWAII**
    VIA SATELLITE (Double LP)   **2/73**   **1**   **2×P**

Also Sprach Zarathustra/See See Rider/Burning Love/Something/You Gave Me A Mountain/Steamroller Blues/My Way/
Love Me/Johnny B. Goode/It's Over/Blue Suede Shoes/I'm So Lonesome I Could Cry/I Can't Stop Loving You/Hound
Dog/What Now My Love/Fever/Welcome To My World/Suspicious Minds/Introductions by Elvis/I'll Remember You/
Long Tall Sally—Whole Lotta Shakin' Goin' On/An American Trilogy/A Big Hunk O'Love/Can't Help Falling In Love

74-0910   Steamroller Blues/Fool   3/73   17

APL1 0283   ELVIS (FOOL) (LP)   **7/73   52**

Fool/Where Do I Go From Here/Love Me, Love The Life I Lead/It's Still Here/It's Impossible/For Lovin' Me/Padre/I'll Take You Home Again, Kathleen/I Will Be True/Don't Think Twice, It's All Right

APBO 0088   Raised On Rock/For Ol' Times Sake   9/73   41

APL1 0388   RAISED ON ROCK/FOR OL' TIMES SAKE (LP)   10/73   50

Raised On Rock/Are You Sincere/Find Out What's Happening/I Miss You/Girl Of Mine/For Ol' Times Sake/If You Don't Come Back/Just A Little Bit/Sweet Angeline/Three Corn Patches

CPL1 0341   ELVIS: A LEGENDARY PERFORMER VOL. 1 (LP) 1/74   43   G

That's All Right/I Love You Because (take 2)/Heartbreak Hotel/Don't Be Cruel/Elvis, excerpt from interview of September 22, 1958/Love Me (6/27/68 8PM)/Trying To Get To You (6/27/68 8PM)/Love Me Tender/(There'll Be) Peace In The Valley (For Me)/Elvis's farewell to his fans/A Fool Such As I/Tonight's All Right For Love/Are You Lonesome Tonight? (6/27/68 8PM)/Can't Help Falling In Love

APBO 0196   I've Got A Thing About You Baby/Take Good Care Of Her   1/74   39

CPL1 0475   GOOD TIMES (LP)   **3/74   90**

Take Good Care Of Her/Loving Arms/I Got A Feeling In My Body/If That Isn't Love/She Wears My Ring/I've Got A Thing About You Baby/My Boy/Spanish Eyes/Talk About The Good Times/Good Time Charlie's Got The Blues

APBO 0280   If You Talk In Your Sleep/Help Me   5/74   17

**CPL1 0606   ELVIS AS RECORDED LIVE ON STAGE   7/74   33
                IN MEMPHIS (LP)**

See See Rider/I Got A Woman/Love Me/Trying To Get To You/Medley: Long Tall Sally—Whole Lotta Shakin' Goin' On—Mama Don't Dance—Flip, Flop And Fly—Jailhouse Rock—Hound Dog/Why Me Lord/How Great Thou Art/ Medley: Blueberry Hill—I Can't Stop Loving You/Help Me/An American Trilogy/Let Me Be There/My Baby Left Me/Lawdy, Miss Clawdy/Can't Help Falling In Love/Closing Vamp

PB 10074   Promised Land/It's Midnight   10/74   14

CPM1 0818   HAVING FUN WITH ELVIS ON STAGE (LP)   10/74   130

(A talking album only. Previously released on the Boxcar label.)

APL1 0873   PROMISED LAND (LP)   **1/75   47**

Promised Land/There's A Honky Tonk Angel/Help Me/Mr. Songman/Love Song Of The Year/It's Midnight/Your Love's Been A Long Time Coming/If You Talk In Your Sleep/Thinking About You/You Asked Me To

PB 10191   My Boy/Thinking About You   1/75   20

ANL1 0971   **PURE GOLD (Midprice LP)**   **3/75**   **2×P**

Kentucky Rain/Fever/It's Impossible/Jailhouse Rock/Don't Be Cruel/I Got A Woman/All Shook Up/Loving You/In The Ghetto/Love Me Tender

PB 10278   T-R-O-U-B-L-E/Mr. Songman   4/75   35

APL1 1039   **TODAY (LP)**   **5/75**   **57**

T-R-O-U-B-L-E/And I Love You So/Susan When She Tried/Woman Without Love/Shake A Hand/Pieces Of My Life/Fairytale/I Can Help/Bringing It Back/Green, Green Grass Of Home

PB 10401   Bringing It Back/Pieces Of My Life   9/75   65

CPL1 1349   **ELVIS: A LEGENDARY PERFORMER VOL. 2 (LP)**   **1/76**   **46**   **G**

Harbor Lights/Interview (1956)/I Want You, I Need You, I Love You (alternate take)/Blue Suede Shoes (6/27/68 8PM)/ Blue Christmas/Jailhouse Rock/It's Now Or Never/A Cane And A High Starched Collar (alt, master takes)/Presentation of awards to Elvis/Blue Hawaii (1/73)/Such A Night (takes 2, 3, master)/Baby What You Want Me To Do (6/27/68 6PM, 8120)/How Great Thou Art/If I Can Dream

PB 10601   Hurt/For The Heart   3/76   28

APM1 1675   **THE SUN SESSIONS (LP)**   **3/76**   **76**

That's Alll Right/Blue Moon Of Kentucky/I Don't Care If The Sun Don't Shine/Good Rockin' Tonight/Milkcow Blues Boogie/You're A Heartbreaker/I'm Left, You're Right, She's Gone/Baby Let's Play House/Mystery Train/I Forgot To Remember To Forget/I'll Never Let You Go/I Love You Because/Trying To Get To You/Blue Moon/Just Because/I Love You Because

APL1 1506   **FROM ELVIS PRESLEY BOULEVARD**
                  MEMPHIS, TENNESSEE (LP)   **5/76**   **41**   **G**

Hurt/Never Again/Blue Eyes Crying In The Rain/Danny Boy/The Last Farewell/For The Heart/Bitter They Are, Harder They Fall/Solitaire/Love Coming Down/I'll Never Fall In Love Again

PB 10857   Moody Blue/She Thinks I Still Care   12/76   31

APL1 2274   **WELCOME TO MY WORLD (LP)**   **3/77**   **44**   **P**

Welcome To My World/Help Me Make It Through The Night/Release Me/I Really Don't Want To Know/For The Good Times/Make The World Go Away (take 2)/Gentle On My Mind/I'm So Lonesome I Could Cry/Your Cheatin' Heart/ I Can't Stop Loving You (6/10/72 Afternoon)

PB 10998   Way Down/Pledging My Love   6/77   18   G

AFL1 2428   **MOODY BLUE (LP)**   **6/77**   **3**   **2×P**

Unchained Melody/If You Love Me/Little Darlin'/He'll Have To Go/Let Me Be There/Way Down/Pledging My Love/Moody Blue/She Thinks I Still Care/It's Easy For You

APL2 2587   **ELVIS IN CONCERT (2LPs)**   **10/77**   **5**   **P**

Also Sprach Zarathustra/See See Rider/That's All Right/Are You Lonesome Tonight?/Teddy Bear/Don't Be Cruel/You Gave Me A Mountain/Jailhouse Rock/How Great Thou Art/I Really Don't Want To Know/Hurt/Hound Dog/My Way/Can't Help Falling In Love/Closing Riff/I Got A Woman—Amen/Love Me/If You Love Me/O Sole Mio—It's Now Or Never/Trying To Get To You/Hawaiian Wedding Song/Fairytale/Little Sister/Early Morning Rain/What'd I Say/Johnny B. Goode/And I Love You So

PB 11165   My Way/America   11/77   22   G

DISCOGRAPHY 1978–1997

This discography represents only releases that include previously unreleased performances.

Cat. no.	Title	Release Date	Top US Chart Position A/B Side	RIAA Status
PB 11212	Unchained Melody/Softly As I Leave You	2/78		
AFL1 2272	**HE WALKS BESIDE ME (LP)**	**2/78**	**113**	**G**

He Is My Everything/Miracle Of The Rosary/Where Did They Go Lord/Somebody Bigger Than You And I/An Evening Prayer/The Impossible Dream/If I Can Dream (take 4)/Padre/Known Only To Him/Who Am I?/How Great Thou Art

CPL1 2901	**ELVIS SINGS FOR CHILDREN AND GROWNUPS TOO (LP)**	**7/78**	**130**	

Teddy Bear/Wooden Heart/Five Sleepyheads/Puppet On A String/Angel/Old MacDonald/How Would You Like To Be/Cotton Candy Land/Old Shep/Big Boots (MO-4)/Have A Happy

ACL 7064	**MAHALO FROM ELVIS (LP)**	**7/78**		

Blue Hawaii (1/73)/Early Mornin' Rain (1/73)/Hawaiian Wedding Song (1/73)/Ku-U-I-Po (1/73)/No More (1/73)/Relax/Baby, If You'll Give Me All Of Your Love/One Broken Heart For Sale/So Close, Yet So Far/Happy Ending

CPL1 3078/3082	**ELVIS: A LEGENDARY PERFORMER VOL. 3 (LP)**	**11/78**	**113**	**G**

Hound Dog/Excerpts from an interview with Elvis and the Colonel from TV Guide/Danny/Fame And Fortune (take 2/Frankfort Special (HO-2)/Britches/Crying In The Chapel/Surrender/Guadalajara (PVX-2)/It Hurts Me (6/68)/Let Yourself Go (6/68)/In The Ghetto/Let It Be Me (2/15/70 Midnight show) [3082 is a picture disc edition of same album]

AQL1 3279	**OUR MEMORIES OF ELVIS (LP)**	**2/79**	**132**	

Are You Sincere (take 1)/It's Midnight/My Boy/Girl Of Mine/Take Good Care Of Her/I'll Never Fall In Love Again/Your Love's Been A Long Time Coming/Spanish Eyes/Never Again/She Thinks I Still Care/Solitaire

CPL8 3699	**ELVIS ARON PRESLEY (8 LPS)**	**8/80**	**27**	**P**

AN EARLY LIVE PERFORMANCE: Heartbreak Hotel/Long Tall Sally/Blue Suede Shoes/Money Honey (Las Vegas, 5/56)
MONOLOGUE: An Elvis Monologue (1962)
AN EARLY BENEFIT PERFORMANCE: Heartbreak Hotel/All Shook Up/A Fool Such As I/I Got A Woman/Love Me/Introductions/ Such A Night/Reconsider Baby/I Need Your Love Tonight/That's All Right/Don't Be Cruel/One Night/Are You Lonesome Tonight?/It's Now Or Never/Swing Down, Sweet Chariot/Hound Dog (Pearl Harbor, 3/61)
COLLECTORS GOLD FROM THE MOVIE YEARS: They Remind Me Too Much Of You (take 1)/Tonight's All Right For Love (takes 3, 4, 7, 8)/Follow That Dream (take 2)/Wild In The Country (take 16)/Datin' (takes 6, 7, 8, 11, 12)/Shoppin'

Around (takes 3, 5)/Can't Help Falling In Love (take 24)/A Dog's Life (takes 4, 5, 6)/I'm Falling In Love Tonight (takes 1, 2, 3, 4)/ Thanks To The Rolling Sea (take 10)

THE TV SPECIALS: Jailhouse Rock (6/68)/Suspicious Minds (1/73)/Lawdy, Miss Clawdy/Baby What You Want Me To Do (6/68)/Blue Christmas (6/68)/You Gave Me A Mountain (1/73)/Welcome To My World (1/73)/Trying To Get To You (77)/ I'll Remember You (1/73)/My Way

THE LAS VEGAS YEARS: Polk Salad Annie (8/13/70 dinner)/You've Lost That Lovin' Feeling (8/7/70)/Sweet Caroline (8/7/70)/Kentucky Rain (2/16/70 dinner)/Are You Lonesome Tonight? (laughing version) (8/26/69 midnight)/My Babe (8/26/69 dinner)/In The Ghetto (8/24/69 midnight)/An American Trilogy (2/15/72 midnight)/Little Sister—Get Back (8/13/70 midnight)/Yesterday (8/24/69 dinner)

LOST SINGLES: I'm Leavin'/The First Time Ever I Saw Your Face/Hi/Heel Sneakers/Softly, As I Leave You/Unchained Melody/Fool/Rags To Riches/It's Only Love/America The Beautiful

ELVIS AT THE PIANO: It's Still Here/I'll Take You Home Again, Kathleen/Beyond The Reef/I Will Be True

THE CONCERT YEARS: Also Sprach Zarathustra/See See Rider/I Got A Woman—Amen/Love Me/If You Love Me (Let Me Know)/Love Me Tender/All Shook Up/Teddy Bear/Don't Be Cruel/Hound Dog/The Wonder Of You/Burning Love/Introductions/Johnny B. Goode/Introductions/Hail, Hail, Rock 'N' Roll/T-R-O-U-B-L-E/Why Me Lord/How Great Thou Art/Let Me Be There/American Trilogy/Funny How Time Slips Away/Little Darlin'/Mystery Train/Tiger Man/Can't Help Falling In Love (May/June 1975, see session data for details)

CPL2 4031   THIS IS ELVIS (2 LPs)   3/81   115

His Latest Flame/Moody Blue/That's All Right/Shake, Rattle And Roll/Flip, Flop And Fly (1/28/56)/Heartbreak Hotel (3/17/56) /Hound Dog (6/5/56)/Excerpt from Hy Gardner interview/My Baby Left Me/Merry Christmas Baby/Mean Woman Blues (movie)/Don't Be Cruel (1/6/57)/Teddy Bear/Jailhouse Rock/Army swearing in/G.I. Blues/Excerpt from Departure for Germany press conference/Excerpt from Home from Germany press conference/Too Much Monkey Business/Love Me Tender/I've Got A Thing About You Baby/I Need Your Love Tonight/Blue Suede Shoes (6/27–29/68)/ Viva Las Vegas/Suspicious Minds (1/73)/Excerpt from JC's Award to Elvis/Promised Land/Excerpt from Madison Square Garden press conference/Always On My Mind (3/30/72)/Are You Lonesome Tonight? (6/77)/My Way/ An American Trilogy (4/9/72)/Memories

AHL1 2347   GREATEST HITS VOLUME ONE   11/81   142

The Wonder Of You/A Big Hunk O' Love (2/17/72 dinner)/There Goes My Everything/Suspicious Minds/What'd I Say (8/23/69 midnight)/Don't Cry Daddy (2/18/70 dinner)/Steamroller Blues (1/13/73)/The Sound Of Your Cry (unedited)/ Burning Love/You'll Never Walk Alone

CPL1 4395   MEMORIES OF CHRISTMAS   8/82   G

O Come All Ye Faithful (take 2)/Silver Bells/I'll Be Home On Christmas Day (6/10/71)/Blue Christmas/Santa Claus Is Back In Town/Merry Christmas Baby (unedited)/If Every Day Was Like Christmas (undubbed)/Silent Night

RCX 7203   THE EP COLLECTION VOL. 2 (EP collection) (U.K. release only)

Your Cheatin' Heart (take 9)/What's She Really Like (take 7)/G.I. Blues (take 7)/Doin' The Best I Can (take 9)/Pocketful Of Rainbows (NO take 2)/His Latest Flame (takes 1 [partial], 3 [partial], 5,6)/Good Luck Charm (take 1)/Judy (takes 1, 3 [partial], 4)/Little Sister (takes 1, 2, 3 [partial], 5,6) (Only outtakes are listed; set also included regular masters)

CPL1 4848   A LEGENDARY PERFORMER VOL. 4   11/83

When It Rains, It Really Pours (takes c, f, e)/Tampa interview 1956/One Night (Of Sin)/I'm Beginning To Forget You/
Mona Lisa/Wooden Heart (takes 3, 4)/Plantation Rock/The Lady Loves Me/Swing Down, Sweet Chariot (10/68)/
That's All Right (6/27/68 8PM)/Are You Lonesome Tonight? (8/26/69 midnight) (laughing version)/Reconsider Baby
(6/10/72 afternoon)/I'll Remember You (6/10/72 afternoon)

PB 3601   ELVIS: THE FIRST LIVE RECORDINGS   2/84   163

Introduction: Elvis and Horace Logan/Baby Let's Play House/Maybellene/Tweedle Dee/That's All Right/Recollections by
Frank Page/Hound Dog (Released on the Music Works label by special arrangement with RCA)

PB 3602   ELVIS: THE HILLBILLY CAT   7/84

Introduction/Elvis Presley with Horace Logan/That's All Right/Elvis talks with Horace Logan/Blue Moon Of Kentucky/
Recollections by Frank Page/Good Rockin' Tonight/I Got A Woman (Released on the Music Works label by special
arrangement with RCA.)

CPM6 5172   A GOLDEN CELEBRATION   10/84   80

THE SUN SESSIONS: Harbor Lights/That's All Right (takes 1,2,3)/Blue Moon Of Kentucky (take a)/I Don't Care If The
Sun Don't Shine (takes a, b, c)/I'm Left, You're Right, She's Gone (take 10)/I'll Never Let You Go (alternate take)/When It
Rains, It Really Pours (takes c, f, e)

THE DORSEY BROTHERS STAGE SHOW: Shake, Rattle And Roll/Flip, Flop And Fly/I Got A Woman/Baby Let's Play
House/Tutti Frutti/Blue Suede Shoes/Heartbreak Hotel/Tutti Frutti/I Was The One/Blue Suede Shoes/Heartbreak
Hotel/Money Honey/Heartbreak Hotel

THE MILTON BERLE SHOW: Heartbreak Hotel/Blue Suede Shoes/dialogue/Blue Suede Shoes/Hound Dog/dialogue/I
Want You, I Need You, I Love You

THE STEVE ALLEN SHOW: Dialogue/I Want You, I Need You, I Love You/introduction/Hound Dog

THE MISSISSIPPI/ALABAMA FAIR AND DAIRY SHOW 9/26/56: Heartbreak Hotel/Long Tall Sally/introductions/I Was
The One/I Want You, I Need You, I Love You/I Got A Woman/Don't Be Cruel/Ready Teddy/Love Me Tender/Hound Dog/
Interviews: Vernon and Gladys/Nick Adams/a fan/Elvis/Love Me Tender/I Was The One/I Got A Woman/Don't Be Cruel/
Blue Suede Shoes/Baby Let's Play House/Hound Dog

THE ED SULLIVAN SHOW: Don't Be Cruel/Love Me Tender/Ready Teddy/Hound Dog/Don't Be Cruel/Love Me Tender/
Love Me/Hound Dog/Hound Dog/Love Me Tender/Heartbreak Hotel/Don't Be Cruel/Too Much/When My Blue Moon
Turns To Gold Again/Peace In The Valley

ELVIS AT HOME IN GERMANY: Danny Boy/Soldier Boy/The Fool/Earth Angel/He's Only A Prayer Away

COLLECTOR'S TREASURES: Excerpt from an interview for *TV Guide*/My Heart Cries For You/Dark Moon/Write To Me
From Naples/Suppose

ELVIS, BURBANK, JUNE 27, 1968: Blue Suede Shoes/Tiger Man/That's All Right/Lawdy, Miss Clawdy/Baby What You
Want Me To Do/monologue/Love Me/Are You Lonesome Tonight?/Baby What You Want Me To Do/monologue/Blue
Christmas/monologue/One Night/Trying To Get To You

AFL1 5418   RECONSIDER BABY (LP)   4/85

Reconsider Baby/Tomorrow Night (edited Sun original)/So Glad You're Mine/One Night (Of Sin)/When It Rains, It Really

Pours/My Baby Left Me/Ain't That Loving You Baby (spliced alternate take)/I Feel So Bad/Down In The Alley/Hi Heel Sneakers/Stranger In My Own Home Town (without some overdubs)/Merry Christmas Baby (long edit without guitar overdub)

6414-1-r THE COMPLETE SUN SESSIONS (2LPs) 6/87

That's All Right/Blue Moon Of Kentucky/Good Rockin' Tonight/I Don't Care If The Sun Don't Shine/Milkcow Blues Boogie/You're A Heartbreaker/Baby Let's Play House/I'm Left, You're Right, She's Gone/Mystery Train/I Forgot To Remember To Forget/I Love You Because/Blue Moon/Tomorrow Night/I'll Never Let You Go/Just Because/Trying To Get To You/Harbor Lights/I Love You Because (takes 1, 2)/That's All Right/Blue Moon Of Kentucky/I Don't Care If The Sun Don't Shine/I'm Left, You're Right, She's Gone (take 9)/I'll Never Let You Go (Little Darlin')/When It Rains It Really Pours/I Love You Because (takes 3, 4, 5)/I'm Left, You're Right, She's Gone (takes 7, 8, 10, 11, 13, 12)
(This double LP was also released as a single CD (6414-2-r), with the following songs omitted: I Love You Because (takes 1, 4)/I'm Left, You're Right, She's Gone (takes 8, 10, 11, 13)

6738-1-r ESSENTIAL ELVIS (LP) 12/86 (Europe);1/88 (US)

Love Me Tender/Let Me/Poor Boy/We're Gonna Move/Loving You (HZ take 10)/Party (A take 7)/Hot Dog/Teddy Bear/Loving You (KX takes 20/21)/Mean Woman Blues (lpa5 5812)/Got A Lot O'Livin' To Do (R take 13)/Loving You (KX take 1)/Party/Lonesome Cowboy/Jailhouse Rock (h2wb 6780)/Treat Me Nice (h2wb 6778)/Young And Beautiful (2004 take sp)/Don't Leave Me Now/I Want To Be Free/Baby I Don't Care/Jailhouse Rock (take 5)/Got A Lot O'Livin' To Do/*Loving You (HZ take 1)/Mean Woman Blues/Loving You (KX take 8)/Treat Me Nice*/Love Me Tender (end) *(Songs in italics on CD only)*

6985-1-r THE ALTERNATE ALOHA (LP) 6/88

Also Sprach Zarathustra/See See Rider/Burning Love/Something/You Gave Me A Mountain/Steamroller Blues/My Way/Love Me/It's Over/Blue Suede Shoes/I'm So Lonesome I Could Cry/Hound Dog/What Now My Love/Fever/Welcome To My World/Suspicious Minds/Introductions by Elvis/I'll Remember You/An American Trilogy/A Big Hunk O'Love/Can't Help Falling In Love/Blue Hawaii/Hawaiian Wedding Song/Ku-U-I-Po

8468-1-r ELVIS IN NASHVILLE (LP) 11/88

I Got A Woman/A Big Hunk O'Love/Working On The Building/Judy/Anything That's Part Of You (take 1)/Night Rider/Where No One Stands Alone/Just Call Me Lonesome/Guitar Man/Little Cabin On The Hill/It's Your Baby, You Rock It/Early Morning Rain/It's Still Here/I, John

9589-2-r ELVIS PRESLEY STEREO '57 (Essential Elvis Volume 2) (LP) 2/89

I Beg Of You (take 1)/Is It So Strange (take 1)/Have I Told You Lately That I Love You (take 2)/It Is No Secret (takes 1, 2, 3)/Blueberry Hill (take 2)/Mean Woman Blues/Peace In The Valley (takes 2, 3)/Have I Told You Lately That I Love You (take 6)/Blueberry Hill (take 7)/That's When Your Heartaches Begin (takes 4, 5, 6)/Is It So Strange (takes 7, 11)/I Beg Of You (takes 6, 8)/Peace In The Valley (take 7)/Have I Told You Lately That I Love You (takes 12, 13)/I Beg Of You (take 12)/*I Believe/Tell Me Why/Got A Lot O'Livin' To Do/All Shook Up/Take My Hand, Precious Lord (Songs in italic on CD only)*

2023-1-r THE MILLION DOLLAR QUARTET (2 LPs) 3/90

You Belong To My Heart/When God Dips His Love In My Heart/Just A Little Talk With Jesus/Jesus Walked That Lonesome Valley/I Shall Not Be Moved/Peace In The Valley/Down By The Riverside/I'm With The Crowd But So Alone/Farther Along/Blessed Jesus/As We Travel Along On The Jericho Road/I Just Can't Make It By Myself/Little Cabin Home On The Hill/Summertime Is Past And Gone/I Hear A Sweet Voice Calling/Sweetheart You Done Me Wrong/Keeper Of The Key/Crazy Arms/Don't Forbid Me/Too Much Monkey Business/Brown Eyed Handsome Man/Out Of Sight, Out Of Mind/Brown Eyed Handsome Man/Don't Be Cruel/Don't Be Cruel/Paralyzed/Don't Be Cruel/There's No Place Like Home/When The Saints Go Marchin' In/Softly And Tenderly/Is It So Strange/That's When Your Heartaches Begin/Brown Eyed Handsome Man/Rip It Up/I'm Gonna Bid My Blues Goodbye/Crazy Arms/That's My Desire/End Of The Road/Black Bottom Stomp/You're The Only Star In My Blue Heaven/(Elvis says goodbye)

2227-1-r THE GREAT PERFORMANCES (LP) 8/90

My Happiness/That's All Right/Shake, Rattle And Roll/Flip, Flop And Fly/Heartbreak Hotel/Blue Suede Shoes/Ready Teddy/Don't Be Cruel/Teddy Bear/Got A Lot O'Livin' To Do/Jailhouse Rock/Treat Me Nice/King Creole/Trouble/Fame And Fortune/Return To Sender/Always On My Mind/American Trilogy/If I Can Dream/Unchained Melody/Memories (The last RCA U.S. vinyl Elvis Presley release. All albums released after 1990 on CD only)

2229-2-r HITS LIKE NEVER BEFORE
(Essential Elvis Volume 3) (CD) 7/90 (Europe);1/91 (US)

King Creole (E take 18)/I Got Stung (take 1)/A Fool Such As I (take 3)/Wear My Ring Around Your Neck (undubbed)/Your Cheating Heart (take 9)/Ain't That Loving You Baby (take 1)/Doncha' Think It's Time (take 40)/I Need Your Love Tonight (takes 2, 10)/Lover Doll (undubbed)/As Long As I Have You (N take 8)/Danny/King Creole (E take 3)/Crawfish (unedited)/A Big Hunk O'Love (take 1)/Ain't That Loving You Baby (takes 5, 11)/I Got Stung (takes 13, 14)/Your Cheating Heart/Wear My Ring Around Your Neck/Steadfast, Loyal And True (M take 6)/I Need Your Love Tonight (take 5)/Doncha' Think It's Time/I Got Stung (take 12)/King Creole (R take 8)/As Long As I Have You (N take 4)

3026-2-r ELVIS PRESLEY SINGS LEIBER & STOLLER (CD) 4/91

Hound Dog/Love Me/Loving You/Hot Dog/I Want To Be Free/Jailhouse Rock/Treat Me Nice/Baby I Don't Care/Santa Claus Is Back In Town/Don't/Trouble/King Creole/Steadfast, Loyal and True/Dirty, Dirty Feeling/Just Tell Her Jim Said Hello/Girls! Girls! Girls!/Bossa Nova Baby/You're The Boss/Little Egypt/Fools Fall In Love/Saved

61021-2 ELVIS NBC TV SPECIAL (CD) 8/91

Trouble/Guitar Man/Lawdy, Miss Clawdy/Baby, What You Want Me To Do/Heartbreak Hotel/Hound Dog/All Shook Up/Can't Help Falling In Love/Jailhouse Rock/*Don't Be Cruel/Blue Suede Shoes*/Love Me Tender/Where Could I Go But To The Lord/Up Above My Head/*Saved/Baby, What You Want Me To Do/That's All Right*/Blue Christmas/One Night/*Tiger Man/Trying To Get To You*/Memories/Nothingville/Big Boss Man/*Let Yourself Go/It Hurts Me*/Guitar Man/Little Egypt/Trouble/Guitar Man/If I Can Dream (This is an expanded version of the original 1968 album Elvis/NBC TV Special [LPM 4088]. New tracks are in italics.)

3114-2-r   COLLECTORS GOLD (3 CDs)   8/91

Disc 1: THE HOLLYWOOD ALBUM

G.I. Blues (take 1)/Pocketful Of Rainbows (takes 22, 17)/Big Boots (M10 take 7)/Black Star (with end title)/Summer Kisses, Winter Tears (takes 1, 14)/I Slipped, I Stumbled, I Fell (take 18)/Lonely Man (take 4)/What A Wonderful Life (takes 2, 1)/A Whistling Tune (7/61)/Beyond The Bend (take 2)/One Broken Heart For Sale (take 1)/You're The Boss/ Roustabout (NOV take 6)/Girl Happy (take 4)/So Close Yet So Far (take 4)/Stop, Look And Listen (take 3)/Am I Ready (take 1)/How Can You Lose What You Never Had (takes 1, 3)

Disc 2: THE NASHVILLE ALBUM

Like A Baby (takes 1, 2)/There's Always Me (take 4)/I Want You With Me (take 1)/Gently (take 3)/Give Me The Right (take 1)/I Met Her Today (take 1)/Night Rider (takes 1, 2)/Just Tell Her Jim Said Hello (take 1)/Ask Me (5/63 take 2)/ Memphis, Tennessee (5/63 take 2)/Love Me Tonight (take 1)/Witchcraft (take 1)/Come What May (take 6)/Love Letters (takes 3, 4, 7)/Going Home (takes 24, 21)

Disc 3: LIVE IN LAS VEGAS (1969)

Blue Suede Shoes (8/25 dinner)/I Got A Woman (8/25 dinner)/Heartbreak Hotel (8/24 dinner)/Love Me Tender (8/22 midnight)/Baby, What You Want Me To Do (8/26 midnight)/Runaway (8/26 midnight)/Surrender (8/21 midnight)/ Are You Lonesome Tonight? (8/26 midnight)/Rubberneckin' (8/26 midnight)/Memories (8/25 dinner)/Introductions by Elvis (8/21 midnight)/Jailhouse Rock—Don't Be Cruel (8/22 midnight)/Inherit The Wind (8/26 dinner)/This is The Story (8/26 midnight)/Mystery Train—Tiger Man (8/22 midnight)/Funny How Time Slips Away(8/25 dinner)/Loving You/Reconsider Baby (8/23 midnight)/What'd I Say (8/23 midnight)

66050-2   THE KING OF ROCK 'N' ROLL:
**   THE COMPLETE 50'S MASTERS**
**   (07863/66050/2) (5 CDs)   6/92   P**

Disc 1: My Happiness/That's All Right/I Love You Because/Harbor Lights/Blue Moon Of Kentucky/Blue Moon/Blue Moon/Tomorrow Night/I'll Never Let You Go/I Don't Care If The Sun Don't Shine/Just Because/Good Rockin' Tonight/ Milkcow Blues Boogie/You're A Heartbreaker/Baby Let's Play House/I'm Left, You're Right, She's Gone/Mystery Train/I Forgot To Remember To Forget/Trying To Get To You/When It Rains, It Really Pours/I Got A Woman/Heartbreak Hotel/ Money Honey/I'm Counting On You/I Was The One/Blue Suede Shoes/My Baby Left Me/One-Sided Love Affair/So Glad You're Mine/I'm Gonna Sit Right Down And Cry/Tutti Frutti

Disc 2: Lawdy, Miss Clawdy/Shake, Rattle And Roll/I Want You, I Need You, I Love You/Hound Dog/Don't Be Cruel/ Any Way You Want Me/We're Gonna Move/Love Me Tender/Poor Boy/Let Me/Playing For Keeps/Love Me/Paralyzed/ How Do You Think I Feel/How's The World Treating You/When My Blue Moon Turns To Gold Again/Long Tall Sally/ Old Shep/Too Much/Anyplace Is Paradise/Ready Teddy/First In Line/Rip It Up/I Believe/Tell Me Why/Got A Lot O'Livin' To Do/All Shook Up/Mean Woman Blues/Peace In The Valley

Disc 3: That's When Your Heartaches Begin/Take My Hand, Precious Lord/It Is No Secret/Blueberry Hill/Have I Told You Lately That I Love You/Is It So Strange/Party/Lonesome Cowboy/Hot Dog/One Night Of Sin/Teddy Bear/Don't Leave Me Now/I Beg Of You/One Night/True Love/I Need You So/Loving You/When It Rains, It Really Pours/Jailhouse Rock/Young And Beautiful/I Want To Be Free/Baby I Don't Care/Don't Leave Me Now/Blue Christmas/White Christmas/ Here Comes Santa Claus/Silent Night/O Little Town Of Bethlehem/Santa Bring My Baby Back/Santa Claus Is Back In Town/I'll Be Home For Christmas

Disc 4: Treat Me Nice/My Wish Came True/Don't/Danny/Hard Headed Woman/Trouble/New Orleans/Crawfish/

Dixieland Rock/Lover Doll/Don't Ask Me Why/As Long As I Have You/King Creole/Young Dreams/Steadfast, Loyal
And True/Doncha' Think It's Time/Your Cheatin' Heart/Wear My Ring Around Your Neck/I Need Your Love Tonight/
A Big Hunk O' Love/Ain't That Loving You Baby/A Fool Such As I/I Got Stung/Interview with Elvis (9/22/58 unreleased)
Disc 5: That's When Your Heartaches Begin/Fool, Fool, Fool/Tweedle Dee/Maybellene/Shake, Rattle And Roll/Blue Moon of
Kentucky/Blue Moon (take 1)/I'm Left, You're Right, She's Gone (take 11)/Reconsider Baby (12/56)/Lawdy, Miss Clawdy
(take 3)/Shake, Rattle And Roll (take 8)/I Want You, I Need You, I Love You (outtake)/Heartbreak Hotel (5/56)/Long Tall Sally
(5/56)/(Blue Suede Shoes (5/56)/Money Honey (5/56)/We're Gonna Move (take 4)/Old Shep (take 5)/I Beg Of You (take
12)/Loving You (slow, HZ take 12)/Loving You (uptempo KX take 13)/Young And Beautiful (2005 take 3)/I Want To Be Free
(2009 sp.)/King Creole (E take 3)/As Long As I Have You (N take 8)/Ain't That Loving You Baby (fast, take 11)

61835-2   DOUBLE FEATURES (4 CDs)   1/93

Disc 1: King Of The Whole Wide World/This Is Living/Riding The Rainbow/Home Is Where The Heart Is/I Got Lucky/A
Whistling Tune/Girls! Girls! Girls!/I Don't Wanna Be Tied/Where Do You Come From/I Don't Want To/We'll Be Together/
A Boy Like Me, A Girl Like You/Earth Boy/Return To Sender/Because Of Love/Thanks To The Rolling Sea/Song Of The
Shrimp/The Walls Have Ears/We're Coming In Loaded/Mama/Plantation Rock/Dainty Little Moonbeams/Girls! Girls!
Girls! (end title version)
Disc 2: Beyond The Bend/Relax/Take Me To The Fair/They Remind Me Too Much Of You/One Broken Heart For Sale
(film)/I'm Falling In Love Tonight/Cotton Candy Land/A World Of Our Own/How Would You Like To Be/Happy Ending/
One Broken Heart For Sale/Fun In Acapulco/Vino, Dinero Y Amor/Mexico/El Toro/Marguerita/The Bullfighter Was A
Lady/No Room To Rhumba In A Sports Car/I Think I'm Gonna Like It Here/Bossa Nova Baby/You Can't Say No In
Acapulco/Guadalajara
Disc 3: Viva Las Vegas/If You Think I Don't Need You/I Need Somebody To Lean On/You're The Boss/What'd I Say/Do
The Vega/C'mon Everybody/The Lady Loves Me/Night Life/Today, Tomorrow And Forever/The Yellow Rose Of Texas/
The Eyes Of Texas/Santa Lucia/Roustabout/Little Egypt/Poison Ivy League/Hard Knocks/It's A Wonderful World/Big
Love, Big Heartaches/One Track Heart/It's Carnival Time/Carny Town/There's A Brand New Day On The Horizon/Wheels
On My Heels
Disc 4: Harem Holiday/My Desert Serenade/Go East, Young Man/Mirage/Kismet/Shake That Tambourine/Hey Little
Girl/ Golden Coins/So Close, Yet So Far/Animal Instinct/Wisdom Of The Ages/Girl Happy/Spring Fever/Fort Lauder-
dale Chamber Of Commerce/Startin' Tonight/Wolf Call/Do Not Disturb/Cross My Heart And Hope To Die/The Meanest
Girl In Town/Do The Clam/Puppet On A String/I've Got To Find My Baby
(4 CD boxed set in metal film canister, sold through mail order only. The following month released as 4 separate CDs:
KID GALAHAD/GIRLS! GIRLS! GIRLS!; IT HAPPENED AT THE WORLD'S FAIR/FUN IN ACAPULCO; VIVA LAS
VEGAS/ROUSTABOUT; HARUM SCARUM/GIRL HAPPY)

66160-2   FROM NASHVILLE TO MEMPHIS: G
THE ESSENTIAL 60'S MASTERS I (5 CDs)   9/93

Disc 1: Make Me Know It/Soldier Boy/Stuck On You/Fame And Fortune/A Mess Of Blues/It Feels So Right/Fever/Like
A Baby/It's Now Or Never/The Girl Of My Best Friend/Dirty, Dirty Feeling/Thrill Of Your Love/I Gotta Know/Such A Night/
Are You Lonesome Tonight?/Girl Next Door Went A'Walking/I Will Be Home Again/Reconsider Baby/Surrender/ I'm
Comin' Home/Gently/In Your Arms/Give Me The Right/I Feel So Bad/It's A Sin/I Want You With Me/There's Always Me
Disc 2: Starting Today/Sentimental Me/Judy/Put The Blame On Me/Kiss Me Quick/That's Someone You Never Forget/

I'm Yours/His Latest Flame/Little Sister/For The Millionth And The Last Time/Good Luck Charm/Anything That's Part Of You/I Met Her Today/Night Rider/Something Blue/Gonna Get Back Home Somehow/Easy Question/Fountain Of Love/Just For Old Time Sake/You'll Be Gone/I Feel That I've Known You Forever/Just Tell Her Jim Said Hello/Suspicion/ She's Not You/Echoes Of Love/Please Don't Drag That String Around/Devil In Disguise/Never Ending/What Now, What Next, Where To/Witchcraft/Finders Keepers, Losers Weepers/Love Me Tonight

Disc 3: Long Lonely Highway/Western Union/Slowly But Surely/Blue River/Memphis Tennessee/Ask Me/It Hurts Me/ Down In The Alley/Tomorrow Is A Long Time/Love Letters/Beyond The Reef/Come What May (take 7)/Fools Fall In Love/ Indescribably Blue/I'll Remember You (unedited)/If Everyday Was Like Christmas/Suppose/Guitar Man/What'd I Say (unedited)/Big Boss Man/Mine/Just Call Me Lonesome/Hi Heel Sneakers (unedited)/You Don't Know Me/Singing Tree/ Too Much Monkey Business/U.S. Male

Disc 4: Long Black Limousine/This Is The Story/Wearin' That Loved On Look/You'll Think Of Me/A Little Bit Of Green/ Gentle On My Mind/I'm Movin' On/Don't Cry Daddy/Inherit The Wind/Mama Liked The Roses/My Little Friend/ In The Ghetto/Rubberneckin'/From A Jack To A King/Hey Jude/Without Love/I'll Hold You In My Heart/I'll Be There/ Suspicious Minds/True Love Travels On A Gravel Road/Stranger In My Own Home Town/And The Grass Won't Pay No Mind/Power Of My Love

Disc 5: After Loving You/Do You Know Who I Am/Kentucky Rain/Only The Strong Survive/It Keeps Right On A-Hurtin'/ Any Day Now/If I'm A Fool/The Fair Is Moving On/Who Am I?/This Time/I Can't Stop Loving You/In The Ghetto (take 4)/Suspicious Minds (take 6)/Kentucky Rain (take 8)/Big Boss Man (take 2)/Down In The Alley (take 1)/Memphis Tennessee (63 take 1)/I'm Yours (take 1)/His Latest Flame (take 4)/That's Someone You Never Forget (take 1)/ Surrender (take 1)/It's Now Or Never (undubbed)/Love Me Tender—Witchcraft (3/60)

66362-2   DOUBLE FEATURES: KISSIN' COUSINS/
CLAMBAKE/STAY AWAY, JOE

Kissin' Cousins (Number 2)/Smokey Mountain Boy/There's Gold In The Mountains/One Boy Two Little Girls/Catchin' On Fast/Tender Feeling/Anyone/Barefoot Ballad/Once Is Enough/Kissin' Cousins/Clambake/Who Needs Money?/A House That Has Everything/Confidence/Hey, Hey, Hey/You Don't Know Me/The Girl I Never Loved/How Can You Lose What You Never Had/Clambake (Reprise)/Stay Away, Joe/Dominic/All I Needed Was The Rain/Goin' Home/Stay Away

66421-2   AMAZING GRACE (2 CDs)   10/94

Disc 1: I Believe/Peace In The Valley/Take My Hand, Precious Lord/It Is No Secret/Milky White Way/His Hand In Mine/ I Believe In The Man In The Sky/He Knows Just What I Need/Mansion Over The Hilltop/In My Father's House/Joshua Fit The Battle/Swing Down Sweet Chariot/I'm Gonna Walk Dem Golden Stairs/If We Never Meet Again/Known Only To Him/Working On The Building/Crying In The Chapel/Run On/How Great Thou Art/Stand By Me/Where No One Stands Alone/So High/Farther Along/By And By/In The Garden/Somebody Bigger Than You And I/Without Him/If The Lord Wasn't Walking By My Side/Where Could I Go But To The Lord

Disc 2: We Call On Him/You'll Never Walk Alone/Only Believe/Amazing Grace/Miracle Of The Rosary/Lead Me, Guide Me/He Touched Me/I've Got Confidence/An Evening Prayer/Seeing Is Believing/A Thing Called Love/Put Your Hand In The Hand/ Reach Out To Jesus/He Is My Everything/There Is No God But God/I, John/Bosom Of Abraham/Help Me/ If That Isn't Love/Why Me Lord (live)/How Great Thou Art (live)/*I, John (3–4/72)/Bosom Of Abraham (3–4/72)/You Better Run (3–4/72)/Lead Me, Guide Me (3–4/72)/Turn Your Eyes Upon Jesus—Nearer My God To Thee (3–4/72)* (songs in italics are previously unreleased)

66482-2   **IF EVERY DAY WAS LIKE CHRISTMAS (CD)**   **10/94**   **94**

If Every Day Was Like Christmas/Blue Christmas/Here Comes Santa Claus/White Christmas/Santa Bring My Baby Back/
I'll Be Home For Christmas/O Little Town Of Bethlehem/Santa Claus Is Back In Town/It Won't Seem Like Christmas/
If I Get Home On Christmas Day/Holly Leaves And Christmas Trees/Merry Christmas Baby/Silver Bells/I'll Be Home On
Christmas Day (alternate version)/On A Snowy Christmas Night/Winter Wonderland/The Wonderful World Of Christmas/
O Come All Ye Faithful/The First Noel/It Won't Seem Like Christmas (take 6)/Silver Bells (take 1)/Holly Leaves And
Christmas Trees (take 8)/I'll Be Home On Christmas Day/Christmas message from Elvis/Silent Night

66557-2   **DOUBLE FEATURES: FLAMING STAR/**
            WILD IN THE COUNTRY/
            FOLLOW THAT DREAM (CD)   **3/95**

Flaming Star/Summer Kisses, Winter Tears/Britches/A Cane And A High Starched Collar/Black Star/Summer Kisses,
Winter Tears (movie version)/Flaming Star (end title)/Wild In The Country/I Slipped, I Stumbled, I Fell/Lonely Man/In
My Way/Forget Me Never/Lonely Man (solo)/I Slipped, I Stumbled, I Fell (alternate master, take 18)/Follow That Dream/
Angel/What A Wonderful Life/I'm Not The Marrying Kind/A Whistling Tune/Sound Advice

66558-2   **DOUBLE FEATURES:**
            EASY COME, EASY GO/SPEEDWAY (CD)   **3/95**

Easy Come, Easy Go/The Love Machine/Yoga Is As Yoga Does/You Gotta Stop/Sing You Children/I'll Take Love/She's
A Machine/The Love Machine (take 11)/Sing You Children (take 1)/She's A Machine (take 13)/Suppose (long ver-
sion)/Speedway/There Ain't Nothing Like A Song/Your Time Hasn't Come Yet, Baby/Who Are You?/He's Your Uncle Not
Your Dad/Let Yourself Go/Five Sleepy Heads/Suppose/Your Groovy Self (Nancy Sinatra)

66559-2   **DOUBLE FEATURES:**
            LIVE A LITTLE, LOVE A LITTLE/
            CHARRO/THE TROUBLE WITH GIRLS/
            CHANGE OF HABIT (CD)   **3/95**

Almost In Love/A Little Less Conversation/Wonderful World/Edge Of Reality/A Little Less Conversation (take 10)/
Charro/Let's Forget About The Stars/Clean Up Your Own Back Yard/Swing Down Sweet Chariot/Signs Of The Zodiac/
Almost/The Whiffenproof Song/Violet/NYU/Clean Up Your Own Back Yard (undubbed)/Almost (undubbed)/Have A
Happy/Let's Be Friends/Change Of Habit/Let Us Pray/Rubberneckin'

66670-2   **WALK A MILE IN MY SHOES:**
            THE ESSENTIAL 70'S MASTERS (5 CDs)   **10/95**

Disc 1 The Singles: The Wonder Of You/I've Lost You/The Next Step Is Love/You Don't Have To Say You Love
Me/Patch It Up/I Really Don't Want To Know/There Goes My Everything/Rags To Riches/Where Did They Go,
Lord/Life/I'm Leavin'/Heart Of Rome/It's Only Love/The Sound Of Your Cry/I Just Can't Help Believin'/How The Web
Was Woven/Until It's Time For You To Go/We Can Make The Morning/An American Trilogy/The First Time Ever I Saw
Your Face/Burning Love/It's A Matter Of Time/Separate Ways

Disc 2 The Singles: Always On My Mind/Fool/Steamroller Blues/Raised On Rock/For Ol' Times Sake/I've Got A Thing
About You Baby/Take Good Care Of Her/If You Talk In Your Sleep/Promised Land/It's Midnight/My Boy/Loving Arms/

T-R-O-U-B-L-E/Mr. Songman/Bringing It Back/Pieces Of My Life/Green, Green Grass Of Home/Thinking About You/Hurt/For The Heart/Moody Blue/She Thinks I Still Care/Way Down/Pledging My Love

Disc 3 Studio Highlights 1970/71: Twenty Days And Twenty Nights/I Was Born About Ten Thousand Years Ago/The Fool/A Hundred Years From Now/Little Cabin On The Hill/Cindy, Cindy/Bridge Over Troubled Water/Got My Mojo Working/Keep Your Hands Off Of It/It's Your Baby, You Rock It/Stranger In The Crowd/Mary In The Morning/It Aint No Big Thing/Just Pretend/Faded Love (unedited)/Tomorrow Never Comes/Make The World Go Away/Funny How Time Slips Away/I Washed My Hands In Muddy Water (long version)/Snowbird/Whole Lotta Shakin' Goin' On/Amazing Grace (take 2)/For Lovin' Me/Lady Madonna

Disc 4 Studio Highlights 1971/76: Merry Christmas Baby/I Shall Be Released/Don't Think Twice, It's All Right (jam edit)/It's Still Here (unedited)/I'll Take You Home Again Kathleen (undubbed)/I Will Be True/My Way/For The Good Times/Just A Little Bit/It's Different Now/Are You Sincere/I Got A Feelin' In My Body/You Asked Me To/Good Time Charlie's Got The Blues/Talk About The Good Times/Tiger Man/I Can Help/Susan When She Tried/Shake A Hand/She Thinks I Still Care (take 2B)/Danny Boy/Love Coming Down/He'll Have To Go

Disc 5 The Elvis Presley Show: See See Rider/Men With Broken Hearts/Walk A Mile In My Shoes/Polk Salad Annie/Let It Be Me/Proud Mary/Something/You've Lost That Lovin' Feeling/Heartbreak Hotel/I Was The One/One Night/Never Been To Spain/You Gave Me A Mountain/It's Impossible/A Big Hunk. O'Love/It's Over/The Impossible Dream/Reconsider Baby/I'll Remember You/I'm So Lonesome I Could Cry/Suspicious Minds/Unchained Melody/The Twelfth Of Never/Softly As I Leave You/Alla' En El Rancho Grande/Froggy Went A Courtin'/Stranger In My Own Home Town

66856-2 ELVIS '56 (CD) **4/96**

Heartbreak Hotel/My Baby Left Me/Blue Suede Shoes/So Glad You're Mine/Tutti Frutti/One-Sided Love Affair/Love Me/Anyplace Is Paradise/Paralyzed/Ready Teddy/Too Much/Hound Dog/Anyway You Want Me/Don't Be Cruel/Lawdy, Miss Clawdy/Shake, Rattle And Roll (alternate take 8)/I Want You, I Need You, I Love You/Rip It Up/Heartbreak Hotel (take 5)/I Got A Woman/I Was The One/Money Honey (CD also available in collector's edition: 07863/66817-2)

64476-2 HEARTBREAK HOTEL (CD Single) **4/96**

Heartbreak Hotel/I Was The One/Heartbreak Hotel (take 5)/I Was The One (take 2)

66866-2 A HUNDRED YEARS FROM NOW
(Essential Elvis Vol. 4) (CD) **7/96**

I Didn't Make It On Playing Guitar/I Washed My Hands In Muddy Water (unedited/undubbed)/Little Cabin On The Hill (take 1)/A Hundred Years From Now (take 2)/I've Lost You (take 6)/Got My Mojo Working—Keep Your Hands Off Of It (unedited)/You Don't Have To Say You Love Me (take 2)/It Ain't No Big Thing (take 2)/Cindy, Cindy (take 1)/Faded Love (country version, 6/4/70, take 3)/The Fool (take 1)/Rags To Riches (take 3)/Just Pretend (take 2)/If I Were You (take 5)/ Faded Love (take 3)/Where Did They Go Lord (take 1)/It's Only Love (take 9)/Until It's Time For You To Go (6/70 master)/ Patch It Up (take 9)/Whole Lotta Shakin' Goin' On (unedited)/Bridge Over Troubled Water (take 5)/The Lord's Prayer

66880-2 GREAT COUNTRY SONGS (CD) **10/96**

I Forgot To Remember To Forget/Blue Moon Of Kentucky/When My Blue Moon Turns To Gold Again/Old Shep/Your Cheatin' Heart (take 9)/A Fool Such As I/Just Call Me Lonesome (take 6)/There Goes My Everything (take 1)/Kentucky

Rain/From A Jack To A King/I'll Hold You In My Heart/I Really Don't Want To Know/It Keeps Right On A-Hurtin'/Green, Green Grass Of Home (take 1)/Fairytale (take 2)/Gentle On My Mind/Make The World Go Away/You Asked Me To/ Funny How Time Slips Away/Help Me Make It Through The Night (take 3)/Susan When She Tried/He'll Have To Go/ Always On My Mind/Guitar Man (1980 remix)

67457-2   AN AFTERNOON IN THE GARDEN (CD)   3/97

Also Sprach Zarathustra/That's All Right/Proud Mary/Never Been To Spain/You Don't Have To Say You Love Me/Until It's Time For You To Go/You've Lost That Lovin' Feelin'/Polk Salad Annie/Love Me/All Shook Up/Heartbreak Hotel/ Teddy Bear/Don't Be Cruel/Love Me Tender/Blue Suede Shoes/Reconsider Baby/Hound Dog/I'll Remember You/ Suspicious Minds/Introductions by Elvis/For The Good Times/American Trilogy/Funny How Time Slips Away/I Can't Stop Loving You/Can't Help Falling In Love

67452-2   LOVING YOU (CD)   4/97

Mean Woman Blues/Teddy Bear/Loving You/Got A Lot O' Livin' To Do/Lonesome Cowboy/Hot Dog/Party/Blueberry Hill/ True Love/Don't Leave Me Now/Have I Told You Lately That I Love You/I Need You So/Tell Me Why/Is It So Strange/ One Night Of Sin/When It Rains It Really Pours/I Beg Of You (alternate master, take 12)/Party (alternate master, A take 7)/ Loving You (uptempo version, KX take 13)/Got A Lot O'Livin' To Do (finale, R take 13) (Expanded version of original LP)

67453-2   JAILHOUSE ROCK (CD)   4/97

Jailhouse Rock/Treat Me Nice/I Want To Be Free/Don't Leave Me Now/Young And Beautiful/Baby I Don't Care/ Jailhouse Rock (movie version)/Treat Me Nice (movie version)/I Want To Be Free (movie version)/Young And Beautiful (movie version, jail)/Don't Leave Me Now (alternate master, 2016)/Love Me Tender/Poor Boy/Let Me/We're Gonna Move/Love Me Tender (end title version)/Let Me (solo S35)/We're Gonna Move (stereo/take 9)/Poor Boy (stereo S12)/ Love Me Tender (stereo) (Expanded version of original LP)

67454-2   KING CREOLE (CD)   4/97

King Creole/As Long As I Have You/Hard Headed Woman/Trouble/Dixieland Rock/Don't Ask Me Why/Lover Doll/ Crawfish/Young Dreams/Steadfast, Loyal And True/New Orleans/King Creole (take 18)/As Long As I Have You (movie version, take 4)/Danny/Lover Doll (undubbed)/Steadfast, Loyal And True (movie version, M take 6)/As Long As I Have You (movie version/N take 8)/King Creole (take 3) (Expanded version of original LP)

66960-2   G.I. BLUES (CD)   4/97

Tonight Is So Right For Love/What's She Really Like/Frankfort Special/Wooden Heart/G.I. Blues/Pocketful Of Rainbows/ Shoppin' Around/Big Boots/Didja Ever/Blue Suede Shoes/Doin' The Best I Can/Tonight's All Right For Love/Big Boots (M10 take 7)/Shoppin' Around (BO take 11)/Frankfort Special (HO take 2)/Pocketful Of Rainbows (NO take 27, 2)/ Didja Ever (take 1)/Big Boots (M10X take 2)/What's She Really Like (GO take 7)/Doin' The Best I Can (DO take 9) (Also available: Collectors Edition 07863/67459) (Expanded version of original LP)

66959-2   BLUE HAWAII (CD)   4/97

Blue Hawaii/Almost Always True/Aloha Oe/No More/Can't Help Falling In Love/Rock-A-Hula Baby/Moonlight Swim/ Ku-U-I-Po/Ito Eats/Slicin' Sand/Hawaiian Sunset/Beach Boy Blues/Island Of Love/Hawaiian Wedding Song/Steppin'

Out Of Line (LO 17)/Can't Help Falling In Love (film version, take 23)/Slicin' Sand (one line sung before take 9 and take 4)/No More (take 7)/Rock-A-Hula Baby (take 3)/Beach Boy Blues (film version, take 3)/Steppin' Out Of Line (film version, take 19)/Blue Hawaii (take 3) (Expanded version of original LP) (Also available: Collectors Edition 07863/67459)

67469-2 PLATINUM: A LIFE IN MUSIC (4 CDs) 7/97 80

Disc 1: I'll Never Stand In Your Way/That's All Right (takes 1,2,3)/Blue Moon (take 3)/Good Rockin' Tonight/Mystery Train/I Got A Woman (alternate take)/Heartbreak Hotel (take 6)/I'm Counting On You (take 13)/Shake, Rattle And Roll Flip, Flop And Fly/Lawdy, Miss Clawdy (take 1)/I Want You, I Need You, I Love You (take 4)/Hound Dog/Don't Be Cruel/Rip It Up (take 15)/Love Me Tender/When The Saints Go Marching In (home, 1956)/All Shook Up/Peace In The Valley (take 4)/Blueberry Hill (1/57)/Teddy Bear/Jailhouse Rock/New Orleans/I Need Your Love Tonight (take 7)/A Big Hunk O'Love (take 4)/Bad Nauheim Medley (I'll Take You Home Again Kathleen/I Will Be True/It's Been So Long Darling/Apron Strings/There's No Tomorrow)

Disc 2: Stuck On You/Fame And Fortune/It's Now Or Never/It Feels So Right (take 3)/A Mess Of Blues (take 1)/Are You Lonesome Tonight?/Reconsider Baby/Tonight Is So Right For Love (take 3)/His Hand In Mine (take 1)/Milky White Way (take 3)/I'm Comin' Home (take 3)/I Feel So Bad (take 1)/Can't Help Falling In Love/Something Blue (take 1)/Return To Sender/Bossa Nova Baby (take 2)/How Great Thou Art (take 2)/Guitar Man (take 5)/You'll Never Walk Alone (take 2)/Oh How I Love Jesus/Tennessee Waltz/Blowin' In The Wind/I Can't Help It/I'm Beginning To Forget You (solo)/After Loving You

Disc 3: I Got A Woman/Tiger Man/When My Blue Moon Turns To Gold Again/Trying To Get To You/If I Can Dream (take 1)/In The Ghetto (take 3)/Suspicious Minds (take 7)/Power Of My Love (take 3)/Baby What You Want Me To Do/Words/Johnny B. Goode/Release Me/See See Rider/The Wonder Of You/The Sound Of Your Cry (take 6)/You Don't Have To Say You Love Me/Funny How Time Slips Away/I Washed My Hands In Muddy Water (7/29)/I Was The One/Cattle Call/Baby Let's Play House/Don't/Money Honey/What'd I Say/Bridge Over Troubled Water (8/11/70)

Disc 4: Miracle Of The Rosary (take 1)/He Touched Me (take 2)/Bosom Of Abraham (take 3)/I'll Be Home On Christmas Day (take 4)/For The Good Times (take 2)/Burning Love (take 1)/Separate Ways (take 25)/Always On My Mind (take 2)/An American Trilogy/Take Good Care Of Her (take 4)/I've Got A Thing About You Baby/Are You Sincere (take 2)/It's Midnight (take 10)/Promised Land (take 5)/Steamroller Blues (3/20/74)/And I Love You So (take 2)/T-R-O-U-B-L-E/Danny Boy (take 9)/Moody Blue/Hurt (take 2)/For The Heart (take 1)/Pledging My Love (take 3) Way Down (take 2)/My Way (5/2/77)/The Jaycees Speech (excerpt)

OUTTAKES

This reference list is meant as a guide to alternate takes of Elvis recordings released by RCA Records. It's not meant to be a complete list of all abnormalities released by RCA worldwide over the years. Varying edits of songs like "Don't Think Twice, It's All Right," stripped-down versions from Joan Deary's *Our Memories* series, later overdubbed masters by producers Felton Jarvis and David Briggs, and outright mistakes such as the version of "I'm Yours" released without its vocal overdub are not all included. Likewise the many outtakes released on bootlegs are omitted. The aim, instead, is to give an overview of the wholly different takes of individual songs that have been released over the years.

A Big Hunk O' Love
(master: splice of takes 3 and 4)
Take 1—Hits Like Never Before (Essential Elvis Vol. 3)
Take 3—The King Of Rock 'N' Roll
Take 4—Platinum—A Life In Music

A Big Hunk O' Love (2/72 live)
2/17 Dinner show—Elvis: Greatest Hits Vol. 1

A Cane And A High Starched Collar
(master: splice of take 6 and instrumental insert take 6)
Take 2—Elvis—A Legendary Performer Vol. 2

A Dog's Life *(master: instrumental take 5; vocal overdub take 9)*
Takes 4, 5, 6—Elvis Aron Presley

(Now And Then There's) A Fool Such As I
(master: take 9)
Take 3—Hits Like Never Before (Essential Elvis Vol. 3)

A Hundred Years From Now
(master: splice of takes 1 and 2)
Take 2—A Hundred Years From Now—Essential Elvis Vol. 4

Ain't That Loving You Baby *(master: take 4)*
Takes 1, 5, 11—Hits Like Never Before (Essential Elvis Vol. 3)

A Little Less Conversation *(master: take 16)*
Take 10—released by accident on Almost In Love

Always On My Mind *(master: take 1)*
Take 2—Platinum—A Life In Music

Amazing Grace *(master: take 5)*
Take 2—Walk A Mile In My Shoes

A Mess Of Blues *(master: take 5)*
Take 1—Platinum—A Life In Music

An American Trilogy (2/72 live)
(master: 2/16 midnight show)
2/15 Midnight show—Elvis Aron Presley

And I Love You So *(master: take 5)*
Take 2—Platinum—A Life In Music

Anything That's Part Of You *(master: take 10)*
Take 1—released by accident on Elvis In Nashville

Are You Sincere *(master: take 4)*
Take 1 (edited)—Our Memories Of Elvis
Take 2—Platinum—A Life In Music

Ask Me (5/63) *(master: 1/64, take 11)*
Take 2—Collectors Gold

As Long As I Have You (movie version)
(master: take 8)
Take 4—Hits Like Never Before (Essential Elvis Vol. 3)

Baby What You Want Me To Do (8/69 live) *(master: 8/25 dinner show)*
8/24 Midnight show—Platinum—A Life In Music
8/26 Midnight show—Collectors Gold

Beyond The Bend *(master: take 4)*
Take 2—Collectors Gold

Beyond The Reef *(undubbed master: take 2)*
Take 2 with 1968 overdubs—Elvis Aron Presley

Big Boots (slow) *(master: edited take 4)*
Take 4 (middle section not master)—Elvis Sings For Children And Grownups Too

Big Boss Man *(master: take 11)*
Take 2—From Nashville To Memphis

Blueberry Hill *(master: take 9)*
Take 5, 2, 7—Essential Elvis Vol. 2 (Stereo '57)

Blue Hawaii *(master: take 7)*
Take 3—Blue Hawaii (1997 CD)

Blue Moon *(master: take 4)*
Take 2—The King Of Rock 'N' Roll
Take 3—Platinum—A Life In Music

Blue Moon Of Kentucky
(master take unknown)
Take 1—A Golden Celebration

Blue Suede Shoes (8/69 live)
(master: 8/25 midnight show)
8/25 Dinner show—Collector's Gold

Bosom Of Abraham *(master: take 6)*
Take 3—Platinum—A Life In Music

Bossa Nova Baby *(master: take 11)*
Take 2—Platinum—A Life In Music

Bridge Over Troubled Water *(master: take 8)*
Take 5—A Hundred Years From Now—
Essential Elvis Vol. 4

Burning Love *(master: take 6)*
Take 4—Platinum—A Life In Music

Can't Help Falling In Love
(master: splice of take 29)
Take 24—Elvis Aron Presley

Cindy, Cindy *(master: take 3)*
Take 1—A Hundred Years From Now—
Essential Elvis Vol. 4

Come What May *(master: take 8)*
Take 6—Collectors Gold
Take 7—From Nashville To Memphis

Danny Boy *(master: take 10)*
Take 9—Platinum—A Life In Music

Datin' *(master: instrumental take 2; vocal overdub take 14)*
Takes 6, 7, 8, 11, 12—Elvis Aron Presley

Didja's Ever *(master: take 2)*
Take 1—G. I. Blues (1997 release)

Doin' The Best I Can *(master: take 13)*
Take 9—The E.P. Collection Vol. 2 (U.K. release)

Doncha' Think It's Time
(master: splice of takes 40, 47, 48)
Splice of takes 40 and 39—Elvis Gold Records Vol. 2

Don't Cry Daddy (2/70 live)
(master: 2/17 midnight show)
2/18 Dinner show—Elvis—Greatest Hits Vol. 1

Down In The Alley *(master: take 9)*
Take 1—From Nashville To Memphis

Faded Love *(master: 6/7/70, take 1)*
6/4/70, take 3—A Hundred Years From Now—
Essential Elvis Vol. 4

Fairytale *(master: take 3)*
Take 2—Great Country Songs

Fame And Fortune
(master: splice of takes 15 and 14)
Take 2—Elvis—A Legendary Performer Vol. 3

Follow That Dream *(master: take 6)*
Take 2—Elvis Aron Presley

For The Good Times *(master: take 4)*
Take 2—Platinum—A Life In Music

For The Heart *(master take unknown)*
Take 1—Platinum—A Life In Music

Frankfort Special (1. version [04-27-60])
Take 2—Elvis—A Legendary Performer Vol. 3

Gently *(master: take 5)*
Take 3—Collectors Gold

G.I. Blues *(master: take 7 with work part ending take 10)*
Take 1—Collectors Gold
Take 7 (master with original ending)—The E.P. Collection Vol. 2 (U.K.)

Girl Happy *(master: splice of take 13 and take 4 of an insert, with new intro)*
Take 4—Collectors Gold

Give Me The Right *(master: take 4)*
Take 1—Collectors Gold

Goin' Home *(master: take 30)*
Takes 21, 24—Collectors Gold

Good Luck Charm *(master: take 4)*
Take 1—The E.P. Collection Vol. 2 (U.K. release)

Green, Green Grass Of Home *(master: take 5)*
Take 1—Great Country Songs

Guadalajara *(master: instrumental takes 1 and 7; vocal overdubs takes 6 and 2)*
Take 2—Elvis—A Legendary Performer Vol. 3

Guitar Man *(master: take 12)*
Take 5—Platinum—A Life In Music
Take 12 (unedited master)—From Nashville To Memphis

Have I Told You Lately That I Love You *(master: take 15)*
Takes 2, 6, 12, 13—Essential Elvis Vol. 2 (Stereo '57)

Heartbreak Hotel *(master: take 7)*
Take 5—Elvis '56
Take 6—Platinum—A Life In Music

Heartbreak Hotel (8/69 live)
(master: 8/25 midnight show)
8/24 Dinner show—Collectors Gold

Help Me Make It Through The Night
(master: splice of take 11 and ending of take 16)
Take 3—Great Country Songs

He Touched Me *(master: take 4)*
Take 2—Platinum—A Life In Music

Hi-Heel Sneakers *(master: take 7)*
Unedited master—From Nashville To Memphis

His Hand In Mine (*master: splice of take 5 and ending of take 4*)
Take 1—Platinum—A Life In Music

(Marie's The Name of) His Latest Flame (*master: take 8*)
Takes 1 (partial), 3 (partial), 5, 6—The E.P. Collection
Vol. 2 (U.K. release)
Take 4—From Nashville To Memphis

Holly Leaves And Christmas Trees (*master: take 10*)
Take 8—If Every Day Was Like Christmas

How Can You Lose What You Never Had (*master: take 6*)
Takes 1, 3—Collectors Gold

How Great Thou Art (*master: take 4*)
Take 2—Platinum—A Life In Music

Hurt (*master: take 7*)
Take 2—Platinum—A Life In Music

I Beg Of You (*master: take 34*)
Takes 1, 6, 8, 12—Essential Elvis Vol. 2 (Stereo '57)

I Don't Care If The Sun Don't Shine (*master take unknown*)
Takes 1, 2, 3—A Golden Celebration

I Feel So Bad (*master: take 2*)
Take 1—Platinum—A Life In Music

If Every Day Was Like Christmas (*master: vocal overdub take 2*)
Without celeste intro—Memories Of Christmas

If I Can Dream (*master: take 5*)
Take 1—Platinum—A Life In Music
Take 4—He Walks Beside Me

If I Were You (*master: take 9*)
Take 5—A Hundred Years From Now (Essential Elvis Vol. 4)

I Got A Woman (*master: take 8*)
Unknown take—Platinum—A Life In Music

I Got A Woman (8/69 live)
(*master: 8/24 midnight show*)
8/25 Dinner Show—Collectors Gold

I Got Stung (*master: take 24*)
Takes 1, 12, 13, 14—Hits Like Never Before (Essential Elvis Vol. 3)

I'll Be Home On Christmas Day
(*master: take 8*)
Take 4—Platinum—A Life In Music

I'll Remember You (*master: splice of vocal overdub takes 3 and 1*)
Unedited master—From Nashville To Memphis

I Love You Because (*master: splice of takes 2 and 4*)
Takes 1, 3, 4, 5—The Complete Sun Sessions
Take 2—Elvis—A Legendary Performer Vol. 1

I'm Comin' Home (*master: take 7*)
Take 3—Platinum—A Life In Music

I'm Counting On You (*master: take 17*)
Take 13—Platinum—A Life In Music

I Met Her Today (*master: take 18*)
Take 1—Collectors Gold

I'm Falling In Love Tonight (*master: take 8*)
Takes 1, 2, 3, 4—Elvis Aron Presley

I'm Left, You're Right, She's Gone (slow version) (*master: take 5*)
Takes 1, 2, 3, 4, 6, 7—The Complete Sun Sessions (Some takes only available on LP)
Take 5—A Golden Celebration

I'm Yours (*master: splice of take 6 and take 2 of a work part for the ending*)
Take 1—From Nashville To Memphis

I Need Your Love Tonight (*master: take 18*)
Takes 2, 10—Hits Like Never Before (Essential Elvis Vol. 3)
Take 7—Platinum—A Life In Music
Take 9—U.K. single

In The Ghetto (*master: take 23*)
Take 3—Platinum—A Life In Music
Take 4—From Nashville To Memphis

In The Ghetto (8/69 live)
(*master: 8/25 dinner show*)
8/24 Midnight show—Elvis Aron Presley

Is It So Strange (*master: take 12*)
Takes 1, 7, 11—Essential Elvis Vol. 2 (Stereo '57)

It Ain't No Big Thing (But It's Growing) (*master: take 9*)
Take 2—A Hundred Years From Now—Essential Elvis Vol. 4

It Feels So Right (*master: take 5*)
Take 3—Platinum—A Life In Music

It Is No Secret (What God Can Do) (*master: take 13*)
Takes 1, 2, 3—Essential Elvis Vol. 2 (Stereo '57)

It's Midnight (*master: take 19*)
Take 10—Platinum—A Life In Music

It's Only Love (*master: take 10*)
Take 9—A Hundred Years From Now—Essential Elvis Vol. 4

It Won't Seem Like Christmas (*master: take 7*)
Take 6—If Every Day Was Like Christmas

I've Lost You (*master: take 7*)
Take 6—A Hundred Years From Now—Essential Elvis Vol. 4

I Want You, I Need You, I Love You
(master: splice of takes 14 and 17)
Take 4—Platinum—A Life In Music
Unknown take—Elvis—A Legendary
Performer Vol. 2
Take 16—The King Of Rock 'N' Roll

I Want You With Me *(master: take 2)*
Take 1—Collectors Gold

I Was The One *(master: take 7)*
Take 2—"Heartbreak Hotel"/"I Was The One"
CD Single

Jailhouse Rock *(master: take 6)*
Take 5—Essential Elvis Vol. 1
Take 6 (master) with movie overdubs

**Jailhouse Rock/Don't Be Cruel (8/69
live)** *(master: splice of 8/26 and 8/24
dinner shows)*
8/22 Midnight show—Collectors Gold

Judy *(master: take 8)*
Takes 1, 3 (partial), 4, 5—The E.P. Collection
Vol. 2 (U.K.)

Just Call Me Lonesome *(master: take 1)*
Take 6—Great Country Songs

Just Pretend *(master: take 3)*
Take 2—A Hundred Years From Now—
Essential Elvis Vol. 4

Just Tell Her Jim Said Hello *(master:
take 6)*
Take 1—Collectors Gold

Kentucky Rain *(master: take 10)*
Take 8—From Nashville To Memphis

Kentucky Rain (2/70 live)
(master: 2/17 midnight show)
2/16 Dinner show—Elvis Aron Presley

King Creole (1. version [01-15-58])
Take 3—Hits Like Never Before (Essential Elvis
Vol. 3)

Lawdy, Miss Clawdy *(master: take 10)*
Take 1—Platinum—A Life In Music
Take 3—The King Of Rock 'N' Roll

Let It Be Me (2/70 live)
(master: 2/17 midnight show)
2/15 Midnight show—Elvis—A Legendary
Performer Vol. 2

Let Me *(Instr. master take 2 and splice of
vocal take 384)*
Take 3, 4—Jailhouse Rock (expanded CD)

Like A Baby *(master: take 6)*
Takes 1 (false start only), 2—Collectors Gold

Little Cabin On The Hill *(master: take 2)*
Take 1—A Hundred Years From Now—
Essential Elvis Vol. 4

Little Sister *(master: take 4)*
Takes 1, 2, 3, (partly 5, 6)—The E.P. Collection
Vol. 2 (U.K.)

(It's A) Long Lonely Highway *(master:
take 2)*
Take 1—released as B-side of "I'm Yours"
single
(47-8657) by accident

Love Letters (5/66)
Takes 3, 4, 7—Collectors Gold

Love Me Tender (8/69 live)
(master: 8/26 dinner show)
8/22 Midnight show—Collectors Gold

Love Me Tonight *(master: take 8)*
Take 1—Collectors Gold

Loving You (main title version 2/14/57)
(master: take 21)
Takes 1, 8, 20—Essential Elvis Vol. 1
Take 13—The King Of Rock 'N' Roll

Loving You (slow farm version 2/14/57)
(master: take 12)
Takes 1, 10—Essential Elvis Vol. 1

Make The World Go Away *(master: splice
of take 3 and work part take 1 of ending)*
Take 2—Welcome To My World

Mama *(master: take 10)*
Take 10 and instrumental part of movie
version—Let's Be Friends

Mean Woman Blues (movie version)
(master: take 7)
Master with movie intro and ending—This Is
Elvis

Memories (8/69 live) *(unknown master
date)*
8/25 Dinner show—Collectors Gold

Memphis Tennessee (5/63)
(master: 1/64, take 6)
Take 1—From Nashville To Memphis

Milky White Way *(master: take 7)*
Take 3—Platinum—A Life In Music

Miracle Of The Rosary *(master: take 4)*
Take 1—Platinum—A Life In Music

My Babe (8/69 live)
(master: 8/25 midnight show)
8/26 Dinner show—Elvis Aron Presley

Mystery Train/Tiger Man (8/69 live)
(8/25 midnight show)
8/22 Midnight show—Collectors Gold

Night Rider (1961) *(master: take 3)*
Takes 1 (partial), 2—Collectors Gold

No More *(master: splice of take 13 and
take 16 ending)*
Take 7—Blue Hawaii (1997 CD)

O Come All Ye Faithful *(master: take 1)*
Take 2—Memories Of Christmas

Old Shep *(master: take 1)*
Take 5—The King Of Rock 'N' Roll

Patch It Up *(master: take 8)*
Take 9—A Hundred Years From Now—
Essential Elvis Vol. 4

(There'll Be) Peace In The Valley (For Me) *(master: take 9)*
Takes 2, 3, 7—Essential Elvis Vol. 2
(Stereo '57)
Take 4—Platinum—A Life In Music

Plantation Rock *(master: incorrect splice of take 17 and unknown take)*
Master corrected to reflect original lacquer—
Double Features (Kid Galahad/Girls! Girls! Girls!) (corrected from the original release on Elvis: A Legendary Performer Vol. 4)

Pledging My Love *(master: take 6)*
Take 3—Platinum—A Life In Music

Pocketful Of Rainbows (4/60)
(master: 5/60, take 2)
Take 2—The E.P. Collection Vol. 2 (U.K.)
Takes 17, 22—Collectors Gold
Take 27—G.I. Blues (Expanded CD)

Polk Salad Annie (1970 live)
(master: 2/18 midnight show)
8/13/70 Dinner show—Elvis Aron Presley

Power Of My Love *(master: take 7)*
Take 3—Platinum—A Life In Music

Promised Land *(master: take 6)*
Take 5—Platinum—A Life In Music

Rags To Riches *(master: splice of take 4 and one line of take 3)*
Take 3—A Hundred Years From Now—
Essential Elvis Vol. 4

Rip It Up *(master: take 19)*
Take 15—Platinum—A Life In Music

Rock-A-Hula Baby *(master: take 5)*
Take 3—Blue Hawaii (Expanded CD)

Roustabout *(master: instrumental take 11, vocal overdub take 17)*
Take 6—Collectors Gold

Runaway (8/69 live)
8/26 Midnight show—Collectors Gold

Separate Ways *(master: take 21)*
Take 25—Platinum—A Life In Music

Shake, Rattle And Roll *(master: take 12)*
Take 8—The King Of Rock 'N' Roll

She Thinks I Still Care *(master: take 17)*
Take 2—Walk A Mile In My Shoes

Shoppin' Around (4/60) *(master: 5/60, take 7)*
Takes 3, 5—Elvis Aron Presley

Silver Bells *(master: take 2)*
Take 1—If Every Day Was Like Christmas

Sing You Children *(master: take 22)*
Take 1—Double Features (Easy Come, Easy Go/ Speedway)

Slicin' Sand *(master: take 19)*
Take 4—Blue Hawaii (Expanded CD)

Something Blue *(master: take 7)*
Takes 1 (intro only), 2—Platinum—A Life In Music

Stay Away, Joe *(master: instrumental take 2; unknown take of vocal overdub)*
Take 17 (with live vocal) released accidentally on Almost In Love

Such A Night *(master: take 5)*
Takes 2 (partial), 3—Elvis—A Legendary Performer Vol. 2

Summer Kisses, Winter Tears *(master: take 20)*
Takes 1, 14—Collectors Gold

Suppose (Nashville version) *(master: 1966; 3/67 overdubs)*
Undubbed 1966 vocal/piano track—A Golden Celebration

Surrender *(master: splice of take 4 and ending work part take 8)*
Take 1—From Nashville To Memphis

Suspicious Minds *(master: take 8)*
Take 6—From Nashville To Memphis
Take 7—Platinum—A Life In Music

Take Good Care Of Her *(master: take 6)*
Take 4—Platinum—A Life In Music

Thanks To The Rolling Sea *(master: take 5)*
Take 10—Elvis Aron Presley

That's All Right *(master: unknown take)*
Takes 1, 2, 3—A Golden Celebration

That's Someone You Never Forget *(master: take 8)*
Take 1—From Nashville To Memphis

That's When Your Heartaches Begin *(master: splice of takes 7 and 14)*
Takes 4, 5, 6,—Essential Elvis Vol. 2 (Stereo '57)

The Fool *(master: take 2)*
Take 1—A Hundred Years From Now—
Essential Elvis Vol. 4

The Love Machine *(master: take 12)*
Takes 4 (partial), 11—Double Features (Easy Come, Easy Go/Speedway)

There Goes My Everything *(master: take 3)*
Take 1—Great Country Songs

There's Always Me *(master: take 10)*
Take 4—Collectors Gold

The Sound Of Your Cry (master: take 11)
Take 6—Platinum—A Life In Music

They Remind Me Too Much Of You
(master: take 9)
Take 1—Elvis Aron Presley

Tonight Is So Right For Love (master:
take 11)
Take 3—Platinum—A Life In Music

Tonight's All Right For Love (master:
splice of R10 take 10 and R20 take 2
[insert])
Takes 3 (partial), 4, 7, 8—Elvis Aron Presley

Way Down (master: take 2)
Take 2—Platinum—A Life In Music

What A Wonderful World (master: take 7)
Takes 1, 2—Collectors Gold

We're Gonna Move (master: splice of
takes 4 and 9)
Take 4—The King Of Rock 'N' Roll
Take 9—Jailhouse Rock

What'd I Say (8/69 live)
(master: 8/25 midnight show)
8/23 Midnight show—Collectors Gold
Edited version released on Elvis—Greatest Hits
Vol. 1

What's She Really Like (master: take 19
and ending work part take 22)
Take 7—The E.P. Collection Vol. 2—(U.K.
release)

When It Rains, It Really Pours
(take 10—not officially a master)
Takes 7, 9—A Legendary Performer Vol. 4

Where Did They Go, Lord (master: take 6)
Take 1—A Hundred Years From Now—
Essential Elvis Vol. 4

Wild In The Country (master: take 19)
Take 16—Elvis Aron Presley

Witchcraft (master: take 3)
Take 1—Collectors Gold

Wooden Heart (master: take 4)
Take 3—Elvis—A Legendary Performer Vol. 4

Words (8/69 live)
(master: 8/25 midnight show)
8/24 Midnight show—Platinum—A Life In
Music

Yesterday/Hey Jude (8/69 live)
(master: 8/25 dinner show)
8/24 Dinner show—Elvis Aron Presley
("Yesterday" only)

You Don't Have To Say You Love Me
(master: take 3)
Take 2—A Hundred Years From Now—
Essential Elvis Vol. 4

You'll Never Walk Alone
(master: splice of takes 8 and 1)
Take 2—Platinum—A Life In Music

Young And Beautiful (master: take 22)
Take splices of 8, 12, 18, 22—Essential Elvis
Vol. 1

Your Cheatin' Heart (master: take 10)
Take 9—Released by accident on Readers
Digest LP also available on Hits Like Never
Before (Essential Elvis Vol. 3)

You're The Boss (master: splice of take
16 and take 3 ending)
Unedited take 16—Double Features (Viva Las
Vegas/ Roustabout)

INDEX